ENCYCLOPEDIA OF
GOVERNMENT AND POLITICS

ENCYCLOPEDIA OF GOVERNMENT AND POLITICS

Volume 2

EDITED BY

Mary Hawkesworth
and
Maurice Kogan

LONDON AND NEW YORK

First published in 1992
by Routledge
11 New Fetter Lane, London EC4P 4EE

Simultaneously published in the USA and Canada
by Routledge
a division of Routledge, Chapman and Hall, Inc.
29 West 35th Street, New York, NY 10001

Typeset in 10/12½pt Ehrhardt Linotronic 300 by Intype, London
Printed in Great Britain by Clays Ltd, St Ives plc

British Library Cataloguing in Publication Data
Encyclopedia of government and politics.
1. Political science
I. Hawkesworth, Mary *1952–* II. Kogan, Maurice *1930–*
320

Library of Congress Cataloging-in-Publication Data
Encyclopedia of government and politics/edited by Mary Hawkesworth and Maurice Kogan.
p.   cm.
Includes bibliographical references and index.
ISBN 0–415–03092–7 (set)
1. Political science—Encyclopedias. I. Hawkesworth, M. E.,
1952–   . II. Kogan, Maurice.
JA61.C66   1992
320'.03—dc20
91–30399
CIP

ISBN 0–415–07224–7 (Volume 1)
ISBN 0–415–07225–5 (Volume 2)
ISBN 0–415–03092–7 (set)

This paper is manufactured in accordance with the proposed ANSI/NISO Z 39.48–199X
and ANSI Z 39.48–1984

CONTENTS

Part IX International relations

Part X Major issues in contemporary world politics

ENCYCLOPEDIA OF GOVERNMENT AND POLITICS

VOLUME 2

PART VIII

POLICY MAKING
AND POLICIES

39

THEORIES OF POLICY MAKING

RITA MAE KELLY AND DENNIS PALUMBO

Theories of policy making are important because they shape definitions, provide guidance in structuring problems, make some types of enquiry more critical than others, and provide normative and empirical standards with which to judge the merit and adequacy of policy. They also legitimate some social consequences while downplaying others. Theories of policy making shape the questions addressed and the values emphasized in policy analysis. They also help set the agenda for public policy as well as for policy enquiry.

There are many theories of policy making, decision making, and policy analysis. These include the familiar theories of rational choice, incrementalism, systems analysis, bureaucratic politics, organizational process and public choice, as well as the somewhat less familiar theories of loosely coupled systems, garbage cans, policy cycle, street-level bureaucrat, top-down versus bottom-up, adaptive and evolutionary implementation. Some of these theories (i.e. rational choice, systems analysis, incrementalism, policy cycle) pertain to policy making; others (i.e. loosely coupled systems, garbage cans, top-down versus bottom-up) are directed more to decision making and/or implementation. Figure 1 categorizes the major theories of policy making and decision/implementation. We do not claim that each theory listed fits exclusively into

Figure 1 Major policy-making theories

POLICY-MAKING THEORIES	
* Rational choice	* Bureaucratic politics
* Incrementalism	* Organizational process
* Policy cycle	* Public choice
* Systems analysis	
DECISION/IMPLEMENTATION THEORIES	
Loosely coupled systems	Adaptive
Garbage cans	Evolutionary
* Top-down v. bottom-up	Street-level bureaucrat

one or the other rubric; the dynamic nature of policy theory does not allow such neat and mutually exclusive ordering.

In the short space available we cannot cover all of these theories in detail. Therefore we will describe the asterisked items in some detail and devote only a brief paragraph to each of the others.

After describing these models, we critique each using several criteria: first, the political, institutional and economic contexts within which each model can most appropriately and effectively be used; second, the cognitive basis of each model; and third, the normative and ideological bias of each model.

THE RATIONAL-COMPREHENSIVE MODEL

As is the case with all models of policy making, there is not just one version of the rational-comprehensive theory of policy making; nor are the range, scope and applicability of rational-comprehensive models appropriate for all levels of the socio-political, economic system. On one level, the rational choice model applies to decision making within organizations rather than to entire political systems. On a broader level, it refers to the synoptic model of the intellectually guided society outlined by Charles Lindblom in *Politics and Markets* (Lindblom 1977) that was associated with the command economies of Eastern Europe and the Soviet Union prior to the Gorbachev reforms.

At this broader level, the synoptic model assumes that humans have the capacity to comprehend reality and the processes of social change so as to guide society in a given direction. Experts, or an elite set of decision makers, can use available knowledge to guide society toward predetermined ends. The co-ordination and implementation of their policies depend on bureaucracies, hierarchies and control over large amounts of data, people and things. Unfortunately, information overload, communication failures, red tape and human failure to absorb, interpret and process decision elements typically reduce the command system to being a policy-making mechanism of 'strong thumbs, no fingers' (Lindblom 1977: 65–75).

This broad societally based version of the rational-comprehensive model has fallen into severe disrepute in the 1990s. By late 1991, the command economies of the USSR and Eastern Europe had moved towards market systems and social interaction/exchange bases for much of their economic decision making.

Although the rational-comprehensive model has not been found to be extraordinarily effective at the broad societal level, it has contributed substantially to organizational decision making. The narrower range of information needed at these levels makes rational-comprehensive strategies more feasible, at least in theory. In management, policy making within this model typically starts by setting the objectives first, as in techniques such as management by objectives.

In this model the policy maker must start with goals, establish priorities among them, and specify the objectives to be obtained, maximized or minimized. Once this step is completed, the options available for achieving those objectives are identified, the consequences and costs/benefits of each determined and, finally, the best means to maximize the desired ends selected (Hogwood and Gunn 1984: 46–7).

The projects developed by NASA to send a person to the moon illustrate a successful application of rational-comprehensive policy making in the United States. President John F. Kennedy announced the goal. Scientists presented plans based on scientific theory as to how to accomplish this goal. Options for implementing the plan were reviewed and a particular means selected. Resources were allocated and invested. Finally, in 1962, the launch was made and the theories were vindicated.

The effort of President Jimmy Carter to have the United States move to 'zero-based budgeting' is an example of how difficult it is to apply the rational-comprehensive model to more complicated social policies. In this type of budgeting, the goals to be obtained are of the utmost concern. All programmes are examined to assess their contribution to those goals and objectives. Expenditures and resources are to be given to those that most effectively maximize these goals and objectives. Under President Carter, the 'zero-based budgeting' effort was found to be too time-consuming and politically controversial and it was abandoned.

An alternative to rational choice is the 'satisficing' model created by Herbert Simon (1957a, 1957b, 1960, 1983). Simon rejected the notion that goals and objectives could be specified up front. As Hogwood and Gunn note, 'The initial specification of objectives may foreclose unduly the courses of action that are considered and the initial focus on objectives may distract attention from the actual situation in which the decisionmaker is placed' (Hogwood and Gunn 1984: 46). Moreover, there are a number of limits to rational decision making. For example, Sorenson (1963) noted five limits on decision making in the White House under John F. Kennedy. These are the limits of permissibility (legality, political acceptability), availability of resources, availability of time, previous commitments, and availability of information. Barnard (1938: 202–5) also notes that it is not always possible to identify what factors can be controlled by decision makers.

Examples of efforts to make the decision making of bureaucrats and administrators more rational include quantitative scheduling models (Gannt Charts, Critical Path Method, and Program Evaluation Review Techniques (PERT)); structural analyses, such as relevance trees, to examine whether a programme or policy includes all needed components and to maximize utility of resource allocation; and decision trees to highlight the interrelationships of given decisions and possible events. In addition, various types of system analyses have been devised to ensure a comprehensive, rational examination of the interdependence and interrelationship of society's components. Simulation models illustrate the effort of systems analysts to formulate a problem, model it, develop an optimal solution, and then implement it. Other techniques, such as sensitivity analysis, allow assessment of which solutions or options posited by a model provide the most optimal strategy for addressing a problem.

Operations research and management science derive from this rational-comprehensive model of decision making. Operations research relies on modelling, sophisticated mathematics and optimal decision making. Linear programming, a mathematical technique for deriving optimal solutions to linear relationship problems, has been widely used to determine appropriate product mixes requiring particular specifications and cost restrictions, optimum product lines and production processes, and optimum transportation routes. Operations research and management science offers techniques that are particularly successful in dealing with any 'problem concerned with maximizing or minimizing some economic quality (e.g., cost) subject to a set of constraints (e.g., human resources, materials, and capital)' (Starling 1977: 161).

Criticisms of the rational-comprehensive model include: the uncertainty and difficulty involved in identifying, structuring, and linking problems with their causes and effects; the lack of time, resources and ability to obtain the information and data needed to decide rationally and comprehensively; the difficulty of dealing with value trade-offs and conflicts; and, finally, the method of systems analysis itself which can become its own end, dwarfing the problem and the original purpose of providing clarity among alternatives and obscuring their likely consequences (Starling 1977: 162–7).

Perhaps the most damning criticism of the rational-comprehensive model is that it requires that a central authority or entity select the values and objectives to be maximized (or minimized). This requirement tends toward centralized, technocratic decision making. Intellectual cognition, on which rational-comprehensive policy making rests, places great credence in the expert and the central planning decision maker. It reduces the role of the average citizen.

In the 1970s and 1980s, this means–end emphasis of the rational-comprehensive model joined with the applied social science movement and scholars promoting the 'experimenting society' to create a policy studies field focused strongly on impact assessment. Lance de Haven-Smith has noted that 'The restriction of policy analysis to policy impacts is based implicitly on a cognitive-instrumental conception of rationality. . . . The cognitive-instrumental conception of rationality leads analysts to ignore policy formulation because it implies that the ways in which policies are formulated have no bearing on their effects' (de Haven-Smith 1988: 84–5).

Between 1970 and 1980 the instrumental conception of rationality prevailed in policy studies. However, in the 1980s strong counter-forces arose. For example, the writings of Jurgen Habermas (see, for example, Habermas 1975) came to be used by policy scholars to challenge the instrumental nature of policy analysis and the negative impact it was having on the quality of not only decision making but also democracy in general (see, for example, Hawkesworth 1988). Habermas became important to this counter-movement not because he was opposed to using the rational-comprehensive model, but rather because of the very extreme instrumental way in which policy analysts and decision makers were applying it. From Habermas's world view, being rational and comprehensive meant more than being instrumental, empirical and 'scientific' as the empiricist and logical positivist traditions required. For Habermas, reason is seen 'as a process not of choosing pathways to given ends but of reaching understanding in a social context. This shifts the analytic focus to policy formulation' (de Haven-Smith 1988: 85).

THE INCREMENTALIST MODEL

Incrementalism as a policy-making theory and its political counterpart – pluralism – were developed to defend liberal democracy from socialism (Lindblom 1959, 1965, 1968). Incrementalism is based on the fragmented and balanced nature of power in liberal democracies and the need to have a policy-making approach that does not concentrate power in the hands of an elite or a ruling class. Lindblom argued that although incrementalism does refer to a series of small adjustments, it does not necessarily imply that these adjustments must always conserve the status quo. Lindblom argues, particularly in *Politics and Markets* (Lindblom 1977), that major changes in policies, ideas and public desires can occur as the result of small changes in key politico-economic mechanisms. Hence, the conservative or radical nature of incrementalism depends on what is changed as well as the quantity of the change.

Incrementalism serves several important functions for decision makers. It minimizes the intellectual investment required to create new policies and programmes, and reduces the necessity and expectation of rethinking basic issues, problems and solutions, thereby making policy and budget making more manageable tasks. The more routine the policy-making task, the more likely the incrementalist model will be used (Jacob 1988).

The essence of incrementalism is presenting policy changes as though they are routine and only minor changes from existing law or funding levels (Jacob 1988). The cloak of the existing law's legitimacy is thus placed around the change proposed, and opposition is disarmed. Traits that characterize incremental policy making include: defining a problem narrowly rather than broadly; following a strategy of exclusion so as to restrict interest group participation; relying on experts to develop policy so as to exclude novices and outsiders; stressing the incremental rather than radical shift in any policy; cloaking the incremental change in the legitimacy of past law and budgets so as to seek acquiescence rather than debate or controversy; highlighting the determinant and minimal nature of any risks associated with the policy so as to ease fears about uncertainty and undebated risks; emphasizing the small impact the change will have on the budget; and keeping the policy making out of the media and public limelight.

Incrementalism is most suited as a decision strategy in situations with low levels of conflict and visibility. These situations tend to exist in distributive policy arenas and to be absent in redistributive arenas. Decisions about distributive policies are typically made with short-run consequences in mind.

Incrementalism also fares well as a policy-making strategy when decentralization exists within the decision-making body, such as a legislature or bureaucracy. Incrementalism allows for minimization of conflicts among participants, thus lowering the likelihood of stalemate and gridlock.

Criticisms of incrementalism come in several forms. First, because policy deals only with marginal changes, it generally does not challenge the status quo. Second, given the narrow focus of data and issues considered in marginal analyses, incremental decisions over a long period of time can create a highly complex 'policy morass', as occurred in US federal income tax policy which by the 1980s had become encrusted with a multiplicity of loopholes. Once such a morass exists, incrementalism must be abandoned and a more rational-comprehensive approach needs to be undertaken. As an issue becomes more controversial and/or the political system itself becomes less stable, resistance to the status quo increases while resistance to change decreases. In order to adapt to rapid change, the only strategy available is to speed up marginal changes (see Mucciaroni 1988).

RATIONALITY, ORGANIZATIONS AND POLICY MAKING

Max Weber's approach to promoting a more rational and efficient policy-making process (Weber 1978) was to establish a hierarchically ordered system, the bureaucracy. Grounded in notions of value-free science, Weber's ideas established a supporting foundation for Woodrow Wilson's argument that politics and administration could be separated. Weber (1978) and Wilson (1885, 1887) emphasized the speed, efficiency and dispatch of bureaucracy. For Weber, bureaucracy was essential for legal, economic and technical rationality; it placed an emphasis on goals, means, ends, rules, guidelines, calculation of consequences, access to and control over information, division of labour, experts and the interchangeability of decision makers and officials.

Herbert Simon (1957a, 1957b, 1960) presented a major challenge to Weber's understanding of bureaucracy by emphasizing the psychology of decision making and by introducing a cost calculus to test the criterion of efficiency rather than simply presume, as Weber and Wilson did, that bureaucracies are efficient. Theories of policy making grounded on bureaucratic and organizational politics arose in conjunction with this challenge. Simon and other behaviouralists emphasized 'reality'. They noted the regularity of goal displacement and bureaucratic dysfunctions. Simon and his followers focused on the problems of 'bounded rationality' and 'zoned authority'. The former highlights the limits of knowledge and the psychology of choice; the latter stressed that authority is of necessity limited rather than comprehensive. The behavioural emphasis on reality and human behaviour, rather than on policy making as an intellectual-cognitive phenomenon, contributed to the development of the bureaucratic politics and organizational process theories of policy making.

Organizations are composed of individuals who are members of groups, committees, subcommittees, bureaux and divisions. According to the bureaucratic politics model, these individuals and groups have interests they pursue, and try to attain through bargaining and negotiating. These actors have varying conceptions of what policies are best; they pursue a multiplicity of goals, and, as Allison writes, 'make government decisions not by a single, rational choice but by the pulling and hauling that is politics' (Allison 1971: 144). Thus, the bureaucratic politics model focuses on different characteristics of organizations than the other models. 'To explain why a particular formal governmental decision was made or why one pattern of governmental behavior emerged,' Allison writes, 'it is necessary to identify the games and players, to display the coalitions, bargains, and compromises, and to convey some feel for the confusion' (Allison 1971: 146).

The players in the game of politics are not convinced to support a policy on the basis of facts or rational argument. Instead, persuasion is the key strategy, and individuals are persuaded by the use of influence, which involves 'deceiving, inveighing, rewarding, punishing, and otherwise inducing' (Banfield 1961: 30). In the political model, actors impose their ideology on the world, ignore the facts and sift the environment only for information that supports their biases. Policies are changed only if they are perceived as liabilities by ruling elites.

The existence of bargaining means that organizations are not fully directed systems. They are multicultural, but power is unevenly distributed. Conflict is therefore inevitable as the groups that have less power struggle to improve their position by proposing policies that will benefit them. But, of course, they rarely succeed, and policy tends to reflect the interests of those in power.

The organizational politics model is considered to be an accurate representation of policy making in democratic political systems such as the United States. It resembles incrementalist theory in a number of ways. Since it is essential to bargain, trade and compromise in the organizational politics model, changes in policy tend to be incremental and supportive of the existing distribution of power. This is inevitable because those with the most power have the greatest amount of political capital with which to influence policy outcomes. Moreover there is little or no consideration of the general public interest.

PUBLIC CHOICE

Public choice theories are counterposed to traditional policy-making and public administration theories that are grounded in or are reactions to the Weberian theory of bureaucracy. Public choice is founded on theories of collective action and public goods, and incorporates elements of microeconomics, political science and public administration. Public choice theory assumes that people will pursue their self-interest. Consequently, they are not likely to pursue collective interests. Thus, the main problem in decision making is how to aggregate individual preferences into a collective choice that is not harmful or non-rational (Arrow 1954). Public choice theory defines the core problem of policy making to be the provision of public goods and services but rejects the notion that one unified governing unit, organization, bureaucracy or set of decision makers is or should be responsible for all public policy making in a given geographical area. 'Bureaucratic structures are necessary but not sufficient for a productive and responsible public service economy. Particular public goals and services may be jointly provided by the coordinated actions of a multiplicity of enterprises transcending the limits of particular governmental jurisdictions' (Ostrom 1989: 17). According to Vincent Ostrom, a viable theory of public policy making is one in which the organizational arrangements (which in his opinion are the same as decision-making arrangements) allow self-interested individuals to pursue optimizing strategies in structuring events yet which permit collectively appropriate policy outcomes to occur. Public choice theorists agree with Simon and the bureaucratic and organizational politics theorists that individual self-interest will lead to goal displacement and risk avoidance in policy making and implementation. However, in contrast to the behaviourists, who assume that this reality is inevitable, the public choice theorists, such as Ostrom, argue that human beings construct their own reality and that they can therefore alter institutional (decision-making) arrangements so as to address these tendencies. Political theory, in conjunction with proper organizational design, will lead to improved policy making, policy implementation and democratic administration. The public choice theorists argue that only through the proper design of institutional arrangements can effective, efficient and responsive public policy making occur.

POLICY CYCLE

The principal model used by political scientists to understand policy making and public policy is a process model (Rodgers 1989). In earlier literature, the focus was on the US Congress and the role of the executive in the formulation stage, during which bills became laws. More recently, a number of additional stages have been identified. These include agenda setting, problem definition, formulation, implementation, evaluation and termination.

Agenda setting is the process by which items become a part of the institutional agenda (Cobb and Elder 1984; Kingdon 1984). This is considered by some to be the most crucial stage; if an issue does not get onto the institutional agenda, no action will be taken. Some scholars (Bachrach and Baratz 1970) argue that the power elite maintain their power by keeping items that would challenge their power and privileges off the agenda.

Problem definition is crucial once an item becomes a part of the institutional agenda (Dery 1984). How a problem is defined determines what kind of solution is likely to be proposed. For example, if abortion is defined as primarily a moral problem, the policy is likely to try to prevent women from having abortions by criminalizing abortion. If, on the other hand, it is defined as a constitutional right to privacy, then abortions are likely to be permitted under some circumstances.

Formulation involves the design of policy when legislatures are considering how to approach or address an issue. The usual interest group, administration and congressional committee interaction occurs during this stage as compromises are reached about how to address an issue.

Generally, policies in American politics are largely symbolic (Edelman 1964, 1989). Thus, they are often vague and general and the actual meanings are attached during the *implementation* stage. Some scholars believe that most policy is made during this stage (Nachmias and Rosenbloom 1978; Meier 1979; Ripley and Franklin 1982). In fact, there is considerable evidence that most *de facto* policy is made by street-level bureaucrats, who are the administrators who interact with clients (Lipsky 1980; Weatherly and Lipsky 1977).

Programme evaluation would take place, ideally, after a programme had been fully implemented, but unfortunately, because of political pressure, this does not always occur (Patton 1979).

Finally, programmes may be *terminated* for a variety of reasons, but most end due to political reasons rather than because they are not working (de Leon 1983). In fact, relatively few programmes are terminated (Kaufman 1976).

The policy cycle has been criticized on the basis that it depicts a neat, sequential process, when in fact policy making is actually complicated and interactive. However, the policy cycle is meant as an analytical device highlighting the various points at which critical policy decisions are made rather than as a description of an actual process for all policies. Similar to all theories, it points to crucial factors in policy making, but it does not purport to describe the actual details of policy making, as is the case with incrementalism.

TOP-DOWN AND BOTTOM-UP MODELS OF IMPLEMENTATION

Implementation research has added greatly to our understanding of the policy-making process. Early implementation research pointed to this stage of policy making as the 'Achilles heel' or 'missing link' (Hargrove 1976). Because of the complexity of joint action in federal programmes that involved a multiplicity of participants and decision points, government programmes were bound to fall short of their intended targets – according to one important study of implementation (Pressman and Wildavsky 1973). Scholars then began to search for conditions under which implementation might be successful. Sabatier and Mazmanian (1979) identified five conditions for effective implementation that later became known as the 'top-down' view. The five conditions are as follows.

1 The programme is based on a sound theory relating changes in target group behaviour to achievement of the desired end state.
2 The policy contains unambiguous policy directives and structures the implementation process so as to maximize the likelihood that target groups will perform as desired.
3 The leaders of the implementing agencies possess the necessary managerial skills and are committed to the statutory goals.
4 The programme is supported by organized constituency groups and legislators throughout the implementation process.
5 The relative priority of statutory objectives is not significantly undermined over time by the emergence of conflicting public policies or by changes in relative socio-economic conditions.

At about the same time the 'bottom-up' model was proposed as a more appropriate policy-making approach (Elmore 1979–80). Since street-level bureaucrats (Lipsky 1980) are the ones who are familiar with the problems with which the policy is trying to deal, they are in a better position to determine what policies and programmes will work. Some scholars found that empowering street-level implementors so that they had a role in policy making produced more effective policy (Musheno et al. 1989). However, the bottom-up approach was criticized on the grounds that the descriptive reality, that street-level implementors have a large impact on policy, should not be turned into a prescription for policy making because they also can be biased and wrong (Linder and Peters 1987). For example, police officers may not be the best ones to make policy about how to deal with the problem of police brutality.

Recently, attempts have been made to integrate the top-down and bottom-up perspectives (Palumbo and Calista 1990); the argument here is that the bottom, middle and upper levels should all have a role in making policy.

Both the top-down and bottom-up approaches can be considered to be rational models in that they assume that goals can be defined and rationally achieved. In contrast, *loosely coupled systems* (Weick 1976) and *garbage-can models* (Cohen *et al.* 1972) do not make this assumption; they posit that goals are discovered by acting, action precedes intent, solutions search for problems, and subordinates specify spheres of work to superordinates. Similar to Chinese baseball, in which the bases are moved after the pitcher releases the ball (Siu 1984), programme goals are adjusted and changed as the policy-making process proceeds. This is similar to adaptive implementation which allows policy to be modified, specified and revised according to the unfolding interaction of the policy with its institutional setting (Berman 1980). A similar model is evolutionary implementation in which organizations learn as they attempt to achieve policy goals. 'When we act to implement a policy, we change it. . . . [A]s we learn from experience what is feasible or preferable, we correct errors' (Majone and Wildavsky 1984: 177).

CONCLUSION

The above theories of policy making reflect changing emphases. The rational-comprehensive theories assume a knowable, objective world, typically where information can be used to reduce uncertainty and where a 'correct', or at least satisfactory, decision can be reached. Cognition, comprehensive knowledge, and experts are highly valued by these theories. Obtaining the 'best', or most cost-effective, cost-efficient policy has priority over other values. Incrementalist theories prefer social-interaction to cognitive-intellectual models of policy making. Denying that public policy making in a democratic society can be made in a comprehensive and systematic way, these theories emphasize pluralism, interest-group politics and marginal change. Underlying incrementalism is scepticism about the wisdom of experts and the scope of solutions they can offer. Although policy expertise is valued, it is only one of many relevant factors to be considered in the policy-making process.

The rise of behaviouralism and the focus on the psychology of individual and collective policy making contributed to both the rise and popularity of bureaucratic politics and organizational process theories of policy making, including the policy cycle and various implementation theories. The emphasis on empirical reality in these theories helps us to understand successes and failures in policy making and implementation and to identify points for improving both policy making and policy implementation.

REFERENCES

Allison, G. J. (1971) *Essence of Decision: Explaining the Cuban Missile Crisis*, Boston: Little, Brown & Co.

Arrow, K. J. (1954) *Social Choice and Individual Values*, 2nd edn, New York: John Wiley.

Bachrach, P. and Baratz, M. (1970) *Power and Poverty: Theory and Practice*, New York: Oxford University Press.

Banfield, E. (1961) *Political Influence*, New York: Free Press.

Barnard, C. I. (1938) *The Function of the Executive*, Cambridge, Mass.: Harvard University Press.

Berman, P. (1980) 'Thinking about programmed and adaptive implementation: matching strategies to situations', in H. Ingram and D. Wann (eds) *Why Policies Succeed or Fail*, Beverly Hills: Sage Publications.

Cobb, R. and Elder, C. D. (1984) *Participation in American Politics: The Dynamics of Agenda Building*, 2nd edn, Baltimore: Johns Hopkins University Press.

Cohen, M., March, J. G. and Olsen, J. P. (1972) 'A garbage-can model of organizational choice', *Adminstrative Service Quarterly* 11: 1–250.

de Haven-Smith, L. (1988) *Philosophical Critiques of Policy Analysis*, Gainseville: University of Florida Press.

de Leon, P. (1983) 'Policy evaluation and program organization', *Policy Studies Review* 2 (4): 631–48.

Dery, D. (1984) *Problem Definition in Policy Analysis*, Lawrence: University of Kansas Press.

Edelman, M. (1964) *The Symbolic Uses of Politics*, Urbana: University of Illinois Press.

Elmore, R. (1979–80) 'Backward mapping: using implementation analysis to structure political decisions', *Political Science Quarterly* 94 (4): 601–16.

Habermas, J. (1975) *Legitimation Crisis*, Boston: Beacon Press.

Hargrove, E. (1976) *The Missing Link: The Study of Implementation of Local Policy*, Washington, DC: Urban Institute.

Hawkesworth, M. (1988) *Theoretical Issues in Policy Analysis*, Albany, NY: SUNY Press.

Hogwood, B. and Gunn, L. (1984) *Policy Analysis for the Real World*, Oxford: Oxford University Press.

Jacob, H. (1988) 'Is routine policy making a special case of incrementalism?', paper presented at the American Political Science Association Convention, 31 August– 3 September, Washington, DC.

Kaufman, H. (1976) 'Are government organizations immortal?', Washington, DC: Brookings Institution.

Kingdon, J. (1984) *Agendas, Alternatives and Public Policy*, Boston: Little, Brown & Co.

Lindblom, C. (1959) 'The science of muddling through', *Public Administration Review* 19: 79–88.

——(1965) *The Intelligence of Democracy*, New York: Free Press.

——(1968) *The Policy Making Process*, Englewood Cliffs, NJ: Prentice-Hall.

——(1977) *Politics and Markets*, New York: Basic Books.

Linder, S. and Peters, B. G. (1987) 'A design perspective on policy implementation: the fallacies of misplaced prescription', *Policy Studies Review* 6 (2): 459–76.

Lipsky, M. (1980) *Street-Level Bureaucracy*, New York: Russell Sage.

Majone, G. and Wildavsky, A. (1984) 'Implementation as evolution', in J. Pressman and Aaron Wildavsky (eds) *Implementation*, 3rd edn, Berkeley: University of California Press.

Meier, K. (1979) *Politics and Bureaucracy: Policymaking in the Fourth Branch of Government*, North Scituate, Me.: Duxbury Press.

Mucciaroni, G. (1988) 'The rise and fall of an "incrementalist paradise": the case of comprehensive tax reform', paper presented at the American Political Science Association Convention, 31 August–3 September, Washington, DC.

Musheno, M., Palumbo, D., Maynard-Moody, S. and Levine J. (1989) 'Community corrections as an organizational innovation: what works and why', *Journal of Research in Crime and Delinquency* 26 (2): 136–67.

Nachmias, D. and Rosenbloom, D. (1978) *Bureaucratic Culture: Citizens and Administrators in Israel*, New York: St Martin's Press.

Ostrom, V. (1989) *The Intellectual Crisis in American Public Administration*, Tuscaloosa: University of Alabama Press.

Palumbo, D. and Calista, D. (1990) *Implementation and the Policymaking Process: Opening Up the Black Box*, Westport, Conn.: Greenwood Press.

Patton, M. (1979) 'Evaluation of program implementation', in L. Sechrest, S. G. West, M. A. Phillips and R. Redner (eds) *Evaluation Studies Review Annual*, Beverly Hills: Sage Publications.

Pressman, F. and Wildavsky, A. (1973) *Implementation*, Berkeley: University of California Press.

Ripley, R. and Franklin, G. (1982). *Bureaucracy and Policy Implementation*, Homewood, Ill.: Dorsey Press.

Rodgers, J. (1989) 'Social science disciplines and policy research: the case of political science', *Policy Studies Review* 9 (1): 13–29.

Sabatier, P. and Mazmanian, D. (1979) 'The conditions of effective implementation: a guide to accomplishing policy objectives', *Policy Analysis* 5 (4): 481–504.

Simon, H. (1957a) *Administrative Behavior*, 2nd edn, London: Macmillan.

——(1957b) *Models of Man*, London: John Wiley.

——(1960) *The New Science of Management Decision*, Englewood Cliffs, NJ: Prentice-Hall.

——(1983) *Reason in Human Affairs*, Oxford: Basil Blackwell.

Siu, R. (1984) 'Chinese baseball and public administration', in E. Chelimsky (ed.) *Program Evaluation: Patterns and Direction*, Washington, DC: American Society for Public Administration.

Sorenson, R. (1963) *Decision Making in the White House*, New York: Columbia University Press.

Starling, G. (1977) *Managing the Public Sector*, Homewood, Ill.: Dorsey Press.

Weatherly, R. and Lypsky, M. (1977) 'Street-level bureaucrats and institutional innovation: implementing special education reform', *Harvard Educational Review* 47 (2): 171–97.

Weber, M. (1978) *Economy and Society*, eds G. Roth and C. Wittich, Berkeley and Los Angeles: University of California Press.

Weick, K. (1976) 'Educational organizations as loosely-coupled systems', *Adminstrative Science Quarterly* 21: 1–9.

Wilson, W. (1885) *Congressional Governments*, New York: Houghton Miffin.

——(1887) 'The study of administration', *Political Science Quarterly* 2 (June): 197–220.

40

ECONOMIC POLICY

ROSALIND LEVAČIĆ

In this essay economic policy is defined to encompass all government actions which affect individuals' welfare and, given it can be defined, the welfare of society. Welfare depends on the kinds and quantities of goods and services people consume, including environmental goods such as air, water and noise. Economic policy refers to government decisions which affect the allocation and distribution of resources. The key instruments are legislation, government expenditure, and its financing by taxation, borrowing or issuing money (Levačić 1987: chapter 1).

Three conceptions of economic policy are considered. The first is the orthodox viewpoint of economists that they are politically neutral experts, drawing upon a corpus of scientific knowledge in order to offer advice on how to achieve specific social objectives. The second conception (Schultz 1982) is that the 'orthodox' view is an ideology which economists should promote in the public interest in order to counter sectional interests. The third (Lindblom 1977, 1987) is that, since the public interest cannot be defined, economics should be openly acknowledged as an input into the competition between different values and interests that is resolved through politics. The orthodox view is used here as the vehicle for presenting the standard 'theory of economic policy'. It is argued that the divergence between the 'theory of economic policy' and its practice has strengthened the case for the second and third conceptions of the relationship between economics and economic policy.

THE PROGRESSIVE VIEW OF ECONOMICS AND POLICY MAKING

Pigou in *The Economics of Welfare* set out a view of the purpose and nature of economics as a policy science which still remains the official stance of economists: 'the goal sought is to make more easy practical measures to promote welfare-practical measures which statesmen may build upon the work of the economist, just as Marconi, the inventor, built upon the discoveries of Hertz' (Pigou 1920: 10). This viewpoint is labelled progressive by Nelson (1987) since it reflects the dominant idea of the progressive movement of the late nineteenth and early twentieth centuries which separated a realm of 'politics', where collective preferences are determined, from the realm of 'administration', where highly trained experts decide and implement the most efficient means for securing politically determined objectives. In the progressive view, economic policy making is a rational activity; its purpose is to maximize social welfare subject to the constraints imposed by economic factors. The role of economics is to produce and apply scientifically verified knowledge that will enable politicians, public sector officials and the electorate to make better decisions about which objectives they wish to pursue and the best means to use. A good exposition of this approach is to be found in Boulding (1959) who makes the characteristic statement that 'It is not the business of the social sciences to evaluate the ultimate ends of human activity' (Boulding 1959: 2).

The objectives of economic policy

The ends or objectives of economic policy are normally classified into three or four key categories. Following Musgrave's three functions of the budget (Musgrave 1957, 1986), these are efficiency, stabilization and equity (or distribution) to which a fourth, freedom (defined as either negative or positive freedom), is often added rather than subsumed within either efficiency or equity. Musgrave's classification is comprehensive as it includes both microeconomic and macroeconomic policies. The latter policies are concerned with aggregate level variables such as national income, unemployment, inflation, the exchange rate and the balance of payments. Thus stabilization refers to the goal of steady economic growth accompanied by high employment and low inflation, unconstrained by difficulties in financing balance-of-payments deficits. Microeconomic policies are concerned with the operation of individual subsectors and markets; examples are competition policy, assistance for industry, and welfare programmes.

Efficiency and stabilization are most typically the specialist concern of economics, efficiency usually being associated with microeconomic analysis and stabilization with macroeconomics. Both are premised on the view that the purpose of economic policy is to benefit society as a whole. This was very clearly the message of Keynesian economics: when resources are involuntarily unemployed, government action can generate additional output at no net cost to society. In the monetarist view, stabilization in the form of reduced inflation also promotes efficiency. Inflation distorts market choices because it misleads people regarding correct relative prices and induces them to hold those assets which preserve their real value during inflation.

657

Efficiency arises from mutual gains as the result of exchange. This may be a market exchange of goods and services at an agreed price or an agreement to act co-operatively, as in providing a public good. In terms of game theory, efficiency is implied by a positive-sum game where all players can benefit, in contrast to a zero-sum or negative-sum game where the winners' gains are matched by the other players' losses. In contrast to efficiency, equity – if interpreted to mean equalizing the distribution of income and wealth – means reducing some people's welfare in order to increase that of others, unless all those from whom wealth is redistributed obtain utility from the transfer. The focus of economists on efficiency gives rise to a crucial difference between the progressive perspective on the conduct of economic policy and that of latter-day political scientists. This is succinctly expressed by Riker: 'Most economic activity is viewed as a non-zero-sum game while the most important political activity is often viewed as zero-sum' (Riker 1962: 174).

Thus economists in the progressive tradition presume that economic policy making, which necessarily involves political choice mechanisms, should be directed at securing mutual gains. The progressive approach has adopted two strategies for sanitizing economic policy from the messy conflicts of values and interests that is the terrain of politics. One is to presume that the objective function will be determined by the political process, informed by economic knowledge, and given to the professional economic policy makers to maximize using their scientific knowledge of the means. The second strategy is to attempt to devise policy criteria which command an overwhelming consensus. The only one to satisfy this condition – leaving aside the thorny problem of equity – is the Pareto criterion: a policy measure is efficient if it benefits one or more persons in society without reducing another person's welfare. The problem with this definition is that it rules out making judgements in favour of most policy changes. The solution has been to develop a public interest criterion, used in techniques such as cost–benefit analysis, whereby a measure is deemed socially beneficial if the losers' losses are estimated to be less than the beneficiaries' gains (Schultz 1982: 62–3). This is frequently not accepted by the losers, as shown by environmentalists' protests over road building, airport extensions and nuclear power reactors.

It has always been recognized that efficiency could be achieved without an equitable distribution of income and that the acceptability of the efficiency criterion depended on a prior (Wicksell 1896) or separate resolution of the equity issue (Bergson 1954; Musgrave 1957). In the progressive conceptualization of the economic policy-making process, equity is left to the political system to resolve. In the period following the Second World War until the middle of the 1970s, this stance was buttressed by a general consensus in favour of an active and expanding state role in redistribution, and this enabled economists to proceed with attempts to apply efficiency criteria to policy making.

The instruments of economic policy

In the progressive view, the means for achieving the objectives of economic policy are determined on a scientific basis using evidence derived from positive economics on what effects particular policy instruments will have. This evidence is obtained from constructing predictive economic theories and ascertaining their validity by testing them against the empirical evidence, mainly in the form of secondary statistical data on recorded past values of variables. In the early days of this methodology there was considerable optimism that it would narrow down differences of opinion, since these were held to be mainly due to disagreements about facts and not about values (Friedman 1953). In the 1940s and 1950s, managing the economy was modelled on controlling a mechanical device, now immortalized at the London School of Economics by the restoration of Phillips's mechanical water-driven model of the Keynesian multiplier. The purpose of economic research was to accumulate knowledge about how the machine worked, what bits needed to be altered and how it could be manipulated to maximize the policy makers' objective function.

This rational approach, with its clear separation of objectives from the means to achieve them, was set out formally as the 'theory of economic policy', as in Tinbergen (1956). The policy makers' objective function is expressed in terms of a number of economic variables, such as national output, unemployment and inflation, and is maximized subject to the constraints imposed by the workings of the economy, captured in key equations which constitute the model of the economy. The objectives of economic policy are necessarily dependent variables; the value of each is determined in the model by the interaction of the other variables. Some of the variables in the model are independent – their values are determined outside the economic system. Those independent variables upon which the government can directly operate are the policy instruments. The usual ones are fiscal policy (tax rates and government spending) and monetary policy (money supply, interest rates and the exchange rate). Tinbergen's work (ibid.) drew attention to the important constraint that if a government is to achieve all its stated objectives then it must have at least the same number of independent policy instruments as it has separate policy objectives. Successful macroeconomic policy requires the simultaneous achievement of internal balance ('full' employment and low inflation) with external balance (balance-of-payments equilibrium). Given the trade-off between inflation and unemployment (Phillips 1958), fiscal or monetary policy has to be assigned to selecting some combination of the two, while the remaining instrument is assigned to external balance. From this perspective insufficient independent policy instruments led to inconsistency and hence disconti-nuity in government policy and was seen as the underlying cause of stop–go cycles in the UK. Prices and incomes policies were tried in the 1960s and 1970s as the solution to the missing third instrument. Monetarists criticized prices and incomes controls for distorting the price mechanism and hence harming efficiency, while practical experience led to the more widely held feeling that such controls did not work in the longer term.

The retreat from the optimistic and mechanistic view of economic manage-ment since the mid-1970s is associated with the attack on Keynesian economics on both theoretical and empirical grounds and with evident failures in demand management. At the micro level, debate over the appropriate instruments of economic policy has revolved around the extent to which government should replace or redirect the market. The progressive view, that this is a pragmatic matter not an ideological one, is not born out in the writings of libertarians and Marxists. The topics of economic management and the respective roles of government and market are now examined further. Although disagreement still rages, there has been a significant shift in opinion since the late 1970s towards lower expectations from demand management and a greater reliance on market forces.

ECONOMIC MANAGEMENT

The theoretical basis of Keynesianism is that the economy is not self-regulat-ing: when there is a fall in aggregate demand, firms do not cut prices so as to increase demand. Keynes (1936) argued that money wages would not fall since workers resist cuts in their money wages because these reduce their wages relative to other workers. However, when there is involuntary unemployment, workers will accept lower real wages provided these come about through general price rises. Thus an increase in demand brought about by the govern-ment would raise the price level and so reduce real money wages causing firms to employ more labour.

Keynes's *General Theory* (Keynes 1936) reflected the key economic features of the 1930s – stable prices and the relative economic autarky brought about by controls and protectionist policies introduced in the First World War and the inter-war Depression. The simple Keynesian models propounded in the 1940s and 1950s reflected these two factors by assuming a closed economy and fixed prices. These models proved unrealistic. The Phillips curve showed a trade-off between inflation and unemployment, while the need to correct balance-of-payments deficits in order to maintain the fixed exchange rates of the Bretton Woods system (1944–71) led to stop–go policies. By later stan-dards, unemployment and inflation remained low in the 1950s and only began creeping noticeably upwards in the late 1960s when the USA had embarked upon Keynesian tax cutting to raise output, together with higher expenditure on social programmes and the Vietnam war.

Though monetarism had begun in Chicago by the late 1940s, carrying on pre-Keynesian traditions, it made a major advance with Friedman's 1968 critique of the Phillips trade-off between unemployment and inflation. Friedman (1968) put forward the now widely accepted theory that this trade-off is only temporary. It only lasts while economic agents' expectations of inflation, which are based entirely on their past experience of inflation, are below the current level of inflation. While these mistaken expectations persist, workers expect real wages to be higher than they turn out to be and so more labour is employed by firms. Once actual and expected inflation are again equal, real wages are perceived at their correct higher level and employment falls back to its equilibrium or 'natural' level. Thus Keynesian demand management only increases employment temporarily above its natural level. This higher level can only be maintained by accelerating inflation, which is ultimately due to too rapid an expansion of the money supply. The monetarist's policy remedy is to stop the futile effort of lowering unemployment by increasing aggregate demand. The way to reduce the natural rate of unemployment is by greater flexibility in the labour market, with larger differentials in wages for different regions and types of work and greater mobility of labour. The unprecedented experience in the 1970s of rising inflation and unemployment, which was not then explained by Keynesian models, increased the credibility of monetarism and it came to dominate official economic thinking. Whereas countries of the Organization for Economic Co-operation and Development (OECD) had responded to the 1973 oil price crisis by expanding demand and subsequently experiencing low or negative growth accompanied by high inflation, they reacted to the 1980 oil crisis by tight monetary policies which produced a sharp downturn followed by a long upswing.

Economists' understanding of how the linkages between economies are transmitted through trade, capital flows and exchange rates proved inadequate in the face of changes in the international monetary order. When the Bretton Woods fixed exchange rate system finally collapsed in 1971, many economists advocated flexible exchange rates. Keynesians thought it would ease the balance-of-payments constraint on domestic demand management, while monetarists thought markets should be better than governments at determining equilibrium exchange rates. The new monetarist approach to the balance of payments (McKinnon 1981) deduced that flexible exchange rates would allow governments to choose their own inflation rate rather than having to accept the world inflation rate. The new theory focused on the demand and supply of stocks of international financial assets in contrast to Keynesian theory which was focused on trade flows. The latter was appropriate for the 1950s when capital flows were highly regulated and small. In the course of the 1960s and

1970s, international capital flows were gradually deregulated and expanded enormously. In 1979 the UK abolished the remaining exchange controls on capital transactions and all the major EC economies were due to have done so by 1990. In the event, the optimism of economists about flexible exchange rates was misplaced. Exchange rates have proved volatile and have been judged to overshoot their equilibrium values, thus casting doubt on the ability of foreign exchange markets to promote smooth economic adjustment. The US trade deficit in the 1980s was therefore accompanied by a high dollar which helped to provoke a spate of protectionism.

Macroeconomic theory has undergone profound changes, many of them in response to economic developments which the majority of economists had not anticipated. But the key issue for macroeconomics is still the one Keynes addressed – the interlinkages between the real economy (goods and services) and the monetary economy (financial assets). To what extent can nominal changes (for example, in the domestic price level and the exchange rate) provoke undesirable real changes and to what extent can they be harnessed to help smooth the adjustment to real changes (for example, a collapse of investment, increased union militancy, a decline in export competitiveness)? These central theoretical questions have their counterparts on the political agenda. How important is containing inflation for the stability and progress of the economy? How important is it to have a fixed exchange rate in order keep inflation low and to foster trade through relative price stability, or is it still important for a government to retain the discretion over the exchange rate? Outsiders listening in on disagreements between macroeconomists may fail to appreciate that most of them work within a common set of models incorporating both Keynesian and monetarist features. One clear impact of monetarism is the acceptance by policy makers that the exchange rate and the money supply are interdependent policy instruments. A country cannot have a fixed exchange rate and an independent monetary policy. If it wants an independent monetary policy then the exchange rate must be allowed to adjust to the level consistent with the country's money supply growth and interest rates.

Now that models are more complicated and encompass more permutations of possible assumptions, a greater variety of predictions is generated. Which results one finds more plausible will depend on how closely one judges the assumptions of the model accord with reality. Keynesians prefer models in which prices are sticky and so markets do not clear; monetarists prefer models with flexible prices. Developments in macroeconomics have shown quite clearly that economics cannot place in the hands of policy makers a set of tools and instructions based on a well-known and tested technology for managing the economy.

MARKETS AND THE ROLE OF GOVERNMENT

The second most significant development in economic policy in the 1980s has been the reduction of the role of government in economic affairs and the increase in the influence of market forces. This has been a worldwide phenomenon, experienced not only in countries such as the USA and the UK, with radical right governments, but also in those under social democratic governments as in France, Australia and New Zealand.

One aspect of the reassertion of market forces has been the move away from Keynesian reliance on demand management, to foster growth in output, to emphasizing the supply side or structure of the economy. The appropriate policy instruments are micro-level ones to encourage increased industrial efficiency through restructuring, research and development, investment, training and greater competition (Levačić 1988). Such structural emphasis is evident in the policy stance of the OECD, the International Monetary Fund (IMF) and the World Bank (see, for example, OECD 1989). There are a number of key features of supply-side policies, in particular privatization and deregulation (Swann 1988; Vickers and Yarrow 1988). Another is concern with the effects of taxation on incentives to work, save, invest and take risks. Governments have lowered the proportion of gross domestic product taken in tax and restructured their tax systems by cutting high marginal tax rates and tax exemptions. Both the supply-side desire to reduce taxation and state control of industry and the monetarist emphasis on the inflationary impact of government budget deficits led to curtailment in the growth of government spending in the 1980s, a condition frequently required by the IMF when providing structural assistance to countries with international debt problems. With the loss of confidence in state bureaucracies to run commercial activities efficiently, there has been a decisive shift towards reliance on markets across the political spectrum. It is now on the agendas of democratic socialists (Le Grand and Estrin 1989) and, most spectacularly, in the former communist states of Eastern Europe for whom the transition to a market or market socialist economy is an uncharted sea.

However, the extent to which this should occur remains controversial. In the progressive view, the appropriate use of markets is a technical issue to be resolved pragmatically with respect to each particular case by applying neo-classical welfare theory (Barr 1987, 1989). This view predominated in the 1950s and 1960s but was increasingly attacked by the libertarians favouring market solutions, which have been well publicized in the UK by the Institute of Economic Affairs. This debate has revealed how both the welfare economics and libertarian perspectives on the case for markets are founded on a different value basis. As Buchanan (1987) has reiterated, neo-classical welfare economics presumes that government is a benign dictator taking decisions in the best interests of society, and so is modelled as maximizing a social welfare function. The libertarian view, developed particularly in the field of public choice economics (Mueller 1989), is that when participating in collective decision making through political institutions, citizens, politicians and public sector bureaucrats act in their own self-interest, aiming to secure government redistributive transfers. Thus politics is a zero- or negative-sum game rather than the positive-sum game presumed in the progressive view. So both neo-classical welfare economists and libertarians are partisan advocates of particular value systems.

An illustration of the use of economics as partisan advocacy of efficiency is environmental policy where neo-classical welfare economists and libertarians have similar views (Beckerman 1990). The latter accept that pollution is an external cost which is not reflected in market prices. Consequently consumers pay less than the full social costs, including pollution, of the goods they consume. Thus the market leads to inefficient resource allocation. There are two types of policies for reducing pollution. The first, and most popular, is physical controls: limits are placed on permitted levels of pollution, and firms may be prosecuted for breaching them. The second is using the price system by taxing the product or charging the firm for licences to discharge pollutants, where the higher the permissible limit the greater the charge. Economists favour pollution taxes because they are more efficient than physical controls, as only those products which consumers value more highly, reflected in the extra price they are willing to pay for pollution rights, will be produced. Production will be cut back far more on those products consumers value less. Outside the economics profession, however, the tax solution to controlling pollution is much less popular than direct controls. To an economist's way of thinking this is due to an irrational dislike of polluters being able to pay for polluting rather than being stopped or limited by a government edict. Thus the advocacy of taxes and licence charges for reducing environmental damage is an example of using economics as a partisan interest. As Nelson remarks, a hallmark of economics as an ideology is 'a conviction that government should be actively used for achieving social goals – preferably by manipulating the competitive market mechanism, rather than command and control methods' (Nelson 1987: 58).

RULES VERSUS DISCRETION IN RELATION TO CURRENT POLICY ISSUES

Whether policy makers should use discretion or abide by rules in the conduct of economic policy has been an overarching issue for many decades and applies to a wide range of policy areas.

Keynesian demand management is a good example of discretionary policy, especially the fine-tuning variety practised in the UK from the 1950s to the 1970s, when government adjusted tax rates and credit conditions as it felt economic conditions required at any time during the financial year. Monetary policy conducted via daily central bank intervention in the money markets is another important area of discretionary policy. In contrast, rules involve the government committing itself to specified actions, often contingent upon particular circumstances prevailing.

The advocacy of policy rules by economists has come from two major sources – constitutional political economy (Brennan and Buchanan 1985) and macroeconomic theory. The constitutionalists link their approach with social contract theorists. Their concern is to protect the citizen from state coercion by having agreed limits on government action. A key argument put forward by Brennan and Buchanan is that precommitment by government is needed to prevent the democratic collective decision-making process being dominated by zero-sum transfers between groups instead of serving its prime function of promoting positive-sum, and hence socially efficient, collective agreements. Government budget deficits and inflation are cited as important examples of concealed means by which governments redistribute income away from certain groups without their consent. Government budget deficits transfer income from future generations to the current one; inflation is the means whereby government uses its monopoly of the issue of money to finance expenditures which benefit some groups at the expense of those whose assets lose value. The constitutionalists argue for a constitutional rule forbidding government budget deficits, especially over a period of years. The Gramm–Rudmann–Hollings Act of 1985 was an attempt to impose such a precommitment on Congress in order to eliminate the US budget deficit gradually. It has so far failed because of loopholes permitting creative accounting.

A significant theoretical development has been the introduction into economic models of rational expectations, whereby economic agents form their expectations on the basis of all available information, including government policy changes. Agents, in money markets in particular, form their expectations about inflation, interest rates and exchange rates on the basis of what they observe governments doing. So if economic agents are not convinced that a government will act to reduce inflation, they will not expect a fall in inflation. They will set prices, including nominal interest rates, assuming higher inflation and so make it more difficult for a government to bring it down. Therefore it is important for governments to establish a reputation for credible policies through precommitment or rules (Kydland and Prescott 1977).

Monetarists in the 1970s advocated rules for limiting the growth of the money supply and these were instituted in a number of countries. Monetary targets proved difficult to implement in the USA and the UK because of instability in the relationships between the money stock and national income and difficulties in defining and controlling the money supply in a period of rapid financial innovation. Economists and policy makers have now turned to the exchange rate as offering a better rule for restraining inflation and promoting stability. Given the unsatisfactory experience of flexible exchange rates since the collapse of Bretton Woods, governments have sought forms of international economic policy co-ordination (Artis and Ostry 1986). The Exchange Rate Mechanism (ERM) or the European Monetary System (EMS) in which EC currencies keep within a fixed band was set up in 1979, though sterling remained outside. The ERM is, in effect, a Deutschmark currency area. The general verdict (Brittan and Artis 1989) is that it has been quite successful in reducing inflation and exchange-rate volatility between the EMS currencies.

The proposals to create monetary union between EC members is a prime example of a rule which will limit governments' discretion. As a common currency is a permanently fixed exchange rate, governments would no longer be able to use exchange rate adjustment to alter the relative price level of their domestic goods *vis-à-vis* those of other member countries and so counteract changes in competitiveness due to non-monetary factors. With a common currency an EC institution to control the supply of monetary assets is needed. For monetarists this central bank must, like the Bundesbank, be constitutionally independent of the government and charged with preserving price stability. This would prevent the excessive issue of monetary assets to finance government budget deficits in response to political pressures for redistributive transfers. It is ironic that the advocacy of discretion with respect to EC policy making is common to both social democrats and UK Conservatives who share a predilection for keeping monetary and fiscal policy in the hands of government politicians.

A return to fixed exchange rates is the adoption of a policy rule which constrains national economic sovereignty in order to achieve, it is hoped, greater stability and so promote economic development. A weaker form of international policy co-ordination is the summits of the Group of Seven finance ministers which, since 1985, have attempted to agree to exchange rate bands supported by mutual action. This form of concerted action still leaves national governments with considerable scope for discretion – and reneging.

CONCLUSION

In focusing on the interrelationship between economics and economic policy, this essay has sketched out in broad terms the major shifts in economic policy concerns and in economic thinking. The verdict of experience over the post-war years is that the progressive view of economic policy making has lost credibility. An important factor in this has been the inability to develop a scientifically robust body of knowledge and the increasing realization that this is due to the nature of the subject rather than to inadequacy of technique. Even though economists still pay frequent lip service to the value-free stance of positivism (for example, Helm 1989: 11), in practice economics is either a partisan advocacy of its particular viewpoint of economic policy as the rational pursuit of the public interest (for example, Henderson 1986) or it is used to bolster particular interests. This state of affairs does not mean that there is no factual or common theoretical basis for the formulation of economic policy; there clearly is, as one can see by the popular shift of opinion away from state administration of commercial activities which is in response to observed events and which confirms the assessment of a broad spectrum of economics. The conclusion must be that making economic policy recommendations is not a purely technical activity; it involves an interaction between economic theory, empirical evidence and political values in which all are mutually affected.

REFERENCES

Artis, M. and Ostry, S. (1986) *International Economic Policy Coordination*, London: Routledge & Kegan Paul.
Barr, N. (1987) *The Economics of the Welfare State*, London: Weidenfeld & Nicolson.
——(1989) 'Social insurance as an efficiency device', *Journal of Public Policy* 9 (1): 59–82.
Beckerman, W. (1990) *Pricing for Pollution*, 2nd edn, London: Institute of Economic Affairs.
Bergson, A. (1954) 'On the concept of social welfare,' *Quarterly Journal of Economics* 68: 233–53.
Boulding, K. (1959) *Principles of Economic Policy*, London: Staples Press.
Brennan, G. and Buchanan, J. (1985) *The Reason of Rules*, Cambridge: Cambridge University Press.
Brittan, S. and Artis, M. (1989) *Europe Without Currency Barriers*, London: Social Market Foundation.
Buchanan, J. (1987) 'The constitution of economic policy', *American Economic Review* 77 (3): 243–50.
Friedman, M. (1953) *Essays in Positive Economics*, part I, Chicago: Chicago University Press.
——(1968) 'The role of monetary policy', *American Economic Review* 58: 1–17.
Helm, D. (ed.) (1989) *The Economic Borders of the State*, Oxford: Oxford University Press.
Henderson, D. (1986) *Innocence and Design: The Influence of Economic Ideas on Economic Policy*, Oxford: Basil Blackwell.
Keynes, J. (1936) *The General Theory of Employment, Interest and Money*, London: Macmillan.
Kydland, F. E. and Prescott, E. C. (1977) 'Rules rather than discretion: the inconsistency of optimal plans', *Journal of Political Economy* 19: 473–92.
Le Grand, J. and Estrin, S. (eds) (1989) *Market Socialism*, Oxford: Clarendon Press.

Levačić, R. (1987) *Economic Policy Making: Its Principles and Practice*, Brighton: Harvester/Wheatsheaf.

———(1988) *Supply Side Economics*, Oxford: Heinemann.

Lindblom, C. (1977) *Politics and Markets*, New York: Basic Books.

———(1987) 'Who needs what social research for policy making?', in W. R. Shadish and C. S. Reichart (eds) *Evaluation Studies Review Annual*, Berkeley: Sage Publications; London: Macmillan.

McKinnon, R. (1981) 'The exchange rate and macroeconomic policy: changing postwar perceptions', *Journal of Economic Literature* 19: 531–57.

Mueller, D. C. (1989) *Public Choice II*, Cambridge: Cambridge University Press.

Musgrave, R. (1957) 'A multiple theory of budget determination', *Finanzarchiv* new series no. 3.

———(1986) *Public Finance in a Democratic Society*, vol. 1, Brighton: Harvester/Wheatsheaf, chapter 2,.

Nelson, R. (1987) 'The economics profession and the making of public policy', *Journal of Economic Literature* 25 (1): 49–91.

OECD (1989) *Report on Surveillance of Structural Policies*, Paris: OECD.

Phillips, A. W. (1958) 'The relation between unemployment and the rate of change of money wage rates in the UK 1861–1957', *Economica* 15: 283–99.

Pigou, A. W. (1920) *The Economics of Welfare*, London: Macmillan.

Riker, W. H. (1962) *The Theory of Political Coalitions*, New Haven: Yale University Press.

Schultz, C. (1982) 'The role and responsibilities of the economist in government', *American Economic Review* 72 (2): 62–6.

Swann, D. (1988) *The Retreat of the State*, Ann Arbor: University of Michigan Press.

Tinbergen, J. (1956) *Economic Policy: Principles and Design*, Amsterdam: North-Holland.

Vickers, J. and Yarrow, G. (1988) *Privatization: An Economic Analysis*, London: MIT Press.

Wicksell, K. (1896) 'A new principle of just taxation', in *Finanztheoretische Untersuchungen*, Jena; reprinted 1967 in *Classics in the Theory of Public Finance*, eds R. Musgrave and A. T. Peacock, New York: St Martin's Press.

FURTHER READING

Artis, M. and Ostry, S. (1986) *International Economic Policy Coordination*, London: Routledge & Kegan Paul.

Barr, N. (1987) *The Economics of the Welfare State*, London: Weidenfeld & Nicolson.

Boulding, K. (1959) *Principles of Economic Policy*, London: Staples Press.

Brittan S. and Artis, M. (1989) *Europe Without Currency Barriers*, London: Social Market Foundation.

Buchanan, J. (1987) 'The constitution of economic policy', *American Economic Review* 77 (3): 243–50.

Dell, S. (ed.) (1988) *Policies for Development*, London: Macmillan.

Ellman, M. (1989) *Socialist Planning*, Cambridge: Cambridge University Press.

Greenaway, D. (ed.) (1989) *Current Issues in Macroeconomics*, London: Macmillan.

Helm, D. (ed.) (1989) *The Economic Borders of the State*, Oxford: Oxford University Press.

Henderson, D. (1986) *Innocence and Design: The Influence of Economic Ideas on Economic Policy*, Oxford: Basil Blackwell.

Hitiris, T. (1989) *European Community Economics*, Hemel Hempstead: Harvester/Wheatsheaf.

Krueger, A. O. (1983) *Exchange Rate Determination*, Cambridge: Cambridge University Press.

Le Grand, J. and Estrin, S. (eds) (1989) *Market Socialism*, Oxford: Clarendon Press.

Levačić, R. (1987) *Economic Policy Making: Its Principles and Practice*, Brighton: Wheatsheaf.

Mueller, D. C. (1989) *Public Choice II*, Cambridge: Cambridge University Press.

Nelson, R. (1987) 'The economics profession and the making of public policy', *Journal of Economic Literature* 25 (1): 49–91.

Pechman, J. (1989) *Tax Reform*, Hemel Hempstead: Harvester/Wheatsheaf.

Swann, D. (1988) *The Retreat of the State*, Ann Arbor: University of Michigan Press.

Vickers, J. and Yarrow, G. (1988) *Privatization: An Economic Analysis*, London: MIT Press.

Wolf, C. (1988) *Markets or Governments: Choosing Between Imperfect Alternatives*, Cambridge, Mass.: MIT Press.

41

EDUCATION POLICY

PASCAL GRUSON AND MAURICE KOGAN

The study of educational policy must take account of both the substantive policy issues and the processes and structures through which they are formed and mediated. Many of the substantive changes in education as they have evolved since 1945 in the most developed countries derive from attempts to meet challenges presented by an environment of social, economic and political change. These changes have taken the form of attempts to modify the curriculum and organizational structures of school and higher education and the politics and government of education. The latter evince characteristics somewhat different from other areas of public policy, although attempts have been made to apply general political and sociological theory to a mass of changing empirical examples.

In this essay some of the substantive policy issues that have emerged in developed countries since 1945 will be related to changes in the modes of educational government and politics. The patterns of change do not match well the somewhat haphazard attempts that have been made to develop theories of educational policy and politics which are mainly concerned to apply explanatory language to complex historical phenomena. These are, however, briefly examined in the later sections of this essay.

SOCIAL, ECONOMIC AND POLITICAL ENVIRONMENT

Educational systems in countries that have attained a high level of economic development have changed considerably since the Second World War. All have had to face demands that have been not only increasingly diverse but also evolving rapidly. Educational growth was the result only in part of population changes which fluctuated greatly in many countries. It was also a response to demands arising from expanding economies and changes in client expectations.

Until the Second World War, education systems could meet the expectations of their social and economic environments. But the demands were limited in scope. All educational systems were binary in nature and offered compulsory education of short duration and longer cycles of education for excellence directed to the elite. Compulsory education had a strong socialization purpose, and provided basic skills that might be topped up, but for the majority often were not, with short vocational or 'on the job' training. Elite education was offered either through humanistic education, or through high level technical training, in order to qualify key staff in the vital sectors of the economy, politics or education. Access was very selective.

As a result of the rapid development of the Western economies after the Second World War, educational expectations were greatly changed. Many countries were slow to meet the new challenge to provide a larger work-force readily adaptable to technical changes. When, however, policy makers began to make the link between economic growth and educational opportunity they also became increasingly concerned with education as a means of equalizing life chances, and of securing social justice. The two themes of economic efficiency and of equality became locked into an unresolved dialectic; some urged that equality of opportunity would improve performance while others asserted the economic need for excellence and selectivity. The conflicting claims of equality and skills for the economy affected educational policy at every turn and became explicit in conflicts over the curriculum, over access to the more esteemed forms of education and over questions of who should control and govern the schools.

There were different stages of policy evolution. Expansion began on the traditional assumption that investment in inputs – teachers, buildings and time spent in school and higher education – would automatically build up a good society and strong economy. As these hopes became increasingly disappointed, attention turned to processes of defined educational ability and knowledge, and to the ways in which the products of education should be evaluated.

Changing institutional structures

Both efficiency and equality policies affected the institutional structures of educational institutions. Western governments at first answered the demands for increased access by enlarging their previously elite systems. But in almost all countries, structures changed to meet the twin demands for access for economic growth and for more equal opportunity. This led, from the beginning of the 1960s, to the creation or expansion of comprehensive schools in Britain, the *Gesamtschulen* in the Federal Republic of Germany and the *Collèges* in France, while in the United States, the public high schools system was to become the sole provider of compulsory schooling until the age of 16 or 18.

In higher education, similar trends could be observed. Both to meet the growing and changing needs of the labour market and to provide wider opportunities, the more traditional forms of higher education were paralleled by new structures. Some were 'binary' in form, allowing for the growth of institutions which provided more directly vocational teaching, research and development in institutions separate from universities: for example, Polytechnics in the UK, the *Instituts Universitaires de Technologie* in France and the *Fachhochschulen* in Germany. In other countries there were attempts to create comprehensive universities, such as the *Gesamthochschulen* in West Germany and the regional arrangements in Sweden. In the USA, the Community Colleges underpinned a diverse structure containing both selective and comprehensive institutions. In the 1990s the trend is towards unitary structures, within which, however, there might be a hierarchy of esteem and resource.

Curriculum and governance

During the period of growth and expansion, roughly from 1945 until the oil crises of the early 1970s, developments were mainly professionally led. Teachers and administrators recruited from teaching felt confident that they could meet the need of the economy for new skills and of society for more equality of provision and opportunity. In some school systems, growth was accompanied by substantial reform of the curriculum intended to make pupils capable of critical reasoning, although, as successive OECD reports on educational systems showed, the majority remained committed to formal and teacher-dominated forms of learning. Whatever the degree of change in educational content, however, criticism grew which was eventually to affect radically concepts and modes of educational governance. Progressive or child-centred education, where it existed, was thought to be advanced at the expense of competence in basic skills and expertise in foreign languages, sciences and other disciplines. These complaints implied a belief in return to the previous selective forms of education.

But a conflicting complaint was that schools and higher education had failed to achieve social equality. In that area of educational objectives, there had been an evolution from the 'soft' or 'weak' concept of educational opportunity which would grant all children the right to compete for the more favoured forms of education, to the 'hard' or 'strong' concept which argued the importance of providing equality of outcomes, if necessary by positive discrimination or affirmative action in favour of the disadvantaged (Crosland 1962). At the same time, sociologists (Jencks *et al.* 1973; Boudon 1973) were raising doubts about the inherent capability of education to cause social change. Were not systems in their very nature contradictory to any democratic process, being only capable of breeding the current social order (Bourdieu and Passeron 1970)? Education was assailed from all sides, right and left, and the very authority of received forms of knowledge and the power of those who transmitted it came under attack from the sociology of knowledge as well as from those seeking the inculcation of instrumental working skills and social discipline.

The changing patterns of belief in educational content and institutional organization affected modes of educational governance. The treatment of the curriculum had always been a political issue but now became more explicitly contentious. Most countries had sustained strong public control of the content and methods of education, sometimes, as in France and the Scandinavian countries, through nationally determined and enforced curricula. But others, particularly the UK and some of the American states, had increasingly allowed schools to pursue 'progressive' forms of learning. In the first and majority group of countries, the tendency was towards devolution of control from the centre to the local authorities and the schools (see, for example, the Norwegian trends described by Granheim *et al.* 1990). Similar trends in higher education towards the liberalization of central control over content in those countries previously most restrictive, but under more complex conditions, became observable in the 1980s (Van Vught 1989; Teichler 1989). Where control over institutions was relaxed, in either the schools or higher education, the demands of employment and of consumers were expected to replace or complement the prescriptions of central government. In some countries however, particularly the UK, the teacher-created curriculum was to be replaced by a national curriculum in which a prescribed core, with periodic testing, was enforced (Maclure 1988).

Changes in assumptions about the requirements for the curriculum, therefore, were being pressed from different directions. The states that had been most prescriptive sought to create modes of steerage in which evaluation and client pressure, sometimes presented through different forms of real or simulated markets, were to be left in the schools and higher education institutions. The more liberal and teacher-centred systems, however, were to find professional dominance replaced by requirements of the centre, to be reinforced by stronger managerial systems.

Models of governance and accountability in school systems

Accompanying these changes were parallel shifts in the processes of accountability and evaluation. In the 1960s and 1970s the bulk of academic literature (for example, House 1980) had endorsed liberal and professionally led forms of accountability in which teachers might evaluate themselves but expect their evaluation to be subject to increased client – as opposed to political or bureaucratic – control. By the late 1970s, however, it was possible to discern four forms of accountability (Kogan 1988).

The four forms were: public or state control and managerialist accountability; professional accountability; and two consumerist modes of account-ability: partnership and free market. The dominant mode was that of public or state control and its associated connotations of managerial forms of governing structure. In those countries where the central ministries remained dominant, a direct line might run from the national authorities to schools or via local or regional authorities. Even in those countries where schools had traditionally been free, there would be lines of accountability between the heads of schools and the public authorities above them, and between heads of schools and teachers. Increasingly it had been noted how head teachers might be both chief executives and leading professionals (see, for example, Hughes 1976), but that was essentially a matter of style and process and did not affect the fundamental authority arrangements. If, however, the lines were managerial, the managers were themselves mainly drawn from the teaching profession and the professionally orientated bureaucrat was the key factor in reconciling professionalism and public accountability.

The professional accountability model (for example, Elliott *et al.* 1981; Sockett 1980) was intended to meet two objectives. The first was to protect schools from demands for product-orientated outcomes and to allow them to engage in self-evaluation and self-report. On the basis of that the laity might then form a judgement. The second objective was claimed to be to achieve greater responsiveness to clients, and it was felt that this could not happen if the structure was managerial. Hence professional accountability led to concepts of self-reporting with or without mechanisms for making that report the basis of accountability.

The third mode of control was that of the consumer, in which it was argued that there should be a 'partnership' between teachers and their clients, as represented by the parents of pupils, and that the relationship between schools and parents must go beyond the metaphors and thinking of the market place (Sallis 1979). Clients should participate in a partnership and not in a relation-ship of dependency on the professional. Indeed, even the metaphors of client and consumer might be thought unsatisfactory in this way of thinking. Essen-tially the model assumed that parents must share responsibility, and hence power, with the school for the education of children. These arguments for changes in control, implying as they did some move towards client or consumer control, were first most cogently argued in those American school systems where there were demands for the decentralization of large school systems, held to be in thrall to teacher unions, towards community control (for example, for Oceanshill and Brownsville in New York City, see Berube and Gittels 1969). In some systems, notably in the UK, provision was made for the control of schools to pass from a local authority to the governing body, on which parents and others were represented, who were to have power to appoint teachers and handle the bulk of their budgets (Department of Education and Science 1988).

A fourth model was that of the consumerist type of control that depended upon free-market analogies. This first surfaced as voucher schemes in which the control would be those of the family over the school (Coons and Sugarman 1978). Public authority monopoly over education should thus be broken. Vouchers could be used to equalize the opportunities of children from different social backgrounds. Whilst explicit voucher schemes remained a rarity, the power of parental choice of school, again potently exemplified in recent British practice and law, and the ability of schools to opt out of local authority control, might have the same effect because they enable schools to flourish or wither according to parental judgements of their competence.

The four forms of control can be viewed in different ways. The professional model is clearly different from all the other three inasmuch as it does assume that education requires esoteric knowledge and the use of legitimate power on the part of the professionals. The other models are all to some degree anti-professional although the state control of education is often in the hands of professionals with delegated power from the state. It has been noted (Wirt 1977) that the control might move in cyclical fashion from professionals to the laity. The professionals retain control until discontent with the distribution of resources and power is felt by enough members of the laity – either politicians or consumers – to demand change. At that point, lay beliefs in the nature of education and its control become dominant. But in time, because educational policies have to become operational through the curriculum and institutional arrangements, power and authority move back to the professionals who may take note of the shift in popular demands.

MODELS OF GOVERNANCE IN HIGHER EDUCATION

Similar changes in the governance of higher education began to emerge in the 1980s (Van Vught 1989; Becher and Kogan 1991). The model of the self-governing or collegial institution, to be found in the most prestigious British and US cases, remains powerful. It essentially implies control by the professionals. It has been taken to imply processes of governance that are non-managerial, based on a political rather than a rationalistic planning mode of behaviour (Baldridge et al. 1978), and conducting themselves as an 'organized anarchy' (Cohen and March 1974).

The traditional, professional model of higher education government is being challenged by governments who seek to supplant it by forms of governance and control in which the central government takes on powerful steerage functions. At the same time, and increasingly during the 1980s, governments and trustees press the case for institutions to behave as actors in a market. Higher education institutions should then look to clients who would pay money for some of their services. At the same time, governments might set up paramarkets through which they require institutions to compete, perhaps even through a formal bidding process as in the UK, for their clients and resources.

At the end of the 1970s, Western economic development was still declining and education was no longer seen as an impregnable fortress of social policies. As the welfare state gave way to radical conservative policies in many countries, so educational policy became more hard edged and product oriented. But the numbers of students were still increasing, as was the demand for graduates. Governments chose, as we have seen, to move away from holistic policies and forms of governance towards systems to be differentiated according to local and market demands on them. Schools and universities were made responsible for their outputs on a new basis. Whilst institutions might become free to play with market forces, at least in some countries, some systems also imposed *dirigiste* policies at the same time. For example, the British government insisted on both the national curriculum and on both schools and higher education institutions operating in market modes which were both a response to the money economy outside (that is, seeking contracts, running short courses and the like) and on paramarket mechanisms by which, for example, higher education institutions had to 'bid' for the student places that they would offer. The French government, too, enlarged the access to university but secured minimum academic requirements through demands on institutions. At the same time, it opened the way to competition between universities, albeit on a rather confused basis, that might undermine its own capacity to keep control.

Education at all of its levels was beginning to form a prominent example of the 'Evaluative State' (Neave 1988). Performance measurement was being imposed on both higher education and on schools in many Western countries. As forms of direction and steerage became more complex, sometimes both more *dirigiste* and more dependent on inducing market behaviour, so the use of evaluation in its many forms of inspection and audit became more prominent (Henkel 1991). These all tended to reduce the power of professional control in the education systems.

ATTEMPTS TO APPLY THEORY

Given the complexities of policy and government described above – and the complexity has been reduced to a selective minimum – it is not surprising that the literature of educational policy began with essentially descriptive or prescriptive attempts to describe structures and how they worked. It was rarely critical of what existed, perhaps because it shared the assumption of those working within the system that education within publicly legitimated systems was an undisputed good. From the 1960s onwards, however, a full range of alternative versions emerged. They were of two kinds: attempts to apply main-line social science concepts to education and, later, attempts to join the anti-positivist movements through the perspectives of Marxists, feminists and the ethnic minorities.

The mainline theoretical treatments included excursions into systems theory, exchange and dependency theory; the operation of micropolitical systems; Marxist interpretations of the role of the state; community power structure; and pressure group theory (Whitaker 1982).

The use of Eastonian systems theory has informed many key attempts to describe analytically how education policy is formed and put into operation (see, for example, Wirt and Kirst 1975 for the USA, and Howell and Brown 1983 for UK higher education). A major, 'unslavish' application was made in Archer's account of the emergence of education systems (Archer 1979), which emphasizes the importance of structure in conditioning, if not wholly determining, behaviour. Each stage of development is described in terms of structure, interaction and elaboration; the process of change is described through the application of exchange theory.

Exchange and dependency theory have proved particularly useful in account-ing for the mysteries of the relationship between central and local government (Rhodes 1981; Ranson 1980). Organizations are dependent on others for resources which are exchanged through patterns of developed relationships. They generate degrees of power as a result of exchange, and from this different patterns of dependency emerge. The dependency of local authorities on the centre for resources and legal legitimacy is seen as reciprocated by its depen-dency on local government for the achievement of national goals.

An adjacent area has been the study of educational interest groups. They fit no rigorous theoretical frame and studies have been concerned to show how, at the national level at least, they might move into confrontational political modes as consensus about national policies breaks down, or as economic policy increasingly moves the locus of power away from their 'own' ministers (Coates 1972). They possess various degrees of legitimacy (Kogan 1975), determining their access to the policy arena. This restricted pluralism substantiates the notion of the policy community (Richardson and Jordan 1979) in which interest groups participate alongside the central bureaucracies. The extent to which they then help make, as opposed to modify, policies remains contentious. A recent account of British educational policy making by the Conservative Party barely refers to them (Knight 1990). At the local political level, by contrast, interest groups have been shown to be progressively less integrated into the policy-making system as local government has become increasingly politicized, that is, subject to the frameworks and oligarchies set up by the political parties (Jennings 1977; Widdicombe 1986).

If the bulk of studies has shifted and turned within pluralistic and systems theory derived assumptions, critique has come from two main sources: those concerned with the role of the state, and those drawing upon the sociology of knowledge to depict the artefactual nature of knowledge and its hold over academic stratification which is implicit in educational systems.

Of the first, British studies have been concerned with unmasking the consensus which obtained for two decades in Britain as part of the way in which capitalism sustained existing distributions of resource and power by rallying alliances of forces that might support it (CCCS 1981). A further version (Salter and Tapper 1981) of similar themes associates a growingly *dirigiste* role for central government with education's capacity to act as an agent of social control and to legitimize inequality through the sponsorship of a dominant educational ideology. This latter description of the immanent power and intentional ideology of central bureaucracy may have become outdated by the arrival of heroic ministers whose impulses cannot be easily related to bureaucratic continuity.

Intermediate between Marxist and pluralist explanations lie the growing number of corporatist accounts of power distribution, although not applied much to explanations of educational government. One version asserts:

> that the governments of liberal democracies have tried to persuade the leaders of many 'producer' groups in the pluralist cosmos to recognise their common interest, with each other and with government, in achieving a stable and long-lasting relationship in which the demands can be bargained and conflict contained.
>
> (McPherson and Raab 1988)

Thus elites move in partly pluralistic ways.

The sociology of knowledge has presented challenges to the more traditional and consensual versions of how education is governed, and in whose interests. Social class differences in educational benefits derive, it is maintained, from the definition of knowledge and of excellence that is incorporated in state and private schooling. This definition is biased against working-class pupils (Young 1971, quoted by McPherson and Raab 1988). Bernstein (1975) maintains that how a society selects, classifies, distributes and evaluates educational knowledge reflects the distribution of power and the nature of social control. Broadfoot (1983) describes a significant change in the basis of control of teaching in the classrooms from one based on structure to one based on ideology. Such versions could be convincingly linked, though no attempt has been made to do so, with the reduced power of teachers and scholars whose claims to command of a world of objective knowledge is thus challenged.

The ways in which policies are made can be further disputed between two perspectives which are particularly contestable in the field of education. The first perspective unites virtually all of the dominant academic traditions, from

Marxist through anti-positivist to traditional institutional studies. Those traditions assume that policies are the product of the action of those who hold power at the national and local levels, whether within government institutions or from the vantage points of the interest groups. Decisions may be made through an elite led system or pluralistically, with the interests of all of the people at heart or in the interests of particular classes. A second perspective is that 'the explanation of policy is not to be found solely in the beliefs, intentions and actions of the policy-makers of the time. A wider reference is required in history, social institutions and the practice of the schools' (McPherson and Raab 1988), a view echoed in some studies of higher education governance (for example, Becher and Kogan 1991). It does indeed seem likely that the most fruitful work in educational politics will come from those who are willing to link studies of content and forms of education with the analysis of the political processes and structures of educational action.

REFERENCES

Archer, M. S. (1979) *The Social Origins of Educational Systems*, London: Sage Publications.

Baldridge, J. V., Curtis, D. V., Ecker, G., and Riley, G. L. (1978) *Policy Making and Effective Leadership*, San Francisco: Jossey-Bass.

Becher, A. and Kogan, M. (1991) *Structure and Process in Higher Education*, London: Routledge.

Bernstein, B. (1975) *Class, Codes and Control*, Vol. 3: *Towards a Theory of Educational Transmission*, London: Routledge & Kegan Paul.

Berube, M and Gittell, M. (eds) (1969) *Confrontation at Ocean Hill Brownsville*, New York: Praeger.

Boudon, R. (1973) *Education, Opportunity and Social Equality*, New York: John Wiley & Sons.

Bourdieu, P. and Passeron, J. C. (1970) *La reproduction*, Paris: Éditions de Minuit.

Broadfoot, P. (1983) 'Central versus decentralized control in education', University of London Institute of Education, *Department of Education in Developing Countries, Annual Workshop*.

CCCS (1981) *Unpopular Education: Schooling and Social Democracy in England since 1944*, Centre for Contemporary Cultural Studies, London: Hutchinson.

Coates, R. D. (1972) *Teacher Unions and Interest Group Politics*, Cambridge: Cambridge University Press.

Cohen, M. D. and March, J. G. (1974) *Leadership and Ambiguity: The American College President*, New York: McGraw-Hill.

Coons, J. E. and Sugarman, S. D. (1978) *Education by Choice. The Case for Family Control*, Berkeley: University of California Press.

Crosland, A. (1962) *The Conservative Enemy*, London: Jonathan Cape.

Department of Education and Science (1988) *Education Reform Act 1988*, London: HMSO.

Elliot, J., Bridges, D., Ebbutt, D., Gibson, R. and Nias, J. (1981) *School Accountability: The SSRC Accountability Project*, Grant McIntyre.

Granheim, M., Kogan, M. and Lundgren, U. (1990) *Evaluation as Policy-Making. Introducing Evaluation into a National Decentralized Educational System*, London: Jessica Kingsley Publishers.

Henkel, M. (1991) *Government, Evaluation and Change*, London: Jessica Kingsley Publications.

House, E. R. (1980) *Evaluating With Validity*, Beverly Hills: Sage Publications.

Howell, D. H. and Brown, R. (1983) *Educational Policy Making: An Analysis*, London: Heinemann Educational Books.

Hughes, M. G. (1976) 'The professional-as-administrator: the case of the secondary school head', in R. S. Peters (ed.) *The Role of the Head*, London: Routledge & Kegan Paul.

Jencks, C. S., Smith, M., Acland, H., Bane, M. J., Cohen, M. and Gintis, H. (1973) *Inequality*, London: Allen Lane.

Jennings, R. E. (1977) *Education and Politics*, London: B. T. Batsford.

Knight, C. (1990) *The Making of Tory Educational Policy in Post-War Britain*, Trowbridge, Wilts: Falmer Press.

Kogan, M. (1975) *Institutional Autonomy and Public Accountability, Autonomy and Accountability in Educational Administration*, London: British Educational Adminstration Society.

——(1988) *Education Accountability*, London: Hutchinson Educational Books.

Maclure, S. (1988) *Education Re-formed*, Sevenoaks: Hodder and Stoughton.

McPherson, A. and Raab, C. D. (1988) *Governing Education*, Edinburgh: Edinburgh University Press.

Neave, G. (1988) 'On the cultivation of quality, efficiency and enterprise: an overview of recent trends in higher education in Western Europe, 1986–1988', *European Journal of Education* 23 (1, 2).

Ranson, S. (1980) 'Changing relations between centre and locality in education', *Local Government Studies* 5: 3–23.

Rhodes, R. A. W. (1981) *Control and Power in Central–Local Relations*, London: Gower.

Richardson, J. J. and Jordan A. G (1979) *Governing Under Pressure: The Policy Process in a Post-Parliamentary Democracy*, Oxford: Martin Robertson.

Sallis, J. (1979) 'Beyond the market place: a parent's view', in J. Lello (ed.) *Accountability in Education*, London: Ward Lock Educational.

Salter, B. and Tapper, T. (1981) *Education, Politics and the State*, Grant Mcintyre.

Sockett, H. (ed.) (1989) *Accountability in the English Educational System*, Sevenoaks: Hodder & Stoughton.

Teichler, U. (1989) *Changing Patterns of the Higher Education System: The Experience of Three Decades*, London: Jessica Kingsley Publications.

Van Vught, F. A. (ed.) (1989) *Governmental Strategies and Innovation in Higher Education*, London: Jessica Kingsley Publications.

Whitaker, T. (1982) 'Politics of Education', in L. Cohen, J. Thomas and L. Manion (eds) *Educational Research and Development in Britain, 1970–1980*, Windsor: NFER–Nelson.

Widdicombe, D. (1986) *The Conduct of Local Authority Business*, Report of the Committee of Inquiry into the Conduct of Local Authority Business (Chairman: David Widdicombe QC), Cmnd 9797, London: HMSO.

Wirt, F. M. (1977) 'Reassessment needs in the study of the politics of education', *Teachers' College Record* 78 (4).

Wirt, F. M. and Kirst, M. W. (1975) *Political and Social Foundations of Education*, Berkley, Calif.: McCutchan.

Young, M. F. D. (ed.) (1971) *Knowledge and Control: New Directions for the Sociology of Education*, London: Collier-Macmillan.

The Chronical of Higher Education (USA), *The Times Higher Education Supplement* (UK), *Le Monde de l'Éducation* (France) are important sources of information about current trends in education.

42

ENVIRONMENTAL POLICY

PETER KNOEPFEL

MAJOR ENVIRONMENTAL PROBLEMS AT THE BEGINNING OF THE 1990s

Highly industrialized Western countries that have been actively pursuing environmental policy since the 1960s, with an emphasis on air and water pollution control, have achieved considerable reductions in sulphur dioxide and dust emissions, and, with the help of large-scale public investment, adequate facilities for waste water treatment have become common. On the other hand, emissions of other, equally relevant pollutants such as nitrogen oxides or heavy metals have not been reduced to the same extent; in the case of hydrocarbons they have even been neglected. Emissions of carbon dioxide, a by-product of combustion processes and considered a prime cause of the greenhouse effect, are increasing dramatically. In spite of major investments, water pollution control has only achieved marginal success. Contamination of ground and drinking water and eutrophication of stagnant surface waters caused by extensive use of fertilizers continue to grow. Constantly increasing amounts of household and, in particular, hazardous wastes also provide reason for alarm, all the more since toxic waste is still being dumped into the sea, stored in inadequate dumps, or shipped to Third World countries. Further matters of concern are the rapid extinction of plant and animal species world-wide and an irreversible destruction of natural areas that continues almost unhindered.

In highly industrialized countries of Eastern Europe, the situation is even worse. There, concentrations of sulphur dioxide and dust in the ambient air have reached levels that are an unequivocal threat to health. It is still quite common to discharge sewage and industrial effluents into surface water with practically no prior purification treatment. Prospective development in the Third World, be it endogenously or exogenously induced, suggest prognoses of dramatic deterioration of ecosystems already out of balance, and, furthermore, an exponential growth in ecological hazards of global proportions before the year 2000 – in particular, disastrous changes in climatic conditions. Within countries of the northern and southern hemispheres, but also between the two hemispheres as such in comparison with each other, ever-widening gaps in the social distribution of environmental quality are discernible: already over-taxed ecosystems are being further polluted while efforts are made to improve conditions in regions where environmental quality is comparatively sound.

All in all this alarming situation is largely the result of the anthropogenic emission of pollutants. The most important groups of emitters are:

1 basic and heavy industry (for example, dust, sulphur dioxide, hydrocarbons, carbon dioxide, nitrogen oxides, toxic substances in solid and liquid waste);
2 transport (for example, nitrogen oxides, lead, noise, waste);
3 agriculture (for example, erosion, damage to flora and fauna, contamination of soil and ground water through excessive use of fertilizers);
4 infrastructural public works and construction (for example, noise, surface sealing of soil, destruction of landscape).

ENVIRONMENTAL POLICY: A GENERAL DEFINITION

The term 'environmental policy' comprises all government measures aimed at: first, assessing the state of environmental pollution; second, evaluating it either in relation to its hazards to human beings (anthropocentric) or ecosystems (ecocentric); and third, controlling pollution by means of regulations, economic incentives and/or training, moral persuasion and information campaigns according to a set of policy goals that are more or less quantifiable, depending, as the case may be, on the existence of precise emission standards or environmental quality standards ('immission' standards). Environmental policy goals can be the reduction of emissions or local immissions, a freeze of current emission or immission levels, or a deceleration of envisaged growth rates. In principle, pollution control can be practised either by means of basic preventive measures (changes in the emission source structure) or by limiting given emitting activities (control of immission levels). Currently, the latter strategy prevails in most industrial nations.

As a rule, formal environmental policy is the administrative responsibility of special departments or ministries of the environment and it normally covers only a part of administrative action relevant to the environment. Many of the activities of other departments, such as energy, agriculture, regional planning, industry and transport, are often complementary to formal environmental policy. Land-use decisions in regional planning policy, for example, establish basic determinants for the structure of anthropogenic emission sources in local ecosystems. In many countries, owing to their ecological indifference, the policy areas mentioned above are, however, undoubtedly responsible for the emergence and growth of various environmental kinds of damage rather than for limiting it.

A BRIEF HISTORY OF ENVIRONMENTAL POLICY

Up to the early 1960s, the term 'environmental policy' was practically unheard of. President Eisenhower's 'fifteen goals for America' in 1960, proclaiming the most important policy objectives for the decade to come, did not even mention environmental problems. Yet only five years later, President Johnson's 'Great Society' programme stated environmental protection as an important issue, and by 1969 the US Congress had enacted one of the first pieces of modern environmental legislation in the world, the National Environmental Protection Act. In 1971 the German federal government passed its first environmental programme. As in many other countries, this programme was prepared in anticipation of the famous UN conference, 'Man and the Biosphere', held in Stockholm in 1972. The conference concluded with a declaration, which, presumably for the first time, made 'the environment' an issue of profound political debate, as it had already been claimed to be by concerned scientists (for example, the Club of Rome) during the 1960s. Prior to this historic date, environment-related policy had merely been concerned with more or less technical measures concerning public health (such as water quality control and clean air measures in notorious smog areas); consumer protection and protection of fair competition (such as legislation pertaining to food and toxic substances); and safety problems (such as safety at work and the prevention of boiler explosions). In addition to this, several measures were taken with regard to natural and 'homeland' conservation (such as the designation of nature sanctuaries and the protection of natural and historical monuments).

Although governments pursued individual and different paths in their attempts at systematic environmental quality control triggered by the Stockholm conference, by the end of the 1980s the state of national environmental legislation had more or less reached a common level. There is, however, great variation concerning the speed with which individual countries have introduced environmental regulations, owing to geographic, topographic and demographic differences as well as differences in environmental conditions (such as high levels of pollution in urban conglomerations) and the structure of national industry. Differences in the perception of environmental problems, in political judgement and in political strength have also influenced the pace of development.

Accordingly, in most West European countries, waste disposal and, in particular, waste incineration were among the first targets of environmental regulation. In the United States, with its vast land resources, the usual practice of waste dumping (landfills) was maintained for a long time, but on the other side of the Atlantic population density is much higher and space for waste dumps has become sparse. Waste incineration therefore became more common and corresponding air pollution measures were called for. In reaction to the smog catastrophes in the 1950s, the United Kingdom (1956), France (1961) and Italy (1966) adopted air pollution abatement measures quite early, while other countries, such as West Germany, did not introduce systematic clean air measures until the 1970s. Central environmental legislation also lagged behind local and regional anti-pollution measures (for example, in Switzerland). In East European countries serious attempts at establishing environmental policy comparable to Western standards only commenced in 1989, shortly before the political unheavals in those countries. These attempts were mostly last-ditch measures hastily taken to appease environmentalist protest, which could no longer be disregarded. As it turned out, this protest was one significant factor leading to the disintegration of the communist regimes.

By the end of the 1970s, a number of organizations established in the wake of the Stockholm conference pursued environmental policy at an international level: for example, the United Nations Environmental Programme (UNEP), the Organization for Economic Co-operation and Development (OECD) and the Economic Commission for Europe (ECE). Meanwhile, several important international conventions were ratified by many countries. These included the Geneva Convention on long-range transboundary air pollution (1979, in force since 1983); the ECE's Helsinki Protocol on the reduction of sulphur dioxide emissions or their transboundary fluxes by at least 30 per cent (1985, in force since 1987); the ECE Protocol on the reduction of nitrogen oxides or their transboundary fluxes (1987, in force since 1990); the Vienna Convention on the protection of the ozone layer (1985) and the Montreal Protocol (1987), both attempts to combat chlorinated fluorocarbons (CFCs) used as propelling agents in aerosols, cooling agents, cleaning agents, blowing agents, etc.; the Basle Convention on the control of transboundary transport of hazardous waste and its disposal (22 March 1989); and the International Convention on the abatement of the greenhouse effect caused by carbon dioxide emissions from combustion (1990).

ENVIRONMENTAL POLITICS

In most Western industrialized nations, traditional political parties discovered the environmental issue long after the first environment-related measures had been launched, i.e. in the late 1970s or even in the 1980s, when grave environmental damage had become manifest (for example, 'Waldsterben', endangered maritime ecosystems, deterioration of soil and biological death of water bodies). Undoubtedly, the environmental issue found its first political articulation not in established political parties but in grassroots movements of the mid-1970s concerned with ecological disputes over infrastructural projects such as nuclear power plants, international airports, highways, etc. Grassroots movements were, and are, characteristic of post-materialist values which had increasingly gained ground and, in surpassing the environmental issue in the narrower sense, led to the development of alternative concepts of human needs. Typical forms are the peace movement, the anti-nuclear movement, the women's liberation movement, and movements promoting ecologically sound urban renewal.

During the late 1980s these opposition movements, dominated by the well-educated new urban middle classes, evolved into new political parties ('green parties'), which have altered and will continue to alter the political party spectrum of most West European countries (as, for example, in Germany, Sweden, Belgium, Ireland, Austria and Switzerland). These new parties are characterized by a loose and strongly decentralized structure with a major emphasis on local and regional activities and an ideology that often runs contrary to traditional left-wing/right-wing classifications. Apart from environmental policy, they have become increasingly concerned with other policy areas, such as energy, transport and peace policy.

Since the revolutionary events of 1989, newly founded political groups and parties in East Europe have included environmental policy as a key element of their programmes. This hardly comes as a surprise in view of the fact that dramatic deterioration of the environment was one reason for the decline of the former communist regimes.

ENVIRONMENTAL POLICIES

Long before the public and traditional political parties recognized the importance of the environmental issue, many central and regional administrations had taken up the struggle against pollution in various ways, in close co-operation with natural scientists and the industries and trades concerned. Pollution abatement measures of the first generation focused on regions with particularly high pollution levels (immissions), first, in order to reduce health hazards and, later on, to limit damage to plants, animals and ecosystems to an acceptable level. What that acceptable level of pollution should be was defined in legislation on environmental quality standards. To comply with these standards, two major strategies were applied: first, measures aimed at reducing emission of pollutants by households, industry and traffic; and second, measures aimed at the dilution or long-range distribution of pollutants in water or air, thereby reducing local concentration levels. The best-known example of the latter strategy is the notorious high-stack policy, which was pursued mainly in the United Kingdom, northern France and the West German Ruhr

686

district. The high-stack policy facilitated long-range transboundary fluxes of air pollution, mainly to Scandinavia, entailing dire consequences. Scandinavian lakes and soil were seriously affected by acidification. This helps explain Scandinavia's leading role in promoting international conventions on the reduction of sulphur dioxide and, more recently, nitrogen oxide emissions. Further examples of such immission-oriented strategies, mostly found in air and water pollution control, are smog regulations or the designation of smog-alarm zones (for example, the French *zones d'alertes*) which provide for a curb on emitting activities during unfavourable weather conditions, but which leave emitters unhindered once these conditions have improved.

All these immission-oriented regulations, confined to a few highly polluted areas, have a great disadvantage: they lower total emission of pollutants only marginally. For that reason, they were progressively replaced by prevention-oriented concepts prescribing the application of state-of-the-art technology in pollution abatement for old and new emitting facilities, irrespective of local immissions. Where such general and nationwide emission cutbacks still fail to meet immission standards, regional and local authorities are called on to implement stricter emission limits. Such an emission-oriented (preventive) concept was first formulated in precise wording and with all its consequences in the Swiss Environmental Protection Act of 1983.

By now, most countries have introduced the principle that the polluter pays, thus passing the costs for environmental protection measures on to those who incur them. Nevertheless, there still are numerous provisions for all kinds of public subsidy, mostly in connection with water pollution control, waste disposal, and, prospectively, noise abatement. In general, however, it is widely agreed that the consequent internalization of costs according to the 'polluter pays principle' enhances environmental protection, although there are various negative effects on income distribution. For example, passing the costs for, say, waste-water purification, waste disposal, air pollution or noise abatement on to the emitters by way of cost-equivalent taxes affects lower-income groups harder in relative terms than middle- or higher-income groups. Aside from financial incentives for emitters to minimize polluting activities, negative repercussions on income are the main reason for granting public subsidies in most areas of environmental policy.

INTERNATIONAL COMPARISONS

National variations in strict standards in environmental legislation, especially for emission and immission, affect the competitive position of enterprises in international markets. Since many kinds of pollution do not stop at national borders, one country's environmental-political measures may affect neighbouring countries. It is understandable, therefore, that administrators, politicians and scientists often make reference to international comparison when evaluating environmental protection measures. Meanwhile, an extensive literature relevant to the subject has indicated the following basic findings.

National environmental quality standards (immission standards) are extremely heterogeneous. It is an established fact that immission standards are easier to implement at the international level than, say, emission limits. Consequently, the EC has set immission standards for several air and water pollutants, despite opposition from a sceptical France, but under pressure from the United Kingdom, which, benefiting from its geographic situation, is strongly in favour of immission standards. According to EC law, member countries may, however, adhere to existing stricter standards.

Environmental quality standards have become an integral part of environmental policy in most Western industrialized countries, but also in some East European countries. There is great variation, however, in terms of strictness, enforcement and effectiveness. This is due to the fact that, above all else and with only a few exceptions (for example, Austria, the Netherlands, Switzerland), governments have failed to base environmental policy on a broad ecocentric concept which would extend the scope of protection objectives to ecosystems as such and to all groups that run a higher risk of being harmed by pollution than the average population. Instead, most countries still make do with an anthropocentric concept of environmental protection. Consequently, the environmental quality standards of these countries are distinctly lower. Heterogeneity of standards is furthermore the result of the varying levels of political importance attached to environmental quality standards, unequal positions of strength among the various actors concerned with, and affected by, environmental protection measures (for example, polluting industries, eco-industry, environmentalist groups, consumer organizations, etc.), and, not least of all, the distinctly varying effectiveness of environmental quality standards themselves. Observed differences in the effectiveness of standards often indicates built-in implementation failure due to insufficient monitoring capacities, incomplete information on monitoring results, or missing legal provisions to make non-compliance actionable.

Cross-national variation is even greater with respect to emission and product-related norms having immediate effect on competition. This is already evident in the various lists of substances placed under regulation. In negotiations at the EC level, the United Kingdom, for example, obstinately fights against emission norms and adheres to the traditional case-by-case application of the best practicable means approach as performed by the Pollution Inspectorate, although most of Western Europe, Japan and the United States enact more and more pollutant-specific emission norms, in particular for air and water pollutants.

In the interest of fair competition, the EC is committed to harmonizing the various existing emission norms, but as yet little progress has been made owing to the opposition of some member states. As things stand, emission norms still are basically a true reflection of the political strength and influence of the different branches within the industrial system concerned.

Furthermore, international comparison reveals that, in spite of great differences in national policy styles underlying programme formulation, the implementation of national environmental programmes by individual regional administrations show both similarities and differences that cannot be explained on the basis of the noted differences in the programmes (standards, etc.) themselves. Rather, the relevant distinguishing factors are the different constellations of actors, local conditions of environmental quality, size of staff, budget, and technical equipment of regional authorities, as well as the strategic choices they make. Accordingly, various empirical studies have identified a certain conformity of implementation impacts, or at least a distinct similarity concerning those variables guaranteeing a certain quality of implementation in spite of the wide variation among environmental political programmes. In the United States, for example, the process of programme formulation is highly controversial, while British or Swedish policy processes aim at mutual consensus and cosy accommodation between government agencies and industry with quite different results. On the other hand, however, implementation effects achieved at the regional level, as measured against emitter behaviour, do not reflect the great differences one might expect considering the differences in the underlying programmes. In environmental policy, as in other policy areas, the decisive factor for successful performance is the political willingness and resolution of responsible authorities to take the necessary measures. Experience has shown that potential impediments at local or regional level cannot easily be dissolved by rigorous national programmes. And, vice versa, weak national (and international) programmes cannot in the long run hold back progressive local or regional authorities. There is valid scientific evidence that regional authorities faced with pressing problems and strong political mobilization can realize environmental policies more successfully than their colleagues within other regions where intervention is successfully blocked and/or the urgency of environmental problems is played down by withholding relevant information in spite of strict national programmes and standards.

CURRENT PROBLEMS OF ENVIRONMENTAL POLICY

One prerequisite for an effective implementation of environmental policy is the systematic monitoring of the state of environmental quality. Monitoring, however, should not be confined to isolated parameters (air and water quality, meteorological parameters, etc.). The whole range of data should be compiled in a national information system and should include integrated ecological monitoring (as in Sweden), along with selected pollution fluxes, information on flora and fauna, land use in open and built-up areas, and anthropospheric aspects (health, economy, politics). In this way it will be possible to pursue continuous, long-term environmental monitoring, necessary not only for a comprehensive evaluation of current environmental policy, but also for a sensible anticipation of future developments with corresponding environmental political readjustments. Furthermore, environmental monitoring data must be available for every interested citizen (as it is in Japan) and for environmental impact assessments. Local citizens and municipalities should be able to participate in environmental monitoring in order to speed up the process between problem perception and remedial action.

Today, at the beginning of the 1990s, most Western industrialized countries have at their disposal a more or less comprehensive legal basis to fight environmental pollution, at least with respect to water, air, waste and (new) chemicals. Environmental-political action based upon this legislation, however, is still largely divided according to individual environmental media. Consequently, intervention frequently takes the form of shifting pollution problems from one environmental medium to another. Fluxes of harmful substances from production to consumption and waste disposal into the soil cannot be dealt with appropriately within such fragmented political administrative arrangements. One important task for environmental policy in the 1990s is to replace sectorial administrative action with an integrated ecological management of pollution fluxes. To this end, natural and social science research is required, studying current substance cycles and the physical, social, economic and legal factors that are responsible for their present state and relevant for future change. It will then be necessary to reform current administrative structures that have been established according to the outdated logic of segmentation in environmental policy and, in many cases, have been responsible for problem-shifting. Instead of hierarchically structured administrations and legal dogmas obliged to linear single causalities, there is a requirement for co-operative administrative networks and legal acceptance of multiple responsibilities (with a corresponding reversal of the burden of proof on the part of the polluter). Such an ecology-based restructuring of administration and management is particularly necessary at the regional level because regional agencies have always had the largest share in implementing the diverse environmental laws and regulations. Moreover, policy implementation will gradually shift its focus towards the performance of environmental impact assessments concerning new and/or old emission sources in specified areas. Thus a considerably stronger linkage between regional planning and environmental policy is called for. In the United States and the United Kingdom this has been an aim for quite a long time, but in most of continental Europe hardly any serious attempts have been made in this direction. Regional planning will have to integrate into its quantitative concepts for land use qualitative concepts and ecological choices, while environmental policy will have to put a stronger emphasis on land-use aspects. All EC member states (according to Directive 85/337) and most other European countries have introduced procedures for environmental impact assessment similar to those provided by the US National Environmental Protection Act as early as 1969. As yet, however, environmental impact assessment still has to pass the test as a crucial instrument in the implementation of land-use-oriented ecological policy.

At the beginning of the 1990s, most scientists and environmental agencies in Western industrialized countries finally seem to be determined to introduce economic instruments in environmental policy. During the 1980s only a few countries, such as Japan and Sweden, and some US states, made broader use of such instruments. The reluctant attitude towards economic instruments in most other countries has multiple causes, including, among others, the anticipation of negative impacts on competition in international markets, assumptions about administrative difficulties and apprehension over negative social impacts. One could also add the fear that government agencies might be forced to pay for their own polluting activities and thus lose face before their voters, and/or the market economy's fear of itself. In East European countries, initiatives for the introduction of economic instruments in environmental policy have largely failed. This could be due to the widespread hostile attitude of the public towards the centralized economy, and the reluctance of state-owned industry.

The most commonly applied economic control instruments are presumably those in waste management (advanced charges for waste disposal) and in clean air policy (limited marketable emission certificates sold in order to accelerate air quality improvement in urban conglomerations).

It is neither realistic nor constitutionally admissible to call for an ecological police state to enforce compliance with environmental regulations. Therefore, a more or less voluntary co-operation between government agencies, industry, agriculture and households becomes inevitable. For this purpose, governments would have to expand and improve information and consulting services. The 1980s have taught that undifferentiated and widely dispersed appeals hardly lead to success. Instead, the required teaching and learning opportunities should be provided by problem-specific consulting, as practised, for example, in the official agricultural advertising services of the Netherlands, France, Germany or Switzerland. Aside from sufficient funds, several other requirements must be met in order to establish effective consulting services, such as the co-operation of interconnected administrative units with industrial federations, immediate transfer of information from ecological research to consulting and practice, and vice versa, the inclusion of the ecological message into operational consulting with a corresponding account of ecological costs, and the continuity, credibility and individuality of consulting which, not least of all, can be guaranteed by a certain independence from policy and adminis-tration. Such structures of consulting services will become necessary in the areas of households (waste, energy), transport (promotion of public transpor-tation), and, of course, industry and trades (along the lines of the British example). Moreover, if consulting services are to be attractive for their clientele, what they teach should be economically utilizable in a broad sense.

All in all, ecology in the 1990s will become a central element of domestic policy in both industrialized and developing countries. Environmental protec-tion will probably therefore lose some of its importance as a policy area of its own standing, but will instead find access to many other single-issue policy areas, above all in regional planning. For economic reasons alone it will hardly be possible to go on and develop independent policies in the areas of infrastructure, energy, agriculture or industry and then afterwards, with great effort and at high cost, make them ecologically compatible. On the contrary, the products of these policies will only find demand on the 'voter and consumer markets' as goods with a 'practical value', if they are conceived and developed in relation to ecological considerations throughout the whole process. In this sense, in Western and Eastern industrialized nations, environmental policy of the 1990s will be linked far more to general industrial and economic policies than the traditional environmental policy of the 1970s and 1980s. Hitherto, environmental policy was more or less doomed to manage the disposal of prefabricated and ecologically detrimental policy products with as little damage as possible. By the late 1990s this type of environmental policy will belong to the past!

ACKNOWLEDGEMENT

The author wishes to thank Dagmar Kollande for assistance in translating this essay.

FURTHER READING

Crenson, M. (1971) *The Un-Politics of Air Pollution: A Study of Non-Decisionmaking in the Cities*, Baltimore: Johns Hopkins University Press.

Dales, J. H. (1968) *Pollution, Property and Prices*, Toronto: University of Toronto Press.

Dierkes, M., Weiler, H. N. and Antal, A. A. (eds) (1987) *Comparative Policy Research: Learning from Experience*, Aldershot: Gower (in particular the contribution by D. Vogel and V. Kuhn, 'The comparative study of environmental policy: a review of literature').

Heidenheimer, A., Heclo, H. and Adams, C. T. (1989) *Comparative Public Policy: The Politics of Social Choice in America, Europe and Japan*, 3rd edn, New York: St Martin's Press.

Ingelhart, R. (1977) *The Silent Revolution*, Princeton: Princeton University Press.

Kennedy, W. V. (1985) *Environmental Impact Assessment and Highway Planning: A Comparative Case Study Analysis of the United States and the Federal Republic of Germany*, Berlin: Edition Sigma.

Knoepfel P. and Weidner, H. (1985) *Luftreinhaltepolitik (stationäre Quellen) im internationalen Vergleich*, 6 vols, Berlin: Edition Sigma.

——————(1986) 'Explaining differences in the performance of clean air policies: an international and interregional comparative study', *Policy and Politics* 14 (1): 71–92.

Lederer, K. (ed.) in co-operation with Galtung, J. and Antal, D. (1980) *Human Needs: A Contribution to the Current Debate*: Königstein/Ts: A. Hain.

Lundqvist, L. (1980) *The Hare and the Tortoise: Clean Air Politics in the U. S. and Sweden*, Ann Arbor: University of Michigan Press.

Majone, G. (1976) 'Choice among policy instruments for pollution control', *Policy Analysis* 4: 589–612.

O'Riordan, T. and D'Arge, R. C. (eds) (1979) *Progress in Resource Management and Environmental Planning*, vol. 1, New York: John Wiley & Sons.

Pearce, D. W. and Nash, C. A. (1981) *The Social Appraisal of Projects: A Text in Cost–Benefit Analysis*, London: Macmillan.

Policy Studies Organization (ed.) (1982) *Policy Studies Journal* 11 (1), Tallahassee: Florida State University.

Schnaiberg, A., Watts, N. and Zimmermann, K. (eds) (1986) *Distributional Conflicts in Environmental-Resource Policy*, Aldershot: Gower.

Tsuru, Sh. and Weidner, H. (eds) (1989) *Environmental Policy in Japan*, Berlin: Edition Sigma.

Weidner, H. (1986) *Air Pollution Control Strategies and Policies in the F. R. Germany: Laws, Regulations, Implementation and Principal Shortcomings*, Berlin: Edition Sigma.

Wildavsky, A. and Douglas M. (1982) *Risk and Culture: An Essay in the Selection of Technical and Environmental Dangers*, Berkeley: University of California Press.

43

HEALTH POLICY

JOHANNES VANG

Since ancient times, the public concern about health has been with the protection of the community against communicable diseases. Religious and health objectives were often inextricably intermingled in dietary laws and rules of hygiene, merging healers, politicians and priests. The provision of clean water, unpoisoned food, sewerage, drainage and waste disposal always was and still is a concern as specified from Leviticus to modern health legislation.

In the past, while the health of the public was dealt with in a collective way, the care of the sick was based on family ties or individual relationships, performed through a mixture of faith and beliefs, knowledge and skills, guided by ethical/religious traditions and some formal demands on the healers.

Health services in their present form are of rather recent date, developing out of the beneficence based in religious charity. With the birth of the welfare state after the Second World War, health care and health services were introduced in terms of justice and rights. Health services became a public good, eventually claiming up to 10 per cent of gross national product, and offering work opportunities to large numbers of the population, particularly women. Health services thereby came to play a substantial role in developing the buying power and independence of women. Health policy gained increased importance, expanded and finally became a major political issue in many countries.

Health policy traditionally meant policy aimed at the prevention, diagnosis and cure of illnesses and included health service policy. With changing views of health, increasing understanding of health as a social stabilizing factor and a social and economical resource, health considerations have penetrated many other fields of policies. Today, talk of 'policies for health' also means agricultural policies supporting the production of healthy food, labour market policies that support occupational health and employment, communication policies that prevent traffic accidents and pollution, educational policies that support health education, etc. Not least as a result of the agreements between member states of the World Health Organization (WHO) on the 'health for all' policy, traditional health policy has been converted into the broader policy for health.

In the following, we shall discuss the factors and actors of health policy and health service policy, the dynamics and the trends, and we shall touch upon 'policies for health'.

ATTITUDES TOWARDS HEALTH AND ILLNESS

The main determining factors for health policy are the attitudes and values which dominate society. These are closely related to cultural tradition and historical background, socio-economic development, economic capacity and social structure, demography and technological development.

There are in essence two ways for humans to interact with nature. One is to submit to the forces of nature and accept the human being as a part of nature. The other one is to try to master nature's forces, to see the human species as the crowning work of creation, created in the image of God, with the right to dominate. The first of the two attitudes is often found in what is known as 'primitive' cultural tradition, while the other one is typical for Judeo-Christian tradition. This second one is the cultural environment in which modern society has developed and of which modern health care systems and health care policies are reflections. The industrial state and modern technology are a function of human ambition to master nature and to use nature to make life safer and more comfortable. The modern health care system in a welfare state could be considered the ultimate response to the human search for security and physical immortality.

In traditional thinking, people are either healthy or ill. With an inherited view of illness as a punishment, illness became the culprit, the one to identify as a disease and to destroy. Health policy became disease-oriented, oriented towards prevention, diagnosis and treatment of diseases. As biological knowledge expanded, medical specialization evolved and health care systems became specialist-oriented in their search for effective means to deal with specific diseases.

The disease-oriented approach to health emerged out of the Cartesian view of body and soul as separate entities, the body being akin to a mechanical machine submitted to wear and tear and breakdowns, which with sufficient biological knowledge and understanding of its function can be repaired. This reductionistic view of life came to dominate medicine and medical practice for several generations within Western culture. It is the background for both the health and educational policies' focus on biological sciences and the development of biological medicine, sometimes called 'scientific' medicine. These policies also gained support because they were rather successful, at least temporarily, in gaining control over many communicable diseases and some non-communicable ones.

This traditional view is now being questioned by people who are frustrated by the fact that the knowledge expansion has been too weak and slow to conquer the problems of ageing and degenerative diseases such as arteriosclerosis and cancer. The makeshift techniques developed by modern medicine to amend these problems within, for instance, modern oncology, cardiovascular and transplantation surgery have proved very costly and only moderately effective, and some of them have been downright failures. Also, apart from the economic problems, they have raised difficult ethical issues. As degenerative diseases are diseases of the aged, these technologies operate in an area between medicine, caring and social support. This demands a broader and multiprofessional approach to problems than 'scientific' medicine can offer. With the advent of HIV and AIDS, the dearth of knowledge about communicable diseases has again become exposed. The absence of an effective causal treatment, the characteristics of the disease, its mode of transmission and the age of the patients underline the needs for psychological and social counselling, and again point to the limits of 'scientific' medicine.

When the costs of medical care rose to levels which could not be dealt with by individuals without creating dangerous inequity, developed societies could not maintain individual economic responsibility for health care. Collective systems were invented, using insurance techniques, either private or public models or tax financing. Although the high expenses of care for those who needed it were now shared by large groups of the population, demography and medical technology developed faster than the development of general and national wealth. Health care, together with all other sorts of collective expenses such as defence, transportation and education, started taking an increasing toll of the gross national product, making the cost of modern medical care increasingly burdensome even for the population collectively. The cost of modern health care systems, and their inability to meet expectations from populations, however irrational, has lead to changing attitudes and brought health care in the modern welfare state to a crossroads.

THE WELFARE STATE AND THE RIGHT TO HEALTH

The welfare state as it developed after the Second World War offered people health care as a social good among others such as education. This created a notion of a 'right to health'. This 'right' is in fact reflected in a declaration of WHO from its Constitution of 1946 which states: 'The enjoyment of the highest attainable standard of health is one of the fundamental rights of every human being without distinction of race, religion, political belief, economic or social condition.' However, WHO sees this right not as a 'natural right' but a right in a social context including some duties of the individual when it comes to lifestyle and of society when it comes to environment and support. The WHO declaration also takes into consideration the economic means and the cultural and social attitudes of society.

Many people, however, still thinking in Cartesian ways, see this right to health as a right to health care regardless of cost and collective sacrifices. From such a perspective health is a commodity delivered by a free health care system, not as an act of beneficence, but as one of justice. Within the same realm of thinking evolved the notion of 'health care needs'. There are no biological needs for a health care system. Humans have survived for millions of years without health care systems and would continue to do so. In fact the major global problem today is one of a geometric population expansion beyond available resources and with severe social and environmental problems as a consequence for both the human species and other species.

As there is no need for a health care system for humanity to survive it can only be a cultural/social manifestation, like the system of transportation and general education. For individuals it is an important one, however, as it is closely connected to fundamental human experiences such as illness and death. The notion of an absolute 'health care need', as developed in the disease-oriented mechanical view of health, was combined with the view that there were a given number of diseases to be cured. If enough hospitals were built and physicians and nurses educated, one would be able to cope with the diseases, and after having overcome the backlog that existed, one would have a health care system in balance. This view was the basis of the development of the British national health system and it was shared by many other countries, such as the Scandinavian countries. For the social engineers of the period after the Second World War, health was only a matter of resources, organization and knowledge development. These views were probably supported by the experiences of the war, when governments took over responsibilities for the production and organization of resources and successfully won the war in doing so.

In planned economies, health care needs can only be seen within a framework of what and how much a society is willing to set aside for this particular purpose. Going outside this framework one enters into the health care market: a commercial field of supply and demand. We shall return to this later (pp. 703–6).

The accelerating costs of care and the 'Medical Paradox' – i.e. that increased resources used on health care increase the complaints of ill health, a paradox only in a mechanical health paradigm – eventually showed this policy untenable. Moreover, many pathological conditions were self-inflicted, as for instance those resulting from smoking, overeating, alcohol or drug abuse or even the abuse of 'scientific medicine'. Violence and accidents came to dominate the panorama in large cities and were dealt with much the same way as in a war: as a medical problem, not a social one. Studies showed large variations in the way people were treated for the same illnesses without this having any influence on the outcome. Obviously ill-health was something much more complicated, and medicine as much art as science. Perhaps medicine belonged as much to the social sciences and humanities as to biology.

A NEW VIEW OF HEALTH

The consequences of the developments mentioned above (p. 697) brought support to a different view of health than the disease-oriented one. In this view of health, the individual is seen as a whole, 'body and soul' are interacting constantly, the individual is constantly interacting with his/her environment, and health and ill health do not form a dichotomous phenomenon but a continuum of degrees of health and illness, where the individual has the power to influence this balance through lifestyle choices and through environmental policies. Man or woman is not a passive person stricken by disease, who passively receives treatment in a paternalistic health care system, but is autonomous and in command.

Such a view of health and ill health focuses on behaviour and on society's policies towards occupational health and environmental health. The individual and society share the responsibility for health and obtaining the individual's health potential becomes the objective of the policy.

Such a view adds new dimensions to the health service. It removes paternalism from health services and establishes them as true service organizations offering help in case of ill health and support in the promotion of good health. Establishing disease diagnosis according to an international classification system is of less importance than the delineation of the patient's problems and their solution. Problem-oriented care comes into the foreground, giving a broader approach to ill health than the medical reductionistic view and therefore demanding a different sort of education for physicians and nurses, who will now have to act in groups, not in a hierarchy, and intersectorally with people with non-medical education with a different frame of reference. Communicative skills become essential. However, medical performances have to be based on a biological knowledge base. The major change is that medicine is seen as applied science, and not as a science in itself but as a humanistic-social enterprise based on biological sciences.

With the sharpening of the individual's own responsibility for health through lifestyle and behaviour, there is a risk of a fundamentalistic health moralism, a return to a view of illness as punishment for bad behaviour. It is particularly important to guard against this in relation to the physically or mentally weak, the uneducated and the uninformed. It also very strongly points from 'health policy' towards 'policy for health', and society's responsibility to make healthy choices easily available and possible.

THE MORAL PHILOSOPHY BEHIND HEALTH POLICY

The objective of health policy is to create a structure for public health service which as far as possible responds adequately to the health problems in that particular country or society, doing so by applying the ethical norms which are characteristic for and acceptable to that society. Health policies are therefore strictly culturally dependent. We cannot speak of an international health policy and it is sometimes difficult even to describe a national policy. Health policy is only transferable within the socio-economic framework in which it has been developed. In that respect health policy is similar to technology.

To discuss health policy and structure we therefore have to look at a spectrum of values. For most people the differences are most clearly shown by comparing a health care system such as the American one, which could be called a libertarian system, with nationalized systems such as those we find in the UK or in Scandinavian countries. To form a basis for this discussion about structure, it might be useful to go beyond health policies *per se* and look at the problem from a moral-philosophical point of view. We shall do this by following a train of thought which has been proposed by the medical philosopher Henrik Wulff.

One can imagine a spectrum of societies based on different values. At one end would be a closely structured society such as a very primitive society or a society living under strong pressure. The ethos is fixed by tradition. Human behaviour is more or less codified, with individuals being born into certain roles in society. At the other and opposite end of that spectrum would be a libertarian society with maximal individualism and a minimum of structure. In this society there are no general rules except the right to self-determination. This means that this is a society of the broadest tolerance except when individual autonomy is violated.

At both ends of the spectrum there would be little reason for health policy debates, or ethical debates for that matter. Most societies exist somewhere in between these two theoretical extremes. Some societies are further towards the libertarian end, some more towards the structured one. In recent years it seems that many countries have been a shifting towards the more libertarian end. The principle of autonomy has come more into focus than the principle of the protective structure of society, such as was developed in early welfare state thinking. We therefore have to analyse briefly and rather superficially what is meant by autonomy.

The principle of autonomy is the belief that a person has a free will and the capacity for making moral choices. One reasoning goes: as the individual has a free will and can make moral choices, then each person has the right to do whatever he/she pleases as long as it does not directly hurt other people.

This right is understood as a 'natural' right given to each person, nobody knows from where or by whom, but it presupposes the supreme value of the human being as mentioned above (p. 695). This right differs from the 'right to the highest obtainable health' talked about in the WHO declaration which discusses a right given in the social context in which the individual lives (pp. 696–7)

Immanuel Kant has a different view of the consequences of autonomy, which is: as an autonomous being, each person has a free will and consequently a duty to behave in a certain way. This way can be tested against a supreme moral principle, a categorical imperative, which very loosely could be formulated so: never treat people merely as means but always as ends, or 'What would happen if everyone acted like this?', or 'Do unto others as you would they should do unto you.'

The characteristics of these two different views of the consequences of autonomy is that the Kantian one emphasizes the relationship amongst people, the duty towards others, while the individual ethic is concerned with the individual in isolation, the ability to chose for oneself, to formulate and carry out individual plans and postures. The polarity in the present health policy debate very much reflects the two different interpretations, which each play a role in the formation of modern health policies.

Traditional Kantian duty ethics carried out at the social level will put its emphasis on distributive justice and consequently force health care systems into a more closely knitted structure, while the humanistic understanding of autonomy as a right will push health care policies towards a libertarian system with less structure and more beneficence characteristics. The degree to which a given society puts emphasis on the right to self-determination or to distributive justice will determine where on the above-mentioned value spectrum (p. 699) the health policy will be found. The United States was originally populated by people who escaped oppression and poverty in Europe. For historical reasons the general inclination is therefore towards individual freedom, and public opinion will tend to attach greater value to self-determination. Countries with traditional centralized governing will praise the high value of social stability and a coherent network of interrelated duties and structure the system more closely.

In societies with a closely knitted structure there is always a risk that the structure may strangle individual freedom. There are numerous examples of the abuse of structuring in European societies in recent history. It is therefore not surprising that with increasing levels of education and affluence the present tendency in Europe today is towards a loosening of the structure: in other words, moving towards the right in the value spectrum. The price of this is a risk of maldistribution of resources and loss of equal access. This risk has been magnified several times by the exploding cost of medical care. With the middle-class revolution and expanding economy of the 1980s, and the advent of the new individualism which modern technology and media made possible, this tendency was sustained throughout this period. The collapse of the socialist societies in Eastern Europe in the late 1980s served to reinforce the trend.

Whichever moral philosophy is behind the different health policies today, all policies have one thing in common: the problem of money.

TECHNOLOGY AND SPENDING

The amount of knowledge has increased with accelerating speed; the last forty years in particular have been characterized by an extremely rapid growth of knowledge, paralleling demographic development. With modern communication technology the dissemination of new knowledge has also become very fast. This again has contributed to the rapid development of new knowledge. It also means that new knowledge becomes common knowledge rapidly, and when it has become common knowledge it is possible for many people to apply and exploit that knowledge, and new technologies therefore evolve with unprecedented speed.

This development of new knowledge is not governed by social rationality. Some people believe, rightly or wrongly, that the application of knowledge, the development of new technologies and the use of those newly available technologies could be governed by social forces. This is the background of technology assessment within policy analysis, which attempts to define and delineate the social usefulness of technologies. Medical technologies have usually understood as drugs, devices, procedures and supportive administrative techniques.

Although many new medical technologies have been useful and have reduced the quantifiable and non-quantifiable costs of disease, both for the individual and for society, they have also created large expectations regarding health care systems, which cannot as yet be lived up to. Moreover, technology is expanding much more rapidly than the prosperity of society. Only very few individuals would be able to pay for the use of the possible health technologies, and no single country could afford to make all technologies available to all its citizens in an equal access policy. The gap between what is possible and what is affordable widens daily, placing a strain on governments promoting health policies that are tax-financed and centred around equal access and equity ideology. In countries where health policy is based on individual responsibilities and cost sharing, either through insurance companies or through a wider agreement between employers and employees, this burden is being pushed around among the actors.

Rationing of care, open or hidden, is appearing in most health care systems, either through queuing or through more parsimonious medical decision making. Where responsibility for payment is divided between the patient and a third party, one approach is to increase the patient's share of payment, and this is a step towards a market system where personal income may determine the technical level of care offered. In the less structured and more libertarian societies this kind of development increases the inequity in the delivery of care to an extent that it may shift the political focus, depending on expectations.

One reason for these problems is that the described dynamics of development make it impossible to calculate the costs of health care in the future. Insurance companies are concerned with risk: not the risk to the patient, but the economic risk for the company. If the cost of the worst outcome, the risk, cannot be calculated, it is difficult to offer insurance. Employers such as General Motors, as well as many national governments, find it difficult to fulfil promises of medical coverage – particularly to the elderly – given at a time when life looked different.

STEERING HEALTH CARE

Health policy is carried out on several different levels in society. The national level, which could be called the macrostructural level, steers the health system. The powers at this level act through laws and regulations, financing rules, etc. Inside the system, amongst institutions and professionals, is the microstructure: rules and work traditions which manage the day-to-day work. In regionalized health systems there may also be intermediate policy structures, interfacing macrostructural and microstructural policies.

Apart from the individual patient and groups of patients, the three main powers in a macrostructural health policy perspective are:

A the legislative body, usually the parliament, which institutes the health and social laws and, through different agencies, makes sure that they are kept;

B the paying authority, which can be a national social insurance system financed through tax or dues from individuals or shared by employers and employees; insurance companies; or non-profit or for profit foundations, either privately owned or owned by a mixture of private enterprise, the state and labour unions;

C providers of care, which can be private foundations, or can be owned by national or subnational authorities.

In democracies the legislative power is, in principle, with the parliament. This can but ought not to be changed. In making health policy reforms at the macrostructural level it will therefore be the characteristics and rules for interaction between the other two powers (B and C) which can be manipulated within the boundaries decided by the legislative power. There are obviously many possible solutions, and various combinations are found throughout the world, which have evolved out of cultural tradition, history, political trends and reforms in the past. There are usually many vested interests within these areas, ideological, economical or political, which make adaptive changes difficult and slow. This has become particularly obvious and frustrating during the last few decades, when the dynamics of the development of technique, economy, attitude and demography have often made previous solutions obsolete and revisions mandatory.

Somewhat simplistically, one can reduce the main question to the degree of coherence between B and C. In very structured and budget-driven systems, B and C may be one and the same authority. This makes hidden rationing very easy and cost containment effective. However, it usually leaves the patient with very little influence except for that afforded by the political vote, if it is a nationalized system, and the possibility to change provider, if it is a Health Maintenance Organization (HMO) type of system in a libertarian health care system. B and C can be separate authorities, either national or private, which in some way establish contracts on how to serve the patient. Such contracts can involve the patient or the patient's employer, or they can be tax financed and the patient can have a co-responsibility for payment.

All the different solutions to the interaction between the powers B and C have difficulties and problems as well as advantages.

BUDGET-DRIVEN VERSUS MARKET-DRIVEN SYSTEMS

In closely structured systems, health care is usually regionalized and budget driven. A region may have a budget for its health care that is distributed to the sub-units of the region according to certain given rules – the cost of care is supposed to stay within the budget limits. In an expanding economy one might accept overdrafts or budget expansions, but the opposite would be so in a recession. The budget will usually follow the means and ambitions of the country: this is a plan-economic model.

In the libertarian system, the money is tied to the patient. Thus the provider of care is paid by the patient or the insurer according to billing, and the limits of care will be determined by the patient's purse or the insurance contract. This is a market model with or without a third-party payer.

In budget-driven cases the health care system will act paternalistically and the patient will be submitted to the medical or administrative bureaucracy, and their values and competence, with little influence of his/her own. The patient's possibility of choice will often be very restricted, and in certain cases there will be no choice at all. With no choice for the patient, there is no competition between providers. This tends to slow down the technical development of health care. On the other hand, however, the quality of care, or lack of quality of care, may be more consistent than in a market-oriented system, at a level depending upon which formal or informal mechanisms are used in safeguarding the quality of care. The lack of concern and amenities for patients in strongly structured systems has been noticed or registered even in the best examples. In Sweden, for instance, the health authorities established a programme called 'the patient in the centre'. This was to a large extent a way of educating health care personnel towards greater patient-oriented care. The limited success of this campaign was probably caused by the fact that there were few incentives to support the educational effort.

The problem of equity and freedom of choice raises the fundamental issue that it is impossible to maximize two competing goals at the same time and therefore one has to more or less settle for a degree of equity and a degree of freedom.

Let us look at the libertarian end of the spectrum. Here the money follows the patient, who has a free choice of provider. There are strong economic incentives to maintain high quality and patient orientation. As there are choices, there is also competition, and, because the money follows the patient, detailed and correct information on the whole decision process during a treatment episode is required to be able to bill the insurance company or the patient correctly. This calls for a substantial administrative apparatus. The cost of marketing in an open market situation is not negligible either, and therefore the cost of the administrative part of health care in such systems is exceedingly high compared with a system that is budget-driven. In the United States 20 per cent of health care money is used for administration, as compared to 5 per cent in Sweden where health care is budget-driven.

The differences between the systems raises the issue of the value of choice and competition. As the patient is not an informed customer, the value of choice may be less than one is lead to believe. Even for the informed consumer there will often be a limit to the choice because of the special circumstances which prevail in cases of illness. Competition, when it comes to matters which are not easily quantifiable, depends on what one is competing for. This is easily recognized when it comes to television stations where a high degree of competition for viewers does not necessarily improve the quality or the selection. Competition in this field, by contrast, seems to limit and streamline the supply. In a free-market health care system there is a risk that the market will streamline the competition and will limit choices, leaving orphan drugs, orphan technologies and orphan diseases in its wake. So the libertarian system, although strictly patient-oriented, offers the risk of inequality in two dimensions, one which relates to economy and maybe geography, and one related to product availability. It is therefore not surprising that in countries with this type of health care there are strong voices recommending a firmer health care system structure. This is particularly true when one considers demographic situations where groups of elderly people dominate the health care scene.

In libertarian systems where the money follows the patient and there is a free health care market, control is at the microstructural level, concentrating on the medical or caring decisions made by physicians or other therapeutic personnel. The control at the microstructural level is carried out through utilization management (diagnosis-related groupings (DRGs), peer review, second opinion, etc.), the objective of which is double: both to ensure quality and to ensure effectiveness and cost control.

Although libertarian systems put great emphasis verbally on physician autonomy, the mode of control described above has limited physicians' freedom of action considerably. In fact, physician autonomy in the highly structured system is much larger since there is little direct control of physicians' actual decisions. For this professional freedom, the physician has traded off freedom in salary options in return for a fixed salary.

The ineffectiveness of physicians and nursing care in the budget-driven system can be obscured by references to inadequate funding. The individual physician cannot usually be singled out as responsible for inadequate or ineffective care, except in cases of major failures. This situation again underlines the lack of power of the consumer in structured systems and it could be said that the consumer has traded off personal influence and choice against the freedom from economical risk to be found in libertarian systems.

Recently, many health policy efforts within structured systems have been devoted to making the clinical decision process more visible and controllable. Development of policies for informatics in different countries has been helpful but development has been slow, with medical decision making relying mainly on the traditional social control between physicians. As physicians' organizations have developed more of the characteristics of traditional labour unions instead of the traditional guild or fraternity qualities that monitor ethics and performance, and as the number of physicians has expanded greatly, it has also become important to establish new organizational models for the social control of medical decision making. It is possible that intelligent information systems may offer considerable help to physicians and nurses in the future by broadening the working knowledge base, improving the general view of the field and sharpening decision logics. This would not only secure quality but would also make the health care process more transparent.

In summary one can say that in the structured models the major steering will be at the macrostructural level, with a weak steering at the microstructural or operational level, at least in the immediate future, and that the opposite is true for libertarian models of health policies. Those actors who are in power in the two different models are therefore two different groups of people: in the structured systems it is the senior administrators and the managers, often in collaboration with politicians and labour union representatives, while in the libertarian systems managers are usually only facilitators and the physicians and their organizations are in power. For example, there appeared at the same time in America and in Sweden, as a result of system flaws, the phenomenon 'Dox in a Box' – a physician who takes care of minor illnesses such as small wounds and common infections, in a setting without bureauratic arrangements such as appointments and waiting lists. In America it was the American Medical Association that was worried and protested about this, whereas in Sweden it was the County Council Association, as the responsible provider, that protested.

CONTROL FROM THE OUTSIDE

Since control in the United States is on the microstructural level – on the medical decision making – the judicial process in terms of malpractice suits is commonly used and plays a major role for physicians' behaviour and the development of 'defensive medicine'. The judicial system acts as the protector of the individual's rights with regard to other individuals – physicians or other responsible health personnel. This has raised the cost of care, partly because of physicians' insurance costs and partly because it provides an excuse for medical actions which are only marginally beneficial for the patient but create preventive safety for the physician and are commercially interesting. In budget-driven systems there are very few malpractice suits, not because malpractice is less usual (it is probably at least as common), but because of the lack of visibility or transparency of the medical decisions in the system and because of the closely knitted common interests of senior physicians, managers and politicians. The patient is up against a system, not an individual. The judicial tradition may be different and individual patients' interests are less well taken care of. From the social point of view and for the common good, some may consider this rational, but from the individual's point of view and that of duty ethics it is a flaw.

A question that can be raised is: who is representing the consumer in the structured system? The interface between the 'system' and the consumer is difficult because there is no consumer in a traditional sense but rather a patient/client and a taxpayer/financier. The agent of the citizen in the first role is supposed to be the physician; in the second, the parliamentary representative. The physician, as an employee of the system, is also supposed to act loyally towards that system, to identify with system objectives such as cost containment. At the same time the physician represents patient interests, which may be in conflict with system interests. This makes the physician the judge of which interests should be given priority, giving a strong management role in the aggregate to physicians' decisions.

Administrative managers constantly complain about physicians not being able to identify with organization goals. In recent years, when cost containment has been a dominant issue, much policy thinking has focused around this conflict. Seminars, courses and formal administrative education have been developed for physicians to strengthen their interest and understanding of system problems. As physicians increasingly transfer their loyalty towards the system, their strength as the 'patients' spokespersons' weakens, and the patients turn to other powers. Usually they find that the parliamentarian also speaks with a 'forked' tongue, being more a provider-representative embedded in and having vested interests in the system, more willing to represent the interests of a tax payer than those of a patient/client. The power left for patients is the media, which in the politicized climate of the structured system serve the same role as the judicial system in libertarian systems. While the judicial system is slow in the specific case and tends to threaten only physicians and medical decision making, the media have a much broader line of attack and can deal with the quality of medical, administrative and policy processes, but with decreasing strength. The media, however, lack the perseverance of the judicial process. After the initial exposure patient issues rapidly lose value for the media, and the follow-up is weak. The system has learned that and knows how to sit tight for a few days.

Still, the media are important. The judicial process can be neutralized through a regulatory approach. Sweden, for instance, has devised a system for compensation to patients for accidents happening in the course of diagnostic and therapeutic activities where no obvious error or negligence can be proven. This is a positive and consumer-oriented step taken by a strong system which would not have to bother. It is also an ingenious step to protect the system against expensive and cost-driving judicial processes. The very low compensation levels may suggest that the protection of the system has had a high priority in developing the concept.

CENTRALIZATION/DECENTRALIZATION

With large expansion and specialization, health care became administratively quite fragmented. The working patterns became complicated and many interdependent functions were supposed to work smoothly together. This is obviously not easy and functional problems became increasingly common and overt in the late 1960s and early 1970s. With the ageing of the population in many countries, the collaboration between health care and other social support systems, particularly with the development of home care, gained importance. For people in productive age groups with occupational diseases, the collaboration between health care systems and employer, rehabilitation organizations and sick funds was important. The functional integration or at least the smooth collaboration of these systems became an urgent priority.

This happened at a time when information technology was not yet fully developed. Computers in health care at the time were primitive mainframe machines delivering administrative production data of very limited value. Personnel were not computer literate and networking was unknown in most countries. Those responsible for the care had neither the knowledge nor the money, nor the visions to deal with it.

The obvious policy solution was to move towards decentralization of health care since it was impossible to maintain an overview of the whole organization. This change began in Western Europe in the early 1970s. Politically it was made possible by a change of climate as a consequence of the 1968 revolution, the 'small is beautiful' movement which developed out of the universities as reaction to positivism, the atomic bomb, the technical society, Vietnam, etc. But the economic imperative in most of the countries with nationalized budget-driven systems, where health care expenses took a high toll on gross national product, was created by the oil crisis. This prompted countries to reduce or freeze budgets, but also to think about new ways for making health care more effective. Decentralization became the magic word.

The decentralization of power in those countries where it was carried out seems to have been successful, and in the structured systems this improved the influence of the consumers/patients by bringing them closer to decision makers. The increasing recognition that problems might vary, not only between countries but also within a country, also underlined the importance of decentralized decision making, both administratively and economically. Health laws were changed to give simple broad goals and directions for health care, in the hope that local authorities or whoever was responsible at the regional or local/district level would operationalize the broad goals of the laws, in accordance with local needs and health problems. This is very much in parallel with WHO's broad goal of Health for All, and the thirty-eight European targets which operationalize the rather ambitious goal.

Decentralization was only an introduction to much wider deregulation, which became the policy magic of the 1980s. Deregulation is supposed to move the patient into focus, to make the health care system 'work for patients'. This philosophy reflects two general convictions: first, that budget-driven health care systems have created a power constellation within health care which is more concerned about the system itself and its conservation than effectiveness as measured by patient outcome and patient satisfaction – in other words the balance of the system's role as a social institution and that as a care system has tipped unduly towards the former; second, the incentives and the management philosophy in the system are inadequate, but when corrected they liberate human resources now being wasted or not brought into use, and also reduce wasteful irrational routines. Opponents of deregulation fear that new and different incentives may create inequality in delivery of care, unduly increase the work-load for health care personnel and create new, less attractive power constellations.

So while deregulation and decentralization have been the keywords in structured, budget-driven health care systems, utilization management on quality assurance programmes, powered by judicial processes, has been the key instrument in the health policies to cut back and control costs and maintain quality in the libertarian systems.

THE SOCIAL MARKET OR MANAGED COMPETITION

At present, health policies from the two ends of the previously described spectrum (p. 699) seem to be moving towards each other or maybe towards a third policy solution, a solution which is sometimes known as the social market. The obvious goal is to try to merge the advantages in equity of the structured system of budget steering with the advantages of the patient-oriented, service-minded, free-choice system. This will probably mean devising some sort of incentives for health care personnel. These could be collective incentives or individual ones, economic incentives or non-economic ones. It would probably mean the development of more freedom of choice and patient independence: in other words, moving more decisions to the patients in the structured systems and reducing physician autonomy in the open systems.

A first step toward the social market, which strengthens the consumer influence in budget-driven systems at the structured end of the spectrum, involves giving the patient choices, both of budget-driven providers and budget-driven third-party payers, but submitting both to the running control of some governmental agency and maintaining some political control over the contracts made between the two, to secure the avoidance of orphan cases. Obviously tax financing needs to be behind such a construction, which would be an example of modifying the steering characteristics at the macrostructural level. As such it might be possible in nationalized systems.

The other end of the spectrum, the one in which the free market is supposed to solve the problems, is moving towards greater structure. The development of DRGs is in a sense a social market. The third-party payer sets an upper limit below which providers may compete as much as they want. HMOs and Preferred Provider Organizations were designed to provide total services through their own facilities and with their own employed staff in order to create better provider structure. As it has turned out, HMOs have become budget holders on behalf of their enrollees and buy services for them. Like everybody else they have underestimated the cost development and many of them have been removed by the fierce competition. The competing hospitals have to act along business economic lines, streamlining their 'products' to those that are profitable. They have entered into what has been termed an 'arms race' in competing on new technology, and need to use marketing techniques, which are perceived by some physicians as unseemly. Those who believed in market steering are as disappointed as those who believed in bureaucratic steering. Clearly we do not yet have solutions which can satisfy both reality and prevailing ideologies.

SHIFTING THE FOCUS FROM DISEASE TO HEALTH

As stated in the introduction to this chapter, health policy deals with health and not just the care of the sick. Behaviour, lifestyle and environmental protection are gaining increasing attention. Young people in the developed world tend to consider present and past health policies as 'cooking dinner when the house is burning'. They are concerned with global warming, ozone depletion, deforestation, water depletion, population explosion, radiation hazards, toxic waste and toxic or allergenic food additives as health hazards. They are brought up to see health in a broader context and are prepared to put pressure on policy makers. Although their views are meeting increasing understanding, present decision makers still talk the language of their own generation and act and react on the fears and issues of the 1960s. Young people in the Third World experience these problems every day, but are so far without political influence. They are just paying the price.

Traditional environmental health was basically sanitary engineering combined with epidemiology. Today environmental health has a much broader scope and deals with clean water and air and waste control. The emphasis on these matters is, however, still rudimentary. Highly developed Western European countries are still polluting the air and the waters with only minimal activities to reduce the problem. The health authorities are swamped by traditional short-term problems and do not have the power, organization, know-how or vision to deal with these matters. It is, however, interesting to note that one major driving force in the recent change in the socialist countries was a deep concern in the population about the devastation of the environment in their countries resulting from a political smoke-stack philosophy.

There is an interesting difference between countries that have been highly structured politically and those that have had the emphasis on self-determination. In the first group one finds severe environmental damage of all possible kinds, while in the other group lifestyle diseases, particularly drug abuse, are a dominant feature, especially amongst those who are socially disadvantaged.

The World Health Organization has moved the focus of the organization's policy from disease to health and from health policy to policy for health. The development of health as stated by WHO depends upon:

1 equality of health and living conditions;
2 health promotion and disease prevention;
3 active involvement of the general public;
4 intersectoral co-operation;
5 health and medical care concentrating on primary care;
6 international co-operation.

At the World Health Assembly in 1986 there was a resolution in which the member states called upon each other:

1 to identify goals of a health policy for development in several sectors of society (for example, agriculture, environment, education, housing) and to endeavour to specify health effects of current programmes in these fields;
2 to specify goals of equality in their national health policy objectives, formulated in terms of improved health for underprivileged groups;
3 to use the health status of the population, especially that of underprivileged groups, as an indicator of the quality of social development.

The objective is to increase people's life expectancy by reducing unnecessary and premature death and to improve life quality.

With decentralization of health care it should be possible for local health authorities to set up specific goals using the WHO targets as guidelines and develop a local health policy which is adapted to local needs and local resources. It would also seem easier to mobilize the participation of the population in both the formulation and implementation of the goals when working at the local level.

The growth of population and the increasing density of population in major cities will tend to increase violence, traffic accidents, pollution, inequity and drug abuse. This will seriously affect health, first in the Third World and then more generally. Deforestation and global warming will affect many countries negatively in the beginning of the next century, causing effects such as those already seen in Africa. This will lead to considerable population movements, poverty, refugees, and consequently cultural interactions, which may influence values more than expected and also influence future health policy substantially. It is therefore important for most countries and international health organizations to develop adequate long-term policies to meet the future.

HEALTH POLICY AND POLICY SCIENCE

Health policy operates in areas with strong political influence. There are conflicting goals, variations in values, different outcomes and seldom any consistently superior solutions to problems. Since the policy analyst works in a highly politicized area, sometimes as a pawn in a power game, and policy analysis seldom presents any major chromium-plated solutions, one has to be satisfied by presenting the options and their limits and leave the rest to the political process. Since political debate even in the health care area is regressing towards the mean and, except in emergencies, tends to deal with problems at least a decade after they have been raised, policy analysis can at best hope for a cumulative effect as part of a protracted process.

The dynamics of development when it comes to knowledge and technical development, as well as cultural phenomena and values, have made traditional planning in the field of health care exceedingly difficult, at both the policy and the operational levels. The planning process has been slowed down by the democratic process, which calls for more people to take part in the decision process, while everything else accelerates. This problem has made the use of the scenario technique popular when discussing major structural problems. This methodology has the advantage of liberating the discussion somewhat from ideological attachments and biases. The technique typically gives a description of the consequences of the extremes and can be used to delineate the area of the politically possible, and one may analyse the consequences of the unlikely but possible event with large consequential impact.

Policy development is not a linear process. The reason for this is that changes – at least in democratic societies – can be made only when views and expectations are broadly shared amongst decision makers. The span of time from idea to a critical mass of shared insight amongst decision makers may be substantial, depending upon the level of change. Nationalized health care systems are not only closely structured but are also often very uniformly shaped at the operational level, particularly if there is a strong centralizing power function. As they are politically governed and bureaucratically steered, there is a built-in short-range stability which makes the system less inclined towards renewal. On the libertarian end the flexibility has created a very complex system, not very cheap or satisfying from an equity point of view, which in a way is just as entangled in its prejudice and bias as the other end of the spectrum.

BIBLIOGRAPHY

Amara, R., Morrison, J. I. and Schmid, G. (1988) *Looking Ahead at American Health Care*, Washington, DC: McGraw-Hill/Healthcare Information Center.

Greer, A. Lennarson and Greer, S. (1986) 'Some consequences of market forces in US hospitals: lessons for the new look NHS?', *Health Service Management* 86: 180–2.

Ham, C. (1988) 'Governing the health sector: power and policy making in the English and Swedish health services', *Milbank Quarterly* 66 (2): 389–414.

Heidenheimer, A., Heclo, H. and Adams C. T. (1989) *Comparative Public Policy: The*

Politics of Social Choice in America, Europe, and Japan, 3rd edn, New York: St Martin's Press.

Jönsson, B. (1989) 'What can Americans learn from Europeans?', *Health Care Financing Review* (Annual Supplement).

Majone, G. (1989) *Evidence, Argument and Persuasion in the Policy Process*, New Haven: Yale University Press.

Milio, N. (1988) 'Making healthy public policy; developing the science by learning the art: an ecological framework for policy studies', *Health Promotion* 2 (3): 263–74.

OECD (1990) *Health Care Systems in Transition: The Search for Efficiency*, OECD Social Policy Studies, no. 17, Paris: OECD.

Otter, C. von and Saltman R. B. (1990) 'Towards a Swedish health policy for the 1990s: planned markets and public firms', *Social Science and Medicine*.

Reinhardt, U. E. (1989) 'Health care spending and American competitiveness', *Health Affairs* (Winter): 5–21.

Saltman, R. B. and Otter, C. von (1990) 'Implementing public competition in Swedish county councils: a case study', *International Journal of Health Planning and Management* 5 (2).

WHO (1990) *Basic Documents*, 38th edn, Geneva: World Health Organization.

44

IMMIGRATION POLICY

GUY S. GOODWIN-GILL

Few subjects attract quite the same degree of emotional debate as does immigration. Community membership sits at the centre of the modern notion of the nation-state: we inevitably define ourselves as a community by contrast with, or in opposition to, other communities (Walzer 1983: 31; Hammar 1986). Practice and policy with respect to immigration reveal most shades of difference: from denial of the right to emigrate to the curtailment of all opportunity to enter elsewhere. The ideal of free movement, which found support among the early writers on international law (Goodwin-Gill 1978: 91–6) and certain nineteenth-century economists, still receives occasional formal acknowledgement, for example in the 1948 Universal Declaration of Human Rights (United Nations 1948: article 13(2)) or the 1966 Covenant on Civil and Political Rights (United Nations 1966a: article 12(2)). In modern times, however, it has never really raised itself beyond the inchoate – a right to leave proclaimed for the individual, but without any correlative duty to admit attaching to any state other than that of origin or nationality; even the latter's duty is often disputed by nations anxious to rid themselves of particular individuals or minorities.

Few analysts today share the views of those who earlier defended both free trade and unrestricted immigration, seeing the latter as essentially self-regulating and market driven (Walzer 1983: 37). Ironically, rigorous immigration controls in fact date from this same period, initially constructed to exclude criminals, but rapidly extended to the potential social charge, the sick and the disabled, and the politically undesirable. Those countries which at that time were principally concerned to attract migrants also, for the most part, incorporated racial bases for exclusion, directed against Asian and Asiatic peoples, and intended to maintain the dominant north European characteristics of societies in, for example, Australia, Canada, New Zealand and the United States (Plender 1988: 66–75). While close attention was given to inadmissible classes, immigration overall none the less played a dominant role in the development of economy and country, serving as an important resource for both skilled and unskilled labour. Those few countries still in the business of immigration today, however, have also come to recognize that it serves to meet the needs and aspirations of resident communities by facilitating the strengthening of family and cultural links; and to satisfy domestic concerns and international obligations with respect to refugees and the displaced.

Today immigration policy is nearly everywhere characterized by controls or restrictions, intended to serve narrowly defined national goals. Europe, in particular, has long tended to see itself as a region of *emigration* – an overpopulated resource for distant communities rich in land and opportunity. While that may have been true in the nineteenth century and up until shortly after the Second World War (Perruchoud 1989: 504; Widgren 1989), thereafter Europe became a continent of internal migration and of immigration (Condé 1986). Economic expansion in northern Italy, for example, drew labour from the country's south and away from traditional overseas alternatives in the Americas and Oceania. Similar developments occurred in Greece and, to a lesser extent, in Spain and Portugal. Condé notes that intra-European migration replaced the transoceanic at a period of economic growth, but also at a time when traditional receiving countries were becoming more selective with respect to migrant labour. In the 1950s and 1960s, Europe's labour needs, particularly those of the primary sector, could not be met from within the region alone. The net of attraction and recruitment spread wider and the intake, together with movements from former colonies, generated a base of the foreign-born who were the vanguard of many of today's reluctantly multicultural societies (Penninx 1986). These flows may have been market driven, but their impact and implications for future movements necessarily escaped the control of market forces (Stahl 1988: 33).

As economic need, underdevelopment and wage differentials served to make or made Western European countries poles of attraction, international labour migration changed from a neighbourly, regional affair to a long-distance, large-scale business (Condé 1986: 33), and to these necessary conditions were now added available transport, information and the support systems that developed out of the first movements and became institutionalized by the chain of migration. These additional elements were still in place and rendered no less effective when Western European countries officially turned off the immigration flow in the early 1970s (Hammar 1985), at a time of economic recession. It has never been officially turned on again, although in practice many European states have had to accept that they are now multicultural societies with attendant and substantial domestic ties overseas (Castles *et al.* 1984; also Council of Europe 1989a, 1989b). At one end, restrictive measures had some obvious success in controlling entry, but they could not, of course, reduce the pressure from below: neither the perpetual crisis of underdevelopment (demographic pressures, falling investment, rising unemployment) and its frequent concomitants (intercommunal strife, ideological struggle, persecution of political and other elites); nor the needs and aspirations of established communities for reunion with family and friends (Stahl 1988: 12).

Latterly, Western countries have been under increasing pressure from mixed migrant/refugee streams, particularly from the South. Uncertain how to deal with the latter, they began in the 1980s to employ a variety of generally ineffective control measures (McDowall 1989; Widgren 1989), while in practice tolerating the absorption of the officially unwanted into the bottom end of the labour market. The real prospect of intraregional freedom of movement within the European Community by the end of 1992 seems likely to have an overall negative or restrictive effect upon overseas access to Western Europe, particularly if it is accompanied by a generally more relaxed approach to rising migration pressures from Eastern Europe.

REGULATION AND INTERNATIONAL ORGANIZATION

National and international laws and regulations continue to play a relatively small role in the field of immigration policy. In 1974, the United Nations World Population Conference Plan of Action recommended that voluntary migration be facilitated, and also that discrimination against migrants in society and the labour market be avoided. This recommendation alone has had little or no significant impact on policy and practice.

The defence of the interests of workers employed abroad is expressly included, in the Preamble to its Constitution, among the objectives of the International Labour Organization (ILO). The ILO has recognized the particularly weak position of migrant workers, formally interpreted to cover those who migrate from one country to another for the purpose of being employed there other than on their own account. They are exposed to hostility and exploitation, and commonly face major problems in assimilation or integration, as well as in the preservation of their national, ethnic and linguistic base (Castles et al. 1984: chapters 5–7; Council of Europe 1989b, 1989d). A recent commentator sees the revival of extremist, anti-foreigner violence as due not to migrants themselves but to 'the attempt to treat migrants purely as economic men and women, and to separate between labor power and other human attributes' (Castles 1986: 776; also Böhning 1984: 123, 141; Cohen 1987) Some groups are especially open to violation of rights, such as those exposed to double discrimination (as refugees or migrants, and as women, or because of religious beliefs or ethnic origin). The situation of women migrants is now only slowly being addressed, with belated recognition, in some countries at least, of the disadvantages that flow, for example, from the inadequate provision of basic services such as language training and orientation (Boyd 1987).

716

If fundamental questions of admission or residence still remain largely within the domestic jurisdiction of states (but see Council of Europe 1989a, 1989c), the promotion of standards of non-discrimination and equal treatment has long been on the agenda of the ILO, which has adopted a variety of conventions and recommendations (Perruchoud 1986; Kellerson 1986; Tardu 1985; Böhning 1988; ILO 1980, 1982; International Labour Conference 1980a, 1980b). The most important instruments promoted by the ILO are the Migration for Employment Convention (Revised) 1949 (no. 97); the Migration for Employment Recommendation (Revised) 1949 (no. 86); the Migrant Workers (Supplementary Provisions) Convention 1975 (no. 143); the Migrant Workers Recommendation 1975 (no. 151). Both Conventions are in force, but the number of ratifications is low and their efficacy correspondingly limited, particularly in the major labour-importing states. ILO standards also recognize the reunification of families (see United Nations 1966a: articles 17, 23; Council of Europe 1990, 1989a, 1989c). The type of migration involved is considered a relevant factor, however, as is its permanent or temporary nature and duration. None of the ILO provisions contemplates any obligation to permit reunion, and the entitlement of migrants to be joined by family members is disputed by many states, particularly those which do not consider themselves as countries of permanent immigration.

Of some general relevance to the situation of migrant workers and policies in their regard are the various ILO Conventions on social security, social policy and discrimination in employment (International Labour Conference 1980b; 44 f., n. 49). ILO Conventions rely on the principle of choice of methods by states, and on the principle of progressive implementation, an approach intended to encourage greater readiness on the part of states with different legal and administrative systems, and at different levels of development, to adopt the standards in question. In practice, the reluctance of many states to limit their policy options by subscribing formally to the ILO's standard-setting processes has led to efforts in other international forums, inspired particularly by sending states in the less developed world. In 1985, the United Nations General Assembly adopted a Declaration on the Human Rights of Individuals Who Are Not Citizens of the Country in Which They Live (United Nations 1985). Even here, however, major differences were apparent between the views of sending and receiving states, particularly with respect to minimum rights (Goodwin-Gill 1989: 539–42). These differences, and the problem of securing agreement in this sensitive area, recurred continuously during the drafting of the UN General Assembly's 1990 Convention on the Protection of the Rights of All Migrant Workers and Their Families (Goodwin-Gill 1989: 541 f.; Hasenau 1990). Greater progress with respect to the protection of migrants' rights can be noted in the activities of regional organizations, such as the Council of Europe (Council of Europe 1989a, 1989d), or in the context of regional mechanisms for the promotion of human rights.

Outside the United Nations system, but involved in many of the practical dimensions of interstate movements, stands the International Organization for Migration (IOM), created in 1951 as the International Committee for European Migration (and later renamed the International Committee for Migration). The initial focus of this organization was on the provision of migration services, particularly for migrants and refugees moving out of Europe. Although membership has been traditionally open to governments committed to the principle of freedom of movement, the organization itself recognizes that immigration standards and criteria are to be decided by states as matters falling within their domestic jurisdiction. Over time the scope of activities has considerably increased, accompanied by a change in geographical emphasis; the IOM has become more and more involved in providing services to those moving between less developed countries, assisting in the orderly planning of migration, with transportation, language training, medical and documentary requirements, and return of talent and reintegration. IOM has also provided a forum for states to discuss measures and co-operation with respect to migration laws and policies (Perruchoud 1989: 501).

MIGRATION/IMMIGRATION

Migration can be classified according to various overlapping characteristics. In part, movements of people occur for demographic reasons, such as population pressures in the countries of the 'South'. Additional economic pressures, in the form of unemployment or underemployment, also have their impact in such circumstances, and economic prospects elsewhere offer an opportunity to satisfy basic needs. But the move may also be generated by more specifically *political* conditions – coercion resulting from conflict or persecution, for example (United Nations 1986) – and by such additional causative factors as ethnic, cultural or family links elsewhere.

People move between states for various and complex reasons; even the simplest of cases reveals mixtures of motive, pressure and desire. The line between voluntary and forced migration is often blurred or indeterminate, and rendered more complex by the varying effects of both proximate and root causes. How causes are perceived varies according to perspective. Major displacements result, of course, from what Zolberg identifies as 'two major historical processes, the formation of new States out of colonial empires, and confrontations over the social order in both old and new States' (Zolberg 1990: 93; also Zolberg *et al.* 1989). These processes are frequently combined, and are just as frequently fuelled by external forces, or influenced by the present state of the international economy, existing relations of dependency and the run-on consequences of social and economic inequity.

For the migrant, the 'realm of possible choices' (Papademetriou 1988: 241) will necessarily be conditioned by the declared policies and practices of potential receiving states, as well as by their relative position in the international economy. A greater number of choices is available today, fuelled by information and the example of others. Communications have grown, and information about other places and other chances is readily available; transport is cheaper, and within the bounds of more family budgets; an industry has emerged, within the interstices of the international migration movements, to assist with travel and documentation. But these facilities are, in many respects, consequential upon a greater failing: the inability of the international community, in many instances, to provide local and lasting solutions to the cycle of underdevelopment. As one commentator puts it, voluntary migration is 'largely a response to social and economic inequalities between nations' (Stahl 1988: 12).

Survival is thus commonly the primary motivation, inspired by the existence elsewhere of protection and assistance, food and shelter. Most usually a variety of factors will be involved, not excluding environmental conditions, such as drought or famine (Essam el-Hinnawi 1985), nor economic and demographic considerations of massive unemployment or population pressure. In such cases, 'choices' are not necessarily the reflection of pure personal convenience or 'pure migratory intent', but flow from circumstances and the nature of things, and from the urgent necessity common to all human beings: to satisfy, or try to satisfy, basic needs (Johansson 1990: 253).

Immigration, as a reflection of opportunity, may be either regular or irregular (Böhning 1984: 47). 'Regular migration' for permanent settlement, as a large-scale, regular process, is generally limited to four countries, Australia, Canada, New Zealand and the United States of America, whose total annual intake is in the region of 850,000 persons. In their respective policies, each of the traditional immigration countries puts first emphasis on *family migration* (see Canada 1989). *Refugees and the displaced* often feature as a second priority, and their need for resettlement will often, in principle at least, determine selection without strict regard to immigration criteria such as economic viability or adaptability. Next comes *economic migration*, considered as the recruitment of those with skills specifically needed in the present state of the economy (and thus leading to fluctuations in the relative value of trades and qualifications). *Investors and entrepreneurs* are also welcome, often as exceptions to general criteria relating to language or recognized skill, but as individuals expected to make a substantial, long-term financial or equivalent contribution to the economy of the receiving state.

Regular *migration for temporary purposes* is more often geared to the short-term interests of the state. It may reflect the business and professional needs of multinational corporations; or the grander physical scale of labour brigades recruited (often on a bilateral basis) for construction of major public works in countries rich in natural wealth but short on skills and labour (Birks and Sinclair 1980; Birks et al. 1988; Böhning 1984: chapters 9, 10). Temporary economic need has likewise played its part in intraregional movements in South America and Africa (Böhning 1984: chapter 8), although persistent underdevelopment may often give such migration a semi-permanent character.

The economic, as opposed to the settlement, objective was also a dominant consideration in the development of guest-worker schemes in Western Europe in the 1950s and 1960s. In large measure, however, these schemes also rapidly acquired a permanent and settled dimension, as the value to employers of a skilled or at least experienced work-force was recognized, and as workers were able, in one way or another, to reunite with family members in the state in which they were employed or as they established firmer links with local communities over time (Castles et al. 1984; Castles 1986; Böhning 1984: chapter 6; Piore 1979; Rogers 1985). Even though the policy objectives of the receiving states may have differed initially from those of traditional immigration countries, the effects in both cases have been similar: the institutionalization of multicultural communities in a climate that is, in many countries, increasingly hostile and discriminatory towards the foreigner. It is generally agreed that successful integration depends on securing the migrant's legal status and on facilitating participation in national economic and social life (Council of Europe 1989b, 1990). However, the multicultural aspects of modern societies would appear to figure as a policy consideration more often in the traditional countries of immigration, such as Australia and Canada, than in European countries or other receiving states concerned principally with migration's economic dimensions.

At an Organization for Economic Co-operation and Development (OECD) Conference on the Future of Migration held in May 1986, one observer noted that there was a trend towards convergence in policy – a tendency for both immigration (non-European) and non-immigration (European) states to orient their admission policies increasingly in favour of family reunification (Miller 1987). However, there was little agreement on migration's economic role. European countries linked migration to the labour market, where demand in turn is considered likely to decrease under the influence of new industrial technology. By contrast, in non-European immigration countries, immigration is perceived much more in terms of national development (see Bach and Meissner 1990). There is far less of a tendency now to link admissions to short-term labour needs (and to curtail entry in times of recession), and longer-term strategies are taking over (Australia 1985; Samuel 1988; Taylor 1987, 1988a, 1988b). Present and future demographic concerns, which might be thought to raise pressing issues in the face of population decline in Western

Europe, are not generally being approached in other than labour-market terms (Taylor 1988b).

CLANDESTINE MIGRATION

The pressures to move and the limitation of opportunity have contributed to the perennial problem of irregular, illegal or clandestine migration (United States Congress 1990; Böhning 1984: 53–7; Passel 1986; Lohrmann 1987). The ILO's 1975 Convention (no. 143) has the objective of suppressing migration in abusive conditions, including illegal migration and illegal employment of migrant workers. The Convention defines migration in abusive conditions to include 'any movements of migrants for employment in which the migrants are subjected during their journey, on arrival or during their period of residence and employment to conditions contravening relevant international multilateral or bilateral instruments or agreements, or national laws or regulations'. States are required to take steps to detect and suppress such activities, and to provide minimum legal protection to migrant workers whose situation is irregular; basic human rights are not conditional upon the circumstances of residence, but the reality is that those in an irregular situation often find it difficult if not impossible to obtain anything but the minimum. At this juncture, international policy and national practice may diverge. Standards of treatment of migrant workers (for example, that those admitted on a permanent basis not be required to return home in the event of incapacity arising from illness or injury subsequent to entry; or that loss of employment not be regarded as putting lawfully resident migrant workers into an illegal or irregular situation) are often ignored in many of the labour-importing countries, where the unemployment of the migrant labour force is seen as a social and economic burden best re-exported to the home state.

Paradoxically, many states and interests within states are still reluctant to introduce measures that might significantly reduce the pool of cheap labour; primary sector labour needs, for example, may have been accommodated by concessions to tolerance, if nothing more, and the acceptance of a floating class of refugees and migrants lacking any defined status in their countries of residence. The recent programme of legalization in the United States of America, for example, was delayed for many years by lobbying against employer sanctions, initiated and encouraged by agricultural interests in the southern states (Böhning 1984: 42–4); even now there is pressure to revoke these provisions of the law. If states are sometimes willing to permit regularization of status or to announce general amnesties for those in an irregular situation, policy makers are also inclined to resist such measures for fear that they will encourage further flows (Papademetriou 1989; Miller 1989). Studies have meanwhile confirmed that ethnic minorities in Western Europe, which is what the migrant labour force has become over time, remain vulnerable to dismissal during recession and generally have high rates of unemployment (Castles *et al.* 1984: 53–4, 70–4, 143–9; Castles 1986: 775–6; Böhning 1986: 108).

The available data are far from clear, both as to the numbers involved and as to the supposed social and economic effects of a clandestine migrant worker population (Passel 1986: 181; Castles *et al.* 1984: 31 f., 47, 51, 179). Developed states, in particular, *perceive* the problem as significant, and justify restrictive practices accordingly. In the developing world, too, particular perceptions of the negative effect of migration have periodically led to drastic measures, such as the mass expulsion of foreigners who have entered for the purposes of employment. Mostly, they are in an irregular situation, their presence and economic activity tolerated for a variety of reasons, particularly in times of growth. When stagnation, recession or crises arrive, the foreign worker must often suffer the further disadvantage of expulsion. The Conventions which protect migrants in such circumstances have secured relatively few ratifications, while their benefits often are limited to those lawfully in the country. Foreign nationals expelled from Nigeria in 1983, for example, were outside the scope of the free travel agreement of the Economic Community of West African States, which was limited to visa-free travel for periods up to three months. Significantly, at a seminar organized by the Intergovernmental Committee for Migration (now the IOM) in April of that year, no agreement was reached on even the fundamental human rights which undocumented or irregular migrants should enjoy. Many participants stressed, too, that acceptance of basic rights should not imply *de facto* recognition of the legality of status.

So far as the recessions of recent years have spilled over into the developing world (where they have generally been compounded by conflict, ecological disaster and massive population displacements), the urge to move further afield has strengthened; the balance between pull and push factors tilted inexorably towards the latter, with resulting increases in clandestine migration. Condé concludes that control measures may have slowed, but have generally failed to stop the inflow; and that, no matter how strict the border controls, 'illegal migration movements will be difficult to check so long as the deep-rooted causes of south-north migration persist' (Condé 1986: 16).

CONCLUSION

Substantial demographic growth is to be expected in the developing world over the next thirty to forty years, especially in the percentage of those of working age (Golini and Bonifazi 1987: 10). Apart from labour at the bottom of the ladder, OECD countries, for example, seem unlikely to generate any great demand for foreign labour. Even if they did, their intake capacity is estimated at but a small proportion of the developing world's employment needs. Golini and Bonifazi estimate that with an activity rate of 55 per cent, some 35–40 million jobs must be created each year in the developing world over the next decade (Golini and Bonifazi 1987). They reckon OECD's maximum capacity (if willing) at one million migrants. Migration is obviously not the answer to underdevelopment, but in present conditions the pressure to move seems hardly likely to conform to the standards of slowness, gradualism and selectivity that some managers would prefer (see OECD 1987: 35: Abadan-Unat, General Rapporteur). Experience shows that where there are controls alternative means of entry will be sought so long as the necessary conditions continue: the push from below – economic, political, environmental, humanitarian, or combined; the ties of attraction; and the gateway of opportunity.

Since the late 1980s, a development-oriented approach to migration and refugee flows has begun to figure in the thinking of capital-exporting states and may be expected to have some effect on the content of future policies (Sweden 1990; Switzerland 1990; Kerll 1990; United States Congress 1990). Recent experience shows that there is little long-term comfort in the adoption of restrictive measures, and that there is a degree of self-delusion in the supposition that arrivals can be checked and problems thereby solved. Such measures may, indeed, serve certain management objectives and be a part of an overall 'solution', but they are not likely to constitute the greater part. Similarly, if entry controls are not the whole answer in a coherent immigration policy, neither are post-entry methods such as deportation or mass expulsion. However, foreigners and resident minorities still find themselves in a precarious position, from time to time, even as slow progress is made in favour of the rights of non-citizens. The damaging impact of xenophobia cannot be discounted in any part of the world where there are migrants. It is often an element, if not the very foundation, of measures against them, which in the suddenness of their application disregard the individualized aspect of basic human rights; experience shows that mass expulsions, for example, always take place in conditions of great hardship, characterized by discrimination and arbitrariness.

The developed world will continue to exercise its attraction on the displaced, and it is hardly likely to lose its role as 'pull' factor, no matter how tough or deterrent it seeks to present itself. Strict policies with respect to admission are difficult to maintain at a constant level of consistency, particularly in the face of changing conditions and well-documented tides of violence, danger and oppression. What is more, the essential value base of Western developed countries is oriented towards protection of the individual, and those values frequently pervade not only national review structures but also influential, if not majoritarian, sections among population and policy makers. None of that is foreseeably likely to change, any more than the pressures to move are likely to disappear.

Some states have begun to recognize the necessity or desirability of co-ordinating policies of control. Issues of concern include the operation of networks for illegal and irregular migration; sanctions on those who employ irregular migrants, and on airlines and other carriers who transport insufficiently documented passengers; and the initiation of common visa policies and practices, with respect to migrants, refugees, asylum seekers and others in need. The prospect and objective of a Europe without internal frontiers by 1993, in particular, has given member states of the European Community a new incentive to reach agreement on such basic issues (Feller 1989; Hailbronner 1990; Meijers 1990).

Prospective migratory movements in the coming decades, it has been suggested, may require a reconsideration of traditional notions of state and sovereignty (Keely 1985). At the same time, migration is not a solution to the problems of underdevelopment, even if it helps to relieve social and political pressures and provides short-term financial assistance to sending states in the way of overseas remittances (Keely and Bao Nga Tran 1989).

The complexity of these issues is only now beginning to be recognized; co-operation is clearly an essential feature of future arrangements, but it is not yet clear that states acting within the existing system of international organizations will be able to settle on unified and effective strategies (compare Widgren 1989). The major policy issues still to be addressed by states on an individual and multilateral basis include the following.

1 The role of migration, and its potential scope, in national development and international assistance plans. This will also encompass an assessment of the extent of immigration's place in meeting short- and long-term local labour requirements, and the contribution which overseas remittances may make to the economies of sending states.

2 The parameters of response (local, regional, multilateral) to humanitarian movements of refugees, displaced persons and other persons in distress (such as victims of natural disaster, drought and famine). This will also link solutions and prevention to the realization of human rights, particularly in the economic, social and cultural domain (United Nations 1966b).

3 The assessment of the 'causes' of migration, on the basis of up-to-date information and analysis of demographic, economic, political and social factors in potential 'sending' states.

4 The development of new and the consolidation of old standards of treatment consistent with recognition of the inherent worth and dignity of individual migrants and their families.

5 The determination, particularly among and by 'receiving' states, of the

process due to non-nationals arriving or present within their borders. Such policies, and the laws which may follow them, will need to take account of the reality of multiculturalism in many states, the problems of 'assimilation' and a balance with cultural identity, as well as basic rights questions, such as the conditions of residence and admission to membership of the community.

6 The revision of existing international institutional arrangements to link coherently and more effectively the various organizations presently concerned with different facets of the phenomenon of people moving between states.

Whether the developed world can address those elements that generate migration in such a way as to open up the possibilities of choice to those who would otherwise move will be the major challenge for the 1990s.

REFERENCES

Australia (1985) Committee for the Economic Development of Australia, *The Economic Effects of Immigration on Australia*, vol. 1, P series no. 26, April.

Bach, R. L. and Meissner, D. (1990) *America's Labor Market in the 1990's: What Role Should Immigration Play?*, Washington, DC: Carnegie Endowment for International Peace.

Birks, J. S. and Sinclair, C. A. (1980) *International Migration and Development in the Arab Region*, Geneva: ILO.

Birks, J. S., Seccombe, I. J. and Sinclair, C. A. (1988) 'Labour migration in the Arab Gulf States: patterns, trends and prospects', *International Migration* 26: 267.

Böhning, W. R. (1984) *Studies in International Labour Migration*, London: Macmillan.

——(1986) 'Basic rights of "temporary" migrant workers: law vs. power', in Tomasi, L. (ed.) *In Defense of the Alien*, vol. VIII, New York: Center for Migration Studies.

——(1988) 'The protection of migrant workers and international labour standards', *International Migration* 26: 133.

Boyd, M. (1987) *Migrant Women in Canada: Profiles and Policies*, report submitted to the Monitoring Panel on Migrant Women, OECD, Ottawa: Employment and Immigration Canada.

Canada (1989) *Annual Report to Parliament on Future Immigration Levels*, Ottawa: Employment and Immigration Canada.

Castles, S. (1986) 'The guestworker in Western Europe: an obituary', *International Migration Review* 22: 761.

Castles, S., Booth, H., and Wallace, T. (1984) *Here for Good*, London: Pluto Books.

Cohen, R. (1987) *The New Helots: Migrants in the International Division of Labour*, Aldershot: Gower.

Condé, J. (1986) *South-North International Migrations*, Paris: OECD.

Council of Europe (1989a) *Human Rights without Frontiers*. Madureira, João. Background Document. *Aliens' admission to and departure from national territory: Case-law of the organs of the European Convention on Human Rights and the European Social Charter*. CE Doc. DH-ED-COLL (89) 4. Original in French. Strasbourg. 30 June 1989.

___(1989b) *Human Rights without Frontiers*. Directorate of Human Rights. Background Document. *Intolerance and Human Rights*. CE Doc. DH-ED-COLL (89) 5. Strasbourg. 20 September 1989.

___(1989c) *Human Rights without Frontiers*. Secretariat of the European Commission of Human Rights. *Refugees and Family Reunion of Immigrants: The Strasbourg case law*. CE Doc. DH-ED-COLL (89) 7. Strasbourg. 30 November 1989.

___(1989d) *Community relations and solidarity in European society*. Committee of Experts on Community Relations. *Interim report on the community relations project*. CE Doc. MG-CR (89) 3 rev. Strasbourg. 1989.

___(1990) *Human Rights without Frontiers*. Colloquy, Strasbourg, 30 November–1 December 1989. Committee of Experts for the Promotion of Education and Information in the Field of Human Rights (DH-ED). *Reports of Workshop Rapporteurs and Summing-Up and Conclusions by General Rapporteur*. CE Doc. DH-ED (90) 2. Strasbourg. 25 January 1990.

Essam el-Hinnawi (1985) *Environmental Refugees*, United Nations Environment Programme, New York: United Nations.

Feller, E. (1989) 'Carrier sanctions and international law', *International Journal of Refugee Law* 1: 48.

Golini, A. and Bonifazi, C. (1987) 'Demographic trends and international migration', in OECD, *The Future of Migration*, Paris: OECD.

Goodwin-Gill, G. S. (1978) *International Law and the Movement of Persons Between States*, Oxford: Clarendon Press.

___(1989) 'International law and human rights: trends concerning international migrants and refugees', in *International Migration: An Assessment for the '90s*, *International Migration Review* (Special Silver Anniversary Issue) 23.

Hailbronner, K. (1990) 'The right to asylum and the future of asylum procedures in the European Community', *International Journal of Refugee Law* 2: 341.

Hammar, T. (1985) *European Immigration Policy*, Cambridge: Cambridge University Press.

___(1986) 'Citizenship: membership of a nation and of a state', *International Migration* 24: 735.

Hasenau, M. (1990) 'Setting norms in the United Nations system: the draft conventions on the protection of the rights of all migrant workers and their families in relation to ILO standards on migrant workers', *International Migration* 28: 133.

ILO (1980) *Migrant Workers: Summary of Reports on Conventions Nos. 97 and 143 and Recommendations Nos. 86 and 151*, report III (part 2), Geneva: International Labour Organization.

___ (1982) *International Labour Conventions and Recommendations, 1919–1981, Arranged by Subject Matter*, Geneva: International Labour Organization.

International Labour Conference (1980a) *Migrant Workers: General Survey by the Committee of Experts on the Application of Conventions and Recommendations*, report III (part 4B), 66th session, Geneva.

___(1980b) *Report of the Committee of Experts, Migrant Workers*, 66th session, Geneva.

Johansson, R. (1990) 'The refugee experience in Europe after World War II: some theoretical and empirical considerations', in G. Rystad (ed.) *The Uprooted: Forced Migration as an International Problem in the Post-War Era*, Lund: Lund University Press.

Keely, C. (1985) 'The myth of uncontrolled borders', *Georgetown Immigration Law Reporter* (January): 6–14.

Keely, C. and Bao Nga Tran (1989) 'Remittances from labour migration: evaluations, preformance and implications in *International Migration: An Assessment for the '90s*, *International Migration Review* (Special Silver Anniversary Issue) 23: 500.

Kellerson, H. (1986) 'International labour conventions and recommendations on migrant workers', in A. Dummett (ed.) *Towards a Just Immigration Policy*, London: Cobden Trust.

Kerll, W. (1990) 'New dimensions of the global refugee problem and the need for a comprehensive human rights and development-oriented refugee policy', *International Journal of Refugee Law* (special issue) 2: 237.

Lohrmann, R. (1987) 'Irregular migration: a rising issue in developing countries', *International Migration* 25: 253.

McDowall, R. (1989) 'Co-ordination of refugee policy in Europe', in G. Loescher and L. Monahan (eds) *Refugees and International Relations*, Oxford: Oxford University Press.

Meijers, H. (1990) 'Refugees in Western Europe: "Schengen" affects the entire refugee law', *International Journal of Refugee Law* 2: 428.

Miller, M. J. (1987) *Draft 1986/87 SOPEMI Report*, prepared for the annual meeting of the OECD Continuous Reporting System in Migration (SOPEMI), Paris, 16–17 November.

——(1989) 'Preliminary results of IRCA legalization at the end of phase 1', *International Migration* 27: 109.

OECD (1987) *The Future of Migration*, Paris: Organization for Economic Co-operation and Development.

Papademetriou, D. (1988) 'International migration in a changing world', in C. W. Stahl (ed.) *International Migration Today*, Vol. 2: *Emerging Issues*, Paris: UNESCO.

——(1989) 'The U.S. legalization program: a preliminary final report', *International Migration* 27: 5.

Passel, J. S. (1986) 'Undocumented immigration', *Annals of the American Academy of Political and Social Science* 487: 181.

Penninx, R. (1986) 'International migration in Western Europe since 1973', *International Migration Review* 20: 951.

Perruchoud, R. (1986) 'The law of migrants', *International Migration* 24: 699.

——(1989) 'From the Intergovernmental Committee for European Migration to the International Organization for Migration', *International Journal of Refugee Law* 1: 500.

Piore, M. J. (1979) *Birds of Passage: Migrant Labour and Industrial Societies*, Cambridge: Cambridge University Press.

Plender, R. (1988) *International Migration Law*, 2nd rev. edn, Dordrecht: Martinus Nijhoff.

Rogers, R. (ed.) (1985) *Guests Come to Stay: The Effects of European Labor Migration on Sending and Receiving Countries*, Boulder, Colo.: Westview Press.

Samuel, T. J. (1988) *Canada's Immigration Levels and the Economic and Demographic Environment, 1967–1987*, Ottawa: Employment and Immigration Canada.

Stahl, C. W. (ed.) (1988) *International Migration Today*, Vol. 2: *Emerging Issues*, Paris: UNESCO.

Sweden (1990) 'A comprehensive refugee and immigration policy', *International Journal of Refugee Law* (special issue) 2: 191.

Switzerland (1990) 'A possible Swiss strategy for a refugee and asylum policy in the 1990s', *International Journal of Refugee Law* (special issue) 2: 252.

Tardu, M. (1985) 'Migrant workers', in R. Bernhardt (ed.) *Encyclopedia of Public International Law*, vol. 8, Amsterdam: North Holland.

Taylor, C. (1987) *Demography and Immigration to Canada: Challenge and Opportunity*, Ottawa: Employment and Immigration Canada.

——(1988a) *The Role of Immigration in Determining Canada's Eventual Population Size*, Population Working Paper no. 11, Ottawa: Employment and Immigration Canada.

——(1988b) *The OECD and Migration: Canadian Perspectives*, Ottawa: Employment and Immigration Canada.

United Nations (1948) Universal Declaration of Human Rights, UN General Assembly resolution 217A(III), December.

——(1966a) International Covenant on Civil and Political Rights, UN General Assembly resolution 2200A(XXI), December.

——(1966b) International Covenant on Economic, Social and Cultural Rights, UN General Assembly resolution 2200A(XXI), December.

——(1985) Declaration on the Human Rights of Individuals Who Are Not Citizens of the Country in Which They Live, UN General Assembly resolution 40/144, December.

——(1986) Group of Governmental Experts, *Report on International Co-operation to Avert New Flows of Refugees*, UN doc, A/41/324, May.

United States Congress (1990) *Unauthorized Migration: An Economic Development Response*, Report of the Commission for the Study of International Migration and Cooperative Economic Development, Washington, DC: US Congress.

Walzer, M. (1983) *Spheres of Justice: A Defense of Pluralism and Equality*, New York: Basic Books.

Widgren, J. (1989) 'Europe and international migration in the future: the necessity for merging migration, refugee, and development policies', in Loescher, G. and Monahan, L. (eds) *Refugees and International Relations*, Oxford: Oxford University Press.

Zolberg, A. (1990) 'The refugee crisis in the developing world: a close look at Africa', in Rystad, G. (ed.) *The Uprooted: Forced Migration as an International Problem in the Post-War Era*, Lund: Lund University Press.

Zolberg, A., Suhrke, A. and Aguayo, S. (1989) *Escape from Violence: Conflict and the Refugee Crisis in the Developing World*, New York: Oxford University Press.

FURTHER READING

Appleyard, R. (ed.) (1988) *International Migration Today*, Vol. 1: *Trends and Prospects*, Paris: UNESCO.

——(1989) 'Migration and development: myths and reality', in *International Migration: An Assessment for the '90s, International Migration Review* (Special Silver Anniversary Issue) 23: 486.

International Migration Review (1989) *International Migration: An Assessment for the '90s, International Migration Review* (Special Silver Anniversary Issue) 23.

Loescher, G. and Monahan, L. (eds) (1989) *Refugees and International Relations*, Oxford: Oxford University Press.

Rystad, G. (ed.) (1990) *The Uprooted: Forced Migration as an International Problem in the Post-War Era*, Lund: Lund University Press.

Teitelbaum, M. (1985) *Latin Migration North*, New York: Council on Foreign Relations.

Tomasi, L. (ed.) (1986) *In Defense of the Alien*, vol. VIII, New York: Center for Migration Studies.

Zolberg, A., Suhrke, A., and Aguayo, S. (1986) 'International factors in the formation of refugee movements', *International Migration Review* 20: 151.

45

THE CONCEPT OF SECURITY

LAWRENCE FREEDMAN

Political units value their security above all else, for this reflects their ability to survive as distinctive entities. Hence 'national security' is presented as the prime responsibility of government. Yet the self-evident importance of this objective has not been matched by a reliable definition of the underlying concept. As a result, it is something to which politicians make regular appeals without being subjected to the rigorous tests of logic and evidence.

The status of security as a controversial political value and its habitual misuse as a rationale has discouraged academic investigation, implying a lack of any intrinsic value as a concept. As a result, security has become, in Barry Buzan's phrase, an 'underdeveloped concept', which deserves to be recognized as 'much more powerful and useful than its current status would suggest' (Buzan 1983: 2).

Buzan lists five possible explanations for its weak conceptual development. First, it defies simple definition and is 'essentially contested' (although as he notes this latter attribute does not prevent other contested concepts such as 'power' and 'the state' generating enormous literatures). Second, for those working within the realist school, which has been pre-eminent in international relations theory, power is the dominant concept and security merely a natural consequence of its effective accumulation and exertion. Third, because security as an (albeit weakly developed) concept is linked to the realist school it has suffered from guilt through association and has thus been neglected by those challenging this school. Fourth, as the critique of realism encouraged new approaches to international relations, of which one of the most significant is the 'interdependence' school, the military dimension with which 'security' is naturally associated has been seen to be increasingly marginal when compared with the economic. Meanwhile strategic studies, in which a military focus is maintained and where security is a central concept, allocates little time to conceptual development, with its energies taken up by new technologies or the latest policy debates. Lastly, Buzan suggests, policy makers are quite happy to

730

keep the concept ambiguous and imprecise – it makes it easier to appeal to it in support of a great variety of objectives.

In one of the most thorough attempts prior to Buzan to analyse the concept, Arnold Wolfers described security as an 'ambiguous symbol' and also noted the potential for the ambiguity to be exploited by policy advocates (Wolfers 1962). Conceptual imprecision can thus have important policy consequences, for recourse to the requirements of 'security' can be used to justify exceptional measures – perhaps as an extension of patriotism as the 'last refuge of the scoundrel'. Censorship can be imposed, political rights suspended, young men conscripted and aliens deported all in the name of security.

Suspicion that security is too readily manipulated by the unscrupulous helps explain why academics have become wary of employing it for analytical purposes, yet the extent to which the concept can perform such a critical political role underlines its broad attraction. It is not necessary to endorse all dubious appeals to recognize that voters expect a government to provide security, and that its simplest meaning – a capacity to cope with threats – is widely understood.

THE CONCEPT

According to Wolfers, 'security, in an objective sense, measures the absence of threats to acquired values, in a subjective sense, the absence of fear that such values will be attacked' (Wolfers 1962: 150). This dual character is reflected in the dictionary definitions of being 'secure' which refer on the one hand to being 'safe against attack, impregnable, reliable, certain not to fail or give way' and on the other to being 'untroubled by danger or apprehension' (*Concise Oxford Dictionary*). It combines a physical condition with a state of mind. It is also negative in that it is achieved when bad things do not happen rather than when good things do. This means that it is often difficult to judge whether actions undertaken in the name of security have made any real difference to the situation.

Translating security as a physical condition into an objective for a state soon raises problems. One might have complete confidence in the ability of a bridge to withstand a certain weight and volume of traffic or of armour to resist specified projectiles. In this sense the bridge and the armour are secure. But the design problem undergoes a step change when the tests to which the bridge and the armour could be subjected are varied by an opponent determined to find their breaking point.

Such a dynamic interaction must be the core of any strategic concept. A key feature of strategy is the interdependence of decision making (Schelling 1963: 3). Thus any provisions for security must always be tested against the potential challenge of an intelligent opponent. There can never be an absolute definition of security because it is an inherently relational concept. One can identify physical conditions that are more or less favourable to a secure existence, but these can only be properly assessed in relation to the capabilities and intentions of possible adversaries.

An analysis of security must therefore be outward in that it depends on an assessment of external threats. It must also be inward. It requires vulnerability before another's hostility can be turned into a threat. This hostility is irrelevant if there are no means through which it can be expressed. The ability to take advantage of another's areas of weakness is a reasonable indication of power. Power is also a relational concept. The production of intended effects (as power is commonly defined – see Russell 1938: 25) requires a match between the resources of one and the weaknesses of another.

A state anxious to resist another's will must therefore look not only to the potential enemy's capabilities but also to its own exploitable vulnerabilities. Much of the analysis of security is concerned with identifying those national weaknesses – from militant trade unions to open borders – which might be manipulated by an enemy. When this is done the next stage is to see how susceptible these vulnerabilities might be to corrective measures. No state can ever be completely invulnerable and so none can ever enjoy complete security. It is always a matter of degree. Security can therefore be defined as the extent of a state's confidence in its capacity to withstand another's power.

VULNERABILITIES

Countries can be vulnerable in a number of ways – for example, supplies of raw materials from distant sources, secessionist movements in a particular region, a long border which is hard to police or major cities within range of enemy missiles. Security policy revolves around judgements concerning the severity of known vulnerabilities and the measures necessary to reduce any risk to an acceptable level. There can, of course, also be *unknown* vulnerabilities which will only be revealed when a clever opponent is able to exploit them.

How does a state identify its vulnerabilities? This is much more than a question of where an enemy might inflict hurt. It involves fundamental values and interests. A revolutionary government will see the revolution itself as something to protect and may assume that it is at risk from those who fear that it will be copied in their own country. An imperial power will see any challenge to its rule in a single colony as a threat to its authority throughout the empire. A trading nation will be anxious with regard to interference with sea routes while one that imports all vital raw materials will be sensitive to possible manipulation by its suppliers.

There is not necessarily a close match between the judgements made within a state as to where an adversary might inflict the greatest harm and those made within the adversary. They will both be working with different value systems and different understandings of political dynamics. Just as a householder may protect with great care a collection of rare books of no interest to a likely burglar while leaving a television unguarded, so a state may concentrate on defending territory that has great symbolic importance even though it is of no practical interest to any predator. This is one reason why the threat from others is often misperceived (Jervis 1978).

Although security is often discussed as solely a question of military policy, the above examples indicate that critical vulnerabilities can be in the economic, social and political spheres as much as the military. The political dimension is especially important because real threats will only arise out of conflicts of interest and not just because another state may see in some weakness a tempting opportunity. Why then the focus on the military? This is because there is often little that can be done, at least over the short term, with regard to patterns of trade, reserves of raw materials and social structure, and any adjustments will require the development of a range of policy instruments that are not normally available. It is fundamental in the sense that it is only through military means that one state can take direct control of another and also that the armed forces are directly under state control and are the only instruments primarily geared to conflict with another state.

A distinction is often drawn between internal and external security. The former is concerned with subversion and challenges from disaffected groups who fail to accept the state's authority, while the latter is concerned with the threats posed by other states. Each is often dealt with by distinct agencies. However, the distinction often breaks down in practice. For many states the key vulnerability that might be exploited by a hostile power relates to a flaw in its political structure. A persecuted minority, a regional uprising, a frustrated group of officers are all liable to make common cause with an outside power who may share their hostility to the ruling group and may be prepared to help subvert it. Few internal challenges may be externally generated and most will have no external links. None the less, the tie-up between internal and external threats is the most dangerous challenge for any state, and it is of note that a significant proportion of modern conflicts are largely concerned with the battle for power within a particular country rather than between countries.

In practice it is important to note the interaction between the various types of vulnerabilities. For example, in the mid-1970s there was an abrupt increase in the price of oil as a result of a successful producers' cartel, and at one point this was combined with an Arab oil embargo in order to put direct pressure on the West to end support for Israel. Over the long term it proved possible to adjust energy policies and develop new sources of supply to ease dependence on Arab oil. In the short term, if the crisis had been chronic the only alternative response would have been military action (supposing a realistic option existed).

Another form of pressure on the West has been terrorist attacks on international communications, especially aircraft. Again the long-term policy of adjustment has been to improve airport security, while in the short term there is a temptation to attack the bases of those believed responsible (as with the 1986 US attack on Tripoli in response to Libyan support for terrorist action).

As there are so many possible areas of vulnerability, a key question in security policy is the degree of risk to assign to each one, to be set against the cost and feasibility of attempts to ease them. As an example we can take a basic vulnerability which is universally shared – the destruction of centres of population by nuclear-tipped missiles. Most countries can do nothing about this vulnerability but do not concern themselves as they can think of no good reason why a nuclear power would attack them in this way. They assign the problem a low risk. Others may see some risk and accept that this means an adjustment in relations with the nuclear power. They must follow non-provocative policies in relation to the nuclear power, or develop their own nuclear power to act as a deterrent, or draw on the deterrent effect of another's nuclear power, or combine all these approaches.

The only additional option would be to seek to remove the threat. This could be done either by a surprise attack on the threatening weapons, or by constructing defence capable of intercepting the weapons before they reach their targets, or by providing shelter for the population if an attack is unstoppable. All these three options have at various times been discussed by the Soviet Union and the United States and, for a variety of reasons including the counter-measures available to the opponent, have been generally judged not to be feasible, although such judgements are always controversial.

An estimate concerning the risk of a particular vulnerability being exploited, which can depend on the sort of risks the opponent is deemed likely to take, can never be objective. The relevant information will always be imperfect and much will depend on calculations of probabilities. Individuals in exactly the same conditions can vary in their sense of security, according to whether they naturally tend to be paranoid or complacent. This is also the case with states. Security is therefore a function of personality as much as circumstance.

The political personality of a state when it comes to security will reflect cultural attributes developed over time (for example, the insularity of an island people, or religious convictions) and past experience of conflict. Neighbours of Germany are still anxious that it might return to its former aggressive ways, while the holocaust continues to influence Israeli policy. Countries regularly involved in wars have quite different expectations from those that have enjoyed periods of unbroken peace. Political personality will also be influenced by the distribution of power within the state. This will determine whether certain groups are able to insist that their interests are protected as a matter of priority, and also who is able to influence the allocation of resources to the various instruments of security policy. Perceptual biases in states reflect distortions in decision-making processes rather than personality defects (unless the decision making is so distorted as to depend solely on an authoritarian leader). A number of explanations can be put forward as to why states might come to exaggerate threats, such as a tendency by the military to indulge in worst-case assessments.

NATIONAL AND INTERNATIONAL SECURITY

A degree of insecurity is an unavoidable product of the nature of the inter-national system. The anarchic nature of this system means that it is always possible that states will attempt to resolve their differences through force of arms. There will always be some doubt concerning the long-term intentions of others, for even if relations with one government are cordial those with a successor might be much cooler. Because intentions change more quickly than capabilities, states will gear their military policies to the tangible attributes of a potential adversary rather than to its proclaimed intentions. It is often sug-gested that arms races set in motion on this basis can aggravate political relations and in turn lead to war. History provides no examples of such a cause and effect, despite some of the explanations offered for the First World War (Rotberg and Rabb 1989). A more useful concept than the 'arms race' is that of the 'security dilemma'. According to this, the efforts of one state to render itself secure, which may have only defensive motives, may be interpreted by another as offensive in intent, so increasing its insecurity and leading it to take its own corrective measures and thereby generating a vicious cycle (Herz 1951; Jervis 1978).

These structural factors indicate that the ultimate answer to the problem of insecurity cannot be found at the state level. This leads to advocacy of an international approach to security able to put conflicts between particular states in perspective. In addition, this is the level at which any attempt to resolve differences can most readily be organized. Thus a wholly 'national' focus to security, providing an inevitably narrow focus, has been rejected in favour of a more holistic, systemic view (Booth 1979). This can also be seen as an attempt to reconcile realist with legalist/idealist approaches to international relations, by pointing to the realists' inability, in their own terms, to provide definitive answers to the problem of national security, and also pointing to the need for idealist approaches, with their stress of international rules and institutions, to address security interests.

Buzan notes that only great powers are in a position to carry out a national security strategy, drawn from within the threatened state. As states get smaller they come to look to other states as allies and protectors. Small, vulnerable states often place their hope in what Buzan calls an 'international security strategy', which depends on the adjustment of relations between states. However, an international security strategy can take a variety of forms.

The 'balance of power' system, within which states build up their strength while making and unmaking tactical alliances, reflects a hope that independent states each pursuing national security strategies will produce a relatively stable equilibrium (in the same way that economists might hope that the 'magic hand' of the market would transform pursuit of individual self-interest into the common good). This was achieved for much of the nineteenth century following the defeat of Napoleon in 1815. As Germany unified and gained in power, the system showed increasing signs of strain until it broke down completely in 1914. (On the 'balance of power' concept, see Wright 1989.)

The horror of the 1914–18 war encouraged not only attempts to prohibit war as a means of resolving disputes but also the establishment of a collective security system, by which all states would accept responsibility for each others' security and take common action against an aggressor.

The 1939–45 war is commonly seen as a failure of a collective security system as much as the previous war was seen as a failure of a balance-of-power system. The experience of the League of Nations suggested that in order to make a collective security system work it was necessary to ensure that all relevant states joined the system, that there were agreed means of determining aggression in particular instances and that collective action would follow almost automatically. The League, however, was weakened by the failure of the United States to join it, out of a desire to avoid further entanglement in European squabbles, and by the League's failure to respond to the challenges posed by Japan, Italy and Germany.

The lack of a supranational authority means that states maintain an independence of action which allows them to respond to particular crises according to their own perceived national interests rather than in terms of the collective interest. The political conditions which make the state so special undermine efforts towards a collective security regime. Even an alliance, which is a form of partial collective security system, can be seen as second-best to a national strategy. Overdependence upon the protection of another creates the risk of being abandoned at the last minute.

On the other hand, the balance-of-power approach can get caught by the shifts of power that result from the rise and fall of states according to their economic prowess, or their ability to cope with purely domestic challenges, or the opportunities for expanding their influence which may arise from the processes of change in neighbouring states. Both the national and the international security strategies thus appear flawed.

SECURITY POLICIES IN THE MODERN WORLD

Following the Second World War there was a drift back towards realist approaches. The previous decades were seen to have provided sobering examples of the dangers of optimism with regard to another's intentions and of allowing aggressive states to go unchallenged, as well as of the limits of international institutions. This tendency was reinforced by suspicion of Soviet totalitarianism and its intentions *vis-à-vis* Europe and the consequent deterioration in relations among the wartime allies. But the potentially catastrophic consequences of total war were now even greater than before and so there were considerable incentives for potential enemies to work together to prevent any conflict getting out of hand. The security policies of the major powers since 1945 have therefore tended to involve a mixture of national and international elements, including both military preparedness and alliances and pursuit of *détente* and measures of arms control. The resulting mixture can be said to have worked, given the absence of a third world war.

One critical feature of the post-war security environment was its bipolarity. Theorists of international relations argued that bipolarity is stable because it leads naturally to a stalemate, while more multipolar systems are always in an unsettling state of flux.

After the Second World War Europe was divided according to the path of liberation from Nazi rule into East and West. The former became socialist states dominated by the Soviet Union, eventually to be gathered together in the Warsaw Pact, while the second remained capitalist and drew closer to the United States, forming the North Atlantic Treaty Organization (NATO). Gradually other regions of the world began to reflect this East–West conflict. In Asia, the success of the communist revolution in China, followed by the attack by communist North Korea on the South, encouraged the view that here too local politics could be understood in terms of bipolarity. The processes of decolonization brought many new states to the fore and there was a degree of competition to encourage them to follow a capitalist or a socialist road. This too reinforced the notion of bipolarity, although many of these states sought to escape from this presumption – under the banner of non-alignment – and in practice most regions other than Europe did not lend themselves to such simplistic interpretations.

Another factor which fortified the sense of a durable stand-off was the arrival of nuclear weapons coincident with the start of the Cold War. By the early 1950s, these weapons were coming to dominate security calculations, yet from the start they had provided clear reason why another war was best avoided. Their enormous destructive power, which underwent a step change as 'city-busting' thermonuclear bombs superseded the first fission 'atomic' bombs, provided an unambiguous warning of the consequences of any repli-

737

cation of the strategic bombing campaigns of the Second World War. During the 1950s the range of these weapons was also extended and by the end of the decade both superpowers were introducing intercontinental ballistic missiles. By the mid-1960s the situation could be described as one of 'mutual assured destruction' (Freedman: 1989).

Although the United States had the lead in nuclear capability for much of this period, the significance of any superiority declined given the devastating impact of only a few Soviet weapons reaching American soil. To the United States, which had long felt protected by the Pacific and Atlantic oceans, long-range Soviet power undermined this presumption of invulnerability (Brodie 1959), although it remained far less vulnerable than others to occupation by a hostile power.

There were two important questions with regard to this nuclear balance. The first related to its delicacy. Might technological breakthroughs allow one side to neutralize the nuclear power of the other? This would involve catching forces on the ground prior to launch in a disarming attack (first strike) or intercepting them before they could reach their targets (active defence). Despite substantial investments in advanced systems the balance remained stable. The increasing use of relatively invulnerable submarines as launch platforms meant that it would be difficult to destroy all means of retaliation in a surprise attack while centres of population remained hopelessly vulnerable. As late as the mid-1980s President Reagan, in his Strategic Defence Initiative, was still toying with the idea of finding a means of defence against ballistic missile attack, but it was evident that such a grand objective was not feasible (Lakoff and York 1989).

The second question raised by the nuclear balance concerned the extent of its deterrent effect. There was good reason to believe that nuclear arsenals deterred each other. But if neither side would gain from initiating nuclear hostilities, what credibility should be attached to a threat to do just that in the face of overwhelming conventional military strength? This was the position adopted by NATO in an effort to deter the superior conventional strength of the Warsaw Pact without the expense of attempting to match this strength. As the immediate risk of war subsided, Western countries sought to reduce their defence burdens to a few per cent of gross domestic product. Reliance on nuclear deterrence allowed this to happen. While it was never wholly credible that NATO would escalate to the nuclear level, in practice the mere possibility that it might came to be seen to have sufficient deterrent effect. This was a bluff that would be extremely risky to call.

Another aspect of the range of the deterrent effect was geographical. By locating nuclear weapons in areas of vital interest, such as West Germany or South Korea, the United States ensured that any aggressor faced a nuclear threat. Where interests became less vital the relevance of nuclear threats became ambiguous. The record of the nuclear age is of an evident unwilling-ness to use nuclear weapons against non-nuclear states, even when engaged in combat (as in Vietnam), and an equally evident reluctance to get into even non-nuclear combat with other nuclear states. In Europe, at least, stable political bipolarity reinforced by elemental fears of war meant that the tensions and harsh rhetoric of the Cold War never came close to a truly hot war.

However, while bipolarity and nuclear deterrence contrived to produce stability at the systemic level, especially as it related to Europe, more basic changes were underway at the level of the state.

Although the state remains the basic unit in international politics, the 'society' of states is in a process of continual development. This is a question not just of individual states rising or subsiding but of changes in the character of states and the relations between them. For example, since 1945 the expan-sion of the international economy and advances in international communi-cations have increased the interdependence of states and also led to a growing role of non-state actors (such as multinational companies) in international affairs. The relations among Western capitalist states have thus matured to a point where it becomes extremely difficult to envisage hostilities breaking out among them. This is especially true of members of the European Community. Given the role of Franco-German hostility in generating war in the past this was no mean achievement. Common security arrangements such as NATO survive in part because they serve a socially and economically coherent group and are not simply a product of tactical convenience. This is the sort of virtuous development envisaged by theorists of interdependence.

However, despite the fact that the rhetoric of interdependence was also embraced in the communist world, integration there was far less marked and economic development much more limited. The consequences of economic failure in the countries of the Warsaw Pact were substantial, in that the communist governments lacked any legitimacy and the close relationship with the Soviet Union was deeply resented. When the point was reached at which economic reform was impossible within the existing political framework, it was the framework which gave way with remarkable speed.

This led to the end of the bipolar system in Europe but without any clarity as to what might take its place. There has been a recent revival of discussion on new collective security structures, now to be based on the Conference on Security and Co-operation in Europe (CSCE). However, the limited achieve-ments of CSCE to date have been based on forging a consensus over a prolonged period, hampered by an insistence on unanimity (thirty-three Euro-pean states plus the United States and Canada) and the lack of a permanent base and secretariat. It can be strengthened, but not necessarily sufficiently to cope with the great variety of challenges that Europe is now likely to face.

These challenges fall far short of the set-piece confrontation which has dominated Western security debates over the past few decades. Rather they may be more typical of those that are found in the Third World. The most striking feature of the Europe that is emerging from communism, in addition to its poor economic state, is the strength of nationalist feeling and the divisions among ethnic groups. These are proving to be particularly intense within the former Soviet Union.

As Western countries address a transformed Europe they must develop a new security policy. As the broad thrust of this article would indicate, the starting point for this effort must be a judgement on vulnerabilities. Even without a strong, hostile power threatening hegemony in Europe, the Western countries might still wish to protect themselves from the consequences of disorder. If the part of Europe which previously knew a rough order imposed by Moscow poses any real security problem to the West, it may be as a result of population movements or economic dislocation. Exactly how that might be done without becoming embroiled in a series of complex and intractable conflicts remains to be seen.

REFERENCES

Booth, K. (1979) *Strategy and Ethnocentrism*, London: Croom Helm.

Brodie, B. (1959) *Strategy in the Missile Age*, Princeton: Princeton University Press.

Buzan, B. (1983) *People, States and Fear*, Brighton: Wheatsheaf.

Freedman, L. (1989) *The Evolution of Nuclear Strategy*, 2nd edn, London: Macmillan.

Herz, J. H. (1951) *Political Realism and Political Idealism*, Chicago: University of Chicago Press.

Jervis, R. (1978) 'Co-operation under the security dilemma', *World Politics* 30 (2): 167–214.

Lakoff, S. and York, H. (1989) *A Shield in Space: Technology, Politics and the Strategic Defense Initiative*, Berkeley: University of California Press.

Rotberg, R. and Rabb, T. (1989) *The Origin and Prevention of Major Wars*, Cambridge: Cambridge University Press.

Russell, B. (1938) *Power: A New Social Analysis*, London: Allen & Unwin.

Schelling, T. (1963) *The Strategy of Conflict*, reprinted 1980, Cambridge, Mass.: Harvard University Press.

Wolfers, A. (1962) 'National security as an ambiguous symbol', in A. Wolfers, ch. 10 of *Discord and Collaboration*, Baltimore: Johns Hopkins University Press.

Wright, M. (ed.) (1989) 'Special issue on the balance of power', *Review of International Studies* 15 (2).

FURTHER READING

The number of books with security in the title is massive, although few do more than discuss national defence policies. In addition to the titles mentioned above, readers wishing to explore this subject further could consult two substantial collections of essays: J. Baylis, K. Booth, J. Garnett and P. Williams (1987) *Contemporary Strategy*, 2 vols, London: Croom Helm; and E. Kolodziej and P. Morgan (1989) *Security and Arms Control*, New York: Greenwood Press. For discussions of contemporary issues see F. Heisbourg (ed.) (1989) *The Changing Strategic Landscape*, London: Macmillan.

46

ETHNIC POLICY

MARTIN MARGER

The development of nation-states and the expansion of Europe beginning in the fifteenth century produced for the first time societies made up of distinct racial and ethnic groups living within a common political and economic system. The emergence of most contemporary multiethnic societies, however, is a more recent historical phenomenon, arising from several global currents. Chief among these are large-scale immigrations throughout the nineteenth and twentieth centuries and the creation of new states in the Third World following the post-Second World War breakup of European colonialism. Few societies today are not, to some extent at least, multiethnic.

With emergent heterogeneity, the overriding questions of ethnic policy in these societies have been concerned with how diverse ethnic groups are incorporated into the polity and other major institutions, how intergroup conflict is mediated, and how societal resources are apportioned among the groups. In a broad sense, social policy can propel a heterogeneous population into one of two trajectories: the integration of diverse groups into a more homogeneous societal unit or the maintenance of group divisions within a context of common citizenship. With each alternative, state policies either challenge or sustain the inequitable distribution of resources among ethnic groups, and regulate, to some degree, the nature and extent of group interaction. Historically, few societies have been consistent in the drift of their ethnic policies, vacillating instead between, on the one hand, promoting absorption of distinct ethnic groups into the social mainstream and, on the other, preserving group boundaries. Similarly, policies pertaining to the distribution of economic and political resources have fluctuated between measures designed to foster ethnic equalization and measures aimed at sustaining group inequality.

At the outset, we must recognize that few nations in the modern world officially differentiate their population by racial or ethnic order. More commonly in multiethnic societies groups are recognized by the state in a *de facto* manner, creating, as a result, issues of ethnic identification and classification.

Given the imprecise and shifting views of the notions of race and ethnicity, societies have employed different criteria, often inconsistently, in categorizing individuals and groups. Omi and Winant (1986) suggest the term 'racial formation' to describe the social flexibility of the race concept and the role of the state in legitimizing specific racial and ethnic categories. In the United States, for example, southern and eastern European groups, such as Italians, Greeks, Jews and Slavs, who earlier in the twentieth century were classified and treated as 'races', are today commonly understood as 'ethnic groups', whose members are distinguishable only on the basis of cultural traits, not phenotypes or genetic features. Even where cultural or physical differences among groups are strongly evident, the state may combine several distinct ethnic categories into one, based on some overarching characteristic like language or geographical origin. The designation of all groups in the United States with Latin American origins as 'Hispanic' is a case in point, as is the growing tendency to treat diverse Asian groups as a single unit. Such classifications have decisive policy implications, dictating the manner in which group members are dealt with by the state and governing social responses to them.

Conceptualizations of race and ethnicity on the part of both policy makers and social scientists have lacked precision and consistency. Moreover, the race concept in particular has generated great controversy. As a result, some have suggested a broad application of the term ethnic group to include groups identified by admixtures of national origin, cultural distinctiveness, racial features or religious affiliation (Ben-Rafael 1982; Gordon 1964; Hunt and Walker 1974). Because each distinguishable group in modern multiethnic societies ordinarily displays features deriving from a combination of these origins, this appears to be a practical solution to a continuously perplexing conceptual problem. Another way of approaching this definitional issue is to specify the varieties of ethnicity. Enloe (1973), for example, classifies tribal, national and racial ethnicity according to the origins of ethnic groups' separate identities. What is critical in any case is that the group's members are recognized by themselves and by the larger society as a distinct social grouping and are set off from others on the basis of certain cultural and/or physical characteristics (Schermerhorn 1970; Shibutani and Kwan 1965). In the following discussion, a broadly based inclusive meaning, incorporating both cultural and racial components, is implicit in references to 'ethnic' or 'ethnic group'.

Most important from the standpoint of policy is that groups in multiethnic societies are arranged in an ethnic hierarchy, in which a dominant group 'has preeminent authority to function both as guardians and sustainers of the controlling value system, and as prime allocators of rewards in the society' (Schermerhorn 1970: 12–13). Other ethnic groups are therefore minority groups, given differential treatment, either legally or customarily, on the basis of their cultural or physical distinctiveness (Wirth 1945). A society's system of ethnic stratification is shaped by the nature of initial contact between groups, the scarce resources for which they compete, and, most importantly, the ability of one to impose its dominance over others (Lieberson 1961; Noel 1968). Dominant–minority relations, then, are power relations which mould the legal and customary framework of group interaction in multiethnic societies. Ethnic policy is therefore shaped within that framework.

Three major patterns have characterized the ethnic policies of multiethnic societies at particular times, each undergirded by a sometimes explicit but more often tacit ethnic ideology: assimilation, equalitarian pluralism and inequalitarian pluralism.

ASSIMILATION

Assimilation, as Yinger defines it, is 'a process of boundary reduction that can occur when members of two or more societies, ethnic groups, or smaller social groups meet' (Yinger 1985: 30). Assimilation, then, can be seen as a homogenizing objective or ideal, toward which multiethnic societies aim, and for which public policies and ideologies are put in place. The goal of assimilationist policies is, in Barth and Noel's terms, 'the biological, cultural, social, and psychological fusion of distinct groups to create a new ethnically undifferentiated society' (Barth and Noel 1972: 336).

If the intent of assimilationist policies is to reduce the cultural and structural divisions among groups, ideally, at the culminating point of the assimilation process, a homogeneous society is forged in which groups are no longer racially or culturally differentiated. Ethnicity therefore no longer serves as a basis for the unequal distribution of wealth and power. Citizens are recognized only as individuals, not as group members, and ethnic groups, therefore, can make no claims against the state. This complete form of assimilation, however, is rarely achieved either for the society as a whole or for specific groups within it. Instead, assimilation is variable in form and degree, as is evident among those societies that have, either in the past or currently, adopted an assimilationist approach to ethnic relations: the United States, Canada, Australia, Brazil, Argentina and Israel. These are societies which have absorbed large populations of voluntary immigrants, the major targets of assimilationist policies. For indigenous or involuntary immigrant groups, however, policies of a noticeably different nature have been instituted. Moreover, in none of these societies have assimilationist policies been applied consistently even to voluntary immigrants.

Cultural and structural assimilation

As a societal process assimilation may be seen as encompassing two dimensions: cultural and structural. The cultural dimension involves the adoption by one ethnic group of another's cultural traits – language, religion, diet and so on. At the end point of the process of cultural assimilation the previously distinct cultural groups are no longer distinguishable on the basis of their behaviour and values.

Although cultural assimilation is ideologically driven by liberal notions of individual choice, weaker (that is, minority) groups almost always take on the major cultural traits of the dominant group. Policies prescribing that groups conform to the dominant culture have been evident in most multiethnic societies. In the United States, for example, periods of large-scale immigration have produced official or quasi-official efforts at imposing language and behavioural styles on entering groups. Policies aimed at 'Americanizing' southern and eastern European immigrants of the late nineteenth and early twentieth centuries, for example, were abetted by notions of Social Darwinism. Native Americans, too, were dealt with in such a way as to impose the dominant cultural traits, though Indian policy fluctuated between the goals of assimilation and cultural self-determination. As for involuntary immigrants, specifically African slaves, the imposition of the dominant culture was a fundamental part of slave policy from the outset.

Whereas cultural assimilation refers to a blending of behaviours, values and beliefs, structural assimilation refers to an increasing degree of social interaction among different ethnic groups. With structural assimilation, members of minority ethnic groups are dispersed throughout the society's various institutions and increasingly enter into social contracts with members of the dominant group. In its ultimate stage, then, structural assimilation involves the elimination of ethnic minority status.

Structural assimilation may occur at two distinct levels of social interaction: the primary, or personal, and the secondary, or formal. At the primary level, structural assimilation implies interaction among members of different ethnic groups within intimate social settings – clubs, neighbourhoods, friendship circles, and, ultimately, marriage. At the secondary level, structural assimilation entails equality of access to power and privilege within the society's major institutions, specifically the economy, the polity and education. To foster secondary structural assimilation, measures may be designed to raise the occupational and educational status of ethnic minorities or, at minimum, to reduce blockages to jobs and schooling. American civil rights legislation of the 1960s, for example, intended to curtail ethnic discrimination in housing, schools and employment, can be understood as an outgrowth of a societal commitment to maximize equality of opportunity in various areas of social life for minority ethnic groups. Similar measures have been instituted in other societies with assimilationist goals. In Brazil, for example, a society which has officially subscribed to policies promoting the blurring of racial and ethnic lines, an anti-discrimination measure, the Afonso Arinos law, was enacted in

1951. The significance of this legislation lay not so much in its subsequent effect (as with any such measure, its enforcement can be frustrated in countless ways) as in the formal recognition for the first time that discriminatory practices did in fact exist. Even more fundamentally, it officially acknowledged ethnic differences in Brazil.

The distinction between primary and secondary levels of assimilation is important, for it is clear that the entrance of ethnic minorities into formal relations with the dominant group must precede those within intimate social settings. Moreover, it is at the secondary level that public policies can be enacted to further assimilation. Thus, integration of minority ethnic groups into mainstream institutions may be facilitated through legal measures, whereas entrance into more personal social groups cannot be dictated by public policies. In the United States, for example, black Americans have been afforded more equitable access to jobs, political authority, and other critical life chances in recent decades through legislative and judicial fiat. Interaction with whites within more personal settings, however, remains limited.

PLURALISM

In a general sense ethnic pluralism is the opposite of assimilation. Like assimilation, pluralism entails several dimensions and forms, but in all cases the retention or even intensification of differences among ethnic groups is presumed. Policies designed to support pluralism, therefore, encourage group diversity and the maintenance of group boundaries. Unlike assimilationist policies, pluralistic policies are founded on the principle of group, not individual, rights. 'The extent to which a state thus institutionalizes group rights as distinct from, and in addition to, individual rights', notes van den Berghe, 'is perhaps the main differentiating factor of ethnic policies' (van den Berghe 1981: 348).

No matter what its degree, ethnic pluralism never entails an absolute separation of groups. In an ethnically pluralistic society a common political or economic system (or both) loosely binds the groups together. Without such an integrated institutional structure there is no multiethnic society *per se* but rather several autonomous societies. Beyond the recognition of common political and economic institutions, however, groups may remain widely divergent.

As with assimilation, several dimensions of pluralism can be delineated, most importantly the cultural and structural. Cultural pluralism implies the preservation of varied cultural systems; structural pluralism connotes not simply differences in culture but also the existence to some degree of segregated racial or ethnic communities within which much of social life occurs. These ethnic subsocieties create institutions – schools, businesses, churches and the like – that duplicate to some extent those of the dominant group.

Two forms of ethnic pluralism are evident in modern multiethnic societies, each sustained by markedly different policies and ideologies. In the first, equalitarian, form, groups maintain cultural and structural autonomy but remain relatively balanced in political and economic power; moreover their separation is mainly voluntary (Barth and Noel 1972; Shibutani and Kwan 1965). In the second, inequalitarian, form, groups maintain structural segregation, and perhaps cultural distinctness as well, but the power arrangement among them is highly disproportionate; moreover, group separation and inequality in such cases are ordinarily prescribed by specific state policy.

EQUALITARIAN PLURALISM

In a multiethnic society guided by equalitarian pluralistic principles, ethnic groups become political interest groups that compete for the society's rewards. Ideally these competitive differences are expressed within the context of a consensually agreed-to set of political rules, thus minimizing serious cleavages. All groups give allegiance to a common political system, participate in a common economic system, and understand a common set of broad ethical values (Petersen 1980; Taft 1963; Williams 1977). Structural and cultural differences among ethnic groups are protected by the state, and institutional provisions are made to encourage an ethnically proportionate distribution of societal rewards. Gordon (1975, 1981) refers to such cases as *corporate* pluralism.

With ethnic parity as their guiding principle, corporate pluralistic systems allocate political and economic power on the basis of an ethnic formula. Thus, in the political arena, legislative seats and other government offices may be apportioned on the basis of ethnicity. Not only is proportionality in the distribution of political benefits assumed, but, most importantly, co-operation prevails among leaders of the significant segments of the ethnically plural society. Moreover, on local matters each group maintains substantial political autonomy. Some have referred to such political arrangements as 'consociational' (Lijphart 1977; McRae 1974). In the economic realm as well, the objective is a distribution of income and jobs among the various groups proportional to their make-up in the national population (Wagley and Harris 1958).

In societies characterized by corporate pluralism, ethnic groups consist mainly of culturally homogeneous, often territorially concentrated peoples who have long historic roots in their native area. They have become part of a larger national society either through conquest or by voluntarily relinquishing sovereignty to a central state in order to secure economic and political benefits. In Switzerland, Yugoslavia and the former Soviet Union, for example, ethnic groups remain geographically distinct, and in Canada over 80 per cent of French Canadians reside in the province of Quebec. Such societies are not similar to multiethnic societies like the United States, Australia, Argentina, Brazil and English Canada, in which ethnic groups have emerged primarily among voluntary immigrants who have severed most of their society-of-origin ties and have dispersed spatially.

A common feature of corporate pluralistic systems is officially sanctioned multilingualism (Gordon 1981). Switzerland, with four language groups, Belgium, with two, and Canada, with two, are perhaps the most evident examples (McRae 1983, 1986). Where cleavage among groups arises, however, it is often language that serves as its catalyst. Canada is a case in point. With its French and English speaking groups, it is officially a multilingual (in this case, bilingual) society. But multilingualism has not been accepted on a widespread basis or without serious problems. Indeed, linguistic rights have been and continue to be the crux of ethnic conflict in Canada.

Belgium, perhaps most clearly, displays a number of the principal characteristics of corporate pluralism. Neither of the two major ethnic communities, Flemish and Walloon, holds political power disproportionately, owing to safeguards provided by the formal political structure. Similar measures protect each group's cultural and linguistic integrity. These have assured, if not a fully equitable system, increasing equality of opportunity to members of the two groups (Lamy 1986; Lijphart 1981). The Soviet Union, whose ethnic diversity was unmatched by any industrial society other than perhaps the United States, was also a case of corporate pluralism, though somewhat different from the Western European type. More than one hundred distinct ethnic groups, perhaps a dozen of major size and importance, maintained a language, heritage and other significant cultural traits, and each enjoyed considerable political autonomy. But there was a noticeable power imbalance among them. The Russians were not only numerically the largest among Soviet ethnic groups (or, as the Soviets preferred, 'nationalities') but were also clearly the dominant group culturally, economically, and, at the national level, politically (Rakowska-Harmstone 1981). In the last few years of the Soviet Union, with the policies of *perestroika* and *glasnost*, the tenuous nature of the Soviet system of pluralism became evident, with ethnic and national movements of self-determination springing up in various areas.

Multiculturalism

In some societies made ethnically diverse mainly through voluntary immigration, formal state policies referred to as *multiculturalism* have sought to provide a framework for corporate pluralism, albeit in a relatively moderate form. Multiculturalism as ideology and policy has been advanced most trenchantly in Canada, Australia and New Zealand. In Canada, the federal government in 1971 announced the policy of 'multiculturalism within a bilingual framework', the purpose of which was to assist ethnic minorities in maintaining their cultural integrity, promote ethnic equality in access to social and economic institutions, and defuse ethnic discrimination at all social levels (Berry *et al.* 1977; Hawkins 1989). Multiculturalism subsequently evolved from *de facto* policy to a set of formalized statutes firmly entrenched in the Canadian constitutional system. It is today an implicit consideration in all policy decisions at the national level.

In addition to demonstrating the discrepancies between its principles and practices, critics have argued that multiculturalism concerns only the most superficial aspects of ethnic relations, namely the retention of cultural traditions and heritages. Left untouched, they argue, are the more significant issues of ethnic inequality and access to political and economic power (Fleras 1984; Kallen 1982). Moreover, some view multiculturalism as basically divisive for the society as a whole and stultifying as well for minority ethnic groups (Porter 1975, 1979; Zubrzycki 1986). Sustaining ethnic pluralism, they maintain, can only hinder the mobility of minority ethnic groups into mainstream institutions, thus perpetuating ethnic stratification.

Preferential ethnic policies

In the United States, Canada and Australia, various preferential policies, termed 'affirmative action', enacted in recent decades are essentially equalitarian pluralistic measures. The intent of such policies and programmes has been to advance the economic and educational status of those ethnic minorities that have been most severely and consistently victimized by past discrimination. In supplying redress they have promoted equality of access to major societal institutions and have sought to create a more proportional distribution of power and wealth among the society's diverse ethnic population. Policies with similar intentions have been instituted in other multiethnic societies including India, Sri Lanka, Indonesia, Malaysia and Nigeria (Horowitz 1985; Nevitte and Kennedy 1986; Srinivas 1966; Weiner 1975). Such compensatory measures have commonly met with controversy regarding their preferential criteria, their fairness, and their effectiveness in raising the collective status of ethnic minority groups (Glazer 1975; Horowitz 1985; Sowell 1989).

Equalitarian pluralistic policies of whatever blend are more a product of group choice than the largely involuntary *de facto* pluralism of racial-ethnic minorities in the United States and Britain, or of inequalitarian pluralistic forms, which will be discussed presently. But if we can judge from contemporary societies that have instituted such policies with the intention of producing ethnic harmony, the results are not always more benign. Cases like Belgium, the Netherlands and Switzerland, where interethnic relations are less discordant, appear to be exceptional, and even in those societies periodic group

749

conflict is evident. The assertion of Wagley and Harris (1958) that pluralistic objectives perpetuate some degree of conflict and the subordination of one group by another is well taken. Indeed, pluralistic policies, no matter how seemingly well intentioned, seem to produce persistent, if fluctuating, conflict.

INEQUALITARIAN PLURALISM

Both assimilationist and equalitarian pluralistic policies are most evident in societies that have blunted to some extent the acuteness of ethnic stratification and have made the reduction of ethnic inequality a commitment of the state. Clearly these are policies that, however effective they have proved, are aimed at reducing the level of ethnic conflict and enhancing equity in the distribution of societal resources. Inequalitarian pluralism, however, connotes outcomes and processes that are clearly inequitable for the society's various ethnic groups. This form of ethnic pluralism is most characteristic of classic colonial societies and racist regimes of the modern era. Some of its features, however, in less extreme form, can also be seen in multiethnic societies where assimilation or equalitarian pluralism is the more prevalent rationale of ethnic policies.

Inequalitarian pluralistic systems are governed by policies that separate ethnic groups structurally and enforce a highly unequal distribution of power and privilege. Whereas equalitarian pluralistic policies are carried out within the context of a system in which the various groups maintain consensual allegiance to a common state, inequalitarian pluralistic policies are enforced mainly through coercion by a state that may not be recognized as legitimate by all groups. Smith (1969: 33) explains that in a plural society of this type, the state is the agent of the dominant ethnic group only. Others have no rights or protection. The majority of people are 'subjects, not citizens'. Whereas equalitarian pluralism assumes a progressive equalization of political and economic power among groups, the assumption here is quite the opposite. Sustained or increased inequality among groups is a built-in feature of ethnic policy, with the dominant group retaining all political authority and the bulk of material wealth.

Racist ideologies promoting beliefs in the innate character of group differences are the philosophical underpinnings of inequalitarian pluralistic policies. Social relations between dominant and minority ethnic groups are typified by extreme polarization, supported by high levels of prejudice and discrimination. Basically it is only within the impersonal confines of the economic and political systems that dominant and minority group members interrelate, and these relations are limited to purely instrumental contacts such as work and government administration. As Kuper and Smith describe it, 'Economic symbiosis and mutual avoidance, cultural diversity and social cleavage, characterize the social basis of the plural society' (Kuper and Smith 1969: 11). In its most extreme form, inequalitarian pluralism resembles a caste system in which segregation is maximally enforced in all areas of social life (Furnivall 1948).

The inequalitarian pluralistic model is most applicable to slave or traditional colonial societies (Rex 1970), neither of which is evident in the contemporary world. South Africa, however, today closely approximates the model. There, the system of apartheid, though attenuated in recent years, has traditionally protected the power and privilege of a sociologically dominant group which is a distinct numerical minority. Indeed, so complete has been white political dominance that 'subordinate ethnics', note Adam and Moodley, 'do not form part of the polity, however differentially incorporated, but are considered noncitizens or, at best, second-class citizens' (Adam and Moodley 1986: 30).

Although inequalitarian pluralistic policies in extreme form are rare in modern multiethnic societies, they are apparent in muted form in some societies in which ethnic divisions are based primarily on racial rather than cultural distinctions. In slave, caste or colonial situations, ethnicity and class are synonymous: one group has almost all the society's power and wealth. As a result it monopolizes the higher status occupational positions. Under conditions of *competitive race relations*, however, characteristic of modern industrial societies, the occupational gap between ethnic groups is narrowed, with each becoming more class diversified (van den Berghe 1978; Wilson 1973).

Because the norms of social distance and economic dominance have so well institutionalized in the paternalistic conditions of slave or colonial societies, there is little need for laws to enforce social segregation and occupational subserviance. With competitive ethnic relations, however, these must be enforced through official as well as customary policies. The Jim Crow system of the post-slavery US South illustrates this well. Following the disengagement of federal troops from southern states in 1876, a set of discriminatory laws was enacted that assured the economic and political subserviance of former slaves and their social segregation from the dominant white population (Woodward 1974). The functions of the South African apartheid system can be viewed similarly, though apartheid has historically been designed to maintain not only physical separation and economic subserviance, but cultural separation of the society's major racial groupings as well (Fredrickson 1981).

Internal colonialism

Internal colonialism is a type of inequalitarian pluralism characteristic of societies like the United States where ethnic relations otherwise follow the assimilation model. Here, particular ethnic groups may be treated in a colonial fashion. In the traditional form of colonialism practised by the European powers in the seventeenth, eighteenth and nineteenth centuries, a conquering group – a numerical minority – established political and economic domination over an indigenous people. Internal colonialism, by contrast, is a condition in which both dominant and subordinate groups are indigenous; moreover, the dominant group is a numerical majority (Blauner 1969).

Using this model, Blauner (1969) and others (Blackwell 1976; Carmichael and Hamilton 1967; Clark 1965) have interpreted the black experience in the United States as basically colonial in nature and the ghetto uprisings of the 1960s as anti-colonial movements. The internal colonial model has been applied to other ethnic groups in the United States, namely Mexican Americans and American Indians (Blauner 1972; Moore 1970; Snipp 1986) and, with some variation, to groups in other multiethnic societies as well (Zureik 1979). A somewhat different application of the idea of internal colonialism is made by Hechter (1975), who describes it as a condition in which a dominant ethnic group in the industrialized core of a nation subjugates an industrially backward ethnic group in the nation's periphery.

Expulsion or annihilation

Inequalitarian pluralism may culminate in the expulsion or even the annihilation of minority ethnic groups. State policies aimed at both of these outcomes have been implemented in recent Western history. Efforts to reverse the flow of immigration commonly result in policies of expulsion. In the United States, for example, the deportation of Chinese immigrants in the nineteenth century and of Mexicans in the 1930s and again in the 1950s were aimed at relieving the society of what was perceived as a threat to the labour dominance of majority ethnic group workers (Estrada *et al.* 1981; Lyman 1974). The internment of people of Japanese ethnic origin in both the United States and Canada during the Second World War (Daniels 1977; Adachi 1976) are other notable examples of expulsion. Such expulsions are ordinarily rationalized by dominant group ideologies supporting the idea of the expelled group's inferiority or depravity.

Policies aimed at annihilation are best illustrated by the destruction of native groups by European settlers in North America, Australia and South Africa in the nineteenth century as well as in Latin America and the Caribbean earlier. A more deliberate and methodical case of annihilation was the genocidal policy of the Nazis, which resulted in the destruction of the European Jews. In the 1930s, German Jews were subjected systematically to an almost complete expulsion from every phase of institutional life. Later, Jews were impelled to leave Germany through a state-supported campaign of terror that included physical attacks and the appropriation of their property. Finally, Nazi policies were consummated in the establishment of death camps to which the German and subsequently other European Jewish populations were sent to be slaughtered (Hilberg 1979).

VARIATIONS IN ETHNIC POLICY

It is important to consider that these three major patterns of ethnic relations and policy are never perfect characterizations of what occurs in any multiethnic society. While societies may display a predisposition to one or the other, in reality features of two or possibly even all three will be evident simultaneously. Discriminatory measures applied to racially distinct (i.e. non-European) groups in the United States, for example, have historically functioned alongside more democratic policies intended for Euro-American groups. In South Africa as well, the apartheid system has existed in conjunction with a democratic participatory system for the dominant white populace.

In addition, none of the three models of ethnic relations and their attendant policies should be seen as inflexible or irreversible. Depending on economic and political circumstances, societies may promulgate disparate ethnic objectives and ideologies, and thus policies, at different times. Canada and Australia are cases in point. Determined to keep out or reduce the numbers of non-Europeans, both societies in the late nineteenth and early twentieth centuries enacted restrictive immigration policies aimed at securing a 'White Australia' and a 'White Canada'. In both societies these racially motivated measures were gradually reversed in the 1960s and 1970s, driven by the decline of racial ideologies and national population needs. In the process, Australia and Canada moved from assimilationist objectives to officially proclaimed ethnic pluralism. A similar shift is evident in the United States, in which a significant revision in immigration policy in 1965 lowered what had been long-established restrictions against non-European groups. In light of the growing, and increasingly politically effective, non-white proportion of the population, some have perceived an emergent change in United States policy and ideology from assimilation to corporate pluralism (Gordon 1981).

Sharp reversals of policy may also be brought about by the manipulation of ethnic relations for political advantage. As Kuper has noted, 'Politicians readily find in racial and ethnic cleavages a resource for political exploitation' (Kuper 1969: 485). Societies that advocate and display harmony and progressive assimilation among ethnic groups may revert to pluralistic policies when political conditions demand. The Nazis, for example, determinedly reversed the quite thorough assimilation of Jews into mainstream German society. Such policy reversals may occur in the opposite direction as well. In the wake of the civil rights movement in the American South, for example, many politicians, ordinarily staunchly supportive of racial segregation, advocated moderately

753

integrationist positions when it became obvious that the black vote might be a decisive electoral factor.

The content and style of ethnic policy in any case are ultimately dependent on the objectives of both the society's dominant and minority ethnic groups. Obviously the two may be at odds. When the objectives of both are congruent, conflict is reduced; when they are in opposition, conflict is unavoidable. Assimilationist intentions of a minority group, for example, may be at odds with the segregationist policies of the dominant group. Such opposing goals and policies have been at the crux of black–white relations for most of the past century in the United States, resulting in continual conflict in one form or another. The reverse situation may also be evident. That is, the dominant group may insist on assimilation and the minority group may resist relinquishing its ethnic culture and institutional structure. The relationship in the United States between American Indians and whites has been typified by this set of incongruent goals and policies. Indians did not seek assimilation but desired to remain on their traditional lands as independent nations. Whites, however, responded to Indian objectives either by destroying the social and economic base upon which their communities were built or by demanding acculturation into white values and lifestyles to which Indians did not aspire.

In the final analysis, all policies of racial and ethnic relations are manifestations of power, especially of the dominant group. Van den Berghe has observed that 'state policies toward ethnic groups, and toward ethnicity as a principle of state incorporation, vary enormously, but most of that variation is explainable in terms of the material interests of the ruling group, as mediated by a multiplicity of ecological, technological, and political factors' (van den Berghe 1981: 346). On the structure of power, then, hinges the eventual nature of relations among groups of a multiethnic society and the shape of policies that govern them.

Ethnic issues will continue to occupy the attention of policy makers in modern societies in the foreseeable future for at least two reasons. First, ethnic loyalties have given no appearance of weakening, despite earlier predictions of their demise as a corollary of industrialization. Second, the forces of ethnic diversity, particularly immigration, do not appear to be relenting. On the contrary, the emergence of global economic organizations and labour markets have stimulated large-scale immigration movements that in size and complexity have rivalled those of the late nineteenth and early twentieth centuries.

REFERENCES

Adachi, K. (1976) *The Enemy That Never Was*, Toronto: McClelland & Stewart.
Adam, H. and Moodley, K. (1986) *South Africa Without Apartheid: Dismantling Racial Domination*, Berkeley: University of California Press.

Barth, E. A. T. and Noel, D. L. (1972) 'Conceptual frameworks for the analysis of race relations', *Social Forces* 50: 333–48.

Ben-Rafael, E. (1982) *The Emergence of Ethnicity: Cultural Groups and Social Conflict in Israel*, Westport and London: Greenwood Press.

Berry, J. W., Kalin, R. and Taylor, D. M. (1977) *Multiculturalism and Ethnic Attitudes in Canada*, Ottawa: Minister of Supply and Services Canada.

Blackwell, J. E. (1976) 'The power basis of ethnic conflict in American society', in L. A. Coser and O. M. Larsen (eds) *The Use of Controversy in Sociology*, New York: Free Press.

Blauner, R. (1969) 'Internal colonialism and ghetto revolt', *Social Problems* 16: 393–408.

——(1972) *Racial Oppression in America*, New York: Harper & Row.

Carmichael, S. and Hamilton, C. V. (1967) *Black Power: The Politics of Liberation in America*, New York: Vintage.

Clark, K. B. (1965) *Dark Ghetto*, New York: Harper & Row.

Daniels, R. (1977) *The Politics of Prejudice: The Anti-Japanese Movement in California and the Struggle for Japanese Exclusion*, 2nd edn, Berkeley: University of California Press.

Enloe, C. H. (1973) *Ethnic Conflict and Political Development*, Boston: Little, Brown & Co.

Estrada, L. F., Garcia, F. C., Macias, R. F. and Maldonado, L. (1981) 'Chicanos in the United States: a history of exploitation and resistance', *Daedalus* 110: 103–31.

Fleras, A. (1984) 'Monoculturalism, multiculturalism and biculturalism: the politics of Maori policy in New Zealand', *Plural Societies* 15: 52–75.

Fredrickson, G. M. (1981) *White Supremacy: A Comparative Study in American and South African History*, New York: Oxford University Press.

Furnivall, J. S. (1948) *Colonial Policy and Practice*, Cambridge: Cambridge University Press.

Glazer, N. (1975) *Affirmative Discrimination: Ethnic Identity and Public Policy*, New York: Basic Books.

Gordon, M. M. (1964) *Assimilation in American Life*, New York: Oxford University Press.

——(1975) 'Toward a general theory of racial and ethnic group relations', in N. Glazer and D. P. Moynihan (eds) *Ethnicity: Theory and Experience*, Cambridge, Mass.: Harvard University Press.

——(1981) 'Models of pluralism: the new American dilemma', *Annals of the American Academy of Political and Social Science* 454: 178–88.

Hawkins, F. (1989) *Critical Years in Immigration: Canada and Australia Compared*, Kingston and Montreal: McGill–Queen's University Press.

Hechter, M. (1975) *Internal Colonialism: The Celtic Fringe in British National Development, 1536–1966*, Berkeley: University of California Press.

Hilberg, R. (1979) *The Destruction of the European Jews*, New York: Harper Colophon.

Horowitz, D. L. (1985) *Ethnic Groups in Conflict*, Berkeley: University of California Press.

Hunt, C. L., and Walker, L. (1974) *Ethnic Dynamics: Patterns of Intergroup Relations in Various Societies*, Homewood: Dorsey.

Kallen, E. (1982) 'Multiculturalism: ideology, policy and reality', *Journal of Canadian Studies* 17: 51–63.

Kuper, L. (1969) 'Ethnic and racial pluralism: some aspects of polarization and depluralization', in L. Kuper and M. G. Smith (eds) *Pluralism in Africa*, Berkeley: University of California Press.

Kuper, L. and Smith, M. G. (eds) (1969) *Pluralism in Africa*, Berkeley: University of California Press.

Lamy, S. L. (1986) 'Policy responses to ethnonationalism: consociational engineering in Belgium', in J. F. Stack, Jr (ed.) *The Primordial Challenge: Ethnicity in the Contemporary World*, New York: Greenwood.

Lieberson, S. (1961) 'A societal theory of race relations', *American Sociological Review* 26: 902–10.

Lijphart, A. (1977) *Democracy in Plural Societies: A Comparative Exploration*, New Haven: Yale University Press.

——(1981) *Conflict and Coexistence in Belgium: The Dynamics of a Culturally Divided Society*, Berkeley: Institute of International Studies, University of California.

Lyman, S. (1974) *Chinese Americans*, New York: Random House.

McRae, K. D. (1974) *Consociational Democracy: Political Accommodation in Segmented Societies*, Toronto: McClelland & Stewart.

——(1983) *Conflict and Compromise in Multilingual Societies: Switzerland*, Waterloo, Ont.: Wilfrid Laurier University Press.

——(1986) *Conflict and Compromise in Multilingual Societies: Belgium*, Waterloo, Ont.: Wilfrid Laurier University Press.

Moore, J. W. (1970) 'Colonialism: the case of the Mexican-Americans', *Social Problems* 17: 463–72.

Nevitte, N. and Kennedy, C. H. (eds) (1986) *Ethnic Preference and Public Policy in Developing States*, Boulder: Lynne Rienner Publishers.

Noel, D. L. (1968) 'A theory of the origin of ethnic stratification', *Social Problems* 16: 157–72.

Omi, M. and Winant, H. (1986) *Racial Formation in the United States: From the 1960s to the 1980s*, New York: Routledge & Kegan Paul.

Petersen, W. (1980) 'Concepts of ethnicity', in S. Thernstrom (ed.) *Harvard Encyclopedia of American Ethnic Groups*, Cambridge, Mass.: Harvard University Press.

Porter, J. (1975) 'Ethnic pluralism in Canadian perspective', in N. Glazer and D. P. Moynihan (eds) *Ethnicity: Theory and Experience*, Cambridge, Mass.: Harvard University Press.

——(1979) *The Measure of Canadian Society*, Toronto: Gage.

Rakowska-Harmstone, T. (1981) 'The Soviet Union', in R. G. Wirsing (ed.) *Protection of Ethnic Minorities: Comparative Perspectives*, New York: Pergamon.

Rex, J. (1970) *Race Relations in Sociological Theory*, New York: Schocken.

Schermerhorn, R. A. (1970) *Comparative Ethnic Relations: A Framework for Theory and Research*, New York: Random House.

Shibutani, T. and Kwan, K. M. (1965) *Ethnic Stratification: A Comparative Approach*, New York: Macmillan.

Smith, M. G. (1969) 'Institutional and political conditions of pluralism', in L. Kuper and M. G. Smith (eds) *Pluralism in Africa*, Berkeley: University of California Press.

Snipp, C. M. (1986) 'The changing political and economic status of the American Indians: from captive nations to internal colonies', *American Journal of Economics and Sociology* 45: 145–57.

Sowell, T. (1989) ' "Affirmative action": a worldwide disaster', *Commentary* 88 (December): 21–41.

Srinivas, M. N. (1966) *Social Change in Modern India*, Berkeley: University of California Press.

Taft, R. (1963) 'The assimilation orientation of immigrants and Australians', *Human Relations* 16: 279–93.

van den Berghe, P. L. (1978) *Race and Racism: A Comparative Perspective*, 2nd edn, New York: John Wiley.

——(1981) *The Ethnic Phenomenon*, New York: Elsevier.

Wagley, C. and Harris, M. (1958) *Minorities in the New World: Six Case Studies*, New York: Columbia University Press.

Weiner, M. (1975) *Changing Conceptions of Citizenship in a Multi-ethnic Society: Migration, Protected Labor Markets, Law, and Citizenship in India*, Cambridge, Mass.: MIT Press.

Williams, R. M., Jr. (1977) *Mutual Accommodation: Ethnic Conflict and Cooperation*, Minneapolis: University of Minnesota Press.

Wilson, W. J. (1973) *Power, Racism, and Privilege*, New York: Free Press.

Wirth, L. (1945) 'The problem of minority groups', in R. Linton (ed.) *The Science of Man in the World Crisis*, New York: Columbia University Press.

Woodward, C. V. (1974) *The Strange Career of Jim Crow*, 3rd edn, New York: Oxford University Press.

Yinger, J. M. (1985) 'Assimilation in the United States: the Mexican-Americans', in W. Connor (ed.) *Mexican-Americans in Comparative Perspective*, Washington, DC: Urban Institute Press.

Zubrzycki, J. (1986) 'Multiculturalism and beyond: the Australian experience in retrospect and prospect', *New Community* 13: 167–76.

Zureik, E. T. (1979) *The Palestinians in Israel: A Study in Internal Colonialism*, London: Routledge & Kegan Paul.

FURTHER READING

Adam, H. and Moodley, K. (1986) *South Africa Without Apartheid: Dismantling Racial Domination*, Berkeley: University of California Press.

Enloe, C. (1973) *Ethnic Conflict and Political Development*, Boston: Little, Brown & Co.

Glazer, N. (1975) *Affirmative Discrimination: Ethnic Identity and Public Policy*, New York: Basic Books.

Gordon, M. M. (1981) 'Models of pluralism: the new American dilemma', *Annals of the American Academy of Political and Social Science* 454: 178–88.

Hawkins, F. (1989) *Critical Years in Immigration: Canada and Australia Compared*, Kingston and Montreal: McGill–Queen's University Press.

Hilberg, R. (1979) *The Destruction of the European Jews*, New York: Harper Colophon.

Horowitz, D. L. (1985) *Ethnic Groups in Conflict*, Berkeley: University of California Press.

Kallen, E. (1982) *Ethnicity and Human Rights in Canada*, Toronto: Gage.

Kuper, L. (1981) *Genocide: Its Political Use in the Twentieth Century*, New Haven and London: Yale University Press.

Lijphart, A. (1977) *Democracy in Plural Societies: A Comparative Exploration*, New Haven: Yale University Press.

McRae, K. (ed.) (1974) *Consociational Democracy: Political Accommodation in Segmented Societies*, Toronto: McClelland & Stewart.

Noel, D. L. (1968) 'A theory of the origin of ethnic stratification', *Social Problems* 16: 157–72.

Omi, M. and Winant, H. (1986) *Racial Formation in the United States: From the 1960s to the 1980s*, New York: Routledge & Kegan Paul.

Schermerhorn, R. A. (1970) *Comparative Ethnic Relations: A Framework for Theory and Research*, New York: Random House.

van den Berghe, Pierre L. (1978) *Race and Racism: A Comparative Perspective*, 2nd edn, New York: John Wiley.

——(1981) *The Ethnic Phenomenon*, New York: Elsevier.

Wilson, W. J. (1973) *Power, Racism, and Privilege: Race Relations in Theoretical and Sociohistorical Perspectives*, New York: Free Press.

Wirsing, R. G. (ed.) (1981) *Protection of Ethnic Minorities: Comparative Perspectives*, New York: Pergamon.

47

SCIENCE AND TECHNOLOGY POLICY

PHILIP GUMMETT

Science and technology policy is a term that refers to public policy concerning science and technology, in the senses both of policies that support those activities and policies that channel them towards the goals of governments. It also refers to the academic study of the interrelations between science, technology, government and the wider society. Although, as we shall see, it had deeper roots, the main flowering of the field dates from the mid-1960s. Its practitioners, in academia and in numerous government organizations around the world, by and large have first degrees in science or technology, often followed by a social science qualification. More recently, training specifically in science and technology policy, especially at graduate level, has become available in several countries.

A more formal definition has been offered by the International Council for Science Policy Studies:

> Science policy studies have as their focus the systematic investigation of scientific and technological activities and their function within society. In particular, they are concerned with policy-making in scientific and technological fields, and with the inter-relationship between policy-making, cultural values and social goals.
> (quoted in Jain 1988: 257)

The shift from the term *science policy* to the term *science and technology policy* occurred between the late 1970s and mid-1980s, the relevant policy and academic communities having seen a need to focus more attention on the technological dimension of the relations between science, technology and society. This shift was driven in particular by growing appreciation of the inadequacies of the simple 'science push' model of technological change, according to which technological innovation starts from scientific discoveries. (For criticism of this, and other linear models of innovation, see Langrish *et al.* 1972.) More modern conceptions, including especially a body of work concerned with evolutionary theories of technical change, saw technology as

759

something that developed primarily within firms, and by no means necessarily with reference to new scientific findings (Freeman 1974; Nelson and Winter 1982; Clark 1985; Georghiou et al. 1986; Coombs et al. 1987; Dosi et al. 1988). This newer thinking also rejected the assumption of neo-classical economics that scientific and technological information moved freely between organizations. On the contrary, evolutionary theorists considered knowledge, especially technological knowledge, to be highly organization-specific in the sense that it grows from the existing competences of the organization, which are unique to it, and therefore cannot transfer easily to other organizations. On this approach, some technologies have been seen as developing largely independently of science, while others have been seen as related to it in a more complex way than linear models suggest. Accordingly, the linguistic convention that 'science' embraced 'technology' became slowly less acceptable. Historical and sociological work (Hughes 1986; Bijker et al. 1987) reinforced the argument for more subtle and complex accounts of the development of technologies.

This essay sketches the historical background to the development of science and technology policy as an identifiable activity. It considers the intellectual basis of science and technology policy as a subject of academic study. And it reviews some of the main questions that have exercised both governmental practitioners and academic students of the subject. If there is a geographical bias in the examples and sources given, towards Britain and Europe, and away from the United States, this is justified by the existence of a valuable earlier review by Sapolsky (1975) which is particularly concerned with the United States.

HISTORICAL BACKGROUND

The relations between science, technology and government stretch back into antiquity. There is, in particular, a long history of technical inventiveness being applied to military affairs, in relation both to weaponry itself and to the supply and support of the fighting forces (McNeill 1983). Closer to our own time, one important tradition grew out of Bacon's New Atlantis (1627), which offered a vision of a Christian civilization which had mastered scientific knowledge. Dedicated to the 'knowledge of causes, and secret motions of things; and the enlarging of the bounds of human empire, to the effecting of all things possible', the Fathers of Salomon's House also took it upon themselves to decide which of their inventions and discoveries should be published, and which kept secret, adding, darkly, that 'some of those we do reveal sometimes to the State, and some not' (Johnston 1965: 175–80). As the coincidentally named French writer Salomon (1973: 8) reminds us, Bacon was not a savant or a practising scientist, but a politician. As a statesman, he saw the links between experimental research and society, and dreamed of a new social order in which organized science would be systematically developed. But the fact that he was a politician makes it the more remarkable that, in a vision which has provided an important model for relations between science and the state up to present times, he leaves so much to the discretion of the scientists.

In our own century, war, or the preparation for it, has been a great stimulant to science–government relations (Edgerton and Gummett 1988). Since the Second World War, it has dominated government spending on science and technology globally, and particularly in the United States (Long and Reppy 1980), the Soviet Union, Britain (Council for Science and Society 1986) and France, with profound but still inadequately understood consequences for technological advance (Gummett and Reppy 1988). Indeed, as various authors have observed (MacKenzie 1986; Mendelsohn *et al.* 1988), the association between science and war in general has been insufficiently studied. This failure can be explained by suggesting that prevailing liberal ideas have seen science and technology as progressive forces, associated with internationalism, and therefore as incompatible with warfare and nationalism (see Haberer 1969). As Edgerton (1988: 110–11) has pointed out, two other important traditions in political thought, German nationalism and Marxism, take a different view. For German nationalists, German technology was in competition with British technology – as an integral part of the struggle and not an aberration. For Marxists, technology would become a progressive force under socialism; but in the meantime, the inevitable tendency of capitalism towards imperialism and war necessarily corrupted science and technology.

In Britain, the First World War saw the establishment of the Department of Scientific and Industrial Research, created in urgent response to British dependence upon Germany for vital war materials such as optical and electrical equipment, drugs, and even dyes for soldiers' uniforms (MacLeod and Andrews 1970; Varcoe 1974). It is worth adding, however, that even with this new emphasis, the scale of scientific activity was tiny in comparison with that of an industrialized country today. In rough terms, the volume of British state-supported science and technology in 1915 would have been about that of, at most, a handful of modern Western universities. This is much the same as the situation that persists today in many developing countries.

It was with the build-up to, and onset of, the Second World War that the relationship between science and government became firmly established in the public mind. Scientists, economists and other specialists were integrated into government administration and planning in ways that they had not been previously. They contributed more than simply inventions, important as were radar, proximity fuses, jet engines, and the work of atomic energy, culminating in the Manhattan Project in the United States. They also developed a powerful new analytical approach – operations research – rooted in the statistical analysis of such matters as bomb damage and attacks upon convoys (Waddington 1973; Clark 1962; Zuckerman 1978). Crucial in all this was a close working relationship between scientists, military officers and civilian officials. Nor were the effects of this relationship one-sided: the experience of large-scale scientific activity, in big teams, changed the conception of how to go about academic physics, with consequences for the scale and organization of post-war research (Galison 1988).

The ground for a closer relationship between science and government had in fact begun to be laid just before the war among the scientific community, as awareness grew of what, in a later period, would be called the social responsibility of scientists. This awareness had, in turn, been part of a wider climate of internationalist intellectual soul-searching generated by the conjunction of the depression and the rise of communism and fascism (Wood 1959). One of the standard bearers among the scientists was J. D. Bernal, who argued in his book *The Social Function of Science* (Bernal 1939) that science should be planned so as to serve social needs. The book was highly controversial (Price 1976; Werskey 1978; McGucken 1978; Baker 1978) and came under attack from the Society for Freedom in Science, which was started in 1940 by, among others, J. R. Baker and M. Polanyi (who, in a much later article, was to argue that 'You can kill or mutilate the advance of science, you cannot shape it' (Polanyi 1968)). Against them, S. Zuckerman (who was to play a major part in science–government relations throughout the war and on into the 1970s (Zuckerman 1978, 1988)) argued that Bernal's position was widely shared among scientists, and misunderstood by his critics (Zuckerman 1939, 1966).

By the 1940s, then, a set of issues and beliefs was in place. Science was seen as a powerful force for change – for good or ill. The modern state would increasingly turn to science for solutions to social and economic problems: science, having helped win the war, was now to help win the peace. But this in turn meant that science needed the support of the state. This raised questions over how, by whom, and to what ends that support was to be dispensed.

Similar sentiments were being expressed elsewhere. In the United States, Vannevar Bush, in his famous report, *Science – The Endless Frontier* (Bush 1945), called for the federal government to provide generous and stable funding for research. He recommended the establishment of a National Research Foundation, run by an independent board of scientists from universities and industry, charged with supporting medical and physical science and military research, and with formulating a national policy for research and scientific education. In the face of argument and delay within the Administration and Congress over the independence of the proposed board, the Office of Naval Research stepped into the breach and established a long-lasting relationship between the military authorities and university research. Another major institution, the US Atomic Energy Commission (which had responsibility for the atomic weapons programme), established in 1946, also began to play a major role in the direction of US science and technology, albeit in the face of major debate about military versus civilian control of atomic energy. (The journal *Bulletin of the Atomic Scientists* and the Federation of American (formerly Atomic) Scientists stem from this controversy; see *Bulletin of the Atomic Scientists* 1985.) When, therefore, what in the end was called the National Science Foundation was finally established in 1950, it was very much the poor cousin alongside the defence agencies, a situation that still obtains today. Moreover, the chance to set up a single central science policy-making body had passed (Price 1954: chapter 2; Greenberg 1969: chapter 6).

In Britain, debate within Whitehall about the form to be adopted for the post-war central co-ordinating machinery for science and technology began in 1943. In 1945, the Committee on Future Scientific Policy (the first use known to me of such terminology) was established to settle this question (Gummett and Price 1977; McAllister 1986: 122–40). It rejected the conservative view that national scientific policy should be left in the hands of the Royal Society and the research councils, as the supposed guardians of freedom in science. It also rejected radical proposals for a strong central organization to oversee the planning of publicly and privately funded research in the civil, military and industrial fields. Instead, the outcome, and that of a parallel debate on defence research and development, was the adoption of an intermediate position in which responsibility at ministerial level remained split between a non-departmental co-ordinating minister and departmental ministers, with an Advisory Council on Scientific Policy to advise on the civil side, and a Defence Research Policy Committee on the defence side. Overtones of the 1930s controversy about freedom versus planning permeated the debate, as did the traditional British resistance to the idea of a strong minister of science, it being argued then (and since) that the appointment of such a minister would cut across the responsibility of departmental ministers for the research and development programmes of their own departments.

By the late 1940s and early 1950s then, science policy, recognized as such, was becoming an accepted part of the machinery of government in industrialized countries. As another example, France set up a complex of institutions in the 1940s and 1950s, beginning with the Commissariat à l'énergie atomique (CEA), and in 1953 setting up a special committee of the planning board to prepare the first plan for scientific research. As Papon has commented, 'belief in the usefulness of long-term budgets for investments in science and technology took root at that time' (Papon 1988: 495). The same was true in some developing countries also: India, in particular, began to integrate a science policy dimension into its national plans from the early 1950s, established a Scientific Advisory Committee to the cabinet in 1956, and promulgated a major statement of intentions and aspirations in the field with its first Scientific Policy Resolution in 1958 (Ahmad 1984: 9).

All this activity was taking place within governments. With a few notable exceptions (Price 1954; Carter and Williams 1957; Dedijer – see Annerstedt and Jamison 1988; and Dedijer 1964) neither the theme of science–government relations nor that of the relations between investment in science and national economic performance was much subjected to independent analysis. Nor was there much general political or wider public interest in these matters during the 1950s. But the position began to change by the early 1960s, as spending on individual programmes increasingly crossed the threshold of political visibility, and as, from about the mid-1960s, a number of academic science policy research centres and other bodies, such as the London-based Science of Science Foundation (now the International Science Policy Foundation) were created (Goldsmith and Mackay 1964).

In Britain, for example, public spending on civil science and technology had reached such a level, and the process through which it was distributed between the research councils and departments had become so evidently unsatisfactory, that the Treasury had begun to press for reforms (Gummett 1980: 40–4). These issues were in turn swept up into wider political debate about the role of science and technology in the modernization of Britain, which came to a head in the 1964 general election, remembered for the Labour Party's promise to forge a new Britain in the white heat of the technological revolution (Vig 1968).

The question of priorities became increasingly urgent as countries began to appreciate that science was growing at a rate far greater than that of national economies as a whole. This fact was quantified by Derek de Solla Price, one of the founding fathers of that branch of science policy studies known as bibliometrics, who showed that the number of scientists globally was doubling every ten to fifteen years, and that the cost of science was increasing as the square of the number of scientists (Price 1963: 92–3).

These questions came increasingly to be addressed by the Paris-based Organization for Economic Co-operation and Development (OECD). In 1960, the Secretary-General of the OECD appointed an *ad hoc* group of independent scientists and economists to advise him on the policy issues of science and technology that were increasingly demanding attention. The group, chaired by the then chief scientist to the French government, Pierre Piganiol, produced in 1961 a report (Piganiol 1961) which in many ways provided the starting point for the discussion, and the definition, of science policy as we now know it.

The Piganiol report stressed the need for all the OECD countries to develop explicit policies and mechanisms for the management and effectiveness of the science system as such, which they called 'policies for science'. But, they noted, additional questions arose with regard to the application of science to the attainment of national objectives. They suggested that, at least in principle, government policies in every field were capable of improvement through the application of new knowledge derived from scientific research. This point was already well accepted in the defence field, but was much less clear in other fields. The report thus argued that the conception of what was meant by 'science policy' should be broadened to include the potential of science to assist in the formulation of policies across the board. This aspect of science policy they called 'science for policy'.

The report recommended that each government should set up some central mechanism for discussing science policy in both its aspects, and that the OECD should convene a meeting of ministers responsible for science policy to continue the debate. When the first such meeting took place, in Paris in 1963, only three of the twenty-two member countries had ministers of or for science; most other countries were represented by ministers of education (King 1974: vii). This situation was to change considerably over the next decade. Also to change was the evidential base for debate, as the OECD began to establish both international comparative statistical series on science policy questions, and detailed reviews of national arrangements for science policy (Freeman 1988).

INTELLECTUAL FOUNDATIONS

From the point of view of academic legitimacy, and perhaps also of wider acceptance within policy communities, we should briefly consider whether science and technology policy is a 'proper' academic subject, or whether it remains, as was once claimed, a 'literature in search of a field' (Denny 1965).

As Sapolsky observed (Sapolsky 1975: 79–80), it is difficult to differentiate science policy studies from policy studies in general: its domain is as general and as changing as the scope of government itself. Hence, work on environmental policy (Rothman 1972), acceptability of risk (Irwin 1985), biotechnology and 'genethics' (Yoxen 1983, 1986), public acceptability of new technology (Williams and Mills 1986), nuclear power decisions (Williams 1980), nuclear trade (Walker and Lonnroth 1983), employment effects of new technology (Green et al. 1980) and policy towards industrial innovation (Pavitt and Walker 1976; Pavitt 1980) has all been done under the umbrella of science and technology policy.

Nor is it any easier to seek the boundary of the subject from a methodological perspective, for no single methodological approach defines the field. Students of the subject would be expected to acquire familiarity with at least some aspects of economics, sociology, history and politics, as applied to science and technology. They would find that work in the economic dimension has reached the point where some broadly synoptic treatments, not focusing upon any particular country, are now available (for example, Freeman 1974; Clark 1985; Dosi *et al.* 1988). Similarly, following the path-breaking work of T. S. Kuhn (Kuhn 1970), a strong tradition of work in the sociology of scientific knowledge (Barnes 1985) and, more recently, in the sociology of technology (Bijker *et al.* 1987) has been established. Along the politics dimension, however, while many works exist describing national science and technology policy systems (for example, the Longman guides and OECD reviews; Gummett 1980, and Kogan and Henkel 1983 on the UK), very little has been done that is rigorously comparative in approach (Brickman 1979; Brickman and Rip 1979; Ronayne 1984; Williams and Mills 1986), or that tries to relate national systems of decision making for science and technology to broader themes and concepts in public policy analysis. (An exception is the application of implementation studies to science policy; see Rip and Hagendijk 1988.) This point is particularly important, given the significance of national differences in policy-making systems and cultures for analysis in any domain of policy studies.

It is easy, therefore, to accept Sapolsky's definitional difficulty. But we might also wish to ask how many of the more established fields of academic activity would pass his tests of having a sharply defined boundary and a distinctive methodology. We could go further, drawing on a large body of work in the sociology of knowledge, and argue that the legitimation of intellectual activities is in any case a socially negotiated process, the history of which is written by the winners. By this token, the fact that science policy is much more firmly institutionalized, and in more countries, than was true when Sapolsky wrote his review indicates growing acceptance of its claim to a place in the academy, even if much remains to be done to systematize the subject.

Nor need we accept Sapolsky's further argument that the key distinction lies in 'the basic assumptions of those who label their studies science policy studies' (Sapolsky 1975: 80). He suggests that these assumptions are, first, the belief that opportunities for progress in technology depend increasingly upon scientific advance, and second, that science and technology are the prime determinants of social change. It is this shared view of the process of social change, says Sapolsky, rather than a shared concern for a particular governmental programme or the shared attraction of a particular methodological approach, that unites the interest in science policy.

In fact, however, and even though many science policy makers have used such assumptions (Averch 1985; Edgerton and Hughes 1989), much of the analytical literature questions them. The *analysis* of the linkages between science and technology (increasingly treated at the level of specific disciplines and industrial sectors), and between science and technology, on the one hand, and social progress, on the other, lies at the heart of much contemporary work in the field. Salomon, in the early 1970s, had resoundingly criticized these assumptions as well as others others that imputed a superior rationality to *science* policy processes (Salomon 1973: chapters 5 and 6). Far from assuming the general primacy of science over technology, or of both over social change, it is precisely the relations between these phenomena that science policy specialists examine. As Salomon put it more recently, 'Technology is a social process among other social processes' (Salomon 1988: 50). What unites these analysts is a belief in the importance of these questions, not a shared view of the underlying processes, nor even of which are the most appropriate intellectual traditions for their analysis. (See also Nelkin 1989.)

ISSUES

Since at least the 1950s, the key question for governments in relation to science has been what science to support and through what machinery. The question has turned on choices of subjects, on machinery for dispensing funds, and on means for holding the recipients accountable. In relation to technology, the key question has been how to develop and maintain international competitiveness in industry (manufacturing and service, and in some cases also including a strong defence sector), while also supporting other policy areas such as health, transport, environment, etc. Associated questions have considered the precise relations between science and technology in specific sectors, and the contribution of technology to competitiveness, bearing in mind the range of other factors (training and education, banking systems, market conditions, trade unions, quality of management, and so on) that are also in play.

The context in which these questions have been raised has, however, varied considerably over the post-war years. Blume, himself drawing upon a widely held view, had distinguished three periods (Blume 1985), and it is convenient here to follow, and embroider, his analysis.

First was a 'golden age' beginning in the 1960s (and I would add, the 1950s in some countries), in which science was seen as the 'motor of progress'. Resources for science and technology grew at an almost unprecedented rate. The focus of science policy was on meeting the needs of science, these needs being determined by bodies of distinguished scientists (often, especially in the United States, physicists; see Greenberg 1969). But by the late 1950s or early 1960s, as we have seen, it had become clear that unlimited resources were not available. Attention was directed to what the British Advisory Council on Scientific Policy called 'the problem of priorities'. Criteria for choice between fields of science began to be developed (Shils 1968). As Blume observes, in these discussions utilitarian reasoning played a part, but not in the sense of determining research programmes by identifiable and immediate needs (Blume 1985: 71). It was rather a case of getting the structures right, and then good science would generate innovation. As the UK Council for Scientific Policy asserted in 1967, 'Basic research provides most of the original discoveries and hypotheses from which all other progress flows' (Council for Scientific Policy 1967: paragraph 45). Technology policy, meanwhile, outside the defence sector, was largely limited to a few high-technology fields, all in fact with strong defence connections, such as nuclear power, aerospace and computers.

The early 1970s saw a reaction against the beliefs which had underpinned the expansionist policies of the preceding two decades. The 'Counter-culture'; (Roszack 1970) and 'Limits to Growth' (Meadows *et al.* 1972) debates, in their critiques of materialism and consumerism, implicated science and technology as prime agents in humankind's harmful domination and abuse of nature. The oil shock of 1973–4 sharpened the debate, bringing issues of energy policy, environmentalism and growth before a wider public. This led, among other things, to the growth of technology assessment and strengthened environmental regulatory bodies. From within the scientific community, radical (left) critics argued that science should not be oriented solely towards the interests of the most powerful in society, which meant in practice towards the strongest economic and military powers, but should be directed towards a more broadly conceived social good (Dickson 1974).

In this context the OECD commissioned the Brooks Report, *Science, Growth and Society* (Brooks 1971), which argued that economic growth was not a sufficient goal for science policy. In Britain, the Rothschild Report (Rothschild 1971), commissioned by a government committed to improving lines of accountability and responsibility (Williams 1973), distinguished between basic and applied research; defined the latter as research which had a social objective in mind; and argued that applied research should, therefore, be done only at the behest of ministers or their delegated officials, on a 'customer–contractor basis'.

While this demand for social responsiveness (at least as defined by governments) was sweeping through science policy, so also was a more measured approach being adopted towards the relations between science and technological innovation. At the pragmatic level, a sense was growing that science had been oversold; at any rate, it seemed not to be delivering the expected economic goods. New academic work was casting further doubt on the so-called 'linear model' of the relations between science and innovation (see Jevons 1973; Langrish *et al.* 1972; Gibbons and Johnston 1974). In contrast to the 'science-push' attitude that had often characterized the rhetoric of science policy-making bodies (see the quotation above from the UK Council for Scientific Policy), the new work emphasized the organic interaction between 'science push' and 'demand pull' in technological innovation, together with the importance of personal and organizational factors within innovating firms.

Blume's third period, in which science is regarded as a source of 'strategic opportunity', began in the late 1970s or early 1980s. In it, radical innovation, involving the development of new high-technology industries, came to be seen as an essential element in industrial strategy. Industrial innovation itself became *the* central priority for R & D. The OECD, meanwhile, had emphasized the *complexity* of modern technology, arguing that innovation today depends upon contributions from science and from multiple and complementary technologies (such as electronics and new materials). Indeed, the OECD believes that the complexity of today's leading-edge technologies demands description as a 'new techno-economic system' (OECD 1987), although this concept raises an interesting question about how to characterize technological advance.

The understanding behind these developments is more subtle than before. As Blume notes, in place of science-push and demand-pull notions, we now have a more complex and iterative understanding. Attention is focused upon university–industry relations and upon the development of 'strategic' research to underpin new fields of technology, often across the boundaries of established disciplines. The science park, he says, has become 'the temple of the modern cargo cult' (Blume 1985: 74). In new fields of technology, the relations between science and technology are also very close. But support for science is also highly conditional upon perceptions of its relevance to technological advance. In Britain, for example, the concept of 'exploitable areas of science' has become important, but also problematical; indeed, it has been claimed that Thatcherism has fundamentally challenged the allegedly 'technocratic' outlook of important sections of scientific opinion and of science and technology policy analysts (Edgerton and Hughes 1989). Cuts in funding for basic research and/or for higher education more generally, rapidly rising costs of research, and structural rigidities leading, among other things, to ageing research communities and a lack of opportunities for young researchers, have led to what the OECD has described as 'the research system under constraint' (Drilhon 1989). Ziman (1987) has further argued that, far from the current difficulties being a tempo-rary or abnormal state, they have become the new norm, so that science policy must now come to terms with 'science in a steady state' – that is, with change being managed within a budget that is a fixed percentage of gross national product. In this context, the call by Rip and Hagendijk (1988) for greater attention to implementation studies is timely.

Two features of the current phase of science policy deserve final reference. These are the emphases upon 'evaluation' and 'foresight'.

'Evaluation' refers to the attempt to assess the value obtained from invest-ment in science and technology, either in terms of the quality of the results or in such other terms as, for example, development of expertise or stronger inter-institutional links. It arises particularly acutely in countries suffering from resource constraints, for it is here that the pressure to free limited funds for new activities is greatest. Cutting existing activities is notoriously difficult, especially if done by traditional peer review methods; hence the desire of governments to have good grounds, supposedly supplied by an evaluation, for so doing.

We cannot here go into details (see Gibbons and Georghiou 1987; Irvine 1988; Raan 1988; Evered and Harnett 1989). But it is worth noting that the very fashionableness of evaluation within governments and other public bodies raises a danger that the decision maker's desire for clear and simple messages will dismiss the caveats with which careful evaluators surround their con- clusions. This is especially so with respect to quantitative conclusions based upon, for example, the bibliometric analysis of citations to papers, using these as a proxy measure of the quality of the papers. Fine-grained quantitative evaluation of research is far from being an exact or an easy science, despite current enthusiasm for it.

The other topical new subject is 'foresight', an activity that is particularly highly developed in Japan. Unlike forecasting, which implies the existence of a single possible future (as if, when reading a book, one attempts to guess the next page), foresight is concerned with reaching an improved understanding of possible developments in science and technology, and the forces likely to shape them. It aims to identify various possible 'next pages' for the book, with a view then to structuring policy so as to steer events in a chosen direction.

Again, we cannot elaborate (see Martin and Irvine 1989; and Irvine and Martin 1984). Suffice it to say that some countries use formal bibliometric methods to try to spot growth points in science, nationally and internationally. Some engage in consultative exercises, involving large numbers of scientists and users of science and technology. Some adapt various tools from forecasting and futurology. Some set up specialist panels on narrow subjects, while others try to take a view of the whole national scene. Some draw on professional analysts, especially in Japan where there is a network of some 300 public and private think-tanks, many of which have levels of expertise in monitoring and forecasting R & D unmatched even by the large US consultancies. Some simply use what in the United States is called the BOGSAT method (Bunch of Guys Sitting Around a Table).

In the end, the fundamental questions remain: what science and technology should be supported; through what machinery; and how should both be related to social and economic goals? We are somewhat better at answering them today than in the past, at least to the extent of being more aware of the inadequacies of earlier approaches. A number of governments share this aware- ness, having burned their fingers on science and technology more than once. There remains, however, in and around some governments, a hankering for a 'scientific' approach to science policy (Comteian rather than Marxist in origin), as expressed in the current vogue for evaluation. Most contemporary science and technology policy analysts, in contrast, would reject such scientistic tend- encies, as they would equally reject simple-minded arguments about science and technology being the single most important driving forces of economic progress. They would resonate instead with Weber's observation that 'Politics is a strong and slow boring of hard boards' (Weber 1970: 128), arguing that this is as true of science policy as of anything else. As the defence orientation of so much post-war science and technology gives way in the 1990s and beyond to renewed concern with environmental and developmental issues (which are much more complex problems), the validity of Weber's dictum will be increasingly recognized.

ACKNOWLEDGEMENT

I wish to thank many friends and colleagues in Manchester and elsewhere for comments on an earlier draft, from which this final draft has greatly benefited.

REFERENCES

Ahmad, A. (1984) 'Science and technology in India: policy, management, implications', in M. Gibbons, P. Gummett and B. Udgaonkar (eds) *Science and Technology Policy in the 1980s and Beyond*, London: Longman.

Annerstedt, J. and Jamison, A. (eds) (1988) *From Research Policy to Social Intelligence*, London: Macmillan.

Averch, H. (1985) *A Strategic Analysis of Science and Technology Policy*, Baltimore and London: Johns Hopkins University Press.

Bacon, F. (1627) *New Atlantis*, reprinted in A. Johnston (ed.) (1965) *Francis Bacon*, London: Batsford.

Baker. J. R. (1978) 'Michael Polanyi's contributions to the cause of freedom in science', *Minerva* 16: 382–96.

Barnes, B. (1985) *About Science*, Oxford: Basil Blackwell.

Bernal, J. D. (1939) *The Social Function of Science*, London: Routledge & Kegan Paul.

Bijker, W. E., Hughes, T. P. and Pinch, R. (eds) (1987) *The Social Construction of Technological Systems*, Cambridge, Mass.: MIT Press.

Blume, S. (1985) *The Development of Dutch Science Policy in International Perspective, 1965–1985*, a report to the Raad van Advies voor het Wetenschapsbeleid, The Hague: Ministerie van Onderwijs en Wetenschappen.

Brickman, R. (1979) 'Comparative approaches to R & D policy coordination', *Policy Sciences* 11: 73–91.

Brickman, R. and Rip, A. (1979) 'Science policy advisory councils in France, the Netherlands and the United States, 1957–77: a comparative analysis', *Social Studies of Science* 9: 167–98.

Brooks, D. H. (1971) *Science, Growth and Society – A New Perspective*, Paris: OECD.

Bulletin of the Atomic Scientists (1985) 41: (December, 40th anniversary issue).

Bush, V. (1945) *Science – The Endless Frontier*, a report to the President on a programme for post-war scientific research, Washington, DC: US Government Printing Office; reissued by the National Science Foundation, July 1960.

Carter, C. F. and Williams, B. R. (1957) *Industry and Technical Progress: Factors Governing the Speed of Application of Science*, London: Oxford University Press.

771

Clark, N. (1985) *The Political Economy of Science and Technology*, Oxford: Basil Blackwell.

Clark, R. W. (1962) *The Rise of the Boffins*, London: Phoenix House.

Coombs, R., Saviotti, P. and Walsh, V. (1987) *Economics and Technological Change*, London: Macmillan.

Council for Science and Society (1986) *UK Military R & D*, Oxford: Oxford University Press.

Council for Scientific Policy (1967) *Second Report on Science Policy*, Cmnd. 3420, London: HMSO.

Dedijer, S. (1964) 'Research policy – from romance to reality', in M. Goldsmith and A. Mackay (eds) *The Science of Science*, Harmondsworth: Penguin.

Denny, B. C. (1965) 'Science and public policy: a literature in search of a field', *Public Administration Review* 25: 239–48.

Dickson, D. (1974) *Alternative Technology*, London: Fontana.

Dosi, G., Freeman, C., Nelson, R., Silverberg, G. and Soete L. (eds) (1988) *Technical Change and Economic Theory*, London: Pinter.

Drilhon, G. (1989) 'The research system under constraint', *STI Review* no. 5, Paris: OECD.

Edgerton, D. (1988) 'The relationship between military and civilian technology: a historical perspective', in P. Gummett and J. Reppy (eds) *The Relations Between Defence and Civil Technologies*, Dordrecht: Kluwer.

Edgerton, D. and Gummett, P. (1988) 'Science, technology and economics in the twentieth century', in G. Jordan (ed.) *British Military History: A Supplement to Robin Higham's Guide to the Sources*, New York and London: Garland Publishing.

Edgerton, D. and Hughes, K. (1989) 'The poverty of science: a critical analysis of scientific and industrial policy under Mrs Thatcher', *Public Administration* 67: 419–33.

Evered, D. and Harnett, S. (eds) (1989) *The Evaluation of Scientific Research*, Chichester: John Wiley.

Freeman, C. (1974) *The Economics of Industrial Innovation*, Harmondsworth: Penguin; rev. edn (1982) London: Pinter.

——(1988) 'Quantitative and qualitative factors in national policies for science and technology', in J. Annerstedt and A. Jamison (eds) *From Research Policy to Social Intelligence*, London: Macmillan.

Galison, P. (1988) 'Physics between war and peace', in E. Mendelsohn, M. R. Smith and P. Weingart (eds) *Science, Technology and the Military*, Dordrecht: Kluwer.

Georghiou, L., Metcalfe, J. S., Gibbons, M., Ray, T. and Evans, J. (1986) *Post-innovation Performance: Technological Development and Competition*, London: Macmillan.

Gibbons, M. and Georghiou, L. (1987) *Evaluation of Research: A Selection of Current Practices*, Paris: OECD.

Gibbons, M. and Johnston, R. (1974) 'The role of science in technological innovation', *Research Policy* 3: 220–42.

Goldsmith, M. and Mackay, A. (1964) *The Science of Science*, Harmondsworth: Penguin.

Green, K., Coombs, R. and Holroyd, K. (1980) *The Effect of Microelectronic Technologies on Employment Prospects*, Farnborough: Gower Press.

Greenberg, D. S. (1969) *The Politics of American Science*, Harmondsworth, Penguin.

Gummett, P. J. (1980) *Scientists in Whitehall*, Manchester: Manchester University Press.

Gummett, P. J. and Price, G. L. (1977) 'An approach to the central planning of British science: the formation of the Advisory Council on Scientific Policy', *Minerva* 15 119–43.

Gummett, P. J. and Reppy, J. (eds) (1988) *The Relations Between Defence and Civil Technologies*, Dordrecht: Kluwer.

Haberer, J. (1969) *Politics and the Community of Science*, New York: Van Nostrand Reinhold.

Hughes, T. P. (1986) 'The seamless web: technology, science, etcetera, etcetera', *Social Studies of Science* 16: 281–92.

Irvine, J. (1988) *Evaluating Applied Research: Lessons from Japan*, London: Pinter.

Irvine, J. and Martin B. R. (1984) *Foresight in Science: Picking the Winners*, London: Pinter.

Irwin, A. (1985) *Risk and the Control of Technology*, Manchester: Manchester University Press.

Jain, A. (1988) 'Science and technology studies in India', in *40 Years of Research – a CSIR Overview*, New Delhi: CSIR.

Jevons, F. R. (1973) *Science Observed: Science as a Social and Intellectual Activity*, London: Allen & Unwin.

Johnston, A. (ed.) (1965) *Francis Bacon*, London: Batsford.

King, A. (1974) *Science and Policy: The International Stimulus*, London: Oxford University Press.

Kogan, M. and Henkel, M. (1983) *Government and Research*, London: Heinemann.

Kuhn, T. S. (1970) *The Structure of Scientific Revolutions*, 2nd edn, London: Chicago University Press.

Langrish, J., Gibbons, M., Evans, W. G. and Jevons F. R. (1972) *Wealth from Knowledge*, London: Macmillan.

Long, F. A. and Reppy, J. (eds) (1980) *The Genesis of New Weapons: Decision Making for Military R & D*, New York: Pergamon.

Longman Guides to World Science and Technology (national or regional guides to science and technology policy around the world), Harlow: Longman.

McAllister, J. F. O. (1986) 'Civil science policy in British industrial reconstruction 1942–51', unpublished D.Phil. thesis, University of Oxford.

McGucken, W. (1978) 'On freedom and planning in science: the Society for Freedom in Science, 1940–46', *Minerva* 16: 42–72.

Mackenzie, D. (1986) 'Science and technology studies and the question of the military', *Social Studies of Science* 16: 361–71.

MacLeod, R. M. and Andrews, K. (1970) 'The origins of DSIR: reflections on ideas and men, 1915–16', *Public Administration* 48: 23–48.

McNeill, W. H. (1983) *The Pursuit of Power: Technology, Armed Force, and Society Since A.D. 1000*, Oxford: Basil Blackwell.

Martin, B. R. and Irvine, J. (1989) *Research Foresight: Priority-Setting in Science*, London: Pinter.

Meadows, D. H., Meadows, D. L., Randers, J. and Behrens, W. W. III (1972) *The Limits to Growth*, London: Earth Island Publications.

Mendelsohn, E., Smith, M. R. and Weingart, P. (eds) (1988) *Science, Technology and the Military*, Dordrecht: Kluwer.

Nelkin, D. (1989) 'Science Studies in the 1990s', paper presented to the Symposium on the Outlook for STS, Program on Science, Technology and Society, Cornell University, Ithaca, NY.

Nelson, R. and Winter, S. (1982) *An Evolutionary Theory of Economic Change*, Cambridge, Mass.: Harvard University Press.

OECD, Reviews of national science policy (various, covering many countries), Paris: OECD.

OECD (1987) *The Contribution of Science and Technology to Economic Growth and Social Development*, Paris: OECD (mimeo.).

Papon, P. (1988) 'Science and technology policy in France: 1981–1986', *Minerva* 26: 493–511.

Pavitt, K. (ed.) (1980) *Technical Innovation and British Economic Performance*, London: Macmillan.

Pavitt, K. and Walker, W. (1976) 'Government policies towards industrial innovation', *Research Policy* 5: 11–97.

Piganiol, P. (1961) *Science and the Policy of Governments: The Implication of Science and Technology for National and International Affairs*, Paris: OECD.

Polanyi, M. (1968) 'The republic of science', in E. Shils (ed.) *Criteria for Scientific Development: Public Policy and National Goals*, Cambridge, Mass.: MIT Press.

Price, D. de Solla (1963) *Little Science Big Science*, New York: Columbia University Press.

Price, D. K. (1954) *Government and Science: Their Dynamic Relation in American Democracy*, New York: Oxford University Press.

Price, G. L. (1976) *The Politics of Planning and the Problems of Science Policy*, Leeds: SISCON.

Rip, A. and Hagendijk, R. (1988) *Implementation of Science Policy Priorities*, London: Science Policy Support Group.

Ronayne, J. (1984) *Science in Government: A Review of the Principles and Practice of Science Policy*, London: Edward Arnold.

Roszack, T. (1970) *The Making of a Counter-culture*, London: Faber & Faber.

Rothman, H. (1972) *Murderous Providence: A Study of Pollution in Industrial Societies*, London: Hart-Davis.

Rothschild, V. (1971) 'The organization and management of government R & D', in *A Framework for Government Research and Development*, Cmnd. 4814, London: HMSO.

Salomon, J-J. (1973) *Science and Politics*, London: Macmillan (originally pub. in French, 1970, Paris: Éditions de Seuil).

——(1988) 'Technology and democracy', in J. Annerstedt and A. Jamison (eds) *From Research Policy to Social Intelligence*, London: Macmillan.

Sapolsky, H. (1975) 'Science policy', in F. Greenstein and N. Polsby (eds) *Handbook of Political Science*, Reading, Mass.: Addison-Wesley.

Shils, E. (ed.) (1968) *Criteria for Scientific Development: Public Policy and National Goals*, Cambridge, Mass.: MIT Press.

Raan, A. F. J. van (ed.) (1988) *Handbook of Quantitative Studies of Science and Technology*, Amsterdam: Elsevier.

Varcoe, I. (1974) *Organizing for Science in Britain: A Case-Study*, London: Oxford University Press.

Vig, N. J. (1968) *Science and Technology in British Politics*, London: Pergamon Press.

774

Waddington, C. H. (1973) *OR in World War 2: Operational Research Against the U-Boat*, London: Elek.

Walker, W. and Lonnroth, M. (1983) *Nuclear Power Struggles: Industrial Competition and Proliferation Control*, London: Allen & Unwin.

Weber, M. (1970) 'Politics as a vocation', in H. H. Gerth and C. Wright Mills (eds) *From Max Weber: Essays in Sociology*, London: Routledge & Kegan Paul.

Werskey, P. G. (1978) *The Visible College*, London: Allen Lane.

Williams, R. (1973) 'Some political aspects of the Rothschild affair', *Science Studies* 3: 31–46.

——(1980) *The Nuclear Power Decisions: British Policies 1953–78*, London: Croom Helm.

Williams R. and Mills, S. (eds) (1986) *Public Acceptability of New Technologies*, London: Croom Helm.

Wood, N. (1959) *Communism and British Intellectuals*, London: Victor Gollancz.

Yoxen, E. J. (1983) *The Gene Business: Who Should Control Biotechnology?*, London: Pan.

——(1986) *Unnatural Selection? Coming to Terms with the New Genetics*, London: Heinemann.

Ziman, J. (1987) *Science in a 'Steady State': The Research System in Transition*, London: Science Policy Support Group.

Zuckerman, S. (1939) 'Science and society', *New Statesman and Nation* 17: 297–8.

——(1966) *Scientists and War*, London: Hamish Hamilton.

——(1978) *From Apes to Warlords: The Autobiography (1904–1946) of Solly Zuckerman*, London: Hamish Hamilton.

——(1988) *Monkeys, Men and Missiles: An Autobiography, 1946–88*, London: Collins.

FURTHER READING

Barnes, B. (1985) *About Science*, Oxford: Basil Blackwell.

Bijker, W. E., Hughes, T. P. and Pinch, T. (eds) (1987) *The Social Construction of Technological Systems*, Cambridge, Mass.: MIT Press.

Blume, S. S. (1974) *Toward a Political Sociology of Science*, New York: Free Press.

——(1981) *Science Policy Research – The State of the Art and Implications for Policy*, a report to the Swedish Council for Planning and Coordination of Research, Stockholm: Forskningsrådsnämnden.

Clark, N. (1985) *The Political Economy of Science and Technology*, Oxford: Basil Blackwell.

Dosi, F., Freeman, C., Nelson, R., Silverberg, G. and Soete, L. (eds) (1988) *Technical Change and Economic Theory*, London: Pinter.

Edgerton, D. and Gummett, P. (1988) 'Science, technology and economics in the twentieth century', in G. Jordan (ed.) *British Military History: A Supplement to Robin Higham's Guide to the Sources*, New York and London: Garland Publishing.

Freeman, C. (1974) *The Economics of Industrial Innovation*, Harmondsworth: Penguin; rev. edn (1982) London: Pinter.

Gummett, P. J. and Reppy, J. (eds) (1988) *The Relations Between Defence and Civil Technologies*, Dordrecht: Kluwer.

Longman Guides to World Science and Technology (national and regional guides to science and technology policy around the world), Harlow: Longman.

Martin, B. R. and Irvine J. (1989) *Research Foresight: Priority-Setting in Science*, London: Pinter.

Mendelsohn, R., Smith, M. R. and Weingart, P. (eds) (1988) *Science, Technology and the Military*, Dordrecht: Kluwer.

OECD, Reviews of national science policy (various, covering many countries), Paris: OECD.

Rossner, J. D. (ed.) (1989) Special Issue on Evaluation of Government Innovation Programmes, *Research Policy* 18.

Sapolsky, H. (1975) 'Science policy', in F. Greenstein and N. Polsby (eds) *Handbook of Political Science*, Reading, Mass.: Addison-Wesley.

Smith, M. R. (1985) *Military Enterprise and Technological Change: Perspectives on the American Experience*, Cambridge, Mass.: MIT Press.

Spiegel-Rösing, I. and Price, D. (eds) (1977) *Science, Technology and Society*, London: Sage Publications.

Williams, R. (1971) *Politics and Technology*, London: Macmillan.

Ziman, J. (1984) *An Introduction to Science Studies*, London: Cambridge University Press.

——(1987) *Science in a 'Steady State': The Research System in Transition*, London: Science Policy Support Group.

48

URBAN POLICY

MICHAEL PACIONE

Urban policy is concerned with the management of urban change. It is a state activity which seeks to influence the distribution and operation of investment and consumption processes in the built environment. It is important to realize, however, that urban policy is not confined to activity at the urban scale. National and international economic and social policies are as much urban policy, if defined by their urban impacts, as land use planning or urban redevelopment. In effect urban policy is often made under another name. Urban policy is dynamic. Its formulation and implementation is a continuing process, not an event. Measures that are introduced cause changes which may resolve some problems but create others for which further policy is required. Furthermore, only rarely is there a simple optimum solution to an urban problem. More usually a range of policy options exist for the consideration of decision makers and urban managers.

Urban policy is the product of the power relationship between the different interest groups that constitute a particular social formation. Foremost among these actors are the state, both local and national, and capital in its various fractions. Capital and state pursue specific goals which may be either complementary or contradictory. For capital, the prime directive is profit maximization. The state, on the other hand, in addition to facilitating the process of accumulation, must also satisfy the goal of legitimation. These political and economic imperatives have a direct influence on the nature of urban policy. Urban policy is also conditioned by external forces operating within the global economic system, as well as by locally specific factors and agents.

It follows that understanding the nature, operation and impacts of urban policy requires a comparative examination of the particular manifestations of urban development processes in various countries and localities, informed by an appreciation of the macropolitical economy.

THE RESTRUCTURING OF URBAN SPACE

Many of the world's cities are currently experiencing social, economic, political and environmental changes of unprecedented magnitude. These changes are the outcome of the interplay of a host of private and public interests operating at a variety of geographic scales. Theorists from both left and right have attached particular importance to the mechanisms of the capitalist mode of production and the rise of a global economic system.

Uneven development is an inherent characteristic of capitalism which stems from the propensity of capital to flow to locations which offer the greatest potential return. The differential use of space by capital in pursuit of profit creates a mosaic of inequality at all geographic levels from global to local. Consequently, at any one time certain countries, regions, cities and localities will be in the throes of decline as a result of the retreat of capital investment while others will be experiencing the impact of capital inflows. At the metropolitan scale the outcome of the uneven development process is manifested in the poverty, powerlessness and polarization of disadvantaged residents. The older industrial cities in the advanced economies have been among the biggest losers in the global investment competition. Cities such as Pittsburgh and Cleveland, Glasgow and Liverpool have experienced the strains of recession and contraction as a result of the new international division of labour and the deindustrialization of traditional economies. In stark contrast, global command cities such as London or Tokyo are booming and experiencing the diverse problems caused by concentration of activities. Centrally planned economies have not been immune to the forces of change emanating from the operation of the global economic system either. In the Third World, as a direct result of the uneven pattern of development within most countries, urban areas are growing at an explosive rate as a consequence of rural–urban migration. Given the comparatively low levels of urbanization and the limited resource base of most Third World states, the urban crisis seems destined to deepen.

The central importance of capital in this process of urban restructuring is axiomatic, but it is important to avoid the fallacy of economic determinism which, paradoxically, is shared by the conservative New Right and the Marxist left. Technical and economic processes, the material forces of production, are not the only determinants of urban growth and decline. The policies of the local and national state can exert at least an equally important influence on urban change. Regulatory and tax policies shape the environments which attract or repel investors, decisions about public investment determine whether infrastructure will be rebuilt or allowed to deteriorate, government procurement policy stimulates the private economy, and intergovernmental transfer payments can prevent the total collapse of a local economy.

A structural interpretation of urban change which emphasizes the omni-

778

potent logic of the capitalist (or any other) mode of production also affords insufficient consideration to the way in which general processes are embedded in and modified by historically specific national and local settings. For example, it is the combination of economic forces with historically specific social and political processes that produces the particular form of uneven development found in the USA. Sprawling suburban development, widespread urban fiscal stress, and extreme class segregation of residential communities are not reproduced in other capitalist states. In Europe, for example, suburban sprawl is less extensive, the central state finances a larger share of local government budgets thereby mediating local fiscal stress, and the upper social strata are less anti-urban in lifestyle and residential location.

The restructuring of urban space is best understood as the outcome of actions taken by both economic and political actors operating within a complex and changing matrix of relations between global and national political-economic forces, and national and local social and political processes.

MAJOR ACTORS IN THE RESTRUCTURING OF URBAN SPACE

The principal agents of urban change are located in both the private sector (various fractions of capital: for example, industrial capital, finance capital) and the public sector (for example, legislation and various public bodies). The former includes property speculators, financial institutions and industrialists.

Property speculators, either individual entrepreneurs or corporations, purchase land in anticipation of profiting from subsequent increases in property values. Such increases may be the direct result of public policy. For example, in the UK the granting of planning permission for a new residential development on land formerly zoned for agricultural use brings an immediate windfall benefit to the landowner. Attempts by Labour governments to impose a betterment tax to capture some of this added value for the public good have not survived a change of government, being antithetical to Conservative philosophy. Speculative activity occurs throughout the capitalist city. In the central areas it can lead to the creation of slums, displacement and the breakup of communities prior to revitalization or gentrification. On the urban periphery the speculative holding of land can encourage leap-frog development and urban sprawl.

Financial institutions have increased their importance in the production of the built environment in both Britain and North America. This is particularly evident in the housing sector with the decline in private rented housing and the growth of home ownership. Financial institutions seek to maximize profits and minimize risks, and, since opportunities are differentiated over an urban area, financiers adopt spatially discriminating lending practices. This will have a significant impact on the location of new construction as well as on mainten-

779

ance and improvements to existing structures. Discrimination has also been practised on the grounds of race. The practice of red-lining areas perceived as poor risks has also been followed by the insurance industry. Given that financial institutions operate within a free market environment it is unrealistic to expect otherwise.

Industrial capital played a key role in the development of urban society first in the UK, then in North America and Europe. The process of de-industrialization has been a major factor in producing high levels of unemployment in the older urban-industrial areas. Traditional manufacturing industry has failed to maintain its international competitiveness. A significant reason has been underinvestment. Finance capital has flowed out of manufacturing into areas offering greater profit, including pension funds and office development. In addition, the leading sector of industrial capital has sought to retain its competitiveness by operating internationally. This has led to the relocation of production facilities and jobs to the low-wage countries of the Third World as part of the new international division of labour. This decline of manufacturing industry has had a disproportionate effect on those cities which were traditional centres of the activity.

In practice the activities of different fractions of capital interact and operate as growth coalitions to foster urban restructuring. However, while the reality of elite coalitions managing urban growth has been validated empirically, the extent of their effects is more difficult to assess. In instances of financially weak cities the business-financial community can exercise close to monopoly control. The fiscal crisis of New York in the mid-1970s is a clear example of how a financial coalition can benefit at the expense of the public. The degrees of freedom which permit growth networks to restructure urban space are provided by the relative autonomy enjoyed by capital. This freedom varies between countries depending upon the extent of state policy, planning and land use controls.

The state – central and local government – exercises both a direct (for example, planning regulations) and indirect (for example, taxation policy) influence on urban restructuring. Recognition of the need for urban planning emerged in the UK and in North America during the late nineteenth century as a response to the problems of the industrial city. But despite the existence of similar urban problems national responses were different. In the USA an ideology favouring private property rights and local autonomy has limited intervention to zoning and minimum land use control, whereas in the UK the public have accepted the implications of the comprehensive system of urban planning initiated by the Town and Country Planning Act of 1947. The basic principle enshrined in the 1947 Act was that of private land ownership but public accountability in use. On balance, the UK planning system has achieved its stated objectives. Post-war urban growth has been contained to the extent that the coalescence of adjacent cities has been prevented and good quality agricultural land protected. By contrast with the situation in Britain, in the USA there is no system of planning in the sense of a common framework with a clearly defined set of physical, social and economic objectives. Planning is not obligatory, as it is in the UK, and together with the fragmented structure of local government – in addition to the federal government and fifty states there are about 8,000 counties, 18,000 municipalities and 17,000 townships each with the power to plan or regulate land use – this means that the content of planning is both local and variable from place to place. In principle a range of techniques for controlling urban growth and change is available, but in practice the major tool employed is land use zoning. Critics of zoning maintain that (a) it is unnecessary since market forces will produce a fair segregation of land uses; (b) the system is open to corruption, particularly in respect of variances or zone changes; (c) it can lead to premature use of resources by owners who fear a zoning change; and (d) it is unequal in its effect since a piece of property zoned for commercial uses within a residential area provides its owner with windfall profits at the expense of neighbours who must bear the costs of negative externalities. The most vociferous criticism, however, has been reserved for the practice of exclusionary zoning. This refers to the legal regulations adopted by suburban municipalities to preserve their territories against intrusion of undesired land uses and population groups. Supporters of zoning argue that it is a flexible tool and an effective means of allowing local residents to determine part of the character of their neighbourhood. Certainly its wholesale use during the past half-century has largely determined the current land use structure of metropolitan America.

FORMS OF URBAN POLICY

Policies vary considerably between countries, reflecting the institutional environment in which they are set and the procedures and instruments selected for implementation. Nevertheless it is possible to distinguish several general forms of urban policy. The first are policies designed to guide urban growth and change at a national scale, i.e. between urban regions. The second are policies to guide urban growth and change at an intraregional or metropolitan scale, i.e. within urban regions. Third, in some federal countries (such as Australia, Canada, Germany, India and the USA) there may be an intervening level of policy development at the state or provincial level. Finally, there are 'non-urban' policies which indirectly and often inadvertently affect urban restructuring.

Two broad kinds of national urban policies may be identified. The first refers to attempts to restrain the growth of core city-regions and promote growth in peripheral regions. These policies have been applied to cities such as London, Paris and Tokyo with varying levels of success. Since the mid-1970s, however, the reduction in economic and population growth in many cities of the developed world and increased concern for declining inner-city areas have questioned the general need for growth constraint policies. The second type of national policy seeks to reshape the settlement system. In the 1960s and early 1970s many countries adopted growth pole strategies (for example, the French *metropoles d'équilibre*), in part as a response to metropolitan restraint policies. By the late 1970s, however, these policies had lost favour because of political opposition from those small and medium-sized towns not designated as growth centres, and the fact that in practice the geographic spread effects of the policy were less than postulated by theory. More recently, governments have employed a range of national policy initiatives to direct investment into declining industrial cities. These have typically included tax concessions, employment incentives, infrastructure improvements, selective public sector procurement policies and creation of special economic zones (such as enterprise zones, simplified planning zones and urban development corporations).

Although not all countries have national urban strategies, most have attempted to influence the form of urban development at the metropolitan scale. For much of the post-war period such policies have aimed to channel development in order to stem the physical expansion of the built-up area, avoid excessive loss of valuable agricultural land, ensure more efficient use of infrastructure and reduce congestion in the urban core. A variety of housing, transport, land use and development control policies have been employed in pursuit of these goals. Since the late 1970s, policy emphasis at the metropolitan level has also turned to the steering of employment and investment into inner urban areas or to new suburban sub-centres using a combination of controls on and inducements to the private sector.

Of at least equal importance as these explicit urban policies, in terms of their influence on urban development, are those national policies which are urban in neither focus nor intent but which significantly affect the form and rate of urban change. These 'non-urban' policies include the following.

1 Fiscal policies such as tax relief on mortgage interest payments affect urban development. In the USA the availability of tax relief and federal mortgage insurance for new single-family dwellings were major stimuli to low density suburban development in the post-war period.

2 Industrial policies including decisions to support certain industries (such as steel production) or expand certain public expenditure (such as defence) have a differential spatial impact since relevant activities are unequally distributed among cities and regions.

782

3 Equalization policies which result in inter-governmental transfers operate in favour of some urban areas above others.

4 Transport policies can have significant urban effects. For example, the US interstate highway programme greatly encouraged post-war metropolitan sprawl and stimulated the growth of cities whose accessibility was enhanced.

5 Even agricultural policies can have an urban impact. Structural policies to promote the capitalization of agriculture directly affect the size of the agricultural labour force and therefore rural to urban migration. This is of particular significance in the Third World today.

6 The impact of immigration policies tends to be concentrated on particular cities. Flows of migrants profoundly affect urban labour markets, housing programmes and social structures. Nowhere is this more evident than in the burgeoning cities of the Third World.

IDEOLOGY AND URBAN POLICY

The form of urban policy employed depends on the problem to be tackled and, most fundamentally, on the ideological position of the state. The outcome of the power relationship between capital and polity can be usefully translated into four ideological regimes. In two of these – the market capitalist (or market conservative), and the corporate fascist – capital as a whole occupies a hegemonic position which enables it to maximize the benefits of state programmes and limit the costs. In the first, the degree of state penetration of the means of production is low, involving, for example, tax reductions, employment subsidies, urban renewal and designation of free trade zones. In the second, state involvement is more direct and may include controls over investment decisions, wage structure, union power and the banking system. The third type of policy regime – the liberal democratic or welfare state liberalism – incorporates working-class interests through the dominance in the governing coalition of a conservative party of the left (such as the British Labour Party or the German Social Democrats). The final ideological position is represented by a social democratic regime dominated by a leftist working-class party favouring direct control of production to channel income benefits to labour rather than to capital. Whichever ideology is dominant in a country largely determines the form of urban policy. During the post-war period, in advanced economies particular attention has focused on the changing strength of market capitalism and welfare state liberalism.

Advocates of market capitalism (as espoused by Reaganomics in the USA and Thatcherism in the UK) view the production of unevenly developed cities and regions as the inevitable outcome of technological change within an economic system that readily adapts to innovation. The negative socio-spatial effects of this restructuring that impinge on disadvantaged people and places are regarded as unavoidable consequences of a process which is of benefit to society as a whole. Since market forces are seen to be the most efficient allocators of capital and labour, state intervention is considered unnecessary. Policies involving social welfare expenditure and government financial aid to declining cities are regarded as harmful because they anchor low-wage workers to sites of low employment opportunity, discourage labour force participation and inhibit labour mobility. Welfare state liberals, on the other hand, while accepting the central role of the market, acknowledge that the institutional and cyclical 'market imperfections' which have left certain people and places in prolonged economic distress must be rectified by compensatory government policies.

The implementation of urban policy under these different ideological regimes can be illustrated with reference to post-war developments in the USA and the UK.

URBAN POLICY IN THE USA

All metropolitan areas of the USA contain blighted areas which undermine the tax base and fiscal viability of their cities, exude negative externalities, and ghettoize minority and disadvantaged groups (such as recent immigrants, low-income elderly and public-assistance recipients). For over thirty years public programmes have been directed at the social and economic regeneration of these distressed areas. This has been the context for federal programmes of Urban Renewal during the 1950s, Model Cities during the 1960s, Urban Development Action Grants and Community Development Block Grants during the 1970s, and Economic Development Administration programmes over several decades. These policies funded public activities such as land assembly, infrastructural investments, subsidized financing for private investment, and job training and employment programmes for the residents of distressed neighbourhoods. Significantly the aid to implement these policies flowed via a direct federal–municipal link which deliberately bypassed the states. Such strategies represented a post-war extension of the New Deal philosophy of the 1930s.

The election of the Reagan administration in 1981 heralded a shift from a liberal democratic policy stance to a market capitalist perspective. This signalled a radical change in urban policy, although there had been clear signs of a federal reassessment of the role of cities towards the end of the Carter administration in response to the worldwide recession. Thus the Presidential Commission on the National Agenda for the Eighties emphasized that policies should promote national economic growth but should be neutral about where that growth took place. This trend was continued by the Reagan administration and translated into a shift away from the practice of targeting distressed or declining cities in urban policy. The guiding principle of the Reagan urban policy (and of the Thatcher government in Britain) was that the future of cities depends upon the strength of the national economy. This philosophy was accompanied by cuts in federal spending; retreat from the close federal-city link that had developed since the 1930s, with correspondingly greater responsibility to the states; and most fundamentally, reliance on market forces rather than on explicit federal urban policy.

The Reagan administration's objective of federal disinvestment from urban policy was substantially achieved during the 1980s. Nevertheless, the cutback in federal urban funding proved less damaging to city budgets than anticipated, partly because after 1982 Congress rejected most proposals for further cuts. In general, throughout the 1980s most city governments continued to balance their budgets by raising taxes, increasing productivity, privatizing municipal services and, in some cases, receiving increased state aid. The federal strategy to 'recapitalize' the economy through tax reductions, deregulation and private business growth also encouraged renewed civic entrepreneurialism. Cities such as Pittsburgh, Baltimore, Portland and New Orleans showed marked improvement in their capacity to compete for a share of national economic growth. The greatest indictment of the market capitalist approach of the New Right, however, stems from its indifference to the socio-spatial effects of its *laissez-faire* urban policy. This has ensured that certain cities, localities and social groups have borne a disproportionate share of the costs of the restructuring of urban space. For many analysts this alone is sufficient justification for more active government involvement in urban policy.

URBAN POLICY IN THE UK

Modern urban policy in the UK dates only from the late 1960s when the experience of riots in US cities, concern over the possible growth of an urban racial problem in Britain, and the rediscovery of the inner-city problem focused attention on urban social problems as opposed to the physical deficiencies that had been the concern of the earlier comprehensive redevelopment strategy. Between 1965 and 1976 the policy emphasis was on supplementing existing social programmes to improve the welfare of disadvantaged individuals and communities. Of particular significance for the subsequent development of urban policy were the Community Development Projects which rejected a social-pathological view of urban deprivation in favour of a structural interpretation of the underlying causes. This was acknowledged in the 1977 White Paper on policy for the inner cities which signalled a more broadly based approach to urban problems, combining economic, social and environmental programmes and involving new organizational arrangements between central and local government to provide a more co-ordinated response. Thus the

1978 Inner Urban Area Act, sponsored by a Labour government, created partnerships between central and local government that attempted to harness private capital interests and investment for urban economic revival. The emphasis on improving the economic environment of cities was also promoted by a shift of attention from new towns to urban regeneration and increased powers to enable local authorities to aid and attract industrial developments. The major vehicle for these measures was the expanded Urban Programme. Since the election of 1979, successive Conservative administrations have endeavoured to reduce central government involvement in urban regeneration, and to shift the policy emphasis from the public to the private sector. As with the Reagan administration in the USA, the main role envisaged for the public sector is to attract and accommodate the requirements of private investors without unduly influencing their development decisions. This perspective underlay a number of new initiatives introduced by the 1980 Local Government Planning and Land Act, the most significant of which were the concepts of enterprise zones (which were also proposed but not enacted by the Reagan government) and urban development corporations (reflecting the approach embodied in the US urban development action grants). The belief of government in the power of the private sector to initiate urban regeneration was also evident in a variety of other schemes including derelict land grants, urban development grants, Inner City Enterprises Ltd, Business in the Community, the Financial Institutions Group, enterprise trusts, and inner-city compacts.

While the market capitalist approach may be a logical policy response in areas where there is significant economic potential, it is unlikely to resolve the difficulties that confront the deprived inhabitants of the most disadvantaged areas. In order to address such problems urban policy must be as much social policy as economic policy. This principle has been at the centre of local economic initiatives introduced by some left-wing councils seeking to moderate the impact of uneven development within their regions by focusing attention on the social costs associated with the unrestrained ability of corporate capital institutions to move investments between global locations in search of maximum profit. Although local economic initiatives are innovative and wide-ranging (including, for example, equity financing of firms, planning agreements between local authorities and companies, and promotion of 'socially useful' production), operating alone they cannot resolve the problems of disadvantaged city dwellers in the face of contrary tendencies originating from the central state and from capital itself.

URBAN POLICY IN THE THIRD WORLD

As we have seen, global restructuring has had major consequences for urban policy in the core countries. Urban development in the Third World is conditioned to an even greater extent by its interaction with the global political economy. Many Third World countries are currently undergoing a form of development which is dependent on the needs of multinational corporations. The urban consequences of a local economy oriented to external demands include a highly polarized class structure in which the mass of the urban population endures the diverse social and economic disadvantages which accompany urban underdevelopment. These generally include high rates of unemployment and underemployment, insufficient housing and shelter, inadequate sanitation and water supplies, overloaded transportation systems, environmental degradation, health and nutritional problems, and municipal budget crises. That urban conditions in the Third World are relatively superior to those in rural areas should afford little comfort for policy makers confronted with limited resources and an urban growth process of unprecedented proportions.

A variety of national, regional and urban policies has been employed in response to the urban crisis of the Third World. As in the developed world, these reflect goals and priorities defined by the dominant political economy. As a result, in most Third World cities to date, policy outcomes have favoured political elites and growth coalitions at the expense of the urban majority. Resolving the social, economic and environmental problems of the urban poor represents the fundamental challenge for urban policy. This will require innovative approaches which recognize the historically specific context of Third World urbanization and the individual complex of problems and opportunities that exist in every country. It is necessary to advance beyond policies and plans based on the urban experience of the developed world. National deconcentration and decentralization policies have generally failed to curb the growth of primary cities. Urban master plans have often been overtaken by events, and housing policies have been unable to provide shelter at costs that the intended beneficiaries can reasonably afford. Such failures have exposed the weaknesses in traditional approaches to planning and encouraged the search for policies that are based on an understanding of what is feasible as well as desirable.

The past decade has highlighted the problems of resource scarcity and the limitations of conventional planning. It has also focused attention on the potential contribution that people can make to urban development in an environment of scarcity. This reappraisal of the role of key elements such as squatter areas and the informal economy suggests that the main objective of urban policies in the Third World should be one of enhancing conditions for self-help and mutual aid, through forms of enabling action in support of locally determined, self-organized, and self-managed settlement programmes. Enabling actions are essentially institutional changes in administrative rules and regulations and typically cover the ways in which funds are allocated, credit generated and disbursed, decisions made and responsibility exercised. With respect to the key question of credit, for example, governments must intervene to provide initial capital and to assist in creating institutions that mobilize the often limited resources of those involved in the self-help and mutual-aid processes. A shift towards enabling strategies implies greater and not less involvement by governments. First, this approach requires governments and public authorities to transfer certain decision-making powers to local organizations. Second, governments must remove obstacles to local initiatives whether in the form of restrictive building codes or conventional, entrenched views on land holding and tenure. Third, enabling strategies imply that those professionals involved in urban development must learn to plan with, rather than for, people. Fourth, and most fundamentally, this strategy requires that governments accept the social demands of communities as legitimate bases for urban policy. These preconditions may be too demanding for some developing countries in which the economic elite also constitute a significant element of the political elite. Nevertheless, radical problems demand radical measures.

PROBLEMS AND PROSPECTS FOR URBAN POLICY

Current trends in world urbanization, the increasing number and size of cities, and the deterioration of many urban environments have placed a particular responsibility on policy charged with the management of urban change. The extent to which policy can meet this challenge depends on a variety of factors including the nature of the problem to be addressed, the organizational, institutional and fiscal framework of the country, the effect of external forces such as 'non-urban' policies and those emanating from the global political economy, and the power balance between capital and polity. The variability of policy environments in the modern world ensures that there is no single optimum approach to the formulation and implementation of urban policy. Despite these differences, however, it is possible to make a number of conclusions and recommendations for future urban policy research and practice.

The increasing scale and impact of the restructuring process affecting the world's urban areas, together with the continuing scarcity of public resources requires a realistic appraisal of the problems and prospects for cities. Rather than attempting to recreate the historic economic base of many old industrial cities, policy must seek to exploit the new opportunities that emerge from the process of economic change. The infusion of a sense of resource-realism into policy formulation is particularly important in the Third World. Past policies aimed at developing a comprehensive national settlement system should be replaced with more sensitive metropolitan level planning and have achievable sectoral policies regarding housing, transport, employment and service provision.

Possibly the greatest challenge for urban policy concerns the distribution of the benefits and costs of urban restructuring. While the problems experienced by people and places marginal to the capitalist development process have deepened over the past decade, urban policy has proved incapable of remedying the situation. At the crux of the matter is the relative importance attached to social and economic priorities in national policy. The resolution of urban poverty and deprivation requires a complementary programme of 'people policies' operating over a long term at the structural level in order to achieve a redistribution of wealth in society, and more immediate local-level 'place policies' to improve the current position of the disadvantaged. The practical difficulties of implementing such policies should not be underestimated, particularly in states where economic and political elites enjoy a symbiotic relationship.

The greatest resource available to many cities, and in particular to distressed urban areas, is the labour and expertise of the residents. This may be mobilized to ease the process of urban restructuring. Particular efforts should be directed towards improved mechanisms for citizen participation in urban policy and planning. People who play a part in the design of a project, for example, are more likely to be willing to assist in implementation and thereafter have some psychological commitment to project maintenance.

The magnitude of the urban crisis in both the developed and developing world is such that the successful restructuring of urban space, and in particular the revitalization of declining cities, requires capital investment from the private sector. Policy makers must strike an appropriate balance between the demands of capital and the needs of people. The aim is for urban policy to work with, not for, capital.

While the problems of Third World urban areas to a large degree result from real resource shortages, the situation is often compounded by ineffective urban management. Effective use of limited resources can only come from policies which are complementary and do not cancel each other. Attention should also be directed to basic managerial activities including reliable data collection, land registration and cadastral surveys.

The administrative structure of an urban region can influence the impact of policy. Metropolitan-wide government can overcome problems of fragmented decision making and via cross-subsidization can aid resource redistribution within an urban region. The merits of public participation, on the other hand, point to increased decentralization of government. The distribution of powers between different levels of government is a key issue. Urban policy makers must be prepared to experiment with new ideas when existing administrative arrangements are proved to be unsatisfactory.

Academic research also has a role to play in forming future urban policy. Several important questions merit analysis. In view of the impact of 'non-urban' policies on cities, consideration could be given to the derivation of a method of urban impact analysis whereby the differential effect of public spending on distressed urban areas might be one component of decisions on whether to implement a particular policy. An important issue at a time of resource scarcity is the cost-effectiveness of policy and, in particular, the extent to which public expenditures succeed in generating private investment. Research might also be directed to the development of a methodology to determine whether the increasing concentration of population and economic development in a limited number of very large cities in developing countries is a result of faulty policies or whether rapid urban concentration is an inevitable part of the development process.

Finally, it is important to realize that contemporary urban problems are long term, multi-sectoral and global in scope. There are clear policy benefits to be derived from greater international co-operation. More systematic observation of cities throughout the world with different types of government, in different cultural realms, and at different stages of technological evolution could reveal recurring themes, uncover innovative policies and practices, and may suggest important new directions for urban planning and governance.

FURTHER READING

Blair, T. L. (1984) *Urban Innovation Abroad: Problem Cities in Search of Solutions*, New York: Plenum Press.

Chatterjee, L. and Nijkamp, P. (1983) *Urban and Regional Policy Analysis in Developing Countries*, Aldershot: Gower.

Cheshire, P. and Hay, D. (1989) *Urban Problems in Western Europe*, London: Unwin Hyman.

Dogan, M. and Kasarda, J. (1988) *The Metropolis Era*, 2 vols, Beverly Hills: Sage Publications.

Fainstein, N. and Fainstein, S. (1982) *Urban Policy under Capitalism*, Beverly Hills: Sage Publications.

Gurr, T. R. and King, D. S. (1987) *The State and the City*, London: Macmillan.

Hamnett, S. and Bunker, R. (1987) *Urban Australia: Planning Issues and Policies*, London: Mansell.

Judd, D. (1984) *The Politics of American Cities: Private Power and Public Policy*, Boston: Little, Brown & Co.

King, R. (1983) *Capital and Politics*, London: Routledge & Kegan Paul.

Kirby, R. J. R. (1985) *Urbanization in China*, London: Croom Helm.

Lawless, P. (1986) *The Evolution of Spatial Policy*, London: Pion.

Linn, J. F. (1983) *Cities in the Developing World: Policies for their Equitable and Efficient Growth*, New York: Oxford University Press.

Morton, H. and Stuart, R. (1986) *The Contemporary Soviet City*, London: Macmillan.

OECD (1983) *Managing Urban Change*, 2 vols, Paris: OECD.

——(1986) *Urban Policies in Japan*, Paris: OECD.

Peterson, P. E. (1985) *The New Urban Reality*, Washington, DC: Brookings Institution.

Peterson, G. E. and Lewis, C. W. (1986) *Reagan and the Cities*, Washington, DC: Urban Institute Press.

Renaud, B. (1981) *National Urbanization Policy in Developing Countries*, New York: Oxford University Press.

Rose, E. A. (1986) *New Roles for Old Cities*, Aldershot: Gower.

Smith, M. and Feagin, J. (1987) *The Capitalist City*, Oxford: Basil Blackwell.

Smith, M. P. (1988) *City, State and Market*, Oxford: Basil Blackwell.

Tolley, G. S. and Thomas, U. (1987) *The Economics of Urbanization and Urban Policies in Developing Countries*, Washington, DC: World Bank.

United Nations Centre for Human Settlements (1987) *Global Report on Human Settlements*, New York: Oxford University Press.

49

SOCIAL WELFARE POLICY

ADAM GRAYCAR

VALUES AND OBJECTIVES

Social welfare policy helps determine how people live. 'Social welfare' is a broad term that describes systems of allocations in any society in which benefits are distributed to individuals and communities so that they may attain a certain standard of living and/or quality of life. This structure of benefits and their distribution is an intensely political predicament, for there is often great disagreement about why anything should be allocated, what is allocated, who the recipients ought to be, how generous the allocation ought to be, who should do the allocating, and how it might be financed.

Traditionally, social welfare has been thought of as those allocations which benefit those deemed to be the poorer, less fortunate, and less capable members of our society, but in recent years broader definitions of social welfare have included 'quality of life' for all citizens. The debate, then, on why an allocation is to be made includes options such as: to provide a basic subsistence standard of living below which no citizen should be allowed to fall; to compensate individuals or communities for personal accidents, injuries or disabilities, or societally induced malfunctions; to make an investment for the future of the society through features such as the education system, preventive health programmes, rehabilitation programmes and so on; to protect the community against both juvenile and adult delinquents; to ensure that people facing short-term crises can be helped over them; to ensure that the work-force (and potential defence forces) are sufficiently healthy and literate to be able to function adequately in their roles; or to redistribute income and resources (as well as life chances) in a society.

These, and many similar aims and objectives, are the conceptual building blocks for a social welfare system, and clearly the final mix of these will be determined by community values and the interplay of political forces.

How people live and how they ought to live are the central concerns of planners and practitioners in the welfare industry. There are numerous systems for interpreting how people live. There are many criteria for measuring how people live. There are countless values, attitudes and prejudices which carry over into the realm of how people *ought* to live. As social policy is concerned with the aims and consequences of social interventions oriented to the enhancement of levels of living, especially for the weak and vulnerable, discussions of how people do live and how they ought to live form the substantive and theoretical underpinnings of this area of study.

It has been argued that:

> The theory and practice of the welfare state rests on the ability of the central government to collect and redistribute a portion of the economic surplus of an advanced industrial society. The economy can make use of its economic surplus for the sheer accumulation of wealth, for investment in further capital-goods expansion, for higher private consumption, or for expanded governmental expenditures, including welfare expenditures. The economic surplus that is available for public welfare expenditure rests on the productivity of the economy, an effective tax system, and a system of social and political control that defines the legitimacy of welfare expenditure.
>
> (Janowitz 1976: 41)

The argument over how the surplus is to be allocated, and according to whose interests it is to be allocated, has for a long time been one of the fundamental arguments in politics, and in recent years has moved significantly into the welfare arena.

Two traditions manifest themselves in writings on social policy. One tradition sees the objectives of social policy as a quest after social improvement, as an exercise in setting desirable social objectives and in organizing the mechanisms of social change to achieve these objectives. It is an optimistic activity, hoping to build a consensus related to solving the gargantuan questions of the theory of benefits and their distribution.

The other tradition focuses on the concept of scarcity – on the premise that demands for services and allocations always exceed the capacity of the society to deliver. Two competing, and together unattainable, demands present themselves – demands for equality, and demands for efficiency. According to some authors (for example, Okun 1975) the central question in social policy is to arrange a trade-off between equality and efficiency.

Efficiency reflects the demands of different historical periods. In the 1930s and again in the 1960s demands for equality were at the forefront. It was regarded as humane and just to allocate to all the people who contributed to society a share of its outputs, and it was in these periods that growth took place in the allocative sector – in the earlier period in response to a crippling depression, and in the latter period in response to unprecedented economic growth and industrial prosperity. The growth in the latter period led to new allocations, new delivery systems and new administrative methods. Not all of these were 'efficient' in the economist's language, and calls for 'better' use of resources became an increasingly significant aspect of political debate which intensified with the economic recessions of the early and mid-1980s.

Two different ethics were in conflict. On the one hand, the thrust for equality meant scattering one's shots and hoping many of the pellets would find their targets. The approach was one of political activism, emphasizing rights, shares and claims. If the central task was the improving of society, then it meant that political institutions would have primacy over economic ones. The welfare state was the fruit of the Fabian socialists' stress on gradual reform and, while it was costly, it was seen as both just and humane, even if it had by no means reached its limit.

While Ralf Dahrendorf has argued that 'whereas the central institutions of the expanding society were economic, those of the improving society are political' (Dahrendorf 1975: 81), Martin Rein goes a step further. Social policy, he says:

> conventionally is thought to be concerned with redistribution and increasing equality, or at least relieving distress and poverty; economic policy is conventionally thought to be concerned with distribution and increasing output. These distinctions are no longer satisfactory. The scope of social policy is now raising questions about the capacity of the economic system to meet the legitimate demands placed upon it while the political system is not capable of redefining these claims.
>
> (Rein 1977: 567–8)

The 1980s have been characterized by different economic times. While some areas of private enterprise have registered record profits, Western economies have been faced with a stark turnaround. Public programmes have had their rates of growth so severely curtailed that many programme proponents despair at the future level of coverage and the quantity and quality of that which is actually delivered.

When economic conditions are tough, one school argues that welfare expenditures need to be cut drastically so that government spending, as it becomes leaner, is better targeted, is not wastefully applied and goes only to those 'in genuine need'. Another school of thought argues that difficult economic conditions impact most severely on those already in poverty, and drag into poverty those who previously had been just out of its clutches. Numbers in poverty invariably grow during economic recession and while many areas of government may be obliged to trim their sails, those dealing with the most vulnerable and dispossessed need continued support and financial strengthening.

In the simplest of terms, all members of a society aspire to an adequate standard of living, an adequate set of community infrastructure supports and adequate human interaction, namely:

1 material provision;
2 effective support services; and
3 close companionship.

There has been, in recent times, a vigorous debate about who is responsible for each of these things and the level at which these should be acquired, provided, or allocated.

Material provision, supportive services and close companionship can be provided in a variety of ways by a variety of operators – the state, community service agencies, commercial enterprises, families and friends and acquaintances. In very crude terms we can identify four service sectors: the public sector, the community sector (often called the 'voluntary' sector), the commercial market sector and the informal sector.

The debate about whether governments should or should not intervene in market activities or in social welfare is *passé*. Governments do intervene, and management of the economy is the first and foremost professed function of all governments, while governments' responsibility for ensuring the well-being of their citizens (and immigrants) is taken for granted. The arguments now revolve around three questions.

1 With what objective in mind should government intervene?
2 In what form of partnership with the other sectors should government intervene?
3 To what financial extent should government contribute to the community's well being?

The delivery of material resources involves a study of government economic and administrative processes. Most people receive an income from the labour market or from returns on capital. People who do not have these forms of income invariably have lower incomes derived from government cash transfers or family transfers. Most income comes from the labour market, but government policy in social security, taxation and incentives for the private pension system profoundly affects standards of living. Income, however derived and however defined, is the currency of living standards.

The market clearly does not ensure an adequate income for all people. Only government has the capacity to meet the non-labour market income maintenance requirements in industrial societies. In most countries that are members of the Organization for Economic Co-operation and Development (OECD), somewhere in the order of 20 per cent of persons 16 years or over have transfer payments as their main source of income. Income maintenance expenditure, as a proportion of gross domestic product (GDP) varies considerably among OECD countries. In 1986, Japan spent 7.3 per cent of its GDP on income maintenance, a little less than Australia at 7.5 per cent, and well below the market leaders, France at 17.9 per cent, Germany at 19 per cent and Denmark at 19.7 per cent.

Very great changes have taken place in the last two decades during which the welfare state at first experienced unprecedented growth and then came under considerable scrutiny as attempts were made to limit expenditures, or at least limit the rate of growth of expenditures. The attempts to limit public sector outlays began in many countries in the mid-1970s and have continued since then, with varied results. Generally, growth in welfare expenditure comes in response to three types of conditions: demographic change, changes in economic circumstances and policy change.

The first, demographic change, has come in general from declining birth rates and an ageing population. In addition to almost universal ageing of populations, changes in family structure and marriage dissolution rates have led to considerably more single parent families. The second of the conditions, changes in economic circumstances, has been notable as the effects of cyclical recessions and the structural changes in labour markets have played havoc with employment. The most significant condition relevant to any country's expenditure growth has been policy change. This is not the place to survey the enormous range of policy changes.

Policy changes invariably result from political pressures and, as in any system of pluralistic interests, claims are made on behalf of parts of the system, and rarely with a view to the integration of the system as a whole. The result has been what some analysts have called an 'overload of demand', that is, increasing and often conflicting claims on the state, which government cannot meet.

The apparatus of the welfare state does not consist of government alone. Non-government welfare organizations (NGWOs) are central components of all welfare states. In Australia, a country of 16 million people, there are in excess of 37,000 NGWOs. (Similar proportions apply in most Western countries.) These organizations perform a wide range of functions. Some provide services to individuals, some provide their wares as a supplement to state welfare, others see themselves as an alternative to the state, some try to fit in between and act as a pressure group in an attempt to have the state provide resources for something more or better or different. NGWOs are under pressure because their tasks are continually being redefined, because their financial resources base is quite insecure, and because their membership structure can never be taken for granted.

NGWOs are, however, important to government as a key vehicle for implementation of public policy; as an information network; as a means of mediation of social issues into 'proper channels'; and as a cheaper and more flexible avenue than alternatives – government itself or the market. There are disharmonies and inconsistencies in the relationship between government and NGWOs (Yates and Graycar 1983). The study of the politics and administration of service activity and service funding, both 'public' and 'private', is a crucial field of social policy analysis.

Close companionship is basically the purview of families, and because of demographic and labour force changes, as well as changing socio-cultural expectations and relationships, the family is under a great deal of pressure. Politicians who stress the virtues of family care are either unaware of the costs to families of providing the care or are cynically expecting a major shift in social provision and social resources, with the result that those least able to provide adequately will find greater burdens thrust upon them. The abilities of families to care for their members depends not only on material resources but also on human resources.

In most industrial societies we are faced with an explosion of care and we can see the traditional care-providing organizations all facing different sorts of pressures. What is very obvious is that no one sector alone can provide all that has to be provided – certainly not government, certainly not voluntary agencies, certainly not families. Different needs are met by different support systems, or the same needs are met by different systems for different groups of people.

Each of these three – governments, NGWOs and families – are under great pressure, and one operationally heuristic tool might be to examine issues of capacity and willingness of the various major actors and delivery systems. It could be hypothesized that there is an inverse relationship between capacity and willingness. If we think of governments, NGWOs and families as in some sort of capacity hierarchy, we can argue that willingness is inversely related to capacity, and that as one moves down the hierarchy the operator in question is less and less able to deflect or reject the claims made. Government with its eligibility requirements can quite dispassionately send claims which it cannot meet onto NGWOs and families. NGWOs likewise can draw lines and pass the excess onto families. Families are the providers both of first and last resort – as extensive research shows, a repository of willingness, but often lacking in capacity. The politics of capacity and willingness forms a fruitful arena of investigation. The relative capacities of the major players are continually being debated.

REDRESSING INEQUALITIES

The most difficult task for social policy – and one which has never been successfully achieved – is to redress inequalities of a market economy. While social policy in the 1960s and part of the 1970s was concerned with seeking initiatives to redress inequalities, and while it was successful in the diversion of considerable sums into welfare coffers, the magnitude of the task was so great that successes were not always clear and apparent. By the early 1980s, a neo-conservative counter-attack was successfully launched. Consequently social policy, which had been on the offensive in earlier decades, was clearly on the defensive – responding to changing fortunes rather than trying to shape social futures; working out how best to pick up pieces, rather than developing comprehensive preventive mechanisms.

If social policy is to succeed in the 1990s as a relevant, credible and humane activity, it must provide a theoretical and empirical basis for social intervention, and interventionist activities must be geared to three things: the creation of a social and economic environment which is conducive to redistribution and which provides substantial investment in human capital, public goods and services; an equitable income support system; and a set of personal social services available to all who need them.

Two decades of rapid economic growth changed base level material standards. The post-Second World War welfare state was a political mechanism built on aspirations which hoped for the elimination of want, ignorance, squalor, disease and idleness. As outlined by Beveridge (1942), the mechanism of the welfare state would temper the inequalities which had persisted for two centuries before. A society characterized by distributive justice, maximum feasible participation and social supports that would maximize self-worth and dignity, minimize stigma and create an equitable and just community was the political ideal. It came in fits and starts, and although there were examples of both stunning and limited success, in general the outcome fell far short of the aims.

The welfare state as a concept of social, economic and political organization in modern industrial societies was very much the product of a synthesis of Keynesian economic theory and the programme for social policy formulated by Beveridge during the Second World War. In this perspective, the role of the state as a regulator of economic activity (Keynes) was extended into the provision of universal health services and income maintenance for those unable to secure adequate income from the market, as well as the provision of universal retirement pensions (Beveridge). Entitlements to those benefits were incorporated into social and political theory as the rights of citizenship by Marshall (1981), and into the principles of social policy by Titmuss (1974).

The 1990s and beyond will probably see more unequal societies with more people reaching new heights of affluence, and at the same time more people excluded from what we see as the mainstream of modern affluent industrial life. The arguments about present and future performance of the welfare state are arguments about claims on the system, about social, political and economic claims – and about the legitimacy of those claims.

The distributional and redistributional functions of the welfare state are of great importance. The distribution may take various forms, with different effects for the recipients of services or benefits, as well as for the society as a whole. Allocation of resources in the form of cash transfers, such as direct payments, taxation concessions and the like, means tangible material benefit to the recipients. On the other hand, allocation of resources to such services as health or education means, first and foremost, creating employment for various occupations, with the eventual service delivered to the recipient being in a more or less intangible form, though described as part of the 'social wage' (see pp. 802–3).

Despite great expenditures in these areas over the past two decades, poverty has not been eliminated, and there remains no consensus on the appropriate distribution of rewards in an industrial society. Controversy reigns about whether the role of the welfare state is to build a protective set of institutions to encourage stability and coherence, social development and self-fulfilment, or whether its role is to pick up the pieces, with maximum skill and efficiency, after people have crumbled. In his analysis of citizenship and social class, T. H. Marshall (1965: 71–134) demonstrated that social allocations were provided, sometimes on the basis of need, sometimes as a result of contribution and sometimes as a result of citizenship.

The questions to be considered relate to whether we have the political and moral commitment, the technology and the management skills to achieve our objectives of social well-being. Do we know how to formulate, implement and evaluate policies and programmes that might assist in achieving our stated objectives? How do we set our targets? How do we plan our strategies? How do we allocate our resources? How do we assess the results? These are the issues with which students of social policy must come to grips.

BALANCING GOALS AND STRATEGIES

The value dimension in social policy distinguishes it from the more general area of public policy. While the methodology and practice of public policy focus on the full spectrum of authoritative decision making within the society, social policy is built on a narrower ideational base. Social policy has in the past been confined to the study of social services and the 'welfare state', although there is a strong argument that social welfare and social well-being affect not only the poor and the vulnerable, but the whole community. The extension of this argument raises questions such as who wins and who loses in social allocation, and who may legitimately make a claim on the system, and what, legitimately, is the structure of claims.

Martin Rein's simple description of social policy (p. 794) as being concerned with a theory of benefits and their distribution alerts the student of social policy to the fact that benefits consist of more than the tangible and obvious hand-outs of the welfare services. It is obvious that if there is a theory of benefits, then the nature of what constitutes a benefit is a matter of debate. The debate focuses on how consciously benefits are planned and allocated. Do direct benefits do more or less 'good' than indirect benefits? What do we mean by 'good'? Whose conception of 'good', as it relates to benefits, is to prevail? How is this to be determined? Is the regular political process, or the free market, the most appropriate venue in which these decisions might be made?

When we look at the distribution aspect of the 'theory of benefits and their distribution' it is obvious that a number of strategic questions about policy implementation come to the fore. What is being distributed? To whom is it being distributed? What are the mechanics of distribution? Is it being done efficiently? One cannot answer any of these mechanical questions without seeing them in the context of the many value questions that shape an understanding of social policy. Such a theory means utilizing a variety of methodological approaches from such disciplines as economics, sociology, geography and philosophy, as well as studying the politics of welfare services.

The policy formulation process requires careful problem identification plus the ability to steer a path somewhere between a statement of general desirability and perceived practical impediments. It is a process that requires philosophical clarity and intellectual resourcefulness as well as careful political appreciation.

Welfare policy is thus concerned with matching values with actions, the values being tempered by economic, social and political constraints, not to mention administrative reality. Skill in this matching process may both widen the scope and impact of social policy and improve the rationality of the policies themselves. As stated, social policy is concerned with formulating and implementing strategies to bring about change that will 'beneficially' affect the welfare of the members of the society. It relies upon value judgements – about the nature of people and the function of society – and upon the existence and integration of economic, social and political resources to achieve these changes.

To date, a great deal of social legislation has been regulatory. Designed to protect weaker members of society, legislation relating to child welfare, factory work and mental health has been negative and full of prohibitions rather than socially innovative. This has occurred because social policy has in the past been regarded as applying only to some groups who must be protected for their own good.

In seeking a more comprehensive philosophical justification for social intervention, T. H. Marshall writing two decades ago posed a tripartite formulation of the aims of social policy (Marshall 1970: 169). These aims were:

1 the elimination of poverty;
2 the maximization of welfare; and

3 the pursuit of equality.

While these may have a dated feel about them they do give the analyst a star to follow.

In pursuing these aims one must move from the general to the specific, taking care to strike a workable balance. It would be trite to assume that the policy formulation process involves no more than the mechanical practice of sitting down and listing a number of generally desirable goals and then proceeding to analyse the feasibility of attaining them. Of course it is necessary to do this, but such action on welfare policy occurs within a political and cultural environment which itself legitimizes certain goals and strategies while outlawing or limiting others.

THE WELFARE BACKLASH

There has always been a 'welfare backlash' in which righteous citizens protest at having to pay taxes for the unemployment benefits of those who 'won't work'; for the pensions of those who have not had the foresight to provide for their own old age; for the 'illegitimately conceived' offspring of others. New Right sentiments of the past decade have developed an anti-welfare hysteria by claiming that the taxpayer has met too many of society's claims and that those who want these services should purchase them in the market, and not expect the general taxpaying public to bear the cost.

There has never been any resolution of the argument about whether social services exchanged through the market (that is, bought and sold) are of a higher quality than those 'given free', or whether they are distributed more efficiently. There have been attempts to develop voucher systems in education, public housing and health services in an effort to have these as pure market activities, but the effects of these experiments remain inconclusive.

One view is that welfare consumers should be given the ability to purchase services in the market, thereby enhancing their bargaining position along with their ability to secure services. The argument is that the poor should be able to compete, without stigma, like everyone else in the community. The market is seen as an efficient regulator which will reduce interventionist policies to a minimum, thus saving massive bureaucratic costs. The sovereignty of the consumer will be high, and shoddy products will be eliminated, because the market will eliminate them.

The counter-argument is that this is simply not so. The free enterprise system has not eliminated shoddy products, as any consumer will testify. Furthermore, health and welfare services are not consumer commodities that can be bought and sold in a market situation like television sets or used cars. In addition, poor people cannot participate on an equal footing in a welfare market. Problems arise as to how a market price is determined, how it finds its level, and how it can ensure that monopolies of delivery skills do not play on consumer ignorance (as is found in free enterprise medicine). Health and welfare services cannot be delivered equitably in a free market situation as the situations that necessitate their usage are usually produced by stress or anguish, rather than by free choice.

One strong argument for the market relates to stigma, and the dignity of the recipient. Despite the fact that there is no such thing as a free lunch, there are many people in our society who cannot afford to pay for certain essential services. The allocation is made on their behalf and no cash payment is expected from the recipient. Is some other sort of 'payment' expected? The answer to this question depends on the distinction one makes between an 'economic' exchange and a 'social' exchange. In the transfer situation, then, the recipient is often regarded as being under an obligation to conform in certain ways, to alter lifestyles and preferences to satisfy the moral one-upmanship that often goes with transfers.

THE SOCIAL WAGE

To those with a commitment to greater social and economic equality, public spending on social security, welfare services, health, housing, transport, urban development and education is a means of broadening the social wage. Many of these services, which some would argue should fall totally within the private sector, are heavily subsidized by government, and many confer greater benefits on those who are not poor than on those who are poor.

With all the best intentions in the world, social benefits do not always fall equitably. Julian Le Grand (1982) has analysed British data to conclude that public expenditure in the UK on health care, education, housing and transport systematically favours the better-off and thereby contributes to inequality in final income, as well as inequality of access. In contrast, Ann Harding (1984) has analysed Australian social wage outlays by income decile and found that social security and welfare outlays, particularly age pensions, invalid pensions and widows' pensions go mostly to very low income earners. So too does expenditure on rental welfare housing. Education expenditure goes mostly for the benefit of those in the highest income deciles. This is particularly so of outlays for non-government schools and tertiary education. Health and medical outlays, according to Harding's analysis, reasonably match income distribution in Australia.

When we analyse the distribution and impact of transfers, goods, and services provided collectively through government spending we are dealing with the 'social wage'. While the social wage reflects general government commitments, its distribution is intensely political.

The social wage is a difficult concept to define because it comprises certain government expenditures that have some value to individuals or families, and one assumes a redistributive component flowing from the expenditure. The social wage is that part of government spending which provides benefits, either in cash or kind, to individuals and families. If these goods and services were not provided by government they would have to be purchased out of private income. These items are a convenient and readily identifiable group of expenditures. The impact of each on individuals and families can be assessed, unlike other indivisible collective expenditures such as defence expenditure, law and order, roads and highways, etc.

The social wage items have a wide range of redistributive objectives. These include alleviating poverty, redistributing resources towards particular stages of the life cycle and providing equal access to certain services.

The four main social wage items differ in the emphasis that they place on these redistribution objectives. Education and health spending are primarily based on the principles of equality of access and opportunity. Most social security and welfare outlays are intended to alleviate poverty. Spending on housing is based on the principle of equality of access, but the programmes are mainly directed at low income earners.

Over the last decade the terms of the welfare debate have changed, but the substance has changed very little. Terminology such as charity, sustenance and stigma has been replaced by social justice, the social wage, markets, efficiency and vertical and horizontal equity.

The reality is that there are people in our modern affluent societies who miss out – people who find they cannot get an income in the labour market; people whose education does not buy them a place in the job market; people whose skills have been undermined by technological change; people whose occupations have been rendered obsolete by structural adjustment; women whose productive value is disregarded and who are confined to a state of dependency; people who have difficulty in achieving satisfaction in housing, services or income; young people who believe they have no worthwhile place in a competitive industrial society; and family heads who receive insufficient infrastructural support to maintain their families. In addition there are many adults who, through loss of a spouse, find themselves in dramatically changed circumstances.

To attack these issues and seek social improvement is the highly political task that confronts social policy in the foreseeable future.

REFERENCES

Beveridge, W. H. (1942) *Social Insurance and Allied Services*, Cmd. 6404–6405, London: HMSO.

Dahrendorf, R. (1975) *The New Liberty: Survival and Justice in a Changing World*, London: Routledge & Kegan Paul.

Harding, A. (1984) *Who Benefits? The Australian Welfare State and Redistribution*, SWRC Reports and Proceedings, no. 45, Kensington: University of New South Wales.

Janowitz, M. (1976) *Social Control of the Welfare State*, New York: Elsevier.

Le Grand, J. (1982) *The Strategy of Equality*, London: Allen & Unwin.

Marshall, T. H. (1965) *Class, Citizenship and Social Development*, New York: Anchor Books.

——(1970) *Social Policy*, London: Hutchinson University Library.

——(1981) *The Right to Welfare and Other Essays*, London: Heinemann.

Okun, A. M. (1975) *Equality and Efficiency: The Big Trade-off*, Washington, DC: Brookings Institution.

Rein, M. (1977) 'Equality and social policy', *Social Service Review* 51 (4): 565–87.

Titmuss, R. M. (1974) *Social Policy: An Introduction*, London: Allen & Unwin.

Yates, I. and Graycar, A. (1983) 'Non government welfare: issues and perspectives', in A. Graycar (ed.) *Retreat From the Welfare State: Australian Social Policy in the 1980s*, Sydney: Allen & Unwin.

FURTHER READING

Bean, P., Ferris, J. and Whynes, D. (eds) (1985) *In Defence of Welfare*, London: Tavistock Publications.

Donnison, D. (1982) *The Politics of Poverty*, Oxford: Martin Robertson.

George, V. and Wilding, P. (1984) *The Impact of Social Policy*, London: Routledge & Kegan Paul.

Glennerster, H. (ed.) (1983) *The Future of the Welfare State: Remaking Social Policy*, London: Heinemann.

Graycar, A. (1979) *Welfare Politics in Australia: A Study in Policy Analysis*, Melbourne: Macmillan.

——(ed.) (1983) *Retreat From the Welfare State: Australian Social Policy in the 1980s*, Sydney: Allen & Unwin.

Graycar, A. and Jamrozik, A. (1989) *How Australians Live: Social Policy in Theory and Practice*, Melbourne: Macmillan.

Morris, R. (1986) *Rethinking Social Welfare*, New York and London: Longman.

50

BUDGETARY PROCESSES

NAOMI CAIDEN

Budgetary processes are the means by which budgets are formulated and carried out. In the most basic sense budgets are simply documents that set out projected income and expenditures for a given period, and budgetary processes are the procedures used to compose these documents. But public budgets and budget processes have a much deeper significance: they represent fundamental aspects of modern democratic government, and their institutionalization reflects crucial concepts in political, administrative and economic thought.

Budgetary processes are political in nature. Budgets are the published expression of commitments of resources raised from the public. Budget processes embrace the institutions and procedures established to resolve the recurring conflicts about the level of resources to be raised and their sources, and the purposes to which they should be devoted.

Budgetary processes thus reflect political processes, but they add to them two distinctive elements. First, budgetary processes are finite in nature: the budget battle is fought every year, and every year must find resolution in the published budget. If it does not, the process breaks down and crisis ensues. The cyclical decision process thus helps shape the rules of the political process adapted to periodic resolution of disputes (Schick 1980: 19–20).

Second, the figures in the budget are not mere declarations of purpose but binding legal commitments that are enforceable against governments. While changes may be made after budgets are passed, such transfers, supplementaries or deferrals may only be carried out according to law. The open publication of appropriations for stipulated and agreed purposes enables audit checks that actual expenditures are carried out as intended. The appropriation-audit cycle lies at the heart of the budget process concept (Roseveare 1973: 72–4). But equally important, the commitments of the budget represent promises, legitimized by constitutional and democratic processes, to groups and organizations. An institutionalized budget process is the antithesis of an arbitrary or dictatorial style of government which keeps secret its revenue sources and expenditures, channels funds to those it favours without check, and refuses to commit its intentions to public debate, enforcement, or accountability.

The promise of budgetary processes remains unrealized unless there are parallel administrative processes that ensure orderly handling of resources, and enable informed decision making. A primary function of administrative budgetary processes is to ensure accountability, that funds are actually expended for stipulated purposes, that programmes are carried out as intended, and that funds, from whatever sources, are not spent on unauthorized activities. Budgetary processes also support managerial functions, tying financial decision making to programme performance. The annual financial decision-making process should be structured to take account of a flow of information which includes projected availability of resources, results of past expenditures, public priorities, projected costs and expected results. Finally, budgetary processes support planning and policy making beyond the annual budget cycle. Plans, whether for public sector capital projects or for broader social and economic objectives, are ineffective unless implemented through budgeted resources. Macroeconomic and fiscal policy making, similarly, find realization in budgetary processes. Conversely, budgetary decision makers at all levels require information about future revenues and costs, in turn heavily dependent on projected economic conditions (Anthony 1965: 16–18; Axelrod 1988: 7–8).

Finally, since economics is the science of scarcity, budget processes are also economic in nature. Just as economics studies individual decision making in conditions of scarcity, public microeconomics focuses on the processes of societal priority setting in the light of economic and political constraints. Budgets represent community choices about what should be publicly and what should be privately financed, and how much and what should be supplied (Ostrom and Ostrom 1971). Both explicitly (as user charges for specific services) and implicitly (in weighing one priority against another), budgets set prices. As government activities reach into more and more areas of economy and society – environment, health, welfare, commerce, technology, public safety – budgets come to regulate not only the public sector but the economy as a whole (Stein 1989: 6–8). Budgetary processes parallel market processes and heavily influence them.

The political, administrative and economic aspects of public budgetary processes have been dominated for nearly two hundred years by a single institutional paradigm: the annual centralized budget process based on the closed cycle of appropriation and audit. Within this paradigm, budgetary processes in different countries have been characterized to some degree by their own historical, constitutional, political, cultural and economic circumstances.

Since the early nineteenth century, budgetary processes have followed a broad line of development. They emerged with constitutional and democratic government in Western Europe from a long period of pre-budgetary financial administration. During the twentieth century, with the growth of government expenditures, the potential of budgetary processes for purposes beyond control and accountability came to be realized. As the field of public finance (both as public microeconomics and Keynesian macroeconomics) developed, government budgets became a focus of concern for economists, policy analysts and managerial experts, who found much to criticize in contemporary budget processes. However, with growing constraints on public revenues in the last quarter of the twentieth century, budgetary processes seem to be undergoing adaptations emphasizing long-term commitments, separate funding arrangements and continuous expenditures that may either enhance or undermine traditional processes (Caiden 1982; Caiden 1988: 43–58).

PRE-BUDGETARY PROCESSES

The simplest form of pre-budgetary processes was the feudal model of private financial administration. Essentially the kings of feudal Europe were dependent on their private estates for revenues, which consisted of feudal payments similar to those of other lords, and proceeds of transactions such as sales of land and timber. There was virtually no accountability, since the king was responsible to no one. But control over the dispersed properties and their resources was so difficult that rulers would often contract out financial functions and use the same agents for payments as well as receipts, in effect turning them into private decentralized treasuries. Even so, the lack of day-to-day control and information required the employment of *ad hoc* and regular commissioners who travelled frequently between the centre and local units.

With the emergence of the nation-state under aggrandizing absolutist monarchs, financial administration became more complex. Increasing ingenuity was devoted to devising and implementing new sources of tax and non-tax revenues. The diversification of the economy, and particularly the growth of towns and trade, gave the state opportunities to profit from the increased wealth. But the state's legitimacy was inadequate to gain the flow of resources it required through direct taxation. Those in whose hands wealth was concentrated paid few or no taxes. Taxation was indirect, regressive and piecemeal in nature. It was also resisted strongly.

This pattern of resource mobilization demanded a complex financial administration. The dispersed system of receipts and expenditures continued and became entrenched as it grew. The state became dependent on independent businessmen and tax farmers (who 'leased' rights to specific tax sources in return for fixed lump sum payments) to maintain cash flow and also for credit. The lack of any clear distinction between public and private capacity encouraged corruption and leakage, which could not be kept under control by periodic trials of the leading practitioners. Because of the limitations of tax revenues the state was continually forced into expedients such as sale of office, borrowing on future specific revenues, fees of all kinds, borrowing on receipts of future borrowing, forced loans, alienation of state lands and so on. Those in control of state finances scrambled from month to month to keep the state solvent, for of course they were not really in control. There was no budget and accounting system that could give them information about the real state of finances (Caiden 1978: 542).

At the end of the eighteenth century these systems broke down: too much was demanded of them, and demands for the accountability of governments burst forth in revolution. But what was to replace them? Two other models had been tried. One was the highly controlled system based on direct legislative control of earmarked funds associated with city-states which had flourished in ancient Greece and medieval Italy and Northern Europe. These cities were ruled by councils of citizens well aware of the need to keep taxes low. Taxation therefore tended to be direct, but at a low level. Financial officials were carefully chosen and, in some cases, rendered audits every few months. Administration also involved a strong voluntary element. But direct control of finance by legislatures was not easy to maintain and depended more on informal or personal relationships than formal control. The pattern re-emerged in the English Republic of the seventeenth century and in the French Revolution, but the difficulty of raising revenues and maintaining controls made it short-lived.

Another alternative was an autocratic pattern, apparent in seventeenth- and eighteenth-century Prussia but best exemplified by the Napoleonic Empire. Gone were the private financial officials, and the tax burden could be kept relatively low because of the availability of outside resources (the sums plundered from invaded countries) which relieved pressure on internal resources. Administration improved with centralization of finances, semi-bureaucratic officials and double-entry bookkeeping, but built-in duplication and the existence of numerous personal and secret funds from which transfers and payments could be made outside normal processes belied administrative efficiency. A modern budget system was still lacking. 'Budgets' were presented late and were more fiction than fact. Internal accountability was lacking, and the inability to forecast revenues and react to shortfalls contributed to repeated financial crises which had to be met through the injection of personal resources, 'loans' and a certain sleight of hand.

The dysfunctions of these patterns form the background to the emergence of modern budgetary processes. But they are also likely to recur, irrespective of what has been learned in the meantime, where appropriate conditions prevail. The feudal models strongly resemble those of states and organizations that draw most of their revenues from non-tax sources. The absolutist monarchy's complex and contradictory pattern of financial administration resembles that of many contemporary poor countries, whose typical features are continuous cash flow budgeting, expedients, fragmented budgets, earmarked revenues, lack of budgetary control, fictional budgets, lack of information on the real financial position, confusion between private and public roles, and high rates of short-term borrowing at disadvantageous terms (see Caiden and Wildavsky 1980). The autocratic pattern is often put forward as a technocratic solution for the financial administrations of poor countries, stressing administrative expertise, but ignoring questions of political accountability and state capacity to tax upon which modern budget systems rest.

CLASSICAL BUDGETARY PROCESSES

During the nineteenth century, an interesting phenomenon occurred: the tax riot as a characteristic form of political expression died out (Ardant 1975: 168). Its demise may be associated with a rising standard of living and less onerous forms of taxation, but it is also reasonable to associate it with the rise of representative government and, specifically, with the development of national budgetary processes.

While certain elements of modern budgeting existed previously (notably the Consolidated Fund in Britain), the first budget in Europe was promulgated in France with the restoration of the monarchy after the Napoleonic Wars (Bruguière 1969: 1). The minister of finance, Baron Louis, announced a complete break with previous financial disorder, expediency and corruption:

> We are going to present the most exact evaluation of our needs possible, the sums necessary to operate the ministerial departments. Then we shall offer a proposal of the ways and means of meeting them. Each ministry is guaranteed the regular employment of the funds put at its disposal. These funds are in the most rigorous proportion possible to its needs for the services performed. If clarifications are necessary, each minister has to place before you all the elements necessary for you to form your opinion.
>
> (Marion 1927–31, vol. 4: 379)

Budget principles involved the annual estimate and prediction of expenditures, consolidation of revenues, controls over payments, and preparation of audited accounts at the end of the financial year (see Stourm 1909).

By the beginning of the twentieth century, the general principles of public budgeting had crystallized into an internationally accepted concept of the executive budget. In cabinet government systems, such as that of Britain, the concept was clear and relatively easy to implement. The budget was in the hands of the executive which presented it to Parliament annually as the cornerstone of its policies which were debated within a fixed period of days by the House of Commons sitting as a committee of the whole. While the entirety might be rejected, members of Parliament might not raise individual appropriations. Unless the legislature was willing to bring down the government, therefore, the executive budget was the budget, and as long as the government was able to command a stable legislative majority, it could command the budget. Budgetary politics, therefore, took place in internal party and cabinet discussions, or through the activities of pressure groups working with politicians or the bureaucracy.

In presidential systems, budgetary processes were more complicated, since executive and legislature share power over budgetary decision making. The United States federal government adopted the executive budget in 1921, but also created a strong Appropriations Committee in Congress. The executive budget was part of the programme of an administrative reform movement which emphasized efficiency and expertise in government. The Report of the President's Commission on Economy and Efficiency in 1912 saw managerial expertise and leadership in the executive as enhancing congressional control. It envisaged a division of labour between Congress and president in which the former retained ultimate power over appropriations and the president took on the role of general manager proposing and implementing decisions of Congress. As long as both executive and legislature acted with restraint, and there was no fundamental disagreement between them, the constitutional separation of powers was not an obstacle to the successful implementation of the executive budget. But with the emergence of an adversarial relationship between executive and legislature in the 1970s and 1980s, budgetary politics became highly unstable, and the executive budget was only the starting point for legislative wrangling (Caiden 1987).

In both cabinet and presidential systems, annual budgets were highly successful in organizing public finances. Budget processes accommodated to the demands of wars, depressions and the growth of the welfare state. But as governments in Western industrialized nations took on increasing functions, a new reform movement emerged emphasizing incorporation of analytical techniques into the regular routines of annual budgeting.

INNOVATIONS

The continuing movement to reform budget processes represents more than a mere tinkering with classifications and procedures. Beyond the details of the different reform agendas lies a distinctive set of ideas about the purposes of government and the ways decisions should be made. Reform proponents see the reorganization of budget processes as realizing the original purposes of budgeting and enhancing administrative capacity toward greater effectiveness. Those who doubt the enterprise view budget processes rather as a reflection of underlying political realities, which in a democratic pluralistic polity shape institutions that in turn serve to structure power relationships. Budget reforms take place in a tension between these two perspectives.

The budgetary reform movement arose from a number of reinforcing and complementary trends, including reactions to traditional budget processes, changes in the role of government, application of micro- and macroeconomic theories to the public sector, and the availability of new analytical tools for decision making. The movement may be traced back to municipal government at the beginning of the twentieth century, but found its strongest expression in the 1960s and early 1970s (Schick 1966).

In some sense the budgetary reform movement was a tribute to the success of the classical budget model which had achieved routinization and stability in many countries. This stability rested on three elements which had become characteristic of budgets. First, budgets were typically organized according to 'line items' or 'objects of expenditure'. The budget was a detailed list of items of expenditure, such as personnel, supplies, and so on. It was a classification designed for control, and particularly suited for a period in which governmental functions were relatively restricted and economy in administration was the primary preoccupation. Second, budget formulation rested on a set of stable bureaucratic routines that emphasized hierarchical relationships and in particular the dominance of the central financial administration (ministry of finance, treasury or budget bureau). Typically, budgets were built up according to set instructions by budget officers in agencies or departments, and were reviewed by budget examiners in the central financial administration, working according to their own rules. Even in countries characterized by acute political instability, bureaucratic dominance of the budget process maintained a measure of stability. Third, budget processes tended to be incremental in nature, building increments each year on the previous year's base. This tendency, particularly evident in the United States, might be reinforced by relatively restricted political access to the budget, and the stable roles of influential participants and institutions (Wildavsky 1988: 78–9; Schick 1980: 20–1).

As governments moved beyond traditional functions to the administration of large-scale complex social programmes, an emphasis on control and economy gave way to one on programme management. There was a need to move beyond controlling inputs to link financial inputs to programme results, to determine the most efficient means to accomplish objectives, to compare performance of different units, to establish service levels. More sophisticated management demanded a more useful flow of information than that provided by the traditional line-item budget, and envisaged the budget as a crucial tool of management.

Overhaul of budget methods also received support from economics, as economic theorists moved from *laissez faire* positions to consideration of the role of government in the mixed economy. In 1942 the eminent political scientist V. O. Key called attention to the lack of a budgetary theory that would answer the fundamental question in public budgeting: 'on what basis shall it be decided to allocate X dollars to Activity A instead of to Activity B, or instead of allowing taxpayers to devote the money to their individual purposes?' (Key 1940: 1137). A decade later, Verne Lewis stated: 'Budget decisions must be made on the basis of relative values. There is no absolute standard of values' (Lewis 1952: 44). Hence, given limited resources, budget makers should employ the concept of marginal utility: 'The method, briefly, is to divide available resources into increments and consider which of the alternative uses of each increment would yield the greatest return' (ibid.: 45). Ultimately, maximum returns will be obtained at the point where 'expenditures are distributed among different purposes in such a way that the last dollar spent for each yields the same real return' (ibid.: 46). Budgetary analysis and decision making should therefore be organized to take explicit account of the effectiveness of public expenditures.

Keynesian macroeconomic theory influenced budget processes in two main ways. Most directly, by emphasizing fiscal policy and the deliberate manipulation of the balance between revenues and expenditures, it elevated budgeting from a somewhat humdrum activity of budget specialists to the sphere of national economic policy making. Budgeting was now about more than financing the government: it was about running the country. More indirectly, since fiscal policy and expenditure policy were but two sides of the same coin, a more systematic approach toward budgeted expenditures appeared.

Reform of budgetary processes did not come all at once, and as successive groups of reformers took on the task they built on the efforts of their predecessors. Allen Schick traces the modern reform movement to the beginning of the century and the efforts of the Bureau of Municipal Research in New York City to add a functional classification based on activities and a work programme setting out costs (Schick 1966). The inability to realize this conception at the time did not spell the end of reform efforts, and similar ideas dominated more widespread reform in the 1950s. Performance budgeting, advocated in the reports of the United States Hoover Commission, emphasized a management perspective. According to Schick, 'its principal thrust is to help administrators to assess the work efficiency of operating units by (1) casting budget categories in functional terms, and (2) providing work-cost measurements to facilitate the efficient performance of prescribed activities' (Schick 1966: 252).

By the 1960s, spurred by new techniques of systems analysis, cost–benefit analysis and strategic planning, the conception of budget reform had moved a further and more ambitious step forward. The aim of Planning, Programming, Budgeting Systems (PPBS or programme budgeting) was to convert not only budget classifications to a new programme basis, but to transform routine budget processes so that budget decisions would be based on the results of policy analysis. Budget information would provide decision makers not only with information on costs of performing activities or the financial requirements of agencies, but would link resources with actual effectiveness of these activities – the health of the population, the cleanliness of the environment, the safety of the cities, the reduction of poverty.

The general concept, not always clearly understood, spread from its original application in the United States Department of Defense to governments all over the world. Variations have been advocated by international agencies and applied across the board to rich and poor countries and to governments at both national and local levels. While results have often been less than optimal and might have been achieved in different ways, the reform attempts have left behind them revised budget formats, possibly clearer understanding of the uses of resources, and much controversy (Premchand 1983: 345).

There is no question that problems of implementation have proved a stumbling block to the achievement of process reforms such as performance and programme budgeting (PBB) as well as later variants such as zero-base budgeting (ZBB, which substitutes incremental decision packages for programmes and uses ranking systems to structure priority setting). Absence of computer capacity and sophisticated software programs made the expanded information handling virtually impossible. The extent of training required by staffs was also underestimated, as was the resistance of those accustomed to the old ways. But the abandonment by the United States federal government of PPB (and later ZBB) did not end the controversies nor the attempts at reform which still continue.

More important than questions of the different kinds of classification or techniques, or details of implementation, are fundamental divergences on the nature of decision making in society. In Allen Schick's words, reform aspired 'to create a different environment for choice' (Schick 1966: 256). Traditional budgeting emphasized moving incrementally from a base, while the reformed budgeting would define its mission in terms of objectives and purposes. Underlying the new processes was the premiss that they would enable a society or a community to chart its future direction according to maximum utility and effectiveness.

The uneasiness of critics lay in ascertaining the place of analysis in setting public priorities: unlike an individual who made choices according to his or her own scale of priorities, there was no single welfare function for society as a whole, nor an accepted scale of indicators that would rank priorities. When it came to measuring costs and benefits of more or less abstract quantities – health, education, defence, environment, community – analysts were often on dangerous ground. The values assigned could not always be justified and bias often crept in. In particular, it was charged, an analytical perspective all too easily ignored distributional questions, and raised the level of societal conflict by clarifying and confronting issues usually blurred by the norms of politics and incrementalism. Against the analytical ideal, the critics placed the realities of politics; the professed neutrality of the analyst confronted the interests of different and often opposing groups.

Theoretical arguments about budgetary innovations, however, faded in the face of more pressing concerns as the economic and political climate changed in the last quarter of the century from one of expansion to one of constraint.

BUDGETARY PROCESSES UNDER PRESSURE

By the mid-1970s, the conditions of economic growth that had prevailed since the Second World War in most Western industrialized countries had changed. Inflation, lagging productivity and economic growth rates, periodic recessions, and economic shocks replaced stability, economic expansion and optimism. As economic conditions deteriorated, resistance to taxation grew, and expanding revenues could no longer be taken for granted. Budgeting could no longer be considered as 'an engine of program and financial expansion' (Schick 1986: 124), and to the extent that budgetary innovations reflected and contributed to the expansion of government programmes it was no longer relevant. The age of incrementalism, in which an annual 'fiscal dividend' was regularly available to fund new programmes and expand old ones, was over. Instead, governments faced massive deficits and the task of reorienting budgetary processes to cope with an era of constrained revenues, and continued urgent pressures for an enhanced role for government (Caiden 1981).

The task was complicated by the legacy of the past. Growth in a variety of entitlement programmes during the 1960s and 1970s, such as health, social security, unemployment benefits and various other allowances, meant that an increasing proportion of budgets was subject to automatic growth. Entitlements are payments to individuals or organizations according to formulas based on eligibility, and often indexed to an outside indicator such as the rate of inflation. These payments lie outside regular budget processes and thus limit their influence: where well over half the budget is subject to automatic advance appropriation (whether from entitlements or long-term contracts), the area left for choice is greatly diminished (Ysander and Robinson 1982). In addition, because the amounts of entitlement payments are dependent on conditions beyond the government's control (numbers of persons eligible and economic conditions), they are a matter of prediction rather than determination. A good part of the budget process has to centre on assumptions about key economic indicators, such as the rate of inflation, economic growth, unemployment and interest rates. Figures that rest on assumptions may not only turn out to be

814

wrong, but are also subject to manipulation. In any case, they lend an uncertain quality to budgets already under stress.

In recent years, the governments of Western Europe and the United States have taken steps to adapt their budget processes from encouraging growth to enforcing restraint. They have moved in two major complementary directions – the imposition of controls from the centre, and a variety of measures to curb programme expansion.

In the past, budgeting has often worked as a 'bottom-up' process, in which agencies and departments initiate the process by sending their requests for the coming year to a central budget agency. Increasingly, the budget process now works as a 'top-down' process, which begins with an enunciation of a 'fiscal norm' or guideline setting limits on expenditures. These limits are often expressed in specific quantitative terms, such as a percentage of the deficit reduction required, the amount expenditures will be allowed to rise relative to gross domestic product, or the extent to which programmes will be allowed to grow to absorb projected inflation. These norms are then translated into targets which may be more or less detailed. To accommodate this analysis, budget preparation is advanced long before the beginning of the budget cycle, even though this may increase uncertainty in making projections.

These targets are of crucial importance to the budget debate. They signify the move from a budget driven by incrementalism to one attempting to achieve decrementalism. In the former, the base, or last year's spending, is the estimate on which requests for new spending are built. In the latter, the baseline budget is the focus of debate. The baseline (also known as the current services estimate) is a projection of what current spending would be if no policy action were taken. It refers not only to the coming year, but several years ahead. Budgetary proposals are routinely calculated and scrutinized as additions or substractions to the baselines for revenues, expenditures and deficits, so that the implications of changes may be traced ahead. Of course, baselines themselves are subject to argument, depending on the assumptions built into them (Schick 1986).

Setting targets or ceilings is one thing: enforcing them is another. While all may be in favour of aggregate limits it is a different matter when it comes to cutting individual programmes. Where entitlements are concerned, cutbacks have been extremely difficult politically, and where they have been undertaken, have required special procedures outside the normal budget process to gain agreement on 'cutback packages' or 'mini-budgets'. A variety of other measures have been implemented to ensure conformity with budget targets. One is cash limits or financial ceilings stringently applied irrespective of circumstances, usually applied only to non-entitlement spending. Another is strict monitoring of expenditures with frequent checks. Somewhat in contrast to the emphasis on centralization is a movement toward decentralization that requires programme managers to manage their own budgets according to performance standards for which they are held accountable (Schick 1988a).

It would be misleading to state that all these measures have led to a dramatic reversal in the growth of government expenditures, though they may have slowed it. The reasons are many. In some cases, the government agenda, in particular for defence or entitlements, has simply opposed any trend towards reduction. In others, the sheer size of deficits has brought about so great an increase in government borrowing that interest costs form a significant and growing part of the budget. Often, budgets themselves do not reflect total government expenditures, omitting credit activities and separate accounts. Cuts are often concentrated in areas which lack strong political supporters, while other areas are allowed to continue to grow. Pressures on government budgets continue from demands for expenditures related to the vulnerability of modern industrial society, a growing gap between rich and poor, environmental conditions beyond the capability of the private sector, and a volatile political situation in many countries. Yet despite these pressures budget processes have been able to adapt within tolerable limits and there has been little evidence of widespread breakdown. Such is not the case in the poorer countries of the world where budget processes face their greatest challenge.

BUDGETING IN POOR COUNTRIES

Budget processes in poor countries follow the same formal lines as those in rich countries, but in practice they reflect the prevailing poverty and uncertainty of their societies. Over the past two decades, some developing countries have been able to improve their position, in some cases dramatically, but where poverty is exacerbated by high levels of debt, inflation, corruption and conflict, budget processes tend to break down and assume different forms.

The combination of a generalized lack of resources and multiple converging uncertainties results in acute tension between those responsible for the financial viability of the government, the central ministries of finance, and those carrying out the programmes of government, the agencies and departments. Ministries of finance seek to conserve resources and to retain them for contingencies that they know are all too likely to occur. Hence they underestimate revenues, cut estimates, and irrespective of budgeted appropriations refuse to commit expenditures in advance. This 'repetitive budgeting', in which the budget is in effect made throughout the year, serves the purpose of always having cash in hand, but undermines the whole concept of budgeting as orderly planning of government finances. Programme managers faced with the unpredictability of repetitive budgeting adopt their own strategies to defeat it – they pad appropriations, create special funds, earmarked revenues and parastatal enterprises that they can control, and seek to withhold information to support their claims. If there is a separate economic planning agency, it strives to maintain control of its own budget, the development budget. The result is budgetary fragmentation, which allows the central ministry of finance even less room to manoeuvre so that it redoubles its efforts to gain control. This vicious circle makes reliable budget information a scarce quality, erodes trust, results in both underspending and wasteful spending, and prevents orderly planning and financial administration (Caiden and Wildavsky 1980). Yet the wealth of literature decrying these practices testifies to their entrenchment and rationality as long as the underlying problems remain.

CONCLUSION

Because budgets are involved in virtually every aspect of government, budgetary processes may be viewed from a number of perspectives. There is no single unified theory of budgeting, and a variety of disciplines focus on budgetary processes as integral elements of their theories. Economists study the processes and outcomes of fiscal policy making, as well as constructing theoretical models of public choice and decision making. Management theorists concentrate on administrative aspects of budgetary processes and financial management to the virtual exclusion of political context. Legal experts investigate constitutional issues, and even anthropologists research budgetary behaviour. Those seeking understanding of budgetary processes need to take account of all these – and many other possible – perspectives.

Political scientists study budgetary processes from the point of view of the political process, and as an aspect of how societal resources are claimed and rationed (Schick 1988b: 63). They explore trends in public expenditures, the workings of political institutions and the roles and interactions of participants. Political processes may be seen as one mechanism of allocating societal resources, complementing alternative means such as the market, inheritance and co-operation. Budgetary processes are a specific way of structuring political conflicts to determine the extent of the public sector, its influence upon other sectors, and the allocation of resources within it.

The formal outline of budgetary processes differs little all over the world, and is based on the classic budgetary principles of annuality, unity, appropriation and audit: a cyclical, comprehensive process of choice. Within the framework, budgetary processes are shaped by decision rules that in turn reflect not only constitutional, political and cultural differences, but the more basic relationships between claimers and rationers. Where revenues have been relatively easy to raise, claimers have been encouraged. Decision rules such as incrementalism or emphasis on programme effects have predominated.

As public revenues have become more constrained, and conflicts have risen, decision rules have adapted to the changed circumstances. Participants have sought to entrench their claims in the budget in advance through entitlements, thus swallowing up future increments. New forms of expenditures, such as loans, loan guarantees and tax expenditures, have been created, subject to different decision processes outside the regular budgetary process. New forms of taxes have emerged, often tying specific revenues to specific expenditures. Governments have attempted to build budgets from the 'top down' rather than from the 'bottom up', to negotiate shifting coalitions to settle particularly difficult issues, and to use multi-year planning to chart the way ahead.

But where constraint and uncertainty become too severe, the annual budget process may disintegrate. Budgets fragment; long-term continuing commitments defeat annual decision making; and repetitive year-round budgeting replaces the planned budget cycle. Financial administration then seems to have more in common with pre-budgetary models than the classic budget process.

Budgetary processes are rarely static. From year to year, changing political configurations make for an ebb and flow in decision making, in which one group or party gains ascendancy and another suffers losses. Over a longer period, gains may become consolidated so that past decisions drive present choices, and budget processes take on a rigidity or uncontrollability preventing much change in direction. At these times budgetary processes seem to take on a life of their own. But overshadowed by the tumult of each year's budget battle, and changes in policies and strategies, lies institutional development. Currently the lines of this development are not clear, and it will take more time and further research to determine whether the budgetary processes of the future will resemble those of the past or whether a new synthesis will emerge to transform them beyond the boundaries of our present conceptions.

REFERENCES

Anthony, R. N. (1965) *Planning and Control Systems: A Framework for Analysis*, Boston: Harvard University Press.

Ardant, G. (1975) 'Financial policy and economic infrastructure of modern states and nations', in C. Tilly (ed.) *The Formation of National States in Western Europe*, Princeton: Princeton University Press.

Axelrod, D. (1988) *Budgeting for Modern Government*, New York: St Martin's Press.

Bruguière, M. (1969) *La Première restauration et son budget*, Geneva: Droz.

Caiden, N. (1978) 'Patterns of budgeting', *Public Administration Review* 38: 539–44.

——(1981) 'Public budgeting amidst uncertainty and instability', *Public Budgeting and Finance* 1: 6–19.

——(1982) 'The myth of the annual budget', *Public Administration Review* 42: 516–23.

——(1987) 'Paradox, ambiguity and enigma; the strange case of the executive budget and the United States Constitution', *Public Administration Review* 47: 84–92.

——(1988) 'Shaping things to come: superbudgeters as heroes (and heroines) in the late twentieth century', in I. S. Rubin (ed.) *New Directions in Budget Theory*, Albany: State University of New York Press.

Caiden, N. and Wildavsky, A. (1980) *Planning and Budgeting in Poor Countries*, New Brunswick: Transaction.

Key, V. O., Jr. (1940) 'The lack of budgetary theory', *American Political Science Review* 34: 1137–40.

Lewis, V. (1952) 'Toward a theory of budgeting', *Public Administration Review* 12: 43–54.

Marion, M. (1927–31) *Histoire financière de la France*, 6 vols, Paris: Rousseau.

Ostrom, E. and Ostrom, V. (1971) 'Public choice: a different approach to the study of public administration', *Public Administration Review* 31: 302–16.

Premchand, A. (1983) *Government Budgeting and Expenditure Controls: Theory and Practice*, Washington, DC: International Monetary Fund.

Roseveare, H. (1973) *The Treasury 1660–1870: The Foundations of Control*, London: Allen & Unwin.

Schick, A. (1966) 'The road to PPB', *Public Administration Review* 26: 243–58.

——(1980) *Congress and Money: Budgeting, Spending and Taxing*, Washington, DC: Urban Institute.

——(1986) 'Macrobudgetary adaptations to fiscal stress in industrialized democracies', *Public Administration Review* 46: 124–34.

——(1988a) 'Microbudgetary adaptations to fiscal stress in industrialized democracies', *Public Administration Review* 48: 523–33.

——(1988b) 'An inquiry into the possibility of a budgetary theory', in I. S. Rubin (ed.) *New Directions in Budget Theory*, Albany: State University of New York Press.

Stein, H. (1989) *Governing the $5 Trillion Economy*, New York: Oxford University Press.

Stourm, R. (1909) *Le Budget*, Paris: Alcan.

Wildavsky, A. (1988) *The New Politics of the Budgetary Process*, Glenview, Ill.: Scott, Foresman & Co.

Ysander, B. and Robinson, A. (1982) 'The inflexibility of contemporary budgets', *Public Budgeting and Finance* 2: 7–20.

FURTHER READING

Axelrod, D. (1988) *Budgeting for Modern Government*, New York: St Martin's Press.

Burkhead, J. (1956) *Government Budgeting*, New York: John Wiley.

Caiden, N. (1990) 'Public Budgeting: the state of the discipline', in N. Lynn (ed.) *Public Administration: The State of the Discipline*, Chatham, NJ: Chatham House.

Caiden, N. and Wildavsky, A. (1980) *Planning and Budgeting in Poor Countries*, New Brunswick: Transaction Publishing.

Hyde, A. C. and Schafritz, J. *Government Budgeting: Theory, Process, Politics*, Oak Park, Ill.: Moore Publishing.

OECD (1987) *The Control and Management of Government Expenditure*, Paris: Organization for Economic Co-operation and Development.

Premchand, A. (1983) *Government Budgeting and Expenditure Controls: Theory and Practice*, Washington, DC: International Monetary Fund.

Premchand, A. and Burkhead, J. (eds) (1984) *Comparative International Budgeting and Finance*, New Brunswick: Transaction.

Public Budgeting and Finance, A journal of practice and ideas, Washington, DC: Public Financial Publications.

Schick, A. (1980) *Congress and Money: Budgeting, Spending and Taxing*, Washington, DC: Urban Institute.

——(ed.) (1987) *Perspectives on Budgeting*, Washington, DC: American Society for Public Administration.

Webber, C. and Wildavsky, A. (1986) *A History of Taxation and Expenditure in the Western World*, New York: Simon & Schuster.

Wildavsky, A. (1985) *Budgeting: A Comparative Theory of Budgetary Processes*, Boston: Little, Brown & Co.

——(1988) *The New Politics of the Budgetary Process*, Glenview, Ill.: Scott, Foresman & Co.

51

PRIVATIZATION

E. S. SAVAS

Privatization is a political and economic phenomenon being adopted today in the West and the East, in developed and developing countries, in democracies and dictatorships, and in capitalist, socialist and communist countries.

Three subtly different and often implicit definitions of privatization are in common use. In the broadest definition, one which emphasizes a philosophical basis, privatization means relying more on the private institutions of society and less on government (the state) to satisfy people's needs. These private institutions include: the market-place and businesses operating therein; voluntary organizations (religious, neighbourhood, civic, co-operative and charitable, for example); and the individual, family, clan or tribe. According to a second and more operational definition, privatization is the act of reducing the role of government, or increasing the role of the private sector, in an activity or in the ownership of assets. The third and most constrained definition considers privatization to be the act of transferring government enterprises or assets to the private sector. It will be seen below that this last definition is too limited to encompass the changes occurring in countries that have had strong state control of economic activity.

The earliest dictionary entry (1983, *Webster's New Collegiate Dictionary*) offers yet another definition: making private, especially changing from public to private control or ownership. This definition is inadequate, however, in view or the most common form of privatization in the United States, namely, contracting for service, where government retains control of and responsibility for the service but delegates the production to a private entity.

FORMS OF PRIVATIZATION

Three broad methods are used to privatize government activities, state-owned enterprises (SOEs), and state-owned assets: divestment, delegation, and displacement. Each of these encompasses several specific approaches which are identified in Table 1 and discussed in turn (Savas 1990).

Table 1 Forms of privatization

I By divestment	A Sale	1 to private buyer 2 to the public 3 to employees 4 to users or customers
	B Free transfer	1 to employees 2 to users or customers 3 to the public 4 to prior owner (restitution)
	C Liquidation	
II By delegation	A Contract	
	B Franchise	1 public domain (concession) 2 public assets (lease)
	C Grant	
	D Voucher	
	E Mandate	
III By displacement	A Default	
	B Withdrawal	
	C Deregulation	

Divestment

Divestment means shedding an enterprise or asset. This requires a direct, positive act by government and is generally a one-time affair (but see p. 823 for an exception). The enterprise or asset is either sold or given away as an ongoing business, or an enterprise may be liquidated (that is, closed down and the remaining assets sold). Where state-owned enterprises are abundant, 'denationalization' is frequently used to mean divestment.

Divestment by sale Table 1 shows that divestment by sale can be carried out in four ways: first, by selling the enterprise (or asset) to a single buyer; second, by issuing and selling shares to the public; third, by selling the enterprise to the managers or, more broadly, to the employees; and fourth, by selling the enterprise or asset to its users or its customers. For example, state-owned land may be sold to ranchers or loggers, and a rural electricity, water or transportation enterprise may be sold to a co-operative of local users.

The sale of an SOE can be partial or in stages, where the government sells only a portion of its holdings at any one time. Unless government cedes majority ownership and control, however, such a sale can be considered merely a form of raising capital, not privatization.

Divestment by free transfer Divestment does not require sale of an enterprise; the latter could be given away, for example, to employees, to users or customers, to the public at large, or to the prior owner. An instance of giving away an enterprise to the employees occurred when the English Channel hovercraft ferry service, formerly owned by British Rail, the state-owned railway, was given to its management, thereby ending the drain on the public purse.

A novel example of giving away an SOE to the public took place in Canada. The proposed sale of an enterprise owned by a provincial government, the British Columbia Resources Investment Corporation, led to a prolonged and bitter political debate. In order to block the sale, opponents questioned the proposed sale price. The dilemma faced by the proponents was that if the price was too low, they would be accused of giving away the people's patrimony; if it was too high, the sale would not succeed. In a stroke of political genius, the provincial premier reasoned that since, in the final analysis, the corporation belonged to the people, and the people had already paid for it once, why should they have to pay for it again? It could be given away to them! Despite the complexity, this bold step was carried out successfully by issuing shares to all residents of the province. Giving away SOEs to the public is an important privatization strategy in Central and Eastern Europe.

Divestment by liquidation Finally, divestment can be carried out by shutting down and liquidating a poorly performing enterprise that is, selling its assets if no buyer can be found for it as a going enterprise and if the prospects are bleak for ever turning it around and achieving profitability.

Delegation

The second broad privatization strategy is delegation, which, like divestment, requires an active role by government. Unlike divestment, however, which is generally a one-time act, delegation requires a continuing active role for government. When privatizing by delegation, government delegates to the private sector part or all of the activity of producing goods or services, but remains responsible for overseeing the result. Delegation is carried out by contract, franchise, grant, voucher or mandate.

Delegation by contract Government can privatize an activity by contracting with a private organization to perform the work. This is the most common form of privatization in the United States. Local governments contract for direct services such as solid-waste collection, street repair, street cleaning, snow removal and tree maintenance. State and federal government agencies often contract for support services such as data processing, loan processing, architecture and civil engineering, training, audio-visual services, food services, mail and file services, libraries, laundry and dry cleaning, facilities maintenance, warehousing and vehicle maintenance.

Delegation by franchise Franchising is another method of privatization. Under a franchise, government awards a private organization the right (often the exclusive right) to sell a service or a product to the public. The private firm usually pays the government a fee.

Two forms of franchising exist. One involves the use of the public domain – airwaves, air space, streets, underground space, etc. For example, broadcasters, airlines, bus and taxi companies, and utilities (electricity, gas, water, telephone) use the public domain in the course of carrying out their commercial activities. This arrangement is often called a concession.

The second form is a lease, in which tangible government-owned property is used by a private lessee to engage in a commercial enterprise. This is one of two important privatization strategies emerging in post-socialist countries. (The other is deregulation, discussed on p. 826.)

Delegation by grant Delegation is also achieved by awarding grants. Instead of government itself carrying out an activity, it arranges for a private entity to do the work and provides a subsidy. In the United States, grants are used for mass transit, low-income housing, maritime shipping and innumerable other activities. Grants are distinguished from contracts in that grants usually involve only the most general requirements (to run a bus service, to build houses that rent at below-market prices, to do research, to promote the arts), whereas contracts are usually specified in great detail for a particular service (sweeping the west side of certain north–south streets between 7 a.m. and 9 a.m. on Tuesdays and Fridays).

Delegation by voucher Governments can also delegate by issuing vouchers to eligible recipients of formerly state-run services. Instead of subsidizing producers, as grants do, vouchers subsidize eligible consumers. Vouchers are used for food, housing, education, health, day care and transportation. Recipients use their vouchers to purchase these services in the market-place.

Delegation by mandate The fifth and final form of privatization by delegation is a government mandate requiring private agencies to provide a service at their expense. Unemployment insurance is a long-standing example of such a mandate in the United States; private employers provide this for their employees.

It should be noted that privatization connotes directionality and therefore mandates, like grants, vouchers, franchises and contracts, can be considered forms of privatization only when they lead to a lesser, not a greater, role for government. Thus if the government-run social security (retirement) system in the United States were replaced by mandatory individual retirement accounts, this would be privatization by mandate, a form of delegation. On the other hand, if market-based health care were replaced by mandatory employer-provided health care, this would be the opposite of privatization, as it would involve a greater rather than a lesser role for government.

Displacement

Besides divestment and delegation, privatization can proceed by displacement, as shown in Table 1. In contrast to the first two methods, which require active efforts by government, displacement is a somewhat more passive process that leads to government being displaced more or less gradually by the private sector – a withering away of the state, so to speak, as markets develop to satisfy the need. Displacement occurs by default, by withdrawal, and by deregulation.

Displacement by default When the public considers government service to be inadequate, and the private sector recognizes the demand and steps in to satisfy it, this can be termed displacement by default. Gradually, the public begins to look to the private sector for the service, and if the service grows over time, and if the government-supplied service continues to be neglected or at least fails to grow in absolute terms, then the private sector plays a larger and larger role as government shrinks. A simple example of this phenomenon is offered by municipal tennis courts and other recreational facilities. Poor maintenance and unreliable scheduling lead many players to avoid public facilities in favour of private ones, as entrepreneurs sense the market demand and fill the void. As more and more users come to rely on private facilities, and as market niches are discovered and served by the private sector, the public facilities lose their patrons and disappear over time. Note that voluntary efforts, and not only for-profit commercial ventures, can come forth to serve a perceived need; this is particularly true of charitable, social, philanthropic and community activities and services.

A somewhat different example is provided by private police. Public dissatisfaction with traditional police protection and the level of public safety in the United States led to the growth of private guard and patrol services. Although the latter have not displaced the former, in the United States the growth has been primarily in the private sector, and so the public sector has shrunk in relative terms.

Yet another example is the growth of private transportation where government-provided surface systems are deemed inadequate by the public. Gypsy cabs, commuter vans, minibus systems and other unofficial or technically illegal transport services have emerged in numerous cities throughout the world.

A similar phenomenon is evident as private firms begin to satisfy infrastructure needs that have been neglected by government agencies. Thus, one sees the private sector financing, building, owning and operating roads, bridges, prisons and sewage-treatment plants, for example, and the Channel Tunnel linking England and France.

Displacement by withdrawal Whereas default is unintended, government can engage in deliberate load shedding, or withdrawal. At one extreme, government can simply shut down a failing enterprise, or it can accommodate private sector expansion into that field while restricting and even shrinking the size and resources of the state enterprise.

Displacement by deregulation State-owned enterprises and government activities often exist because they have monopoly status and competition by the private sector is prohibited.

Deregulation is a method of privatization if it enables the private sector to challenge a government monopoly and even displace it altogether. In the United States, express mail services offered by competing companies have grown rapidly, but the US Postal Service vigorously defends its exclusive right to handle first-class mail and it prohibits competitors from depositing mail in recipients' mail boxes. The regulations are under attack and their repeal has been advocated by the President's Commission on Privatization (1988).

In countries where state-owned agriculture marketing boards are monopsonies – the only authorized buyers of agricultural products, to which all farmers must sell – deregulation allows private markets to develop and displace those SOEs.

The former Soviet Union and other post-socialist countries are reviving their moribund economies by repealing laws that prohibit private ownership, thereby encouraging entrepreneurs and allowing market mechanisms to prevail. 'Marketization' is another term recently introduced as a label for this process which aims to achieve economic efficiency through exposure to market discipline. It refers to deregulation that is intended to have this effect.

The end result of deregulation is the emergence of demand-driven, market-based arrangements to satisfy unmet needs.

HISTORY

Reliance on what today is called the private sector is, of course, as old as the family and older than government. As a deliberate policy to reduce the role of government and expand the role of the private sector, however, it appears that privatization was first suggested (and the word, in the form 'reprivatize', first used) by the Austrian-born American management professor, Peter F. Drucker (1969). At the same time, E. S. Savas, a New York City official, was independently promoting privatization as a pragmatic policy to improve the cost-effectiveness of municipal services (Phalon 1971; Savas 1971; 1985: vii-ix, 69–77; 1987: 291). Research and writing in the 1970s by Savas (1974: 473–500; 1977a, 1977b, 1977c, 1977d, 1979), Poole (1976), Spann (1977), Rothbard (1978), and Fisk et al. (1978), among others, strengthened the case for privatization, and privatization of municipal services, by contracting, was already widespread in the United States by 1980. Policy advocates in Britain, notably at the Adam Smith Institute, were actively promoting privatization in the late 1970s. Strong opposition was expressed by public employee unions as early as 1977 in the United States and later in Britain (Savas 1987: 122).

The elections of Margaret Thatcher as prime minister in Britain and Ronald Reagan as president in the United States, in 1979 and 1980 respectively, gave high visibility and a pronounced ideological impetus to what became the privatization movement. A dramatic series of denationalizations – privatization by sale of state-owned companies – took place in Britain: British Petroleum (1979), British Aerospace (1981), Britoil (1982), National Freight Corporation (1982), Cable & Wireless (1983), Jaguar (1984), British Telecom (1984), British Aerospace (1985, final portion of holdings), British Gas (1986), British Airways (1987), Rolls Royce (1987), and British Airports Authority in 1987 (Bishop and Kay 1988: 5, 6). Water utilities followed in 1989 and electric utilities in 1990. Compulsory tendering (inviting competitive bids) of local government services in Britain was mandated in 1989.

Despite President Reagan's efforts, relatively little privatization by sale took place at the federal government level, in part because the United States has relatively few state-owned enterprises. Considerable contracting out of support services (for example, data processing, food service, building maintenance and guard services) was carried out, however, by federal government agencies, and privatization by contracting continued to grow in local governments both for support services and for direct services to the public (waste collection, street cleaning, ambulance service and park maintenance, for example).

In the 1980s many industrialized Western nations embarked on privatization programmes, no doubt stimulated by the British example (Bishop and Kay 1988; Ramanadham 1988), and so did many developing nations (Candoy-Sekse 1988), pushed in part by Western donor nations and by international agencies that had grown impatient with the poor performance of state-owned enterprises that they had financed. The exceptionally strong economic perform-ance of the newly industrializing countries of East Asia, which relied extensively on private enterprise and a market orientation, also provided a stimulus and served as a model worthy of emulation by the developing countries that had relied on state enterprises and were falling behind at an alarming rate. In Latin America, by the end of the 1980s, Mexico, Brazil, Chile and Argentina had all elected presidents who adopted strong privatization policies.

Among the socialist countries, China was the first to embrace privatization, beginning with agriculture in 1978. Eliminating state-owned and collective farms and allowing what was, in effect, private farming, resulted in greatly increased food production and an end to the famines that had characterized the period before. Private sector industrial and retail operations were allowed in the 1980s as part of China's economic reform programme, but were usually presented as involving multi-ownership, that is, co-operatives, joint ownership, joint ventures, local collectives, partnerships and stockholder-owned enterprises. The collapse in 1989 of the socialist bloc in Eastern Europe promptly led to privatization in Hungary, Poland and Czechoslovakia. The Soviet Union changed its legal framework in 1990 to allow private ownership of the means of production, opening the door to privatization there. The Baltic states, Bulgaria, Romania and Slovenia are doing the same. Vietnam, in desperate economic straits, allowed private enterprises to emerge, and Cuba began selling public housing to the tenants, something Britain had started doing a decade earlier.

EXTENT OF PRIVATIZATION

Comprehensive, worldwide data on the extent of privatization are sketchy, although major divestments are reported and so is the extent to which privatization by contracting for services has taken place in the United States. An international study by the World Bank found that eighty-seven countries had completed 626 privatization transactions, and 717 additional such transactions were planned or under way (Vuylsteke 1988). During 1988, major privatizations by divestment were carried out in seventeen countries, with total proceeds of $39.2 billion. Of this total, $8.3 billion was by private sale and $30.9 billion was by public offer of shares; $22.8 billion of the latter was due to the Japanese sale of 9.6 per cent of Nippon Telegraph and Telephone (*Privatization International* 1989). During 1989, major divestments took place in twenty-four countries, with total proceeds of $24.8 billion, $18.5 billion by public offer and $6.2 billion by private sale (*Privatization International* 1990). The largest single sale was that of the water industry in the UK, for $8.4 billion (*Privatization International* 1990).

Information about divestments in developing countries is more difficult to obtain, but the proceeds would generally be modest and therefore not likely to affect reported dollar totals very much. Information about privatization by displacement is inherently difficult and even impossible to obtain, as this form involves gradual change and rarely a single identifiable act.

Privatization by delegation is also difficult to capture statistically on an international basis; this is particularly true of grants. Contracting and franchising of municipal services in the United States, however, have been measured and reported. A survey of more than a thousand cities, covering forty-eight common municipal functions, shows that virtually every city contracts for at least one function, with the average city contracts for 20 per cent of them in whole or in part (Morley 1989). The most commonly contracted services are vehicle towing and storage, street-light maintenance, waste collection and disposal, street repair and tree planting and trimming. The same study found that the average city used franchises for 9 per cent of the forty-eight services.

REASONS FOR PRIVATIZATION

Four major forces propel the privatization movement: pragmatic, ideological, commercial and populist. The goal of the pragmatists is greater efficiency in the production of goods and services. The goal of those who advocate privatization on ideological grounds is less government, one that plays a smaller role in relation to the private sector. The goal of commercial interests is to do more work at a profit. The goal of populists is to achieve a better society by giving people greater power, through the market-place, to satisfy their needs while diminishing the power of large public and private bureaucracies.

The principal reason for privatizing SOEs is the widespread dissatisfaction with their performance. Substantial evidence supports the contention that SOEs generally perform poorly (Monsen and Walters 1983; United Nations 1984, 1986; Gantt and Dutto 1968; Aharoni 1986). Poor management is often cited as the reason for poor performance, but the fundamental reasons are:

1 the monopoly nature or permanently protected status of SOEs (Kay and Bishop 1989);
2 the ambiguity and multiplicity of objectives – due to political interference – imposed on SOEs; and
3 the lack of effective ownership rights in SOEs and therefore the absence of owners who manage their enterprise well in order to maximize its value (Savas 1989).

The objectives for privatizing any particular SOE may be to:

1 reduce government expenditures;
2 raise efficiency;
3 improve quality and responsiveness;
4 increase government revenues;
5 broaden ownership of economic assets;
6 decentralize the economy;
7 accelerate economic development;
8 attract new investment;
9 satisfy foreign lenders;
10 gain popular support;
11 punish political opponents; or
12 reward political allies.

The first three objectives are also the major reasons for privatizing public services by contracting. Indeed, there is overwhelming evidence that contractors can provide services of at least equal quality at a substantially lower cost, even allowing for the cost of administering the contract and monitoring the contractor's performance.

RESULTS OF PRIVATIZATION

There is ample persuasive evidence as to the results of contracting for services. Surveys of local governments in the United States that contract for services show a high degree of satisfaction among their public officials. Three-quarters of them cite cost savings as an advantage; 40 per cent report savings exceeding 20 per cent (David 1988). Comprehensive evaluations of agencies in the United States with numerous contracts for support services show savings of about 30 per cent (Savas 1991). Finally, careful comparative studies in several countries find savings that average 25 to 30 per cent with no drop in quality (Savas 1987: chapters 6 and 7).

With respect to divesting SOEs, it is more difficult to arrive at similarly compelling evidence. Divestment in the UK can be judged successful in terms of the government's objectives of, first, selling shares of stock to the public (the number of shareholders rose from 5 per cent to 20 per cent of adults) and, second, obtaining sizeable sales proceeds (£15,160 million up until 1987) (Ramanadham 1989: 64–5). It is not so clear that a third objective, promoting competition in order to increase efficiency, was realized; some of the large entities that were privatized were left relatively intact and were not subjected initially to effective competition or regulation (Ramanadham 1988: 25–9).

Because every divestment is unique, one cannot point to increased sales or profits as unambiguous measures of success; they may result from favourable treatment by the government, monopoly privileges, or an economic recovery in that sector, for example. One cannot conduct large-scale comparative studies of many privatized telephone companies, for example, or vehicle manufacturing enterprises, because there are very few cases and each is unique, whereas, as noted above, such studies have been done for many local services that are ubiquitous, similar and relatively easy to measure. Millward (1988) cautions that there is only scattered evidence that productivity is lower in the public sector, but studies of SOEs in Africa, for example, 'present a depressing picture of inefficiency, losses, budgetary burdens, poor products and services, and minimal accomplishment' (Nellis 1986: ix).

DISADVANTAGES

One of the principal arguments raised against privatization, particularly of public services, is that it weakens the local political order and accelerates the decline of citizenship and community. Co-operative endeavor is essential to social progress, so the reasoning goes, and privatization limits or interferes with such co-operation: In particular, the use of market forces for welfare ends loosens the bonds of community. Purchased services and vouchers drain public programmes of those who can absorb economic risks; thus the poor, the sick, the less educated and the unskilled became increasingly segregated and thus more vulnerable politically. In short, privatization's preoccupation with efficiency, competition and market forces may overlook interests and issues vital to the public social well-being (Morgan and England 1988).

Another argument against privatization of public services is that the most influential and articulate segment of the public will eschew the public service and opt for the private provider, thereby seriously weakening any effort to reform and improve the public services; in Hirshman's terms they will exercise 'exit' rather than 'voice' (Hirschman 1970). This argument is clearest with respect to education vouchers. Parents who would make the effort to examine various schools and select the one they deem best for their children are the ones most needed to stay within the public school system, it is argued, in order to bring pressure for much-needed reform. The same point is made about neighbourhood associations of homeowners who, dissatisfied with local public services, abandon reliance on them and choose instead to contract jointly for refuse collection, street cleaning, street repair, snow removal, tree trimming and street patrols, for example.

The counter-argument is that concerned parents who have the means will move to other jurisdictions that have better public schools, or will enrol their children in private schools. Their 'voice' for reform is already lost, it is reasoned, and privatization by vouchers merely extends the same freedom of choice to all parents. Similarly, contracting for municipal services may bring the benefits of better services to all neighbourhoods, not only those with the ability to organize and make their own arrangements.

Another basic argument against privatization is that by reducing the role of government, the ability to redistribute wealth is impaired. The counter-argument is that contracting, vouchers and grants are privatization techniques that permit any desired degree of redistribution, but opponents fear that although this is theoretically possible, public resources will not in fact be allocated for this purpose after privatization.

A special concern in the United States is the effect of privatization on the minority black population. Inasmuch as a larger function of employed blacks work for government, compared to the fraction of employed whites, privatization would appear to cause disproportionately more job losses among blacks than among whites; however, blacks gained employment with contractors under privatization at about the same rate as they had been employed by government (Suggs 1989).

LIMITATIONS AND OBSTACLES

Every form of privatization has its limits. For example, contracting can be used effectively only where it is possible to specify precisely the work to be done and to measure and monitor the resulting performance. Moreover, contracting requires a truly competitive environment with multiple providers. Ideally, franchising has the same requirements, but in the absence of competition regulation is commonly undertaken. Divestment poses a problem if the net effect is to transform a public monopoly into a private one. This is a particular problem in small, developing countries where even a straightforward commercial enterprise, such as a brewery, may be a monopoly because the country is too small to support two breweries. The remedy in this case, rarely taken, is to allow foreign competition to restrain the domestic monopoly.

One can reasonably ask whether *all* government activities can be privatized. Clearly, making laws and judging that people should be deprived of life, liberty or property are functions reserved for the state. Any goods-producing activity can be divested to the private sector, but services are more complicated. Depending on whether the service in question is a public or private good, some privatization forms may be appropriate and others not. Other inherent characteristics of the service also determine the mode of possible privatization (Savas 1982: chapters 4 and 5).

With respect to implementation, the principal barriers are ideological opposition, the problem of dealing with redundant workers, concern about what is said to be a loss of control over the 'commanding heights of the economy' or over public services, the belief that 'government can do it cheaper because it doesn't make a profit', fear of corruption and of 'cream skimming', the instinctive feeling that the poor will suffer under privatization, and the assumed shortage of capital with which to buy SOE's in developing countries. Each is discussed in turn.

Sometimes there is ideological hesitancy concerning privatization, particularly where there is a significant socialist tradition or where the word 'privatization' evokes the image of a small, ruling elite and a large lower class. In such cases, political leaders often choose other, less controversial terms for the process, hence 'reconstruction' (*perestroika*) in the USSR, 'economic reform' in China, 'renovation' in Vietnam, 'renewal' in Hungary, 'people-ization' in Sri Lanka, 'people's capitalism' in Latin America, 'socialist privatization' in Spain, 'de-statization' in Greece, etc.

The most serious practical problem is how to deal with the excessive number of employees that is so typical of SOEs and public services. Common approaches are hiring freezes together with gradual absorption of the redundant employees into the remaining state agencies and enterprises, severance pay, unemployment insurance, early retirement, retraining, loans to start small businesses, sale of shares at a discount to workers, and even giving away an enterprise to the workers.

Loss of control is obviously a barrier with respect to enterprises involved in national defence, and also with so-called natural monopolies, such as gas, electricity, water and telecommunications. Regulation is required to control such monopolies if they are privatized. In the case of social and other services for which precise contractual terms cannot be specified, contracting and franchising may not work well; vouchers and competitive grants may be better.

The argument that 'government can do it cheaper because it doesn't make a profit' is a rhetorical claim that is belied by the evidence cited above.

Corruption – real or alleged – is an ever-present danger that can best be dealt with by the following open and fully 'transparent' privatization procedures and, whenever possible, competitive bidding practices. It is also well to remember that quite similar forms of corruption can be found entirely *within* the public sector, as when employees are forced to kick back a portion of their wages or to pay for promotions.

'Cream skimming' is often cited as an argument against privatization; that is, only the best and most profitable activities will be assumed by the private sector, leaving the public sector saddled with the most difficult and expensive segment of a service and without the possibility of cross-subsidies from the more lucrative, privatized segments. This fear, commonly raised to thwart the privatization of transportation services, has been effectively refuted (Cervero 1988; Savas 1987: 284). The 'cream' of rush-hour service is bad for an agency's fiscal health because it requires staffing and equipping the agency for peak conditions, thereby saddling it with extra employees and buses during most of the day.

If one assumes that privatization is synonymous with market prices for all goods and services, to be paid directly by consumers (for example, for elementary education), then the plight of the poor would indeed be worsened. It was noted above, however, that several forms of privatization can be used for redistribution and can reduce to zero the price of services to eligible poor recipients.

The shortage of capital and the paucity of financial institutions and capital markets makes privatization of SOEs by public sale of shares difficult to do in developing countries; however, even in such cases, 'mattress money', 'flight capital', expatriates, and informal lending societies can be important sources of capital.

In sum, there are many factors to consider and obstacles to overcome when undertaking a programme of privatization, to assure public support for the move and to achieve the desired results.

REFERENCES

Aharoni, Y. (1986) *The Evolution and Management of State-Owned Enterprises*, Cambridge, Mass.: Ballinger, pp. 174–90.

Bishop, M. and Kay, J. (1988) *Does Privatization Work?*, London: London Business School.

Candoy-Sekse, R. (1988) *Techniques of Privatization of State-Owned Enterprises*, Vol. III: *Inventory of Country Experience and Reference Materials*, technical paper no. 90, Washington, DC: World Bank.

Cervero, R. (1988) 'Transit service contracting: cream-skimming or deficit-skimming', Berkeley: University of California, Institute of Urban and Regional Development, December.

David, I. I. (1988) 'Privatization in America', *Year Book*, Washington, DC: International City Management Association, Table 5/2.

Drucker, P. F. (1969) *The Age of Discontinuity*, New York: Harper & Row.

Fisk, D., Kiesling, H. and Muller, T. (1978) *Private Provision of Public Services: An Overview*, Washington, DC: Urban Institute.

Gantt, A. H. and Dutto, G. (1968) 'Financial performance of government-owned corporations in less developed countries', in *Staff Paper* 15 (1): 102–48. Washington, DC: International Monetary Fund.

Hirschman, A. O. (1970) *Exit, Voice and Loyalty*, Cambridge, Mass.: Harvard University Press.

Kay, J. A. and Bishop, M. R. (1989) 'Privatization and the performance of public firms', in *Role and Extent of Competition in Improving the Performance of Public Enterprises* (Proceedings of United Nations Seminar, New Delhi, April), New York: United Nations.

Millward R. (1988) 'Measured sources of inefficiency in the performance of private and public enterprises in LDCs', in P. Cook and C. Kirkpatrick (eds) *Privatization in Less Developed Countries*, Hemel Hempstead: Harvester/Wheatsheaf.

Monsen, R. J. and Walters, K. D. (1983) *Nationalized Companies: A Threat to American Business*, New York: McGraw-Hill.

Morgan, D. R. and England, R. E. (1988) 'The two faces of privatization', *Public Administration Review* 48: 979–87.

Morley, E. (1989) 'Patterns in the use of alternative service delivery approaches', in *The Muncipal Year Book*, Washington, DC: International City Management Association.

Nellis, J. R. (1986) 'Public enterprises in sub-Saharan Africa', *World Bank Discussion Paper* 1 (November).

Phalon, R. (1971) 'City may use private refuse haulers', *New York Times* 6 April: 1.

Poole, R. W., Jr (1976) *Cut Local Taxes Without Reducing Essential Services*, Santa Barbara, Calif.: Reason Press.

President's Commission on Privatization (1988) *Privatization: Toward More Effective Government*, Champaign: University of Illinois Press.

Privatization International (1989) 'Sales of government assets and enterprises worldwide reach nearly $40 billion last year', *Privatization International*, no. 4 (January): 18–19.

——(1990) 'Sales of state-owned enterprises worldwide reach nearly $25 billion last year', *Privatization International*, no. 16 (January): 18–19.

Ramanadham, V. V. (ed.) (1988) *Privatisation in the UK*, London: Routledge.
——(ed.) (1989) *Privatisation in Developing Countries*, London: Routledge.
Rothbard, M. N. (1978) *For a New Liberty: The Libertarian Manifesto*, New York: Collier Macmillan.
Savas, E. S. (1971) 'Municipal monopoly', *Harper's* 243 (December): 55–60.
——(1974) 'Municipal monopolies versus competition in delivering urban services', in W. D. Hawley and D. Rogers (eds) *Improving the Quality of Urban Management*, Beverly Hills: Sage Publications.
——(1977a) (ed.) *Alternatives for Delivering Public Services*, Boulder, Colo.: Westview Press.
——(1977b) *The Organization and Efficiency of Solid Waste Collection*, Lexington, Mass.: D. C. Heath.
——(1977c) 'An empirical study of competition in municipal service delivery', *Public Administration Review* 37: 717–724.
——(1977d) 'Policy analysis for local government: public versus private refuse collection', *Policy Analysis* 3 (1): 49–74.
——(1979) 'How much do government services really cost?', *Urban Affairs Quarterly* 15 (1): 23–41.
——(1982) *Privatizing the Public Sector*, Chatham, NJ: Chatham House.
——(1985) 'Privatization from the top down and from the outside in', in J. C. Goodman (ed.) *Privatization*, Dallas: National Center for Policy Analysis.
——(1987) *Privatization: The Key to Better Government*, Chatham, NJ: Chatham House.
——(1989) 'Improving the performance of public enterprises through competition', in *Role and Extent of Competition in Improving the Performance of Public Enterprises* (Proceedings of United Nations Seminar, New Delhi, April), New York: United Nations.
——(1990) 'A taxonomy of privatization strategies', *Policy Studies Journal* 18 (2): 343–55.
——(1991) 'Privatization and productivity', in M. Holzer (ed.) *Public Productivity Handbook*, New York: M. Dekker.
Spann, R. M. (1977) 'Public versus private provision of governmental services', in T. E. Borcherding (ed.) *Budgets and Bureaucrats: The Sources of Government Growth*, Durham, NC: Duke University Press.
Suggs, R. E. (1989) *Minorities and Privatization*, Washington, DC: Joint Center for Political Studies Press, p. xvi.
United Nations (1984) *Performance Evaluation of Public Enterprises in Developing Countries*, New York: United Nations, pp. 206–33.
——(1986) *Economic Performance of Public Enterprises*, New York: United Nations, pp. 51–6.
Vuylsteke, C. (1988) *Techniques of Privatization of State-Owned Enterprises*, Vol. I: *Methods and Implementation*, technical paper no. 88, Washington, DC: World Bank.

FURTHER READING

American Federation of State, County and Municipal Employees, AFL–CIO (1983) *Passing the Bucks: The Contracting Out of Public Services*, Washington: AFL–CIO.

Butler, S. M. (1985) *Privatizing Federal Spending: A Strategy to Eliminate the Deficit*, New York: Universe Books.

Finley, L. K. (ed.) (1989) *Public Sector Privatization: Alternative Approaches to Service Delivery*, New York: Quorum Books.

Fitzgerald, R. (1988) *When Government Goes Private: Successful Alternatives to Public Services*, New York: Universe Books: International City Management Association.

ICMA (1989) *Service Delivery in the 90s: Alternative Approaches for Local Governments*, Washington, DC: International City Management Association.

Kamerman, S. B. and Kahn, A. J. (eds) (1989) *Privatization and the Welfare State*, Princeton: Princeton University Press.

Kay, J., Mayer, C. and Thompson, D. (eds) (1986) *Privatization and Regulation: The UK Experience*, Oxford: Clarendon Press.

LeGrand, J. and Robinson, R. (eds) (1984) *Privatization and the Welfare State*, London: Allen & Unwin.

Marlin, J. T. (ed.) (1984) *Contracting Municipal Services*, New York: John Wiley.

Pirie, M. (1988) *Privatization: Theory, Practice and Choice*, Aldershot: Wildwood.

President's Commission on Privatization (1988) *Privatization: Toward More Effective Government*, Champaign: University of Illinois Press.

Ramanadham, V. V. (ed.) (1988) *Privatisation in the UK*, London: Routledge.

——(ed.) (1989) *Privatisation in Developing Countries*, London: Routledge.

Rehfuss, J. A. (1989) *Contracting Out in Government*, San Francisco: Jossey-Bass.

Roth, G. (1987) *The Private Provision of Public Services in Developing Countries*, Oxford: Oxford University Press.

Savas, E. S. (1987) *Privatization: The Key to Better Government*, Chatham, NJ.: Chatham House.

Steele, D. and Heald, D. (eds) (1984) *Privatizing Public Enterprises*, London: Royal Institute of Public Administration.

Veljanovski, C. (1987) *Selling the State*, London: Weidenfeld & Nicolson.

Vernon, R. (ed.) (1988) *The Promise of Privatization: A Challenge for American Foreign Policy*, New York: Council on Foreign Relations.

Vickers, J. and Yarrow, G. (1988) *Privatization: An Economic Analysis*, Cambridge, Mass.: MIT Press.

Specialized periodicals:
Privatization International, (monthly), London.
Privatization Watch (monthly), Santa Monica, Calif.
Privatization Review (quarterly), Washington, DC.

PART IX

INTERNATIONAL RELATIONS

52

WORLD POLITICS THEORY

JOHN VASQUEZ

Theory is a discourse that seeks to identify out of all that happens the significant and learn from it. Because of the nature of our cognition, humans do this automatically; the self-conscious construction of theory is an attempt to perform this function as rigorously as possible. Historically, there have been two different ways of doing theory and defining what it is in the study of politics. The first has been to see theory in the tradition of political philosophy. In this instance, theory is meant as a guide to practice, and 'significant' is defined as what will aid practice. From this approach, theory is done by withdrawing from the press of events, reflecting upon their underlying order, and distilling that reflection so that practitioners will know how to survive and shape history. Throughout history most international relations theorizing has been devoted to this *practical theory*.

With the development of the scientific revolution, the idea of a social science increasingly influenced thinking about world politics, including that of classical realists who adopted a positivist conception of history as basically unchanging and subject to a few laws that not only could be apprehended, but had to be followed in order to avoid failure. Classical realism, although influenced by the language of science, still saw the attempts to understand the empirical primarily as a way of guiding practice. With the onset of the behavioural revolt in political science, a sharp separation was made between empirical and normative analysis, with empirical analysis restricted to description and explanation and subject to scientific methodology, while normative analysis was left to fend for itself, often with the implication that since it had no methodology it could not be an activity of serious scholarship. With this movement came a new conception of theory in world politics: *scientific theory*.

In both the physical and social sciences, scientific theory is used in two senses. In one sense, scientific theory can be defined as 'a set of linked propositions that purport to explain behavior' (Mansbach and Vasquez 1981: xiv). In this usage, a theory can be either true or false, and no connotation is

839

given that the theory in question is the same as a confirmed and accepted theory. When analysts speak of theories of world politics or of psychology, they are using theory in this broad sense. The second sense of theory is more technical and is used only to refer to a systematically organized body of knowledge. In this usage, a theory explains a set of documented empirical generalizations through propositions that have been tested and accepted. While such theories exist in the physical sciences, there are no theories of this calibre in international relations inquiry. At best, there are candidates for such a theory, but it is more accurate to say that theory in the second sense of the term is the goal of research and theorizing. It is the final aim of a particular intellectual project that makes certain epistemological assumptions and institutionalizes a set of practices to guide inquiry. It is the playing out of part of the larger modernist project that began with the 'Enlightenment'. In all social sciences, theory came to mean scientific theory, which was exclusively empirical, even though there was a rich history of practical theory.

CRITERIA FOR GOOD THEORY

Within international relations inquiry, theorizing is an activity that has evolved certain rules and norms as to what is good theory, how it can be distinguished from bad theory, and how the practices of scholars should be disciplined to produce research and analyses that will eventually result in good theory.

All criteria of adequacy for scientific theory are based on the fundamental principle that good theory must be true, that it must constitute knowledge. The philosophy of science has attempted to establish principles of inquiry that would form an Archimedean leverage point which would irrefutably demonstrate that what it said was knowledge. Just as other areas of the modernist project attempted to establish within their particular domain that their way was the best way, the most optimal way, indeed the only way toward progress, the philosophy of science attempted to show that its principles were the optimal, best, and only way to proceed. It has become increasingly clear, however, that no such epistemology can be philosophically established, and all of the social sciences have now entered a post-positivist era. Rather than having established its position through irrefutable logic, it now appears that, historically, science won a battle with other discourses for the right to control belief and language in certain domains.

One of the benefits of the post-positivist era is the restoration of practical theory as a legitimate scholarly activity. One of the dangers, as Lapid (1989) argues, is that a proliferation of scientific theories and explanations without any criteria for theory appraisal raises the spectre of relativism. The way out is through the creation and justification of criteria of adequacy. Such criteria are essential if the field is to have any way of selecting among competing views. But can criteria in a post-positivist era be anything but arbitrary?

Just because there may be no single eternally valid standard (or standards) of knowledge does not mean that there are no standards whatsoever. Scientific criteria for knowledge must be seen as *norms* of inquiry that are *justified* in the same rationalist manner as is any norm or ethical rule.

At the heart of the scientific spirit is a commitment to the truth. Truth is not simply a semantic concept (Tarski 1949), but a value that guides inquiry. To say that truth is the primal value means that theories and beliefs are accepted or rejected solely on the basis of their ability to be consistent with the evidence and not because their acceptance will have beneficial consequences, promote a particular economic or political interest, be consistent with a preconceived revealed doctrine, or provide an enabling function that allows a society to shape the world by controlling people and resources. These other considerations, one or more of which are often important criteria in ethics, religion or public policy for the acceptance of statements, are in competition with the scientific spirit. Science insists that for empirical questions its conception of the truth must be taken as guiding, and its practices privileged as the best way of attaining knowledge. In non-empirical matters, it is willing to give way.

For scientific theorizing, a set of propositions is accepted as if they are true if they consistently pass a set of reasonable and valid tests. Although theories are never proved and science is an open-ended process, theories whose propositions have passed tests can be seen as satisfying a *criterion of accuracy* and tentatively accepted as accurate, or at least not inaccurate. Because testing is such an important step in determining whether a theory is true, Popper (1959) maintains that, in order for a set of statements to be considered a scientific theory, it must specify in advance (or at least at some point in time) what evidence will falsify them. If theories (or a set of statements) do not satisfy this *criterion of falsifiability*, then Popper (ibid.) would reject them as inadequate to begin with. When two theories have passed tests and are vying for the allegiance of the scientific community, the *criterion of explanatory power* maintains that the theory that resolves puzzles and anomalies that could not be explained before, and predicts or explains new phenomena, is superior. In addition, good theories should be *fruitful* and *productive*. They should give rise to research programmes and new avenues of inquiry that advance knowledge and promote its cumulation, rather than constantly face anomalies and puzzles to be resolved through *ad hoc* explanations. In Lakatos's terms (Lakatos 1970: 118), problem shifts should be progressive rather than degenerative. Lastly, theories should be consistent with one another. The purported knowledge in one area should not contradict the purported knowledge in another area. The *criterion of consistency* lays out the ultimate goal of the scientific project, the construction of a single unified theory within domains of inquiry and perhaps across them.

These are some of the main criteria by which theories are evaluated in scientific inquiry. Only after such basic criteria are fulfilled are other criteria, such as parsimony and elegance, applied. The problem with inquiry about world politics, however, is not so much a problem of comparing theories and selecting the best one as it is of finding any theory that has passed the tests. In this sense, the field of world politics is very much in a theory-constructing stage, trying to document a set of empirical generalizations that can then be explained.

Not all aspects of theory construction within world politics deal with empirical analysis, however. Most of the history of reflection on world politics has been devoted to enabling practitioners to survive in and shape the world. Theory as a philosophy of practice, to the extent that it has an empirical domain, can be evaluated by some of the criteria for scientific theory, but clearly other criteria will be needed as well. It would be a mistake to think that no criteria can be developed and justified for non-empirical questions (see Kratochwil 1988).

Since one of the main purposes of traditional theory in world politics is to guide practice, then criteria can be centred on the extent to which the theorizing provides an *enabling* function; that is, the extent to which it provides an adequate guide to practice. Just as scientific theories are tested by propositions, so a philosophy of practice can be tested by the policies (and actions) to which it gives rise.

The most fundamental test of a practical theory is to determine whether the purpose and consequences of its practices are considered *good*, where good is defined and determined (or contested) by the larger ethical, religious, professional or organizational goals guiding the group. Goodness is only a prerequisite; ideas must be put into practice and that is very difficult given the constraints of the world. There is always a slippage between what philosophy and policy look like on paper and what they look like in practice. This gap between theory and practice (George and Smoke 1974: 503) provides a way of evaluating the adequacy of practical theory on the basis of the *criterion of practicability*.

Being able to implement a policy, or practise a way of life, is a way of testing a practical theory, but it is very costly. Discourse needs ways of evaluating new ideas before they are put into practice. The *criterion of completeness* admirably satisfies this demand. The more precise and detailed the advice and recommendations offered by a practical theory, obviously the more useful it will be. Theories that simply postulate 'follow the national interest' or 'be rational', without providing a theory that will permit practitioners to determine what is the national interest or what is rational in a given situation, are flawed. They are too vague and are plagued by ambiguity.

A good practical theory, however, must do more than just provide detailed advice. An adequate practical theory must provide guidance on the most difficult policy dilemmas of the day. A theory that can do that is satisfying an important need and a theory that is unable to do that is clearly *irrelevant*.

The *criterion of completeness* and the *criterion of relevance* are two ways in which a practical theory can be evaluated before it is put into practice. The third way it can be evaluated before it is tried is to examine its *anticipated costs*. Costs here must be defined not only in material terms, but also in terms of intangible costs such as moral costs, costs to the prevailing character and structure of a society, costs to internal and external relationships, and the general decision costs in adopting a new practice. These costs must then be compared with anticipated benefits and the probability of success. Many of the techniques of policy evaluation can be fitted into this *criterion of anticipated utility* so long as this is done not in a narrow technocratic manner but within a broad humanistic perspective.

Nevertheless, there are real limits to the extent to which a practical theory can be evaluated before it is put into practice. In actuality, theories are evaluated by their *success* or *failure*. Jervis (1976: chapter 6) has shown that approaches to foreign policy are evaluated by whether they appear to succeed or fail. Nothing will discredit a foreign policy (and the practical theory underlying it) faster than a dramatic failure. Idealism was displaced by realism precisely because of this. Conversely, avoidance of dramatic failure can permit a theory to command adherence even in the absence of many successes, and even in the presence of convincing intellectual criticism.

The critical test for practical theories is their ability to deal with the great political questions of the time. If the prevailing theory is associated with a great catastrophe, then it is replaced by the alternative most critical of it, best able to explain the failure, and most likely to produce a modicum of success if it is adopted. The mere association of ideas with a catastrophe, even if this association is coincidental or even bogus, can bring about a theory's downfall. The result of using the *success–failure criterion*, as Jervis (1976: 281–2) points out, is often to learn the wrong or exaggerated lessons. In order for this powerful criterion to be a more adequate guide to theory appraisal, the standards for success and failure must be defined more precisely and the grounds for inferences must be rigorous.

Finally, since a large component of practical theory is its latent (and sometimes explicit) empirical theory of how the world works, most of the critera applied to scientific theory can be applied to the empirical aspects of the practical theory. Obviously, a practical theory that is based on a set of empirical

843

assumptions and propositions that are found to be false or questionable is not as good a practical theory as one that is consistent with accepted knowledge.

THE STATE OF WORLD POLITICS THEORY

The dominance of the realist paradigm

The criteria for scientific and practical theory can be used to gain a sense of the current state of world politics theory. Within the West, the *realist paradigm* has dominated inquiry on world politics since the Second World War (Vasquez 1983; Smith 1987). It came to dominate by pushing aside the idealist paradigm that had produced the structure of world order associated with Versailles and the League of Nations. The clear failure of this structure to preserve the peace and the resulting war were seen as a failure to understand and employ power properly in the world. Realism and power politics theory were developed from a synthesis of traditional wisdom – including Thucydides, Machiavelli, Hobbes, and Prussian *realpolitik* theorists – to uncover the fundamental laws of international politics. Hans Morgenthau (1948) best expressed and synthesized the realist perspective an entire generation of thinkers was struggling to formulate. By all accounts, his work was the single most important vehicle for transforming the field from idealist advocacy to realist analysis (Olson 1972: 19–20). In doing so, his work became the exemplar for the field and provided it with a paradigm (Vasquez 1983).

In order to explain the failure of idealism to prevent a second world war, Morgenthau attempted to delineate those realistic laws of behaviour that the idealists had ignored to their, and the rest of the world's, peril. He maintained that all politics was a struggle for power, that nations strove to protect their national interest, and that the power of one nation could be most effectively limited by the power of another nation (Morgenthau 1948: chapters 1 and 11). In delineating these general 'laws', Morgenthau provided a view of the world the international relations scholar was investigating, and provided answers to the major questions any field must answer before it can begin a collective inquiry: what are the fundamental units that compose the world; how do they interact; what conception of the world should be employed to answer these questions? Morgenthau's *Politics Among Nations* (Morgenthau 1948) was such an exemplar of analysis that its most fundamental assumptions became the paradigm for the field.

Morgenthau's answers to the most pressing political questions of the time presented a practical theory with a strong empirical component that provided a view of the world that made three fundamental assumptions:

  1 Nation-states or their decision makers are the most important actors for understanding international relations.

2 There is a sharp distinction between domestic politics and international politics.

3 International relations is the struggle for power and peace. Understanding how and why that struggle occurs and suggesting ways for regulating it is the purpose of the discipline. All research that is not at least indirectly related to this purpose is trivial.

(Vasquez 1983: 18).

These assumptions have guided most theorizing and research in the field. They have exercised a disciplinary force on thinking, telling scholars and practitioners what is important to focus on and what is irrelevant.

Morgenthau provided many answers, but he did not provide all the answers. After Morgenthau's landmark work, there were fewer and fewer attempts at 'grand theory' and more investigations of limited topics originally delineated by Morgenthau and the early realists as legitimate research areas. From the 1950s to the present, this division of labour, which is often confused with competing schools of thought, can be seen as attempts to articulate the realist paradigm (see Kuhn 1970: 10–11, 23–4) and make its picture of the world more detailed and accurate. One of the major contributions of the realist paradigm to the field has been to permit the field to develop a common research agenda and follow it more systematically and cumulatively. Within the realist paradigm there are many theories (or candidates for theories), mostly at the mid-range level, with some closer than others to the power politics centre outlined by Morgenthau. All, however, can be considered within the paradigm so long as they do not violate any of its three fundamental assumptions.

The power of the realist paradigm, and specifically of Morgenthau's realism, can be seen by how it satisfied the various criteria of adequacy for a practical theory. Its initial ascendency was based on the criteria of success–failure and of relevance; it claimed that it could and would have succeeded where idealism failed. The tremendous explanatory power of realism is seen through Morgenthau's use of the concept of national interest to explain foreign policy. The concept, as he noted, allowed one to put oneself in the shoes of decision makers and trace as well as anticipate their moves. Since it was a general law that nation-states act in terms of interest defined as power, almost any foreign policy action that was taken could be given a plausible explanation. This high degree of generalizability allowed leaders, especially those of relatively new and inexperienced states like the USA, to have a rule of thumb by which the ship of state could be steered in a world of unfamiliar countries.

This concept, particularly when compared with idealist goals and democratic messianic tendencies, also provided a standard for the conduct (and evaluation) of policy. Foreign policy making, realists asserted, could be rational and was a matter for experts. Morgenthau provided not only an explanation of foreign

845

policy, and a way of predicting other states' moves, but also a philosophy of practice. In these ways, realism provided an explicit framework for assessing costs and benefits as well as the probability of success of a policy. Its explanatory power, generalizability, relevance and utility, coupled with the catastrophic failure of idealism, carried the day. This was particularly the case since power politics had had a long tradition within Europe, and the main other alternative paradigm, apart from idealism, was the Marxist paradigm – the paradigm of the West's alleged enemy. This political fact, along with the need of a new state to justify its goals ideologically and combat isolationists, made realism irresistible.

At the scholarly level, the realist paradigm's continuing ability to evolve and grow by drawing insights from other fields and making them conform to its three fundamental assumptions illustrate its fruitfulness and productivity as a guide to research. Its ability to articulate theories on nuclear deterrence and political economy is a tribute to the richness of its research programme and its ability to meet the challenges of the major events of its time. To some, the culmination of this effort is the neo-realist synthesis of Waltz (1979) who has transformed much of classic realism into an elegant and parsimonious structural explanation of international politics. This effort, when combined with Krasner's discussion of foreign policy (Krasner 1978), Gilpin's explanation of war and peace and political economy (Gilpin 1981, 1987), and Keohane's analysis of hegemony and its institutions (Keohane 1984), appears to bode well for the paradigm and theory construction. This is particularly the case since rational-choice approaches are enjoying a theoretical heyday with some explicitly tied to realism (see Jervis 1978) and others compatible with the paradigm's assumptions but critical of power politics *per se* (for example, Bueno de Mesquita 1981b).

While such a conclusion would be widely accepted within the United States, this says more about the power of the paradigm to dominate thinking than it does about the power of the paradigm and its theories to adequately explain behaviour and guide policy. During the last ten years, the paradigm's three fundamental assumptions have appeared increasingly flawed and inaccurate. The most rigorous empirical research within the field continues to raise questions about the assumptions (see Vasquez 1983: chapter 7). Adherents to the paradigm must constantly give ground to conceptual critiques, which suggests that the paradigm is always being saved by *ad hoc* explanations in gross violation of the criteria of falsifiability and productivity. The ending of the Cold War and attempts to build a new world order that would preserve the peace raise the prospect that a competing paradigm based on a more interdisciplinary synthesis may be more relevant and accurate. To see how this might be the case, some of the defects in realist explanations of foreign policy and interstate behaviour, and the inadequacy of its three assumptions, can be examined.

Foreign policy and the rational actor model

One of the weakest areas within realist analysis is the use of the concept of national interest. For realists, the interests of all states are the same. The protection of a state's territorial integrity and national sovereignty are matters of survival. Morgenthau (1952) recognized, however, that beyond these minimal requirements the national interest also included the whole gamut of actions logically compatible with these minimal goals. These could pose a potential danger in that the elastic elements might swallow up the logically minimal elements so that in the end all sorts of things might be justified in the name of the national interest. Morgenthau was not particularly concerned about this, because for him it was clear that US interests lay in being internationalist and not narrowly isolationist, but at the same time not being so internationalist that it followed the supranationalist interests of a United Nations instead of its own national interests.

Morgenthau and other realists were fairly successful in the early years in avoiding these two shoals, even though they did not like the official justification given for the Korean war. It became obvious, however, that the concept of national interest, or national security, was based on a very ambiguous conceptualization and an inaccurate explanation of foreign policy. Wolfers (1952), in a prescient essay, pointed out many of these defects. Empirically, states did not strive just for security, but for other values as well, particularly wealth. Nations did not aim just to survive, but to survive well. Of course, this should have come as no surprise to careful observers, since there was always a contradiction between the realist 'law', that nation-states act on the basis of interest defined by power, and Morgenthau's, Kennan's, and other realists' strident criticisms of the USA and other states for failing to follow their national interest.

One of the reasons such criticisms were necessary was that the elastic elements were in fact constantly swallowing up the minimal elements, so that in the end all sorts of things could be justified in terms of national security. Wolfers warned that national security was such an ambiguous symbol that its main use was not analysis, but as a symbol by which decision makers could justify whatever action they wanted. Long before Watergate and the Vietnam war, he anticipated the kinds of actions that would be justified by the concept.

This ambiguity is further aggravated by the fact that the concept does not provide a very *complete* guide to policy. It does not tell policy makers how to define the national interest in specific situations, thereby providing little guidance in choosing various options. Nor does it provide any guidance in *how* to achieve the goals of the national interest. In addition, while it is able to explain almost any action after the fact, it does this so well that its *post hoc* reasoning violates the criterion of falsifiability. Reliance upon it and its associate, the rational actor model, to anticipate events has often led policy makers astray and produced more than one surprise and 'intelligence failure'. Ultimately, the concept and the explanation turned out to be fine rhetoric, but grossly inaccurate as an explanation and incomplete as a guide to policy. Although most scholars have abandoned it as a tool of analysis, it persists within the realm of practice because no other single concept has been developed to provide a standard for the evaluation and conduct of foreign policy.

As the problems of national interest explanations became evident, early behaviouralists attempted to resolve some of the defects. Snyder, Bruck and Sapin provided a framework that would identify the factors that actually influenced foreign policy decision making (Snyder *et al.* 1954). In doing so, they sought to create a theory of foreign policy that explains the foreign policy of any state, thereby following the direction of classical realists of moving the field away from explaining the foreign policy of individual states through national histories. At the same time, Snyder *et al.* solved the problem that early realists had of anthropomorphizing the nation-state. The focus on individual decision makers and those who influenced them provided a kind of operationalization of the state concept that permitted it to be observed. The problem with Snyder *et al.*, however, was that their conceptual framework was an 'everything-is-related-to-everything-else' theory, which fails to identify and order a relatively few variables. The main contribution of Rosenau (1966) was to do precisely this, which gave rise to the comparative foreign policy movement that attempted to create a unified scientific theory of foreign policy (Rosenau 1971). After some initial successes (Rosenau 1974; East *et al.* 1978), this movement has faltered, primarily because of an inability to reach a consensus over what constitutes valid data and a general malaise that more findings have not been produced. Recent work on artificial intelligence holds open the possibility of new breakthroughs, but on the whole what is needed is to integrate findings into a meaningful theoretical explanation (see Hermann *et al.* 1987), and that is not likely to happen until there are considerably more findings.

Meanwhile, practical theory has relied on a rational actor model in order to explain and make foreign policy. Later generations have amplified the first assumption of the realist paradigm to argue that nation-states are not only the most important actors in international relations but are also rational unitary actors. This model as employed by power politics theorists assumes that decision makers will behave in a similar fashion and will be affected not by personal or other idiosyncratic factors, but only by the nature of the situation and/or the structure of the global system (Wolfers 1959; Waltz 1979). Foreign policy analysts have then gone on to argue that foreign policy can be explained by deducing how decision makers pursue their interest through a calculation of costs and benefits.

Even though the rational actor model employed by theorists is a more sophisticated version of the rational decision-making model discussed in public administration, it has been undercut by recent research. The first argument against the model is that individuals and groups generally do not make decisions in a rational manner, because they process information not on the basis of logical rules but on a basis of a set of psychological principles which do not necessarily correspond to logical reasoning (see Jervis 1976; Janis and Mann 1977; Kahneman *et al.* 1982). Jervis (1976) argues that decision makers process information in terms of images they have developed of other actors and of the environment. These images are a product of past interactions and particularly of intense learning during traumatic experiences (see Deutsch and Merritt 1965; Wayman 1984). These lessons of the past are often over-generalized, producing inappropriate analogies (Jervis 1976: chapter 6; May 1973). New information that conforms to existing images tends to be emphasized and information that is discrepant with the images is often unseen, ignored or explained away (Jervis 1976: chapters 5 and 7). Especially during crisis situations, overreliance on images and analogies to what worked in the past plays an important role in decision making (Jervis 1976: chapter 6; see also C. F. Hermann 1972; Holsti and George 1975).

The second argument against the rational actor model is that, since certain types of individuals and specific kinds of groups behave differently, it is incorrect to assume that they would all behave rationally. This means that a state's foreign policy cannot be deduced on the basis of a rational national-interest (or cost–benefit) calculus, because personal factors affect individual behaviour and internal structural characteristics affect group decision making (see Guetzkow and Valadez 1981: chapters 7 and 8; M. G. Hermann 1974; Etheredge 1978; C. F. Hermann 1978). All of this suggests that a more appropriate way to study foreign policy decision making is through the use of learning theory and the construction of cognitive maps (Axelrod 1976; Shapiro and Bonham 1973). Such an approach would make for an accurate description, but still would need to be converted into a theoretically significant explanation (Holsti 1976).

A third argument against the rational actor model comes from taking a bureaucratic politics and organization theory perspective. As Allison and Halperin (1972) point out, foreign policy is the product not simply of external politics but of internal political pressures and fights. This implies that personal, sub-national or organizational interests, not solely the national interests, govern foreign policy making. Quantitative analysis by Phillips and Crain (1974), Tanter (1974) and McCormick (1975) has shown that, except in crises, the foreign policy actions of states do not correlate as strongly with the actions others take toward them (reciprocity), as they do with their own previous actions. Such evidence is consistent with the view that, in general, foreign policy making is a function of bureaucratic inertia and unchanging images. It does not follow, however, that in crises the bureaucracy can be completely side-stepped. Allison (1971) has shown that, even in a nuclear crisis, bureaucratic and organizational factors have a critical influence.

The response of adherents to the realist paradigm to these arguments is to speak of 'bounded rationality' (see Keohane 1984). Yet, at best, this is an *ad hoc* explanation meant to save the model. It is clear that decision making is bounded, but it is not at all clear in what sense it is rational. Labelling it as 'bounded rationality' tells us little and obscures a variety of flaws. Under this rubric, many analysts still employ rational-choice models that treat states as unitary actors and black-box domestic factors (see Bueno de Mesquita 1981b). Rather than subsuming psychological variables, like uncertainty and risk taking, within an overall cost–benefit calculation, it is probably more accurate to treat these and other psychological and organizational factors as separate variables in their own right. One way to do this would be to identify the various decision-making calculi (psychological as well as cost–benefit) and then explain under what conditions leaders or groups are apt to employ each calculus (see Mansbach and Vasquez 1981: chapter 6). This is not to say that cost–benefit analysis cannot explain some kinds of behaviour, but only that rational choice theorists have failed to specify the range of behaviour to which it is applicable.

What is likely to occur is that as empirical research within world politics and the other social sciences continues, it will produce a unified theory of how decision making takes place in a variety of situations, cultures and historical eras. It is upon such an empirical base, rather than upon the overly generalized, indeed normative, base of rational choice that an adequate explanation of foreign policy will be built. Such a unified theory will undoubtedly involve a paradigm shift (see Burton 1984). Empirical research and conceptual analysis have been trying to tell scholars that there are fundamental problems in the first two assumptions of the realist paradigm. Rather than continue to patch over these problems through *ad hoc* explanations, many have felt it is time to take a different perspective (Banks 1985).

Interstate politics, anarchy, and the struggle for power

For the realist paradigm, world politics is international politics. It has not only a very state-centric bias, believing that states are the most powerful actors and therefore the most important, but also a very nationalist bias, believing that states are best formed around nations, as opposed to cities or multinational empires. These perspectives are not an accident, but reflect the fact that the realist perspective is a product of the formation of the modern Western nation-state system that began at the end of the fifteenth century. Realist ideas must be seen not only as a reflection of that new structure, but as a set of ideas that evolved and helped institutionalize that system, particularly at the time of the Peace of Westphalia. As such, realist thought must be seen as providing a social construction of modern global reality. A practical theory could claim no greater success. The idealist domination, then, must be seen as a brief interlude before the return of a resurrected realist tradition.

Throughout the past five hundred years, the nation-state focus has served not only as an empirical description but also as a prescriptive guide to what the system should be. The ideas of nationalism aided the formation of new major states, like Italy and Germany, in the nineteenth century, and legitimated the anti-colonial revolts of the mid-twentieth century. As Marxists, as well as others, were quick to point out, however, the focus on nation-states often obscured power realities. Many nation-states were legal fictions because of their penetration and dependence on other states or even non-state actors (see, respectively, Rosenau 1966; Cardoso and Faletto 1979). The first assumption of the realist paradigm obscured the importance of revolutionary groups as well as, in recent times, multinational corporations and international institutions, such as the International Monetary Fund. Realist theories had a difficult time recognizing, let alone explaining, imperialism and neo-imperialism, seeing it simply as a form of power no different now from that of ancient systems (contrast Morgenthau 1948 and Waltz 1979, on the one hand, with Galtung 1971, on the other). The neglect of the importance of capitalism and the general role of economics in the historical evolution of a world-system (Wallerstein 1974) made realist theories of international politics seem ahistorical, unable to explain fundamental social change at the global level (see Ruggie's 1983 criticism of Waltz 1979). Seeing history as fundamentally unchanging, realists were unable to explain where the structure of world politics came from in the first place and were unable to apprehend that the immutable 'laws' of the system that they were seeking to uncover might merely be the social constructions of a particular epoch.

From the fifteenth century on, one of the premier 'laws' realists 'discovered' to explain and guide world politics has been the balance of power. Throughout this time, the balance-of-power concept has been cited as a justification for policy and has been lauded by some as the only realistic proposal for maintaining peace and the independence of states. Nevertheless, it has been fraught with problems. At the practical level, it has not provided a very permanent solution to the problem of war; wars have occurred throughout the last five hundred years. Those who have argued in favour of the balance of power have maintained that these wars occurred when the balance was disrupted. Even if this contention were empirically true, which is dubious, it concedes that the balance may be difficult to implement at the point at which it is needed most – when war threatens. Thus, this argument by its very defence of the balance of power raises questions about its practicability. Conversely, others have argued that the balance can be implemented, but that it will not prevent war; states will fight each other whether they are equal or unequal in capability.

At the conceptual level, the idea of the balance of power has difficulties because it means different things. Some, such at Waltz (1979), see it as an automatic and natural phenomenon, like Adam Smith's invisible hand; if one nation increases in power, one or more other nations will move to match and counter that power. Others view it as a conscious policy that decision makers must meticulously follow if it is to work. Still others see it as a popular symbol with which to marshal support and rationalize a position that has been motivated by other concerns. With the exception of Waltz (1979), most twentieth-century scholars (for example, Morgenthau 1948; Haas 1953; Organski 1958; Claude 1962) find the concept problematic, as did David Hume and Johann Heinrich Gottlob von Justi in the eighteenth century.

Regardless of whether, in Haas's words, it is a prescription, an empirical concept, or propaganda (Haas 1953), it is unclear why the balance of power should prevent war. Thucydides and other ancients commented that if one state gained too much power there would be nothing to stop it from subjecting all others. This certainly points out a potential danger, but it does not follow that peace will be produced from a balance. All a balance will prevent is an easy victory. War often does occur between relative equals. This has led many scholars to argue that security can be attained not through a balance of power, but only through a preponderance of power (see Organski 1958). The other side will only be prevented from attacking if it knows it will lose the war. While this argument makes sense, what is to prevent the preponderant power from attacking?

These theoretical problems help explain the balance of power's limited historical success. Scientific research has shown that sometimes a balance in the system or the dyad is associated with peace and at other times with war (see Bueno de Mesquita 1981a; Singer et al. 1972), which suggests that the relationship is random. In fact, it can be argued that neither a balance of power nor a preponderance of power is associated with peace, but rather each is associated with different types of war! From this perspective, the balance of power has been associated with total wars like the Peloponnesian War, the Punic Wars, the Thirty Years' War, the Napoleonic Wars, and the First and Second World Wars. These were wars of rivalry among relative equals. Conversely, a preponderance of power has been associated with imperial wars of conquest. A balance of power may prevent the latter wars in the short run, but in so doing often produces conditions that lead to wars between rivals.

With the advent of nuclear weapons, balance-of-power thinking was supplanted by the idea of nuclear deterrence. The nuclear balance of terror, although horribly frightening, seemed to achieve the positive aspects of both the balance of power and the preponderance of power without the negative aspects. As long as each side was able to absorb an initial attack and to retaliate, power was relatively equal, as in the balance of power. Thus, wars of conquest resulting from inequality could be prevented. Conversely, the tremendous destructive capability of nuclear weapons ensured that both sides would lose a nuclear war. As long as this mutual assured destruction was in place, each side had, in effect, a preponderance of power. Thus, wars of rivalry could be prevented.

By the late 1950s and early 1960s, a group of American scholars (Brodie 1945: Kahn 1960; Schelling 1960; see also Kissinger 1957) examined issues concerning nuclear weapons and developed what, in light of public pronouncements by John Foster Dulles and Robert McNamara, became an American doctrine of deterrence. Yet, for obvious reasons, this was a very deductive theory without an empirical base. As empirical and conceptual analyses (Russett 1963; Huth and Russett 1984; Morgan 1983) were conducted, questions about the accuracy of deterrence and the logical validity of its inferences were raised. Comparative case studies of actual American practice also raised serious questions. George and Smoke's review of American actions (George and Smoke 1974) showed that deterrence theory provided decision makers with insufficient guidance and that decision makers often deviated from the guidance that was provided. If deterrence theory is unable to describe accurately and explain the actions of American decision makers, then it is doubtful that it could predict how the Russians or Chinese would react in a nuclear confrontation. Yet it is precisely this information that it purports to provide.

This raises the possibility that the absence of nuclear war between the USA and USSR was due not to nuclear deterrence but to other factors (Kugler 1984; Mueller 1989). Of much more crucial importance might have been such irenic factors as the general absence of Soviet–American territorial continuity, tolerance of the status quo, the raising of the provocation threshold by the experience of the two world wars, and the creation of rules of the game along with conscious efforts at crisis management and arms control. If this is the case, then nuclear proliferation is even more dangerous than had been thought, because it is not likely that these irenic factors will be present among other states.

Both the balance of power and deterrence are based on the assumption that peace can only come out of the exercise of power. Neither place much credence in the role of rules and institutions, because they see the heart of international politics as consisting of a struggle for power within anarchy. Waltz's reformulation of classical realism (Waltz 1979), in particular, places great emphasis on the structural anarchy of the system for explaining behaviour. Yet is the system fundamentally anarchic? If one means by anarchy the absence of hierarchical domestic-type government, then it is, but if one means the absence of all governance and order, then it is not. Despite the analogy to domestic government, most realists, including Waltz, *use* the term 'anarchy' to mean not simply the absence of hierarchical government, but the presence of a Hobbesian state of nature.

In the modern global system since 1495, anarchy, while present at times, has not been as pervasive as Waltz would have us believe. As Bull (1977) has shown by taking a Grotian perspective, global society has evolved certain rules and customs that have patterned behaviour, including the way force and war may be used (see also Alker, forthcoming). Global society does not permit states to go to war for just any reason; it identifies either through law or through intellectual argumentation the *casus belli* and legitimate reasons for war. The presence of war does not mean that there is no order in the world, that all is a Hobbesian anarchy; rather, the strength of order in a global society is reflected in how it makes war. A true anarchy is not characterized by war (which is a socially constructed invention) but, as Bull (1977: 185) notes, by a 'more ubiquitous violence'.

One of the reasons why Waltz underestimates the amount of order in the system is that he treats the anarchy–order distinction as a dichotomy, when it is better seen as a continuum. Major wars have given rise to world orders (although not world governments) and most wars are not fought in conditions of anarchy, but within a regional or global order that shapes the way in which the war is fought. The kind of anarchy that Waltz and Hobbes talk about only emerges with the complete breakdown of a political system, which occurs only during world wars in the global system and civil wars and social revolutions in domestic systems.

In fact, as Campbell (1989: 104) astutely observes, the defining characteristic of the international system since the sixteenth century has been capitalism, not anarchy. To see the modern global system as 'anarchic' is to hide the historical fact that an arbitrary system of organization (i.e. nation-states and a capitalist world economy) evolved at a particular period of history and has been guided by clear principles that make this system much more of a society than a state of nature. Anarchy as a state of nature never was an eternal truth of world politics.

There are two basic responses to the thrust of this criticism. One is again to save the paradigm by *ad hoc* analysis. Just as one talked of 'bounded rationality', now some scholars speak of 'bounded anarchy'. A second response is to take the Grotian perspective to its logical conclusion and, unlike Bull, reject the third assumption of the realist paradigm: namely, that world politics is a struggle for power.

The third assumption of the realist paradigm poses a picture of the world, and as such it is very difficult to determine whether it, as opposed to some other picture, is a useful guide to inquiry. A major claim that can be made against the assumption is that realist explanations of interstate relations do not provide an empirical theory of world politics, but merely an image that decision makers can have of the world. Power politics is not so much an explanation as a description of one type of behaviour found in the global political system. If this is correct, then power politics behaviour itself must be explained; it cannot explain.

As an image of the world employed by policy makers, power politics promotes certain kinds of behaviour and often leads to self-fulfilling prophecies (see Vasquez, forthcoming: chapter 3). An adequate theory of world politics would seek to discover when policy makers adopt a power politics image of the world, what kinds of behaviour this image fosters, and when such behaviour results in war. It should be possible to find non-power politics behaviour and to develop a theory of what conditions promote power politics and non-power politics behaviour, and how a system or issue area characterized by one mode of behaviour might be transformed to the other. Such an approach would provide an authentic alternative to the realist paradigm because it would not only explain everything the realist paradigm purports to explain, but would also discover and explain a vast area of behaviour that the realist paradigm ignores.

The most obvious areas that the image of anarchy and power struggle have had difficulty explaining are those of peace, conflict resolution, co-operation, and the creation of regimes. The early call of Keohane and Nye (1972) for a new paradigm that would look at how behaviour varied by issue area, and their comparison of realism and complex interdependence (Keohane and Nye 1977), recognized this. The latter framework, however, was insufficiently broad to compete effectively with the realist paradigm. The world society paradigm of Burton et al. (1974) provided an authentic alternative, rejecting the division between domestic and international politics and seeing power politics and coercion not only as empirically inaccurate but also as an inadequate guide to practice that was creating a host of intractable problems for which it had no solutions (Burton 1984; see also Banks 1984). Burton's world society paradigm, however, is still a sketch and needs to be more fully developed. Here the work on regimes (Young 1980; Haas 1980; Krasner 1983) and the issue approach (Coplin et al. 1973; Mansbach and Vasquez 1981; Randle 1987) offer specific explanations and testable hypotheses. If such work were linked to aspects of the historical-structural analysis of the world system (for example, Braudel 1966; Wallerstein 1974; Modelski 1978; Thompson 1988; Cox 1981), then a much more complete picture of world society could be drawn with important implications for practical theory.

Existing research in world politics not only raises questions about the empirical accuracy of realist theories (see Vasquez 1983), but points to areas where more promising avenues of inquiry might be pursued. With the emergence of a post-Cold War era and the attempt to create a new world order, the answers the realist paradigm has provided seem less and less relevant to the pressing needs of the day.

THE FUTURE OF WORLD POLITICS THEORY

The construction of a theory of world politics has never been done in isolation from the intellectual developments of other disciplines. At the century's end, post-modernist and post-structuralist currents have been sweeping through the social sciences and the humanities. The importance and relevance of such work, particularly that of Foucault (1972, 1980) and Derrida (1978), to world politics has led a new generation to question the modernist project (Ashley 1987, 1988; Der Derian 1987; Der Derian and Shapiro 1989; Shapiro 1981; Walker 1984). Within international relations inquiry the very way in which we think and write about theory is being changed by these scholars. At the same time, feminist scholars are using post-structuralist analysis to unmask the gendered nature of the realist construction of reality (see Cohn 1987; Tickner 1988) and are beginning to tell her-story within world politics (for example, Elshtain 1987). The implications of Berger and Luckmann's constructivism for world politics (Berger and Luckmann 1966) are only beginning to be seen in light of the post-modernist critique.

It is clearer than it ever was before that science cannot uncover the one true way because all ways are constructed. There can be no doubt that the ideas of political *development* and economic *development* were modernist conceits. The replacing of traditional society by modern society must be seen not as a progressive inevitable movement of history, but as an act of imposition and hegemony (Ashley 1987). In this manner, modern science has played a very hegemonizing role, but that does not mean that the scientific spirit has played no liberating role or is unable to be self-critical. Traditionalism, itself, is hegemonizing. Likewise, just because there is no teleology guiding history, this does not mean that humans cannot learn and cannot improve their lot.

The best hopes for doing so still reside in the use of the scientific method. As has been seen, practical theory can be no better than the empirical theory upon which it rests. Although attempts to study world politics scientifically have not produced quick answers, rigour has made a difference (Huth and Russett 1990). One of the problems with traditional theorizing has been the attempt to explain empirical generalizations that were never fully documented. This has been the main flaw in Waltz's and Gilpin's elegant analyses (Waltz 1979; Gilpin 1981). Generating empirical findings is still essential despite the feeling of some that the creation of a science of world politics is an 'elusive quest' (Ferguson and Mansbach 1988). Nevertheless, until the findings are put together and integrated into a theory, they are of little use. Therefore, the creation of a scientific theory, whether through induction or deduction, remains a pressing task (compare Singer 1972; Zinnes 1976). Such an enterprise is best done at the mid-range level using important research in the areas of war, arms races, negotiation and bargaining, decision making, crisis, imperialism, political economy, conflict resolution and peace to develop islands of theory. Guetzkow's vision that such islands of theory could be cumulated and eventually connected (Guetzkow 1950) remains a project worth pursuing. What is needed in a post-modern and post-positivist era is not less science but more critical and emancipatory science (Alker 1988). This is particularly the case in a field that has been dominated by a flawed paradigm.

REFERENCES

* Recommended for further reading.

Alker, H. R., Jr (1988) 'Emancipatory empiricism: toward the renewal of empirical peace research', in P. Wallensteen (ed.) *Peace Research*, Boulder, Colo.: Westview Press.
____(forthcoming) 'The presumption of anarchy in world politics', in H. Alker and R. Ashley (eds) *After Neorealism*.
Allison, G. T. (1971) *Essence of Decision: Explaining the Cuban Missile Crisis*, Boston: Little, Brown & Co.
Allison, G. T. and Halperin, M. H. (1972) 'Bureaucratic politics: a paradigm and some policy implications', *World Politics* 24 (supplement): 40–89.
* Ashley, R. K. (1987) 'The geopolitics of geopolitical space: toward a critical social theory of international politics', *Alternatives* 12 (4): 403–34.
____(1988) 'Geopolitics, supplementary, criticism: a reply to Professors Roy and Walker', *Alternatives* 13 (1): 88–102.
Axelrod, R. (ed.) (1976) *Structure of Decision*, Princeton: Princeton University Press.
Banks, M. (ed.) (1984) *Conflict in World Society*, Brighton: Wheatsheaf.
____(1985) 'The inter-paradigm debate', in M. Light and A. J. R. Groom (eds) *International Relations: A Handbook of Current Theory*, London: Frances Pinter.
Berger, P. L. and Luckmann, T. (1966) *The Social Construction of Reality*, New York: Doubleday.
Braudel, F. (1966) *The Mediterranean and the Mediterranean World in the Age of Philip II*, New York: Harper & Row.
Brodie, B. (1945) 'The atomic bomb and American security', memorandum no. 18, New Haven, Conn: Yale Institute of International Studies.
Bueno de Mesquita, B. (1981a) 'Risk, power distributions, and the likelihood of war', *International Studies Quarterly* 25 (4): 541–68.
____(1981b) *The War Trap*, New Haven: Yale University Press.
* Bull, H. (1977) *The Anarchical Society*, New York: Columbia University Press.
* Burton, J. W. (1984) *Global Conflict: The Domestic Sources of International Crisis*, Brighton: Wheatsheaf.
Burton, J. W., Groom, A. J. R., Mitchell, C. R. and de Reuck, A. V. S. (1974) *The Study of World Society: A London Perspective*, Occasional Paper no. 1, International Studies Association.

Campbell, D. (1989) 'Security and identity in united states foreign policy: a reading of the Carter Administration', unpublished Ph.D. dissertation, Australian National University.

Cardoso, F. H. and Faletto, E. (1979) *Dependency and Development in Latin America*, Berkeley: University of California Press.

* Claude, I. L., Jr. (1962) *Power and International Relations*, New York: Random House.

Cohn, C. (1987) 'Sex and death in the rational world of defense intellectuals', *Signs* 12 (4): 692–99.

Coplin, W. D., Mills, S. L. and O'Leary, M. K. (1973) 'The PRINCE concepts and the study of foreign policy', in P. McGowan (ed.) *Sage International Yearbook of Foreign Policy Studies*, Vol. I, Beverly Hills: Sage Publications, pp. 73–103.

Cox, R. W. (1981) 'Social forces, states and world orders: beyond international relations theory', *Millennium* 10 (2): 126–55.

Der Derian, J. (1987) *On Diplomacy*, Oxford: Blackwell.

* Der Derian, J. and Shapiro, M. J. (eds) (1989) *International/Intertextual Relations: Postmodern Readings of World Politics*, Lexington, Mass.: Lexington Books.

Derrida, J. (1978) *Writing and Difference*, Chicago: University of Chicago Press.

Deutsch, K. W. and Merritt, R. L. (1965) 'Effects of events on national and international images', in H. Kelman (ed.) *International Behavior*, New York: Holt, Rinehart & Winston.

East, M., Salmore, S. and Hermann, C. (eds) (1978) *Why Nations Act*, Beverly Hills: Sage Publications.

Elshtain, J. B. (1987) *Women and War*, New York: Basic Books.

Etheredge, L. S. (1978) *A World of Men: The Private Sources of American Foreign Policy*, Cambridge, Mass.: MIT Press.

Ferguson, Y. H. and Mansbach, R. W. (1988) *The Elusive Quest: Theory and International Politics*, Columbia: University of South Carolina Press.

* Foucault, M. (1972) *The Archaeology of Knowledge*, New York: Pantheon.

——(1980) *Power/Knowledge: Selected Interviews and Other Writings, 1972–1977*, New York: Pantheon.

Galtung, J. (1971) 'A structural theory of imperialism', *Journal of Peace Research* 8 (2): 81–119.

* George, A. L. and Smoke, R. (1974) *Deterrence in American Foreign Policy*, New York: Columbia University Press.

Gilpin, R. (1981) *War and Change in World Politics*, Cambridge: Cambridge University Press.

——(1987) *The Political Economy of International Relations*, Princeton: Princeton University Press.

* Guetzkow, H. (1950) 'Long range research in international relations', *American Perspective* 4 (Fall): 421–40; reprinted in J. Vasquez (ed.) (1986) *Classics of International Relations*, Englewood Cliffs, NJ: Prentice-Hall.

* Guetzkow, H. and Valadez, J. J. (eds) (1981) *Simulated International Processes: Theories and Research in Global Modeling*, Beverly Hills: Sage Publications.

* Haas, E. B. (1953) 'The balance of power: prescription, concept, or propaganda?', *World Politics* 5: 442–77.

——(1980) 'Why collaborate? Issue-linkage and international regimes', *World Politics* 32 (3): 357–405.

858

Hermann, C. F. (1972) 'Threat, time, and surprise: a simulation of international crisis', in C. F. Hermann (ed.) *International Crises: Insights from Behavioral Research*, New York: Free Press.

——(1978) 'Decision structure and process influences on foreign policy', in M. East, S. Salmore and C. Hermann (eds) *Why Nations Act*, Beverly Hills: Sage Publications.

Hermann, C. F., Kegley, C. and Rosenau, J. (eds) (1987) *New Directions in the Study of Foreign Policy*, Boston: Allen & Unwin.

Hermann, M. G. (1974) 'Leader personality and foreign policy behavior', in J. Rosenau (ed.) *Comparing Foreign Policies*, New York: Halsted Press.

* Hoffmann, S. (1959) 'International relations: the long road to theory', *World Politics* 11 (3): 346–77.

Holsti, O. R. (1976) 'Foreign policy viewed cognitively', in R. Axelrod (ed.) *Structure of Decision*, Princeton: Princeton University Press.

Holsti, O. R. and George, A. L. (1975) 'The effects of stress on the performance of foreign policy-makers', in C. Cotter (ed.) *Political Science Annual*, Vol. 6, Indianapolis: Bobbs-Merrill.

Huth, P. and Russett, B. M. (1984) 'What makes deterrence work? Cases from 1900 to 1980', *World Politics* 36 (1): 496–526.

——(1990) 'Testing deterrence theory: rigor makes a difference', *World Politics* 42 (4): 466–501.

Janis, I. I. and Mann, L. (1977) *Decision Making*, New York: Free Press.

* Jervis, R. (1976) *Perception and Misperception in International Politics*, Princeton: Princeton University Press.

——(1978) 'Cooperation under the security dilemma', *World Politics* 30 (2): 167–214.

* Kahn, H. (1960) *On Thermonuclear War*, Princeton: Princeton University Press.

Kahneman, D., Slovic, P. and Tversky A. (eds) (1982) *Judgement Under Uncertainty: Heuristics and Biases*, Cambridge: Cambridge University Press.

* Keohane, R. O. (1984) *After Hegemony*, Princeton: Princeton University Press.

Keohane, R. O. and Nye, J. S., Jr (eds) (1972) *Transnational Relations and World Politics*, Cambridge, Mass.: Harvard University Press.

——(1977) *Power and Interdependence: World Politics in Transition*, Boston: Little, Brown & Co.

Kissinger, H. A. (1957) *The Necessity for Choice*, New York: Harper.

Krasner, S. (1978) *Defending the National Interest: Raw Materials Investments and US Foreign Policy*, Princeton: Princeton University Press.

——(ed.) (1983) *International Regimes*, Ithaca NY: Cornell University Press.

Kratochwil, F. (1988) 'Regimes, interpretation and the "science" of politics: a reappraisal', *Millennium* 17 (2): 263–84.

Kugler, J. (1984) 'Terror without deterrence', *Journal of Conflict Resolution* 28 (3): 470–506.

Kuhn, T. S. (1970) *The Structure of Scientific Revolutions*, 2nd edn, enlarged, Chicago: University of Chicago Press.

Lakatos, I. (1970) 'Falsification and the methodology of scientific research programmes', in I. Lakatos and A. Musgrave (eds) *Criticism and the Growth of Knowledge*, Cambridge: Cambridge University Press.

Lapid, Y. (1989) 'The third debate: on the prospects of international theory in a post-positivist era', *International Studies Quarterly* 33 (3): 235–54.

McCormick, J. M. (1975) 'Evaluating models of crisis behaviour: some evidence from the Middle East', *International Studies Quarterly* 19 (1): 17–45.

Mansbach, R. W. and Vasquez, J. A. (1981) *In Search of Theory: A New Paradigm for Global Politics*, New York: Columbia University Press.

Masterman, M. (1970) 'The nature of a paradigm', in I. Lakatos and A. Musgrave (eds) *Criticism and the Growth of Knowledge*, Cambridge: Cambridge University Press.

May, E. R. (1973) *'Lessons' of the Past: The Use and Misuse of History in American Foreign Policy*, New York: Oxford University Press.

Modelski, G. (1978) 'The long cycle of global politics and the nation-state', *Comparative Studies in Society and History* 20 (2): 214–35.

* Morgan, P. (1983) *Deterrence: A Conceptual Analysis*, 2nd edn, Beverly Hills: Sage Publications.

* Morgenthau, H. J. (1948) *Politics among Nations*, 3rd edn 1960, New York: Knopf.

* ____(1952) 'Another "Great Debate": The National Interest of the United States', *American Political Science Review* 46: 961–88.

Mueller, J. E. (1989) *Retreat from Doomsday: The Obsolescence of Major War*, New York: Basic Books.

Olson, W. C. (1972) 'The growth of a discipline', in B. Porter (ed.) *The Aberystwyth Papers: International Politics 1919–1969*, London: Oxford University Press.

* Organski, A. F. K. (1958) *World Politics*, New York: Knopf.

Phillips, W. R. and Crain, R. C. (1974) 'Dynamic foreign policy interactions: reciprocity and uncertainty in foreign policy', in P. McGowan (ed.) *Sage International Yearbook of Foreign Policy Studies*, Vol. II, Beverly Hills: Sage Publications, pp. 227–66.

Popper, K. (1959) *The Logic of Scientific Discovery*, London: Hutchinson.

Randle, R. F. (1987) *Issues in the History of International Relations*, New York: Praeger.

Rosenau, J. N. (1966) 'Pre-theories and theories of foreign policy', in R. Farrell (ed.) *Approaches to Comparative and International Politics*, Evanston, Ill.: Northwestern University Press.

* ____(1971) *The Scientific Study of Foreign Policy*, New York: Free Press.

____(ed.) (1974) *Comparing Foreign Policies*, New York: Halsted.

Rosenau, P. (1990) 'Once again into the fray: international relations confronts the humanities', *Millennium* 19 (1): 83–110.

Ruggie, J. G. (1983) 'Continuity and transformation in the world polity: toward a neo-realist synthesis', *World Politics* 35 (2): 261–85.

Russett, B. M. (1963) 'The calculus of deterrence', *Journal of Conflict Resolution* 7 (2): 97–109.

Schelling, T. C. (1960) *The Strategy of Conflict*, New York: Oxford University Press.

Shapiro, M. J. (1981) *Language and Political Understanding*, New Haven: Yale University Press.

Shapiro, M. J. and Bonham, G. M., (1973) 'Cognitive process and foreign policy decision-making', *International Studies Quarterly* 17 (2): 147–74.

Singer, J. D. (1972) *The Scientific Study of Politics: An Approach to Foreign Policy Analysis*, Morristown, NJ: General Learning Press.

Singer, J. D., Bremer, S. and Stuckey, J. (1972) 'Capability distribution, uncertainty, and major power war, 1820–1965', in B. Russett (ed.) *Peace, War, and Numbers*, Beverly Hills: Sage Publications.

Smith, S. (1987) 'Paradigm dominance in international relations: the development of international relations as a social science', *Millennium* 16 (2): 189–206.

Syder, R. C., Bruck, H. and Sapin B. (1954) *Decision-Making as an Approach to the Study of International Politics*, Princeton: Foreign Policy Analysis Project Series, no. 3, Princeton University.

Tanter, R. (1974) *Modelling and Managing International Conflicts*, Beverly Hills: Sage Publications.

Tarski, A. (1949) 'The semantic conception of truth', in H. Feigl and W. Sellars (eds) *Readings in Philosophical Analysis*, New York: Appleton-Century-Crofts.

Thompson, W. R. (1988) *On Global War: Historical-Structural Approaches to World Politics*, Columbia: University of South Carolina Press.

Tickner, J. A. (1988) 'Hans Morgenthau's principles of political realism: a feminist reformulation', *Millennium* 17 (3): 429–40.

* Vasquez, J. A. (1983) *The Power of Power Politics: A Critique*, London: Frances Pinter.
____(forthcoming) *The War Puzzle*, Cambridge: Cambridge University Press.

Walker, R. B. J. (1984) 'World politics and western reason: universalism, pluralism, hegemony', in R. B. J. Walker (ed.) *Culture, Ideology, and World Order*, Boulder: Westview Press.

* Wallerstein, I. (1974) *The Modern World-System: Capitalist Agriculture and the Origins of the European World Economy in the Sixteenth Century*, New York: Academic Press.

* Waltz, K. N. (1979) *Theory of International Politics*, Reading, Mass.: Addison-Wesley.

Wayman, F. W. (1984) 'Voices prophesying war: events and perceptions as indicators of conflict potential in the Middle East', in J. D. Singer and R. Stoll (eds) *Quantitative Indicators in World Politics*, New York: Praeger.

* Wight, Martin (1966) 'Why is there no international relations theory?', in H. Butterfield and M. Wight (eds) *Diplomatic Investigations: Essays in the Theory of International Politics*, London: Allen & Unwin.

* Wolfers, A. (1952) ' "National security" as an ambiguous symbol', *Political Science Quarterly* 67 (4): 481–502.
____(1959) 'The actors in international politics', in W. T. R. Fox (ed.) *Theoretical Aspects of International Relations*, South Bend, Ind.: University of Notre Dame Press.

Young, O. (1980) 'International regimes: problems of concept formation', *World Politics* 32 (3): 331–56.

Zinnes, D. A. (1976) *Contemporary Research in International Relations: A Perspective and a Critical Appraisal*, New York: Free Press.

53

INTERNATIONAL LAW

EDWARD MCWHINNEY

International law, like national law, reflects the particular eras in which its main principles and processes originated – the values and aspirations of the key political elites and their supporting legal skill-groups, and the compromises and balancing among competing societal interest groups that they have felt it expedient to make. This symbiotic relation between law and society is the key to understanding the role and mission of international law in periods, like the present, of fundamental change and transition in the world community and in the world public order system.

Contemporary international law displays co-existence and sometimes outright conflict between different bodies of legal rules and principles and institutions, inherited from different time periods in international relations; and also between different, competing political-ideological conceptions or visions of the direction and purposes to be given to the international law-making process in shaping the future course of International Society. The antinomy is sometimes made for these purposes between a postulated 'old' international law (usually referred to as 'classical' international law), and a 'new' international law which, by definition, will be universal or at least representative, in trans-cultural, trans-systemic terms.

Classical international law flowed from the mid-seventeenth century political settlement in Europe at the end of the Thirty Years War. It was the creation of those new Western European states, founded on the rise of commerce and on the new doctrines of state sovereignty, that were the main heirs of the political system created by the Treaty of Westphalia of 1648. Elements of the modern system of world public order created by the state practice of those new, succession states (customary international law), and by the treaties that they made between themselves (treaty law), and by the theoretical rationalizations and justifications prepared for them by their professional legal advisers and learned text-writers (legal doctrines), certainly drew upon earlier Roman law and other principles. However, most of the law emerging from the mid-seventeenth century onwards was created *de novo*, responding to considerations of comity and good neighbourliness and business efficacy between the Western European states, usually determined on a basis of mutual and reciprocal self-interest, though, failing any such consensus, always capable of being resolved and imposed by resort to force and direct action.

Classical international law, because of the effective monopoly of political and economic power by the Western European states in the post-Westphalia era in international relations, and also because of the intellectual dominance of Western European jurists and text-writers, was heavily relativist in cultural as well as socio-economic terms. It was Eurocentrist, in contemporary legal language. This undoubted historical truth, together with the frequent naked-ness of the response of classical international law to the self-interest of the Western-European-trading commercial powers involved, have been the prime grounds of attack upon its principles and rules in the post-Second World War era.

With the dissolution, by force-of-arms if need be, of the European colonial empires overseas in the wave of decolonization and national self-determination of the late 1940s, 1950s and early 1960s, the world community and its main public arenas – the United Nations and its specialized agencies, but also general diplomatic negotiating conferences – had to be opened up to the flood of 'new' Asian, African and Caribbean states formed out of the remnants of European imperialism. These new countries were, understandably enough, intolerant of an international law that they viewed as having sanctioned or legitimated the erstwhile imperial powers' seizure of their lands and spoliation of their natural resources ('acquisition of territorial title by discovery and occupation, sovereignty over natural resources'). The new countries were resistant to the body of inherited legal rules (customary international law) in whose creation and subsequent elaboration those new countries themselves had by definition (as legal non-members of the world community at the relevant historical stages) never participated. The opposition by the new states, newly admitted to the United Nations and to the other main international law-making arenas, to classical international law brought, in high-level, doctrinal-legal terms, the demand for elaboration of a 'new', post-Classical international law; and, more importantly perhaps, in more low-level, concrete legal terms, the search for new arenas and new processes for law making as a method of re-making international law in contemporary terms (sources of international law). With the rapid transformation of the United Nations from the mid-1950s onwards, as decolonization and independence were progressively achieved, the countries newly admitted to the United Nations soon achieved an effective voting majority within the United Nations General Assembly, which they then proceeded to use, so long as they themselves remained in coalition, to legislate, in the form of General Assembly resolutions, revolutionary changes or additions to traditional international law.

Among these projects was that of a New International Economic Order. This was sponsored by three programmatic resolutions adopted by the General Assembly in the early 1970s and designed to restore national sovereignty over foreign-owned economic resources to the newly decolonized countries, and also, more generally and more vaguely, to ensure a more equitable participation of those new countries in the processes, and also the resultant material gains, of international trade and commerce. UN General Assembly-based activism by the new, 'Third World' countries was also the direct stimulus of a series of General Assembly resolutions designed to interdict nuclear weapons and their testing and dissemination or proliferation, so as to make up for a certain dragging of feet on nuclear and general disarmament by the two great political-military blocs, Soviet and Western, after 1945. Revived or vestigial Cold War ideological conflicts between the two superpowers in the late 1970s and early 1980s threatened the step-by-step, problem-oriented, treaty-making approach to nuclear and general disarmament inaugurated by Nikita Khrushchev and his US counterparts in the early 1960s in the then new era of 'big power, peaceful co-existence' (later *détente*).

The Third World majority in the United Nations, and their supporting jurists, argued that the General Assembly resolutions – adopted, as they invariably were, by overwhelming majorities, with only a few Western states holding out in the form of negative votes or abstentions – effectively made new law. UN General Assembly resolutions would qualify, thereby, as new sources of international law, side by side with traditional or classical sources. As an abstract, *a priori* legal issue, this debate over the new sources remains unresolved. Western and Soviet jurists have conceded, equally, that resolutions of the General Assembly, if adopted unanimously or at least with substantial intersystemic consensus – Western bloc, Soviet bloc and Third World – may acquire normative legal quality in their own right. This has clearly become the case by now, with most of the great General Assembly resolutions on decolonization and self-determination of peoples, sovereignty over natural resources, and nuclear and general disarmament, however intransigent the last-ditch resistance of predominantly Western members may have been at the actual time of their adoption.

Where such resolutions have been followed up, as they usually have been – for example, in the area of nuclear and general disarmament, and in space law – by UN General Assembly-sponsored specialized treaty making or international codification drafting conferences, then the 'new' sources of international law rejoin the 'old' sources through the form of the final, finished treaty product. In fact, the discovery of the international treaty, whether bilateral treaty or multilateral convention, and the marked exponential increase in recourse to treaties in the post-Second World War era have facilitated a graceful and speedy transition from a corpus of essentially custom-based, 'old', out-dated international law to a genuinely contemporary system. This can be said not only for new fields like air and space law but also for 'old' fields like the Law of the Sea where technological change and a heightened sense of distributive justice and equity have demonstrated, starkly, the inadequacies of the response of the old, pre-existing, classical rules to contemporary world community expectations and demands.

The contemporary multilateral convention, which is necessarily dependent for its successful conclusion on intersystemic consensus, has proved the prime mechanism of change in international law in the post-Second World War era. It has been estimated, in fact, that many more treaties have now been signed since 1945 than were completed in the three centuries from the Treaty of Westphalia in 1648 up to that time. Even when state signatures to a treaty are not promptly consummated by the last, formal legal stage of state ratification of the treaty – as happened, for example, with the comprehensive and, in so many respects, radically innovatory United Nations Convention on the Law of the Sea, signed in December 1982 – the treaty text may still operate, according to some contemporary juristic thinking, as authoritative evidence of what international law, in its contemporary evolution, has come to be. It may thus acquire normative-legal status *qua* new customary international law, binding equally on states that have signed and ratified the treaty and on states that have done neither. Judge (and later President) Lachs of the International Court of Justice provided the intellectual way for this striking doctrinal-legal advance in his rightly celebrated dissenting opinion in the *North Sea Continental Shelf* case in 1969 (ICJ 1969).

The International Court itself has undergone a remarkable political-legal transformation from the mid-1960s onwards. In its earliest era, between the two world wars, the Court reflected the political balance of power of the times and the then League of Nations (of which it was the principal judicial organ) in being an essentially Western European institution. Its agenda was limited, for practical purposes, to European cases, many of which arose out of the peace settlements at Versailles in 1919. Immediately after 1945 the Court, newly reconstituted as the judicial arm of the new United Nations, continued as an essentially Western-dominated institution, reflecting the prevailing political majority within the United Nations itself over the same time period. It was not until the post-decolonization era and the marked expansion of UN membership as a whole that the Court, with the new states using their new voting power to produce that result, was finally to become, and also to be seen as being, fully representative in ethno-cultural and legal-systemic terms. The transition from 'old' Court to 'new' Court was helped, paradoxically, by the Court's single-vote-majority decision (rendered only on the second, tie-breaking vote of its (Western) President) in *South West Africa, Second Phase* in 1966 (ICJ 1966). There the Court majority, on technically refined and rather precious, abstract procedural grounds, refused to intervene to prevent the extension of the legal regime of apartheid by the white minority government of South Africa to its former League of Nations mandate and now UN Trust Territory, South West Africa (Namibia). The wave of bitterness within the UN General Assembly and elsewhere, over what was seen at the time as a 'white man's' decision rendered by a Western-dominated tribunal, brought a general crisis of confidence and credibility in the Court and, as a direct consequence, a dwindling away in its case-load.

However, with the incremental changes in the Court's membership that were effected through the regular, periodical elections of judges by the UN General Assembly and Security Council, the Court's jurisprudence (case law) began to change too. A new judicial activism, oriented towards the progressive development of International Law in accordance with UN Charter principles rather than to an unimaginative restatement of old law, brought a new popularity for the Court and, by the end of the decade of the 1980s, a very full agenda of cases. By then the Third World states that had once spurned the Court for its perceived Eurocentrism and Western political fixation had become the Court's principal client states. In marked contrast the United States – the principal champion of the Court and of an affirmative, policy-making role for its judges in the earlier, post-Second World War years when Western states dominated the UN General Assembly and its main institutions – angrily walked out of the continuing Court proceedings in *Nicaragua v. US*, in 1984 (ICJ 1984 a, b). The United States followed this up by terminating the US government's general acceptance of the Court's compulsory jurisdiction, in reaction to what it characterized as 'an overreaching of the Court's limits, a departure from its tradition of judicial restraint, and a risky venture into treacherous political waters' (US State Department 1985). This US action was not, however, followed by any other state, and the Court's final judgement in the *Nicaragua* case, in which it ruled against the US government on the main substantive-legal complaints advanced by the Nicaraguan Government, was rendered by a 12-to-3 vote, with three of the four Western judges on the Court, apart from the United States itself, voting against the United States.

What had happened over what President de Gaulle had called the 'post-post-war' period, from the 1960s onwards, was that the United Nations and its main institutions, including the International Court, had lost their original, predominantly Western political flavour or colouration. They had increasingly taken on a universalist character, representative of the larger, more inclusive world community that had emerged with the completion of the historical process of decolonization and self-determination of peoples and with the opening up of all main international legal arenas to the new succession states.

The resultant new Third World majority in the UN General Assembly may sometimes have shown a politically unrealistic, even naïve optimism in its belief in the power of changing international society by general fiat, unaccompanied by concrete, empirically based follow-up measures – as with the legislative triad of General Assembly Resolutions of 1974–5 on the establishment of a New International Economic Order. It is a fact, however, that pragmatic, trial-and-error experience has brought an increasing political-legal sophistication as to the use of the United Nations and its main institutions to produce genuinely operational legal solutions to new world community problems.

In the result, the United Nations itself has been transformed from a limited, treaty-based organization that would be limited strictly to its original treaty-defined competences (the long-time Soviet and Soviet bloc conception, and a latter-day US view) to something approaching a constitutional system of world order, operating autonomously through its own parliamentary-style legislating organs and its co-ordinating executive and judicial institutions. This progressive constitutionalizing of the international law-making process has meant that the bulk of contemporary international law can be be traced back to UN sources, whether General Assembly resolutions, Court decisions, or UN-convened or UN-sponsored diplomatic negotiating conferences charged with the elaboration of multilateral codifying conventions.

In the process of transition from old custom and bilateral treaties to this new, UN-based corpus of legal norms, the content of those same norms has revealed far more continuity and far more tendency to build incrementally upon the old, classical international law than might have been expected from the sharpness of the verbal confrontations and interactions between Western states and Soviet bloc states and new, Third World states between the end of the 1950s and the 1980s. This has been because, in very many concrete cases, the Western states have responded, in timely enough fashion, to the 'winds of change' – political, social and economic – in the world community and acquiesced gracefully in legal updating and modernization. The new, Third World states, for their part, soon discovered (as in the OPEC oil pricing crisis of the early 1970s) that they themselves were characterized as much by practical diversity of wealth and economic opportunity and consequent national interest as by an original, *a priori* conceived homogeneity of foreign policy positions.

Awareness of these new truths produced political cross-currents in the coalition building inherent in parliamentary bodies like the UN General Assembly and in diplomatic negotiating conferences. It also brought an increasing recognition that much of the old, essentially custom-based international law – responding as it had, historically, to the particular interests and demands of the dominant social forces of earlier eras in international relations – nevertheless still continued to make good sense. It only needed some more intellectual imagination and wit in its adaptation to contemporary societal needs and interests. The change in attitudes was reflected in the measured comment of the great Soviet jurist of the post-Second World War era, Gregory Tunkin, that what was called for was not *a* 'new' international law, which would necessarily involve the complete discarding of all the 'old', but 'new' international law, in the sense of a process of incremental, step-by-step updating and modernization of the old, classical rules in concrete cases and problem situations (Tunkin 1963). As this particular operational approach has become accepted, classical international law has given way increasingly to contemporary international law, fusing the old and the new. By the same token, special 'regional' bodies of international law like the so-called Socialist (Soviet) International Law and Latin American International Law – whose main *raison d'être* and intellectual justification was always the postulated inequity and outdatedness of classical international law has a historical response to European or Western political self-interest – have tended to recede as their main imperatives have been progressively incorporated into the emerging norms of contemporary international law.

By the close of the 1980s, Soviet President Mikhail Gorbachev, in formulating the international legal points of his general *perestroika* programme, reversed traditional, long-held Soviet international law attitudes of the era between the two world wars and of the post-1945 period by calling for the acceptance of the United Nations as the prime arena for international conflict-resolution and for increased acceptance of the compulsory jurisdiction of the International Court. At the same time, in its concrete proposals for substantive-legal action, Gorbachev's *perestroika* programme in international law signalled the switch in the last decade of the twentieth century from the peace–war continuum, which had been the basic premise (*Grundnorm*) of international law and relations of the post-1945 era, to a new international law emphasis on co-ordination and co-operation across the old political-ideological frontiers of yesterday. This would embrace, most importantly, international trade and commerce, but also common problem-solving ventures directed towards conservation of the earth's natural resources and global environmental protection. It would also involve the common attempt at reduction of the extreme inequalities in wealth and social opportunities currently existing between the advanced, post-industrial societies (whatever their different national political ideologies) on the one hand and the developing countries (the North–South division) on the other.

BIBLIOGRAPHY

Alvarez, A. (1959) *Le Droit international nouveau*, Paris: Editions Pedone.
Anand, R. P. (1969) *Studies in International Adjudication*, Delhi: Vikas Publications.
Bedjaoui, M. (1979) *Pour un nouvel ordre économique international*, Paris: UNESCO

(published in English as *Towards a New International Economic Order*, New York: Holmes & Meier).

Brierly, J. L. (1963) *The Law of Nations*, 6th edn, Oxford: Clarendon Press.

Dupuy, R.-J. (1974) *The Law of the Sea*, Dobbs Ferry, NY: Oceana/Dordrecht: Martinus Nijhoff.

Elias, T. O. (1988) *Africa and the Development of International Law*, 2nd edn, Dordrecht: Martinus Nijhoff.

Gorbachev, M. (1987) *Perestroika: New Thinking for Our Country and the World*, New York: Harper & Row.

ICJ (1966) *South West Africa: Second Phase*, ICJ Reports 1966, p. 6, The Hague: International Court of Justice.

ICJ (1969) *North Sea Continental Shelf*, ICJ Reports 1969, pp. 3, 228–9, The Hague: International Court of Justice.

ICJ (1984a) *Nicaragua v. USA, Provisional Measures, Order of 10 May 1984*, ICJ Reports 1984, p. 169, The Hague: International Court of Justice.

ICJ (1984b) *Jurisdiction and Admissability, Judgment*, ICJ Reports 1984, p. 392, The Hague: International Court of Justice.

Lachs, M. (1972) *The Law of Outer Space*, Dordrecht: Martinus Nijhoff.

McDougal, M. S. and Feliciano, F. P. (1961) *Law and Minimum World Public Order*, New Haven: Yale University Press.

McDougal, M. S., Lasswell, H. D. and Associates (1960) *Studies in World Public Order*, New Haven: Yale University Press.

McNair, L. (1961) *The Law of Treaties*, Oxford: Clarendon Press.

McWhinney, E. (1970) *Conflit idéologique et ordre public mondial*, Paris: Éditions Pedone.

——(1984) *United Nations Law Making*, New York: Holmes and Meier (published in French as *Les Nations Unies et la formation du droit*, Paris: Éditions Pedone/ UNESCO).

Oda. S. (1977) *The Law of the Sea in our Time*, Dordrecht: Martinus Nijhoff.

Oppenheim, L. (1955) *International Law*, Vol. 1: *Peace*, 8th edn, London: Longmans, Green & Co.

——(1955) *International Law*, Vol. 2: *Disputes, War and Neutrality*, 7th edn, London: Longmans, Green & Co.

Rousseau, C. (1953) *Droit international public*, Paris: Recueil Sirey.

Schwarzenberger, G. (1965) *The Inductive Approach to International Law*, London: Stevens & Sons.

Sen, B. (1988) *A Diplomat's Handbook of International Law and Practice*, 3rd rev. edn, Dordrecht: Martinus Nijhoff.

Sepulveda, C. (1964) *Curso de Derecho Internacional Publico*, 2nd edn, Mexico: Editorial Porrua.

Singh, N. and McWhinney, E. (1989) *Nuclear Weapons and Contemporary International Law*, Dordrecht: Martinus Nijhoff.

Stone, J. (1958) *Aggression and World Order*, Berkeley: University of California Press.

——(1954) *Legal Controls of International Conflict*, New York: Rinehart & Co.

Tunkin, G. I. (1963) Letter to *The Times* (London), 25 February.

——(1967) *Ideologicheskaia borba i mezhdunarodnoe pravo*, Moscow: Izdatelstvo 'Mezhdunarodnie Otnosheniaia'.

——(1983) *Pravo i sila v mezhdunarodnoi sisteme*, Moscow: Izdatelstvo 'Mezhdunarodnie

Otnosheniaia'; published in English, 1985, as *Law and Force in the International System*, Moscow: Progress Publishers.

US State Department (1985) 'Statement of Department of State on U.S. withdrawal from Nicaragua Proceedings, 18 January 1985', *American Journal of International Law* 79: 438, 441.

Visscher, C. de (1963) *Problèmes d'interprétation judiciaire en droit international public*, Paris: Éditions Pedone.

Wengler, W. (1964) *Völkerrecht*, Vols 1 and 2, Berlin: Springer Verlag.

54

INTERNATIONAL INSTITUTIONS

ROBERT O. KEOHANE AND CRAIG N. MURPHY

Institutions are persistent and connected sets of rules (formal and informal) that prescribe behavioural roles, constrain activity and shape expectations. Social scientists use this broad definition to refer both to generic categories of human relations, such as sovereign statehood, diplomacy or war, and to specific arrangements, such as the Roman Catholic Church, the Second International or the General Agreement on Tariffs and Trade. The discussion of international institutions in this essay will focus principally on specific international institutions: governmental and non-governmental organizations and regimes whose activities and rules relate principally to activities taking place across state boundaries.

International institutions, thus defined, may conveniently be classified into four categories:

1 bureaucratic intergovernmental organizations (IGOs) such as the United Nations Educational, Scientific and Cultural Organization (UNESCO) or the World Health Organization;
2 international non-governmental organizations (INGOs) such as the International Committee of the Red Cross or the International Council of Scientific Unions;
3 international regimes, such as the international trade regime, which are sets of rules created by explicit agreements among states; and
4 conventions – informal norms and practices, such as reciprocity, that shape the expectations and therefore the behaviour of actors.

When most people think of 'international institutions', they think only of IGOs and, among those, only the IGOs that almost all states join. The first modern organization of this sort, the International Telegraph Union – now the International Telecommunication Union (ITU) – was founded in 1865 to facilitate agreements on standards for international telegraphic transmission. By the end of the First World War almost fifty IGOs existed, rising to about seventy-five at the end of the Second World War, 200 by the early 1960s, and to over 300 by the early 1980s (Jacobson 1984: 37, 40). Throughout this period, with the brief exception of the years immediately following the Second World War, the largest number of international organizational activities have been designed, as was the ITU, to facilitate commerce.

Second in number of activities (first in the period after 1945) has been the issue area of regulating diplomatic and conflict-oriented relations between states, although by 1980 it had been overtaken by development activities. IGOs also have maintained significant involvement on issues concerning agriculture, labour and – especially in recent years – human rights. In 1980 the most active IGOs were led by the central organs of the United Nations, followed by the International Labour Organization, World Bank, International Monetary Fund, UN High Commissioner for Refugees and UNESCO (Murphy 1986). Although most major international organizations have virtually universal membership, industrialized countries are much more heavily represented in IGOs than their less economically developed counterparts.

International non-governmental organizations (INGOs) predate IGOs and are more numerous. The first INGO by contemporary criteria, the Rosicrucian Order, dates from the seventeenth century, and in the nineteenth century a number of INGOs, such as the Anti-Slavery Society, were formed. The Union of International Associations counted over 4,000 INGOs in 1980. INGOs are in general smaller organizations than IGOs, and they have less opportunity to mobilize state power for their objectives. Their membership patterns are even more biased toward the economically industrialized and politically pluralistic part of the world than are those of IGOs (Jacobson 1984: 53).

International regimes are institutions with explicit rules, agreed upon by governments, that pertain to particular sets of issues in international relations (Krasner 1983; Keohane 1984). IGOs help manage and revise international regimes. Indeed, some international regimes revolve around single organizations – such as the International Labour Organization, the ITU or the International Atomic Energy Agency. In these instances we can think of the regime as an overall set of rules and practices, and the IGO as the purposive bureaucratic organization that monitors and reacts to activity. In a sense, the IGO is the spider and the regime the spider's web.

For other international regimes, however, the rules reflect the activity of several international organizations as well as states acting bilaterally or in *ad hoc* ways. The international regime governing exchange rate management, for instance, has involved bureaucracies from the Organization for Economic Cooperation and Development (OECD), the Bank for International Settlements (BIS), and the institutionalized annual summit meetings among seven industrialized countries, as well as the International Monetary Fund (IMF). The international food regime includes both the World Food Programme and the

Food and Agriculture Organization; the development regime involves the IMF, the United Nations Conference on Trade and Development and the World Bank, as well as many other specialized agencies of the United Nations system.

No single spider spins these webs but all are able to co-ordinate their work. Conventions are the institutions, with implicit rules and understandings, that shape the expectations and behaviour of actors. They enable states, non-governmental organizations and secretariats of international organizations to co-ordinate their behaviour on the basis of common practices. They are not only pervasive in world politics but are logically and temporally prior to international regimes, INGOs or IGOs. Indeed, both international regimes and international organizations depended on the existence of widely understood conventions that make negotiations possible (Keohane 1989: 4).

INSTITUTIONALIZATION IN WORLD POLITICS

Much behaviour in world politics is recognized by participants as reflecting established norms, conventions and rules, and indeed could not be interpreted accurately without a knowledge of these institutionalized practices. In this sense, modern world politics has been institutionalized to some extent ever since the early seventeenth century, when the doctrine of sovereignty became widely accepted, along with two corollaries: institutionalized toleration for the 'little islands of alien sovereignty' represented by embassies; and international law, which was required, Grotius argued in 1625, if states were to be preserved (Mattingly 1955: 241, 255). World politics is 'anarchic' only in the sense that it lacks common government, with the power to enforce its decrees on states. International society is not anarchic, if this were to mean chaos, an absence of regularized norms of behaviour, or the Hobbesian 'war of all against all'. As Hedley Bull expressed the point, an international society exists when a group of states 'conceive themselves to be bound by a common set of rules in their relations with one another, and share in the working of common institutions' (Bull 1977: 13).

In world politics, decentralization of power and the institutionalization of common rules and practices co-exist. But the mixture of decentralization and institutionalization is not constant from region to region, issue to issue, or over time. Institutionalization all but collapsed, with the exception of practices of diplomatic immunity and certain laws of war, during the total wars of this century: influence was exercised through the application of force. By contrast, relations among Western European states since 1950 have been highly institutionalized, with increasingly elaborate sets of rules governing relations among the countries of the European Community and to some extent between them and their neighbours. Among the advanced industrialized democracies, an unprecedented set of international institutions has arisen since the Second

World War, involving international regimes and organizations as well as informal and formal conventions.

The increasing institutionalization of aspects of world politics is indicated not only by the growth in numbers and activity levels of international organizations but also by the increased scope of international regimes. After the Second World War, international regimes were established to deal with issues of exchange rates, trade, reconstruction, food and agriculture, and airline transportation, among others; in the 1950s the conception of economic development led to a proliferation of organizations devoted to it, and hopes for peaceful uses of nuclear energy led to the International Atomic Energy Agency; recently we have witnessed the emergence of highly elaborated regimes governing debt, the oceans and, increasingly, the global environment. This pattern is not one of linear growth: for instance, the liberal non-discriminatory trade regime that came to fruition after the Kennedy Round in the 1960s has eroded in a number of areas. Institutionalization is uneven by issue area: for instance, there is still no global international regime for petroleum production and marketing, much less for energy or raw materials in general.

Furthermore, since international institutions reflect the interests of influential states and non-state actors, they are often morally contestable: the ITU can be viewed not as an exemplar of international co-operation but as an international cartel of telecommunications agencies; the international debt regime of the 1980s can be seen as a network of rules and norms that protect bank profits by limiting the ability of indebted governments to default on their obligations. To observe that the institutionalization of world politics has increased does not imply that progress in a normative sense has necessarily been made.

The study of international institutions is significant for world politics because international institutions have increasingly become a major locus of public policy formulation at the international level. States seek to use international institutions to achieve their purposes; so, increasingly, do multinational corporations, international advocacy groups and professional associations. In formulating international public policy, IGOs are crucial. Working with conventions rooted in the institution of sovereignty, these organizations serve both as targets for states and non-state actors seeking to capture them and as forces trying to transform their own environment. The results of these struggles are international regimes. Since IGOs are the active, purposive element in international institutionalization, in an essay such as this one they deserve pride of place.

THE HISTORICAL EVOLUTION OF
INTERGOVERNMENTAL ORGANIZATIONS

The idea of intergovernmental organizations would have made no sense before the institutionalization of state sovereignty in the early seventeenth century. Until the fifteenth century at any rate, the Christian West thought of itself as a single society, with Roman antecedents, whose 'public good' it was the responsibility of ambassadors to seek (Mattingly 1955: 15–44). Only after the collapse of the unity of Western Christendom was it seen as necessary to begin to reconstruct international society, as Hugo Grotius sought to do in the early seventeenth century. Accepting the principle of sovereignty, Grotius developed a sophisticated conception of international law, which was a precondition for international organization.

The direct inspiration for both the League of Nations and the United Nations Security Council can be traced to authors of the Enlightenment, including William Penn (1644–1718) and the Abbé de Saint-Pierre (1658–1743), and particularly Immanuel Kant (1724–1804), whose *Eternal Peace* remains a classic statement of liberal internationalism. Kant argues that in view of the evils of human nature, 'war itself does not require a special motivation, since it appears to be grafted upon human nature' (Kaut 1949: 451). Hence the problem of international organization is to establish arrangements that will keep order 'even for people of devils, if only they have intelligence' (ibid.: 453). Order would be established on the basis of an association of free states with republican constitutions, which would follow publicly avowed rules of toleration towards one another. Kant's view is distinctly modern, since it not only rejects world government but bases the proposed association on premises of rational self-interest rather than idealistic concern for the common good. His vision is so broad, and his arguments so multi-faceted, that *Eternal Peace*, although less than fifty pages long, could provide the intellectual justification for all the major subsequent plans for world order through international organization.

Kant had declared that 'it is the spirit of commerce which cannot co-exist with war' (Kant 1949: 455). If this had been true, the first set of international organizations to be founded, the Public International Unions of the nineteenth century, would have made a great contribution to peace. These organizations began with the ITU and the Universal Postal Union, and were followed, after the start of the 'Great Depression' in the 1870s, by agencies concerned with perfecting a European rail network, setting measurement and industrial standards, protecting intellectual property and reducing trade restrictions. Later agencies were established, designed to strengthen the power of European agricultural producers, to improve health standards and fight international transmission of disease. Although the activities of the Public International

Unions were largely technical, they had political implications. The Unions served the interests of some of those who benefited from the expansion of international commerce, such as the new industries producing chemicals and drugs, packaged foodstuffs and electrical equipment. In contrast, the International Institute of Agriculture also helped protect European farmers from the results of the technological progress of the railway and steamship, which had made it possible for farmers in Kansas to meet Europe's demand for bread.

The cataclysm of the First World War brought an end to the social order served by the Unions. After the war, the world's attention focused on the Versailles Treaty and the League of Nations, which also had its roots in Enlightenment thinking, as articulated by Kant. Woodrow Wilson shared Kant's emphasis on republican government and open diplomacy, but he made Kant's union of free states more specific, in his proposals for a League that would be able to use military force as well as economic sanctions and moral persuasion against aggressive states (Northedge 1986: 25–45). The United States never joined the League, and Britain and France failed, during the 1930s, to pursue consistent policies of collective security.

Thus the League's collapse before and during the Second World War could be seen by its adherents as reflecting not the inadequacy of collective security as a doctrine but rather the fact that the major powers were unwilling to rely upon an unproven new system and continued to act upon older doctrines as well. The result was incoherent and unsuccessful because the principles of collective security conflicted with fundamental practices of balance-of-power politics, which counsel restricting a state's commitments to its power capabilities, and forming alliances against powerful states that would be capable of threatening one's vital interests. For Britain and France, the first principle implied non-intervention against Japanese attacks on Manchuria in 1931, and the second principle suggested alignment with Mussolini against Hitler rather than sanctions against Italy over its attack on Ethiopia. Collective security depended on a suspension of disbelief in its effectiveness, which could hardly have been demanded of British and French policy makers in the 1930s, with their economies depressed and without assurance of support from the United States (Claude 1962; Northedge 1986).

Less publicized than collective security was the system of formal, international institutions established by the League, or brought under its auspices, to cope with commercial and social issues. Even before the war, the European powers, sometimes with American and Asian states as partners, began to establish formal conventions to regulate labour and interstate conflicts. Both conventions and international bureaux were established to deal with emerging communication and transportation technologies (radio, aircraft, vehicles) before 1914. After the war the impetus behind the labour conventions remained, with the International Labour Organization (ILO) emerging as a minor partner in the construction of the welfare coalitions in many industrial states after the beginning of the Depression, and remaining today as the most important legacy of the League of Nations era. The League also established and operated the first refugee regime, which made an impact on subsequent thought and action on human rights and basic needs.

The United Nations Charter constructed an elaborate system under which the Security Council can take action, including the use of military force, against states threatening world peace. However, the great power veto made it impossible to weild force consistently on behalf of the United Nations either against members of the major blocs or against any other states. After experimenting with the use of force in Korea between 1950 and 1953, and sporadically in the near-anarchy of the Congo (1960–4), the United Nations has emphasized 'peacekeeping' operations, conducted with the consent of the parties on whose soil they are deployed. Peacekeeping forces seek to monitor previously negotiated agreements and keep incidents from escalating into major conflicts. (For more detail, see the entry on the United Nations, pp. 887–99.)

Even more than the League of Nations, the United Nations spawned an array of specialized agencies, each with a distinct set of functions, including food (Food and Agriculture Organization), aviation (International Civil Aviation Organization), care for refugees (UN High Commissioner for Refugees), education (United Nations Educational, Scientific and Cultural Institution – UNESCO) and health (World Health Organization). After the failure of an attempt to created an International Trade Organization, the 'provisional' General Agreement on Tariffs and Trade (GATT), first established in 1947, became the principal international institution dealing with world trade.

The most innovative activities of the United Nations were not anticipated at its founding. The UN has played an important role in decolonization and development, a role which has helped to integrate the less-developed African, Asian and Latin American states into the post-Second World War Western system. The UN role in decolonization developed as an extension of the requirements for monitoring developments in mandates and later UN 'trusteeships', mostly the colonies of powers defeated in the Second World War, to all non-self-governing territories. The United Nations became the principal international forum for movements for national interdependence and a source of strength for them. On development matters, the 'Bretton Woods Twins' – the International Monetary Fund (IMF) and the World Bank, devised at the Bretton Woods Conference in 1944 – have been the instrument of choice for the rich countries. Voting in these organizations is roughly proportional to financial contributions rather than on the principle of one state, one vote. As these organizations have dominated the scene with their financial resources, governments of economically less-developed countries have pleaded, on the whole ineffectively, for the expansion of the development responsibilities of the central organs of the United Nations, where the Third World has a clear majority.

The United Nations, and its loosely affiliated economic organizations, such as the IMF, World Bank and GATT, do not exhaust the array of major IGOs in the last decade of the twentieth century. Contemporary alliances, particularly the North Atlantic Treaty Organization (NATO), have undergone an unprecedented degree of institutionalization over the years. NATO has a complex organizational structure involving a Council of states, a military command structure, production and logistics organizations, and an array of Council Committees (Plano and Olson 1982). The OECD is a major institution seeking to co-ordinate the economic policies of advanced industrialized countries. Perhaps most institutionalized of all, and furthest on the path toward supranational decision making including qualified majority voting, is the European Community (EC), encompassing twelve West European countries in a common internal market with agricultural, transportation, monetary, social and regional policies, and with revenues coming not from governmental subventions – the usual source for IGOs – but from a value-added tax on transactions taking place within the Community area. In a fragmented world, the most effective international organizations are not those with universal membership, but organizations linking like-minded states, usually in the West. Regional organizations elsewhere have had a much more chequered history.

Intergovernmental organizations have certainly affected the agenda of world politics during the last half-century, but they have rarely been decisive in influencing the course of war or peace. The more optimistic Enlightenment and post-Enlightenment thinkers have repeatedly been disappointed by the results of their handiwork. The nineteenth-century Anglo-American citizens' 'peace movement', which encouraged scholarship on 'international organization' (an expression coined in 1867 by University of Edinburgh Professor of International Law, James Lorimer) and which supported the Hague Conferences before the First World War, had expected much faster results. When Andrew Carnegie established the Carnegie Endowment for International Peace in 1910, he thought that war could soon be abolished, and that after this had been achieved the trustees should seek to eradicate 'the next most degrading remaining evil or evils' (Fabian 1985: 43) whose banishment would advance the human cause. Even in the 1960s, scholars in the international legal tradition still sought *'World Peace through World Law'* (Clark and Sohn 1958), although the ranks of those who believed in this vision had greatly declined since its heyday before 1914.

EXPLANATIONS OF INTERNATIONAL INSTITUTIONS

The idealist interpretation of international institutions as motivated by a desire to achieve the public good has not been able to survive the cynicism of the twentieth century. States control whether international institutions thrive or wither; the behaviour of states is accounted for more reliably by their interests, and their power positions in world politics, than by the rhetoric of their leaders or their intellectuals. E. H. Carr (1946) and Hans J. Morgenthau (1948) effectively won their 'great debate' with the idealists and legalists who had dominated the Anglo-American study of international relations until the onset of the Second World War.

From a realist standpoint, however, international institutions may seem to be anomalous. If states relied entirely on self-help, on their own power, and if world politics were a Hobbesian state of war, we would observe neither the extensiveness of international institutions nor their rapid pattern of growth, especially since 1945. Putting aside idealism of the international legalists, what could account for the institutionalization that we observe?

The most persistent and persuasive answer to this question emphasizes the functions performed by international institutions in a situation of interdependence. Like other doctrines of international organization, this viewpoint has its roots in the Enlightenment, although it is late eighteenth- and early nineteenth-century figures – Jeremy Bentham and James Mill in Britain, Saint-Simon and Comte in France – who can be considered its originators.

The functionalists begin with Adam Smith's conclusions that prosperity increases with the division of labour and the division of labour increases with the extent of the market. The British founders of this tradition emphasized the utility of international co-operation to form a world market. The French, observing the early factory system and the apparent role of scientists and engineers in perfecting the division of labour, imagined something more: a unified, prosperous, productive world fostered by 'technical' co-operation, co-operation designed to do specific things (functions) with the least effort, under the eye of a benign technological elite.

One of the earliest detailed formulations of the combined perspective, in all its complexity, was an 1851 tract by an Englishman, John Wright, entitled (without brevity or modesty) *Christianity and Commerce, the Natural Results of the Geographical Progression of the Railways* or *A Treatise on the Advantage of the Universal Extension of Railways in our Colonies and Other Countries, and the Probability of Increased National Intercommunication Leading to the Early Restoration of the Land of Promise to the Jews* (Wright 1851). Wright proposed that international co-operation to establish a universal rail network would naturally lead to popular demands to establish a worldwide free market, assuring prosperity and the development of industrial economies throughout the world. In this world of riches most of the grounds for war would disappear and the efficient organization of the whole system would demand that long-oppressed peoples be given the space, resources and dignity for self-determination.

Since Wright's time the claims of functionalist scholars have been made a little less grandly, but the logic has remained similar. Around the time of the First World War, scholars reflecting on the experience of decades of functionalist co-operation in Europe made the link from expanding transportation and communication networks to larger markets, greater prosperity and the greater possibility of peace (for example, Reinsch 1911; Hobson 1915; Woolf 1915; Follett 1918).

Between the inter-war years and the 1970s the towering figure in functionalist scholarship, David Mitrany, used the functionalist argument to offer an alternative to what he considered a not particularly fruitful search for ideal 'constitutional' principles for international peace, as embodied by the League and UN charters and by proposals to reform them. He wished to separate power from welfare in order to reunite them later in a higher, more fruitful, synthesis. Socially valuable functions would gradually be extracted from the state system and assigned instead to a growing network of international functional agencies. Ultimately, these agencies would encourage individuals to transfer their loyalties from their national states to a broader international community. A 'working peace system' could, he thought, only be constructed incrementally: 'Sovereignty cannot in fact be transferred effectively through a formula, only through a function. By entrusting an authority with a certain task, carrying with it command over the requisite powers and means, a slice of sovereignty is transferred from the old authority to the new; and the accumulation of such partial transfers in time brings about a translation in the true seat of authority' (Mitrany 1943: 2).

Among the advanced industrialized democracies after the war, particularly in Europe, attempts both to follow and to amend the functionalist logic abounded. 'Neo-functionalists' sought to explore the ways in which supranational processes of decision making could emerge – what Ernst Haas called 'a cumulative pattern of accommodation in which the participants refrain from unconditionally vetoing proposals and instead seek to attain agreement by means of compromises upgrading common interests' (Haas 1964b: 66). Like those of Mitrany, the neo-functionalist arguments were premised on a view of politics that stressed the role of material interests and groups representing those interests. Citizens and corporations in industrialized countries would find that to achieve increased welfare they must progressively centralize public policy making at the regional rather than national level. Yet for the neo-functionalists, this process of regional centralization would be neither smooth nor conflict-free. Power was not seen as separate from welfare; on the contrary, welfare policy was highly politicized. States would not wither away in a fit of absence of mind; instead, government leaders would have to be placed in situations where their own interests in retaining power would lead them to transfer state functions increasingly to the regional level. The experts on which Mitrany relied would have to be politically sophisticated in order to benefit from far-sighted actions of high-level politicians at crucial junctures; only in pluralistic democracies would individuals be likely to consider transferring their loyalty to regional or global levels (Haas 1964a: 47–50).

The neo-functionalist integration process was characterized by conflict rather than harmony. Dissatisfaction rather than contentment would generate demands for greater regional centralization. Nor was neo-functionalist integration expected to be automatic: far-sighted state leaders must take advantage of opportunities created by the process of 'spillover', in which incremental centralization in one issue area would lead to demands for greater centralization elsewhere, and to increasing willingness to delegate powers to supranational institutions. The supranational 'hybrid', it was argued, was neither purely intergovernmental nor truly federal, but was expected to lead to increasing integration, the consequences of which would be 'plainly federating in quality' (Haas 1958: 527).

In the late 1960s and early 1970s, as students of regional integration became disillusioned with their subject, first in the Third World, then even in Europe, the optimism of neo-functionalism began to fade. Ernst Haas declared neo-functionalism 'obsolescent', because the conditions for its successful operation were not met, although he was careful to argue that under specified conditions the processes that it outlined would still take place (Haas 1976). Students of international interdependence, critical of what they regarded as neo-functionalism's teleological and regional orientation, sought to adapt its precepts to understand the emergence and growth of international regimes (Keohane and Nye 1975, 1977).

Eventually, the theory that emerged from this inquiry adopted a truly functionalist standpoint in the sense that the word is normally used in the social sciences: it sought to explain the existence of institutions in terms of ends that they helped to achieve. Since the theorists recognized the crucial role played by states in world politics, they in effect accounted for international institutions by pointing out how they served the ends of powerful actors – thus using realist principles to explain growing institutionalization. Most international institutions, according to this argument, do not challenge authoritative rule by states. In contrast to the expectations of neo-functionalist students of regional integration, no new centralization of authority at the international level is anticipated. Instead, international regimes, and the organizations that operate them, are seen as facilitating mutually beneficial agreements among states principally by reducing uncertainty, which they do by providing information to participants, stabilizing mutual expectations through the development of common standards, and monitoring compliance with international agreements. These 'neo-liberal institutionalist' theories seek to synthesize three elements: a realistic respect for state power; an appreciation of the incentives that international interdependence creates for co-operation; and an understanding of how established institutions themselves affect states' perceptions of their self-interests, by affecting the costs and benefits of alternative courses of action (Keohane 1984, 1989).

What might be called 'neo-Marxist institutionalist' theories share some of these concerns, but emphasize ends served by international institutions in the world economy as a whole rather than in its political structure, the state system, alone. Neo-Marxists see many contemporary international institutions as key parts of the post-war Western 'historical bloc', Antonio Gramsci's term for a complex of economic, political and cultural institutions which enable the social development characteristic of a period (Cox 1982, 1987). Similarly, the Public International Unions of the late nineteenth century could be considered a fundamental part of the historical bloc that Keynes (1971: 10) called an 'economic Eldorado', the European social order from 1870–1914.

The analyst who wants to determine if specific international institutions are fundamental constitutive elements of a particular historical bloc needs to consider not only the immediate 'functions' of the institutions within the society of states (as a neo-institutionalist liberal analyst would) but also the ways in which institutions affect political, economic and cultural relations at all levels of analysis, to the benefit of some social groups and not to the benefit of others.

Many international institutions, in fact, may have played little or no role of this sort, and that may be one reason why they became moribund or disappeared. Still, attempts to create or maintain any international institution can be understood as part of the process of creating or maintaining a historical bloc. The history of the League era can be interpreted as the first, failed attempt to create the Western system finally established after the Second World War (Pijl 1984).

Thus, the Gramscian, like the neo-functionalist, sees conflict at the centre of the process of political integration, and, like the neo-functionalist, the Gramscian puts great emphasis on the need for political leadership and political learning. Gramscians, along with many neo-functionalists, emphasize that people do not immediately act on the basis of the abstract 'interests' that an observer may see as inherent in a particular role; they act on the basis of learned aspirations and world views which may, at times, be related only imperfectly to their interests.

THEORIES OF INSTITUTIONS AND IGO ACTIVITIES

These various theories are compatible in other ways as well, and each illuminates some aspects of the activities of contemporary IGOs better than the others do. At the most fundamental level, formal bureaucratic international institutions are, as the realists would emphasize, clubs of national governments. Yet, as functionalists and neo-functionalists would be more apt to point out, most state members of most IGOs provide themselves with little opportunity for overseeing their day-to-day activities. Governmental oversight of IGOs typically becomes significant only when some members are pushing for innovation in long-standing routines or when a budgetary crisis looms, which most often assures, as the neo-liberal synthesis of realist and neo-functionalist arguments would predict, that IGOs remain 'functional' to state interests.

When budgetary crises do not loom and when innovation is not on the agenda, IGO staffs routinely provide services similar to those provided by relatively professionalized, autonomous and non-political agencies of national or sub-national governments. Research is their most typical activity – investigating development projects, reporting on different national legal practices, suggesting how the next generation of technology (from weather satellites to computer reservation systems) might be best used. Organizing and staffing intergovernmental and transnational conferences is their other most typical activity.

It is in such conferences (or, perhaps more especially, in the domestic political discussions and diplomatic meetings leading up to them and following upon them) that formal, bureaucratic international institutions accomplish their tasks. They provide a more efficient means for transacting the co-operative business of their nation-state members and their constituents than would be provided by informal, bilateral diplomacy and the play of domestic politics without the decision point of an international meeting. Their result can be tacit or formal co-ordination of state or sub-national policies, which makes international affairs – and, of course, often international commerce and investment, and, sometimes, even the relations between citizens and their national governments – a bit more predictable. IGOs thus make the continuation of co-operative arrangements a bit more likely, as the neo-liberals argue.

Some IGO staff also monitor compliance with conventions reached under an agency's auspices. The monitoring done by UN troops is probably the most dramatic form of this activity. Typically, those employed by international agencies share this responsibility with national governments and with particular domestic constituencies within different member states. For example, the staff of GATT keeps track of the 'openness' of international trade, but the most significant monitoring of compliance with GATT agreements is probably done sector by sector by competitors from different countries and by panels set up by GATT on their initiative.

Similarly, although the few IGOs which provide services or resources, like the IMF and the World Bank, may have some ability to retaliate when international conventions have been violated by a state member, the strongest sanction that most have is the ability of the professional staff (rarely) or the membership as a whole (typically) to call upon some or all members to retaliate. This lack of 'enforcement power' does not mean, of course, that international institutions are somehow inherently 'ineffective' in shaping or affecting world politics. It simply means that, for the most part, IGOs only serve an intermediary or intervening role in the *coercive* shaping of international politics and world society. If anything, the few constraints they place on state members serve to preserve the power of those who are already powerful. The few coercive powers of the IGOs can help bind together a historical bloc, not transform it.

This does not mean, however, that IGOs, and even their bureaucratic staffs alone, have no ability to shape world society by building consensus among states. As the neo-functionalists and some Gramscians would argue, that, in fact, is often their role. Moreover, that role need not always be carried out in the immediate interests of the most powerful states or their most powerful constituencies, but can involve the creation of new, co-operative coalitions organized against status quo powers. Much of the history of the UN system revolves around exactly this anti-status quo potential (Murphy 1984). The UN system became the site of origin and one of the primary supporters of the 'Third World' coalition, the Afro-Asian-Latin American alliance concerned with 'development'. While it should be clear that this alliance failed to achieve its central goal – the establishment of international institutions that would make the increasing wealth of industrialized market states contingent upon a more rapid advance of those that were less industrialized – its impact has not been inconsequential. The rapid pace of post-war decolonization and the emergence of 'development' as a central issue of world politics have been its major legacies.

CONCLUSIONS

While the capacity of IGOs to transform world society is inherently limited and a function of the potential for co-operation among national governments, it would be unwarranted to conclude that the role of international institutions is marginal. International politics has always been institutionalized and cannot be understood apart from the conventions that help constitute the society of states, at the very least. In the last century and a half, international politics has been increasingly institutionalized; the scope of formal regimes and IGOs, not to mention that of INGOs, has grown tremendously since the Industrial

Revolution. It is difficult to understand periods of relative prosperity and peace since then (the late nineteenth century in Europe and the post-Second World War era in the West) without taking the effectiveness of international institutions into account. And it is difficult to understand periods of relative austerity and violent conflict (the first half of this century) without considering the ineffectiveness of international institutions.

Not surprisingly, over the same long period the study of international institutions, rooted in the political economy of the Enlightenment, has many of the characteristics of a long-standing progressive research programme. Arguably, our knowledge of international institutions has grown, and contemporary theories have built directly upon the strongest foundations provided by their predecessors. Perhaps somewhat more surprisingly, the central tradition of scholarly reflection on international institutions, going back to Kant and Smith, has continuously influenced the development of actual international institutions as well.

BIBLIOGRAPHY

Augelli, E. and Murphy, C. N. (1988) *America's Quest for Supremacy and the Third World*, London: Pinter.

Bull, H. (1977) *The Anarchical Society: A Study of Order in World Politics*, New York: Columbia University Press.

Carr, E. H. (1946) *The Twenty Years' Crisis, 1919–1939*, 2nd edn, London: Macmillan.

Clark, G. and Sohn, L. B. (1958) *World Peace Through World Law*, Cambridge, Mass.: Harvard University Press.

Claude, I. L. (1962) *Power and International Relations*, New York: Random House.

Cox, R. W. (1982) 'Production and hegemony: toward a political economy of world order', in H. K. Jacobson and D. Sidjanski (eds) *The Emerging International Economic Order: Dynamic Processes, Constraints and Opportunities*, Beverly Hills: Sage Publications.

——(1987) *Production, Power, and World Order: Social Forces in the Making of History*, New York: Columbia University Press.

Cox, R. W. and Jacobson, H. K. (eds) (1974) *The Anatomy of Influence: Decision Making in International Organization*, New Haven: Yale University Press.

Deutsch, K. W. *et al.* (1957) *Political Community in the North Atlantic Area: International Organization in Light of Historical Experience*, Princeton: Princeton University Press.

Fabian, L. L. (1985) *Andrew Carnegie's Peace Endowment*, New York: Carnegie Endowment for International Peace.

Follett, M. P. (1918) *The New State: Group Organization the Solution of Popular Government*, New York: Longmans, Green & Co.

Haas, E. B. (1958) *The Uniting of Europe*, Stanford: Stanford University Press.

——(1964a) *Beyond the Nation-State*, Stanford: Stanford University Press.

——(1964b) Technocracy, pluralism and the new Europe', in S. R. Graubard (ed.) *A New Europe*, Boston: Houghton Mifflin.

_____(1976) 'Turbulent fields and the theory of regional integration', *International Organization* 30: 173–212.

Hobson, J. A. (1915) *Towards International Government*, London: Allen & Unwin.

Jacobson, H. K. (1984) *Networks of Interdependence: International Organizations and the Global Political System*, 2nd edn, New York: Alfred A. Knopf.

Kant, I. (1949) 'Eternal peace' (1795), in C. J. Friedrich (ed.) *The Philosophy of Kant*, New York: Modern Library.

Keohane, R. O. (1984) *After Hegemony: Cooperation and Discord in the World Political Economy*, Princeton: Princeton University Press.

_____(1989) *International Institutions and State Power: Essays in International Relations Theory*, Boulder, Colo.: Westview Press.

Keohane, R. O. and Nye, J. S. (1975) 'International interdependence and integration', in F. I. Greenstein and N. W. Polsby (eds) *Handbook of Political Science*, Vol. 8, Reading, Mass.: Addison-Wesley.

_____(1977) *Power and Interdependence: World Politics in Transition*, Boston: Little, Brown & Co.

Keynes, J. M. (1971) *The Economic Consequences of the Peace* (1920), New York: Harper & Row.

Krasner, S. D. (ed.) (1983) *International Regimes*, Ithaca, NY: Cornell University Press.

Mattingly, G. (1955) *Renaissance Diplomacy*, Boston: Houghton Mifflin.

Mitrany, D. (1943) *A Working Peace System: An Argument for the Functional Development of International Organization*, London: Royal Institute of International Affairs.

Morgenthau, H. J. (1948) *Politics Among Nations*, New York: Knopf.

Murphy, C. N. (1984) *The Emergence of the New International Economic Order Ideology*, Boulder, Colo.: Westview Press.

_____(1986) 'State interests and the design of world government as it is', Department of Political Science working paper, Wellesley, Mass.: Wellesley College.

Northedge, F. S. (1986) *The League of Nations: Its Life and Times, 1920–1946*, New York: Holmes & Meier.

Nye, J. S. (1971) *Peace in Parts: Integration and Conflict in Regional Organization*, Boston: Little, Brown & Co.

Pijl, K. van der (1984) *The Making of an Atlantic Ruling Class*, London: Verso.

Plano, J. C. and Olson, R. (1982) *The International Relations Dictionary*, 3rd edn, Santa Barbara: ABC–CLIO Press.

Reinsch, P. S. (1911) *Public International Unions: Their Work and Organization*, Boston: Ginn & Co.

Taylor, P. and Groom, A. J. R. (eds) (1988) *International Institutions at Work*, London: Pinter.

Woolf, L. (1915) *International Government*, London: Fabian Society.

Wright, J. (1851) *Christianity and Commerce, the Natural Results of the Geographic Progression of the Railways*, London: Dolman.

55

THE UNITED NATIONS

PETER R. BAEHR

The United Nations (UN) is an intergovernmental organization that emerged from the Second World War. It was, in fact, the successor to the League of Nations, which was widely considered to have been a failure. In a series of conferences during the Second World War, the allied powers prepared the outline of a new organization which was meant to do the job that the League of Nations had failed to do: the preservation of international peace and security. These conferences culminated in a major meeting in San Francisco, where in June 1945 the representatives of fifty victorious states signed the United Nations Charter. The Charter entered into force on 24 October 1945. Forty-six years later, the organization still exists and has meanwhile grown to 166 members.

The main purpose of the organization is to maintain international peace and security. In addition, the Charter mentions three other purposes: to develop friendly relations among nations, based on respect for the principle of equal rights and self-determination of peoples; to achieve international co-operation in solving international problems of an economic, social, cultural or humanitarian character and in promoting and encouraging respect for human rights; and to be a centre of harmonizing the actions of nations in the attainment of these common ends.

This essay deals with a number of issues which illustrate the major problems that the UN is currently facing and that are likely to shape its position in the years to come.

MAINTENANCE OF INTERNATIONAL PEACE AND SECURITY

The founders of the UN wanted the new organization to be more effective than its predecessor in the maintenance of international peace and security. Under chapter VI of the Charter ('pacific settlement of disputes'), conflicting parties are obliged to try to find a peaceful solution to their dispute. They are forbidden to threaten or to use violence, but told to employ negotiation or inquiry to develop more information. Furthermore, the Charter lists methods of mediation, conciliation and arbitration. Arbitration and judicial settlement may result in a legal decision that is binding on the parties. If the parties fail to reach a settlement, the conflict may be submitted to the Security Council, which can recommend a return to any of the listed techniques or select observers for an inquiry, or a mediator, or a conciliation group. The Security Council consisted originally of eleven – now fifteen – members, including the United States, the Soviet Union, the United Kingdom, France and China as permanent members. It is permanently in session and, in the case of an actual outbreak of armed conflict, it is meant to dispose of military and other means in the application of enforcement measures. The members of the United Nations are obliged to help the Security Council in the execution of such enforcement measures under chapter VII of the Charter ('action with respect to threats to the peace, breaches of the peace, and acts of aggression'). This system is commonly referred to as 'collective security'.

A precondition for this system to be effective was continued co-operation among the major wartime allies, in particular between the United States and the Soviet Union. It soon turned out, however, that this precondition was not to be met. The major powers could not, for instance, agree on the size and the composition of the military forces to be put at the disposal of the Security Council, which meant that the Council lacked the teeth that its originators had intended. Moreover, during the Cold War between East and West, decision making in the Council was often paralysed by the right of veto, which the five permanent members can use on matters of substance. Although many political and security matters were put before the Council, it only seldom succeeded in solving them. Its activities at the outbreak of the Korean war (1950) were only made possible through special circumstances: the Soviet Union was boycotting the meetings of the Council to protest against the continued presence of the delegate of the Nationalist Government as the official representative of China. That was the reason why the Security Council could adopt the United States proposal to call on member states to give military support to South Korea. The UN forces, fighting under a United States military commander, succeeded in restoring the situation that existed before the hostilities broke out. Due to Chinese military intervention on the side of North Korea, however, efforts to reunite Korea by military force failed. To this day, United States and South Korean forces operate in Korea under the flag of the United Nations. Still awaiting reunification, the two Koreas became members of the United Nations in late 1991.

For many years, the Security Council was only marginally successful in contributing to the maintenance of international peace and security. For example, in spite of considerable efforts, it was not able to establish a lasting peace between Israel and its Arab neighbours (formal peace between Israel and Egypt was the result of efforts by the United States rather than by the United Nations). However, more recently, thanks to the improved relations between East and West, the role of the Security Council has gained renewed importance. It adopted military sanctions and made possible the successful military operation to end the Iraqi conquest of Kuwait in 1990–1. It played a significant role in the withdrawal of Soviet military units from Afghanistan, in the creation of an effective ceasefire which brought the Gulf War between Iran and Iraq to an end, and in the preparation of Namibian independence. In those instances the Council relied on peacekeeping operations to help carry out its resolutions. These operations lack a formal legal basis in the Charter, though joking reference has been made to 'chapter six-and-a-half', as they fall somewhere between the provisions of chapters VI and VII of the Charter.

PEACEKEEPING OPERATIONS

The Secretary-General – the chief executive officer of the United Nations – progressively developed an important role as a mediator in international conflicts. Article 99 of the Charter gives him or her the right to bring to the attention of the Security Council any matter which in his or her opinion may threaten the maintenance of international peace and security. This means that, from the beginning, the Secretary-General was expected to fulfil a political role. In particular, the second Secretary-General, Dag Hammarskjöld from Sweden (1953–61), made use of what he called 'quiet diplomacy': operating behind the scenes to bring conflicting parties together. He also gave impetus to so-called peacekeeping operations by the United Nations: relatively small, lightly armed military units which, with the approval of the conflicting parties, are stationed in the disputed territory, with the task, among others, of supervising truce agreements or maintaining law and order. In territories such as the Middle East, the Congo (now Zaïre), Cyprus and Namibia these units have fulfilled a useful role. Peacekeeping units were deployed for the first time in the Suez Crisis of 1956: the United Nations Emergency Force (UNEF) took over the positions evacuated by the British and French and the Israeli forces; later, UNEF was stationed along the Egyptian–Israeli border until they were withdrawn in 1967 at the request of Egypt's President Nasser. Hammarskjöld's successor, Secretary-General U Thant, was criticized for acceding to this demand, but he had in fact no alternative: if the host state is no longer willing to accept UN forces on its territory, there is little the UN can do about it. This illustrates one of the major weaknesses of this type of operation. Another problem is to secure the necessary funds. The improved relations between the United States and the states of the former Soviet Union – who themselves have never directly participated in peacekeeping operations – may help to create better conditions for making such operations feasible.

SYMBOLIC ROLE

The UN plays a considerable symbolic and psychological role for the states that have emerged since the Second World War. The UN has, in fact, played a major role in the decolonization process in the former European colonies in Africa and Asia. Nearly all of the territories that were placed under UN trusteeship after the Second World War have reached full political independence. The principle of self-determination and the Declaration Regarding Non-self-governing Territories contained in chapter XI of the Charter laid the foundation for the independence of the other colonies. The former German colony of South-West Africa – nowadays called Namibia – is the most recent example of such attainment of independence.

During the forty-six years of the UN's existence, the nature of its membership has changed from one dominated by states on the European and American continents (71 per cent in 1945) to one consisting of a majority of states from Asia and Africa (54 per cent in 1991). For the latter, the UN symbolizes their legal equality with the older established states. One of the first things for the government of any newly established state to do is to apply for membership of the UN. Having its flag raised in the long row on United Nations Plaza in front of the UN buildings in New York, and taking its seat as an equal partner in the General Assembly, gives physical expression and recognition to its newly acquired status.

What may be seen as a solution of a problem to these states means the creation of a problem to others. The General Assembly is now dominated by a majority of poor nations, many of which have only a very small population. Every year this majority adopts a large number of resolutions on a variety of subjects, against the objections of older, richer – mainly Western – states, such as the United States and the United Kingdom. Although these resolutions are not legally binding, they have the symbolic power of representing the views of a majority of the nations of the world. Among these resolutions there are always a number condemning South Africa's policy of apartheid and Israeli policy in the occupied territories, and urging the Western nations to make greater contributions to improve the position of the poor nations in the world or condemning the West for its supposedly 'neo-colonial' or 'imperialist' attitudes. To the United States this has been especially disconcerting, as during the early years of the UN's existence it was accustomed to dominating decision making in the General Assembly itself. At the beginning of the 1970s, things changed radically and the United States often found itself in the minority – sometimes even a minority of one. At the same time, the United States is still expected to pay the highest assessed annual contribution, amounting to 25 per cent of the UN budget. This situation led to a waning of support by the United States, which used to be one of the most enthusiastic supporters of the UN. The United States Congress has at times withheld contributions and has also adopted the Kassebaum Amendment, which ties US contributions to a demand for a change in the voting system in UN organs to be based on the principle of weighted voting on matters of budgetary consequence, giving each state a number of votes proportional to its financial contribution. Proposals for weighted voting have often been discussed at the UN, but not adopted so far, as the smaller and poorer nations are not inclined to give up their acquired right to an equal voice.

A related problem is that of 'politicization'. This term is used to indicate the emphasis put on political aspects of what would seem at first sight to be mainly technical problems. Thus in functional organizations such as the United Nations Educational, Scientific and Cultural Organization (UNESCO) or the World Health Organization, Arab states are likely to introduce the Arab–Israeli conflict; African states will refer to South Africa's policy of apartheid. This was one of the principal reasons – next to failures of management and irritation over the proposal for a 'New World Information Order', which was seen as a restriction of the freedom of the press – which caused the United States to leave UNESCO in 1985. (It was later followed by the United Kingdom and Singapore.)

The accusation of 'politicization' is usually levelled by those who do not like specific political activities. It should be emphasized, however, that specialized agencies, like the UN itself, are political organs, the members of which are states. It is not surprising, therefore, that in such organs political discussions take place. It would, admittedly, be different if these were bodies composed solely of non-governmental experts.

SOCIO-ECONOMIC CO-OPERATION

From the beginning it was envisaged that the United Nations, unlike the League of Nations, was to have a strong role in the field of socio-economic co-operation. To this end the Economic and Social Council (ECOSOC) was created as a main organ of the organization. The Charter gives it broad jurisdiction related to the general welfare, which is presumed to comprise underlying conditions of peace. Its main tasks include undertaking and initiating studies and reports with respect to international economic, social, cultural, educational, health and related matters. It is also intended to co-ordinate the work of the specialized agencies, some of which, such as the International Labour Organization, the Universal Postal Union and the World Metereological Organization, already existed at the time of the League of Nations.

Yet in reality, ECOSOC has never developed into the major agency in the field of international economic co-operation it was intended to be. The developing nations consider it too much 'a rich men's club', whereas the industrialized nations tend to concentrate their efforts in specialized agencies such as the World Bank and the International Monetary Fund (IMF), where, on the basis of large capital subscriptions and related weighted voting, they can dominate. Although the specialized agencies have to report to ECOSOC, they are in fact autonomous. The directors-general of these agencies head small fiefdoms of their own, with little fear of undue interference by ECOSOC. Aside from the World Bank, the main development programmes are co-ordinated through the United Nations Development Programme, while the developing nations tend to concentrate their efforts on creating a more equitable economic position in the world in the United Nations Conference an Trade and Development (UNCTAD) and the United Nations Industrial Development Organization, which they consider more as organizations of their own. The major post-Second World War international economic problems were not dealt with by ECOSOC; they were handled by *ad hoc* systems such as the Marshall Plan, or by special agencies such as the General Agreement on Tariffs and Trade (GATT), the World Bank or the IMF. The seven major industrialized nations in the world have set up their own series of annual meetings, outside the UN framework. Regional economic systems such as the European Economic Community and the Council for Mutual Economic Aid (COMECON) were developed entirely outside the UN.

UNCTAD, which was founded in 1964, provides the main forum for negotiations between industrialized and developing nations to reach agreement on the goals of development policy. Its task is to promote international trade as an important aspect of general economic development and formulate policy principles on international trade and related issues of economic development. It must also promote the adoption of multilateral trade agreements and serve as a centre for harmonizing trade and related development policies of governments and regional economic groupings. Since the 1960s, the UN has established 'development decades' to speed the development of developing countries. Goals were set for a minimum growth rate for developing nations and for a minimum percentage of gross national product from the industrialized nations to be spent on development aid. These programmes cannot be said to have been singularly successful, but it should be added that the economic problems of the developing world are staggering and it would be rather unfair to blame the UN for not being able to solve them.

HUMAN RIGHTS

From the beginning, the issue of human rights has played an important role in the United Nations. In 1948, the General Assembly adopted the Universal Declaration of Human Rights, which in its preamble is called a 'common standard of achievement for all peoples and all nations'. Though not legally binding, it has become the foundation for establishing obligatory legal norms to govern international behaviour with regard to rights of individuals. About ninety states have acceded to the two international covenants – on civil and political rights and on economic, social and cultural rights, respectively – adopted in 1966 and based on the Declaration.

The Commission on Human Rights is the most important UN organ that deals with human rights. It meets annually for a six-week session in Geneva and is composed of fifty-three states, elected for three-year terms by the Economic and Social Council. It has a broad mandate touching on any matter relating to human rights. The Commission carries out studies, prepares recommendations to governments, and drafts international instruments relating to human rights for ratification by governments. It investigates allegations of violations of human rights and receives and processes communications related to such violations. It has appointed 'thematic' rapporteurs on issues such as torture and summary or arbitrary executions, and a working group on enforced or involuntary disappearances. Unique among UN organs is the presence on the floor of about 120 non-governmental organizations which take an active part in the debates (albeit without a vote) and which may submit proposals for adoption by the Commission. Among these non-governmental organizations are well-known defenders of human rights, such as Amnesty International and the International Commission of Jurists.

The Commission on Human Rights has been criticized for having among its members some notorious violators of human rights. For example, the 1990 term of the Commission included among its members China, Ethiopia, Iraq, Peru, Somalia and Sri Lanka – countries whose governments have been cited for gross violations of human rights. These states, as well as non-member governments that attend the sessions of the Commission as observers, make frequent use of their 'right of reply' whenever they find themselves criticized for failing to live up to international human rights standards. It would not, however, be feasible and probably not even advisable to exclude such countries from the Commission: not feasible, as the members of the Commission are elected by the Economic and Social Council on a political and geographical basis; not advisable, as these countries in the Commission can be confronted with the norms they claim to adhere to – such confrontation has at times led to improvements in the situation.

The Commission on Human Rights is a political body, as are most UN organs. So far, Western states have occupied a disproportionately high percentage of its seats – ten out of forty-three. At the behest of the non-aligned nations, the General Assembly decided in 1989 to expand the number of members of the Commission to fifty-three. This would bring the composition of the Commission in line with that of other UN bodies. This will have its effect on decision making as well, as Commission members tend to vote along bloc lines.

An important development in the late 1980s was the increasingly constructive role played by the Soviet Union, which in human rights matters often aligned itself with Western States. It remains to be seen, however, whether the coalition of West and East European states will be able to repulse the onslaught on the functions of the Commission by certain non-aligned governments. The United States has not shown itself inclined to take the lead in that defence, but opted to concentrate on some political concerns of its own, such as the situation in Cuba, which has received a disproportionate part of its attention.

HUMAN ENVIRONMENT

In 1968, the General Assembly called for the organization of a conference on the protection of the human environment. That conference, which took place in Stockholm in 1972, resulted in a Declaration on the Human Environment and in a UN Environment Programme (UNEP) through which most UN activities in this field are channelled.

Concern for environmental issues first arose in the Western industrialized states. Many developing nations originally saw environmental pollution chiefly as a concern and consequence of production and consumption patterns in the West. However, gradual agreement has been reached that a synthesis must be sought between environmental demands and the need for economic development of the poor nations in the world. While the developing nations are expected to make the protection of the human environment part of their development planning, the industrialized states should guarantee that their concern for environmental problems should not be at the expense of economic progress in the less developed world.

The United Nations Environment Programme has remained rather modest in terms of operational and financing capacity. It was never conceived as an executing agency, but more as a catalytic organization which should provide a survey of environmental problems and should try to facilitate and promote international co-operation in the environmental field. Specialized agencies such as the World Health Organization and the Food and Agriculture Organization are engaged in specific environmental programmes such as combating water pollution and the protection of tropical forests, respectively. A great deal of attention has been paid to the progressive development of environmental law. This programme has served as a basis for many of the present conventions concluded or in progress regarding worldwide environmental problems such as the transportation of hazardous waste, the protection of the ozone layer and the protection of regional seas.

In 1987, the World Commission on Environment and Development (1987), commonly known as the Brundtland Commission, published its report *Our Common Future*. In its report, the Commission pointed to the limits of the carrying capacity of our planet to sustain human activities. It introduced the notion of 'sustainable development' in international politics, which it defined as development meeting 'the needs of the present without compromising the ability of future generations to meet their own needs' (ibid.:43). The Commission advocated a new approach to economic growth based on this concept. The relief of poverty should have top priority in this connection, as it can be both a cause and a consequence of environmental degradation. Furthermore, the Commission proposed institutional and legal changes within the UN system and its specialized agencies, including the drafting of a Universal Declaration and a Convention on Environmental Protection and Sustainable Development, reorienting the policies of the multilateral development and financing institutions and searching for new sources of revenue and automatic financing of environmental policies.

Some institutional reform of UN-dealing with environmental issues is clearly needed. To strengthen existing institutions is always easier than setting up an entirely new organ. Proposals for reform will most likely be discussed at the major UN conference on environment and development to be held in 1992. Twenty years after the conference of Stockholm the problems remain similar, but the principal issues have changed, ranging from the international debt problem to holes in the ozone layer and climate change. Many of these problems can only be solved – if at all – by international co-operation on a world scale. The UN would seem to provide the proper framework for such international co-operation.

CHANGE OF ATTITUDE OF THE SOVIET UNION

For many years, the Soviet Union took a rather negative attitude towards the United Nations. While carefully protecting its interests, it avoided constructive initiatives. It was symbolized by Foreign Minister Andrei Gromyko's nickname 'Mr Njet', referring to the many vetoes cast by him in the Security Council in the course of a few years. The Soviet Union did little to develop the activities of the UN and was critical of its expenditures and the level of salaries paid to UN staff members. It consistently opposed the stationing of UN peacekeeping forces and refused to pay its assessed contributions for these 'illegal' operations, the costs of which, in its opinion, should have been borne by the 'aggressors'. Well-known is the Russian *troika* proposal which was intended to undercut Secretary-General Hammarskjöld's position by replacing him by a group of three officials representing the West, the East and the non-aligned world.

With the coming to power of Mikhail Gorbachev this situation changed. In September 1987, he published a major article in the Soviet press setting out his views about the UN. The article contained a plea for closer multilateral co-operation within the framework of the UN. One of his proposals was to establish a UN centre for lessening the danger of war. Wider use should be made of UN military observers and UN peacekeeping forces in disengaging the troops of warring sides, observing ceasefires and armistice agreements. States should be encouraged to co-operate within the framework of the UN in combating international terrorism.

Other proposals by Gorbachev concerned closer co-operation among states to establish economic as well as ecological security. He pleaded for strengthening the role of the UN in the field of human rights and proposed the establishment of a special fund for humanitarian co-operation. He argued that the role of the International Court of Justice should be upgraded and that the international community should encourage the Secretary-General in his mission of good offices, mediation and reconciliation.

The cited proposals were not necessarily very new or revolutionary. But what was entirely new was the fact that they were put forward by the leader of a major power which in the past had never shown much enthusiasm for ideas to strengthen the role of the UN. The article set the tone for a complete change of attitude on the part of Soviet representatives in UN bodies. By 1991 they could be counted among the more staunch defenders of the United Nations and had tabled numerous proposals to strengthen its role.

CONCLUSION

If the United Nations did not exist – it has often been said – it would have to be invented today. The reason for this lies not so much in the actual 'decisions' of its political organs. Many of these decisions take the form of resolutions that are formulated chiefly for the benefit of the home audiences of the governments that sponsor them. Many of them – for example those adopted by the General Assembly and the Security Council on South Africa or on Israel – are ritually repeated year after year, without much consequence. (If things are changing in South Africa, that is only marginally due to actions taken by the UN.)

In the technical field, important work is being done mainly by the staff employed by the Specialized Agencies of the UN. Regular international mail service would be unthinkable without the agreements reached in the framework of the Universal Postal Union. The World Health Organization offers important services in the fight against contagious and other diseases and is rightly proud of its victory over smallpox. UNESCO is continuing its struggle to stamp out illiteracy. The Food and Agriculture Organization has had some success in its work against the occurrence of famine, though especially in Africa too many people still die of starvation. Many of these organizations also take part in the assistance projects set up under the auspices of the United Nations Development Programme.

These examples show where the strength of the UN lies: on those issues where governments are clearly and directly in need of international co-operation. So far, they have not yet been able to agree on solutions to the problems affecting the human environment. Cynics may observe with some truth that the dangers to the environment must become much greater before governments will be prepared to accept the guidance of an international supervisory agency. Industrial pollution of the rivers, the seas and the atmosphere, the rapid disappearance of tropical rainforests, the erosion of the soil and desertification are all growing at such a rate that before long these phenomena may be considered as equally dangerous to the survival of the human race as nuclear war and the spread of disease.

The UN offers an important forum for political leaders to discuss matters of mutual concern. All governments, with the exception of Switzerland, have opted for UN membership. (Switzerland remains outside the UN mainly for domestic political reasons and ostensibly because it fears that UN membership might impair its traditional neutrality; however, the Swiss government offers important services to the UN, providing many UN bodies with their permanent seats on Swiss soil.) Before the existence of the League of Nations and the United Nations, politicians would meet only occasionally to discuss international problems. Now, the UN provides a useful permanent forum for such meetings. If the UN did not exist, each contact among national representatives would have to be organized specially. Contacts arranged at the UN can preserve the confidentiality governments sometimes demand. Smaller and poorer nations that cannot afford to send diplomatic representatives to all national capitals are well served by 'multilateral diplomacy' at the UN.

The UN also serves a useful function in providing 'collective legitimization' to acts of governments. For that purpose, it is important to note that UN organs try more and more to reach consensus rather than decide by a majority vote. A consensus is seen as representing the view of the whole international community and thus carries greater authority. Efforts to reach such consensus often take much time and are usually carried out beyond the glare of publicity. For instance, the public meetings of the Security Council are nowadays often used to give its stamp of approval to a consensus view that has been reached in private negotiations. This may be a far cry from Woodrow Wilson's famous dictum of 'open convenants of peace openly arrived at', but it is probably more effective, as issues of national prestige and the fear of losing face are less at stake in private than in public meetings.

Proposals for UN reform have been manifold. There has been and continues to be a steady flow of proposals by committees and experts, as well as by academic writers and political figures, on how to change procedures in, and the powers of, UN bodies or on how to change the UN Charter. Such proposals are inspired by the fact that a structure designed for fifty members is not necessarily effective for a body of more than three times that many, whose character is less homogeneous than that of the founders.

Yet formal change in the structure of the UN presents a great number of difficulties. To change the Charter, a two-thirds majority of the membership is needed, including the five permanent members of the Security Council. So far, the Charter has been changed only three times, once to enlarge the membership of the Security Council from eleven to fifteen and twice to enlarge the Economic and Social Council from its original eighteen to the present fifty-four members.

On the whole, governments have appeared extremely reluctant to adopt major changes in the structure or procedure of the UN, for fear of losing their established privileges. National independence rates higher than efficient co-operation or effective authority. Thus, for example, the creation of a permanent UN force for peacekeeping operations has, so far, not been possible. No member state has been willing to give the UN the authority to call on it to make a contribution to peacekeeping forces whenever and wherever the organization may decide to use them.

It has often been proposed to increase the number of permanent seats on the Security Council. It is a somewhat anachronistic anomaly that the United Kingdom and France still hold permanent seats, and that countries such as Germany, Japan, India and Brazil do not. However, for such a change the consent of all present permanent members would be needed, and they are not very likely to give such consent. The same applies to the elimination of the veto, which has often been proposed but which never has had a serious chance of adoption.

Another set of suggestions deals with financing. If the UN had its own independent sources of income, at least some of its difficulties might be overcome. The Secretary-General would then no longer have to solicit donations in order to support peacekeeping operations. But, in fact, the lack of finances is more a symptom than a cause of the weakness of the organization. If member states were prepared to strengthen the organization, the necessary finances would follow.

Although it appears to be very difficult to reach agreement on proposals for reform, this does not mean that the UN has been a failure. Its continued existence forty-six years after its foundation, with a membership that is close to universal, testifies to a degree of success. National governments have created the UN for international co-operation and negotiation. Serving that purpose, in spite of all its shortcomings, it fulfils a most useful function.

ACKNOWLEDGEMENT

The author thanks Monique Castermans, Leon Gordenker and Dick Leurdijk for their comments on an earlier version of this paper.

FURTHER READING

Baehr, P. and Gordenker, L. (1984) *The United Nations: Reality and Ideal*, New York: Praeger.

Bertrand, M. (1989) *The Third Generation World Organization*, Dordrecht: Martinus Nijhoff.

Claude, I. L., Jr. (1965) *Swords into Plowshares: The Problems and Progress of International Organization*, 3rd edn, London: University of London Press.

Finkelstein, L. S. (ed.) (1988) *Politics in the United Nations System*, Durham, NC, and London: Duke University Press.

Forsythe, D. P. (ed.) (1989) *The United Nations in the World Political Economy: Essays in Honour of Leon Gordenker*, Basingstoke: Macmillan.

Franck, T. M. (1985) *Nation Against Nation: What Happened to the UN Dream and What the US Can Do About It*, New York and Oxford: Oxford University Press.

Kaufmann, J. (1988) *Conference Diplomacy: An Introductory Analysis*, 2nd edn, Dordrecht: Martinus Nijhoff.

Puchala, D. J. and Choate, R. A. (1989) *The Challenge of Relevance: The United Nations in a Changing World Environment*, Academic Council on the United Nations System.

Roberts, A. and Kingsbury, B. (eds) (1988) *United Nations, Divided World: The UN's Roles in International Relations*, Oxford: Clarendon Press.

Russell, R. B. (1958) *A History of the United Nations Charter*, Washington, DC: Brookings Institution.

Taylor, P. and Groom, A. J. R. (eds) (1988) *International Institutions at Work*, London: Pinter.

World Commission on Environment and Development (1987) *Our Common Future* (the Brundtland Report), Oxford and New York: Oxford University Press.

56

THE INTERNATIONAL COURT OF JUSTICE AND OTHER INTERNATIONAL TRIBUNALS

LORI FISLER DAMROSCH

Antecedents of modern tribunals for international dispute settlement can be found in the distant past, but it was in the nineteenth century that the current forms began to take shape. The United States and Great Britain created successful mechanisms to resolve a number of disputes growing out of the American Revolution, the War of 1812 and the American Civil War, and thereby built momentum for dispute settlement through arbitration. By the end of the nineteenth century, support was growing for the establishment of permanent machinery to resolve disputes pursuant to standing commitments. The Hague Peace Conferences of 1899 and 1907 resulted in the creation of the Permanent Court of Arbitration, which was not really a 'court' but rather a panel of arbitrators available for selection in particular cases. In a pattern of treaties in the early twentieth century, many states agreed to submit their disputes to arbitration, conciliation or other means of settlement.

A true 'permanent court' took shape following the Treaty of Versailles, when the Permanent Court of International Justice (PCIJ) was established at The Hague. The PCIJ was highly active in the inter-war period. Forty-two states (of fifty-two that were members of the League of Nations at one time or another) accepted the PCIJ's jurisdiction for part or all of its effective life (1922–39) (Gross 1987: 21). In sixty-six cases that were submitted to it over eighteen years, the PCIJ rendered thirty-two judgements, twenty-seven advisory opinions and an additional number of substantive orders; some of these decisions were of high political and legal significance, including ones involving interpretation of the peace treaties of 1919 (Rosenne 1989: 15–18).

In 1945, with the creation of the United Nations, the PCIJ was reconstituted as the International Court of Justice (ICJ) and became 'the principal judicial organ of the United Nations' (UN Charter, Article 92). The ICJ, like the PCIJ before it, is often called the 'World Court'.

As an organ of the United Nations, the ICJ serves as one of various methods developed by the international community for the resolution of disputes between states. Article 2 (3) of the UN Charter obligates states to settle their disputes peacefully; and Article 33 enumerates a variety of peaceful means, including negotiation, inquiry, mediation, conciliation, resort to regional agencies, arbitration and judicial settlement. In contrast to the other enumerated methods (which facilitate resolution of disputes through diplomacy), arbitration and judicial settlement entail submission of a dispute to the binding decision of a third party on the basis of law. Arbitration – resolution of the dispute by one or more individuals selected under procedures agreed between the parties – enables the parties to retain relatively more control over the selection of the tribunal and over the procedures and substantive law applicable to the dispute than is the case in judicial settlement. Judicial settlement, also known as adjudication, involves submission of the dispute to an existing court, such as the ICJ, under procedures and rules of law that are often largely outside the control of the parties.

The jurisdiction of the World Court is based on the consent of states, which may be expressed either in advance or after a dispute has arisen, and may be unconditional or limited to particular kinds of disputes. In the present state of international law, a state cannot be compelled to arbitrate or adjudicate a dispute unless it has consented to do so, either in advance or in the context of a particular case.

COMPOSITION OF THE ICJ

The composition of the ICJ has concerned all states that might participate before it, because of the need to ensure confidence in its impartiality and objectivity. The Court's Statute establishes that judges are to be selected from among the most highly qualified jurists and that they are to be independent of any government (Article 2). They are elected by the UN General Assembly and the UN Security Council on the basis of nominations from national groups that are themselves theoretically independent from governments (Articles 4–12). The Court consists of fifteen judges (Article 3); in electing them the UN organs are to take into account 'that in the body as a whole the representation of the main forms of civilization and of the principal legal systems of the world should be assured' (Article 9). Judges serve nine-year terms and may be re-elected (Article 13). In cases where no judge of the nationality of one or more of the parties sits on the Court, those parties may designate a person to sit as a judge *ad hoc* (Article 31).

In practice, issues concerning the composition of the ICJ have plagued it from its inception and have given rise to recurring concerns about the objectivity of the judges and balance in the system as a whole. Socialist and developing countries long viewed the Court as dominated by the West, although these concerns have been alleviated somewhat by greater diversity recently in the selection of judges. What has evolved *de facto* is a system in which the five permanent members of the Security Council are likely to succeed in having judges of their nationality appointed to the Court. Judges from France, the Soviet Union, the United Kingdom and the United States have sat on the Court virtually continually since 1945, and a judge from China (first the Republic of China; now the People's Republic) has held a seat for much of the relevant period. The remaining ten seats are distributed among European, Latin American and Caribbean, Asian and African (including Middle Eastern) jurists.

It has been a cause for concern in some quarters that certain judges come from states that have not themselves accepted the jurisdiction of the Court, as was the case, for example, of the Soviet Union at the time of the *Case Concerning Military and Paramilitary Activities In and Against Nicaragua* (*Nicaragua v. USA*) (ICJ Reports 1984: 392; 1986: 14). Others respond that by virtue of the principle of independence of judges codified in Article 2 of the Court's Statute, a judge's nationality should be irrelevant; but in the perception of many states, nationality can hardly be disregarded.

Various studies have analysed the voting records of ICJ judges to attempt to ascertain whether there are patterns that might cast doubt on the objectivity of the Court. A statistical analysis of all ICJ decisions up until 1986 concluded that the data do not support inferences of bias or of bloc voting; the author found no evidence of significant alignments, on a regional, political or economic basis (Weiss 1987: 123–34). None the less, some governments and observers remain sceptical about whether the Court as a whole, or individual judges serving on it, can be counted on to decide cases fairly.

In recent years, states have taken increasing advantage of a procedure available under the Court's Statute for submission of disputes to a chamber of the Court consisting of three or more (usually five) judges instead of the full fifteen-member tribunal. This procedure was first used in the *Gulf of Maine Boundary* case between the United States and Canada (ICJ Reports 1984: 246) and has subsequently been used in a variety of other cases, including disputes between two African states (Burkina Faso and Mali, 1986) and two Central American states (El Salvador and Honduras, pending as of 1991). A perceived benefit of the chambers procedure is to give the disputing states some say in the selection of judges (or in the elimination of judges viewed as biased against them). Critics of the chambers concept argue that it dilutes the universality and authority of the Court, since judgements rendered by five rather than fifteen judges may not be as fully representative of the interests of the whole international community. Despite these objections, it is likely that the chambers procedure will gain wider acceptance as a means of overcoming concerns about the composition of the Court. In 1989 the United States and the Soviet Union joined in a proposal to support greater use of the Court through chambers.

JURISDICTION OF THE ICJ AND LEGAL EFFECT OF ITS DECISIONS

Only states may be parties in cases before the ICJ (1945 Statute, Article 34). Thus, individuals and companies may not bring cases directly before the ICJ, in contrast to some other tribunals; however, the state of their nationality may bring a claim on their behalf, under a procedure known as diplomatic protection (which may be invoked after the aggrieved private party has exhausted all remedies available in the respondent state).

The ICJ's jurisdiction is founded upon two basic principles: consent and reciprocity. Consent may be expressed in one of several ways, including:

1 by a treaty clause;
2 by special agreement after a dispute has arisen;
3 by means of the so-called 'optional clause' of Article 36 (2) of the Court's Statute, under which states declare unilaterally in advance that they submit to the jurisdiction of the Court in any case or in defined categories of cases;
4 by indicating consent implicitly, such as by responding on the merits without raising a jurisdictional objection.

By virtue of the principle of reciprocity, the Court will not entertain a case unless both claimant and respondent have consented to the Court's jurisdiction over the claim. Accordingly, the respondent is entitled to invoke reciprocally any limitations that the claimant has placed on its own consent.

The Court also has jurisdiction to render advisory opinions at the request of certain international organizations, and has done so in a number of important cases, including ones involving membership, budget and peacekeeping activities of the UN, relations between an international organization and its host state, and the rights of international civil servants. Some of the advisory opinions concern issues going well beyond the internal law of international organizations and have touched on such highly political matters as decolonization of the Western Sahara, the office of the Palestine Liberation Organization in New York, and the legal status of South-West Africa (Namibia).

There is much misunderstanding over whether the Court's decisions are binding on parties concerned with them. Two treaty provisions clearly establish that decisions are indeed obligatory between states that are parties to a particular case. Article 94 (1) of the UN Charter provides that 'Each Member of the United Nations undertakes to comply with the decision of the International Court of Justice in any case to which it is a party', and Article 59 of the Court's Statute provides that a decision of the Court 'has no binding force except between the parties and in respect of that particular case'. In addition to establishing that the Court's decisions do bind the parties to a case, Article 59 is intended to exclude the rule of *stare decisis* that is generally applied in common law but not in civil law countries, under which a court will treat its own precedents as controlling in future cases raising the same issues. Notwithstanding Article 59, the Court has generally tended to respect its own precedents (with some notable exceptions, as in the *South-West Africa* cases discussed below, p. 907); and its decisions are widely viewed as authoritative statements of international law even though they cannot directly bind non-parties. There is a high degree of continuity between the jurisprudence of the PCIJ and the ICJ, with the latter often relying on the former's decisions as precedent.

Advisory opinions requested by international organizations are formally non-binding (in other words, the states concerned with them are not under a legal obligation to abide by them), but those opinions generally enjoy a high degree of authority.

PATTERNS OF ACCEPTANCE OF JURISDICTION AND USE OF THE ICJ

The ICJ's Yearbook lists more than 250 international agreements under which states have accepted the jurisdiction of the ICJ to resolve disputes arising under those agreements. In fact the number is even greater, because pre-1945 agreements accepting the jurisdiction of the PCIJ apply to the ICJ under the latter's Statute (Article 37). In addition, about fifty declarations under the optional clause were in force at the beginning of the 1990s.

It has become common practice for states to qualify their acceptances with reservations under which they exclude or purport to exclude certain categories of disputes. For example, the US declaration, which was in effect from 1946 to 1986 (when it was terminated in the wake of the *Nicaragua* case) contained a provision known as the 'Connally Reservation', exempting matters 'essentially within the domestic jurisdiction of the United States of America as determined by the United States of America' (ICJ Yearbook 1984–5: 99–100). This reservation, and particularly its self-judging feature, provoked much criticism, because it was viewed as substantially negating the effect of the commitment to the Court on the part of the United States and the other states that followed the US model. Another controversial form of reservation excludes the Court's jurisdiction with respect to actions involving armed hostilities; still others limit jurisdiction concerning other categories of disputes.

The ICJ's case-load has been modest in comparison both to average work-loads of national courts and to the aspirations of the ICJ's supporters. For considerable periods of time the Court has had only one or two cases on its docket; from 1963 to 1970 and again from 1975 to 1980, for example, it entered only about one order per year. On the other hand, some of its cases have been extraordinarily complex and difficult, giving rise to weighty volumes of pleadings and judgements of hundreds of pages.

Why are states so reluctant to entrust their disputes to the World Court? Concerns over the composition of the Court are part of the answer, but probably only a small part. Litigation of any sort entails risks for the parties to the dispute – not only that they might lose the particular case, but also that a judicial opinion could enunciate unwelcome legal principles, or that the very process of litigating the case could exacerbate rather than mitigate the tensions underlying the lawsuit. These risks are especially acute as regards litigation before the ICJ. Because of the uncertain nature of the international law that the Court applies, states cannot confidently predict the outcome of a case, nor are states always willing to have their conduct governed by that law. In the view of many states (especially from the developing world), international law is outdated, and the ICJ is perceived as an institution likely to preserve the status quo rather than to promote desirable change. Furthermore, litigation before the Court is often time-consuming and expensive. It is thus no surprise that many governments prefer to let diplomacy run its course rather than to surrender control over a dispute to an unfamiliar and possibly unsympathetic tribunal.

As the 1990s begin, there are hopeful signs of increased interest in the ICJ and possibilities for its revitalization. Although the Court remains severely under-utilized, its case-load is higher than at any time in the past (eleven cases on its docket as of 1991, as compared to three in 1980). One important change is in the attitude of developing countries: after many years of viewing the Court as inhospitable, the developing countries of Africa and Latin America are now accounting for a growing share of the Court's business. Moreover, the Soviet Union recently reversed its long-standing position of rejecting virtually all forms of ICJ dispute settlement: in 1987 Mikhail Gorbachev gave a major speech encouraging resort to the Court, and in 1989 the Soviet Union accepted the Court's jurisdiction under several important human rights treaties. The United States and the Soviet Union formulated a joint proposal for increasing the use of the Court in resolving treaty-based disputes, under conditions that would allow disputes to be submitted to chambers and that would require specific consent if armed activities were at issue. It remains to be seen whether other states will join in this approach.

MAJOR DECISIONS OF THE ICJ

The Court has been asked to rule on a wide variety of important international issues. Although the major powers have not yet looked to the Court to resolve disputes implicating their vital security interests, some of the Court's decisions have touched on matters of high political sensitivity.

Areas in which the Court has had great success include the delimitation of boundaries and the development of the law of the sea. Key cases resolving maritime boundary disputes include those involving the North Sea and Mediterranean continental shelves and the Gulf of Maine. Beyond clarifying principles of maritime boundary delimitation, the Court has enunciated other important principles of the law of the sea in decisions on fisheries zones and on navigation in international straits. Cases involving conflicting claims to land territory have included disputes between France and the UK, Belgium and the Netherlands, Cambodia and Thailand, Honduras and Nicaragua, El Salvador and Honduras, and Burkina Faso and Mali. The decisions in boundary cases have been accepted and applied by the states concerned to a greater degree than in other categories of cases, and the Court's decisions on the law of the sea have exerted a considerable influence over subsequent developments.

More controversial have been cases in which the Court has been asked to render judgement on the legality of policies or practices which the respondent state has viewed as implicating its national security or other vital interests. An example is the *Nicaragua* case, in which the Court decided (among other things) that the United States had violated international law by laying mines in Nicaraguan waters and by training, arming and financing counter-revolutionaries (*contras*) who sought to overthrow the government of Nicaragua (ICJ Reports 1986: 14). In the initial stages of the case, the USA contended that the Court lacked jurisdiction over Nicaragua's claim and that disputes involving armed hostilities were inappropriate for resolution by the ICJ. In the US view, the primary role of the UN Security Council in preserving the peace and the inherent right of states to individual and collective self-defence should have excluded the Court from any involvement in an ongoing armed conflict. When the Court rejected these arguments (ICJ Reports 1984: 392), the United States refused to participate further in the proceedings and also terminated its declaration under the optional clause that the Court had relied on as a jurisdictional basis in the case.

The United States was claimant in the *Case Concerning US Diplomatic and Consular Staff in Tehran* (*USA v. Iran*), which sought release of the US diplomatic and consular personnel who were being held hostage in Iran in violation of several international treaties (ICJ Reports 1979: 7; 1980: 3). Iran refused to participate in the case, claiming that the hostage matter could not be divorced from a larger political context, including years of US interference in

Iran's affairs. The Court maintained a position that it had adopted in previous cases (and would soon again apply in the *Nicaragua* case), to the effect that political considerations do not prevent the Court from resolving legal questions that are otherwise properly before it. Accordingly, the Court ordered Iran to release the hostages (ICJ Reports 1979: 7; 1980: 3). Iran flouted these orders but did eventually resolve the hostage question in the Algiers Accords concluded with the United States in January 1981. While the case was pending, the United States attempted to rescue the hostages through an unsuccessful military mission. In its judgement the Court criticized this action as 'of a kind calculated to undermine respect for the judicial process' (ICJ Reports 1980: 43).

In the *Nuclear Tests* cases (*Australia and New Zealand v. France*), the claimants contested the legality of atmospheric testing of nuclear weapons in the South Pacific. After the case was brought, the French government announced that it had completed its series of tests and did not intend to test further. Rather than deciding whether the testing violated international law, the Court dismissed the case, stating that because of the statements of the French authorities the claimants' applications 'no longer had any object' (ICJ Reports 1974: 253, 457). The episode prompted France to withdraw its declaration accepting the Court's jurisdiction under the optional clause (Gross 1987: 48).

The ICJ dealt with issues concerning South-West Africa (Namibia) on several occasions, beginning in 1950 when it rendered an advisory opinion entitled *International Status of South-West Africa* (ICJ Reports 1950: 128). Later, using the state-to-state procedure, Ethiopia and Liberia claimed that South Africa had violated obligations under its mandate from the League of Nations with respect to South-West Africa, by virtue of its maintenance of a system of apartheid within the territory. In a preliminary ruling the Court found by a close margin (8-to-7) that it had jurisdiction over the matter (ICJ Reports 1962: 319), but following a small change in the composition of the Court, the case was dismissed a few years later, with the Court's president (who had dissented from the previous judgement) breaking a tie (ICJ Reports 1966: 6). This series of events cast serious doubt on the credibility and objectivity of the Court and contributed to perceptions of the Court as politicized and as a defender of the status quo. Widespread dissatisfaction with the Court's performance caused a number of states to shun the Court thereafter, but also prompted the United Nations and the Court itself to consider ways to repair the damage to the Court's image.

In 1971, at the request of the UN Security Council, the Court rendered an advisory opinion dealing with some aspects of the status of Namibia under international law, including the obligation of states to give effect to a Security Council resolution declaring the continued presence of South African authorities in Namibia to be illegal (*Legal Consequences for States of the Continued Presence of South Africa in Namibia (South-West Africa) Notwithstanding Security Council Resolution 276)* (ICJ Reports 1971: 16). Although the substance of the Court's 1971 advisory opinion was welcomed in the international legal community, South Africa continued to occupy Namibia in defiance of the ruling until 1990. South Africa's flouting of the ruling (albeit a ruling of advisory rather than binding character) contributed to the perception of the Court as ineffectual.

IMPLEMENTATION

The record of compliance with the ICJ's decisions has been mixed and appears less satisfactory than that of the PCIJ or of international arbitration. The actions of Iran in the *Tehran hostages* case (p. 906) and the USA in the *Nicaragua* case (p. 906) are but two of a number of instances of non-participation and non-compliance that could be cited. States are most likely to comply with a judgement when their consent to the Court's jurisdiction is given or renewed after the dispute arises, but are relatively less likely to comply when the jurisdiction of the Court is founded on past rather than present consent (Charney 1987: 299–309).

A perennial concern is how to improve implementation of the Court's decisions. The only method of enforcement provided for by the UN Charter and ICJ Statute is through the Security Council (UN Charter: Article 94), which has power to decide upon enforcement measures such as economic sanctions. The availability of the veto to the five permanent members of the Security Council has frustrated this possibility. For example, the United States vetoed a Security Council resolution to enforce the *Nicaragua* judgement. Security Council enforcement can be blocked not only by formal veto but also by the threat of its use and other less formal means, even in cases when no permanent member's interests would be adversely affected. Thus the Security Council failed to exercise its enforcement power in the *Tehran hostages* case because of US–Soviet tensions in the wake of the Soviet invasion of Afghanistan.

With the Charter's enforcement scheme having proved ineffective, states have looked for other ways to compel recalcitrant respondents to comply with the Court's judgements. In the present stage of evolution of international legal institutions, the mechanisms of compulsion to enforce these (or any other) legal obligations are few and weak. States have attempted various forms of self-help and have tried to enlist the assistance of third countries in imposing economic and other sanctions against non-complying respondents, but such efforts have not produced tangible results. It is sometimes suggested that judgements could be enforced in domestic courts, such as by obtaining local judicial orders to seize assets of the respondent state. Efforts on behalf of

Nicaragua to enforce the 1986 judgement against the United States in US domestic courts were unsuccessful.

Despite the obvious inadequacy of compulsory means of enforcing the ICJ's judgements, many observers of the Court believe that the Court has a vital role to play in mobilizing world public opinion against violators of international law. This function may have long-term effects in shaping state behaviour and should not be overlooked or minimized.

OTHER INTERNATIONAL TRIBUNALS

Many see the ICJ's value as more symbolic than practical: it represents the aspirations of the world community toward the rule of law but has had only a marginal impact on the actual behaviour of states. In contrast, other international tribunals have been more active in terms of numbers of disputes actually resolved, or more effective in terms of voluntary or compelled compliance. Two types will be considered here: *ad hoc* arbitration tribunals; and regional and other specialized tribunals, including those for the enforcement of international human rights.

Ad hoc arbitration tribunals are established to resolve a specific dispute or specified categories of disputes. Typically, an arbitral tribunal consists either of a single arbitrator agreed upon by the parties, or of an uneven number of arbitrators (usually three or five) selected through agreed procedures. The parties agree on the question to be answered by the tribunal and also specify the rules of procedures to be followed and sometimes even the rules of law that the tribunal should apply. Because of these elements of party control, arbitration is often seen as less risky than submission to the jurisdiction of a permanent tribunal.

Many exceedingly important questions have been decided by international arbitration, among them issues of sovereignty over territory, redress for use of force, protection of nationals and environmental pollution. The record of compliance with decisions of international arbitral tribunals is quite favourable – higher than that of compliance with decisions of the World Court (Charney 1987: 299–309). Moreover, many more disputes have been submitted to international arbitration than to settlement by the World Court.

Among *ad hoc* arbitrations in recent years, an especially noteworthy example is the Iran–United States Claims Tribunal, established in the aftermath of the Iran hostage crisis of 1979–81. The Algiers Accords that resulted in the release of the hostages also provided for creation of an arbitral tribunal to resolve claims of the United States and Iran against each other and of their nationals against the two states (excluding claims of the hostages themselves and certain other categories of claims). The tribunal consists of nine members, of whom three are appointed by Iran, three by the United States, and three by a selection process that purports to be neutral. (In fact, much to Iran's chagrin, that process resulted in the selection of West European jurists as the supposedly neutral arbitrators, but Iran's attempts to challenge or change the process were unsuccessful.) More than two thousand cases have been submitted to the tribunal, involving breach of contract, expropriation, injury to persons and property, military sales, interpretation of the Algiers Accords themselves and various other matters. Enforcement of the tribunal's awards is ensured through several means, the most important of which has been the establishment of a security fund in the initial amount of US $1 billion, derived from assets of Iran that had been frozen by the United States during the hostage crisis. The aggregate amount of awards approved by the tribunal and paid pursuant to the Algiers Accords has already exceeded $1 billion, making it by far the largest arbitration in history, and the proceedings are still continuing. During more than a decade in which Iran and the United States have had few diplomatic or other contacts, the existence of the tribunal has served as an important channel of communication between two otherwise hostile governments.

Among regional tribunals, the following deserve special mention: the Court of Justice of the European Communities; the European Court of Human Rights and the Inter-American Court of Human Rights.

The Court of Justice of the European Communities is the judicial organ established to ensure observance of law and justice in the interpretation and application of the Treaty of Rome. Its jurisdiction includes disputes submitted by the EC Commission and Council, member states, national tribunals and private parties (individuals and companies). An important function of the Court is to ensure uniformity in the interpretation of Community law. The Court has established that European law is the higher law of all member states and prevails over national law in the event of conflict. Decisions of the Court are enforceable in member states under conditions prescribed by the Treaty of Rome. Because of the relatively advanced process of European integration, the European Court of Justice has more in common with supreme courts in federal systems than with the ICJ.

The European Court of Human Rights was established by the European Convention for the Protection of Human Rights and Fundamental Freedoms as part of an elaborate institutional framework for implementation of the rights guaranteed by that treaty. Before being submitted to the Court, cases are investigated by the European Commission of Human Rights, which first attempts to reach a friendly settlement and thereafter may take claims to the Court. As to applications from states, or from individuals whose cases are referred to the Court by the Commission, the jurisdiction of the Court and the admissibility of the petition depend on whether the states involved have agreed to these forms of enforcement.

The Inter-American Court of Human Rights has jurisdiction to interpret and apply the American Convention on Human Rights and other instruments protecting human rights within the American states. Individuals may not bring cases directly to the Court; only the Inter-American Commission on Human Rights (an investigatory and quasi-judicial organ) and states that have accepted the Court's jurisdiction may do so. Until very recently the Inter-American Court's principal decisions were advisory opinions on questions put to it by member governments and by the Inter-American Commission. In 1988 the Court held in a landmark contentious case, initiated by the Inter-American Commission, that Honduras was responsible for the disappearances of certain individuals within Honduran territory; the Court ordered Honduras to pay compensation to the immediate families of the victims.

In the category of specialized procedures, the dispute settlement provisions of the 1982 United Nations Convention on the Law of the Sea are worthy of attention. The convention (which is not yet in force) emphasizes the principle that the parties to a dispute have the right to settlement by any peaceful means of their own choice; it also specifies 'Compulsory Procedures Entailing Binding Decisions' should the parties be unable to resolve their dispute otherwise. The convention contemplates submission of disputes to one or more of the following tribunals: the ICJ; arbitral tribunals; or a new International Tribunal on the Law of the Sea, which will have a Sea-Bed Disputes Chamber to handle disputes involving exploration and exploitation of the deep sea-bed (Merrills 1984: 117–40).

CONCLUSION

Quantitative indicators (such as numbers of cases) are incomplete measures for evaluating an international tribunal's achievements. In the case of the ICJ, account should also be taken of its contributions in clarifying and developing principles of international law, as well as of the possibility that the availability of an international court may encourage states to resolve some disputes short of litigation.

The evolution of other forms of third party dispute settlement to complement the ICJ is salutary. It makes sense to have regional courts to resolve disputes among states with close links of geography, history or culture, as well as specialized courts to handle technical issues. As experience grows with judicial resolution of international disputes before a variety of tribunals, it may be possible to develop a greater degree of consensus than now exists about the sorts of disputes that should be resolved by the ICJ. Some assert that the ICJ should gradually build a record of successful resolution of small, quintessentially 'legal' disputes, before states ask it to tackle issues of war and peace; others argue to the contrary that the Court's most important role is educative or visionary, and that it should be activist in promoting the objectives of the international community as a whole (Falk 1986: 96, 173–92). Whether the 'big case' strengthens or weakens an international tribunal is a question on which opinions may surely differ, and one that is not likely to be speedily resolved.

REFERENCES

Charney, J. (1987) 'Problems of non-appearance, non-participation, and non-compliance', in L. F. Damrosch (ed.) *The International Court of Justice at a Crossroads*, Ardsley-on-Hudson, NY: Transnational.

Falk, R. A. (1986) *Reviving the World Court*, Charlottesville: University Press of Virginia.

Gross, L. (1987) 'Compulsory jurisdiction under the optional clause: history and practice', in L. F. Damrosch (ed.) *The International Court of Justice at a Crossroads*, Ardsley-on-Hudson, NY: Transnational.

ICJ (annual) *Reports*, The Hague: International Court of Justice.

——(annual) *Yearbook*, The Hague: International Court of Justice.

——(1945) *Statute*, The Hague: International Court of Justice.

Merrills, J. G. (1984) *International Dispute Settlement*, London: Sweet & Maxwell.

Rosenne, S. (1989) *The World Court: What It Is and How It Works*, Dordrecht: Martinus Nijhoff.

United Nations (1945), *Charter*, San Francisco.

Weiss, E. B. (1987) 'Judicial independence and impartiality: a preliminary inquiry', in L. F. Damrosch (ed.) *The International Court of Justice at a Crossroads*, Ardsley-on-Hudson, NY: Transnational.

FURTHER READING

Damrosch, L. (ed.) (1987) *The International Court of Justice at a Crossroads*, Ardsley-on-Hudson, NY: Transnational.

Elias, T. O. (1983) *The International Court of Justice and Some Contemporary Problems*, The Hague: Martinus Nijhoff.

Falk, R. A. (1986) *Reviving the World Court*, Charlottesville: University Press of Virginia.

Fitzmaurice, G. (1986) *The Law and Procedure of the International Court of Justice*, Cambridge: Grotius.

Franck, T. M. (1986) *Judging the World Court*, New York: Priority Press.

Gamble, J. K. and Fischer, D. D. (1976) *The International Court of Justice: An Analysis of a Failure*, Lexington, Mass.: Lexington.

Gross, L. (ed.) (1976) *The Future of the International Court of Justice*, Dobbs Ferry, NY: Oceana.

Lauterpacht, H. (1958) *The Development of International Law by the International Court*, London: Stevens.

McWhinney, E. (1987) *The International Court of Justice and the Western Tradition of International Law*, Dordrecht: Martinus Nijhoff.

Merrills, J. G. (1984) *International Dispute Settlement*, London: Sweet & Maxwell.

Rosenne, S. (1985) *The Law and Practice of the International Court of Justice*, Dordrecht: Martinus Nijhoff.

____(1989) *The World Court: What It Is and How It Works*, Dordrecht: Martinus Nijhoff.
Wetter, J. F. (1979) *The International Arbitral Process: Public and Private*, Dobbs Ferry, NY: Oceana.

57

THE WORLD BANK

BAREND DE VRIES

Owned by 151 nations, the World Bank Group is a family of institutions of which the International Bank for Reconstruction and Development (IBRD), the International Development Association (IDA) and the International Finance Corporation (IFC) are the best known. All three lend to promote economic development – in 1989 (the fiscal year ending June 1989) this totalled US $23.1 billion, of which $16.4 billion was lent by the IBRD, $4.9 billion by IDA and $1.7 billion by the IFC.

The basic strength of the IBRD rests on the scope and flexibility of its charter, the Articles of Agreement. The Bank was set up to be an efficient intermediary for the transfer of resources at the global level. Governments were to commit capital to the Bank, although only a small portion would be paid in. Most of the capital would remain on call, as a guarantee for the Bank's bonds. These bonds, to be sold in markets around the world, would be the main source of the Bank's finance. As stated in Article 1 of its charter, the Bank's objectives were broad: to finance reconstruction, promote foreign investment and international trade, to guarantee lending by others, or to lend itself for the 'more useful and urgent projects'.

The IBRD and IDA are administered as a single institution, commonly called the World Bank. All loans by both bodies are made either to governments or to entities with the guarantee of their governments. But the terms of these loans – their repayment period and interest cost – differ greatly between the two agencies and reflect the different sources of finance. The IBRD obtains most of its funds from selling bonds in the capital markets of the industrial countries, backed by the Bank's capital and reserves ($124 billion in June 1989). IDA, on the other hand, gets its fund by means of recurring cash contributions ('replenishments') from governments, mostly from those of industrial countries. IBRD loans must be repaid over ten to fifteen years, and carry interest rates that reflect the rates the IBRD pays on the bonds it currently issues in the market. IDA loans, or 'credits' as they are normally called, have a repayment period of thirty to forty years (forty years for the poorest borrowing countries), and carry an interest ('service') charge of only 0.75 per cent, while in the first ten years no repayments are made at all.

Both IBRD and IDA loans are for specific 'projects' (investments) or 'programmes', and both institutions apply the same standards of loan preparation and implementation. But the IDA lends only to the poorest countries – those with per capita incomes below $730; in fact, some 90 per cent of IDA credits are committed to the poorest countries with a per capita income below $400, such as Bangladesh, China, India and many sub-Saharan African countries. Countries with per capita incomes above $730, such as Brazil, Thailand and Turkey, borrow from the IBRD. As countries gain in economic strength they 'graduate' from IDA to the IBRD; a number of countries receive a blend of loans from both institutions. Eventually, when a country's per capita income exceeds about $3,000 the IBRD itself phases out its lending (de Vries 1987: 8–11).

In addition to finance, the World Bank provides considerable technical assistance in the areas of its expertise. It works with other sources of finance: for example, by organizing and chairing aid co-ordinating groups and obtaining co-financing for its projects. Underlying its activities are considerable programmes of development research, and country economic and sector studies.

HISTORY

The origin of the IBRD goes back to the July 1944 United Nations Monetary and Financial Conference held in Bretton Woods, which also set up the Bank's sister institution, the International Monetary Fund (IMF). (Membership in the IMF is a precondition for joining the Bank.) The conference was attended by the allied and other free nations, including the Soviet Union, which later decided not to join. Many less developed countries (LDCs), including China, India and most Latin American countries, also attended and participated in the deliberations. Some of those present, such as India and the Philippines, were not yet independent. In 1956 the IFC was established to help finance private enterprise. Four years later IDA was organized to provide assistance to the weakest and poorest of the LDCs.

Successive presidents have left their marks on the World Bank. By tradition they have been American; but they have been advocates of development first and have reflected their nationality only in that their advocacy has often had to be directed to their fellow Americans. After the initial years following the start of operations in 1946, Eugene Black took the helm in 1949, and like Robert S. McNamara after him, remained for thirteen years. He helped establish the Bank's operating procedures and defined the role of the executive directors in guiding policy and approving individual loan proposals put forward by management. He built up the Bank's credit and credibility, opening markets for its bonds. Under his guidance the Bank took initiative on major multinational projects, of which the development of the water resources of the Indus river basin was the most spectacular.

George D. Woods (1963–8) took many new initiatives, including aid co-ordination, a build-up of economic work, and an international process of assessing development issues (first under Lester B. Pearson of Canada). He broadened the base for IDA and established more effective relations with the United Nations. He extended Bank lending beyond large-scale infrastructure to small-scale agriculture, education and water supply.

Robert S. McNamara (1968–81) gave the strong direction needed for the Bank to adapt to new conditions and was able to deal with the often adverse conditions of that period. He extended Bank activities into the development of human capital through programmes for education, training, health and nutrition. He deepened the Bank's concern with population growth and social and economic inequality. During his tenure, lending commitments increased thirteen times, annual lending operations four times and staff threefold.

During A. W. (Tom) Clausen's presidency (1981–6) the Bank further adapted to changes in the international environment, including sub-Saharan African development and restructuring of the heavily indebted countries (HICs). Under his management the Bank greatly increased policy-based lending (i.e. programme loans associated with agreed policy reforms). Under Clausen's successor, Barber Conable, the Bank undertook a major reorganization and cutback in staff and obtained a general capital increase needed for continued expansion of lending. Conable also led the Bank in paying greater attention to both women in development and environmental problems.

STRUCTURE AND FINANCE

Under the Bank's charter all its powers are vested in a board of governors, consisting of one governor for each member country, which meets once a year. The governors have delegated their powers to twenty-two executive directors who perform their duties full-time at headquarters in Washington. Five of these directors are appointed by the five countries with the largest number of capital shares (the United States, Japan, Germany, the UK and France). The rest are elected by the governors representing the other members.

The executive directors exercise annual oversight over the Bank's financial and operating programmes and administrative budgets, review specific policy proposals (for example, allocation of net income or the Bank's lending terms), approve individual lending operations and review evaluation of completed projects. They also deal with issues fundamental to the Bank's operational priorities and strategies such as poverty alleviation, debt strategy, the environment and private sector development. The operations-evaluation department works outside the Bank's staff structure and reports directly to the executive directors.

The Bank's staff is headed by the president, who is also chairman of the board of executive directors. Four senior vice-presidents supervise lending operations, finance, policy planning and research, and administration. The president and senior vice-presidents, together with the general counsel and the secretary, form the president's council which meets regularly to discuss policy matters.

The financial structure of the Bank is of importance in understanding its operating policies. The level of the Bank's capital is critical to its ability to expand operations since the total of loans outstanding and disbursed cannot exceed its subscribed capital and reserves. Since the capital can only be increased after approval of the Bank's shareholders (members), they can keep control over the pace of Bank expansion. (In June 1989 loans outstanding and disbursed were $77.9 billion, and subscribed capital and reserves were $124 billion. The total authorized capital was $171.4 billion, of which $115.7 had been subscribed; of the subscribed capital $8.6 billion was paid in, leaving $107.1 billion callable, i.e. available for backing IBRD bonds and permitting an increase in loans outstanding.)

An even more stringent limitation on Bank operations results from the policy of keeping the Bank's own debt (i.e. the net total of its outstanding bond obligations) below the 'usable' portion of the Bank's 'callable' capital and to increase the capital when this limit comes in sight; the 'usable' portion is the share of the industrial countries which themselves have AAA rating in the capital markets. If this limit were exceeded, the quality of IBRD bonds would suffer and hence the cost of borrowing and lending would tend to rise. The quality of the Bank's bonds, of interest both to the Bank's shareholders and to its borrowers, is influenced by the full coverage of the bonds by the usable portion of the IBRD capital and its reserve assets, the IBRD's own cautious financial and operating policies and the Bank's preferred position in debt restructuring – i.e. the tacit understanding that, in the case of borrowing countries' debt restructuring, loans owed to the IBRD will not be affected. Net proceeds from the sale of bonds provide about 70 per cent of Bank funding, the rest mainly coming from internal cash generation, capital subscriptions and the sale of loans. In the fiscal year ending June 1989, the Bank's net borrowing was $9.3 billion and net income $1.1 billion, of which $100 million was allocated to IDA and the rest to reserves. The Bank's earnings result from the spread in the cost of borrowing and the interest charged on its loans, as well as the return on investing its liquid resources ($19.4 billion in June 1989) needed to meet obligations on undisbursed loans and as a reserve in the timing of its borrowing operations.

The financial structure and operations of IDA are simpler than those of the IBRD. Most of the resources for the grant-like (concessionary) credits by IDA come from contributions by the industrial countries, normally made in three-year instalments. Additional sources are the reflux of amortization payments (rising rapidly in the 1990s) and annual transfers from IBRD profits. In recent years, regular IDA operations have been supplemented by special assistance for Sub-Saharan Africa.

IDA has been the most important single source of low-interest loans to poor countries. In the 1970s, IDA commitments grew by 11 per cent in real terms, as against 4 percent for all concessionary assistance from industrial countries. However, in the 1980s, government contributions to IDA stagnated, mostly because of the reluctance of the United States to continue increasing its assistance; IDA commitments stayed at about the same level ($3.3 billion per year) until 1988 and 1989 when they averaged $4.7 billion (including special operations in Africa).

The poorer countries in Asia and Africa have been IDA's principal beneficiaries. Total IDA credits outstanding amounted to $52.8 billion, of which $17 billion was in Africa and $29 billion in Asia (of which $16 billion was in India and $4.7 billion in Bangladesh).

FUNCTIONS

The World Bank's lending operations have been associated with technical assistance, policy advice and assistance as well as co-ordinating activities and research. As a result of its research, the Bank has become the largest single source of development publications, including annual *World Development Reports* which focus on different topics of special interest to the developing countries, such as agricultural policies (1986), capital markets (1985), public finance (1988), population and health (1980 and 1984), and environment policies (1992).

In addition to its global studies, the Bank carries on country-oriented research. Economic reports on individual countries highlight such issues as how to improve balance between public and private sectors, constrain urban growth, encourage rural employment, rationalize industrial development and strengthen domestic financial markets.

While each lending operation entails technical assistance to the borrower, the Bank provides additional assistance through special grants, technical assistance loans and direct financing, and by contributions to projects of the United Nations Development Programme (UNDP) for which the Bank acts as executive agency. The work of the Bank's staff on economic, sector and project reports is the backbone of much of the Bank's technical help. The Bank also

918

provides technical assistance indirectly through the training it provides at its staff college, the Economic Development Institute (EDI).

The diversity of the Bank's operations is reflected in the broad composition of loans. Lending for investment in agriculture and rural development has been the most important, followed by energy. Transportation and urban development each receive 9–10 per cent of total commitments. During the 1980s, education, health and nutrition received steadily increasing operational attention.

In the agricultural sector, the Bank has given special attention to the development and modernization of small-scale agriculture, and the development of new products, methods and technology. Recognizing the importance of research, it initiated a special grant programme and, in 1971, established the Consultative Group for International Agricultural Research (CGIAR). The group is co-sponsored by the UNDP and the Food and Agriculture Organization (FAO). In recent years the Bank has given special attention to help strengthen African agriculture. In 1985 the CGIAR called a special meeting to consider new initiatives for solving Africa's food problems; in that year thirty-eight donor members contributed $175 million for research, of which $28 million was given by the Bank. In 1988 the members of CGIAR provided $212 million in research grants.

OPERATIONS POLICIES

Bank loans fall in three different categories, of which project loans are the most important. These finance specific investments: the borrower is usually an operating entity such as an electric power company, a school system or a manufacturing enterprise. Loans of the second category are sector loans made to finance activities in a single economic sector, as, for example, the modernization of an industry, a nationwide irrigation programme or electric power distribution. A third category consists of loans that cut across several economic sectors and addresses broad economic problems such as public investment management, trade policy and economic incentives. These 'programme' or 'structural adjustment' loans are permitted under the Bank's charter under 'exceptional' circumstances. Associated with these programme loans are loans for reconstruction, under the Bank's earliest mandate, such as loans to assist in rebuilding an economy after a civil war or an earthquake. Policy-based loans for structural adjustment became increasingly important during the 1970s and 1980s as the Bank assisted in the restructuring and policy reform of LDCs associated with changes in energy prices, slow-down of demand for LDC exports and the debt crisis. Adjustment loans are typically disbursed over one- or two-year periods during which a government agrees to undertake a number of specific measures.

The conditions or understandings included in World Bank loans vary with the objective of the loan. They can concern project performance, but as the objectives of lending have broadened, the conditions are increasingly related to a country's economic policies.

Although the Bank's conditions are sometimes criticized as being too intrusive (see Hayter 1971; Payer 1983), the large extent to which they are accepted in practice by borrowers is testimony to the close working relations between the Bank and the borrowers and the caution with which projects and programmes are prepared. In general discussions on bank lending policies, LDC representatives have often sought to limit the Bank's conditions and avoid cross-conditionality with the IMF. On the other hand, several creditor governments have demanded conditions with greater emphasis on the adoption by LDCs of more market-oriented policies.

One major objective of the Bank's loan conditions is that its loan funds be well spent. Indeed, in specific investment loans the Bank does not disburse any funds without knowing the precise purpose of the expenditure. This requirement has had the effect of setting a standard for prudent management in the public sector generally. In a broader sense, World Bank loan conditions aim at increasing savings and improving resource allocation, for example by channelling expenditures towards purposes from which the country can achieve the greatest benefits. Savings are increased by the Bank's insistence that user charges and prices charged by public enterprise are set at levels where operating and maintenance expenditures are covered and the project shows a return on investment. In this way public enterprises can be more autonomous and financially independent of the central government. The Bank's insistence on 'sound' pricing policies can be controversial, and some LDC policy makers may feel it interferes unduly in internal affairs.

In the process of project preparation and loan negotiations the Bank carries on a dialogue with borrowers. This dialogue is based on studies of the entire economy as well as of individual sectors and specific projects and their sponsoring institutions. The Bank's economic studies are basic to its discussions with country officials on development management, the level and terms of long-term external finance and an external lending strategy for the country. The Bank's close operational links with country officials and its ongoing economic and project studies enable it to provide assistance effectively when countries face difficult problems of change.

The Bank's studies of country economies and external lending strategy also form the basis for co-ordination with other lenders. Co-ordination is often carried out in the framework of aid groups or 'consultative groups' of lenders, which meet when needed (sometimes annually). At such meetings officials of the borrowing country present their economic programmes, projects and external borrowing needs. The consortium for India has been meeting annually since 1958, followed by similar groups for Pakistan and Bangladesh; the first 'consultative group' was held for Columbia in 1963. Fifteen such aid co-ordinating group meetings were held in 1989. In addition to working with other official lenders, the World Bank has collaborated with non-governmental organizations (NGOs) in a large variety of community-based projects concentrated in agriculture, education, health and urban development.

The Bank also co-operates with other lenders, both public and private, through co-financing of projects. Co-financing increased substantially in the 1980s. In 1989 co-financing of bank projects by other agencies and banks totalled $9.9 billion for 131 projects: the World Bank contributed $11.8 billion.

A major operational objective has been the development and strengthening of the private sector. The Bank has a direct impact on the private sector through its infrastructure loans and through loans for domestic development banks which re-lend their loan funds to small and medium-sized enterprises. The Bank's sector work on domestic financial policies, capital markets and trade incentives encourage more rational policies for private sector development. It has helped set up a number of institutions with a specific mandate in the private sector: the IFC (1956), the Center for the Settlement of Investment Disputes (ICSID, 1965) and the Multilateral Investment Guarantee Agency (MIGA, established in 1988). ICSID provides mutually acceptable procedures for settling investment disputes between foreign investors and their host countries. It has a steadily increasing membership which in 1989 reached ninety-one countries. MIGA was set up to encourage equity investment and other direct investment flows to developing countries through the mitigation of non-commercial investment barriers. It offers guarantees against non-commercial risks and advises on the design and implementation of policies, programmes and procedures related to foreign investments. By June 1989, seventy-three countries had signed the MIGA convention. The IFC makes loans and equity investments in private companies operating in developing countries. Unlike the World Bank, it does not receive LDC government guarantees for its loans and investments. In the year ending June 1989 the IFC made investments of $1.7 billion, of which $314 million had been provided by over sixty participating banks. In June 1989 the IFC held a total of $4 billion in loans and investments; its paid-in capital was $948 million and its accumulated earnings $635 million.

THE POLITICS OF THE BANK

The World Bank has been subjected to criticism from both the left and the right. Some critics believe that the Bank has been insensitive to the political concerns of the LDCs, that it primarily represents the views of industrial countries and acts as a new kind of imperialist power. Other critics believe that the Bank should be more responsive to market forces; they argue that the

Bank has been too detached from the private sector and the political interests of the industrial countries. To some extent the attacks on the Bank have formed part of a wider attack on 'foreign aid'.

The 'aid is imperialism' school argues that the Bank imposes too many conditions in its lending and that the borrowing countries have too little voice in the Bank's decision-making process (Hayter 1971; Torrie 1984; Payer 1983). These critics are correct in that Bank staff have sometimes under-estimated their impact on the local scene or have been perceived as arrogant. Given the Bank's role in these countries, the demands for a greater LDC share in decision making are well founded and have, in fact, been acted upon. The Bank has substantially increased the representation of developing countries in management and staff. But representation on the Bank's executive board continues to be based on shares in the Bank's capital. In June 1989 the United States had 16.3 per cent of the voting rights in the IBRD, Japan 9.4 per cent, the Federal Republic of Germany 7.3 per cent and the UK 7.0 per cent. What is important, however, is that the operating and policy decisions on the board are in practice made by consent and discussions, in which the representatives of the LDCs fully participate.

P. T. Bauer, a leading advocate of market forces, criticizes aid agencies and the Bank for transferring wealth to governments, not to the people and least of all the poorest who need the assistance most, for politicizing life in the recipient countries and for supporting heavy industries rather than small firms using indigenous technology (Bauer 1981, 1984). Most Bank economists would agree with Bauer on the importance of using market incentives for efficient resource allocation. However, little of the criticism of foreign aid by Bauer and others apply to the World Bank. The Bank normally designs its loan projects to meet sound banking standards and its conditions presume, or help establish, efficient policies which may not always be possible under govern-mental bilateral aid. Furthermore, while the Bank substantially increased its lending for poverty alleviation during the 1970s, this lending was not a mere transfer of wealth, but instead was aimed at improving the productivity of the poor through investment in irrigation, water conservation and basic services (de Vries 1987: 1–7).

In practice, criticism is muted by the fact that the Bank and the LDCs share many common objectives, such as the strengthening of economic and financial ties, resumption and maintenance of a new growth momentum, widening of markets and an increase in capital flows.

Some critics doubt that governments can control the allocation of funds contributed to multilateral institutions (Bauer 1981). However, the non-politi-cal character of the Bank, envisaged in its charter, facilitates cost-effective and efficient mobilization and allocation of resources. Moreover, the Bank's lending policies over the years have been in tune with the thinking in donor governments. Representatives of both industrial countries and LDCs have many channels for making their views known and exerting influence on the Bank, as in executive board discussions, in loan negotiations and during discussions about capital increases in the Bank and in IDA replenishment negotiations.

The radical right in the United States urges that the Bank should be more exposed to market forces and has proposed that government support for Bank bonds be removed by winding down its callable capital (Phaup 1984). Such a policy would severely cut back the Bank's lending and other functions, quite contrary to the interest of the developing countries, especially the poorest.

Public opinion in the United States assigns a low priority to foreign assistance. Foreign policy is a concern not of the average person but rather of the elite, the relatively rich and the educated. Moreover, the World Bank does not have the support of any broad public interest organization such as that which the United Nations enjoys in the UN Associates established in many countries.

THE FUTURE OF THE BANK

The World Bank has grown into the single most important development institution in the world and most likely will continue to be so. Even the conservative winds of the 1980s did little to change the Bank's course, except perhaps to slow down its expansion somewhat.

The pace of IBRD lending and other operations will be subject to many influences and often opposing political and economic forces. In the 1970s and 1980s the Bank's lending, both gross and net of amortization, increased in relation to total official and multilateral lending to the LDCs. However, in recent years the IBRD's net transfer (i.e. gross disbursements minus loan repayments and interest) has turned negative, even in the highly indebted countries, and this negative trend is likely to put pressure on the IBRD to continue expanding its new lending for some years to come. The operations of the IDA are likely to be under continuous constraint by the reluctance of the major donor governments to expand their contributions in real terms.

Among the critical issues facing the Bank are the continuing plight of the poorest countries, especially in Africa; the need for restructuring in many middle-income countries; and the resolution of the debt problem. In the years immediately following the debt crisis of 1982, the Bank was reluctant to use its technical and financial resources for formulating a comprehensive strategy for resolving the debt problem. Since the mid-1980s it has greatly expanded its lending to the highly indebted countries and it is likely to continue collaborating with new initiatives for reducing debt and debt service. However, its role will be circumscribed by its own cautious management and its desire to maintain a high standing in the capital markets where its bonds are traded.

The Bank has demonstrated a strong ability to adapt itself to changing circumstances, and in the future it is likely to change the emphasis and composition of its lending as the needs of its diverse membership warrant and the views of donor governments change. The emphasis on combating environmental degradation and the development of human resources, especially women, are relatively new and open up opportunities for considerable innovation and change.

REFERENCES

Bauer, P. T. (1981) *Equality, the Third World and Economic Delusion*, Cambridge, Mass.: Harvard University Press.

——(1984) 'Remembrance of studies past: retracing first steps', in G. Meier and D. Sears (eds) *Pioneers in Development*, New York: Oxford University Press.

de Vries, B. A. (1987) *Remaking The World Bank*, Washington, DC: Seven Locks Press.

Hayter, T. (1971) *Aid as Imperialism*, Harmondsworth: Penguin.

Payer, C. (1983) *The World Bank: A Critical Analysis*, New York: Monthly Review Press.

Phaup, E. D. (1984) *The World Bank: How It Can Serve US Interests*, Washington: Heritage Foundation.

Torrie, J. (1984) *Banking on Poverty: The Global Impact of the IMF and the World Bank*, Toronto: Between the Lines.

FURTHER READING

Alter, G. M. (1978) 'World Bank goals in project lending', *Finance and Development* 15 (2).

Ayers, R. L. (1983) *Banking on the Poor*, Cambridge, Mass.: MIT Press.

Baum, W. C. and Tolbert, S. M. (1985) *Investing in Development: Lessons of World Bank Experience*, New York: Oxford University Press.

Clark, W. (1981) 'McNamara at the World Bank', *Foreign Affairs* 60 (1): 167–84.

Collier, H. (1984) *Developing Electric Power: Thirty Years of World Bank Experience*, Baltimore: Johns Hopkins University Press.

de Vries, B. A. (1987) *Remaking the World Bank*, Washington, DC: Seven Locks Press.

Feinberg, E. *et al.* (1986) *Between Two Worlds: The World Bank's Next Decade*, Washington, DC: Overseas Development Council.

Kamarck, A. M. (1982) 'McNamara's Bank', *Foreign Affairs* 60 (4): 951.

Mason, E. S. and Asher, R. E. (1973) *The World Bank Since Bretton Woods*, Washington, DC: Brookings Institution.

Please, S. (1984) *The Hobbled Giant: Essays on the World Bank*, Boulder, Colo.: Westview Press.

World Bank, *Annual Reports*, Washington, DC: World Bank.

——(annual) *World Development Reports*, New York: Oxford University Press/World Bank.

58

THE INTERNATIONAL
MONETARY FUND

STEPHANY GRIFFITH-JONES

The International Monetary Fund (IMF) was originally designed to influence
the world economy in the monetary sphere. As expressed in its Articles of
Agreement, the Fund's objectives include:

1 to facilitate the expansion and balanced growth of international trade and
   to contribute thereby to the promotion and maintenance of high levels of
   employment and real income and to the development of the productive
   resources of all members as primary objectives of economic policy;
2 to promote exchange stability, to maintain orderly exchange arrangements
   among its members, and to avoid competitive exchange depreciation;
3 to give confidence to members by making the general resources of the Fund
   temporarily available to them under adequate safeguards, thus providing
   them with the opportunity to correct maladjustments in their balance of
   payments without resorting to measures destructive of national or international prosperity.

Walter Robichek, a senior Fund official, has summarized the Fund's objectives
in one sentence: 'The IMF was founded to avert worldwide economic
depressions' (Robichek 1984).

   In practice, the prime functions of the Fund are to provide the machinery
for advice and collaboration on international monetary problems; to supervise
the overall functioning of the international monetary system by promoting a
proper balance between adjustment and financing in all member countries;
and to make resources available to members in order to support the measures
they are taking to correct temporary maladjustments in their balance of payments.

   The Fund and the World Bank, as well as the overall system created at
Bretton Woods, represented a bold attempt to promote multilateralism in a
universal system. It contributed to post-war reconstruction and to the remarkable growth of world production and trade in the 1950s and 1960s, leading

to a degree of international co-operation that was significantly greater than that achieved in earlier periods.

However, the gaps in the Bretton Woods System and the small and (relative to the world economy) declining size of its main institution – the Fund – eventually led to contradictions, which, particularly since the early 1970s, made its contribution to the growth of world output and trade more ambiguous. Several thoughtful analysts have suggested that, had the Fund been created along the lines suggested before and during Bretton Woods by Keynes, its contribution to the sustained growth of the world economy would have been greater and more permanent (see Williamson 1983a). It is noteworthy that suggestions for major reforms of the Bretton Woods System (such as the Triffin Plan, the suggestions of the Committee on the Reform of the International Monetary System and Related Issues (the Committee of Twenty), and proposals in the Brandt Commission reports) contain crucial elements that are similar (or are based on similar principles) to those in the original Keynes plan – in particular the proposals for a far larger Fund, for a larger role for the international currency it issues, and for effective mechanisms to exert pressure on surplus countries (for Keynes's proposals, see Keynes 1969). Naturally, not all – and perhaps not even most – of Keynes's detailed proposals for an International Clearing Union would be relevant in today's significantly different world. Similarly, many of the current difficulties with the operation of the international financial system and of the Fund are not only due to the original limitations and gaps in the system, but also to its slowness to adapt to the rapid and drastic economic and political changes that have occurred in the last forty (and particularly the last fifteen) years.

There are four major changes in the world economy that are relevant to the discussion of the present and future role of the Fund. First, the increased economic, and particularly financial, interdependence that exists in the world today. This is reflected in the very rapid growth that has taken place in world trade and international labour flows, and, particularly since the early 1970s, the dramatic expansion of private financial flows. The internationalization of private financial flows was (especially in 1973–82) far faster than the internationalization of the relevant regulations, and faster than the expansion of official international lending – including the Fund's. Indeed, many of the proposals discussed below would expand the Fund – as well as other public international institutions – as much as the private sector has already expanded. Some analysts are even beginning to draw a parallel between the development of national central banks that followed the growth of commercial banks, and the gradual evolution of the Fund into an embryonic world central bank following the growth of international private banking (see Cooper 1983). At another level, greater international interdependence also implies a need for more co-ordination among countries in the management of their macroeconomic policies – a process in which the Fund, given its mandate, experience and influence, would inevitably play a key role.

Second, the larger and different payments problems of today constitute another major change. During the 1970s and early 1980s international financial intermediation became much more difficult due to the dramatic increase in the size of current account imbalances that occurred as a result of major variations in the price of internationally traded goods (particularly but not only oil), recessions in the industrial countries and – in the early 1980s – major increases in international interest rates. Particularly problematic and severe was the large increase in current account deficits of oil-importing developing countries, which grew especially sharply, from $11.3 billion in 1973 to $109 billion in 1981 (International Monetary Fund 1980, 1984b).

Though positive, the response of official international institutions – and particularly of the Fund – to the magnitude and severity of the balance of payments problems of oil-importing developing countries was clearly insufficient. It has perhaps not been stressed enough in the literature that between 1973 and 1982 the Fund through all its facilities financed only 3.1 per cent of the current account deficits of non-oil-importing developing countries (see Table 1). Clearly, the responsibility for the very marginal role in funding deficits that the Fund played until 1980 is not mainly carried by the institution itself, but by the governments of its member countries. For example, the expansion in the Fund's resources could have been more rapid; the ratio of Fund quotas in relation to world imports in fact declined particularly sharply (from 12 per cent in 1970 to 3 per cent in 1982) when current account imbalances grew fastest in the world economy.

It is true that the Fund did take important steps in response to changes in the international economy during the 1970s. Among these, and of particular

Table 1   Current account deficits and net use of fund credit, non-oil developing countries, 1973–83 (In billions of US dollars)

	Current accounts deficits	Net use of fund credit
1973	11.3	0.1
1974	37.0	1.5
1975	46.3	2.1
1976	32.6	3.2
1977	30.4	−0.2
1978	42.3	−0.3
1979	62.0	0.2
1980	87.7	1.5
1981	109.1	6.1
1982	82.2	7.1
1983	56.4	10.2

Source: International Monetary Fund, *World Economic Outlook* (various issues)

importance in this context, was the creation of the low conditionality oil facility, the extended Fund facility (EFF), the Trust Fund, the Subsidy Account, the Supplementary Financing Facility, and the enlarged access policy. But, given the tremendous and unprecedented magnitude of the deficits that needed to be met, the official response was insufficient and contributed – particularly by omission – to the problems in some countries (especially the low-income nations) in the 1970s, and in most developing countries in the early 1980s. The evaluation of past mistakes made in response to changes in the international environment is important – not to apportion blame (an insider with the benefit of hindsight would be presumptuous even to attempt that), but to extract lessons for the future.

As the financing needs of most developing countries increased dramatically, and as the expansion of official liquidity, development assistance and private direct investment failed to keep pace, the gap was in large part filled by lending by the international private banks. This was the third major change in the world economy. This lending was highly concentrated, helping to sustain economic activity in particular developing countries (such as the middle-income ones) and thus directly to sustain economic activity worldwide. The low-income countries, mostly considered uncreditworthy by commercial bankers, did nót, however, have significant access to this new source of liquidity, even in the 1970s. Thus, as the main source of international liquidity for financing developing countries became market determined, the distribution of this liquidity among developing countries became less equitable than it had been, when aid and official flows played a relatively larger role, as in the 1960s.

Private bank lending also created other problems. As became evident in the early 1980s (but should have been clear to anyone with at least a superficial knowledge of economic history), private international lending is unpredictable and may often become procyclical; there was and still is no assurance that levels of future net lending flows will be related to past levels, since they are to an important extent influenced by bankers' perceptions of countries' creditworthiness, which deteriorates precisely in periods of world recession. Not only has new commercial lending itself become procyclical, but the interest payments on a large proportion of debts contracted earlier have varied according to international interest rates. This variable interest rate debt, which helped fund a high proportion of the deficits of some developing countries in the 1970s (contributing to their sustained economic activity), became an additional and important new channel for the transmission of international disturbances.

Price instability, which has for long been perceived as an important source of instability in earnings from the commodity-exporting developing countries, also became a characteristic of the transfer of financial resources. As Massad put it: 'Interest rates, terms of trade and the supply of lending interact perversely in the international transmission of disequilibria' (Massad 1984). The 'perverse' interaction between high interest rates and the supply of private lending even led in 1982 and 1983 to significant net negative transfers of financial resources from most Latin American countries (their net payments of profits and interest being greater than net capital inflows), and from Latin America as a whole, and there are risks that such a situation could occur even from some low-income countries (see United Nations Economic Commission for Latin America 1984). Although it may be desirable that in the medium term some developing countries may 'graduate' to a position of becoming net exporters of capital, this seems clearly premature and undesirable at this stage, not only for the low-income but also the middle-income countries attempting to emerge from the impact of a major world recession.

The combined effect of the second large increase in oil prices, the prolonged recession of the early 1980s and the dramatic rise in international interest rates – and, for some countries, seriously inadequate economic management – led in the early 1980s to the fourth major change: widespread debt crises in developing countries. The Fund played a major and vital role in preventing these crises from having a destructive effect on the private international financial system.

The role the Fund played went far beyond its greatly expanded direct role in financing developing countries' current account deficits, although the Fund's lending did increase significantly in value and as a proportion of financing current account deficits, and also became more widespread. As Jacques de Larosière, the Fund's Managing Director, pointed out, 'since the debt crisis erupted in the middle of 1982, the Fund has lent some $22 billion in support of adjustment programs in nearly 70 countries' (Larosière 1984). Particularly important in times of financial distress has been the Fund's key role in assembling rescue packages; these have included an upper credit tranche programme with the Fund, the rescheduling of maturing debts, and the arrangement of new finance from banks. The latter has often been largely 'involuntary' as the Fund has placed considerable pressure on banks to increase lending (usually to meet interest payments).

In these packages the Fund's financing was made conditional for the first time, not only upon policy changes in the debtor country but also upon the extension of new credit by private international banks. Furthermore, whereas before 1982 the Fund 'restricted an area of competition and reduced the possibility of "excessive" private lending and borrowing' (Eckaus 1982), as its programme included a limit on countries' foreign borrowing that set the size of a particular market for private lenders, since 1982 the Fund has to some limited extent 'created' a market by encouraging or even pressing private banks to lend when they did not necessarily wish to. These changes in the relations between the Fund and the private capital markets have not been sufficiently stressed in the literature, nor have their present and future implications been fully examined.

The major and effective role which the Fund has played in debt crisis management has been widely acclaimed as having been of immediate benefit, not only to the banks, but also to the debtor countries and to the international economy. Not only has the influence of the Fund greatly increased, but also its prestige as the institution at the centre of the international monetary system has been significantly enhanced. There is also a rather widespread view that as much or more creativity and energy as was involved in debt crisis management should now be used to design an international monetary system that would contribute to making those crises less likely and less damaging both to the world economy and, particularly, to the developing countries.

ISSUES IN THE REFORM OF THE FUND

Given the recent changes in the world economy – some of which have been very briefly sketched in the previous section – and the new problems that these have generated, important alterations should perhaps also be made to the Fund's role and *modus operandi* to help it achieve the purposes for which it was established. Perhaps the Fund itself, given its experience, its aims, and its increased leverage and prestige, should initiate proposals for international monetary reform (including significant changes in its own role), rather than leave this initiative to outside observers or individual member governments.

There seem to be two broad types of possible reform of the Fund. First, there are those proposals that have already been explored in the literature (in some but not all cases exhaustively). These proposals may need some important adaptations due to recent changes, but the main impediment to implementing them seems to be a combination of a lack of political will among the particularly influential national governments and some institutional inertia within the Fund itself. This type of reform includes improving the co-ordination of national policies, increasing the Fund's contribution to global liquidity, expanding the Fund's existing financial facilities, and modifying the conditionality attached to its resources.

The second type of reform involves new issues that have become significant more recently, mainly as a result of changes in the world economy. Further technical clarification of these issues may still be a necessary though obviously not a sufficient condition for future change. It is worth exploring two issues in this latter category: the future relations among the Fund, other official international institutions and the private international banks; and the possible need for special measures to support both countries and groups of people most vulnerable to international instability.

The shocks and instabilities that have characterized the world economy in the past twelve years imply the need within a reformed international system to improve stabilization and contracyclical policies, and the protection of those most affected when instabilities and shocks nevertheless persist. In the past, national instability has generally increased recognition of the role of automatic stabilization devices for national economies. But there has been little parallel use of automatic stabilizing mechanisms at the international level, although the need for more international action to avoid recessions is perceived as essential by economists belonging to different schools of thought. Important elements in automatic or quasi-automatic international stabilization have to do with the provision of stable and adequate international liquidity, and the maintenance of stable and above all predictable flows of international capital. These topics will be examined later (pp. 933–4, 939–40). This section will concentrate on the other key tool of international stabilization: the more effective co-ordination of national stabilization policies.

There are clear difficulties in achieving total agreement among governments of varying powers, political persuasion and economic interest on what optimal economic policies are, whether national or international. It may, however, be possible to develop arrangements in which the international implications of domestic policies are more explicitly and systematically taken into account at the national level. As a fairly recent Commonwealth Secretariat Report points out:

> Multilateral participation in macro-economic consultations and coordination efforts, even when the main issues relate to policies of relatively few major economies, is necessary because the effects of whatever policies are agreed have ramifications far beyond the borders of the industrialized countries.... The most obvious existing multilateral forum for macro-economic consultation is the IMF.
>
> (Helleiner 1983)

One way to achieve such co-ordination effectively would be for the Fund to take a view on a viable global pattern of current account deficits and surpluses (or on a set of current account targets), and, through the different mechanisms at present at its disposal, to attempt to guide and co-ordinate the policies of both deficit and surplus countries to achieve those targets. As Killick pointed out in the Commonwealth Secretariat Report quoted above, the Committee of Twenty agreed in the mid-1970s that the system would develop in this direction; furthermore, this type of evolution was also clearly implicit in Keynes's proposal for an international Clearing Union. More recent suggestions in a related field, such as Harold Lever's scheme to sustain commercial lending to developing countries by expanding government guarantees, are also linked to a set of current account deficit targets that the Fund would define and monitor (see Lever 1983).

It would be of key importance, if the Fund is to play such a central part in policy co-ordination, that its role should take account of one of its main purposes established in its Articles of Agreement: 'to facilitate the expansion and balanced growth of international trade, and to contribute thereby to the promotion and maintenance of high levels of employment and real income and to the development of the productive resources of all members as primary objectives of economic policy'. If such objectives were not clearly pursued, there would be a risk, although presumably a small one, that policy convergence could even lead to a stronger deflationary bias than has characterized economic policies during some recent periods.

Nevertheless, a more global perception of countries' adjustment might *de facto* reduce deflationary (or indeed excessively inflationary) biases in policy making. It has increasingly been pointed out that if deflationary policies are simultaneously pursued by a number of deficit countries, the total impact of such policies may contribute to a world recession or to a reduction of world economic growth without necessarily improving the imbalances on the current accounts of individual countries (see, for example, Griffith-Jones and Harvey 1985). Focusing only on individual deflationary adjustments without accounting for the aggregate impact of those adjustments on world trade implies a certain 'fallacy of composition'. In fact, international institutions that can look at national adjustment from a global perspective should be able to avoid such a fallacy of composition and their advice should tend to have far more expansionary implications than policy makers who see adjustment only from a national perspective.

The fact that programmes designed with the assistance of an institution like the Fund do not in practice have an expansionary bias toward growth may be partly explained by its lack (in this aspect of its work) of such a truly global perception. It is very interesting that the senior official of the Fund mentioned earlier, Walter Robichek, has expressed this problem in a very clear and illuminating manner:

> Let it be admitted that the IMF now faces a certain dilemma. Although it has increasingly adopted a global analytical framework, foremost within the context of its rather elaborate annual world economic outlook exercise, it is not at present well equipped to deal operationally with balance of payments problems except on a country-by-country basis. The unfortunate consequence of the IMF's country-specific operations is that there is a risk that it may become an accomplice to the very beggar-my-neighbour policies that it was created to avert.
>
> (Robichek 1984: 74)

The practical implication may be that the Fund should attempt to increase its influence over industrial economies, and to do so from a global perspective; however, this task – although essential in terms of economic logic – may be frustrated in the short term by the political difficulty of influencing countries that do not need to borrow from the Fund. This is confirmed by the limited impact that the Fund has managed to exercise through its regular consultation and surveillance procedures. It may therefore be more fruitful for the Fund to begin by applying a more global analytical framework, at least when dealing with countries that do request its credit. At a minimum it should consider the interactions of the policies it recommends to different countries.

The Fund should, for example, assess the impact on the trade and current balances of all countries of the policies it evaluates or recommends for individual countries, and particularly of devaluation and constraint on demand expansion. Given the large number of countries with upper credit tranche arrangements with the Fund now, and the importance of some of them in world trade, assessing the global effects of programme policies (even though a second best to a global view of the adjustment of all countries) could be very important. For example, on 30 April 1984, as reported in the Fund's *Annual Report* (IMF 1984a), thirty-five countries had upper credit tranche arrangements with the Fund, including such very large economies as Brazil and Mexico. Given the large number of upper credit tranche Fund programmes at present existing in Western hemisphere countries (ten), and the significant volume of intra-Latin American trade, an initial attempt could be made to consider the interactions within that area. Particularly if this broader view is accompanied by other measures, some of which will be discussed below, such a change in analytical framework could imply a far more global perspective for the Fund, and reduce the bias in its recommendations toward deflation.

The insights, methodology and experience gained in such partial global analysis may be useful for developing a truly worldwide approach toward adjustment, which may become politically more feasible; indeed, the political feasibility of a more global influence of the Fund on adjustment may be enhanced by a successful experience on a partial or regional basis.

It has traditionally been held that a crucial area of international monetary policy relates to ensuring an adequate and appropriately distributed supply of international liquidity. It is a key element in assuring a stable, non-inflationary growth path for the world economy, and thus is intimately linked with the issue of greater global co-ordination of countries' macroeconomic policies, discussed in the preceding section of this essay.

It should be stressed that in the 1970s the trend toward floating currencies and a multi-currency reserve system, combined with the great expansion of international bank lending, gave a new meaning to international liquidity. For a time, the gross supply of international liquidity became, for the creditworthy industrial and middle-income countries, open ended. As a result, international control of liquidity became largely a function of the market. Thus, even after the creation of the special drawing right (SDR), Fund-created liquidity – either through its low conditionality lending or through the issue of SDRs – played a very small role in global liquidity; moreover, control by – or even the influence of – the Fund did not significantly affect the explosive expansion of market-based liquidity that did occur.

As the creation of market-based liquidity clearly slowed down in the 1980s (and as it is widely perceived that even in the 1970s the creation of liquidity through the market was often procyclical and frequently inequitable), the need to increase stability and predictability in the provision of international liquidity and to link it explicitly to the requirements for stable, non-inflationary growth in the world economy became far greater. It is therefore even more essential than in the past to increase significantly the influence of the Fund over the supply of international liquidity, which is one of the purposes for which the Fund was created, and to increase the size of its multilateral creation of liquidity through SDR issues. In the 1970s it may have been difficult – or even superfluous, as some maintain – for the Fund to assert its influence over the magnitude of international liquidity; in the 1990s there seems little choice but for a greater role for the Fund, both direct and indirect, to avoid the possibility that international financial intermediation might impose a deflationary bias on the world economy. At the same time, thought should be given to the currently less urgent need to create mechanisms for supervising and regulating excessive expansion of private international liquidity in the future.

ADAPTING THE FUND'S FACILITIES

Just as the role of the Fund in international co-ordination and in the generation of international liquidity needs to adapt to changing international circumstances, the same is true of the lending facilities through which the Fund provides credit to its member countries. This section will not deal with the creation of new facilities, but with the more feasible adaptation and expansion of two existing Fund facilities: the compensatory financing facility (CFF) and the EFF.

There emerged rather widespread professional consensus in the early 1980s on the need for an expansion and adaptation of the Fund's CFF in response to the increased instability in the international environment. An expanded CFF is favoured both by those concerned primarily with reducing the impact of instability in the world economy on individual developing countries (Dell and Lawrence 1980) and by those who see in the CFF the main mechanism through which the Fund does play – and could play – a significantly larger role in global economic stabilization (Cooper 1983). To these arguments could be added the contribution that the CFF (and particularly an expanded one) could make to the stability of international banking by breaking the set of vicious circles of poor trade performance, high interest rates and financial distress that emerged in the early 1980s.

The main purpose of the CFF was spelled out in a special Fund pamphlet on the subject: 'Ideally, the facility would enable a member to borrow when its export earnings and financial reserves are low and to repay when they are high, so its import capacity is unaffected by fluctuations in export earnings caused by external events' (Goreux 1980: 3). In the late 1970s and early 1980s, the CFF became a major facility through which the Fund provided payments assistance to developing countries; compensating for shortfalls in export earnings in a low-conditional and agile manner. Its capacity for lending has been enhanced through several modifications, the last of which (in 1981) also allows for compensation for temporary excesses in the cost of cereal imports.

However, different studies showed that borrowings under the CFF have been relatively modest, given the magnitude of the deterioration in the terms of trade in the early 1980s of a large number of developing countries: in particular, some studies (see, for example, Williamson 1983b) stressed the inadequacy of the CFF in compensating for the terms of trade deterioration in sub-Saharan Africa during that period. The main problems with the existing *modus operandi* of the CFF were generally identified as the quota limits on maximum drawings (clearly the most important constraint), the calculation of export shortfalls in nominal rather than real terms, and a formula for repayments not linked to the recovery of export earnings (see Griffith-Jones 1983).

Different liberalizations of the CFF have been suggested to provide full (or at least larger than existing) coverage of export shortfalls, either by eliminating the link between the size of a drawing and the drawing country's quota, or by increasing the limit. With the emergence of widespread debt crises in the early 1980s, the proposal was made in many circles that the CFF should also provide loans to offset fluctuations in interest rates (see *The Economist* 1983; Cline 1984). This modification would have the merit of reducing the impact of one of the key new sources of international economic instability.

A CFF thus modified would be able to stabilize import capacity and compensate for externally caused fluctuations in export prices, import prices and interest rates in cases of balance-of-payments need. It would be a very powerful counter-cyclical instrument, and be able to make a potentially major contribution not only to reducing the impact of shocks in the international economy on individual developing countries, but also to dampening instability in the world economy as a whole. Since one of the main features of the world economy since the early 1970s has been increased instability in key variables, and since this instability and the resultant uncertainty are seen as having negative effects by different types of economic agents and different schools of economic thought, measures to enhance prospects for stability could have broader support than the potentially more controversial issue of systematically increasing financial flows to developing countries.

It seems, therefore, particularly regrettable that suggestions of the type outlined above have not been followed up. In fact, the limits on drawings under the CFF as proportion of quotas have been reduced, although the quotas themselves are higher. Of greater concern is the fact that, in September 1983, the Fund's Executive Board passed a Decision (no. 7528–(83/140) which significantly altered the conditions under which the CFF drawings could be made. (See IMF (1984a: 187) for the text of the resolution, and Dell (1985) for a criticism of it.) Until September 1983, the first half of CFF drawings required only willingness on the part of the country 'to cooperate with the Fund in an effort to find, where required, appropriate solutions for its balance of payments difficulties', which implied that in practice it had very little conditionality attached to it and that it could therefore be granted semi-automatically and speedily. The modified resolution says now that readiness to co-operate:

> implies a willingness to receive Fund missions and to discuss, in good faith, the appropriateness of the member's policies and whether changes in the member's policies are necessary to deal with its balance of payments difficulties. Where the Fund considers that the existing policies . . . are seriously deficient or where the country's record of cooperation in the recent past has been unsatisfactory, the Fund will expect the member to take action that gives, prior to submission of the request for the purchase, a reasonable assurance that policies corrective of the member's balance of payments problem will be adopted.
>
> (IMF 1984a: 187)

The fact, therefore, that a country has experienced a temporary export shortfall (as defined by the Fund) for reasons beyond its control is no longer sufficient ground for a CFF drawing. The Fund can send out a mission and require the country to make changes in domestic policies (which are not the cause of that particular balance of payments need) even before a request for a drawing is submitted to the Executive Board.

As Dell points out: 'a further blow has been struck at the competence and responsibility of the IMF by depriving it of the major part of its low-conditional resources' (Dell 1985). There is in fact little left of the Fund's low-conditional resources except for the (unconditional) reserve tranche and the first credit tranche, given the non-renewal of the Trust Fund and other low conditionality facilities established in the 1970s. As a result, the ratio of low and high conditional facilities has been dramatically changed since the mid-1970s, with what seems too severe a bias toward high-conditional facilities, particularly given the fact that unstable and unpredictable external events cause such a large part of developing countries' balance-of-payments problems.

A related area of concern is that the Fund seemed with this decision to have gone back on a clear distinction (expressed in its pamphlet on Fund conditionality by Guitián) between 'deficits stemming from adverse transitory factors [which] typically call for temporary resort to financing', for which mechanisms such as the CFF were devised and 'imbalances . . . due to permanent factors', for which 'appropriate measures of adjustment must be taken to remove them' (Guitián 1981: 4). The distinction now appears blurred, and it seems possible that, even in cases where balance-of-payments needs arise from temporary pressures (outside a government's control), an effort of adjustment may nevertheless be required.

The larger payments imbalances facing developing countries since the early 1970s, as well as their different nature, have prompted many analysts to suggest the need for a facility more appropriate to the new situation. The Fund responded by creating the EFF in 1974. The rationale for the facility is clearly expressed in Fund documents. For example, the pamphlet on conditionality that appeared in the early 1980s had this to say: 'The payments imbalances facing many members in the early 1970s required adjustment over longer periods than were provided for under stand-by arrangements at that time, and, therefore, required larger amounts of assistance than could be made available under such arrangements' (Guitián 1981: 19). A similar analysis was made of the early 1980s:

> There was general agreement that the imbalances that currently existed were structural and therefore not amenable to correction over a short period of time. Adjustments to such disequilibria were likely to require extensive changes in members' economies ... if the restoration of viability to their balances of payments was not to jeopardize their development and growth prospects over the medium-to-long term. ... These considerations led the Fund to move toward a relatively long time frame for the adjustment effort to allow for changes in the patterns of production and demand – changes that can only be effected gradually.
>
> (Guitián 1981: 25)

Many analysts welcomed this adaptation of Fund practice to changes in the international environment. The Fund's own assessment seemed positive. For example, Guitián, in the pamphlet quoted above, wrote that 'in its formulation and administration, the extended facility has proved to be particularly beneficial to developing countries' (Guitián 1981). A major study evaluating the Fund's impact (Killick 1984) concludes that though both stand-by and EFF arrangements frequently broke down, EFFs seem to have led to more satisfactory results of growth and inflation. More broadly, the EFF was welcomed as a genuine attempt to move towards long-term and more structurally oriented programmes.

MODIFYING FUND CONDITIONALITY

The issue of Fund conditionality is the aspect of the Fund's role most frequently and extensively debated in the academic literature, as well as in far wider circles. Although the subject was widely discussed in the 1970s in the academic literature, its relevance increased significantly in the early 1980s for the following reasons. First, a far larger number of countries than in the past were borrowing from the Fund. Second, the proportion of the Fund's high-conditionality lending had dramatically increased since the mid-1970s. Finally, private and public lenders increasingly made new flows or the rescheduling of previously contracted debt to a particular country conditional on an upper credit tranche agreement with the Fund.

As a result of these changes, it is to be hoped that the Fund will take note of the growing and increasingly respectable body of critique of its conditionality by adapting its practices somewhat. It is certainly encouraging that the Fund has engaged in some dialogue with several of its critics and given outsiders greater access to information on its relations with countries that borrow from it. Clearly more studies are required, particularly more evaluations of Fund programmes after 1982 in middle-income countries and generally on pro-grammes in low-income countries. However, the knowledge and analysis already accumulated makes it feasible to pass from a phase of critical evaluation of existing Fund conditionality to proposals for constructive change through the discussion of alternatives to current practices. This would require a major intellectual effort both from the Fund staff and from its critics in academic circles as well as in governments negotiating with the Fund.

Serious discussion of an alternative form of conditionality requires, first, an explicit recognition by governments (and by the social and political groups that support or elect them) that their economy must be adjusted in the medium term in such a way that the current account deficit is not larger than the net flows of capital that other governments or international financial institutions – be they public or private – are willing to supply. Incidentally, this recognition is not only crucial for governments negotiating with the Fund but even more so for those that do not wish to turn to the Fund. Furthermore, the need for a consistent and realistic adjustment package is equally – if not more – relevant for socialist or reformist governments than for more conservative ones (see Griffith-Jones 1981).

Second, the discussion of alternative conditionality would seem to require a recognition by the Fund that its legitimate conditionality is basically related merely to ensuring that a particular improvement in a balance of payments will be achieved by some consistent and feasible set of policy changes. Focusing only on the external balance would also have the advantage of making agree-ments easier to reach; their definition is very straightforward, and the need for balance in the external accounts is compelling. The definition of appropriate 'internal balances' (including levels of inflation, employment and income distri-bution) is much more problematic. The Fund would need to recognize explicitly that the precise path by which governments wish to adjust towards a particular level of external balance should basically be decided by them; this should not only ensure that government's objectives and philosophy are taken into account but should also make it more likely that the programme will be adhered to.

NEW ISSUES

Since 1982 the Fund has in certain countries (mainly the large debtors) contributed to create a market, by encouraging or even pressing particular private international banks or groups of banks to increase their lending beyond levels they may have wished to provide spontaneously. Two crucial types of questions arise from this experience and from the broader context that made the Fund decide such action. First, once the acute debt crisis has been alleviated, should the Fund (and other national as well as international official institutions) continue to influence, guide or control private financial flows? If so, how should this be achieved? Second, should the Fund also expand significantly its 'catalytic' role by co-operating with official donors to help raise funding for adjustment programmes which it is negotiating with low-income countries? Would it be feasible, as has been suggested (Cassen 1986) for the Fund (or the country's government with the Fund's support), while it is carrying out negotiations with a country, simultaneously to be conducting parallel negotiations with the World Bank, and other bilateral as well as multilateral donors? Such a framework would potentially allow a greater harmony among measures required for short-term stabilization and those for long-term development, which at present are sometimes in unnecessary conflict. It would also clarify significantly the expectations of additional financial inflows if a low-income country has a programme with the Fund, as opposed to relying on very rough estimates of likely flows that may turn out to be unrealistic, as occurs in many cases (even though the Fund and particularly the World Bank have recently begun to perform a valuable catalytic role for official flows for low-income countries).

Returning to the first and possibly more complex question, there is an important body of professional opinion that supports the view that the Fund – as well as other official institutions, both national and international – should continue to guide or even broadly control the magnitude and distribution of private international lending, and ensure that the instruments used for this lending are such that they do not put debtors or creditors unnecessarily at risk. Such an intervention would of necessity be at the same time less specific than some of the Fund's interventions have been since 1982, but more pervasive. The rationale for such action is based on the perception of the increased need in today's interdependent world of defining a target or range of international liquidity which would contribute to stable, non-inflationary growth in the world economy. To meet such a target or range, government institutions (both national and international) would need to take measures which would simultaneously restrict private lending during periods of excessive expansion and contribute to sustain private lending in periods of contraction. The latter could possibly (though clearly not necessarily) be linked to some guarantee, insurance, or lender of last resort facility granted either by industrial countries' governments or by an institution such as the Fund or the World Bank.

It is noteworthy, for example, that Johannes Witteveen, former Managing Director of the Fund and currently Chairman of the Group of Thirty, has proposed such a broad initiative (Witteveen 1983), by calling for the creation of a facility within the Fund that would insure bank loans against political risks in debtor countries complying with Fund programmes, accompanied by a major initiative in supervision (via measures such as international reserve requirements under the Fund's control and solvency ratios) to curb excessive credit growth in the future. Even more ambitious proposals have been made, and are summarized in Griffith-Jones and Harvey (1985). These would, for example, imply national governments' guarantees to commercial lending within a set of current account deficit targets that the Fund would define and monitor. Such guarantees are unlikely to be granted by industrial countries' governments at present, but the broader principles and the analysis behind such proposals may be, or become, acceptable to a wide range of governments. Also relevant in this context is the discussion about an appropriate mix of instruments through which private financial flows would be channelled to developing countries (proposing, for example, a greater proportion of fixed interest rate lending or the introduction of quasi-equity arrangements). It would seem that bankers and other economic agents may be more open to debating and accepting new modalities for operation. It is interesting that many of the proposals for new lending mechanisms, new ways of dealing with the debt overhang, or new forms of interaction between the international public and private financial institutions have come from bankers.

It would be particularly valuable if the Fund itself took a lead in the debate on the Fund's future relations with international capital markets, within the context of a broader range of relations that would also involve national regulatory and supervisory authorities, as well as international institutions, such as the Bank for International Settlements. The Fund's opinion and initiatives would carry particular weight on this issue, given the prestige and experience it gained during the phase of debt-crisis management.

The particular problems of the poorest countries seem to require special attention in the context of stabilization assistance, given their unmet rights to uniform treatment in the international economic system. This has become more evident and more widely perceived as a result of the particularly damaging impact that the recent dramatic changes in the international environment have had on most of their economies. Although undoubtedly a large part of the massive problems of the poorest countries can be attributed to mistaken government policies, there is important evidence that what has differentiated individual country growth experience in sub-Saharan Africa has been the magnitude of exogenous shocks rather than domestic policies (see Wheeler 1984); equally there is firm evidence that instability in import volumes is significantly correlated with economic growth (see Helleiner 1984). These results strengthen the case for priority being given by the international community to the stabilization of import volumes in low-income countries, and thus for the provision of liquidity rather than long-term finance. Appropriate levels of short-term finance for low-income countries clearly would not, by themselves, guarantee improvements in their macroeconomic performance, but would make it feasible and considerably more likely. The Structural Adjustment Facility established in 1986 was intended to provide concessional financial assistance to low income members who faced serious balance-of-payments difficulties and who needed to undertake programmes of structural adjustment (Russell 1990).

As noted, the strongest justification for special measures for, and flexibility towards, low-income countries by institutions like the Fund is vulnerable groups (and particularly children) in many developing countries, and this concern has been reflected in political circles. It is perhaps not sufficiently widely known that the US Congress approved in 1980 an amendment to the US Bretton Woods Agreement Act – still in effect – which requires US representatives to the Fund to work for changes in Fund guidelines, policies and decisions, and, in approving adjustment programmes, to: 'take into account the effect... on jobs, investment, real per capita income, the gap in wealth between rich and poor, and social programs, such as health, housing, and education, in order to seek to minimize the adverse impact of those adjustment programs on basic human needs.'

In this connection, it should be noted that the Fund's focus shifted in 1989 from an approach relying mainly upon debt rescheduling to one including possible debt and debt-service reduction in support of adjustment. This would involve a great deal of co-operation between all the parties concerned (Russell 1990).

Given an increased public and political awareness, it would seem to be an appropriate time for the Fund to begin exploring general and concrete ways in which its policy advice could contribute to maintaining or improving nutrition levels, health standards, and real incomes among the poorest sections of the population of countries with which it is negotiating adjustment programmes, and to avoid – wherever possible – policy advice that may be detrimental to the welfare of those groups. The Fund itself is clearly best qualified for deciding the best way in which this could be achieved. Possible measures would seem to include: research in the Fund (or in conjunction with specialized institutions) on measures to maximize welfare of poor people in the context of stabilization; some change in the terms of reference, procedures, and possibly even composition of Fund missions; closer collaboration with other sources of external assistance so as to mobilize additional external resources; and some form of public statement, which would make explicit the Fund's concern with – and the priority it attaches to – the need to protect vulnerable groups in the course of adjustment programmes.

REFERENCES

Cassen, R. (1986) *Does Aid Work?*, Oxford: Oxford University Press.

Cline, W. R. (1984) *Internationl Debt: Systemic Risk and Policy Response*, Washington: Institute for International Economics.

Cooper, R. N. (1983) 'The evolution of the International Monetary Fund towards a world central bank', background paper to G. K. Helleiner (ed.) *Towards a New Bretton Woods: Challenges for the World Financial and Trading System*, London: Commonwealth Secretariat.

Dell, S. (1985) 'Fifth credit tranche', *World Development* 13: 245–49.

Dell, S. and Lawrence, R. (1980) *The Balance of Payments Adjustment Process in Developing Countries*, New York: Pergamon Press.

Eckaus, R. S. (1982) 'Observations on the conditionality of international financial institutions', *World Development* 10: 767–80.

The Economist (1983) 'Facility to finance the balance of payments deficit caused by the rise in interest rates', 2 April.

Goldstein, M. (1986) *The Global Effects of Fund-Supported Adjustment Programs*, Occasional Paper no. 42, Washington, DC: IMF.

Goreux, L. M. (1980) *Compensatory Financing Facility*, IMF pamphlet series no. 34, Washington, DC: IMF.

Griffith-Jones, S. (1981) *The Role of Finance in the Transition to Socialism*, Totowa, NJ: Allenheld, Osman.

——(1983) 'Compensatory financing facility: a review of its operations and proposals for improvement: report to the group of twenty-four', UNDP/UNCTAD project INT/81/046, Geneva: United Nations.

Griffith-Jones, S. and Harvey, C. (eds) (1985) *World Prices and Development*, Aldershot: Gower.

Guitián, M. (1981) *Fund Conditionality: Evolution of Principles and Practices*, IMF pamphlet series no. 38, Washington, DC: IMF.

Helleiner, G. K. (ed.) (1983) *Towards a New Bretton Woods: Challenges for the World Financial and Trading System*, London: Commonwealth Secretariat.

——(1984) 'Outward orientation, import instability and African economic growth, an empirical investigation', mimeograph.

Horsefield, J. K. (ed.) (1969) *The International Monetary Fund 1945–1965*, Washington, DC: International Monetary Fund.

IMF (1980) *World Economic Outlook*, Washington, DC: IMF.

——(1984a) *Annual Report of the Executive Board for the Financial Year Ended April 30*, Washington, DC: International Monetary Fund.

____(1984b) *World Economic Outlook, September 1984*, Occasional Paper no. 32, Washington, DC: International Monetary Fund.

Keynes, J. M. (1969) 'Proposals for an International Clearing Union', in J. K. Horsefield (ed.) *The International Monetary Fund 1945–1965*, Vol. 3, Washington, DC: International Monetary Fund.

Killick, T. (1963) 'The reform of the International Monetary Fund', background paper to G. K. Helleiner (ed.) *Challenges for the World Financial and Trading System*, London: Commonwealth Secretariat.

____(ed.) (1984) *The Quest for Stabilization: The IMF and the Third World*, London: Gower/Overseas Development Institute.

Larosière, J. de (1984) 'Text of address to Council on Foreign Relations', *IMF Survey* 13: 377–80.

Lever, H. (1983) 'International debt threat: a concerted way out', *The Economist* 288: 14–16.

Massad, C. (1984) 'Implications of the external debt for international finance', *Development* 1: 26–9.

Robichek, E. W. (1984) 'The IMF's conditionality re-examined', in J. Muns (ed.) *Adjustment, Conditionality and International Financing*, Washington, DC: International Monetary Fund.

Russell, R. (1990) 'The new rules and facilities of the IMF', *IDS Bulletin* 21 (2).

United Nations Economic Commission for Latin America (1984) *Adjustment: Policies and Renegotiation of the External Debt*, UN document E/CEPAL/G 1299, Santiago de Chile: United Nations.

Jolly, R. and Cornia, A. (eds) (1985) *The Impact of Recession on Children in Developing Countries*, New York: Pergamon Press/UNICEF.

Wheeler, D. (1984) 'Sources of stagnation in sub-Saharan Africa', *World Development* 12: 1–23.

Williamson, J. (1983a) 'Keynes and the international economic order', in G. D. N. Worswick and J. A. Trevithick (eds) *Keynes and the Modern World*, Cambridge: Cambridge University Press.

____(1983b) 'The lending policies of the International Monetary Fund', in J. Williamson (ed.) *IMF Conditionality*, Washington, DC: Institute for International Economics.

Witteveen, J. (1983) 'Developing a new international monetary system: a long-term view', *IMF Survey* 12: 319–21.

59

TRANSNATIONAL ORGANIZATIONS AND ACTORS

DAVID KOWALEWSKI

Students of international organizations (IOs) usually distinguish international non-governmental organizations (INGOs or simply NGOs) and transnational organizations (TNOs or simply TOs) from international governmental organizations (IGOs) (Jacobson 1984). NGOs are most often defined as those international organizations which have at least one private (non-state) actor as member. A more restrictive definition stipulates that these organizations must represent only private actors of several countries. Accordingly, some scholars propose a 'hybrid' IO category between pure IGOs and pure NGOs for those organizations having both governmental and private representation (for example, the International Telecommunications Satellite Consortium or INTELSAT, the International Council of Scientific Unions).

Since scholars normally require that IGOs and NGOs be truly associational and not centrally directed by nationals of only one country, they propose a special category, TOs, for those organizations with special ties of authority to a single nation. Such organizations are not true 'associations' of groups coming together from several nations to form a new collectivity. Rather, they originate and extend their authority abroad from one country. Three major types of TOs are usually distinguished: transnational religions (such as the Roman Catholic Church), transnational foundations (such as Ford and Rockefeller) and business international non-governmental organizations (BINGOs). The last grouping, more commonly called transnational enterprises (TNEs), are usually divided into transnational corporations (TNCs) and transnational banks (TNBs). These companies are also called 'multinational' enterprises (MNEs, including multinational corporations or MNCs and multinational banks or MNBs). Yet this designation is misleading. Usually the majority of stock in the firm is owned by nationals of one country. The major decisions for the foreign subsidiaries in host countries are made by managers in the headquarters of the parent company in the home country. Hence, the term 'transnational' is more appropriate than 'multinational'.

The plurality of NGOs have economic purposes. These are followed closely in number by NGOs pursuing health and science objectives. Some of the larger ones have become well known to the world's citizenry. These NGOs usually have purposes which reflect mass-based interests: for instance, environmental (such as Greenpeace and Friends of the Earth), humanitarian (such as Amnesty International and Oxfam), economic (such as the Club of Rome), cultural (such as the World Council of Churches) and fraternal (such as the International Boy Scouts). Regional NGOs outnumber global NGOs by a ratio of about three to one. The average NGO has a budget of US $1 million and a staff of ten.

Depending on one's definition, the number of NGOs today ranges from 3,000 to 10,000. Their growth in the twentieth century has been remarkable, indeed exponential. By the beginning of 1990s they outnumbered IGOs by a ratio of at least ten to one.

While many scholars accord NGOs little importance in international politics, others are less sanguine. In particular, theorists of the pluralist and functionalist schools assert that NGOs are having a major, albeit slow and incremental, political impact (Jacobson 1984).

Pluralists view NGOs as international private 'interest groups' pressing their demands on IGOs. Thus, NGOs operate much like lobbyists in national political systems. As such, if the pressure exerted by NGOs is persistent, skilled and strong enough, they will shape to some degree the decisions made by IGOs.

Certainly this theory has some basis in fact. Many IGOs accord NGOs a special 'consultative status'. This status may include the rights to send observers, attend meetings, submit agenda items and written briefs, and present testimony at hearings. Although consultative status does not include voting rights, it would be naïve to suppose that IGO officials are unaffected by NGO pressures. Indeed, given the limited budgets of IGOs, and the technical expertise of NGOs, the former would generally seem well served by these 'international registered lobbyists'.

Indeed, consultative status did not merely come about through an informal and haphazard process. It was formally institutionalized after the Second World War by the United Nations (UN). Article 71 of the UN Charter authorized the Economic and Social Council (ECOSOC) to make arrangements for consultation by NGOs. Today, at least 500 NGOs have such status with ECOSOC. Many others are represented at meetings of UN-affiliated IGOs, such as scientific associations at the Food and Agriculture Organization (FAO). Hundreds more have consultative status at regional IGOs, in particular the European Economic Community (EEC) and the European Free Trade Association (EFTA). Economic NGOs tend to have the greatest representation. Most notable among these are the International Chamber of Commerce, World Confederation of Labour, and the International Federation of Agricultural Producers.

Functionalists claim that the proliferation of NGOs represents a historical trend which will ultimately contribute to some kind of global political authority. According to this view, NGOs signify the internationalization of the private sphere of everyday life. Their connections with IGOs strengthen the 'supra-nationalization' of politics, the flow of power from national governments to an international one. In the short term, special-purpose IGOs and their affiliated NGOs will become increasingly active in exerting pressure on national governments. In the long term, the activities of IGOs and NGOs will 'spill over' into some form of world government. As such, they function as global political integrationists. Thus, while perhaps few citizens of the world have heard of the Campaign for a World Constituent Assembly, a political NGO, some scholars believe that its aim is less idealistic than conventionally imagined.

Still, although NGOs collectively may have long-range political consequences, only a few (such as Greenpeace and Amnesty International) become embroiled in political controversy. Such cannot be said of TNEs. Virtually every aspect of their operations has come under close scrutiny and attack in recent decades.

The globalization of national economies has been largely a function of the growing marketing activities and foreign direct investment (FDI) of TNEs from the First World (North America, Japan, Western Europe). (Comparatively few TNEs emanate from the Second World or the larger Third World nations such as India and Brazil.) FDI has been greatly facilitated by First World governments, who provide research, low-cost insurance, low-interest loans, and foreign tax-credits and depletion allowances. Today some 10,000 corporations have investments in some 35,000 subsidiaries in foreign countries. They employ some 70 million people abroad. The total production of these TNCs represents about two-fifths of the Gross World Product. However, a mere fifty account for about one-half of global FDI, and only 200 account for four-fifths. Among the top twenty TNCs, the international oil industry has the largest representation through its 'Seven Sisters' (Exxon, Royal Dutch Shell, and others). Most FDI (about three-quarters) is made in other First World nations, with the remainder largely in Third World countries. Increasingly, however, TNEs have signed joint-ventures and similar arrangements with Soviet enterprises. The de-Sovietization of Eastern Europe will undoubtedly contribute to a growth of FDI in that region during the coming decades.

FDI has increased substantially since the Second World War, a trend that is likely to continue. Generally, profits from FDI are greater than those from equivalent domestic investments. Although most TNEs (about one-half) are

US-based, corporations from Japan have recently shown the greatest growth of FDI, particularly in Asian host nations but also in the United States, Brazil and the Middle East. The expansion of the Japanese economy, and its heavy dependence on foreign raw materials, foreshadows even more FDI in the future.

Some decline in agricultural FDI, however, is evident. TNCs have been forced to respond to nationalist hostilities against the foreign ownership of land. Many TNC landholdings have been expropriated by nationalist governments. TNCs have also found that 'contract farming' with large landowners in host nations can secure the commodities they need while the many risks of agriculture can be shifted onto the shoulders of local producers.

This decline in agricultural FDI, however, has been more than offset by the dramatic growth in the number of manufacturing subsidiaries. About a half of TNCs are manufacturing firms. Most remarkable has been the establishment of special manufacturing sites or Free Trade Zones (FTZs), particularly in Asia. (These centres are also called by other names, such as 'Export Processing Zones'.) In these zones, dozens of TNCs group together to share utilities, roads and other infrastructure. Manufacturing TNCs have increasingly taken advantage of technological mobility as well as the low wage rates and incentives offered by Third World governments. By the early 1990s, about a hundred FTZs had been established across the Third World.

Little controversy surrounds FDI by TNCs in the host nations of the First World. True, some nationalist resentment has been expressed against TNC ownership of land and cultural enterprises (such as newspapers and film studios) and against possible distortion of the political process. However, host nations of the First World have economies independent enough, and political and social institutions strong enough, to prevent TNEs from doing serious damage. FDI represents only a small proportion of the total capital-stock of First World economies. Domestic firms and labour unions exert far more effective political pressure than do TNEs. Indeed, FDI in the host economies of the First World appears to have a net beneficial impact.

There is also little controversy about FDI in the Second World. Some ultraconservatives attack the benefits – military and economic – which communist regimes might derive from TNCs. As such, they believe, the totalitarian Soviet regime will continue the threaten the free world. However, this is a minority view. Most observers feel that FDI has a liberalizing effect, or none at all, on authoritarian Second World governments.

FDI in the Third World, however, has raised a storm of controversy. TNCs themselves, and generally the conservative and liberal scholars of the modernizationist school, tend to view such operations as benevolent. On the other hand, scholars of the Marxist, dependency and world-system schools, as well as numerous social groups, have a far less sanguine theory.

947

The benevolent view can be summarized easily (Freeman 1981; Madden 1977). FDI promotes macro-level economic growth in regions of the world which need it most. The stimulus of FDI flows, multiplier effects, reinvestment of profits and tax contributions will enable Third World economies to 'take off' and ultimately catch up with those of the First World. FDI creates jobs in the Third World, where unemployment normally ranges around 30 per cent. TNEs transfer technology, which will eventually enable local firms to develop and compete in the global market-place.

According to critics, however, these claims concerning macro-level contributions are overstated, if not false. The term 'foreign' direct investment is a misnomer. The typical TNC in fact brings in little foreign currency to Third World economies. Rather, on the average, TNCs raise some 80 per cent of their investment capital from local sources, often from subsidiaries of TNBs. Thus, they actually absorb local capital, removing its availability from local firms and making it more difficult for them to grow and compete. Local businesses also suffer from the marketing power and political influence of TNCs. Many local businesses go bankrupt.

Multiplier effects are exaggerated because of limited, if not non-existent, forward and backward linkages. FDI has a high import content; TNCs purchase few inputs from local firms. Their output is usually exported too, often in the form of raw materials for further processing, to other TNCs in the global economy. Few downstream contracts are generated for local firms.

TNEs reinvest only a small proportion of their profits. Usually, over one-half of profits are repatriated to the parent company in the First World directly, or indirectly by way of fees for patents and licences, 'loans' and transfer pricing. The remainder often goes in higher dividends and salaries for board members and managers (who spend the income on luxury goods produced in the First World), or towards the purchase of local firms. As such, TNEs in fact 'decapitalize' the Third World.

Their tax contribution is also less than usually assumed. TNEs often receive 'tax holidays' of ten to fifteen years from Third World governments. Taxes are easily avoided through manipulation of accounting procedures and connections with mailbox 'subsidiaries' in tax-haven countries.

TNCs, like all economic enterprises, do create jobs. The initial contribution to employment, especially in construction, cannot be denied. Yet, TNCs are far more capital-intensive than local firms. In terms of number of employees per unit of assets, they employ far fewer workers (up to a half less) than equivalent local firms. Since they often drive local enterprises out of business, further unemployment is generated. Since TNCs become increasingly capital-intensive over time, jobs are gradually lost. Mechanization of the countryside for export crops has an especially deleterious impact on employment. The paucity of forward and backward linkages means little generation of related jobs. Finally, the geographical mobility of TNCs makes these jobs unstable. Frequently, TNCs 'run away' to other countries whenever confronted by higher wages or taxes or other profit-threatening conditions, leaving workers unemployed with little advance notice.

Minimal technology transfer occurs. TNCs often have patent monopolies and guard them jealously. Most of the technical experts of the firm are expatriate managers and few TNCs have local programmes for technical training. Sophisticated equipment is imported from First World firms rather than produced or purchased locally. Some TNCs go as far as to import entire 'turn-key' or 'screwdriver' plants, which do little to enhance the productive skills of the local populace.

In sum, as a number of recent empirical studies have demonstrated, FDI flows may provide the economies of the Third World with short-term spurts in rates of growth. The long-term effect of FDI stocks, however, is a lowering of growth rates (Bornschier and Chase-Dunn 1985).

Critics list additional adverse effects: income disequalization, corruption of the political process, social degradation, health hazards, environmental damage and cultural displacement. Cross-national evidence suggests that TNEs have a negative impact on income distribution. Nations with a higher ratio of TNC investment stocks to total capital stocks have greater income inequality than those with a lower ratio (Bornschier 1979). The more dependent the nation's economy is on TNCs, the greater the gap between rich and poor. Higher-income strata benefit from joint-ventures, interlocking directorates, managerial jobs and contract farming with TNEs. Lower-income strata, however, suffer from low wages, often at the bare subsistence level; dangerous working conditions; forced overtime; union-busting practices; evictions from their land; and overfishing in coastal waters by high-tech TNC trawlers. Women and infants are especially disadvantaged (Ward 1985; Wimberly 1990).

TNEs contribute to the corruption of political systems. Bribery of host nation officials, especially military officers, is common. Bribes of half a million dollars are not unusual. Large campaign contributions to candidates of pro-TNE political parties unfairly disadvantage the more nationalist ones. The hiring of former state officials ('exit revolving doors') further distorts the political process. All these practices support 'export-oriented' regimes of 'state-compradors', who become increasingly geared toward the global market rather than local needs. They tend to bolster authoritarian elements, with adverse consequences for human rights. TNEs, in return for their largesse, are able to operate in a 'favourable investment climate', i.e. one with low duties for imports and exports, provision of infrastructure, leases of government land, tax holidays, few environmental restrictions, subsidized utility rates, favourable terms of profit repatriation, curtailment of labour militancy and other benefits. If nationalist parties come to power and threaten profits (as, for example, in

Chile and Jamaica during the 1970s), TNCs engage in destablization practices. They attempt to disrupt these governments directly by means of cutbacks in production, or indirectly through pressure on the states of the First World to apply economic and political sanctions.

Discrimination by TNEs has been assailed by ethnic and feminist groups. Prejudice in hiring, job assignment and promotion has been attacked. The resort facilities and beaches of tourist TNCs are usually off-limits to non-white citizens. Sexist employment practices, such as lower pay and economic coercion for sexual favours, have been criticized. The provision of prostitutes for the clients of tourist TNCs has been publicly attacked in Thailand, South Korea and elsewhere in Asia.

The marketing practices of TNCs have generated extensive criticism. TNC sales of several products – pesticides, pharmaceuticals, baby foods, alcohol and tobacco, armaments and nuclear reactors – have become political issues. Dangerous pesticides, some of which have been outlawed in the First World, have been 'dumped' in Third World countrysides. Often the labelling on such products is non-existent or inadequate, or of little use to illiterate farmers. It appears that chemical TNCs have actively encouraged unnecessary overspraying in order to enhance their profits. The health hazards to farmworkers are evident in high rates of poisoning.

Similar controversy surrounds the marketing practices of pharmaceutical TNCs. Basic drugs are overpriced, putting them out of the reach of the poor – those who need them most because of poverty-related illnesses. Sales of unsafe pharmaceuticals cause additional health problems.

The greatest negative publicity about the marketing practices of TNCs derives from sales of baby milk. The product is heavily promoted by mass-media advertising, free samples in hospitals offered by TNC-employee 'milk nurses', and several other means. Not only are most women in the Third World able to feed their babies with breastmilk, which costs nothing and has more nutritional benefits, but if mothers do not breastfeed their infants soon after birth, they become totally dependent on the high-price formula. The purchase of baby milk formula by poor parents, in turn, may take food out of the mouths of other family members. To make the product last, mothers dilute it with water, thereby inadvertently contributing to the infant's malnutrition. Since the water supply available to poor families is rarely pure, the health of infants is put at risk.

Similar adverse effects on health are caused by the promotion of alcohol and tobacco. By contributing to addiction and health problems in regions which need them least, TNCs are behaving unconscionably. Sales of armaments to dictatorial regimes support authoritarianism and contribute to violations of human rights.

The aggressive marketing of nuclear reactors in the Third World – largely because of a sharp drop in orders in the First World – constitutes a transfer of 'inappropriate technology'. Reactors require a huge capital outlay, which usually means additional foreign indebtedness. Since the construction of nuclear plants is largely in the hands of First World contractors, and since the technology is capital intensive, few economic benefits ensue. If reactors in the First World are plagued by safety problems, the problems in the Third World are even more numerous. Third World economies lack the technical expertise, and Third World states lack the resources, to manage and control a reactor safely. Their capacity for dealing with any serious disaster is severely limited. The possibility of diverting plutonium from the reactors to produce weapons (as in India and Pakistan according to some observers) encourages nuclear proliferation across the Third World.

The negative effects of TNC operations on Third World environments have come under increasing attack. Pollution of oceans, rivers and land has been caused by the marketing of dangerous pesticides and herbicides, spills and leaks from oil supertankers, and slag from mining operations. The destruction of coral reefs and mangrove swamps has brought extensive hardship to coastal residents. The disaster of Bhopal, India, where thousands were killed by an accidental emission of dangerous chemicals, was caused by inadequate procedures for inspection and control, excessive labour overtime and shortage of skilled personnel, and defective safety and operating equipment. Logging, mining and agricultural TNCs have been held responsible in part for the massive deforestation of the Amazon and other rainforests, which may have long-range negative effects on the world's climate. The multinational consortia of TNCs which have formed to mine the ocean floors for manganese nodules are being closely watched by critics. Their operations may have unknown destructive effects on the biology of the ocean floor, where scientists are finding life to be more prolific than heretofore recognized.

TNCs have been accused of damaging the cultures of the Third World. Aggressive and sophisticated advertising has undermined local cultures by means of 'Coca-colonization'. The provision of infrastructure such as roads and dams for TNCs in remote regions of Third World countries, as well as the disruptive practices of mining and logging TNCs, have displaced indigenous tribal peoples and threatened the survival of their cultures.

TNBs have been criticized as well. The largest of these enterprises have up to 150 foreign affiliates and derive up to 80 per cent of their earnings from abroad. They have been attacked for their financial support of dictatorial regimes, especially South Africa. Their responsibility for the Third World's foreign debt of US $1 trillion (one-half of which is owed to 1,000 TNBs) has been assailed. In particular, their high interest rates, short maturities and strict repayment conditions have contributed to the world financial crisis. TNB pressure on the International Monetary Fund (IMF) to impose austerity programmes on Third World nations, in return for the rescheduling of their debts, has been criticized for imposing serious hardships on the poor and leading to 'IMF riots' against the deprivation.

TNEs have also been seen as partly responsible for the prevalence of political violence in the Third World. TNEs increase inequality, which in turn breeds outbreaks of social unrest (London and Robinson 1989). TNCs are increasingly the targets of terrorist attacks; the socially most irresponsible firms are often the victims. Increasingly, therefore, TNEs are implementing security programmes, contracting with consultants for 'terrorist risk assessments', and enhancing their insurance coverage for such eventualities. Less militant actions against TNEs have been conducted by religious groups in the First World, who bring stockholder resolutions to annual meetings to challenge the corporation's social irresponsibilities. Increasingly, labour unions are taking international actions, such as strikes and boycotts, against TNCs which are regarded as abusive to their workers. Universities, local governments and religious groups have divested their stock from TNEs that do business with the apartheid regime of South Africa.

The controversy surrounding TNEs has certainly raised many issues of political economy and, to some extent, brought them to the awareness of the global citizenry. Social scientists and citizens alike are perhaps more enlightened about the international connections between economics and politics. It is difficult, however, to assess and compare the evidence provided by the two sides to the debate. Certainly, each side charges the other with a certain amount of propagandizing, subtle or not so subtle. And each side is, to some degree, probably guilty as charged.

But more sophisticated methodological issues are evident. First, there is the general problem of securing information on TNEs. Second, the debate is real enough, but rarely is it ever really joined. Differences in the level of analysis, and in the issues considered, result in difficulties of comparative assessment.

First, it is simply difficult to do systematic, especially quantitative, global research on the impact of TNEs. Several problems immediately present themselves. The global reach of the largest – and most important – TNEs makes research without substantial funding very laborious. Case studies are possible but often lack generalizability. Funding institutions tend to shy away from the more sensitive – and therefore more politically interesting – research questions. TNEs are private establishments and, unlike many governments, feel justified in withholding information from the public. They often claim the right to privacy or industrial security as reasons for lack of full disclosure. Recently, however, as a result of public pressure, some TNEs have become more amenable to granting access and providing information. In addition to the secrecy of TNEs one should mention the secrecy of many Third World governments, especially of authoritarian regimes.

Second, methodological differences make comparative evaluation difficult. A basic difference lies in levels of analysis. Generally, those with a benevolent view of TNEs stress the aggregate, macro-level contribution to development. Rarely are problems at the more disaggregated, grassroots level, such as wage discrimination or pollution of local rivers, considered. Although critics have provided a few excellent rebuttals of some pro-TNE claims regarding growth and disequalization at the more macro level, most criticism is based on non-systematic micro-level data. Such anecdotal information is invariably scarce and scattered. Some popular and semi-popular publications provide information on these issues at this lower level (for example, *Multinational Monitor* published monthly by Essential Information in Washington, DC, and *Corporate Examiner* published monthly by the Interfaith Center on Corporate Responsibility in New York). Yet such publications are hampered by limited funds.

Another methodological difference lies in types of issues examined. The apologist for TNEs usually emphasizes their economic contribution and tends to avoid environmental, social and other issues. When non-economic issues are considered, they are narrowly conceived. For example, political scientists often analyse TNE–government relations. Yet usually the research question concerns the bargaining process between TNEs and host-nation officials regarding restrictions on operations. Equally important political issues, such as the bargaining relationship between TNEs and workers and the intervention of host governments in labour disputes, go virtually untouched. Public opinion on TNEs is rarely discussed, let alone systematically examined. The fact of TNE bribery is well known; TNE managers admit as much. Yet it is a fact that is rarely considered by scholars. The issue has a host of scholarly implications. Can we put much faith in studies of the bargaining between TNEs and host governments if the possibility of bribery is not introduced as a control variable? How can one assess the degree to which the nationalist rhetoric of host regimes is authentic? If bribery is extensive, does it imply some kind of 'transnational class alliance' between elites of First and Third World nations? To what degree does it limit national sovereignty?

The position on such issues that citizens eventually choose will determine, in large part, their attitude toward the political control of TNEs. Three major questions require consideration. First, should TNEs be controlled? Second, if they should, how can they be? Third, if they can be, by whom?

On the first question, that of desirability, one finds little agreement; even the pro-TNE camp is divided. TNEs themselves favour few if any restrictions. Attempts at control will only result in high bureaucratic and production costs for the sake of regulating only a few deviant corporations, who will then find alternative means to continue their behaviours. TNEs are responsible for the growth of the global economy; regulation damages the international 'geese that lay the golden eggs'. Indeed, excessive control by Third World governments drives TNEs from locales where investment is needed most. By contrast, ultra-conservatives, as suggested above, favour tight restrictions on TNE operations and sales in the Second World, conservatives accept only minimal regulation, and liberals favour additional regulations when serious abuses are evident. Critics of TNEs favour tough controls, including nationalization, deconcentration of ownership, and strict regulatory measures and enforcement.

The second question, concerning the possibility of regulation, is answered in the affirmative by critics. Yet even they admit that the power of TNEs has grown so great that it surpasses that of most governments who are supposed to do the regulating. They also acknowledge that the globalization of TNEs and their mobility make complete control almost impossible at present. On the other hand, since most FDI is made by only a handful of TNEs, control at the source, if not at the branches, is achievable.

The final question, concerning the agency of regulation, finds apologists for TNEs favouring self-regulation by the firms. Among the critics, however, little consensus can be found. Most agree that Third World regimes have few resources available for a large regulatory apparatus. Control must be exercised at least in part by First World governments. Many critics, moreover, favour the institutionalization of grassroots power over the firm. The forms that such control might take include community representation with voting rights on boards of directors and managerial committees, shared ownership and management by workers, and other forms of popular power.

A few critics even assert that TNEs, like IGOs, represent a historical trend of globalization of national economies. The transcendence of economic life beyond the jurisdiction of national states will eventually contribute to some kind of global political authority that will regulate the international economy. From this institution will evolve a body of international economic law. To some extent the activities of TNEs are already constrained by international legal instruments (for example, TNEs in the global communications industry by the International Telecommunication Union). Indeed, the fact that regulation can bring international order out of chaos, and thus enhance profits, will eventually reduce a good deal of TNE resistance to global controls.

Some IGOs have already taken an active stance in attempting to regulate TNE behaviour. In 1975 the UN Commission on TNCs, a body with members from forty-eight nations in First, Second and Third Worlds, established a permanent Secretariat, the UN Centre on TNCs, as an autonomous body within the UN Secretariat. The Centre has a staff of thirty-five and a budget of US $5 million. It has three objectives: first, to strengthen the negotiating capacity of Third World nations in their dealings with TNEs (by establishing an information system and publishing the semi-annual *CTC Reporter* in New York); second, to conduct research on the impacts of TNEs; and third, to formulate a (non-binding) International Code of Conduct for TNCs.

The Centre has been the focus of intensive lobbying by a number of NGOs, including the International Chamber of Commerce and international labour unions. Whether it can resolve the many issues concerning TNEs is problematic. One can predict, however, that TNEs, and NGOs concerned with their impact, will play an increasingly visible role in global politics for some time to come.

REFERENCES

Bornschier, V. (1979) 'Income inequality: a cross-national study of the relations between MNC penetration, dimensions of the power structure, and income distribution', *American Sociological Review* 44: 487–506.

Bornschier, V. and Chase-Dunn, C. (1985) *Transnational Corporations and Underdevelopment*, New York: Praeger.

Freeman, O. (1981) *Multinational Company: Investment for World Growth*, New York: Praeger.

Jacobson, H. (1984) *Networks of Interdependence: International Organizations and the Global Political System*, New York: Knopf.

London, B. and Robinson, T. (1989) 'The effect of international dependence on income inequality and political violence', *American Sociological Review* 54: 305–8.

Madden, C. (1977) *The Case for the Multinational Corporation*, New York: Praeger.

Ward, K. (1985) 'Social consequences of the world economic system: the economic status of women and fertility', *Review* 8: 561–93.

Wimberly, D. (1990) 'Investment dependence and alternative explanations of Third World mortality: a cross-national study', *American Sociological Review* 55: 75–91.

FURTHER READING

Archer, C. (1983) *International Organizations*, London: Allen & Unwin.

Barnet, R. and Muller, R. (1974) *Global Reach: The Power of the Multinational Corporations*, New York: Simon & Schuster.

Billerbeck, K. and Yasugi, Y. (1979) *Private Direct Foreign Investment in Developing Countries*, Washington, DC: World Bank.

Chase-Dunn, C., Rubinson, R. and Bornschier, V. (1978) 'Cross-national evidence of the effects of foreign investment and aid on economic growth and inequality: a survey of findings and a reanalysis', *American Journal of Sociology* 84: 651–83.

Collins, J. and Lappe, F. M. (1979) *World Hunger: Ten Myths*, San Francisco: Institute for Food and Development Policy.

Crough, G. J. (1979) *Transnational Banking and the World Economy*, Sydney: Transnational Corporations Research Project, University of Sydney.

Feld, W. (1980) *Multinational Corporations and UN Politics: The Quest for a Code of Conduct*, New York: Pergamon.

George, S. (1980) *Feeding the Few: Corporate Control of Food*, Washington, DC: Institute for Policy Studies.

Goodrich, L. and Kay, D. (1973) *International Organizations: Policy and Process*, Madison: University of Wisconsin Press.

International Labour Office (1973) *Multinational Enterprises and Social Policy*, Geneva: International Labour Office.

——(1976) *The Impact of Multinational Enterprises on Employment and Training*, Geneva: International Labour Office.

Jacoby, N., Nehemkis, P. and Eells, R. (1977) *Bribery and Extortion in World Business*, New York: Macmillan.

Kumar, K. (1980) *Transnational Enterprises: Their Impact on Third World Societies and Cultures*, Boulder, Colo.: Westview Press.

Ozawa, T. (1979) *Multinationalism: Japanese-Style*, Princeton: Princeton University Press.

Snow, R. (1977) 'Dependent development and the new industrial worker: the case of the export processing zone', unpublished Ph.D. dissertation, Harvard University.

Spero, J. (1981) *Politics of International Economic Relations*, New York: St Martin's Press.

Sturm, H. and Wormuth, F. (1959) 'International power elite', *Monthly Review* 11: 282–7.

Union of International Associations (1984–5) *Yearbook of International Associations*, Munich: K. G. Saur.

UN Centre on Transnational Corporations (1981) *Transnational Banks: Operations, Strategies, and Their Effects in Developing Countries*, New York: United Nations.

——(1983) *Transnational Corporations in World Development*, New York: United Nations.

UN Commission on Human Rights (1982) *Study of the Problem of Discrimination Against Indigenous Populations*, New York: Subcommission on the Prevention of Discrimination against Indigenous Populations, United Nations.

UN Department of Economic and Social Affairs (1974) *The Impact of Multinational Corporations on Development and on International Relations*, New York: United Nations.

US Congress (1980) *Marketing and Promotion of Infant Formula in Developing Countries*, Washington, DC: Committee on Foreign Affairs, US House of Representatives.

——(1980) *Tropical Deforestation: Overview, Role of International Organizations, and Role of Multinational Corporations*, Washington, DC: Committee on Foreign Affairs, US House of Representatives.

Vernon, R. (1971) *Sovereignty at Bay*, New York: Basic Books.

Weir, D. and Schapiro, M. (1981) *Circle of Poison: Pesticides and People in a Hungry World*, San Francisco: Institute for Food and Development Policy.

60

REGIONAL ASSOCIATIONS: ECONOMIC

ALBERT HARRIS

In the most basic sense, regional economic associations (REAs) are entities designed to promote an accelerated but balanced economic growth of the member states. There is also a conscious effort to enhance social progress, cultural development and quality of life in general for the populations of the member states. Beyond this, these organizations can diverge widely in their purposes, ranging from the establishment of a simple free-trade area, where the effort is to reduce internal customs tariffs with the eventual aim of their elimination, to a common market where the effort is towards the elimination of all barriers to the free movement of persons, goods, services and capital between the members, as well as the establishment of a common tariff and commercial policy relative to third countries.

What is meant by the term 'region' and 'regional organization' has been the subject of intense debate. In one view, a region is a matter of self-definition, established by the voluntary actions and public statements of nation-state representatives and the behaviour or activities of states who choose to associate. In another view, some degree of spatial or geographical proximity among a group of states (a subgroup of the entire universe of states) is necessary to constitute a true region. Other factors such as economic interdependence, and social, cultural and linguistic homogeneity, may also be relevant to defining a region (Russet 1967: 11–12). Typically, states come to be viewed as a political region (by themselves as well as by 'outside' states) through the group's practices, including the conclusion of treaties and other formal agreements between the group's members (Padelford 1955: 25–7).

In the post-Second World War era, REAs have proliferated around the globe. Yet in pursuing economic benefit, even within the confines of an association, individual nation-states sometimes find that their interests are not advanced to the same degree as those of other member states. There is often a degree of 'unevenness' within REAs in the economic development of the members of the group. Disparities in economic position among member states

957

may result from differences in natural resource endowments, population size and distribution, access to seaports and other factors. In some cases, the style of colonial occupation by the metropole may have influenced a population's literacy rate, level of indigenous technological advancement and the like. Thus, to achieve balanced economic growth, REAs must deal with existing differentials in the economic condition of member states and cope with the disputes that arise in relation to such issues. In addition, there is also a possibility that some members may be injured, either by another individual member state's pursuit of its welfare or through the efforts of two or more other members' attempts to improve their collective benefit. REAs must therefore cope with conflict generated by the fact that all member states do not benefit equally from REA policies.

REAs are commonly constructed with mechanisms designed to minimize any harm accruing to an individual member as a result of the joint efforts of other members' actions to improve their economic condition. Since their goal is to 'maximize' the total group benefit, REAs are structured to promote cooperation and to achieve dispute resolution. They seek to mediate conflicts by helping members to identify the central issues underlying a dispute. They also attempt to facilitate negotiation by fostering agreements that can be maintained with minimal or no coercion by outside parties or by disputants (Burton 1969: 171; Walton and McKersie 1965: 144–61). Yet given the difficulty of the issues that arise among members, how successful are REAs in settling disputes? What are the consequences for a regional economic association if it fails to resolve a conflict among its members?

The following sections will attempt to shed some light upon such questions by examining conflicts that arose within the Central American Common Market (CACM), the Andean Common Market (ANCOM) and the East African Community (EAC).

CENTRAL AMERICAN COMMON MARKET (CACM)

In 1969 the 'Soccer War' erupted between El Salvador and Honduras, both members of the Central American Common Market (Golbert and Gingold 1980: 191–2). The main issue in the dispute between the two states was the evolution of a particular factor, labour mobility, which most regional economic associations would regard as conducive to the basic goal of the REA, regional growth. In this case, the problem insofar as Honduras viewed it was too large an influx of labourers from El Salvador into the Honduran labour market, many of them on a permanent basis (Cable 1969: 658–9).

El Salvador is a much more densely populated country than Honduras, and the former, although the more heavily industrialized of the two, had a surplus labour problem even before the advent of the CACM. Many of the individuals who migrated to Honduras were more highly skilled than their Honduran counterparts and so increased the competition for higher wage-paying jobs in Honduras. The Honduran trade unions were quite vocal in protesting this immigration, much of it the illegal, 'squatter' variety (Golbert and Gingold 1980: 191). It is not clear how much effort the El Salvador government had put into a land reform movement in order to lessen the number of landless peasants. There is some question as to how much the government could do, given the rather oligarchic structure of land holding in El Salvador (Cable 1969: 659–60). Decreasing the number of landless peasants would have presumably reduced the numbers migrating into Honduras.

In any case the El Salvador government denied any direct blame for the injury Honduras declared it was suffering as a result of Salvadorian immigrants residing in the latter's territory. El Salvador indicated it was not that it was unwilling but that it was unable to stem the flow of its unemployed citizens. Additionally, El Salvador attempted to raise the point that labour mobility should have been a prominent desire of CACM in the movement towards regional integration (Schmitter 1972: 44–5). El Salvador's argument seemed to be that although the migrant cross-border flow had not been conscious policy, the fact of its occurrence was not counter to regional integration theory, and should be viewed in that light by all concerned parties, including the CACM.

Dissatisfied with this response, Honduras then instituted a land 'reform' programme of its own, directed against the immigrants (Golbert and Gingold 1980: 191). El Salvador followed by issuing accusations against Honduras of mistreatment of the 'squatters'. The dispute reached a crescendo on the occasion of a soccer match between the two countries held in El Salvador in mid-June 1969. Honduras lost the match, but only because (at least partially) Salvadorian supporters had harassed Honduran team players. When the reports of this mistreatment reached Honduran communities, the reaction was to attack a number of the illegal immigrants from El Salvador, some of whom were killed. El Salvador denounced these attacks and demanded reparations. As no such 'reparations' were forthcoming, a few days later El Salvador launched a military attack against Honduras (Cable 1969: 662).

For CACM the breach in relations between the two countries after what turned out to be a four-day war had ominous repercussions. Honduras withdrew from formal association membership, thus removing an important internal market for the exports of the more industrialized states of El Salvador, Costa Rica and Guatemala. Subsequently, however, Honduras moved to establish separate bilateral trading agreements with Costa Rica, Guatemala and Nicaragua, while the economic relationship between El Salvador and Honduras remained severed for an extended period (Gordon 1978: 27).

The optimism that once was expressed concerning the prospects for the

CACM have never been fulfilled. 'The CACM has demonstrated in the first few years of its existence that wide-ranging co-operation even in the highly volatile political atmosphere of Central America is a practical possibility once realistic priorities are established and tangible benefits ensured. . . . It has initiated, in spite of the over-ambitious institutional structure, an "irreversible" process of regional integration that, if consolidated, must play a major part in transforming relationships within the entire inter-American region' (Simmonds 1967: 929–30).

The El Salvador–Honduras immigration or 'labour mobility' dispute certainly contributed to the inability of the CACM to reach the 'wide-ranging' co-operation alluded to above. The CACM lacked the channels of communication capable of placing the governments of El Salvador and Honduras in a direct negotiating context that was any more effective than those that existed normally outside the CACM context. The primary issue was the surplus labour from El Salvador distorting the Honduras labour market.

But the less diversified Honduran economy was already serving as a major export market for El Salvador's much more industrialized economy. Honduras had experienced a deficits problem with its fellow CACM states because the bulk of its exports to those countries were agricultural and timber products, while a significant proportion of Honduran imports from its CACM partners was manufactured products (Cable 1969: 669–70). The perception by Honduras was that the benefits of CACM membership were much less visible than the deprivations.

States want to advance their economic development through improved trade patterns resulting from a regional association membership (Gordon 1978: 9). But this is not the only incentive for developing countries to enter such associations. They also hope to expand and diversify their economies, particularly in the manufacturing sector. Trade creation through participation in a regional association can do this, but if it occurs only through a greater volume of traditional exports to association member states, diversification of the economy does not ensue (Lizano and Wilmore 1975: 294–5). This was precisely the complaint of Honduras, and the influx of immigrants from El Salvador contributed greatly to the former's perception that the disparities within the CACM were continuing.

At its inception the CACM instituted two mechanisms, the Central American Bank and the Integration of Industries Agreement, which were designed to channel the location of investment, particularly foreign, in ways promoting region-wide investment distribution (Cable 1969: 670). But these proved to have only a marginal effect because new investment during succeeding years continued to be attracted to traditional industrial sites in Costa Rica, El Salvador and Guatemala. These sites had the initial infrastructure, trained labour force, transportation networks and the like, which provided investment incentives that the Central American Bank and the Integration of Industries Agreement could not match.

In effect, Honduras believed it was already bearing excessive costs, which were not offset by the benefits it was able to accumulate, before the immigration dispute surfaced. Specifically, 'in the CACM no procedures were set up to examine the problem of disparities among countries, to estimate the costs and benefits of the integration process, or to insure an equitable distribution of those costs and benefits' (Lizano and Wilmore 1975: 294). At the time of the immigration dispute there was no institutional apparatus designed to promote negotiated dispute resolution. The Executive Council had responsibility for applying and administering the General Treaty, but it relied on arbitration to locate solutions to disagreements.

Chapter IV of the CACM *Regulation on Procedures for Settlement of Disputes* (produced in October 1968) does call for direct negotiations of disputes, and the Permanent Secretariat is instructed to facilitate such an effort by undertaking a type of conciliatory role (*International Legal Materials* 1969: 634–5). Article 17, however, addressing how negotiations are to be initiated, simply called for 'telephonic, telegraphic or other written communications', or for a 'meeting which the parties have agreed to hold'. This was clearly not sufficient in the El Salvador–Honduras immigration dispute.

ANDEAN COMMON MARKET (ANCOM)

The original five member nations of the Andean Common Market (sometimes known simply as the Andean Group) signed the founding document, the Cartegena Agreement, in May 1969, partially because as concurrent members of the Latin America Free Trade Association (LAFTA), they believed themselves, at that time, ill-prepared to compete with the dominant LAFTA members, Brazil, Argentina and Mexico (Valdez 1972: 2–3). LAFTA has since been superseded by the Latin American Integration Association (LAIA). The latter is designed to be more of a common market with economic preferences for the members relative to outside states than was LAFTA, which was primarily only a region with member states able to conduct trade freely among themselves.

The original five ANCOM members (Colombia, Ecuador, Bolivia, Chile and Peru – Venezuela joined the group only in 1973) believed, barring some joint action on their part, that they would simply continue to serve as export markets for the three large Latin American states, Brazil, Argentina and Mexico, while not receiving equivalent benefit from the system of tariff concessions devised by LAFTA (Danino 1976: 637–8). The ANCOM states made it clear, however, that they did not intend to work in opposition to the

LAFTA arrangement, but rather to work towards strengthening their own positions, thereby enhancing the long-term viability of LAFTA.

The primary objectives of the ANCOM states include the harmonization of economic and social policies, increased trade liberalization, the acceleration of national industrialization, and eventual adoption of a common external tariff. This last goal has been particularly difficult to attain, not least because it conflicts in part with an additional intent, which is to grant Bolivia and Ecuador preferential treatment within the organization owing to their recognized less developed status. ANCOM has been exceptional, relative to regional economic associations generally, in its determination to make explicit efforts towards the elimination of development disparities among the members (Sanchez 1977: 140–1).

But perhaps more than anything else, ANCOM has been guided by a belief in the need to establish a foreign investment standard in order to pull apart the web of dependency within which the member states have generally perceived themselves to be enmeshed (Abbott 1975: 319–30). ANCOM countries consciously set out to free themselves from dependency status relative to the world's developed states, particularly the United States. A major way this dependency status had occurred was through the operations of transnational corporations (TNCs) with headquarters in developed countries. A number of influential academics, politicians and government advisers within ANCOM countries believed that the direct foreign investment of these corporations had, in the past, helped to create domination and *dependencia*.

> Such domination is asserted to have been implemented within each peripheral country through the fostered formation and growth of a minority ruling class which acts as an intermediary for the achievement of the interests of the center country, and which achieves a concentration of wealth and power. It thus dominates the vast majority of the population and is believed to have generated within each peripheral country the existence of two societies in clearly different stages of development, one modern and the other primitive. Their relationship is causal interdependency: the modern society developed and continues to develop through dominating the primitive society, and the primitive society remains underdeveloped because of that dominance. In the international sphere, the same kind of relationship is believed to be reproduced: the center-country maintains its condition through dominating its peripheral countries, and the peripheral countries remain underdeveloped because of that dominance.
>
> (Danino 1976: 636–7)

American foreign investment had exerted a particularly strong influence over the ANCOM state economies for decades, holding roughly five billion dollars worth of equity position in ANCOM domestic markets when the Cartegena agreement was initialled (Goldbert and Gingold 1980: 195). To reduce American and other foreign influence the ANCOM countries in 1971 issued

Decision 24 of the Commission of the Cartegena Agreement, otherwise known as the Andean Foreign Investment Code (*International Legal Materials* 1972: 126). This complex and wide-ranging document regulates areas that include foreign investment, foreign private loans and technology transfers which enter ANCOM from third-country states.

Included among the Code's major provisions (Horton 1982: 44–5) were:

1 a divestment stipulation in which locally organized companies with over 50 per cent foreign ownership, and foreign firms generally, must have a majority of their stock or equity acquired by local firms within a fixed time frame; exceptions are allowed for those foreign firms conducting over 80 per cent of their business outside of ANCOM;

2 tight controls are imposed on the transfer of technology, including the administration of contracts;

3 restrictions on the rate of repatriation of earnings for foreign firms, a rate which initially was 14 per cent, but which was later modified as a result of the Chilean crisis to 20 per cent.

It was this last provision of the Code which helped precipitate the dispute that led to Chile's eventual departure from ANCOM, although it grew from the fact that Chile, through a change of economic philosophy brought about by a change of government, became extremely uncomfortable with the general thrust of the entire measure. The Code only establishes a minimum standard for the regulation of foreign investment in each ANCOM state. Each country is free to establish its own stricter norm if it so desires. This is precisely what the Chilean government, under Salvador Allende as President, pursued as policy (Fouts 1975: 543–4).

The foreign investment policies of the Allende government, which was in place when the Code was ratified by Chile (although the preceding government of Eduardo Frei had actually signed the Cartegena Agreement), were more stringent than called for in the Code. But with the fall of the Allende government and subsequent installation of the Pinochet regime, the Code suddenly became antithetical to Chile's view toward foreign investment. Whereas the Allende government had been an advocate of state ownership of the most important sectors of the economy, the new military regime signalled its determination to adopt University of Chicago-style classical economic theory as the bedrock of Chilean economic policy (Horton 1982: 45).

Decision 24, especially the section referring to a limitation on the repatriation of profits, was believed overly burdensome to the new government's efforts to attract foreign capital. Chile was also concerned that the level of the common external tariff not be set at a level that would prevent foreign capital having reasonable access to the Chilean market. The key element of the dispute between Chile and the rest of ANCOM, however, was the profit remittances section of the Code. Chile decided to enact Decree Law 600 in July 1974, requiring new foreign investors to negotiate contractual obligations with a Committee on Foreign Investments (Horton 1982: 45–6). A particularly grating aspect of Decree Law 600 for the other ANCOM states was Article 19, which made allusions to the possibility that Decision 24 did not apply, at least not fully, in Chile (Fouts 1975: 548). Negotiations between Chile and other ANCOM members ensued during the autumn meeting of the ANCOM Commission.

In the round of negotiations during the autumn of 1974, Chile relented and passed Decree Law 746, which recognized the application of the Andean Code in Chile (Horton 1982: 46). At the same time Chile gave notice that it remained dissatisfied with the Code and would continue to work for its moderation. The point about Decree Law 600 which so raised the ire of ANCOM states was that it established 'only that the contract between the investor and the Foreign Investment Committee will set the manner and opportunity of repatriating the foreign investments, profits, or legally distributed dividends' (Sanchez 1977: 161). Moreover, Decree Law 600 set no exact ceiling on remittance levels, leaving the parties to bargain over this rate.

Discussions between Chile and ANCOM continued during 1975 and the first half of 1976. ANCOM offered certain concessions in an apparent effort to mollify Chile, although there is some thought that the concessions were more to benefit other ANCOM members rather than Chile, because the ANCOM states were experiencing serious downturns in investment and trade. A major ANCOM concession was the Declaration of Boyoca, a measure designed to allow profit remittance levels to increase from 14 to 20 per cent (Vargas-Hidalgo 1978: 406). Other concessions included an offer to reduce the common external tariff to 26 per cent, but Chile demanded a more severe reduction, to 12 per cent.

In any event, Chile was not persuaded to sign Decision 100, the protocol amending the Cartegena Agreement, instead preferring to leave ANCOM altogether in October 1976 (Livingston and Newman 1977: 179–80). The effort by the ANCOM Commission to find a solution to the dispute through an invoking of the Andean Group's Consultative Committee did not succeed. Partly as a consequence of the Chilean withdrawal, ANCOM's commission adopted Decisions 103 and 109, which modified Decision 24, particularly in the area of profit remittances, allowing rates above 20 per cent under certain circumstances (Vargas-Hidalgo 1978: 406).

Negotiations on a fairly direct basis did take place in this dispute. The ANCOM Commission supplied the Junta, or Board, with the means to conciliate discussions between member states. Board members travelled to Chile in October 1974 to discuss Decree Law 600, and these discussions resulted in Decree Law 746, which 'expressly stated that Decision 24 was part of the

Chilean legal system' (Vargas-Hidalgo 1978: 406). But all of this seemed not to do more than delay what may have been an inevitable outcome after the Chilean change of government.

EAST AFRICAN COMMUNITY (EAC)

The East African Community was brought into being by the Treaty for East African Co-operation, signed at Kampala in June 1967; its goals were to 'strengthen and regulate the industrial, commercial and other relations of the Partner states to the end that there shall be accelerated, harmonious and balanced development and sustained expansion of economic activities the benefits whereof shall be equitably shared' (*International Legal Materials* 1967: 932). Although the EAC member states, Kenya, Uganda and Tanzania, had as their eventual intent the free movement of labour, capital and goods among their respective markets, from the outset it was clear this objective would be slow in realization.

In levels of economic development, the advantaged position of Kenya was clearly recognized even before the formation of the EAC. In a measure similar to that seen in our other cases, there were steps taken at the inception of the EAC to moderate these advantages so that the existing disparity between Kenya and its two partners would dissipate over time. The East African Development Bank was instituted with a mandate to distribute funds among the organization's membership in a discriminatory fashion favouring Uganda and Tanzania (Leistner 1975: 263). Certain internal EAC tariff barriers were allowed to remain in place in a fashion deliberately designed to protect Ugandan and Tanzanian 'infant industries' against competition from better capitalized Kenyan firms. These internal tariffs were labelled 'transfer taxes' because their intent was to lessen the inequalities in trade within the community and increase growth in Uganda and Tanzania (Hughes 1975: 40–1). Kenya was initially not allowed to utilize this tax, but the Community had in essence dropped it by 1973.

After a number of years in operation it became apparent that such steps were not sufficient to arrest a disturbing pattern of Kenyan 'dominance' in trade, finance and other sectors, including transportation. The benefits of EAC membership appeared to be accruing disproportionately to Kenya. There were competing explanations for the manner in which growth was unfolding within the Community, one of which was spoken of only in muted tones early on, if at all. This was the suggestion that it was Ugandan political instability, and Tanzania's decision to nationalize all key sectors, which perhaps made foreign investors choose to place their capital in the Kenyan free-market economy. Amon Nsekala, at one time a member of the East African Assembly (the EAC's legislature), chose to phrase it the following way:

The explanation for this is that profit maximization dictates that advantage be taken of external economies with the result that areas with a slight economic advantage succeed in attracting successively more and more enterprises. These then form their own market which draws further enterprises; they build up superior economic, social and cultural facilities which have even more drawing power. Other areas become increasingly less attractive and soon begin to lose the dynamic members of their labour force to the advanced centers, their relative disadvantage thereby being exacerbated.

(Mugomba 1978: 265)

It is against this background that the dispute, which according to some signalled the demise of the EAC, should be seen. Part of the original charter of the EAC was devoted to economic co-operation between the members beyond lowered internal tariffs and a common external tariff. A critical area of emphasis comprised the East African Corporations, jointly owned enterprises (there were four major ones) with operations in all three states and headquarters dispersed throughout the Community. One of these corporations was East African Airways (EAA), an international airline which also served as the Community domestic carrier, based in Kenya (Hughes 1975: 38–9).

East African Airways had been reorganized in 1972 because of financial problems caused in part by low passenger volume. There then followed a period of solvency, but eventually the corporation began to experience difficulties again in 1975 and 1976 for a variety of reasons. A high proportion of the international traffic for the airline was tourist traffic to Kenya and Tanzania, with some significant additional business traffic to Kenya. With time this traffic seemed to 'gravitate' more toward Kenya, leaving Tanzania with principally its less profitable domestic routes, while a similar situation existed for Uganda. Although the political unrest in Uganda was certainly a significant factor in passenger traffic levels, both Tanzania and Uganda argued that Kenya's advantage as a business and tourist attraction was an 'accident' of the colonial period (Hughes 1975: 39).

In an effort to remedy what they believed to be an unfair circumstance, the government of Tanzania constructed a major international airport, meant to serve as an alternative to Nairobi as the primary point of entry to the region. This strategy proved to be something less than a resounding success with traffic patterns not changing significantly, at least not before the collapse of EAA. It must be said that after the dismantling of EAA, and the division of its operations between the three successor national airlines, Tanzania Airways managed to have some initial success with European connections, partially owing to Kenya's decision to ban connecting flights from Nairobi to Dar Es Salaam (Green 1978: 128).

Before EAA ceased operations, however, negotiations did ensue principally between Kenya and Tanzania, concerning various options for sustaining the enterprise. In addition, the World Bank, as well as Nigeria and Liberia, offered their good offices in an attempt to resolve the dispute. These discussions could not be held at the highest levels (the Authority, composed of the three heads of state) because the Tanzanian President, Julius Nyerere, would not sit across the table with General Amin, the Ugandan leader. Negotiations were conducted at a lower level, through the joint Finance and Communications Councils (Amin 1975: 6). These discussions, as General Amin noted in an address to the EAC Assembly, were not successful, but his hopes for the Authority to provide a solution also came to no avail.

Why these negotiations failed may be understood more effectively after having viewed the comments of President Nyerere concerning the Corporations of the EAC generally.

> The East African Corporations are jointly owned by the peoples of East Africa through the three governments of East Africa. Their properties are East African properties, wherever they happen to be located. Decentralisation of control in the Corporations, and the geographical dispersion of the different Headquarters, was agreed in the Treaty. But each corporation is a single entity; as such it has responsibilities to each of the three partner states, and commitments on behalf of all its parts to international organisations and institutions. Further, each of the three partner states has responsibilities towards each of the Corporations, regardless of where the Headquarters is located.
>
> (Nyerere 1975: 6).

One may be safe in presuming that President Nyerere's comments were in part directed towards the EAA dispute. But Kenya's immediate concern in that dispute was the cash-flow problem of the EAA. Attempts to negotiate a rescheduling of the airline's debt through the Finance and Communication Councils' discussions failed in January 1977 (Green 1978: 125).

The financial shortcomings of the airline had begun to reach crisis proportions in 1976. Kenya had begun to make demands on the other two states for payment of due bills (in cash) for landing services at Nairobi airport. Tanzania had claimed in December 1976 that it had indeed made the requisite payment (*Africa News* 1977: 11). This obviously did not satisfy Kenya, as the airline was grounded in Nairobi at the end of January 1977. Because East Africa Airways was the last remaining East African Corporation, the last joint venture, its expiration contributed a great deal to the demise of the East African Community itself (Mugomba 1978: 264).

With the grounding of the airline by Kenya, the response from Tanzania was to close the border with Kenya in February 1977. The manner in which Tanzania undertook this action, which included the detention of Kenyan truck crews, effectively ended any immediate possibility of a resumption of negotiations over the EAA dispute (Green 1978: 126). Thus, although negotiations did have a role in this dispute, the degree of 'directness' possible within the EAC Finance and Communication Councils is open to argument. In any event, here was clearly an effort at dispute settlement, or management, rather than resolution. Since any attempt towards resolution would involve making concessions on values neither side was willing to accept, the EAC Councils decided to work toward the lesser goal of settlement; however, even that aim proved elusive.

CONCLUSIONS

Regional economic associations exist to promote the mutual advantage of their members. As the case studies reviewed above suggest, this is often an extremely difficult objective to achieve. In each of these instances, the REA was not successful in achieving a settlement or a resolution of the dispute in question. For the EAC the consequence of failure culminated in the demise of that REA; for the CACM one result was the Honduran decision to leave the organization (although Honduras did eventually return to the fold), and another was the deterioration of the organization into a quiet period (with the change of government in Nicaragua, the CACM appears to be somewhat reinvigorated); and for ANCOM, despite a modification in disputed policies by the organization, Chile decided not to remain within the group (and to date has not returned).

Failure is not the only possible outcome of REA mediation of intractable conflicts among members. As the record of the European Community in moving toward a unified market attests, REA accomplishments can also be profoundly impressive. But understanding the limits of REA effectiveness in settling disputes provides a means of evaluating their future role in accelerating the economic growth and development in regions characterized by uneven economic development.

When disputes arise under such conditions, the REA can at best perform a consultative function, providing a 'process oriented diagnosis, helping the parties think about their perceptions and attitudes, thus stimulating self-diagnosis of the conflict' (Fisher and Keashky 1988: 385). Acting in a consultative role, the REA must be less interested in extracting concessions from the disputing parties and more absorbed with ensuring that each party's perceptions of the other's position is an accurate reflection of that position. By using its institutionalized position to help the parties to understand the specific issues that divide them, the REA may help manage the dispute and may illuminate the direction in which a solution may be found. Such a consultative role may keep the dispute from escalating, but it cannot guarantee a solution. Indeed, the case studies examined here suggest that the likelihood for successful dispute settlement between members of the REA increases as the level of economic disparity which existed among members prior to REA inception is reduced. Given the numerous obstacles that REAs in the Third World face in eliminating uneven development, it could reasonably be concluded that the economic problems confronting developing nations cannot be remedied through collective self-reliance alone.

REFERENCES

Abbott, F. M. (1975) 'Bargaining power and strategy in the foreign investment process: a current Andean Code analysis', *Syracuse Journal of International Law and Commerce* 3 (2): 319–62.

Africa News (1977) 'East African Airways grounded', *Africa News* 8 (1): 11–12.

Ajomo, M. A. (1976) 'Regional economic organisations – African experience', *International and Comparative Law Quarterly* 25 (1): 58–101.

Amin, I. (1975) 'Opening the EA Legislative Assembly in Kampala', *Africa Currents* 2: 5–6.

Burton, J. W. (1969) *Conflict and Communication: The Use of Controlled Communication in International Relations*, London: Macmillan.

Cable, V. (1969) 'The "Football War" and the Central American Common Market', *International Affairs* 45 (4): 658–71.

Danino, R. (1976) 'The Andean Code after five years', *Lawyer of the Americas* 8 (3): 635–85.

Fisher, R. J. and Keashky, L. (1988) 'Third party interventions in intergroup conflict: consultation is not mediation', *Negotiation Journal* 4 (4): 381–93.

Fouts, S. C. (1975) 'The Andean foreign investment code', *Texas International Law Journal* 10 (3): 537–60.

Golbert, A. S. and Gingold, Y. N. (1980) 'Latin American economic integration: an overview of trade and developments in the Andean Pact, the Central American Common Market, and the Latin American Free Trade Association', *Syracuse Journal of International Law and Commerce* 7 (2): 183–211.

Gordon, M. W. (1978) 'The CACM nations, Panama and Belize: prospects and barriers to trade with the United States and the Caribbean Basin', *International Trade Law Journal* 4 (1): 20–35.

Green, R. H. (1978) 'The East African Community: death, funeral, inheritance', *Africa Contemporary Record* 10: 125–37.

Horton, S. (1982) 'Peru and ANCOM: a study in the disintegration of a common market', *Texas International Law Journal* 17 (1): 39–61.

Hughes, A. (1975) 'Community of disinterest', *Africa Report* 20 (2): 37–43.

International Legal Materials (1967) 'Treaty for East African Co-operation', *International Legal Materials* 6 (4): 932–1057.

——(1969) 'General Treaty of Central American Integration', *International Legal Materials* 8 (3): 629–46.

——(1972) 'Decision 24 of the Commission of the Cartegena Agreement', *International Legal Materials* 11 (1): 126–46.

Leistner, G. M. E. (1975) 'Economic cooperation on a regional basis', *Africa Institute Bulletin* 13 (7): 262–74.

Livingston, E. M. and Newman, R. D. (1977) 'Latin American integration', *Lawyer of the Americas* 9 (1): 179–81.

Lizaro, E. and Wilmore, L. N. (1975) 'Second thoughts on Central America: The Rosenthal report', *Journal of Common Market Studies* 13 (3) 280–307.

Mugomba, A. T. (1978) 'Regional organizations and African underdevelopment: the collapse of the East African Community', *Journal of Modern African Studies* 16 (2): 261–72.

Nyerere, J. (1975) 'Report to East Africa Legislative Assembly', *Africa Currents* 3: 4–9.

Padelford, N. J. (1955) 'Recent developments in regional organizations', *Proceedings of the American Society of International Law*, pp. 25–7.

Russet, B. M. (1967) *International Regions and the International System: A Study in Political Ecology*, Chicago: Rand McNally.

Sanchez, E. B. (1977) 'Chile's rejection of the Andean Common Market regulation of foreign investment', *Columbian Journal of Transnational Law* 16 (1): 138–73.

Schmitter, P. C. (1972) 'Central American integration: spill-over, spill-around, or encapsulation?', *Journal of Common Market Studies* 9 (1): 1–48.

Simmonds, K. R. (1967) 'The Central American Common Market: an experiment in regional integration', *International and Comparative Law Quarterly* 16: 911–45.

Valdez, A. L. (1972) 'The Andean foreign investment code: an analysis', *Journal of International Law and Economics* 7 (1): 1–19.

Vargas-Hidalgo, R. (1978) 'An evaluation of the Andean Pact', *Lawyer of the Americas* 10 (2): 401–24.

Walton, R. E. and McKersie, R. B. (1965) *A Behavioral Theory of Labor Negotiations*, New York: McGraw-Hill.

FURTHER READING

Andemicael, B. and Nicol, D. (1984) 'The OAU: primacy in seeking African solutions within the UN Charter', in Y. Al-Ayouty and I. W. Zartman (eds) *The OAU After Twenty Years*, New York: Praeger.

Cox, R. and Jacobsen, H. (1973) *The Anatomy of Influence*, New Haven: Yale University Press.

Miller, L. H. (1970) 'Regional organizations and subordinate systems', in L. J. Cantori and S. L. Spiegel (eds) *The International Politics of Regions*, Englewood Cliffs, NJ: Prentice-Hall.

Taylor, P. (1978) 'A conceptual typology of international organization', in P. Taylor and A. J. R. Groom (eds) *International Organisation: A Conceptual Approach*, London: Pinter.

United Nations (1988) *Yearbook of International Organizations*, Brussels: Union of International Associations.

61

REGIONAL ASSOCIATIONS: CULTURAL

PAUL F. DIEHL

There are many activities that expose people to the cultures of other countries: viewing a foreign film, sponsoring an exchange student, attending a ballet performance, reading a new book by a foreign author and sampling ethnic food at an international festival are but a few examples. For most citizens in developed countries, and even for many in less developed countries, these activities are daily, weekly or monthly occurrences. What those people may not realize is that some of these cultural activities were directly organized by or facilitated by regional organizations dedicated to the promotion of cultural understanding and interaction.

Although foreign cultural offerings are frequent happenings in most countries, regional organizations such as the Nordic Cultural Fund, the Inter-American Music Council and the Asian Cultural Council, which are responsible for such activities, are virtually unknown among the general public. Better known is their global counterpart, the United Nations Educational, Scientific and Cultural Organization or UNESCO. That organization was in the headlines throughout the 1980s because of accusations of financial mismanagement and 'politicization' (a charge particularly damaging to an organization confined to non-controversial missions such as promoting world literacy). The controversy led to the withdrawal of the United States and the United Kingdom from the organization. Meanwhile, regional cultural associations have been quietly promoting many of the same activities, albeit on a regional rather than a global level. It might be argued that given the scope and volume of activities of regional cultural organizations they are more significant than their more visible counterpart at the global level.

This essay is divided into four sections. First, there is a description of the range of interests and activities performed by regional cultural associations. The second section is devoted to the kinds of structures and funding in those organizations, focusing on those that are primarily governmental organizations versus those that are privately run. The third is a discussion of the importance of regional cultural organizations with a focus on the theoretical tenets of functionalism. Finally, controversies surrounding cultural exchanges and information dissemination are discussed.

AREAS OF INTEREST AND ACTIVITIES

Regional cultural associations encompass a wide variety of topic areas and concerns, including those related to education, the arts, language and ethnic identity. In these areas the organizations perform many functions and sponsor an array of useful activities, including cultural exchanges and workshops.

It is difficult to classify the areas of concern that fall under the broad category of culture. Nevertheless, the concerns of regional cultural organizations can roughly be categorized in the following way: scholarly, educational, language related, the arts, and a miscellaneous category. Many regional associations are concerned with the study of academic topics. Such topics include art, drama and literature, or those directly related to the culture of a given area or ethnic grouping. Regional organizations promote the scholarly exchange of information among teachers and professionals at educational institutions and research organizations in their native countries. Typical of such an association is the Association of Arab Historians, which has a membership of over 12,000. This group encourages the study of Arab history and traditions and facilitates the exchange of ideas among its members and other scholarly groups within and outside of the Middle East. There are other scholarly groups whose focus is not on cultural issues *per se*, but can be classified in this grouping because the promotion of scholarship and exchange of ideas can be considered a component of culture. The Latin American Congress of Radiology is an example of such a group.

Another category of regional cultural associations is those that promote educational goals, but to a wider audience than scholars in a specific academic discipline. In particular, such organizations sponsor research and teaching on certain subjects. The Southeast Asian Ministers of Education Organization (SEAMEO), established in 1965 among states in that region, sponsors regional centres on various topics, some leading to graduate and post-graduate degrees. One such centre is the SEAMEO Regional Centre for Education in Science and Mathematics hosted by the Government of Malaysia.

A third related category concerns promotion of languages indigenous to the region. Scholarly and educational associations have stronger institutional ties and seek to foster co-operation and understanding primarily among students and scholars in university and other professional settings. Regional associations devoted to language target the broader general public and concentrate on increasing the use of language and are less interested in scholarly concerns.

Union Latine, for example, sponsors instruction of neo-Latin languages, with regional offices in both Europe and South America.

Perhaps the largest collection of regional cultural associations is concerned with the arts, a concern that may include paintings, music, dance and drama. Many travelling exhibitions of art or foreign dance company performances are arranged through the relevant regional cultural organization. A popular concern is with paintings and historical artefacts. Several regions have associations of museums that foster exchanges in the region. These include the Scandinavian Union of Museums and the Union of Latin American and Caribbean Museums. Such organizations allow people to view art or experience the culture of their neighbours without having to travel long distances to the country of origin.

A final category of associations includes so many different purposes and concerns, and there is perhaps only one in each region, that they cannot be easily classified with other organizations. These miscellaneous groups may be those that seek to promote a particular ethnic identity or a hobby (for example, stamp collecting). Others are directed more toward culture in a broader sense of the term. Europa Nostra works for European government and public recognition of the threats against sites of natural beauty and of architectural or historic interest and calls for their preservation.

The activities performed by regional cultural associations are also varied. The activities most in the public eye relate to cultural exchanges. These involve reciprocal presentations of art, student and faculty visits, and cultural and ethnic festivals. The Asian and Pacific Cultural Association, among other activities, facilitates the exchange of prominent scholars and artists in the region and sponsors an art festival. The Nordic Choral Committee puts together a triennial music festival celebrating the songs and traditions of that geographic region. What may be less known is that regional associations also sponsor workshops, seminars and conferences for specialized groups. For example, the Pan-African Foundation for Economic, Social and Cultural Development sponsors conferences for women and youth at the sub-national, national and regional levels.

Although exchanges, public events and specialized seminars and workshops are the most visible of the activities of regional cultural associations, they also conduct many other activities. One important activity is advising governments and making recommendations on policies related to culture. In these actions, the goal is to make sure that government agencies promote cultural understanding when designing their policies. This ensures that all such efforts are not merely private concerns or the direct results of other association activities. There is an implicit recognition that cultural understanding and the expansion of cultural activities across borders requires the co-operation of the governments in the region. The Nordic Council of Ministers performs this function in advising the governments of Denmark, Finland, Iceland, Norway and Sweden.

Among the other functions of regional cultural associations is serving as a contact point or conduit for cultural and scholarly contacts. On most occasions this involves facilitating communication between members, or sponsoring joint programmes for members in different countries. The European Cultural Foundation, for example, encompassing both Western and Eastern European countries, co-ordinates a network of research institutes and sponsors a grant programme for its projects.

Finally, some regional cultural associations are directly involved in the transmission of culture and language to individuals. The European Language and Educational Centres are non-profit organizations that teach foreign languages to adults in the places where they are spoken. This helps ensure that visitors and those staying in a foreign country for an extended period can learn the local language and take full advantage of their stay in the country. Such instruction also helps the assimilation process and promotes understanding of the previously unfamiliar surroundings.

Overall, regional cultural associations are involved in a number of concerns that extend beyond art and music; it might be reasonably argued that the range of concerns is considerably greater than that encompassed by regional institutions in the economic and security realms. Promoting educational exchanges, teaching foreign languages, and allowing for the distribution of new literary works are just a few of the activities carried out. For the most part, however, regional cultural associations play the role of facilitator of cultural understanding rather than assuming a primary or direct role in the process. Regional associations work with national organizations and individuals to promote cultural understanding. They do not as a rule play a role independent of their membership; that is, primary responsibility for implementing activities lies with local or national organizations (an exception is the language instruction activity). Yet, without a regional association to bring together different parties and co-ordinate joint projects, national and local organizations would be unable to benefit from the exchange of ideas and culture with similar groups in other countries.

TYPES AND FUNDING

A traditional distinction among international organizations has been between governmental and non-governmental types. The former consist of organizations whose members are states and whose delegates represent the views of their home government. Non-governmental organizations have memberships that might consist of private associations or individuals; even when membership is divided according to states, the delegates of the members do not necessarily represent the views of their national governments. In practice, there have been difficulties with this distinction given that some organizations have characteristics of both types with respect to membership and funding. Nevertheless, this scheme is useful in identifying general types of regional cultural associations.

Some regional associations are governmental entities, especially those whose functions include advising governments on cultural affairs. Several of the organizations are agencies of broader, multi-purpose regional organizations such as the Organization of American States or the Organization of African Unity. The Arab League Educational, Cultural and Scientific Organization, for example, sponsors seminars and professional training courses and also publishes books in its areas of concern. Other governmental groups are free-standing organizations composed of state representatives. The Nordic Council of Ministers, mentioned above (p. 974), was created under a treaty of cultural co-operation among its members.

Other associations are strictly private organizations whose membership consists of national groups or individuals. The European Association of Conservatories is a group of music academies, schools and colleges interested in music education. The Council of Nordic Dental Students is an example of an association with individuals as members; many scholarly organizations share this characteristic.

Funding for governmental associations comes primarily from assessments made on the member governments as a part of a regular budget process. Non-governmental associations must usually depend on grants from charitable foundations, membership dues and proceeds from activities (such as fees from language instruction courses). The European Cultural Foundation depends in part on funds from a lottery and football pool in the Netherlands. Yet it is a mistake to generalize too much about funding for these organizations. Governments will occasionally subsidize private groupings and even governmental organizations do not operate solely on the contributions of member states. It is difficult to classify regional cultural organizations solely on the basis of funding sources.

The governmental versus non-governmental distinction and differences based on sources of funding are blurred even further when focusing on regional cultural associations that mix various elements of the other types. The European Cultural Centre has both individuals and organizations as members, and some of the organizations, although not formally government representatives, have followed the directions of their home governments, especially those in Eastern Europe. The Centre's funding is also a mix of public and private contributions. Similarly, Europa Nostra has a mixed membership of individuals, local government authorities and international, regional and national bodies. Funding comes from a grant from the European Community, membership subscriptions and a corporate grant.

Thus, unlike regional security organizations, for example, regional cultural associations are not necessarily composed of or funded by state members. Such diversity parallels national efforts to promote cultural exchanges and understanding. For example, the United States Information Agency is a government-controlled entity, whereas the British Council is an autonomous entity. The Cultural Relations Department in the Federal Republic of Germany is a mixture of government control and autonomy. When it comes to cultural relationships across national boundaries, there is a wide variety of activities in many areas carried out by a diverse collection of associations.

THE IMPORTANCE OF REGIONAL CULTURAL ASSOCIATIONS

It is somewhat difficult to assess the contribution of regional cultural associations to the global community. Unlike regional or international organizations concerned with economic issues, the benefits derived from an organization are not as tangible as might be the case with increasing trade ties between states. Furthermore, cultural interactions receive less public attention, perhaps because they are perceived as less important, than activities of military or political organizations such as NATO. In this section, the contributions of regional cultural associations are reviewed with a focus on the relative importance of the activities conducted, the role of regional versus other arrangements in this area, and the contribution of such organizations to world co-operation as viewed through the theoretical lenses of functionalism.

Unlike organizations that promote the security of states or aid in world hunger relief, regional cultural associations are concerned with the improvement of the quality of life, rather than basic human needs. They also focus more heavily on individual citizens, rather than states as a whole. It is perhaps because of this emphasis that cultural activities are not considered as important in the world as are weapons and trade imbalances. In many ways, it is difficult to argue with such logic. The spectre of nuclear annihilation and widespread death from hunger and disease makes an art exhibit or a scholarly exchange seem trivial. States and individuals concern themselves with maintaining life before they devote time and resources to its cultural enhancement. Regional cultural associations do not therefore receive the attention nor have the impact on world events that organizations in the economic and security fields do. This is not to say that the activities are unimportant, but rather that they are less significant than other international interactions.

Although regional cultural associations do not have the same importance as NATO or the Organization of Economic Co-operation and Development (OECD), they do contribute to the betterment of the world community. Their main contribution is in the promotion of cultural understanding among peoples.

Such an achievement assists in the development of common experiences and tolerance for diversity; these may make co-operation in other endeavours possible to the benefit of all parties. This is the basis of functionalist thought described below (p. 978).

Beyond cultural understanding, these associations contribute by enhancing the personal and professional experiences of participants in their programmes. In many cases, scholarly pursuits may be enhanced by the acquisition of foreign language skills, new research methods, or merely the exposure of new ideas from foreign colleagues. Less academically oriented is the enjoyment gained by people who otherwise would not have had the opportunity to view a piece of art or visit a historic monument. This may be difficult to describe or quantify, but this should not diminish its value. Regional cultural associations expand the benefits that accrue from exposure to arts and literature and from greater familiarity with people of other cultures.

Without describing all the esoteric and other benefits of broadening one's cultural horizons, it is sufficient to say that regional cultural organizations contribute to this process. Yet there are national government entities (some examples of which are mentioned on p. 976) and international organizations that are designed to perform the same functions. How important are regional organizations relative to these institutions and what can regional organizations offer that the others cannot? First, it might be noted that international inter-actions are the primary domain of states, not individuals and private groups (although this is changing). Consequently, most cultural exchanges (especially in authoritarian countries) take place on a bilateral basis under the aegis of state governments. Thus, regional cultural groupings play only a secondary role in the process.

At the international level, UNESCO and other agencies co-ordinate attempts by states to co-operate on more than a bilateral basis. There are several reasons why regional organization activities are necessary or desired in addition to global efforts. First, regional organizations involve states that are geographically proximate, allowing greater ease of exchange among its members. Programme costs, including transportation, are much less, and more exchanges can be sponsored for less money and effort. A similar pattern is notable for international trade in that states trade more with their neighbours than with states in other regions.

Second, there is a natural tendency toward regional co-operation based on the homogeneity of interests, tradition and values of a group of states in the same region. Such homogeneity among African or Latin American states, for example, may seem contrary to the purpose of broadening horizons through cultural exchanges; it would seem that cultural exchanges would be best among the most heterogeneous of peoples and cultures. Yet many states feel more comfortable in dealing with their neighbours, many of which share the same level of development and traditions (and hence there is little fear of cultural imperialism – see (p. 979). Furthermore, states in a region may also share one or two languages, which facilitates the exchange of ideas. Exchanges between the Soviet Union and Brazil may seem like a good idea, but the contacts are limited by the inability of large numbers of people to speak both Portuguese and Russian. Although people enjoy being exposed to different cultures and benefit by doing so, they may not be willing to experience art and music dramatically different from their own; Islamic societies, for example, would be intolerant of foreign films that involve nudity or perceived improper behaviour by women.

Third, it may be that regional associations serve as a bridge to future global co-operation on cultural affairs. At this stage of international relations and public education, it may be unrealistic to expect states and their citizenry to be open to all cultures. In a future time of profound global interdependence, some regional associations may give way or combine to form new global counterparts.

Regional cultural associations have a potentially important role to play in promoting world peace and co-operation according to the theoretical framework of functionalism. Functionalism suggests that it is easier for states to co-operate in relatively non-controversial areas, such as health care or cultural exchanges, than 'high politics' areas such as arms control and security matters. It is also assumed that co-operation across states is most easily achieved between private groupings of individuals or so-called technical or professional experts rather than between governments. Ideological and other hostilities are thought not to inhibit the exchange of information between such professionals.

Regional cultural associations seem ideally suited for the initial co-operation efforts envisaged in functionalism. Most cultural activities carried out are relatively non-controversial (for example, an art exhibition), and those involved in the activities or those who arrange them (such as scholars or museum curators) are professionals who usually have no overriding political purpose for doing so. Non-cultural activities, such as the promotion of health care, are also envisaged as the first steps in functionalist theory. The key point about functionalism is that the initial co-operation in non-controversial areas by technicians and professionals will expand and eventually spill over into government co-operation on more controversial matters, including security issues. The logic is that with greater understanding and co-operation among peoples there will be more popular support for international organizations and the desire to go to war will be lessened. Thus, regional cultural associations can be one component toward the construction of a global community (and perhaps a regional or world government).

One should recognize, however, that regional cultural associations would only be a small part of the initial co-operative efforts between states. In addition, another school of thought, neo-functionalism, argues that co-oper-ation will not spill over from non-controversial areas to controversial subjects; rather, initial co-operative efforts must be directed at solving the major differ-ences between states (i.e. political conflict). In that view, cultural exchanges become a consequence of the improvement of relations between states, not a causal factor. The evidence for either view is mixed. The success of the European Community might be a testament to neo-functionalism. Yet the growth of international organizations and global interdependence is evidence that functionalist propositions have some validity also.

CONTROVERSIES

Perhaps one of the reasons that regional cultural associations receive so little attention is that their activities are relatively non-controversial and therefore not the subjects of intense political debate. These organizations have also received little or no attention in the academic community. Nevertheless, cul-tural activities across borders have been the subject of two types of contro-versies: those charging activities to be political propaganda, and claims of 'cultural imperialism'.

At first glance, most of the activities carried out by regional cultural associ-ations seem apolitical. Yet films and books on particular subjects may be regarded as supporting a political viewpoint that recipient governments find offensive. During the 1980s, the United States stopped the distribution of two Canadian films that concerned themselves with acid rain and nuclear war. It was argued that such films were political propaganda by a foreign state and therefore not suitable for importation as a part of a cultural exchange pro-gramme. Literature that glorifies or criticizes religious, political or cultural values in contradiction to official government policy may also be rejected by states. According to Western values, such restrictions go against the principles of a free exchange of ideas. Yet, as much as states may support cultural understanding, they will not tolerate activities they regard as insulting to their values or critical of existing government policy.

Although governments encourage cultural exchanges, they do not want foreign activities or programmes to supplant domestic ones. There have been occasions when states have complained that other countries have sought to control cultural development just as they might seek political (colonialism) or economic (neo-colonialism) domination; hence, this is referred to as cultural imperialism. Cultural imperialism may take many forms. In some countries, television programmes may be primarily produced in a foreign country. The popularity of American drama shows in Latin America is an example. News might also be drawn from one or two foreign sources, such as Reuters or the Associated Press. Foreign cultural and information exchanges may stifle the development of domestic institutions and activities. More threatening is the possibility that such activities will replace or dilute efforts to foster and preserve one's own cultural heritage. The risk is that promoting understanding of other cultures will harm efforts to do the same for one's own traditions.

The risk of cultural imperialism seems greatest in bilateral relationships in which one side is a dominant partner in the relationship. Many accusations have been directed at the United States for its news organizations and television distribution companies (for example, the *Dallas* television programme is very popular in some parts of the world). Britain and France have also come under fire for the strong influence they exercise in their former colonies in Africa and Asia. As a result, many states prefer that activities be carried out under the auspices of an international organization, which will not attach the same political conditions to interactions, so that states can operate on a more equal footing. In this way, regional cultural association activities are less vulnerable to charges of cultural imperialism than those stemming from bilateral arrangements. Furthermore, regional associations are also preferable in this regard to global organizations. Because regional associations already have some homogeneity among their membership, there is a greater likelihood that activities may be complementary to the home state's culture rather than a threat. States are also more likely to be similar in terms of national development and political power within regional associations, thereby preventing any one state or national grouping from dominating activities. Nevertheless, in organizations in which one state plays a hegemonic role, such as those in the Western Hemisphere dominated by the United States, there is still the risk that the cultural exchanges will be asymmetrical and that domestic cultural activities will be supplanted.

CONCLUSION

Regional cultural associations are likely to increase in numbers and activities in the coming decades. As states become more interdependent and communication across borders increases, there will be greater impetus for co-ordination of efforts in the cultural area. There will also be greater opportunity for interactions among peoples of different states as illiteracy rates decline and there is more exposure to other cultures through communications technology. Much of the increased activity among regional cultural associations is likely to take place in the private sector as governments will exercise less control over what people hear or see through media outlets. Nevertheless, although regional cultural associations may play a more prominent role, they will remain secondary, at least in the foreseeable future, to contacts facilitated through bilateral state relations and also to economic and security organizations at the regional level.

FURTHER READING

Bennett, A. L. (1988) *International Organizations: Principles and Issues*, 4th edn, Englewood Cliffs, NJ: Prentice-Hall, chapter 14.

Culture (quarterly journal) Montreal.

Fisher, G. (1990) *Mindsets: The Role of Culture and Perception in International Relations*, Yarmouth, Me.: Intercultural Press.

Girard, A. (1972) *Cultural Development: Experience and Policies*, Paris: UNESCO.

Haas, E. (1964) *Beyond the Nation-State: Functionalism and International Organization*, Stanford: Stanford University Press.

Intercultural Studies (annual journal) Japan.

Jacobson, H. (1984) *Networks of Interdependence: International Organization and the Global Political System*, 2nd edn, New York: Random House.

Koek, K. (ed.) (1989) *Encyclopedia of Associations*, Vol. 4: *International Organizations*, Detroit: Gale Research.

Mitchell, J. M. (1986) *International Cultural Relations*, London: Allen & Unwin.

Mitrany, D. (1966) *A Working Peace System*, Chicago: Quadrangle Books.

UNESCO (1981) *Cultural Development: Some Regional Experiences*, Paris: UNESCO.

Union of International Associations (ed.) (annual) *Yearbook of International Organizations*, Brussels: Union of International Associations.

62

REGIONAL ASSOCIATIONS: POLITICAL

SAMUEL S. KIM

International organization can be viewed as an institutional expression of a conflict management process at the international (more accurately interstate) level. It is a process of forming and developing a common framework for facilitating multilateral co-operation within the context of the multi-state system. While acknowledging both conflict and co-operation as basic features of international life, it represents, in theory at least, an affirmative collective response to the question of whether international peace is possible through multilateral co-operation in the absence of a supranational Leviathan. Indeed, what distinguishes the post-1945 international system is the extent to which international organizations have become prominent and permanent parts of a complex, increasingly interdependent global system. The games the nation-states play have lost much of the realist simplicity of the struggle for power, if for no other reason than that different conceptions of power and legitimacy and different types of international organizations have emerged on a global scale during the last four and a half decades in response to a multitude of challenges and crises of a nuclear-ecological age.

International organization, for classification purposes, is the generic term referring to both international governmental organizations (IGOs) and inter-national non-governmental organizations (INGOs). Although international organization first appeared in the nineteenth century, its phenomenal growth is largely a post-Second World War development. Both IGOs and INGOs have multiplied at an unprecedented rate in the post-war era, with their numbers reaching an all-time high in 1985 at 378 and 4,676, respectively, and then tapering off to 300 and 4,621 in 1989. In 1989, there were 223 regional IGOs, constituting 74.3 per cent of the total IGO population (UIA 1989: 1596-7). Regional IGOs as a percentage of all IGOs increased steadily from 28 per cent in 1815-1914, to 37 per cent in 1915-44, to 60 per cent in 1945-55, to 73 per cent in 1956-65, and to 74.3 per cent in 1989 (Nye 1971: 4; UIA 1989: 1596).

Although the post-war international system has also witnessed the proliferation of regional organizations of every sort, the types and numbers of 'regional political organizations' are difficult to specify because one can divide the world of regional organizations in any number of ways – by function, membership, size, geographical contiguity and other criteria. Different definitions and criteria of 'region' and nomenclature based on different analytical purposes will produce different typologies and numbers of what we call here 'regional political organizations'. Nye (1971: 9) counts eight 'macro-regional political organizations'; Miller (1973: 421) four 'co-operative' regional organizations; Haas (1986: 82–7) four 'regionals'; Zacher (1979: 2–3) three 'regional collective security organizations'; and Bennett (1988: 357) ten regional 'multipurpose organizations.'

In this essay the term 'regional political organizations' (RPOs) will be used to refer to those *organizations*, not *systems*, first, whose membership is restricted on the basis of geographical contiguity; second, whose structures embody institutionalized forums of periodic diplomatic interactions, based on formal agreement among independent governments; third, whose day-to-day administration is assisted by an international secretariat; and fourth, whose principal orientation and aims are of a general political character, as opposed to a specific single-issue military, economic, social or cultural orientation. Still, this definition somewhat skates over the fact that the distinction between 'high politics' and 'low politics' – and between 'political' and 'functional' organizations – is more easily made in theory than found in practice in the contemporary global system. As will soon be apparent, this definition is suggested as one of analytical convenience rather than one of descriptive accuracy. This definition leaves us with nine of the ten 'multipurpose' regional organizations that Bennett (1988: 357) counted (as against his regional 'alliance systems' and 'functional organizations') in the following chronological order of their establishment: the League of Arab States (1945); the Organization of American States (1948); the Council of Europe (1949); the Organization of Central American States (1952); the Nordic Council (1952); the Organization of African Unity (1963); the Common Afro-Mauritian Organization (1966); the Association of South-East Asian Nations (1967); and the Andean Group (1969). For our analytical purposes as well as for reasons of even geographical representation and space limitation, we will limit our discussion to five of the most prominent RPOs: the League of Arab States (LAS); the Organization of American States (OAS); the Council of Europe (CE); the Organization of African Unity (OAU); and the Association of South-East Asian Nations (ASEAN).

THEORETICAL PERSPECTIVES

The idea of regionalism, embodied in regional organizations, provides a social laboratory in which to test various models, theories, and alternative approaches to world order (Falk and Mendlovitz 1973; Haas 1973; Nye 1971). Standing as a sort of half-way house between nationalism and globalism – and between the Hobbesian world of anarchy and the thoroughly integrated global community – regional development can be observed and analysed in delineating the limits and possibilities of building a peaceful human community at this intermediate level of human social organization.

Regional development is theoretically fertile, posing many intriguing questions and hypotheses in international relations research. What is the relationship between the levels of political organization in the global system? Under what conditions, and to what extent, does regionalism have an impact upon the scope and character of sovereignty at the state level? Is regional development a primarily sovereignty-diluting, sovereignty-shifting, sovereignty-sharing, or sovereignty-expanding phenomenon? What about its compatibility with, and impact upon, the primary functions of the United Nations (UN) of maintaining international peace and security? Have RPOs proved to be useful supplements or obstructive alternatives to UN action?

Both in theory and practice an assessment of whether regionalism in general, and any RPO in particular, is a success or failure requires various comparisons. Theoretically, what is the relationship between regionalist peace propositions and major international peace theories? For such a comparative analysis, international peace theories can be distinguished between 'peacemaking' approaches designed to deal with long-term underlying causes of war and 'peacekeeping' approaches designed to cope with immediate catalysts of armed interstate conflict (Lebow 1981). The former include federal, functional and neo-functional approaches to world order, while the latter refer to the collective security and various peacekeeping and conflict-controlling systems and devices.

Through the centuries, the idea has persisted in Western political thought that a viable world order required nothing less than the replacement of the sovereignty-centred international order with the formation of some species of world government. The pre-modern federal approach to world order, as embodied in the writings of Pierre Dubois, Erasmus, Sully, Emeric Cruce, William Penn, Abbé de Saint-Pierre, Rousseau, Bentham and Kant, argued for federalism through a panoply of constitutional and institutional changes. Most of the proposals for federalism in the post-Second World War era have emanated from the United States and their leading proponents have been American (for example, Clarence K. Streit, Nicholas Murray Butler, Maynard Hutchins, Grenville Clark, Emery Reves and Louis Sohn). Hanna Newcombe (1974) identified no less than sixteen federal approaches, all proceeding from two key premisses: that law is a substitute for violence and that law is also an expression of the essential unity of humankind. Of all the twentieth-century proposals for world federalism, however, *World Peace Through World Law* by Grenville Clark and Louis Sohn (1966) remains the most comprehensive, detailed, rigorous and influential. Regional organizations have only a marginal and supplementary role in the Clark–Sohn federal model, as it seeks to transfer some functions, capabilities and resources from national governments to a restructured set of global institutions needed to transform the UN into a more effective, albeit limited, world federal government.

The fundamental premiss of the Clark–Sohn federal model is based on the questionable Hobbesian dichotomy of authority or anarchy: either there is world peace based on world authority (and world law) or there is world anarchy and war emanating from state sovereignty. A world without a central authority is a Hobbesian world bereft of restraints to endless warfare. World law is assigned a mission impossible. Yet the remedy proposed is simply more law, world law. Paradoxically, the alternative to the state system emerges as an amplification of the state system to a global scale, a world state. Just as its conceptual origin, key participants and pedagogical materials were all American, so has its legal and structural design for world order reflected the rather unique historical experience of the United States with its largely successful transition from the relatively decentralized condition of 'state' sovereignty under the Articles of Confederation to a 'more perfect union' under a new federal system. The influence of the Clark–Sohn model was confined to the first stage of world order studies (1961–8). The establishment of the world order models project (WOMP) in 1968 marks the initiation of the second stage of the development of world order studies and a break away from the Clark–Sohn federal model (Kim 1984: 83–4).The Clark–Sohn model never found its way to global law-making activities.

Even in the West European setting the regional federalists, fearing that functionalist incrementalism would be too little to overcome the political fragmentation of Europe into warring sovereign states, pressed hard for a united Europe before the post-war *idealpolitik* impulse dissipated. Functionalist incrementalism is an anathema to a federalist system-transforming approach. 'The worst way to cross a chasm', in their view, 'is by little steps' (Nye 1971: 50). The federalist necessity of replacing state sovereignty with central institutions by means of a great constitutional leap forward manifested itself in numerous national and international non-governmental movements for European unity (for example, the United Europe Movement, the European Union of Federalists, and the Economic League for European Co-operation), leading to the formation of the 'International Committee of the Movements for European Unity' in 1947 and a 'Congress of Europe' at The Hague in May 1948. Faced with this clear and present federalist threat, the governments launched a pre-emptive strike. In conceptional and institutional design, the Statute establishing the CE in 1949 was a triumph of an indirect and incremental functional approach to European unity over a direct federal approach (Bowett 1975: 149–51).

Despite various usage (Haas 1964: 3–8; Kim 1979: 335; Groom and Taylor 1975: 284–338), the term 'functionalism' as stated by its leading exponent, David Mitrany (1966), is, in essence, a prescriptive proposition for a welfare-oriented approach to world order. The term has also been used as a synonym for 'non-political', or even 'non-controversial', however misleading such a usage might be in terms of diachronic change in the functional sector of the UN system (for example, the specialized agencies). Mitrany argued:

> Peace will not be secured if we organized the world by what divides it. But in the measure in which such peace-building activities develop and succeed, one might hope that the mere prevention of conflict, crucial as that may be, would in time fall to a subordinate place in the scheme of international things, while we would turn to what are the real tasks of our common society – the conquest of poverty and of disease and of ignorance.
>
> (Mitrany 1966: 96).

In short, the nation-state would be subverted by stealth and made irrelevant through the intricate networks of transterritorial social and economic interdependence. While committed to world peace as the ultimate end, functionalism attacks underlying social and economic causes of war through an incremental 'peace by pieces' approach. Indeed, functional arrangements without any territorial borders are conceptualized as constituting 'organic elements of a federalism by installments' (Mitrany 1966: 83). The logic of functionalism is that the promotion of welfare slowly but surely leads to the prevention of warfare.

Regionalism is regarded as problematic in the functional approach to world order. To design a structure at the outset based on any criteria other than functional utility is to rigidify the incremental process of community building. The functionalists thus assume that forms and structures will vary according to their functions in the course of the community-building process. Institutions follow, not precede, functional needs. Technical self-determination is the logic of the functional approach – international institutions based on function, not on any national or regional territoriality. The functionalists therefore see the regional fallacy in Europe in the dynamics of a united Europe becoming more and more a 'closed' system turning its back on its open cosmopolitan civilization. This is not an escape from the nation-state system but its enlargement on a larger but still enclosed regional scale. It is a *detour* from a wider global functional unity. A Europe preoccupied with the creation of a federal union would most likely generate a parochial brand of regional patriotism, virtually closing itself to second-order, global, functional integration movements. A federalizing Europe, having little normative incentive or energy left, would tend to be incapable of initiating or participating in global functional tasks for tackling global problems (Mitrany 1966: 180–7). Central to the functional approach is the notion of gradual functional transformation of the nation-state system into a global, not a regional, community to achieve a 'working peace system'.

Like the functionalists, the neo-functionalists also stress the primacy of incrementalism over grand world order visions and designs. Neo-functionalism is, to a degree, a synthesis of federalism and functionalism. Still, neo-functionalism can be distinguished from functionalism in three respects. First, neo-functionalism is a classical global functionalism revised and reduced to a regional scale. The euphoria génerated by the European integration process in the 1950s gave birth to neo-functionalist theory, not as a vindication but as a down-graded reformulation of functionalism in a specific West European setting. According to its chief theoretician, neo-functionalism became 'one of the most promising modes of analysis' in international relations (Haas 1958: 3–4); the emerging United States of Europe was seen as 'a new center, whose institutions possess or demand jurisdiction over the pre-existing ones' (ibid.: 16).

Second, the neo-functionalists argue that high politics and low politics cannot be separated. Technical self-determination without the support of geopolitics and political interest groups can generate little spillover; it merely leads to triviality and political irrelevance. The Schuman Plan is cited as an example of how the political game can still be played by selecting a politically important functional sector (coal and steel) as a way of attacking state sove-reignty by an incremental and expansive functional process rather than a dramatic constitutional act. The Continental neo-functionalists are character-ized as 'federalists in functionalist clothing, pursuing federal ends through what appeared to be functionalist means' (Nye 1971: 51). Jean Monnet is a quintessential federalist in functionalist clothing as he is represented as believ-ing that 'the very disequilibrium produced by the integration of one sector and the nonintegration of the surrounding ones, the pressures from the central institutions and from the new community-wide political processes, will result in an ascending spiral of integration' (Hoffmann 1963: 530). Third, neo-functionalism differs from functionalism in its deliberate espousal and design of institutions that would lead to further integration through 'the expansive logic of sector integration' (Nye 1971: 51).

However, in the wake of the 1965 European Community crisis and the challenge posed to supranationalism by de Gaulle's high politics, it was Haas who began to retreat from his neo-functional 'pre-theorizing.' By 1975, Haas had pronounced that the neo-functional theory of regional integration was obsolescent because its core assumptions had become less and less relevant to the behaviour patterns of key state actors in regional organizations.

> Regional integration in Western Europe has disappointed everybody: there is no
> federation, the nation-state behaves as if it were both obstinate and obsolete,
> and what once appeared to be a distinctive 'supernational' style now looks more
> like a huge regional bureaucratic appendage to an intergovernmental conference
> in permanent session. . . . Integration theories are becoming obsolete because
> they are not designed to address the most pressing and important problems on
> the global agenda of policy and research.
>
> (Haas 1975: 6, 17).

With this authoritative pronouncement, international organization research has shifted decisively from regionalism to globalism, from regional integration to the issues of 'complex global interdependence' and their management in international regimes.

Regional organizations, especially regional political organizations, can also be observed and analysed in terms of their performance in coping with the proximate causes and catalysts that trigger international war. This second set of peacekeeping and conflict-controlling 'theories' is of more recent origin – an offspring of two global wars in the twentieth century. The collective security system that first came into being with the League of Nations and later with the UN – and the subsequent transition from the paralysed Charter-based collective security system to *ad hoc* consensual peacekeeping – can all be subsumed under the second set of peace 'theories' designed to cope with the immediate causes of international violence. From the beginning the UN was confronted with the challenge of establishing regional–global equilibrium for its principal objective of maintaining international peace and security. The best the San Francisco Conference could do in 1945 was merely to reconcile the conflicting claims of regionalist and universalist peace approaches in the form of an ambiguous compromise recognizing the legitimacy of existing and prospective RPOs as adjuncts to the UN, while at the same time subjecting them to the general direction and control of the world organization through Articles 52, 53 and 54 of the UN Charter (Claude 1971: 114; Bowett 1975: 143–4). Of course, such a superordination–subordination principle is easier promised than performed.

The idea that regionalism is better suited than globalism as a way of main-taining international peace is expressed diversely as 'arguments', 'claims', or 'theories'. The hegemonial regionalist world order, the notion of a world order backed up by regional superpowers, was first advanced by Walter Lippmann and E. H. Carr during the Second World War (Yalem 1973: 223) and then later found its theoretical articulation by Liska in the 'theory of great powers orbits'. The theory of great powers orbits is based on the premiss that smaller countries 'are hardly able to contrive regional integration and stability on their own; a more promising alternative might be regional groupings anchored in the superior resources of a nuclear Great Power' and that 'regional groupings of small states ought to cluster around the local Great Power and pool military, economic, and other resources in peace and war' (Liska 1973: 236). The theory of great powers orbits as a regionalist world order approach also rests upon several additional but unstated wishful assumptions: 'the ability of great powers to insure regional security; the compatibility of interests between the regional great power and small states; and the disposition of great powers to develop policies of restraint toward their lesser allies' (Yalem 1973: 223).

Other regionalist peace propositions are generally advanced in terms of regionalism's putative comparative advantages over those of globalism. First, the regionalists stress the importance of the size factor in international co-operation. 'Small' regionalism may not necessarily be more beautiful but it is certainly more cohesive and co-operative than 'big' universalism because its capacities are assumed to be more realistically fitted to its objectives. It is also claimed – and there is some evidence supporting this proposition (Oye 1986) – that international co-operation may be more difficult to obtain as the number of participating state actors increases. Second, consensus formation is said to be easier to obtain in a regional setting than in a global one because of a closer identification of greater commonality among its member states sharing similar economic and social systems and closer geographical, cultural and religious affinities. Third, the regionals are claimed to be better situated to pursue 'preventive diplomacy' at early stages of conflict formation and escalation; that is, they can better contain and prevent local disputes from becoming enmeshed with extra-regional insoluble problems. In other words, the regionals are better situated or better able to make peace divisible either by an early preventive intervention or by 'fractionating' interstate conflicts. Such a conflict-controlling and fractionating process is 'far more likely to take place in regional discussion than at a centralized forum comprising one hundred nations' (Burton 1962: 138). Some Eurocentric regionalists generalize about the positive spillover effects for a peaceful world order that would flow from broader emulation of this essentially West European model in other regions of the world (Nye 1971: 15). Fourth, the regionals are viewed as subordinate but burden-sharing agents of the world organization in the service of international peace and security or even as second-line back-up systems should the world organization fail in its primary functions. In addition, the regionals are conceptualized as the more desirable and feasible forerunners of an integrating global community.

A DEVELOPMENTAL PROFILE

Like moving targets of undetermined and unpredictable trajectories, most RPOs have experienced an uneven course of development. Contradictory pressures for integration, disintegration and reintegration explain their turbulent growth, non-growth and even decline. Certain pressures predominated at one period only to be superseded by others in subsequent periods, exacerbating the elephant/blind problem in the study of the regionals. From the perspective of late 1991, with the European Community (EC) poised to move beyond a single unified market in 1992 towards serious discussion about monetary and political union, it seems that the regionalist scholars in the 1950s and early 1960s committed the fallacy of premature optimism, just as the regionalist scholars in the 1970s and early 1980s committed the fallacy of premature pessimism. An assessment of regionalist developments in terms of various theories and propositions sketched above (pp. 984–9) should therefore be tentative in spirit and provisional in form, subject to periodic revisions. Diachronic, issue-area, and region-by-region differentiations seem critical to such a provisional assessment of regional developments.

Of all the theories, federalism stands on the shakiest empirical ground. There are no recent cases of international federalism comparable to the classic federalism of the United States. The federalist approach of directly confronting and replacing the factual attributes of state sovereignty with supranational procedures and institutions of decision making and conflict resolution has not worked, or perhaps more accurately has not been given a chance to work. The phenomenal growth of IGOs in the post-war period has little to do with any federalizing urge to move beyond state sovereignty. Far from undermining state sovereignty, RPOs are created as another way of enhancing the capability of national governments and consolidating state sovereignty. At most, regional and global IGOs can influence national elites' perceptions of external systemic constraints and opportunities and the redefinition of national interests. RPOs without an integrating mission and supranational decision making are little more than standing assemblies of, by and for the participating nation-states. In an overall assessment of 'historical profile of change' in fourteen 'major regional organizations', Haas (1990: 158) concluded that very few regionals have managed to escape 'turbulent non-growth', giving the rating of 'turbulent non-growth' to four of our five RPOs (LAS, ASEAN, CE, OAU) and the rating of 'decline' to OAS.

In early post-war Europe, the Continental federalists were the original driving force behind the establishment of the CE in 1949. As noted earlier, the governments quickly joined this non-governmental federalist drive, beating the non-governmental federalists at their own game: the CE was endowed with a measure of supranationalism in form but not in substance. With the failure of two frontal attempts to bring about a federal Europe – a revitalized CE in 1949–51 and the European Political Community in 1952–4 – European federalism ground to a halt. Some federalists switched to the neo-functionalist approach of 'community-building' through politically important economic integration as the catalyst for the functional spillover process. In 1985, West European governments again preferred the path of a single market by 1992 to the straight federalist path of political integration, even though the Draft Treaty establishing the European Union favoured by Altiero Spinelli, who founded the European Federalist Movement in 1943, was endorsed by the European Parliament in 1984 (Lodge 1986; Hoffmann 1989).

There is no evidence of ASEAN, the LAS, the OAS or the OAU following the EC prototype of creeping supranationalism. The forces working against federal, functional or neo-functional integration in the Third World are so overwhelming that it is difficult to be sanguine about the future of any integration (Mace 1988). To be sure, pan-Africanism, whose original motivation was to reduce Balkanization and to transcend nationalism in order to create a United States of Africa, dates back to the beginning of this century. It was a dominant theme for several African leaders, most notably for Kwame Nkrumah of Ghana. Yet such pre-independence support for the ideal of pan-Africanism evaporated among the leaders of newly sovereign states whose foremost concern was to preserve and consolidate whatever state sovereignty they had. The OAU was a triumph of state sovereignty over pan-Africanism. While the preamble of the OAU Charter makes a token bow to 'the inalienable right to all people to control their own destiny', the OAU soon became the most effective instrument for quashing the right of self-determination in the pursuit of a sovereignty-based African territorial order through the collective legitimation of the norm of state sovereignty. Despite the widely recognized arbitrariness of the African 'national' borders that the European colonialists established in the late nineteenth century, there has not occurred 'one significant boundary change in Africa since the dawn of the independence era in the late 1950s, and not one separatist movement has succeeded in establishing a new state' (Herbst 1989: 675–6). Indeed, sovereignty for African leaders can be said to have become a sword to fight internal secessionist threats and a shield to ward off external supranational schemes so as to strengthen any shaky statism they have inherited.

Likewise, what brought about and bound ASEAN together was not functional interdependence or cultural and geographic affinity, let alone any federalizing impulse, but rather the perception of threat to political and territorial sovereignty first emanating from China in the late 1960s and then from Vietnam between 1978 and 1989. With the Cambodian issue fast fading as a common thread for ASEAN unity, the search for new rallying points has become more vital and open-ended than at any other time in the history of its 'turbulent non-growth'. By any conventional expectations and measures, a federal South America or a federal league of Arab states is a long way off.

By the logic of functionalism, political IGOs *ipso facto* disqualify themselves as a testing ground for the functional approach to world order. At the same time, 'functional' international organizations are expected to follow the logic of technical self-determination working above and away from politics. At the core of functionalism is the separability-priority assumption – that the functional and the political can indeed be separated and that the former can be given priority to transform the latter. Yet, the idea that the supremacy of state sovereignty can be tamed by functionalist stealth flies in the face of the wide disparity between the capacity of the nation-state and the capacity of international organizations to satisfy the welfare and identity needs of the citizen. In practice, 'political' and 'functional' IGOs following the functional path few and far between, as the politicization of all issues and all types of international organizations is the norm, not an exception, in our times. Based on an empirical inquiry into the practice of the International Labour Organization, a functional global IGO, Haas (1964: 456) concluded that the functionalist assumption of the spillover process was much less pronounced at the global welfare level than at the regional (European) level, thus scaling down the implication of the automaticity process in functionalism. Likewise, Sewell (1966: 295) in his careful study of dynamics in the World Bank rebuts the assumption of technical self-determination as being both insufficient and misleading. It is politics that is the driving force behind the origin and growth of most World Bank programmes. Other examples of politics defining the limits of the possible and the permissible in functional IGOs abound.

While the expansive logic of functionalism made comparatively few inroads, four of our five RPOs have adopted economic welfare as one of their principal missions, upgrading various social and economic programmes. To varying degrees and extents, ASEAN, the LAS, the OAS and the OAU and Third World IGOs have all sought to make their organizations anti-dependency agents in the context of North–South relations. Lacking interdependencies within and between the Third World regions, the struggle for a New International Economic Order (NIEO) of reforming global economic organizations has taken the lead over demands for regional integration or South–South co-operation (Kim 1979: 242–333). This is not to suggest that they have been successful in this elusive and now abandoned quest, but simply to question the validity of the functional approach in both political and functional IGOs. The problems engulfing the Third World are not easily amenable to improvement through collective self-reliance (South–South co-operation).

There has now been a sufficient number of cases referred to regional political organizations and to the UN over a sufficiently long period of time that we can identify some trends in the overall performance of political IGOs in managing international conflicts and crises that threaten international peace and security (Falk *et al.* 1991; Haas 1986; Nye 1971; Zacher 1979). Although the number of disputes referred to the UN and RPOs has generally kept pace with the number of international and civil wars, the effectiveness of these IGOs in various modes of conflict management progressively declined until 1987–8 when the world organization suddenly demonstrated its usefulness, even its indispensability, in relation to a series of difficult regional conflicts. For the period 1945–84, Haas (1986: 9) identified a total of 319 'disputes' of which 137 were referred to the UN, 30 to the OAS, 27 to the OAU, 24 to the LAS, 5 to the CE, and 96 to none. Generally, there is a connection between the number of 'successes' and the number of referrals. The UN was most active – and 'effective' – in a certain mode of conflict management in 1955–65, but its effectiveness began to decline in 1965, reaching an all-time low in 1980–6; in contrast, the RPOs were generally effective in abating and isolating disputes during the 1960s and the early 1970s but began to follow the UN downward trend after 1975. Since 1980, regionals have received the lowest share in their history of the global conflict management load (Haas 1986: 20), and this decaying trend shows no sign of reversal to date.

When international conflict management is categorized in terms of various modes of conflict resolution but still on an unweighted basis, the RPOs have been most effective in *isolating* conflicts among their members (74 per cent of the referred cases), somewhat less effective in *abating* conflicts (58 per cent of the cases), even less effective in ending conflicts (44 per cent of the cases) and least effective in *settling* conflicts (32 per cent of the cases). This performance record of the RPOs compares favourably with that of the UN only on an unweighted basis because the UN receives the most difficult and serious cases. When assessed by the intensity and seriousness of hostilities, however, the effectiveness of the RPOs is generally limited to conflicts of low intensity involving minimal fighting; conflicts in which there was a threat to the organization's consensual norms; conflict abatement and isolation rather than conflict settlement; interstate conflicts threatening the consensual norm of state sovereignty with virtually no impact on intrastate conflicts; and conflicts in limited sub-regional geographical scope involving smaller and weaker member states (Haas 1986: 17, 33; Nye 1971: 169–75; Zacher 1979: 213).

There are important differences in the conflict control and peacekeeping performance of the five RPOs. As the only non-Third World RPO, the CE has received only five minor disputes: three disputes of 'very low intensity', one dispute of 'low intensity' and one 'insignificant' dispute (Haas 1986: 87). Of the remaining four RPOs, the OAS on an unweighted basis played a most active and effective role, and the OAU a slightly less active and effective role, compared to the poor performance of the LAS and non-performance of ASEAN. When assessed on a weighted basis there are still striking differences between the relative success of the OAS and the OAU and the failure of the LAS in cases involving hostilities. Yet the conflicts that engulfed the LAS were more serious in intensity and magnitude than those of the OAS, but the organizational will and power were much less (Nye 1971: 170). That ASEAN is excluded from all major studies of the conflict resolution performance of regional political organizations (Nye 1971; Zacher 1979; Haas 1986) speaks

993

directly to the fact that conflict resolution or peacekeeping is minimal in this loose subregional association of six Third World states. Although its principal aim was 'to establish a firm foundation for common action to promote regional co-operation in South-East Asia in the spirit of equality and partnership and thereby contribute toward peace, progress and prosperity in the region' (ASEAN Secretariat 1986: 23), ASEAN is little more than a loose forum of consultation and an affirmation of good intentions.

The RPOs' performance record, especially since the late 1970s, gives little support to most of the regionalist peace propositions. The regional–global equilibrium notion of the RPOs as useful, even indispensable adjuncts to the world organization is intuitively appealing, but it has not worked most of the time or in most of the cases in the Third World regions. Practically all of the most intense and intractable disputes that have engulfed the UN and have caused a chronic financial crisis have involved intraregional, not interregional, wars, involving fellow members of RPOs. Between the late 1970s and 1989 Vietnam served as the glue that held ASEAN together. Yet ASEAN 'solved' the Indo-China conflict by exporting it to the UN politics of collective legitimation and delegitimation. For the first time, the OAU decided in 1980 to establish an OAU peacekeeping force to cope with the Chadian crisis. And yet, both in the case of Chad and the proposals for Western Sahara, the OAU called upon the UN for financial, logistic and other resources in the unrealistic belief that the world organization would give such assistance to a regional peacekeeping force without central control. The OAS did indeed function in the 1950s and 1960s as an effective agent of intraregional conflict management, but this effectiveness was more a result of United States hegemony rather than of the peacekeeping efficiency of the organization. Gradually, the relationship between the OAS and the UN had been transformed from one of compatibility to one of incompatibility, as the United States used the organization as multilateral legitimizing cover for essentially unilateral action (Etzioni 1970: 90–218). Even the most successful case of the OAS, as Claude concludes in his influential study, 'confirms the proposition that the original project of permitting and encouraging regional agencies to operate within a framework of United Nations supervision and control had broken down' (Claude 1973: 297).

More dramatically, the turnaround in UN performance in 1987–8, symbolized by the awarding of the 1988 Nobel Peace prize to the UN Peacekeeping Forces, challenges the proposition that regional organizations enjoy comparative advantages over, or at least complement, the world organization in international conflict management. In the shadow of another cycle of superpower rivalry during the second phase of the Cold War (1980–6), the image of the world organization as an irrelevant and useless talking shop reached a climax. Helped by the muting of East–West tensions in the international climate, growing combat fatigue among warring Third World states, the active leadership of the UN Secretary-General, and global awareness of the inability and unwillingness of the RPOs to resolve their regional disputes, the UN as the world organization suddenly recovered its lost credibility in 1987–8 as an indispensable instrument in settling intractable regional conflicts in deeply troubled and wounded areas of the world. To varying degrees, UN diplomacy in 1987–90 facilitated various formal agreements to end the eight-year-old Iran–Iraq War and the fifteen-year-old Western Saharan War, to arrange for Soviet withdrawal from Afghanistan, to promote discussions about future arrangements for Kampuchea and Western Sahara, and to secure the independence of Namibia and the phased withdrawal of foreign forces from southern Africa (Falk *et al.* 1991). In addition, this turnaround tends to reverse the proposition that the success or failure of global peacekeeping efforts is likely to influence regional prospects – 'the greater the global success at cooperation, the less likely the regional development' (Falk and Mendlovitz 1973: 433).

This leaves the CE's conflict-management role unexplained. The CE members have not only not exported any of their intraregional disputes to the world organization but have also imported some of the Third World's disputes turned into global problems by making substantial contributions to UN peacekeeping operations. In a sense, then, the CE stands out as the only RPO complementing the world organization. At the same time, the CE's inactivism in peacekeeping can be accounted for by the fact that Western Europe had long been an island of peace since 1945. Besides, the Statute of the CE specifically states in Article 1 that 'matters relating to National Defence do not fall within the scope of the Council of Europe' (Bowett 1975: 152). The main political activities of the CE involve matters of political concern, such as East–West and North–South relations, UN activities, the promotion of human rights, increasing co-operation with the EC and Eastern European countries, and drawing up multilateral conventions and agreements. By September 1989 a total of 133 such multilateral treaties had been concluded under the CE's auspices (EWYB 1990: 130), the most important being the European Convention for the Protection of Human Rights and Fundamental Freedoms, concluded on 4 November 1950, and four Protocols.

In the Western European setting, then, the functionalist notion of a working peace system through economic interdependence still remains to be fully tested. How can we explain the fact that Europe has moved from being a major war zone to one with such a long period of peace since the Second World War? Haas, who can hardly be accused of being a classical functionalist, offers an essentially functionalist explanation for the long post-Second World War peace in Europe (and the Western Hemisphere) by stating:

> there is an impressive correlation between the decline of warfare and the growth of economic interdependence, as reflected in statistics on foreign trade, as well

as in the growth of every type of interstate and intergroup contact through the medium of the increasing number of regional organizations.

(Haas 1987: 117).

However, studies of international crisis management show that there is no direct link between the underlying social and economic causes and the proximate political causes of war (Lebow 1981; Snyder and Diesing 1977). An alternative non-functionalist explanation is that liberal democracies simply do not fight against each other (Doyle 1986).

The theory of great powers orbit does not apply to four of the five RPOs in our sample. As the only regional political organization having one of the superpowers as a member and having by far the greatest material capacity, the OAS offers a unique case of testing the hegemonic regionalist world-order theory. The OAS has had a greater number of disputes referred to it and a greater number of 'successes' in conflict control management performance than any other RPO, and the Western Hemisphere as a whole has enjoyed a 'long peace' too. To the extent that we can claim, as Nye does, that 'the effectiveness of the OAS is in large part the effectiveness of imperial hegemony' (Nye 1971: 154), the theory of great powers orbit is confirmed. But Nye quickly adds that 'it is not that alone'; international organization also 'makes a difference' (ibid.). If the record of the OAS supports the first assumption of the theory of great powers orbit – that the hegemonic power has the capacity to ensure regional peace – it lends little support to the second and third assumptions of compatibility of interest between great and small states and self-restraint of the hegemonic power.

The problem with the theory of great powers orbit is the tendency of great powers to manipulate and control weaker allies for their own global geopolitical interests disguised in appealing 'world order' rhetoric. The presence of great powers in a region offers particular difficulties for the development of a truly autonomous regional organization. The memory of Japan's 'Greater East Asia Co-Prosperity Sphere' is still vivid enough in the minds of many Asian leaders to hamper the establishment of a regional organization in East Asia. The use of the OAS as a legitimating fig leaf for imposing US geopolitical interests in certain selective situations of conflict in the Western Hemisphere suggests a less than convincing example to reconcile a hegemonic world order at the regional level with the blessing of the United Nations. In reality, the OAS served as another instrument of the United States in the global struggle against communism. The OAS's 'successes' in earlier years in peacekeeping, involving the smaller states of Central America and the Caribbean, greatly weakened the legitimacy of the organization and hampered its growth in subsequent years. The OAS's 'collective security system' failed to function where a communist state was the victim, but it worked with remarkable vigour where the victim was a non-communist state (Zacher 1979: 109). If the OAS has witnessed 'turbulent non-growth,' in recent years, the ability of the United States to use the OAS as a legitimizing instrument for its unilateral action has shown signs of progressive weakening too, as more and more Latin American states assert greater independence from US hegemony. The OAS's condemnation of the US invasion of Panama in December 1989, by a vote of 20 to 1 with the United States the only dissenter, as a violation of the consensual norm of non-intervention is a good example.

Although the experience of the EC and OAS lends some credence to the notion that international co-operation would be easier in regional organizations composed of states with similar cultural traditions, especially as made evident in the remarkable progress in the promotion of human rights in Western Europe and the Western Hemisphere, the lack of organizational progress in peacekeeping in the other regional political organizations gives little support to the proposition. It is worth recalling in this connection that internal conflicts have been more resistant than interstate conflicts to international conflict management, that four divided polities (for example, two Chinas, two Koreas, two Vietnams and two Germanies) turned into the major zones of superpower rivalries during much of the post-war era, and that three of the four major zones of conflict were, and still are, under the cultural shadow of Chinese civilization.

By and large the record of ASEAN, the LAS and the OAU does not support the proposition that the regionals are better able to maintain international peace by fractionating regional conflicts. More often than not, regional conflicts are allowed to escalate beyond the point of organizational capability and then exported to the UN as extraregional conflicts threatening international peace and security. This is what is meant by the statement that the UN only receives the hardest regional conflicts. Unlike any RPO the UN is hypersensitive to any shift in the global correlation of forces, with its primary function in the war/peace area instantly reflecting gathering pressures towards one or other of the competing approaches to world order. With the momentous changes and events sweeping all over the world in 1987–90, the UN's peacekeeping success curve began to rise sharply. The nature and scope of UN peacekeeping have also been expanded, and the distinction between peacekeeping and peace-making has become blurred in the past several years with the world organization's greater active involvement in monitoring and supervising elections in Namibia, Haiti and Nicaragua; such involvement may yet extend to Afghanistan, Angola, Cambodia and Western Sahara. The idea that international consensus formation and co-operation is simpler with a smaller number of regional state actors in the game is intriguing. The performance record of the five RPOs is inconclusive. The most that can be said about this proposition is to add an essential caveat – 'all other factors being constant and equal'. ASEAN, with only six member states, has not produced greater international co-operation than the CE, with twenty-three member states, or the OAS, with thirty-two member states; and the CE is no less co-operative today than it was in 1949 when it had only ten member states. When the Big Five in the Security Council suddenly demonstrated unanimity for Security Council Resolution 598 on 20 July 1987, calling a cease-fire in the Iran–Iraq War, this was something that the same Big Five had failed to achieve in all preceding forty-two years of their permanent membership in the Council. At the same time, now that the EC, whose membership has increased from six to twelve, seems poised to move towards political union, there is the growing insistence that further 'widening' would endanger further 'deepening' as well as the growing concern that the more integrated the EC becomes the harder it is to let in new members.

FUTURE RESEARCH

The study of regionalism started in the latter half of the 1950s with a big neo-functionalist bang and died with a whimper in the mid-1970s. International regimes suddenly became new buzz words in international relations research and have remained the dominant mainstream focus of international organiz-ation scholarship.

It seems fair to say that the study of regionalism was too closely keyed to the stop-and-go development of European integration. Understandably, it lost its *raison d'être* during the long dark decade of the EC. Instead of being excessively concerned with measuring the scope and depth of integration taking place, a more appropriate and ambitious undertaking should be concerned either with how best to promote peace, economic well-being, human rights and environmental quality within the region, or with what the implications of a regional approach to world order are for the resolution of these basic human problems at the global level. Another major issue concerns the impact that multipolarization might have on regional development or the relationship between regionalism and multipolarism. Opinions vary as to whether US hegemonic decline and multipolarization is a fact, a myth or a wrong question. One notion of a multipolarizing world envisages a trilateral world economic order resting upon three large regional blocs (Europe, the American Hemi-sphere and East Asia). What is the feasibility and desirability of such a trilateral regionalist world economic order? The recent developments of the EC suggest a point of departure for this line of enquiry. Regionalism still seems made to order for providing one approach to the study of international co-operation. As well, it is an alternative to both *realpolitik* and *idealpolitik* for students concerned about the shape of things to come in international life.

REFERENCES

ASEAN Secretariat (1986) *ASEAN Document Series 1967–1986*, 2nd edn, Jakarta: ASEAN Secretariat.

Bennett, A. L. (1988) *International Organizations: Principles and Issues*, 4th edn, Englewood Cliffs, NJ: Prentice-Hall.

Bowett, D. W. (1975) *The Law of International Institutions*, 3rd edn, London: Stevens & Sons.

Burton, J. (1962) *Peace Theory*, New York: Knopf.

Clark, G. and Sohn, L. (1966) *World Peace Through World Law*, 3rd edn, Cambridge, Mass.: Harvard University Press.

Claude, I. L. (1971) *Swords into Plowshares: The Problems and Progress of International Organization*, 4th edn, New York: Random House.

——(1973). 'The OAS, the UN, and the United States', in R. A. Falk and S. H. Mendlovitz (eds) *Regional Politics and World Order*, San Francisco: W. H. Freeman.

Doyle, M. (1986) 'Liberalism in world politics', *American Political Science Review* 80: 1151–69.

Etzioni, M. M. (1970) *The Majority of One: Towards a Theory of Regional Compatibility*, Beverly Hills: Sage Publications.

EWYB (1990) *The Europa World Year Book 1990*, Vol. 1, London: Europa Publications.

Falk, R. A. and Mendlovitz, S. H. (eds) (1973) *Regional Politics and World Order*, San Francisco: W. H. Freeman.

Falk, R. A., Kim, S. S. and Mendlovitz, S. H. (eds) (1991) *The United Nations and a Just World Order*, Boulder, Colo.: Westview Press.

Groom, A. J. R. and Taylor, P. (eds) (1975) *Functionalism: Theory and Practice in International Relations*, London: University of London Press.

Haas, E. B. (1958) *The Uniting of Europe*, Stanford: Stanford University Press.

——(1964) *Beyond the Nation-State: Functionalism and International Organization*, Stanford: Stanford University Press.

——(1973) 'The study of regional integration: reflections on the joy and anguish of pretheorising', in R. A. Falk and S. H. Mendlovitz (eds) *Regional Politics and World Order*, San Francisco: W. H. Freeman.

——(1975) *The Obsolescence of Regional Integration Theory*, Berkeley: Institute of International Studies, University of California.

——(1986) *Why We Still Need the United Nations: The Collective Management of International Conflict, 1945–1984*, Berkeley: Institute of International Studies, University of California.

——(1987) 'War, interdependence and functionalism', in R. Vayrynen (ed.) *The Quest for Peace*, Beverly Hills: Sage Publications.

——(1990) *When Knowledge is Power: Three Models of Change in International Organizations*, Berkeley: University of California Press.

Herbst, J. (1989) 'The creation and maintenance of national boundaries in Africa', *International Organization* 43: 673–92.

Hoffmann, S. (1963) 'Discord in community: the North Atlantic area as a partial international system', *International Organization* 17: 521–49.

——(1989) 'The European Community and 1992', *Foreign Affairs* 68: 27–47.

Kim, S. S. (1979) *China, the United Nations, and World Order*, Princeton: Princeton University Press.

____(1984) *The Quest for a Just World Order*, Boulder, Colo.: Westview Press.

Lebow, R. N. (1981) *Between Peace and War: The Nature of International Crisis*, Baltimore: Johns Hopkins University Press.

Liska, G. (1973) 'Geographic scope: the pattern of integration', in R. A. Falk and S. H. Mendlovitz (eds) *Regional Politics and World Order*, San Francisco: W. H. Freeman.

Lodge, J. (ed.) (1986) *European Union: The European Community in Search of a Future*, London: Macmillan.

Mace, G. (1988) 'Regional integration in Latin America: a long and winding road', *International Journal* 43: 404–27.

Miller, L. H. (1973) 'Regional organizations and subordinate systems', in R. A. Falk and S. H. Mendlovitz (eds) *Regional Politics and World Order*, San Francisco: W. H. Freeman.

Mitrany, D. (1966) *A Working Peace System*, Chicago: Quadrangle.

Newcombe, H. (1974) 'Alternative approaches to world government, II', *Peace Research Review* 5: 1–94.

Nye, J. S. (1971) *Peace in Parts: Integration and Conflict in Regional Organization*, Boston: Little, Brown & Co.

Oye, K. (ed.) (1986) *Cooperation Under Anarchy*, Princeton: Princeton University Press.

Sewell, J. P. (1966) *Functionalism and World Politics*, Princeton: Princeton University Press.

Snyder, G. H. and Diesing, P. (1977) *Conflict Among Nations*, Princeton: Princeton University Press.

UIA (1989) Union of International Associations, *Yearbook of International Organizations 1989/90*, Vol. 2, 7th edn, Munich: K. G. Saur.

Yalem, R. (1973) 'Theories of regionalism', in R. A. Falk and S. H. Mendlovitz (eds) *Regional Politics and World Order*, San Francisco: W. H. Freeman.

Zacher, M. W. (1979) *International Conflicts and Collective Security, 1946–1977: The United Nations, Organization of American States, Organization of African Unity, and Arab League*, New York: Praeger.

FURTHER READING

Andemicael, B. (ed.) (1979) *Regionalism and the United Nations*, Dobbs Ferry, NY: Oceana Publications.

Cantori, L. J. and Spiegel, S. L. (eds) (1970) *The International Politics of Regions: A Comparative Approach*, Englewood Cliffs, NJ: Prentice-Hall.

El-Ayouty, Y. and Zartman, I. W. (eds) (1984) *The OAU After Twenty Years*, New York: Praeger.

Feld, W. (1976) *The European Community in World Affairs: Economic Power and Political Influence*, Port Washington, NY: Alfred Publishing.

Gauhar, A. (ed.) (1985) *Regional Integration: The Latin American Experience*, London: Third World Foundation.

Kihl, Y. W. (1989) 'Intra-regional conflict and the ASEAN peace process', *International Journal* 44: 598–615.

Krafona, K. (ed.) (1988) *Organization of Africam Unity: 25 Years On*, London: Afroworld Publishing.

Leifer, M. (1989) *ASEAN and the Security of South-East Asia*, London: Routledge.

Luke, D. F. (1986) 'Regionalism in Africa: a short study of the record', *International Journal* 41: 853–68.

Nye, J. S. (ed.) (1968) *International Regionalism*, Boston: Little, Brown & Co.

Onwuka, R. I. and Sesay A. (eds) (1985) *The Future of Regionalism in Africa*, New York: St Martin's Press.

Russett, B. M. (1967) *International Regions and the International System*, Chicago, Rand McNally.

Saunders, C. T. (ed.) (1983) *Regional Integration in East and West*, New York: St Martin's Press.

Sesay, A., Ojo, O. and Fasehun, O. (eds) (1984) *The OAU After Twenty Years*, Boulder, Colo.: Westview Press.

Shaw, T. M. (1989) 'The revival of regionalism in Africa: cure for crisis or prescription for conflict?', *Jerusalem Journal of International Relations* 11: 79–105.

Simon, S. (1988) *The Future of Asian–Pacific Security Collaboration*, Lexington, Mass.: Lexington Books.

Taylor, P. (1983) *The Limits of European Integration*, New York: Columbia University Press.

63

REGIONAL ASSOCIATIONS: ALLIANCES

OLE R. HOLSTI

Alliances have been variously considered as techniques of statecraft, international organizations or regulating mechanisms in the balance of power. To grasp the central features of alliances, however, requires only that participating states' decisions to collaborate be made by formal agreement – open or secret – and that the collaboration be directly concerned with security issues. Thus, an alliance is a formal agreement between two or more nations to collaborate on national security issues.

It is far simpler to define alliances than to explain the forces that generate, sustain and destroy them. Why do nations choose to undertake or shun commitments? Is the choice primarily a response to the exigencies of the external environment, including such considerations as the distribution of power in the international system, geopolitical configurations, or the level of conflict and threat among nations? To what extent do alliance policies reflect attributes of nations? Are some nations 'alliance-prone' while others are likely to remain free of external military ties? When faced with alternatives, why do nations elect to join a particular coalition in preference to others? Are nations with important characteristics in common more likely to align than those that are dissimilar? Are alliances merely the pragmatic expression of transient, albeit urgent, interests, rather than the international manifestation of ties arising from common ethnic, cultural, ideological or other attributes? A number of theories have been offered to answer these central questions. The strengths and weaknesses of various efforts to explain alliance formation, alliance performance and the effects of alliances will be considered below.

THEORIES OF ALLIANCE FORMATION
Alliances and the balance of power

Among the oldest explanations of alliances are those derived from balance-of-power, or equilibrium, theories, in which the emphasis is on the external environment, including the structure, distribution of power, and state of relations among units of the system. These are often closely linked to the 'realist' approach to international politics (Morgenthau 1959; Waltz 1979; Gilpin 1981). Nations join forces as a matter of expediency in order to aggregate sufficient capabilities to achieve certain foreign policy goals or to create a geographically advantageous position (for example, to create buffers or isolate a potential adversary). Among the most important motives is preventing any nation or combination of countries from achieving a dominant position. The classic examples that illustrate these principles are the Quadruple Alliance which defeated Napoleon in 1814–15, and the 'Grand Alliance' of the Second World War which defeated German and Japanese attempts to establish domination over Europe and Asia, respectively.

Balance-of-power approaches thus locate the motivations for alliance formation primarily in the attributes of the international system and the situation – the distribution of power, threats to the balance of power, and the like. They tend to deny that alliance policies are significantly affected by national characteristics. Alliance partners, moreover, are chosen on the basis of common goals and needs, not for reasons of shared values, shared institutions or a sense of community. Aside from the examples provided by the coalitions of the Napoleonic Wars and the Second World War, the Nazi–Soviet Pact of 1939 is often cited to illustrate the point that the wellspring of any given alliance is the calculus of interest rather than sentiments of community.

Balance-of-power reasoning relies upon assumptions that are analogous to those of classical free-market economics. Central to both is the notion of the 'invisible hand' – that is, if individuals (institutions or nations) pursue their own interests rationally, an equilibrium is established which serves the general good. Just as the intelligent pursuit of profit in a competitive free market is intended to serve the welfare of the community by ensuring low prices and high quality, so the disciplined pursuit of the national interest maintains international stability while permitting sufficient change to prevent the system from becoming overly rigid. Alliance policies play a central role in the analogy. If any member of the system threatens to become dominant, the interests of the community require some form of collective action; in international politics the alliance is the traditional means of preventing hegemony. According to balance-of-power theories, nations should be more likely to join the weaker coalition to prevent formation of a hegemonic one ('balancing') rather than join the dominant one in order to increase the probability of joining the winning side ('bandwagoning') (Waltz 1979). Several case studies found support for the 'balancing' hypothesis (Walt 1987). But permanent alliances are themselves as detrimental to the system as oligopolies or monopolies, and must therefore be avoided. As Nicholas Spykman noted:

He who plays the balance of power can have no permanent friends. His devotion can be to no specific state but only to balanced power. The ally of today is the enemy of tomorrow. One of the charms of power politics is that it offers no opportunity to grow weary of one's friends.

(Spykman 1942: 103–4)

Balance-of-power formulations are a useful point of departure for understanding some of the motivations underlying alliance policies, at least for some periods or regions. But the number of deviant cases is sufficiently large to raise serious doubts that these formulations can provide a general theory of alliances (see, for example, Dawson and Rosecrance 1966).

Coalition theories and the 'size principle'

In contrast to balance-of-power explanations of alliance formation, aspects of which can be found in some of the earliest known writings on politics, coalition theories are of very recent origin. Central to coalition theories is the 'size principle', according to which 'coalitions will increase in size only to the minimum point of subjective certainty of winning' (Riker 1962: 32–3).

The basic elements of coalition theory are drawn deductively from 'game theory' rather than inductively from historical evidence, yet they share a number of characteristics with balance-of-power, or equilibrium, models. Both place heavy emphasis on calculation of advantage, adequate information and rationality in alliance formation. They also tend to assume that national attributes other than power are of little importance in the calculations leading up to alliance formation. But on one point they appear to differ. Whereas an important goal of 'ideal' balance-of-power systems is to prevent the rise of a dominant nation or group of nations, the primary motivation in game approaches is to form just such a coalition. The politicians in a balance-of-power system must simultaneously pursue policies of self-extension and self-restraint, while in coalition theories they are assumed to be motivated by the single goal of winning, and doing so under conditions that maximize their share of the gain – with enough partners to ensure victory and without any additional ones who would claim a share of the spoils.

Coalition theories are elegant and intuitively appealing. There are, moreover, a large number of experimental studies as well as less formal investigations of political coalitions in elections, conventions, multi-party legislatures and the like, which have often provided empirical substantiation for predictions drawn from coalition theories. But a number of difficulties arise when this approach is applied to international politics.

The first problem is the premiss that whatever an alliance wins must be divided competitively between its members. If war offers the prospect of winning territories, indemnities or other forms of tangible and divisible rewards, there are evident advantages to forming an alliance no larger than is necessary to gain victory. But the zero-sum assumption is not applicable to all coalitions. Even in redistribution alliances the interests of the partners may be complementary, permitting a non-competitive division of rewards. More importantly, alliances are often formed for purposes of defence or deterrence. In that case the success of the alliance is measured by its ability to prevent conflict, not by the territorial or other gains derived from successful prosecution of a war. Instead of dividing the rewards competitively, each member gains from the collective ability to deter an aggressor, and any increase in the security of one nation accrues to the benefit of all. For purposes of deterrence, large alliances may actually serve the common interest better by reducing the probability of miscalculation on the part of a potential aggressor.

A second difficulty, one that is shared with balance-of-power theories, is the demanding requirement that politicians be able to measure capabilities with sufficient precision to define a minimum winning coalition. In an election, convention or legislature this rarely poses a severe problem. Moreover, although pre-voting influence may be unequally distributed among convention delegates or legislators, at the voting stage each person wields equal power and the definition of 'winning' is usually unambiguous. There is thus little difficulty in defining a 'minimum winning coalition'. But these conditions rarely obtain at the international level. Important elements of strength such as morale and popular support for the regime, whether of allies or adversaries, cannot often be assessed with complete accuracy; even the tangible components of power may elude precise measurement. One answer to this criticism is that the size principle is based solely on subjective estimates of capabilities. But if it is thus limited, the size principle appears to lose most of its explanatory power.

Several other considerations may reduce the significance of coalition theories for the contemporary international system. As the number of independent nations increases, so does the difficulty of defining a winning coalition. Moreover, the predominant form of warfare today is that in which conventional measures of power, even rather sophisticated ones, may be inadequate. Finally, when international politics are characterized by intense ideological conflict for which domestic energies and mass emotions are mobilized, the process of alliance formation is unlikely to be dominated solely by calculations of capabilities.

These limitations are sufficiently important to suggest that coalition theories and their central size principle are probably an inadequate base from which to construct a general theory of alliance formation. Nevertheless, one important normative element does emerge from the notion of minimum winning coalitions. It is a reminder that bigger is not necessarily better insofar as alliances are concerned, and that some commitments may entail more costs than benefits. In this respect the prescriptions of coalition theorists converge with those of the 'realist' school of international politics.

National attributes and alliance participation

A clear contrast to the balance-of-power and minimum winning coalition theories is provided by those that emphasize national attributes – other than power or capabilities – as important considerations in alliance policies. These approaches do not deny that calculations of national interest or power influence alliance formation, nor do they rule out the effects of systemic or situational considerations. Virtually all of them agree, for example, that, irrespective of national attributes, nations faced with an external threat are more likely to seek allies than those in a benign situation. They also emphasize that we cannot treat nations as undifferentiated units if we wish to understand either their propensity to use alliances as instruments of foreign policy (as opposed to such alternatives as neutrality) or their choice of alliance partners when there are available options. The common denominator is a suspicion that foreign-policy orientations reflect motives that draw upon many sources, some of which may be related to national attributes.

A nation's historical experience may affect its alliance policies. For example, Swedish and Norwegian policies after the Second World War reflected their past experiences with efforts to remain neutral during the two world wars (Burgess 1967). Newly independent nations often avoid alliances. Most of the states which have achieved independence since 1945 have chosen policies of 'neutralism', although not necessarily neutrality, with respect to Cold War conflicts. American experience is also illustrative. For a century and a half after independence from Great Britain was gained, the warnings of Washington and Jefferson against entangling alliances represented the core of conventional wisdom on matters of foreign policy. However, history is not devoid of counter-examples. Nations which gained independence in 1918 as the German, Austro-Hungarian, Russian and Ottoman Empires collapsed did not as a rule shun alliances; witness the creation in 1920–1 of the Little Entente between Czechoslovakia, Yugoslavia and Romania, and the formation of the looser Balkan Entente by Yugoslavia, Greece, Turkey and Romania in 1934. Moreover, in several instances involving European nations it has been necessary to obtain formal agreement of the major powers to guarantee the new state's neutrality. Article VII of the settlement by which Belgian independence from Holland was recognized in 1839 declared Belgium to be a 'perpetually neutral' state under the collective guarantee of the European powers. A similar stipulation was attached to the treaty by which Austria was freed from four-power occupation in 1955. These examples suggest that newly independent states are most likely to avoid alliances when they are geographically removed from the centres of great-power conflict.

Political stability is sometimes associated with a propensity to join alliances, and instability has been seen as an impetus to go beyond non-alignment and pursue a policy of 'militant neutralism'. On the other hand, a leadership group faced with domestic instability may actively court allies in the hopes of gaining external support for a tottering regime. According to purely utilitarian criteria, small, poor and unstable nations are relatively unattractive alliance partners. Nevertheless, such nations have often been sought as allies, and they have even become the focal point of acute crises; twentieth-century examples include Bosnia (1908–9), Serbia (1914), Cuba (1961 and 1962) and Vietnam (1965–73).

Given a propensity to seek allies, does the choice of partners reflect a discernible pattern of preferences? 'Affinity theories' approach alliance formation from a sociometric perspective, addressing themselves to the similarities and differences of two or more nations as an element in their propensity to align. The premise that nations are likely to be selective in their choice of allies, exhibiting a preference for partners with whom they share common institutions, cultural and ideological values or economic interests, is intuitively appealing. It has, however, received limited support in studies of pre-1945 alliances (Russett 1971; Holsti *et al.* 1973).

ALLIANCE PERFORMANCE

Palmerston once noted that nations have neither permanent enemies nor allies, only permanent interests. More recently Edwin Fedder (1968: 82–3) has asserted that they are not 'particularly viable' components of the international system. It is true that the longevity of most alliances can better be measured in years than decades or centuries, but these observations do not explain why some are cohesive and effective, whereas others are not. Is it because some types of states are particularly unsuitable alliance partners, lacking resources, internal cohesion or coherence of interests? Or is it because the alliance itself is structurally or otherwise unsound, or because the conditions which gave rise to the alliance have passed, rendering it superfluous? Is it because the alliance was unable to bridge the chasm of fundamental differences in goals and values? Why do some coalitions endure for relatively long periods, whereas others are stillborn virtually from the moment of conception? Can alliances survive success (eliminating or outliving the threat) any better than failure (defeat by the adversary)? A range of theories has been advanced to explain alliance performance and longevity: some emphasize the attributes of the member nations; some, the character of the alliance itself; and others, the nature of the international system.

Attributes of alliance members

Open and closed polities   The relative merits of open and closed polities have been debated in many treatises, but without consensus. To some, open polities are inferior allies on two counts: by definition they experience relatively frequent changes in ruling elites, with the consequence that commitments to allies may also change; and the demands of domestic politics may take precedence over the requirements of alliances. Other observers take a kinder view of democracies, finding that when under attack they are more likely to expand alliance functions, that they tend to turn alliances into communities of friendship, and that they are less likely to renege on commitments by seeking a separate peace (Liska 1962: 50, 52, 115). But history is filled with enough examples of ineffective or perfidious alliance performance to lend some weight to the arguments of those who maintain that neither democracies nor dictatorships are markedly superior in this respect.

Domestic instability   Political instability is often associated with poor alliance performance. Unstable regimes may experience radical changes in elites which in turn result in shifting patterns of alignment. Unstable regimes may also be more willing to run high risks on behalf of their own interests but not those of allies. A classic example is Austria-Hungary in 1914. Fearing that the multinational Dual Monarchy would be torn apart by demands for autonomy from various ethnic groups, Vienna pursued a punitive policy toward Serbia, initially with the full support of Germany but later with little attention to advice emanating from Berlin.

Some of the most dramatic cases of realignment or alliance defection, however, have occurred in nations with well-entrenched elites. Nazi–Soviet relations offer numerous illustrations. The Nazi–Soviet Pact was inconsistent with the Franco-Soviet alliance of 1935 and the Anti-Comintern Pact, of which Germany was the leading member. After Hitler turned on his erstwhile ally in 1941, the Soviet government agreed with its new allies – Britain and the United States – that it would not enter into a separate peace with Germany. Yet there is evidence that it attempted to do precisely this in 1943.

Bureaucratic politics   Another line of reasoning suggests that differences in national bureaucratic structures and processes may be an increasingly important barrier to co-ordination of alliance strategies. Its proponents emphasize that national security policy is the product of constant intramural conflict within highly complex and varied bureaucratic structures (Neustadt 1970; Allison 1971). As a result, even close allies may fail to perceive accurately both the nuances in the bureaucratic politics 'game' as it is played abroad and how the demands of various constituents may shape and constrain alliance policies.

Recognition that bureaucratic conflict may affect foreign-policy choices may usefully supplement perspectives that regard alliance policies solely as a matter of rationality and calculation.

Alliance attributes

Alliances differ in many ways, including the circumstances under which their provisions became operative (*casus foederis*), the type of commitment, the degree of co-operation and geographical scope. The ANZUS (Australia, New Zealand and United States) Treaty called only for consultations in case of certain contingencies, and it had a rather minimal bureaucratic apparatus. NATO, on the other hand, commits its members to joint military action in clearly specified circumstances (an armed attack on any one of them) and, unlike the ANZUS pact, has an elaborate political and military infrastructure. NATO is also of broader geographical scope. Other alliance attributes of interest include purpose and ideology, size, structure, capabilities and quality of leadership.

Alliance purposes and ideology The examination of alliance formation centres on nations that choose to undertake or avoid external commitments, and on the sources of their motivations for doing so. Varied as these motives may be, presumably all nations prefer to join alliances that offer them an effective role in determining goals, strategy and tactics; that provide a 'fair' share of the rewards without undue costs; and that offer the maximum probability of success in achieving their goals.

Redistribution alliances might be expected to achieve fewer successes and to break up more easily than those whose primary motives are deterrence and defence. Failure to achieve goals has a disintegrative effect and, other things being equal, it is easier for an alliance of deterrence to succeed; it is sufficient to deny the enemy a victory or to maintain the status quo. A redistribution alliance, on the other hand, must not only be able to avert defeat; it must also win a victory if it is to be successful. Even if it achieves a victory, there are potentially disintegrative elements in the situation. The rewards of an offensive alliance can be shared non-competitively only when the goals of each nation are limited and do not overlap with those of its allies. We might expect even greater friction between allies when distribution of the rewards is delayed until the end of the war. In contrast, the more security an alliance of deterrence provides for one nation, the more secure all of the others are likely to feel. It remains to be seen, however, how long an alliance such as NATO can survive widespread feeling among the public in some nations that the demise of the Warsaw Pact in 1991 symbolized the elimination of the threat to be deterred, and in others that alliance burdens are unequally shared.

The generality or scope of an alliance tends to be inversely related to its durability. It is easier to maintain co-operation for specific purposes in geographically limited areas than in global alliances that make a substantial claim on resources and freedom of action. This is quite consistent with the 'realist' position which tends to argue that alliances are, and should be, instruments of policy entered into to achieve specific and limited goals. In direct contrast is the view that an alliance is more likely to endure through crises if it has a rationale for existence that goes beyond some immediate, concrete problem.

The role that ideology may play in sustaining or dissolving alliance bonds involves two questions. First, does a similarity in values and world views add to the durability and effectiveness of alliance? Even those who minimize the importance of ideology in alliance formation would tend to answer in the affirmative, because a shared ideology may ensure that issues are defined in similar terms, and it should also facilitate intra-alliance communication. The second question concerns the presence of ideology as a salient component of the *raison d'être* for the bloc. A common ideology may sustain alliances, but only as long as its tenets do not themselves become an issue. When they do, alliances in which doctrinal questions are highly salient are less likely to endure than those in which they are of marginal importance. When ideology is taken seriously, issues arising therefrom have a quality that makes them particularly likely to exacerbate relations between those who interpret the faith differently. Concrete alliance problems such as the level of military contributions can almost always be resolved by compromise but it is a good deal more difficult for true believers to split their differences on questions of 'fundamental truth'.

Size Large alliances are usually less cohesive than small ones. There are several reasons why this would seem true. First, the larger the alliance, the smaller the share of attention that nations can give to each other ally. Second, as the size of the alliance increases, the number of relationships within the alliance rises even faster. Not only do the problems of co-ordination increase, but so do the opportunities for dissension. Finally, the larger the alliance, the less important the contributions of any single member (especially minor partners), and the easier it is for any partner to rationalize the argument that failure to meet all alliance obligations will not really make a significant difference – the 'free rider' problem.

The 'size principle' postulates that alliances will only be as large as necessary to win. Coalition theorists recognize that under some circumstances – for example, when information is inadequate – alliances will in fact exceed this optimal size. A natural extension of this theory is that the alliance is unlikely to survive without changes after the discovery that the size principle has been violated. However, a study of nineteenth- and twentieth-century alliances found that they broke up at a constant rate independent of size (Horvath and Foster 1963).

Alliance structure: decision making and the distribution of influence   Alliances differ widely in the kinds of political and administrative arrangements that govern their activities. Two nations may undertake wide-ranging commitments to assist each other under given circumstances and yet fail to establish institutions and procedures for communication and co-ordination of activities. This tended to characterize the alliance between Germany and Austria-Hungary during the years leading up to the First World War (Craig 1965; Williamson 1969). The Warsaw Pact may perhaps be used to illustrate the other extreme. Basic alliance decisions were made in Moscow, and all key positions in the alliance were filled by Russians.

The consequences of alternative decision-making structures are less clear. One line of reasoning suggests that hierarchical and centralized alliances are likely to be more cohesive and more effective in coping with the external environment because they can mobilize their resources better and can respond more quickly to threats and opportunities. The view that pluralistic and decentralized alliances are likely to enjoy greater solidarity, vitality and effectiveness also has its advocates. A comparison of French and Chinese alliance policies suggests that autocratic alliances may be more cohesive and effective as long as there are no issues that might seriously challenge the established order within the coalition, but once such issues develop they are likely to poison all facets of relations between the contending partners. Conversely, although pluralistic alliances will not be free of disagreements, even differences on central concerns are likely to remain confined to the single issue at stake rather than 'spill over' into other issue areas (Holsti *et al.* 1973).

The allocation of functions may also affect alliance unity. The position that influence and benefits in an alliance reflect the distribution of capabilities and burdens among its members appears to fit common sense, historical examples can be adduced in support, and some supporting evidence may be found in both small-group and experimental studies (Morgenthau 1959; Gamson 1961; Torrance 1965). The preponderant influence of the United States and the Soviet Union in NATO and the Warsaw Pact seems to support this view.

Despite the intuitive appeal of the proposition that influence is proportional to strength, it may not always be valid. Under some circumstances weakness may actually be a source of strength in intra-alliance diplomacy. The stronger nation is usually the more enthusiastic partner, it has less to gain by bargaining hard, and it can less credibly threaten to reduce its contributions. The weaker nation may also enjoy disproportionate influence within an alliance because it can commit its stronger ally, which may be unable to accept losses resulting from the smaller partner's defeat (Lall 1966; Olson 1965; Olson and Zeck-hauser 1966; Rothstein 1966).

Because historical examples can be adduced in support of both viewpoints on intra-alliance influence, it may be useful to suggest the circumstances under which each of the opposing views is likely to be valid.

1 The 'tighter' the international system, the greater the likelihood that weaker allies will enjoy disproportionate influence within the alliance.
2 The more pluralistic the alliance, the greater the likelihood that small allies will enjoy disproportionate influence within the alliance.
3 Small nations are more likely to achieve disproportionate influence in an alliance composed of democratic states than in one of authoritarian nations.

Alliance capabilities Each state brings both assets and liabilities to the alliance. The conventional manner of assessing the capabilities of the coalition is to sum the assets of the member nations. The alternative and perhaps more realistic view is that the capabilities of an alliance are rarely equal to the sum of its parts. Under some circumstances the whole may exceed the total contribution of member nations. Given close co-ordination, similar equipment, skillful leadership, and complementary needs and resources, economies of scale may be achieved. This may sometimes be the case for alliances of deterrence. But if there is an actual requirement to carry out military operations, alliance capabilities are probably less – perhaps substantially less – than those of the individual nations combined. Sources of weakness may include poor staff co-ordination, mistrust, incompatible goals, logistical difficulties, dissimilar military equipment and organization, and many others. This is what Napoleon had in mind when he stated, 'If I must make war, I prefer it to be against a coalition' (Padelford and Lincoln 1967: 402). A century later Marshal Foch remarked, 'My admiration for Napoleon has shrunk since I found out what a coalition was' (Rothstein 1968: 125).

Virtually every alliance faces the problem of ensuring the credibility of its commitments. The problem is most serious for alliances of deterrence. If adversaries possess serious doubts on this score, the alliance may serve as an invitation to attack. Equally important, if allies themselves have doubts about the assurances of their partners, the coalition is unlikely to be effective or to survive for long. Nuclear weapons have introduced and nurtured precisely this type of question about the viability of contemporary commitments.

The capabilities and competence of the alliance leader are of special importance. A powerful and wealthy bloc leader is capable of offering economic aid and other types of side payments (private goods to supplement public ones) to smaller partners, which may in turn render the alliance more effective. A prosperous nation can do so without disrupting domestic programmes, whereas a less affluent bloc leader may be tempted instead to drain the resources of its allies. Moreover, according to the economic theory of 'collective action', alliances that supplement public benefits (those that are shared by all members) with private or non-collective ones are more cohesive than alliances that provide only collective benefits. A study of NATO supports this proposition (Olson and Zeckhauser 1966). Conversely, a decline in the strength of the leader makes the alliance especially vulnerable to erosion. America's catastrophic Vietnam undertaking and its relative economic decline, symbolized by budget and trade deficits, raised doubts about both American material power and the political wisdom of its leadership. The successful Persian Gulf War and American leadership of the anti-Iraq coalition no doubt enhanced its reputation, but it will do nothing to arrest its relative economic decline.

Alliance leadership: coping with intra- and inter-alliance diplomacy

Except in a pure conflict situation there are always some tensions between the requisites of alliance cohesion and broader global concerns. If the alliance is to cope effectively with these tensions, it requires effective leadership from its leading member or members. One strategy is to give top priority to alliance maintenance, even if doing so may entail some potential lost opportunities for reducing or resolving inter-alliance conflicts. John Foster Dulles adopted this approach during much of his tenure as US Secretary of State. The Nixon–Kissinger strategy was almost diametrically opposite to that pursued by Dulles. Maintaining harmonious relations with allies took a back seat to the search for *détente* with China and the Soviet Union.

Alliance relationships involve other kinds of tensions and fears. Members must decide whether or not to support their partners. They also face the fears of abandonment when their own interests are at stake, and of entrapment when those of others are threatened (Snyder 1984). Perhaps the ultimate test of alliance leadership comes during an international crisis when the leading partner may be forced to resolve serious tensions between alliance management (intra-alliance diplomacy) and crisis management (inter-alliance diplomacy). In a crisis the alliance leader may face a number of critical tasks:

1 to convey to the adversary: (a) evidence of a determination to maintain existing commitments; and (b) sufficient reassurance to reduce motivations for significant military escalation and, possibly, to permit bargaining on crisis issues;
2 to convey to allies: (a) assurances that their vital interests will not be sacrificed in seeking accommodation with the adversary (assuaging fears of abandonment); (b) assurances that they will not be drawn into a general war over issues of peripheral interest to the alliance as a whole (assuaging fears of entrapment); and (c) a resolve not to be drawn into a strategy of escalation

on behalf of an ally which is willing to run unduly high risks in the pursuit of purely parochial interests.

It will be difficult for any nation to co-ordinate its diplomatic efforts in a way that will simultaneously meet these objectives. The most obvious strategy for coping with these tensions is to tell allies one thing and adversaries something else, but this ploy is difficult to use in an era of public pressures for 'instant history' and of often leaky bureaucracies and communication channels.

It is sometimes suggested that 'irrational' alliance commitments may be undertaken as part of an overall strategy of increasing the credibility of deterrence (Maxwell 1968: 8). For example, a nation may undertake a vast commitment of resources in a peripheral region to support a minor ally of far less value than the costs of the commitment. This strategy is intended to convey to the adversary – and to other allies – that if the alliance leader is willing to expend vast resources to protect areas of little strategic value, then it should be clear that an even greater effort will be made to defend other allies. But like other strategies of buttressing credibility by 'irrational' commitments, this one entails risks. Such pledges may ultimately force the alliance leader to choose between two unpalatable alternatives: reducing the commitment under . threat, thereby seriously eroding one's credibility in the future, or backing the promise to the hilt, with the possibility of becoming a prisoner of the ally's policies. New or expanded pledges of support to small allies may also complicate rather than facilitate the resolution of crisis situations by introducing further issues into crisis negotiations.

History also reveals a number of other instances in which major powers initiated or expanded commitments of support to allies in a crisis, only to discover later that their policy options had been restricted to a far greater degree than they had foreseen. The German pledge of support to Austria-Hungary in 1914, given only a week after the assassination of Franz Ferdinand, is a case in point. Germany's leaders were faced with a cruel dilemma. Having accurately judged that Italy was a weak and perfidious member of the Triple Alliance and that Romania could not be counted on either, Berlin knew that Austria-Hungary was Germany's only real ally. This fact was also appreciated in Vienna, and it was used to generate considerable diplomatic leverage. German intent in its 'blank cheque' commitment to Vienna is still debated among historians. Less open to question is the fact that Austro-Hungarian leaders interpreted German support as unconditional. As a consequence they kept Berlin poorly informed on many policy developments during subsequent weeks, including the details of the ultimatum to Serbia.

Lest this discussion has left the impression that the requirements of alliance management invariably clash with those of crisis management, it is worth making two further distinctions: pre-existing commitments should be distinguished from those that are suddenly undertaken during the course of a crisis, in a desperate effort to bolster one's credibility. Similarly, pledges of support to nations able and willing to make a serious effort to defend their own security should be distinguished from those offered to nations whose illusions are surpassed only by the absence of will, capabilities and popular support to sustain action on their own behalf.

The international system

External threat   It is widely asserted that alliance cohesion, efficacy and maintenance depend upon an external threat and that they decline as the danger is reduced. A closely related view is that as the world becomes relatively war-free it is also likely to become relatively alliance-free. These propositions are, of course, an extension of several major themes: that alliances are formed primarily *against* something and only secondarily *for* something, and that they tend to reflect shared interests in a specific situation rather than a sense of community arising from common values, culture and the like.

Although an external threat tends to create internal cohesion, this generalization must be qualified. If only part of the alliance membership feels threatened, if the threat strikes at the basis of alliance consensus, or if it offers a competitive solution (one which sets off the interests of one ally against those of another), severe divisions may arise. Large alliances such as NATO are almost certain to experience circumstances which are perceived as a dangerous threat only by one or two members. The Suez crisis of 1956 and the Yom Kippur War of 1973 are good illustrations. The Polish uprising in 1956, the offshore island crisis of 1958, and the Sino-Indian border conflict of 1962 were situations in which Moscow and Peking differed rather sharply in their estimate of the threat. But the consequences of such divisive events have been quite different for NATO and the Sino-Soviet alliance.

Similarly, unless the external danger creates an equitable division of labour among alliance members, cohesion and effectiveness are likely to suffer. Although wartime alliances obviously face considerable external threat, they may sometimes experience tensions because military operations rarely result in burdens of an equal magnitude upon the partner nations. Relations among the United States, Great Britain and the Free French forces – to say nothing of the Soviet Union – were not always harmonious during the Second World War, even during the early days of the conflict when the Japanese and Germans achieved spectacular military successes. As long as the threat seems to call for a co-operative solution cohesion will probably be enhanced, but should a solution which favours one ally at the expense of others appear, the alliance may not only lose unity but disintegrate. Finally, an alliance confronting an external threat for which there is no adequate response may also experience reduced cohesion or dissolution.

A related line of reasoning suggests that external conflict may enhance cohesion for the short run while creating longer-range problems of internal unity. Threat may create organizational rigidities in alliances and reduced tolerance for diversity, whereas declining international tensions may give rise to more flexible and less hierarchical arrangements. Some consider rigid alliances as less likely to remain cohesive.

Nuclear weapons Expanding membership in the 'nuclear club' has generated an extensive debate on the likely consequences of nuclear weapons for alliances. Most analysts stress their negative effects. One reason is that contemporary military technology has permitted nations to gain preponderant power without external assistance. Another strand of the argument is that nuclear deterrence will be less than credible if it takes the form of one alliance member's providing a 'nuclear umbrella' (extended deterrence) for the others. Put in its starkest form the question is: what nation will risk its own annihilation by using its nuclear capabilities as a means of last resort to punish aggression against its allies? Any doubts on that score may stimulate a search for an alternative form of security policy. For some nations the answer is neutralism; for others, such as France, it has been disengagement from alliances, combined with self-reliance. India provides an example of a still different strategy. It has portrayed itself as a leader of neutralism on Cold War issues, allied itself with a superpower (the Soviet Union) to gain a position of regional hegemony, and developed its own nuclear capabilities, becoming the sixth nation to test an atomic bomb.

The other side of the argument is the fear that one may unwittingly become a nuclear target as a result of an ally's quarrels. Here is another of the many paradoxes of the nuclear age. Doubts about the credibility of the ally's pledges of assistance seem to encourage disengagement from alliance commitments; but fear that the alliance commitments will actually be honoured, resulting in a nuclear war, may lead to the same conclusion – that it is safer to withdraw from external military ties.

Another aspect of the problem focuses not on the *existence* of nuclear weapons, but on their spread to junior alliance members. The view that nuclear proliferation will result in disintegration of coalitions appears grounded in a strictly utilitarian view of alliances. The opposing thesis seems to follow from the position that because other considerations may be important in the life of an alliance, sharing nuclear capabilities will add to the sense of equality and co-operation among allies. Advocates of the first position can point to the *de facto* defections of France and China from their alliances; it is not clear which came first, however, the decision to acquire an independent nuclear deterrent or strains between Paris and its NATO partners and between Moscow and Peking. The latter viewpoint receives support from Great Britain's continued adherence to NATO after becoming the world's third nuclear power.

Disarmament   Paradoxically, effective agreement on disarmament measures has also been associated with the dissolution of alliances. Given the premiss of substantial disarmament, one might be led to any of several conclusions. Those who assume that present levels of military arsenals are the major source of international tensions might conclude that a disarmed world would be free of the kinds of external threat which have so often given rise to alliance formation. Alternatively, some might argue that with disarmament it would be possible, indeed likely, for nations to establish some sort of genuine collective security arrangement. Such a system would rule out alliances because it would require nations to give up all binding security agreements save one – the commitment to assist the victims of aggression and to punish the aggressors. The premiss of disarmament can lead to still other conclusions about the fate of alliances, however. It might be equally reasonable to predict that because there will always be differences in the capabilities of political units, the weak may always perceive the necessity for collaborative action.

INTERNATIONAL EFFECTS OF ALLIANCES

The foregoing discussion has been concerned solely with the causes and conditions of alliances and their performance. We now turn our attention to their *effects* on the international system and on the nations which join or shun them.

Alliances and the balance of power

Alliances are intended to play a central role in maintaining the balance of power. They provide the primary means of deterring or defeating nations or coalitions that seek to destroy the existing balance by achieving a position of hegemony. But even advocates of balance-of-power diplomacy attach a number of important qualifications. Alliances among great powers contribute to insta- bility. Not only are great power alliances potentially strong enough to destroy the existing balance; they also reduce the number of nations which may act in the role of 'balancers', nations which, according to the theory, are supposed to remain uncommitted until there is a threat to the balance, at which time they are to join a coalition against any potentially dominant nation or group of nations. Finally, alliances must be shifting, *ad hoc* arrangements, formed for the purpose of meeting a specific problem, or to mitigate the consequences of inevitable changes in the relative capabilities of nations. During the period since the Second World War, alliances have not generally met these requirements. All of the 'major powers' have joined alliances, no non-aligned nation or group of nations could aspire to the role of balancer in conflicts involving the Cold War coalitions, and few nations have actually shifted alliances. Alliances are also supposed to perform other stabilizing functions. They reduce uncertainty, and nations that might pursue impetuous or aggressive policies may be restrained by their alliance partners.

Alliances and war

According to balance-of-power theories, then, alliances are accorded a major function in conserving the basic structure of the system, while also adding flexibility by providing a mechanism that will compensate for inevitable changes in capabilities and interests. Balance-of-power reasoning has not gone unchallenged, however. Critics point out that such systems always contain the seeds of their own destruction (a point which even the most sanguine will not completely deny), and that alliances are a major source of instability and war in all types of international system, including balance-of-power systems. These arguments have gained special favour during the twentieth century. The First World War led many, including Woodrow Wilson, to point to the alliance system of pre-war Europe as the primary cause of the war. Ironically, it was the fear that Article X of the League of Nations Covenant would permanently 'entangle' the United States in the seemingly endless quarrels of Europe – just as would joining an alliance system – that led some Senators to oppose Wilson's hopes that the League would act as a collective security system, rendering alliances unnecessary. After a hiatus of some twenty-five years (roughly 1940–65), during which the stabilizing effects of alliances were often stressed, there has been a rehabilitation of the thesis that alliances are a major source of international tensions and violence.

Critics of alliances follow several lines of reasoning. One is that alliances merely breed counter-alliances, thereby leaving no nation more secure, while at the same time contributing to polarization and a rise in international tensions. For this reason Quincy Wright (1965: 774) offers the suggestion that international stability is better served by efforts to break up dangerous coalitions, rather than merely offsetting them with counter-alliances. A further argument against alliances is that they are incompatible with collective security because collective security requires every nation automatically to assist the victim of aggression; alliance commitments can thus place a nation in a position of having a conflict of interest. But it does not necessarily follow that in the absence of alliances nations will develop an effective collective security system. Indeed, a more persuasive case can be developed for the proposition that alliances may arise from disappointed hopes for collective security. Elimination of alliances may be a necessary condition for collective security, but it is not sufficient.

A somewhat different line of reasoning concludes that once alliances are formed they come to be valued as ends rather than as instruments, and the requirements for strengthening and maintaining them may be incompatible with simultaneous efforts at *détente*. Indeed, alliances may seek, or even create, outside enemies where none exist in order to preserve internal cohesion.

Critics of alliances also suggest that they act as conduits to spread conflict to regions previously free of it. They can point to historical instances in which alliances have had this result, as can those who stress that alliances serve a deterrent function. But Liska (1962) has come to the conclusion that alliances neither cause nor prevent conflict, nor do they expand or limit it. Another set of studies of all international alliances during the period between the end of the Napoleonic Wars and the outbreak of the Second World War incorporates two premises. First, the greater the number of independent units, the more peaceful the international system, because nations can concentrate less of their attention on any other country (Deutsch and Singer 1964). Second, the maximum freedom of interaction between nations enhances international stability because cross-pressures on each country are increased. Hence international cleavages tend to be cross-cutting rather than reinforcing, with the result that bargaining rather than war will be used to resolve differences. However, note that these premises directly contradict Waltz's propositions (Waltz 1979) that fewer major actors and rigid alliances, by minimizing uncertainty, reduce the dangers of war miscalculation. The Deutsch–Singer assumptions have an evident relationship to several prominent alliance theories. They are quite consistent with theories of integration which postulate that co-operative activity on one issue tends to nurture co-operation in others. They are also related to classical balance-of-power theories, the central argument of both being that entangling commitments tend to reduce the freedom of action necessary to maintain system stability.

Results based on a system-level analysis of 118 alliances indicate that alliance formation and international conflict are positively correlated for the twentieth century, but the relationship for the nineteenth century is negative (Singer and Small 1968; Bueno de Mesquita and Singer 1973). These studies have been subjected to an an impressive critique on both logical and methodological grounds (Moul 1973). The Singer–Small data set has also been used extensively by others to study the alliance–war relationship. In an analysis of 265 conflicts of the 1815–1965 period, Siverson and Tennefoss (1984) found that equality of power, supplemented by alliance with a major power for weak nations, tended to restrain the likelihood of escalation. Kegley and Raymond (1982) concluded that peace is best preserved when the structure of alliances is moderately flexible and when alliance commitments are considered binding.

In some cases the data have yielded somewhat contradictory conclusions. For example, whereas Zinnes (1967) supports the finding that there is a positive correlation between the level of alliance commitment in the system and the outbreak of war, Ostrom and Hoole (1978) came to a different conclusion. Moreover, we may not yet be in a position to rule out the possibility of a spurious relationship between alliances and war. That is, could both alliance commitments and international conflict be the product of some common underlying factor? Finally, some of these studies were undertaken at a systems rather than a national level, and thus their results do not lend themselves to valid inferences about state behaviour. Even if the number of alliances in the international system is positively correlated to the level of international violence, this does not tell us whether the nations in alliance were also more likely to engage in war.

Alliances and integration

Another strand of theory, not necessarily incompatible with either of the above, sees alliance as a possible step in the process of more enduring forms of integration. This view begins with the premiss that effective co-operation among units in one sphere of endeavour gives rise to collaboration in others and, in the long run, to institutionalization of the arrangements. Presently available evidence appears to support those who doubt the integration potential of alliances. A study of ten political communities in the North Atlantic area revealed that alliances were neither necessary nor sufficient for integration (Deutsch *et al.* 1957). A detailed study of NATO supports these findings. Not even in areas thought to be especially promising – armaments, infrastructure and science – was there evidence of integration (Beer 1969). Others have similarly concluded that co-operation in security-related matters has a lower potential for 'spillover' than collaboration in issue areas such as economic relations (Etzioni 1962).

Finally, alliances may be related to changes in the structure of the international system. For example, the more cohesive the alliances on matters of substance and strategy, the more polarized the international system. But propositions of this form are of fairly limited interest as they tend to be true by definition; that is, a polarized system is usually defined as one in which alliances are cohesive and rigid. Thus we are impelled to ask other questions; for instance, under what circumstances are alliances in balance-of-power or loose bipolar systems likely to become rigid, thereby transforming the nature of the system?

NATIONAL EFFECTS OF ALLIANCES

Alliances have traditionally been regarded as an instrument of policy by means of which a nation may augment its own capabilities. Among the benefits that should accrue from alliance membership are enhanced security from external threat, reduced defence expenditures, and possible side benefits such as economic aid and prestige. For a regime with shaky popular support, a strong ally may be a necessary condition for survival. But benefits rarely come without attending costs. Alliances may be a net drain on national resources; they may distort calculations of national interest if allies become wedded to 'inherent good faith' models of each other; and they may lead to a loss of decision-making independence. And, if alliances merely trigger off counter-alliances, they may leave everyone poorer and less secure.

A rather different argument is that alliances tend to have significant consequences for domestic politics. It scarcely needs to be stated that the American alliance with South Vietnam resulted in deep domestic divisions within both countries. The establishment of NATO during the later 1940s triggered an often bitter debate between proponents of an isolationist 'Fortress America' concept of defence and the internationalists and, as the alliance was celebrating its fortieth anniversary, questions about how NATO should respond to Soviet arms-reduction proposals had a significant impact on the domestic policies of several members.

It is not clear whether the domestic consequences of alliance participation will differ according to the nature of the political system. One view is that in an era of mass politics when there are widespread demands that one's allies be purer than the driven snow, the internal consequences of alliances will continue to increase. Some evidence suggests that democratic nations are likely to be more sensitive to feedback from alliance politics. There are also advocates of the opposite position, however, who suggest that the domestic effects of alliances are likely to be especially intense in hierarchical coalitions composed of authoritarian regimes.

PROSPECTS

The third quarter of the twentieth century has been called 'the age of alliances'. It was ushered in by the formation of NATO in 1949 and by the Sino-Soviet Security Treaty in 1950. Within a half decade the Warsaw Pact, SEATO, CENTO and a multitude of other alliances were formed. As we enter the last decade of the century, we find that some of the Cold War alliances are dormant if not dead (SEATO, CENTO, the Sino-Soviet Pact); others have been beset with internal difficulties, owing in part to differences about the extent of external threat and proper allocation of burdens (NATO, ANZUS); and still another was kept intact until its formal dissolution in 1991 by arrangements that were a blend of empire and alliance (Warsaw Pact). But even if alliances play a declining role during the remaining years of this century, it would be premature to state that they will disappear. As long as the international system is characterized by independent political units, alliances are likely to persist as a major instrument of statecraft.

REFERENCES

Allison, G. T. (1971) *Essence of Decision: Explaining the Cuban Missile Crisis*, Boston: Little, Brown & Co.

Beer, F. A. (1969) *Integration and Disintegration in NATO: Processes of Alliance Cohesion and Prospects for Atlantic Community*, Columbus: Ohio State University Press.

Bueno de Mesquita, B. and Singer, J. D. (1973) 'Alliances, capabilities, and war: a review and synthesis', in C. P. Cotter (ed.) *Political Science Annual: An International Review*, Vol. 4, Indianapolis: Bobbs-Merrill.

Burgess, P. M. (1967) *Elite Images and Foreign Policy Outcomes*, Columbus: Ohio State University Press.

Craig, G. (1965) 'The World War I alliance of the central powers in retrospect: the military cohesion of the alliance', *Journal of Modern History* 37: 336–44.

Dawson, R. and Rosecrance, R.N. (1966) 'Theory and reality in the Anglo-American alliance', *World Politics* 19: 21–51.

Deutsch, K. W. and Singer, J. D. (1964) 'Multipolar power systems and international stability', *World Politics* 16: 390–406.

Deutsch, K. W. *et al.* (1957) *Political Community and the North Atlantic Area: International Organization in the Light of Historical Experience*, Princeton: Princeton University Press.

Etzioni, A. (1962) 'The dialectics of supranational unification', *American Political Science Review* 56: 927–35.

Fedder, E. H. (1968) 'The concept of alliance', *International Studies Quarterly* 12: 65–86.

Gamson, W. A. (1961) 'A theory of coalition formation', *American Sociological Review* 26: 565–73.

Gilpin, R. (1981) *War and Change in International Politics*, New York: Cambridge University Press.

Holsti, O. R., Hopmann, P. T. and Sullivan, J. D. (1973) *Unity and Disintegration in International Alliances*, New York: John Wiley.

Horvath, W. J. and Foster, C. C. (1963) 'Stochastic models of war alliances', *Journal of Conflict Resolution* 7: 110–16.

Kegley, C. W. and Raymond, G. A. (1982) 'Alliance norms and war: a new piece in an old puzzle', *International Studies Quarterly* 26: 572–95.

Lall, A. (1966) *Modern International Negotiation*, New York: Columbia University Press.

Liska, G. (1962) *Nations in Alliance: The Limits of Interdependence*, Baltimore: Johns Hopkins University Press.

Maxwell, S. (1968) *Rationality in Deterrence*, Adelphi Paper no. 50, London: Institute for Strategic Studies.

Morgenthau, H. J. (1959) 'Alliances in theory and practice', in A. Wolfers (ed.) *Alliance Policy in the Cold War*, Baltimore: Johns Hopkins University Press.

Moul, W. (1973) 'The level of analysis problem restated', *Canadian Journal of Political Science* 6: 494–513.

Neustadt, R. E. (1970) *Alliance Politics*, New York: Columbia University Press.

Olson, M., Jr. (1965) *The Logic of Collective Action: Public Goods and the Theory of Groups*, Cambridge, Mass.: Harvard University Press.

Olson, M., Jr. and Zeckhauser, R. (1966) 'An economy theory of alliances', *Review of Economics and Statistics* 48: 266–79.

Ostrom, C. W. and Hoole, F. W. (1978) 'Alliances and wars revisited: a research note', *International Studies Quarterly* 22: 215–36.

Padelford, N. J. and Lincoln, G. A. (1967) *The Dynamics of International Politics*, 2nd edn, New York: Macmillan.

Riker, W. H. (1962) *The Theory of Political Coalitions*, New Haven, Conn.: Yale University Press.

Rothstein, R. L. (1966) 'Alignment, nonalignment, and small powers: 1945–1965', *International Organization* 20: 397–418.

——(1968) *Alliances and Small Powers*, New York: Columbia University Press.

Russett, B. N. (1971) 'An empirical typology of international military alliances', *Midwest Journal of Political Science* 15: 262–289.

Singer, J. D. and Small, M. (1968) 'Alliance aggregation and the onset of war', in J. D. Singer (ed.) *Quantitative International Politics: Insights and Evidence*, New York: Free Press.

Siverson, R. M. and Tennefoss, M. R. (1984) 'Power, alliance and the escalation of international conflict, 1815–1965', *American Political Science Review* 78: 1057–69.

Snyder, G. H. (1984) 'The security dilemma in alliance politics', *World Politics* 36: 461–95.

Spykman, N. (1942) *America's Strategy in World Politics*, New York: Harcourt, Brace.

Torrance, E. P. (1965) 'Some consequences of power differences on decision making in permanent and temporary three-man groups', in A. P. Hare, E. F. Borgatta and R. F. Bales (eds) *Small Groups*, New York: Knopf.

Walt, S. M. (1987) *The Origin of Alliances*, Ithaca, NY: Cornell University Press.

Waltz, K. N. (1979) *Theory of International Politics*, Reading, Mass.: Addison-Wesley.

Williamson, S. T., Jr. (1969) *The Politics of Grand Strategy: France and Britain Prepare for War, 1904–1914*, Cambridge, Mass.: Harvard University Press.

Wright, Q. (1965) *A Study of War*, 2nd edn, Chicago: University of Chicago Press.

Zinnes, D. A. (1967) 'An analytical study of the balance of power theories', *Journal of Peace Research* 3: 270–88.

FURTHER READING

Beer, F. A. (1970) *Alliances: Latent War Communities in the Contemporary World*, New York: Holt, Rinehart & Winston.

Bueno de Mesquita, B. and Singer, J. D. (1973) 'Alliances, capabilities, and war: a review and synthesis', in C. P. Cotter (ed.) *Political Science Annual: An International Review*, vol. 4, Indianapolis: Bobbs-Merrill.

Degenhardt, H. W. (1986) *Treaties and Alliances of the World*, 4th edn, Detroit: Gale Research.

Deutsch, K. W. *et al.* (1957) *Political Community and the North Atlantic Area: International Organization in the Light of Historical Experience*, Princeton: Princeton University Press.

Friedman, J. R., Bladen, C. and Rosen, S. (1970) *Alliance in International Politics*, Boston: Allyn and Bacon.

Gulick, E. V. (1955) *Europe's Classical Balance of Power*, Ithaca, NY: Cornell University Press.

Holsti, O. R., Hopmann, P. T. and Sullivan, J. D. (1973) *Unity and Disintegration in International Alliances*, New York: John Wiley.

Liska, G. (1962) *Nations in Alliance: The Limits of Interdependence*, Baltimore: Johns Hopkins University Press.

——(1968) *Alliances and the Third World*, Baltimore: Johns Hopkins University Press.

Naidu, M. V. (1974) *Alliances and Balance of Power: In Search of Conceptual Clarity*, Delhi: Macmillan Company of India.

Neustadt, R. E. (1970) *Alliance Politics*, New York: Columbia University Press.

Olson, M., Jr. (1965) *The Logic of Collective Action: Public Goods and the Theory of Groups*, Cambridge, Mass.: Harvard University Press.

Olson, M., Jr. and Zeckhauser, R. (1966) 'An economic theory of alliances', *Review of Economics and Statistics* 48: 266–79.

Osgood, R. E. (1968) *Alliances and American Foreign Policy*, Baltimore: Johns Hopkins University Press.

Riker, W. H. (1962) *The Theory of Political Coalitions*, New Haven, Conn.: Yale University Press.

Rothstein, R. L. (1968) *Alliances and Small Powers*, New York: Columbia University Press.

Singer, J. D. and Small, M. (1966) 'Formal alliances, 1815–1939', *Journal of Peace Research* 3: 1–31.

Snyder, G.H. (1984) 'The security dilemma in alliance politics', *World Politics* 36: 461–95.

Walt, S. M. (1987) *The Origin of Alliances*, Ithaca, NY: Cornell University Press.

Williamson, S. R., Jr. (1969) *The Politics of Grand Strategy: France and Britain Prepare for War, 1904–1914*, Cambridge, Mass.: Harvard University Press.

Wolfers, A. (ed.) (1959) *Alliance Policy in the Cold War*, Baltimore: Johns Hopkins University Press.

64

DIPLOMACY

TOM FARER

'Unlike tangible realities, such as a dog,' William Zartman writes, 'concepts have no clear beginnings and ends, no unambiguous middles' (Zartman 1989: 237). Diplomacy, being a concept, cannot shake this boundary problem.

Harold Nicholson, in his celebrated little discourse on the subject, follows the *Oxford English Dictionary* in defining diplomacy as 'the management of international relations by negotiation; the method by which these relations are adjusted and managed by ambassadors and envoys; the business or art of the diplomatist' (Nicholson 1950: 15). Leading contemporary writers take a slightly wider view of the subject. Adam Watson, like Nicholson a practitioner and scholar, sees the substance of diplomacy as a 'dialogue between independent states' including 'the machinery by which their governments conduct it, and the networks of promises, contracts, institutions and codes of conduct which develop out of it' (Watson 1983: 14). James Der Derian, a theoretician, refers both to 'a mediation between estranged individuals, groups or entities' and to 'a system of communication, negotiation and information' (Der Derian 1987: 6–7).

FORCE AND THE TELEOLOGY OF DIPLOMACY

The principal boundary virtually all writers have tried to demarcate in their varying ways is between diplomacy and brute force. They have chosen that line in part out of respect for common usage, but primarily out of a conviction that diplomacy, while less than the totality of foreign policy, is more than its passive instrument; that it has a 'reconciliatory nature' (Der Derian 1987: 7), 'a built-in bias toward cooperation and the search for the maximum advantage to all the participants' (Watson 1983: 200), and that its 'central task is the management of change, and the maintenance by continual persuasion of order in the midst of change' (Watson 1983: 223). But, as all of them concede, their effort is hounded by the indissoluble relationship of persuasion and force, a relationship suggestively summarized in Frederick the Great's aphorism that diplomacy without power is like an orchestra without a score.

Frederick, of course, was a practising Realist in that he proceeded from the assumption that shifts in the distribution of national power create a powerful momentum towards the redistribution of other values (such as wealth and prestige); in other words, power drives change. From that perspective, diplomacy's role is to smooth the way. Diplomatists manage change first by persuasively identifying what the relative losers in the power game must yield and what the relative winners may reasonably claim and by identifying the range of adjustments likely to leave both parties better off than they could reasonably hope to be in the event of reliance on the arbitrament of war.

What makes the role immensely problematical is the unavailability of a political seismograph able to record shifts in the balance of power, much less their extent. National power, being the aggregation of volatile factors many of which – such as internal cohesion, generational memory, administrative competence, strategic astuteness and political will – are insusceptible to precise measurement, will rarely induce a common perception among governments and other key actors. The inherent softness of the data and the absence even of an agreed matrix for processing it leave political leaders ample room to adopt an assessment of relative power most consistent with their interests and passions (Friedberg 1988: 3–303).

Uncertainty about the costs of proposed adjustments will often be no less than uncertainty about the outcome (that is, the relative costs) of a trial by arms. Uncertainty can open the door to negotiation. It can equally well encourage those who are asked to yield some quantum of existing advantage (or, as they may see it, acquired 'rights') to stand fast. Other means of persuasion having failed, the party seeking change may then have recourse to what the German military theorist Clausewitz called 'an act of violence intended to compel our opponent to fulfill our will' (Watson 1983: 58). But long before that point, the very possibility of one side or the other injecting force into the diplomatic argument shadows and often lubricates the discussion. Hence it is misleading to represent war as 'standing in polar opposition to diplomacy' (ibid.: 59) as if the latter were properly defined as bargaining free from the pressures of compulsion. Rather, both 'are inseparably joined under the common heading of means by which states, in pursuit of their interests, bring their power to bear on one another' (ibid.)

The brooding presence of force at many negotiating tables makes it paradoxical but not ironic to speak of 'coercive diplomacy'. Conventionally defined, in Craig and George's words, as the 'strategy of [employing] threats or limited force to persuade an opponent to call off or undo an encroachment' (Craig and George 1983: 189), it is, they suggest, distinguished from 'pure coercion' precisely by the fact that its author seeks to persuade (through a demonstration of resolution), rather than to bludgeon, an opponent into submission (ibid.). Nor is it oxymoronic to speak of 'wartime diplomacy'. For if force not infrequently accompanies the diplomat, then the diplomat is an invariable companion of the rational warrior: first to probe for mutually acceptable conditions of conflict termination and then, although perhaps not until one side has been decisively beaten, to negotiate a new relationship between the belligerents to resolve the precipitating conflict of interest, no doubt in favour of the victor but in the form most likely to be endured by the vanquished.

Polar opposition is central to our apprehension of things whether they be material or conceptual. If not coercion *per se* even in the extreme form of war, then what is diplomacy's antipode? In the work of main-line theorists such as Nicholson and Watson, one can see the antipode assuming both micro and macro forms. In its former guise it is a strategy of naked aggression: the imposition of one state's desires on those of another without claim of right grounded in widely accepted norms. In its macro guise it is any political strategy stemming from opposition to a system of states enjoying a monopoly of authority (that is sovereignty) within their respective territories and conceding to each other reciprocal rights and obligations. Where that opposition informs policy, the reality is anti-diplomacy (Der Derian 1987: 134–67).

Mere ruses, such as assurances of peaceful intentions on the eve of an invasion, are generally characterized and studied not as instances of anti-diplomacy but rather as facets of military strategy indistinguishable in principle from any other trick designed to weaken the belligerent capabilities of an enemy. Anti-diplomacy is not logically compelled to express itself through military aggression, although it often does. Its defining characteristic being rejection of the game of nations, it is nicely exemplified by any evangelical elite subordinating the search for common ground between national communities to the promotion of a human solidarity transcending communities, an elite whose purpose is not to moderate but to exorcise estrangement. (In practice, however, anti-diplomacy normally mutates into 'neo-diplomacy' (Der Derian 1987: 168–98), as what Edmund Burke called the 'Empire of Circumstance' (Watson 1983: 15) forces revolutionary regimes to seek temporary *modus vivendi* with conservative states.)

ORIGIN AND EVOLUTION

If diplomacy is conceived as a process of institutionalized communication between politically organized communities that accept each other, however grudgingly, as more or less permanent bargaining partners, then it appears in a full-blown form no earlier than the fifteenth century, first among the city states of Italy, then spreading through the rest of Europe, particularly after the Thirty Years War (1618–48) extinguished the universalistic pretensions of the Habsburg Emperors. But its precursors extend far back before the birth of Christ.

In the fourteenth century BC, the Hittite King and the Egyptian Pharaoh maintained an episodic correspondence growing out of contact between merchants from the two kingdoms and disputes over border lands. Stylized and cautious, this correspondence has a premonitory ring of elaborate *politesse*, as for example where the King, having received a payment of gold bricks that proved less than solid, chose to express his concern by warning the Pharaoh that he must have a dishonest steward in his retinue (Watson 1983: 84–5). But the closest approximation of the modern phenomenon appears in Greece and Asia Minor during the fifth and fourth centuries BC. Propelled by a dense network of political, military, and commercial relationships, the Greek city states conducted a sustained dialogue with each other and with the Persian Empire through special envoys.

Diplomatic exchanges were particularly intense within the shifting alliances the city states organized to challenge the periodic bids for dominance by one or another of them and to resist Persian expansion. Even at the apogee of their military power relative to the Greeks, the Persians for their part were inclined to the subtleties of coercive diplomacy rather than outright war. By the fourth century BC, with their power conspicuously on the wane and the leading Greek states more inclinded to reduce the incidence of conflict among themselves and with the Persians, the stage was set for the staging of multinational congresses at which men empowered to act on behalf of the city states and the Persian Emperor attempted to settle outstanding issues and to limit the emergence of new ones by laying down mutually acceptable norms of conduct (Watson 1983: 86–7).

A much more recent precursor (and/or, as Der Derian suggests, prototype for the 'feudal' system which may now be evolving on a global scale behind the forms of sovereignty (Der Derian 1987: 70, 76–80)) is the institution of the *missi*, special envoys employed by the Carolingian Empire in the early Middle Ages to assert imperial authority and to sort out or mediate the problematical relationships stemming from the 'confusing complexity of overlapping ties between the emperor and the pope, between feudal princes and the incipient national monarchs, and between the rising townsmen and the rural landowners in general' (Der Derian 1987: 72–3). Initially drawing their authority entirely from their position as envoys of the emperor, enjoying personal inviolability and a right to demand hospitality from vassals of all ranks, they used their formal duties as the transmitters of reciprocal oaths of fealty to promote internal cohesion and homogeneity against the external threat of the Saracens. But once they acquired heritable benefices and hence a measure of personal power, they shifted from being linchpins of the system to additional forces of fragmentation.

Despite the status of the *missi* as the Holy Roman Emperor's personal representatives engaged in reconciliatory activities, Der Derian is persuasive when he argues that the institution is best seen not as a seed of or blueprint for modern diplomacy, but as a distinct paradigm for bridging estrangement, appropriate to a system marked on the one hand by a hierarchical arrangement of power and on the other by a 'diffused' sovereignty 'constantly beset by both external and internal challenges' (Der Derian 1987: 76). The post-modern moment – with its diverse transnational institutions (for instance, the European Community, the International Monetary Fund, commercially and ideologically driven criminal organizations, the Moonies, Amnesty International) acting across, around and through, arguably subverting, the integrity of theoretically supreme states – might witness, Der Derian suggests, the invention of analogues to what he calls the 'proto-diplomatic practices' of the Middle Ages: not only the *missi*, but also the arbitration of disputes among vassals and the dynastic mergers, both of which the *missi* apparently facilitated, which helped to constrain violence and maintain a greater semblance of order than the Emperor could have achieved by military force alone (ibid.: 75–80).

Most of the distinctive institutions of modern diplomacy – resident missions, professional diplomats (and that network of relationships among them in each capital which constituted its *corps diplomatique* defending their professional status and privileges and facilitating mutual appreciation of each embassy's perspectives and interests), and diplomatic immunity – were well established in Europe before the end of the seventeenth century. The eighteenth century's principal addition to the pattern of European diplomacy was the foreign ministry – a bureaucracy, led by a confidante of the Head of Government, collecting and collating information and orchestrating implementation of the government's foreign policies.

Each institution had antecedents of varying antiquity. Centuries before the Italian city states began practising the diplomatic arts, the Byzantine emperors employed a special department of government for dealing with external affairs and training professional negotiators to serve as their ambassadors in foreign courts (Nicholson 1954: 25). As early as the ninth century, the Venetians organized state archives to preserve in systematic form the instructions given to, and the official despatches received from, ambassadors who were, however, not professionals but citizens sometimes dragooned into accepting for a time what was then an expensive and not infrequently dangerous duty. Diplomacy as a recognized profession comes much later. Traders frequently doubled as envoys. But more eccentric choices were not remarkable. According to Nicholson, 'Louis XI sent his barber on a mission to Maria of Burgundy, Florence sent a chemist ... to Naples, and Dr de Puebla, who for twenty year represented Spain in London, was so filthy and unkempt that Henry VII expressed the hope that his successor might be a man more fitted for human society' (Nicholson 1954: 34).

Also relatively late in developing was unqualified and general acceptance of the resident envoy as a good thing. As late as the seventeenth century, governments actively discouraged contact between envoys and local citizens on the assumption that they were potential, if not functioning, spies. The Swiss Minister accredited to Cromwell reported that any Member of Parliament who spoke to a foreign ambassador was liable to be deprived of his seat (Nicholson 1954: 35).

The persistence of suspicion about the functions of the diplomat corresponded logically to the persistence in European politics of strong predatory instincts. For all the respected competence of French diplomacy under Louis XIV – personified by the envoy François de Callieres to whom is attributed the first manual for the profession (Watson 1983: 102) – its function was to further Louis's inexpiable hunger to dominate Europe, which his memoirs almost lyrically record:

> The love of glory assuredly takes precedence over all other [passions] in my soul. . . . La Gloire . . . is not a mistress that one can ever neglect; nor can one be ever worthy of her slightest favors if one does not constantly long for fresh ones.
>
> (Craig and George 1983: 6)

His bid for hegemony, moreover, followed almost immediately on the final defeat of the Habsburgs. Their successive defeats had demonstrated a powerful instinct among European governments for balance-of-power politics, an instinct recorded in the settlement of Utrecht's explicit subordination even of the right of hereditary succession to the preservation of 'a just balance'. But the commitment of the European sovereigns to survival clearly did not imply a parallel commitment to peace. If they either could or would not imagine destroying each other, they could nevertheless envisage tasty enhancements of power, prestige and wealth. The balance provided a safety net. One could say that from the point of view of the larger states, it made Europe safe for limited (but, for the poor wretches who fought them, thoroughly sanguinary) wars.

No one saw this more clearly than Frederick the Great: flautist, correspondent of the *philosophes*, student of poetry, and ruler determined to *corriger la figure de la Prusse* (correct the shape of Prussia) so that its hereditary leaders 'could cut a good figure among the great of this world and play a significant role' (Craig and George 1983: 19). A solemn commitment to respect the Austrian succession did not deter him when in 1740 he saw a chance to seize Silesia. Seize it he did, initiating eight years of war that, for all the Prussian blood it shed, made Prussia a player of the first rank. On the eve of the French Revolution, Europe's rulers still seemed to think that the natural condition of interstate relations was appropriation often by force or its threat of every opportunity for immediate gratification that did not clearly jeopardize the overall balance. Diplomacy, therefore, was the companion of war in the unilateral search for advantage.

But though unilateral, it was of course not unlimited. The shared consciousness of limitation; the strongly institutionalized diplomacy required for the adjustments a 'just balance' entailed and for the economic pursuit of national interest; the developing body of reciprocally accepted norms adumbrating the rights and privileges of sovereignty; the common manners and convictions of the elite; and the perception among rulers of joint descent and estrangement from a once unified Christendom: these things together led scholars and diplomats and presumably all elements of the governing classes to imagine themselves as members of what Burke called 'a federative society, or in other words a diplomatic republic', the *res publica christiana*, the commonwealth of Christendom (Watson 1983: 15).

This sensation of living not in a brutish state of nature but in a civilized association of competitive but not blindly ferocious sovereign polities achieves a clear voice only when 'the society confronts the first major threat to its fledgling existence' (Der Derian 1987: 107). From its perilous encounter with Napoleon and in the midst of its despair, the system achieves full consciousness. Looking backward in 1809 and writing 'upon its ruins', the Hanoverian historian A. H. L. Heeren describes the system he thinks utterly destroyed as 'the union of several contiguous states, resembling each other in their manner, religion and degree of social improvement, and cemented together by a reciprocity of interests' (Heeren 1873: vii).

Informed by its brush with disaster, the European powers did more than re-establish the boundaries and governments swept away by Napoleon and the principle of the 'just balance', which, they rightly saw, required acceptance of France minus Napoleon as one of its pillars. In addition they recognized the need for, and soon established, collective machinery, the Concert of Europe, primarily to maintain but also to amend the settlement where necessary. '[I]n retrospect,' Watson writes, '[t]he Vienna settlement appears ... as the high point of practical achievement of the European diplomatic system' (Watson 1983: 109). The maturing of consciousness about the nature of their collective relationship and the conditions for its survival placed concern for the system (*raison de système*) alongside national interest (raison d'état) as the wellsprings of policy. The resulting self-restraint, along with the opportunities for projecting rivalries into the vulnerable societies of Africa and the Near and Far East, facilitated the diplomatic adjustments that for a century helped keep Europe free of general war.

THE FAILURE OF EUROPEAN DIPLOMACY

If post-Napoleonic Europe was a renewal of the 'diplomatic republic' temporarily incapacitated by the little Corsican's success in harnessing revolutionary nationalism, and if (as the conventional wisdom would have it) diplomacy reached its self-conscious apogee in the early decades of the nineteenth century, how did Europe slide into the abyss of the First World War? Did diplomacy in the form of the assumptions and practices of the European states in their mutual relations fall because of faults intrinsic to it or was it perniciously transformed by the insinuation of new elements? No one seems seriously to doubt that both bear the responsibility for Europe's fall.

Nicholson, a eulogist of European diplomacy, concedes that its practice always expressed two conflicting elements or 'theories'. One, which he calls 'the warrior or heroic' theory and sees as a feudal survival, was concerned with 'national prestige, status, precedence, and glamour.' The other, the 'mercantile or shopkeeper theory [which] arose from the contacts of commerce . . . tended towards profit-politics, and was mainly preoccupied with appeasement, conciliation, compromise, and credit' (Nicholson 1950: 51). Not only are the aims of the warrior theory predatory, he argues, but as a consequence of its search for absolute victories it views and uses diplomacy simply as a tactic to that end. There is no place for the authentic 'give and take of civilian intercourse'. There are, rather, all the elements of military campaigns: surprise, deception, stealthy infiltration, intimidation, and ruthless exploitation of every perceived weakness (ibid.: 52–3).

The civilian theory, on the other hand, 'is based on the assumption that a compromise between rivalries is generally more profitable than the complete destruction of the rival, that negotiation is not a mere phase in a death-struggle, but an attempt by mutual concession to reach some durable understanding . . . and that questions of prestige should not be allowed to interfere unduly with a sound business deal' (Nicholson 1950: 54).

To the extent that the warrior spirit (whatever its etiology) infused powerful elements of European society, as Nicholson claims, then despite the commonality of 'manner, religion, and degree of social improvement' (Heeren 1873: vii) among the contiguous nations of Europe, their 'system' perpetually risked extinction in the event of the warriors acquiring ascendency in a state with the means to subordinate its neighbours. And the nineteenth century's 'peace' (that is, nothing but small, short wars) looks less like a triumph of diplomacy than a confused and uneasy pause before the vagaries of History recreated a fatal disproportion of power.

At times Nicholson writes of the warrior theory as if it were a self-animated force in human affairs, a norm in itself, rather than a point of view, a form of discourse, subject to appropriation by interested parties with ulterior motives.

As the nineteenth century lurched towards disaster, such parties and motives accumulated. The existence of states created opportunities for ruling elites to displace class tensions. Against socialism's image of a transnational community of workers struggling for justice within national societies, they could invoke the ideal of a national community struggling for glory, dignity and interest within international society. The spread of literacy and the print mass media that literacy induced provided an audience and a vehicle for a dramaturgy of foreign affairs.

Merchants, bankers and industrialists were as threatened as kings by the growing mobilization of the lower classes. Many had acquired powerful financial interests in the preparation for war, if not in war itself. The continuing rationalization of public administration; the penetration of the nerves of government into every corner of society; the extraordinary acceleration of movement by land; the refinement of the technology of mass production and the means for systematically improving its products – all these developments occurring within an international political system where each state was the only assured guarantor of its rights, its interests, its very survival, seeded a tremendous potential market for military products.

In addition, the still steeply unequal distribution of income in domestic society and its concentration in those persons with a lower marginal propensity for present consumption, together with the political barriers to the movement of capital and goods, made political control of people and territory outside Europe seem desirable on commercial grounds alone. Thus, without any sudden conversion to the feudal views of the warrior, the *haute bourgeoisie* in England and France could oppose the accretions of presence and influence that Germany sought in light of its heightened power, while their German counterparts had corresponding incentives to support demands for adjustment, and important elements among the bourgeoisie in all countries had good reason to applaud the preparations for war, because they did not appreciate how those preparations would help lock all parties to the cliff-bound European express. From its fall the European elite would emerge broken and bitter, their civility in ruins, their graveyards choked, ready if only they knew for a second ride over the cliff.

CONTEMPORARY DIPLOMACY

Despite the stunning changes in the character of international relations that have occurred since diplomacy's golden age – let us say from the Treaty of Utrecht in 1713 until the French Revolution, and from the Congress of Vienna until the dismissal of Bismark in 1890 – its larger purpose remains unchanged, namely to mediate among estranged political communities whose continuance is a function of their estrangement. Estrangement is a necessary condition of the state system because without the 'other', that which is not one of us and hence alien, there are no boundaries. Without effective boundaries, there are no states. On the day when the well-being of Costa Ricans seems as important to the average American as the well-being of other Americans, the subjective basis for the nation-state system will have vanished. A broadening of the individual's sense of solidarity is only one theoretical approach to the end of estrangement. Coercion is another. At this point, however, one can see neither the preconditions nor possible candidates for the exercise of global hegemony.

And so diplomacy endures, but under conditions dramatically changed from those which marked its Golden Age. The tapestry of change in the conditions of diplomacy has been unfolding for a century. Writing on the eve of the Second World War, Harold Nicholson noted without enthusiasm the increasing democratization of foreign policy (Nicholson 1950: 80–103). Effective diplomacy required, in his judgement, general acceptance of the proposition that elected officials set the broad outlines of policy, leaving its implementation to professional diplomats. If he could have anticipated the powerful role played particularly in the United States by well-organized private groups and by Congressional organs in the management of international relations, he doubtless would have viewed the future with profound pessimism.

Another trend, one whose encroaching shadow he could just barely apprehend, was a vast enlargement in the agenda of diplomacy. Increasing economic interdependence, Nicholson conceded, required expansion of diplomacy's concerns to include questions of trade (ibid.: 162–6). But he does not appear to have doubted the enduring centrality of 'high diplomacy', that is, questions of national security.

As a Marxist was better equipped than a high Tory like Nicholson to foresee, market capitalism has produced a tightly integrated global economy in which forces set in motion, sometimes unintentionally, by public and private actors ripple across national frontiers, galvanizing employment and production in one place, depressing it in another. While that would be reason enough for the electorate and its most immediate representatives to demand a voice both in setting and implementing the foreign policy agenda, it is reinforced by the technological revolution in locomotion and communication that has opened the globe to mass cognitive appropriation. The symbolic power of the nation-state inhibits but cannot deny to its citizens feelings of affection, sympathy or revulsion for clusters of persons beyond its borders. Like material conditions, those feelings fuel the electorate's involvement in the foreign-policy decision process. Little as the traditionalists may like it (Kennan 1985: 1–14), complicating as it may be for successfully mediating conflicts of economic and security interests, the way a government treats its own citizens appears now (along with other moral issues) as a fixture on the diplomatic agenda.

However persuasive the *a priori* case for an oligarchy of decision makers in the field of foreign policy, the empirical data gives grounds for doubt. After all, the still high concentration of decision-power before the First World War did not avert that disaster. Popular emotions may have been consequential in producing its successor, both by encouraging Britain and France to impose harsh terms on Germany in the Versailles Peace Treaty and by discouraging a continuous US political-military presence on the European scene. But it is by no means clear that, if freed from electoral pressures, the leading political figures of the post-war era would have followed a very different course. For instance, French Prime Minister Clemenceau knew that only through the enforcement of harsh restraints could the power of Germany be held at a level the French could match. Is it therefore likely that, freed from all electoral pressure, he would have urged a reconciliatory peace?

If the global trend towards representative government continues largely unchecked, those who see war as a failure of diplomacy may reasonably regard the democratization of foreign policy as a positive development. For it would appear – albeit on the basis of a necessarily limited number of cases – that liberal democracies are disinclined to resolve their differences through the medium of force (Doyle 1986: 1151–69). While they are capable of contemplating each other as potential foes (Friedberg 1988: 185), they rarely come to blows. Indeed, among democracies at comparable levels of economic development, we have no unambiguous example of discord deteriorating into war. The occasionally cited conflict of 1812–14 between the United States and Great Britain can be distinguished on the grounds that in the latter country the great majority of adults were still disenfranchised. The Afrikaner Republics with whom Britain fought at the turn of the century of course denied the vote to their black population. Different levels of national economic development and the secret and proxy character of the United States' effort distinguish the successful subversive war waged by the United States in 1954 against the elected government of Guatemala.

Assuming the truth of theories about the war-averse character of democratic states in their relations *inter se*, then the spread of democracy should reinforce the normative and technological restraints on general war between major powers that sprang up after the Second World War. While the former – embodied in the United Nations Charter, the Nuremberg Principles and other solemn legal texts – are arguably epiphenomenal, the latter in the form of nuclear weapons have plainly insinuated caution into great-power competition. Whether, as nuclear and other weapons of mass destruction proliferate, they will have the same inhibiting effect on new club members remains to be seen.

The existence of the alternative of force has generally been seen by leading authorities on diplomacy as what 'gives diplomatic negotiation its reality and its ability to persuade' (Watson 1983: 219). Should war, for one or another reason, become an implausible option not only in the case of the superpowers, the two great legatees of the Second World War, but for all significant state actors, what then will be the fate of diplomacy?

Within the compass of this brief essay, we can only sketch a response. One answer – that the possibility of war will never cease to haunt interstate relations and hence to lubricate negotiations – is too global a generalization. Both mass and elite in developed capitalist democracies appear to have lost belief in war as a conceivable means of resolving conflict of interests among them. No belief, no lubricant. What remains, however, are other means for exercising influence such as wealth and, sometimes with the aid of wealth, the penetration of another state's decision-making processes. While these means have existed in the past, the prospects for their effective exercise has increased probably in rough proportion to the increased permeability of all active participants in the world economy.

A consequence of permeability, and the consequent normalization of alien presence in virtually all social realms, is that strategies which would in the past have looked subversive, for instance funding opinion-moulding activities in another country, can appear equivocal or even benign. Not only can they *appear* benign, they may on balance *be* benign. As long as the principal dimension of any interstate relationship is the security one, the relationship tends towards zero sum, because power is relative. But when security concerns are submerged and the relationship is primarily one of economic exchange, the distribution of gains becomes less important because both states can be better off than either would be on its own. Hence the effort of one state actor to influence the decisions of the other are much less threatening in appearance and often in fact.

The outward form of our global system is one of states co-operating to increase the production of social values and simultaneously competing for larger relative shares. However, the situation is not quite as it appears from the outside, and hence such a view falls short of reality. Often behind these familiar forms, transnational coalitions of social groups – linked by material interests, ideals or communal identity – are struggling to make public institutions agents of their ends. Wherever the security dilemma has been effectively banished by states in their mutual relations, participants in these coalitions can easily believe that they serve the national as well as their particular interests. In a world where the accelerating spillage of people across frontiers helps confuse the distinction between citizens and aliens, where the state's bureaucratic establishment and political leadership can rarely satisfy popular aspirations and evidence limited control over events, where the globalization of the media permit like-minded strangers to bond across frontiers, where complex transactional webs obscure cause and effect, in such a world people are remarkably free to invent the national interest.

Conceived as a mediator among states, Nicholson's conventional diplomatist seems doomed to a smaller role in the drama of international relations – smaller but not trivial. For unless and until the large island of semi-reconciled polities now formed by the capitalist democracies and their satellites expands to cover the globe, the question of security will still haunt the race, states will retain a certain integrity, and the classical search for the adjustment of differences against a backdrop of possible violence will go on. The age of diplomacy is not yet over.

REFERENCES

Craig, G. and George, A. (1983) *Force and Statecraft*, Oxford: Oxford University Press.

Der Derian, J. (1987) *On Diplomacy*, Oxford and New York: Basil Blackwell.

Doyle, M. (1986) 'Liberalism and world politics', *American Political Science Review* 80: 1151–69.

Friedberg, A. (1988) *The Weary Titan*, Princeton: Princeton University Press.

Heeren, A. H. L. (1873) *A Manual of the History of the Political System of Europe and its Colonies*, London: Bohn.

Kennan, G. (1985) 'Morality and foreign policy', *Foreign Affairs* 64: 1–14.

Nicholson, H. (1950) *Diplomacy*, 2nd edn, Oxford: Oxford University Press.

——(1954) *The Evolution of Diplomatic Method*, London: Constable & Co.

Watson, A. (1983) *Diplomacy*, Philadelphia: Institute for the Study of Human Issues.

Zartman, W. (1989) 'Prenegotiation: phases and functions', *International Journal* 44: 237–53.

FURTHER READING

Bull, H. (1977) *The Anarchical Society*, London: Macmillan.

Butterfield, H. and Wight, M. (eds) (1966) *Diplomatic Investigations*, London: Allen & Unwin.

Craig, G. and George, A. (1983) *Force and Statecraft*, Oxford: Oxford University Press.

Der Derian, J. (1987) *On Diplomacy*, Oxford and New York: Basil Blackwell.

Donelan, M. (ed.) (1978) *The Reasons of States: A Study in International Political Theory*, London: Allen & Unwin.

Doyle, M. (1986) 'Liberalism and world politics', *American Political Science Review* 80: 1151–69.

Hinsley, F. (1963) *Power and the Pursuit of Peace*, Cambridge: Cambridge University Press.

Kennan, G. (1951) *American Diplomacy 1900–1950*, Chicago: University of Chicago Press.

——(1985) 'Morality and foreign policy', *Foregin Affairs* 64: 1–14.

Kissinger, H. (1964) *A World Restored*, New York: Universal Library.

Lauren, P. (1979) *Diplomacy: New Approaches in History, Theory, and Policy*, New York: Free Press.

Mattingly, G. (1955) *Renaissance Diplomacy*, London: Jonathan Cape.

Morgenthau, H. and Thompson, K. (1985) *Politics Among Nations: The Struggle for Power and Peace*, New York: Knopf.

Nicholson, H. (1950) *Diplomacy*, 2nd edn, Oxford: Oxford University Press.
——(1954) *The Evolution of Diplomatic Method*, London: Constable & Co.
Paarlberg, R. (ed.) (1978) *Diplomatic Dispute: US Conflict with Iran, Japan, and Mexico*, Cambridge, Mass.: Harvard University Center for International Affairs.
Rosecrance, R. (1973) *International Relations: Peace or War?*, New York: McGraw-Hill.
Stein, J. (1989) 'Getting to the table', *International Journal* 44: 231–504.
Watson, A. (1983) *Diplomacy*, Philadelphia: Institute for the Study of Human Issues.

65

WAR

ØYVIND ØSTERUD

THE PHENOMENON OF WAR

War is organized violence between groups of people. This may be the only observable factor common to the class of events called 'war'. As organized collective violence, war is embedded in very diverse socio-political conditions, ranging from the ritualized vendettas of tribal society to the revolutionary guerrillas of modern times. The medieval war of knights has very little in common with the industrialized world war, or even with the violent merchant rivalries in post-Renaissance Europe. In the feudal world, war was an integral part of political life; it was an expression of the chivalrous ethos, and was firmly imprinted on the ideological horizon. Warfare in the early modern epoch was ritualized to resemble the military parade, until the total war of the Napoleonic campaigns endangered the existence of states. Yet war was still regarded as a normal way of resolving diplomatic tension right up to the outbreak of the First World War in 1914. Even today, of course, war remains a chameleon, ranging from post-colonial border clashes to the potential of a global nuclear holocaust.

The range of events called war is often organized in conceptual clusters, with specific categories for different types of war. There is, however, no universally fruitful system of classification: should the types be defined in accordance with different motives (wars of conquest, pre-emption, missionary zeal, etc.); in accordance with international conflict patterns (bipolarity, multi-polarity, hegemonic transition, etc.); or in chronological order, with specific conceptualizations for war in different epochs? This notional effort is unsettled and as old as any reflection of war.

THE STUDY OF WAR

The systematic study of war has developed with the evolution of the social and behavioural sciences. New methods and new academic disciplines could benefit from the descriptions and generalizations already presented by the historians of diplomacy and war. Modern scholarly approaches to war also have their distinct ancestors in the history of ideas.

Modern balance-of-power thinking, for example, has granted a notable renaissance to Thucydides and his account of the Peloponnesian War. When 'what made war inevitable was the growth of Athenian power and the fear this caused in Sparta', we realize that the motives sprang from power and insecurity, while a shifting balance between contending parties triggered off the campaign. Hobbes's conception of the anarchic state of nature equally anticipated the realist school: the war-prone insecurity of sovereign states in a system with no transnational authority. These basic premises are shared between an entrenched school in diplomatic history and a growing body of formal analyses employing the mathematical theory of games (Nicholson 1989).

There is an alternative liberal tradition originating in nineteenth-century thought, with a political, an economic and a sociological argument. The political argument is basically that interstate war has domestic roots, with aggression emanating from dictatorships and authoritarian structures; a system of democratic republics would eventually constitute an international peace zone. The economic argument stressed the interdependence emanating from commercial exchange and the harmony of interests in the growth of the world market. The sociological argument saw industrial society as alien to militarism and violent conquest, with imperialism and aggression as relics of pre-industrial structures and feudal values. The modern study of war has revolved extensively around these arguments. Neo-liberal scholars have also stressed the importance of transnational institutions in world affairs – norms, organizations and codes of conduct.

The Marxist study of war is equally diverse, with war reflecting the contradictions of an exploitive mode of production at the core. Even so, Marxist analyses have proliferated on quite different interpretations of imperialism, capitalist development, and the influence of economic forces (Shaw 1984).

Methodological approaches are cutting across these intellectual traditions, with statistical analyses of quantitative data on the one hand, and in-depth case studies or broad historical explorations on the other, with systematic comparative investigations in between. Quantitative behaviourism became particularly dominant in the United States from the 1950s, while British and European scholarship retained a stronger traditionalist bent. The academic study of war has definitely displayed various national characteristics, although the lines of geographic delineation should not be drawn too neatly (Smith 1985).

The modern study of war has also employed new techniques such as systems analysis in defence planning, and war-gaming and simulation for both heuristic and operational purposes.

Some high-profile approaches after the Second World War defy traditional categorization. The peace research movement originated as a cross-disciplinary blend of idealist internationalism and quantitative methods, but soon revealed an internal tension between liberal, Marxist and Third Worldist factions. Peace research has been explicitly globalist and value-oriented, as the intellectual branch of popular peace movements, in particular contrast to realist assumptions.

THE CONDUCT OF WAR

The evolution of warfare is also a story of technological and demographic change (McNeill 1983). There have been long periods of strategic and technical stability in military history, broken by sudden transformations of the means and conduct of war.

Striking examples of the impact of technological innovation are legion. The invention of the stirrup around the year AD 600 made knightly tactics with concentrated force in close-in combat possible, and also increased the effectiveness of steppe cavalry by stabilizing the archer in gallop. There is a direct link between the rise of heavy armoured cavalry as a superior warrior elite and the decentralized power system called 'feudalism' in medieval Europe.

During the Middle Ages there was a technological race between offensive and defensive weapons, between crossbow design and armour, until the use of guns and cannons gradually became more effective and undermined the system of local fortifications. Small sovereignties and city-states were doomed as the military revolution made consolidated powers on a bigger scale essential. Centralized state formation, the royal absolutism of early modern Europe, emerged as firearms and new military tactics led to standing armies far beyond the capacity of local barons.

The offensive use of massive manpower during the Napoleonic campaigns was prepared by the revolutionary principle that everybody owed military service to the nation. The French revolution changed the moral and political variables of war; it heralded a 'total war' with the survival of states at stake. Wars conducted with the full force of national energy frightened the European powers into the balance-of-power system at the Congress of Vienna. When the system was shattered during the second half of the nineteenth century, warfare was also rapidly industrialized. The railway revolutionized military transport and changed the strategic terms of land power, as did the iron battleship in naval warfare. Steamships and railways not only meant rapid mass mobilization to the battlefront, but also allowed European powers to unify and dominate the globe. The colonial advances from the 1880s onwards were facilitated by the development of high explosives, rifle magazines, cartridges and belt-fed machine-guns.

The intensified industrialization of warfare in the late nineteenth century also meant new modes of interaction between military politics and economic interests, with the weapons industry as a strategic growth sector and a factor in the arms race.

The new revolutions of military technology during the twentieth century are symbolized first by the airplane, and then by the nuclear bomb followed by intercontinental missiles. The employment of air bombers meant that civilian populations increasingly became a military objective: civil society no longer enjoyed immunity from combat, even in principle. This obliteration of the duality between mobilized armies and civil society is pushed to extremes by the strategy of nuclear weapons, with civilian populations on a massive scale held as hostages in mutual deterrence.

The balance of terror between the superpowers operates on the premiss that both parties are vulnerable to a devastating nuclear response. Technological developments are still influencing the subtleties of nuclear strategy. Innovations such as satellite surveillance have removed some of the uncertainties about antagonist weapons systems, while the deployment of multiple-warhead rockets and cruise missiles might have worked in the opposite direction. The relative accuracy of ground-launched versus submarine-launched missile forces are also supposed to imply different targeting strategies.

Military strategy is not only conditioned by technological developments. War is conducted in other dimensions as well. The Clausewitzian perspective differentiates between the operational and logistical aspects of warfare. Negligence of logistics has in the past often meant failure for the most elaborate operational strategy. This aspect also has a social dimension, since the conduct of war depends on civilian support and the social basis of mobilization (Howard 1983: 105).

The importance of military–civilian relations is most clearly demonstrated in revolutionary war and guerrilla tactics. The clandestine hit-and-run tactics of insurrectionary guerrillas is the warfare of the military underdog. However, it depends heavily on sanctuaries or civilian support, and it may be decisively facilitated by modern technology – the radio and the airborne supplies for the wartime Resistance in Europe; the Landrover units of the Polisario Front; the Stinger missile of the Afghan Mujaheddin.

Revolutionary warfare often combines regular troops and informal partisans, and at the political level the anti-colonial war of national liberation is its most prominent modern expression. Below the superpower balance of terror the crisis of the states system has, paradoxically, implied a more anarchic conduct of war.

THE ORIGINS OF WAR

The roots of war may be found at every conceivable level of life – biological nature, individual psychology, group dynamics, political regime, economic system, cultural tradition, right up to religion and cosmology. There are several war theories at each of these levels, or for combinations of them. Three different levels may be singled out as fundamentally different.

The individualist explanation ranges from the biological foundations of human nature to the social-psychological mechanisms of aggression or misperception. The biological perspective on war is often derived from ethology, and concentrates on innate behaviour or instinctive characteristics. Since war is an intermittent phenomenon, however, it is hardly explained by the universality of human nature. If human nature was the cause of war in 1914, it was also the cause of peace in 1910, since nature had not changed decisively in the space of four years (Waltz 1959: 28). Similar problems arise with psychological explanations of war. Oedipal and other murderous impulses may well explain violence, but not the fluctuations of organized group violence called war, and still less the origins of specific wars in history. Psychological mechanisms like displacement (in-group loyalty), projection (self-hate lavished on others) and transformed aggression (scapegoating) may be endemic in human society, but large-scale war is still as intermittent a phenomenon as peaceful co-operation. Likewise a student of misperception in war – convincingly shown to be important – modifies the generalizations by admitting freely that 'war has so many causes . . . and misperception has so many effects . . . that it is not possible to draw any definitive conclusions about the impact of misperception on war' (Jervis 1989: 101). Further, national leaders on a war footing may well act as illustrations of psychopathological categories, but, again, it is no accident which leaders are emerging in particular contexts and the scope of action granted them.

The explanations for war have also been found in the characteristics of individual states. There has recently been renewed interest in the Kantian proposition that democracies are inherently peaceful, while authoritarian regimes are more war-prone and externally aggressive. This thesis of liberal pacifism has been pursued both empirically and theoretically. The empirical correlation analyses have so far been partly inconclusive. While liberal-democratic states seem to form a zone of peace among themselves, they have engaged in numerous wars with non-democratic states, and as often as not have started these wars (Levy 1989). Kant's theoretical argument was that the citizens ruling in a democratic republic would not engage in wars from which they would inevitably suffer badly. Likewise, Schumpeter argued in 1919 that only war profiteers and military aristocrats would gain from wars, and that they thus should be explained as relics of a pre-capitalist or early capitalist society: democratic capitalism would lead to peace (Schumpeter 1919). Liberal pacifism on these terms was a counter-argument to the Leninist theory of war as a result of imperialist rivalry at the advanced stage of capitalism.

The liberal theory of economic integration and mutual advantage in trade – as a barrier against war – has been revived in neo-liberal institutionalism: war is an aberration from the harmony of interests in international institutions and division of labour.

There is a notable discrepancy between the theoretical arguments on war and domestic structure on the one hand, and the quantitative empirical analyses on the other. Individual wars may be tied closely to domestic factors, but exceptions are numerous.

Neo-realist theory explains the recurrence of war by the structure of the international system. The argument is that sovereign states in an anarchic order are basically insecure in relation to each other, and must provide for their security by military power or alliance politics. An uneasy 'security dilemma' arises when measures to increase one state's security diminish the security of others. The responsive stockpiling of weapons confirms the first state's worry, while pacifism might increase the temptation of adversaries. The dilemma is derived from the organizational fact of international anarchy, and might explain arms races as well as pre-emptive war.

The neo-realist paradigm, further, connects the likelihood of war to changes in the international system. While anarchy is an organizational condition, the distribution of power is a variable feature. A multipolar balance of power may have qualities of order and instability different from hegemonies or bipolar systems. There is a continuous argument about the relation between such structural characteristics and war, on theoretical and historical terms, but there is no conclusive evidence.

The neo-realist model explains the recurrent propensity of war in the international system, but it does not explain the occurrence of particular wars.

In sum, different explanations of war may be partly to the point. At the macro level, war is embedded in society and requires a broad and historically specific analysis. At the micro level, war definitely involves political and military decisions that are manifestations of more general determinants of behaviour. Behavioural parameters are central to classical balance-of-power theory as well as to modern theories of nuclear deterrence and crisis resolution. If the decision to go to war involves an element of self-preserving rationality, then factors such as a nuclear deterrent raise the threshold considerably. Fruitful explanations of wars must link decision making to the historical context of warfare. War, in short, not only has causes, but is also triggered off by intentional conduct and series of motivated acts.

THE CONSEQUENCES OF WAR

Warfare was probably the dominant public expense in post-feudal Europe, and general taxation originates from the need to finance the crusades of the High Middle Ages. Preparation for war was crucial in early state formation, when the technology of warfare surpassed decentralized feudalism. War is intrinsic to the evolution of the modern states system.

The process of nation-building has also been intimately linked to the experience of war. Compulsory conscription was often the most efficient way to mould primordial identities into the framework of the nation-state, and the common destiny of war experience has recurrently made pre-war cleavages irrelevant.

War has rearranged power relationships at the international level, and shifted the correlates of hegemonic position. Great Britain entered the Second World War as a virtual superpower, but emerged as a medium great power despite an undisputed victory. The long-term processes of history accelerate in war, and sometimes take a new turn.

The economic and technological consequences of previous wars are literally unlimited, ranging from models of planning and management to the most specific consumer goods. When so much destruction and suffering bring innovation and new starts, war is a recurrent illustration of Bernard Mandeville's ironic paradoxes in *The Fable of the Bees* from the early eighteenth century.

THE CONTEMPORARY CONTEXT OF WAR

The Second World War heralded the new superpower rivalry between victorious allies. The Cold War has been a fluctuating evolution of tension and *détente* within an overall balance of terror, with occasional crises and local wars by proxy, and with mutual stop–go arms-control policies. The Cold War as an international system includes the traditional great-power rivalry under overall anarchic conditions, where European and Asian vacuums of power had to be filled after 1945, in a scramble for spheres of influence, alliances and new rules of the game. It includes a rivalry between contradictory social systems, with ideological competition freezing the power blocs. It includes an arms race with mutual perceptions as important as the actual challenge; a geopolitical rivalry for influence in third areas in general and in the Third World in particular; and, finally, the domestic needs in each camp for a high-profile external challenge.

The Cold War has meant polarization of power, with the mechanisms of mutual deterrence regulating the central balance. The strategic forces directly confronting each other have not been unleashed, in an unprecedented period of clear-cut tension without direct war. The nuclear deterrent has most definitely contributed to the long period of peace, and it has been stabilized by tacit understandings such as mutual respect for informal spheres of influence, avoidance of direct military confrontation in the periphery, and reluctance to exploit the regional setbacks for the adversary too provocatively (Gaddis 1987).

The other side of the coin is a peripheral zone of war. Superpower rivalry has induced a series of military interventions within the respective spheres of influence and also in more peripheral arenas. The support of local allies in regional conflicts – with weapons, logistics, instructors – has been endemic during the Cold War years, while direct deployment of troops consistently has defined areas of acute crisis – from Vietnam to Afghanistan.

When superpower *détente* of the 1970s was an architectural aim for a stable international structure regulated by arms control, the peripheral rivalry in the Third World remained a blind spot. *Détente* concealed the fact that both parties tried to gain unilateral advantage in the periphery. Soviet projections in Africa and elsewhere were consistent with the idea of peaceful co-existence as offensive global competition without a central war. The ambiguity of superpower accommodation has evolved around the relationship between arms control and regional conflicts: is tension in one field linked to tension in the other, or is arms control basically a device to prevent third-area conflict from slipping into a major confrontation? (See Garthoff 1985.)

This peculiar dialectic of central peace and peripheral war stems from the paradoxical quality of the balance of terror. On the one hand, it entails the prospect that any conflict and crisis might destabilize the gothic arch of countervailing nuclear forces, so that any potential zone of disagreement should be regulated co-operatively between the superpowers. On the other hand, it entails the promise of a hindmost defence against minor conflicts escalating out of control, so that the scope for assertiveness and conflict behaviour at lower levels increases. This paradoxical ambiguity finds expression in the pendulum swing between superpower tension and accommodation.

There is, finally, an external war zone outside the co-ordinates of interbloc rivalry. A wide range of contemporary armed conflicts spring from boundary disputes, irredentist claims, ethnic division and religious clashes. The modern states system, including the geographical boundaries inherited from colonialism, faces a widespread legitimacy crisis. Terrorist movements and irredentist or civil war are the manifest expressions of this crisis, where state boundaries entrap national minorities or cut across ethno-national groups. In extreme cases, the legitimacy crisis of established states leads to dissolution of authority and the endemic war of anarchy, as in Lebanon since the mid-1970s.

The superpowers might be involved in these wars, but they are often dragged reluctantly into them without a clear purpose and without a firm grasp on the outcome or the implications. This pattern demonstrates, again, the relative irrelevance of military superpower in some of the wars actually taking place in the contemporary world.

THE KNOWLEDGE OF WAR

The evidence concerning the roots of war remain uncertain despite an enormous amount of theorizing and research. Different explanations may be partly to the point, since war involves individual action and strategic decision making at one level, since it is pursued by political regimes at another, and since it also takes place within a specific international mode of organization.

The lack of clear-cut scientific answers to the question of war is partly due to the fact that the problems involved are intrinsically political in nature. The evaluation, for instance, of a smaller risk in the short run against a greater risk in the long run – the daily triviality of deterrence policies – has decisively a non-scientific element. Several questions of war and peace involve uncertainty, with little prospect of a certain answer. Adversaries may be avoiding aggression because of mutual deterrent postures, or they might have avoided aggression in any case. The counterfactual hypothesis as to the preservation of European peace after 1945 is untestable. Theorizing might supply cues for rational choice under uncertainty; research might explain how vital decisions in the past were actually made; but theorizing and research cannot remove uncertainty.

War is rather, as we have seen, a collection of very different phenomena. No simple theory is likely to account for all. Like disease, war has many roots and operates through many mechanisms, even if the parallel is otherwise somewhat misleading. Here is the scientific contribution. Scholarly analyses have contributed greatly to the breaking up of exceedingly broad questions into manageable and meaningful portions. This is a critical contribution with wide implications. But the big question of policy remains unanswered: is a *para bellum* strategy – to prepare for war – the best guarantee of peace, or should unilateral disarmament be trusted?. We do not know under what conditions it is possible to stimulate progress towards mutual disarmament by means of controlled one-sided rearmament, or whether unilateral arms reductions tend to move the adversary in the same direction. This is an aspect of the security dilemma in an anarchic environment. The reactions of political actors are never completely predictable. That is the little unstable core in the study of war.

BIBLIOGRAPHY

Aron, R. (1962) *Paix et guerre entre les nations*, Paris: Calmann-Levy, 1984.

Blainey, G. (1973) *The Causes of War*, London: Macmillan.

Gaddis, J. L. (1987) *The Long Peace*, New York: Oxford University Press.

Garthoff, R. L. (1985) *Détente and Confrontation: American–Soviet Relations from Nixon to Reagan*, Washington, DC: Brookings Institution.

Gilpin, R. (1981) *War and Change in World Politics*, New York: Cambridge University Press.

Halliday, F. (1983) *The Making of the Second Cold War*, London: Verso.

Howard, M. (1976) *War in European History*, London: Oxford University Press.

——(1983) *The Causes of Wars and Other Essays*, London: Temple Smith.

Jervis, R. (1976) *Perception and Misperception in International Politics*, Princeton: Princeton University Press.

——(1989) 'War and misperception', in R.I. Rotberg and T.K. Rabb (eds) *The Origin and Prevention of Major Wars*, Cambridge: Cambridge University Press.

Levy, J. S. (1983) *War in the Modern Great Power System, 1495–1975*, Lexington, Mass.: Lexington Books.

——(1989) 'Domestic politics and war', in R.I. Rotberg and T.K. Rabb (eds) *The Origin and Prevention of Major Wars*, Cambridge: Cambridge University Press.

McNeill, W. H. (1983) *The Pursuit of Power*, Oxford: Basil Blackwell.

Nicholson, M. (1989) *Formal Theories of International Relations*, Cambridge: Cambridge University Press.

Østerud, Ø. (ed.) (1986) *Studies of War and Peace*, Oslo: Norwegian and Oxford University Press.

Paret, P. (ed.) (1986) *Makers of Modern Strategy*, Oxford: Clarendon Press.

Rotberg, R. I. and Rabb, T. K. (eds) (1989) *The Origin and Prevention of Major Wars*, Cambridge: Cambridge University Press.

Schumpeter, J. A. (1919) 'Zur Sociologie der Imperialismen', *Archiv für Sozialwissenschaft und Sozialpolitik*, published in English, 1952, as *The Sociology of Imperialism*, New York: Kelley.

Shaw, M. (ed.) (1984) *War, State and Society*, London: Macmillan.

Singer, J. D. *et al.* (1979–80) *The Correlates of War*, 2 vols, New York: Free Press.

Smith, S. (ed.) (1985) *International Relations: British & American Perspectives*, Oxford: Basil Blackwell.

Wright, Q. (1942) *A Study of War*, 2 vols, Chicago: University of Chicago Press.

66

REVOLUTION

JACK A. GOLDSTONE

A revolution is an illegal, usually violent, seizure of power that produces a fundamental change in the institutions of government. However, the concept of 'revolution' has been used in many ways, with some variation in meaning. 'Revolution' is sometimes used to describe *any* fundamental change, whether or not it was violent or sudden. In this sense we speak of the 'Industrial Revolution' or the 'Scientific Revolution'. Fundamental changes in government that occur through elections, rather than violent seizures of power, are also sometimes described as revolutions: for example, the 'Nazi revolution' in Germany which followed Hitler's electoral victory in 1933.

In most revolutions, the seizure of power depends on uprisings by urban crowds or rural peasants. Such popular action is generally considered an essential feature of the process we call a 'revolution'. In some cases, however, popular groups do little, while an individual or small elite group seizes power and implements sweeping political changes (for example, the Turkish Revolution under Atatürk in 1921, or the Egyptian Revolution under Nasser in 1952). Such events are often described by the qualified terms 'elite revolution' or 'revolution from above' (Trimberger 1978).

Revolutions vary in their scope. Those that change only government institutions are sometimes labelled 'political revolutions'. Those that also change the distribution of wealth and status in a society – for example, by destroying the privileges of a nobility – are often called 'social revolutions' or 'great revolutions'. When groups seeking fundamental change attempt to seize power, but that attempt fails, we speak of 'unsuccessful' or 'failed revolutions', such as the Revolution of 1848 in Germany. (An attack on a government that seeks only to change the ruling personnel or policies, but makes no attempt at fundamental change in institutions, is usually called a 'revolt' rather than a 'revolution'.)

Properly speaking, revolution is a process rather than an event. There is an initial period in which criticism of the state mounts and opponents of the government strive to gain support. There then ensues a period of contention between the government and its opponents; this may entail a long guerrilla war, or a sudden explosion of popular tumults. If the government falls, there follows a period in which revolutionary leaders contend with each other and with adherents of the old regime; this period commonly includes both civil and international wars, and often a period of domestic 'terror' against opponents of the revolution. A successful revolution then leads to the consolidation of power and the construction of new political institutions. Because this process may take decades, the dating of revolutions is frequently imprecise. However, for convenience, revolutions are typically dated by the year in which the old regime falls – for example, the French Revolution of 1789, the Chinese Communist Revolution of 1949 – even though revolutionary struggles and state reconstruction may continue for decades afterwards.

The concept of revolution as fundamental change is a strictly modern development. From ancient Greece to the Renaissance, 'revolution' meant a cyclical motion, such as the revolution of the planets. In politics the term 'revolution' therefore also implied a cyclical pattern, a movement from aristocracy to democracy to tyranny and back in an endless circle. Only in the eighteenth century, particularly after the French Revolution of 1789, did the term 'revolution' come to refer to a permanent and fundamental, rather than cyclical, change.

The concept of revolution is often used with moral, as well as descriptive, overtones. Many authors, particularly those inspired by Karl Marx, use the term 'revolution' to imply change that is valuable and progressive. In politics, this usually means reducing inequality and providing greater justice; it may also imply replacing an authoritarian regime with a more democratic one, or providing a higher standard of living. These authors view revolutions as necessary to provide social progress; indeed, they often argue that revolution is the only way to overthrow established ideas or institutions.

Others, however, use the term revolution to imply a time of chaos, of unfettered struggle for power with destructive consequences. They see revolution as a violent and dangerous departure from the normal course of political life. These thinkers consider revolutions as something to be avoided and advocate that desired social change should be brought about through gradual reform.

This argument is long-standing and far from settled. Different writers continue to view revolutions with optimism or pessimism, depending on their individual judgement whether the benefits of revolutionary change are worth the costs.

Additional debates over the nature of revolutions have centred on two issues: why do revolutions occur, and what have they accomplished?

THE CAUSES OF REVOLUTION

Thinking about the causes of revolution has grown more sophisticated through-out the twentieth century. Early writers, such as LeBon (1913), focused chiefly on crowds, seeing revolution as the product of uncontrolled and spontaneous popular enthusiasm. Such crowd action might be triggered by a burst of economic hardship, or a particularly flagrant act of government corruption or oppression.

In the 1920s and 1930s, writers sought a more systematic description of revolutionary origins and processes. This 'natural history' school (Edwards 1927; Pettee 1938; Brinton 1938) outlined several stages common to the development of major European revolutions:

1 the transfer of allegiance by intellectuals from the state to opposition move-ments;
2 unsuccessful attempts by the state to resolve fiscal and leadership problems by reforms;
3 an acute political crisis that reveals the weakness of the state;
4 an initial taking of power by moderates;
5 a split in the revolutionary forces, with extremists mobilizing popular groups against the moderates;
6 a seizure of power by extremists, involving coercive terror against both moderates and supporters of the old regime;
7 the rise of populist, often military, dictatorship; and
8 a return to a more pragmatic, less ideologically intense post-revolutionary society.

Although more than fifty years have elapsed, these writers' works – especially that of Brinton – are still valuable. Not only do these stages still offer a largely accurate description of the cases from which they were drawn – the English Revolution of 1640, the French Revolution of 1789 and the Russian Revolution of 1917 – but these stages can also be found, with some variation, in the development of the Chinese Revolution of 1911 and the Iranian Revolution of 1979.

None the less, the contribution of the natural history school has two major drawbacks. First, their account of revolution is descriptive rather than causal, providing no explanation for why revolutions should occur in certain countries at certain times but not in others. Second, their account applies best to social revolutions in large, fairly autonomous countries with established traditional governments; their description applies far less well to revolutions from above and revolutions in small countries with recently established semi-modern governments, both of which have been far more common in the latter half of the twentieth century.

In the 1960s and early 1970s, various attempts were made to provide a causal theory of revolutions. These theories grew out of concerns that revolutions would occur widely in countries undergoing a shift from more traditional to more modern patterns of economic and political life. In these decades, revolutions were commonly viewed as resulting from extreme levels of popular discontent. Scholars therefore sought to identify general conditions that would lead to increased popular discontent. Descriptions of such conditions included 'relative deprivation' (Gurr 1970), 'multiple social dysfunction' (Johnson 1966), and 'lagging political institutionalization' (Huntington 1968). These scholars' research emphasized surveys of large numbers of states – dozens or even hundreds – seeking simple correlations between measures of social stress and measures of political violence. (Much of this research is summarized in Gurr 1980.)

By the 1970s, however, particularly as a result of the work of Tilly (1973, 1978), Paige (1975) and Popkin (1979), scholars had become aware that revolutionary behaviour did not simply follow from popular discontent. Instead, revolutionary activity was seen to require leadership, organization and mobilization in pursuit of political objectives. This 'resource-mobilization' view led scholars to seek the causes of revolutions in shifts of resources among politically active groups. Thus analysts of revolution turned away from general theories of popular sentiment, and focused more closely on the precise conditions of state organization and resource distribution that had led to revolutions in specific historical cases.

The most important work in this vein was that of Skocpol (1979). Skocpol built on the earlier work of Moore (1966), who had sought to create a historically specific theory of revolutions by close study of a few cases of revolutionary and non-revolutionary social change. However, whereas Moore had concentrated on the conflicts and coalitions among social classes to explain revolutionary processes, Skocpol insisted that conflicts between classes must be viewed in the context of the efforts of autonomous states to maintain and extend their authority. In Skocpol's view, the fundamental cause of revolutions was a failure of rulers to obtain the resources needed to cope with international military competition, owing to either elite efforts to block the state's control of resources, or a backwards economy, or both. If state failure occurred in the context of peasant communities that were sufficiently well-organized to press their own claims for freedom from landlord control, the result would be a social revolution. Skocpol's work produced a fundamental reorientation of studies of revolution, placing the emphasis on state vulnerability, the organization of popular groups, and the careful comparative examination of a handful of cases as the best method of research.

Goldstone (1991) accepted Skocpol's emphasis on state vulnerability and followed her method of careful study of a small number of cases. He argued, however, that international competition was not a sufficient explanation of the pressures on states. Military competition was a virtually constant feature of early modern history; yet states dealt better with such pressures in some periods than in others. Goldstone pointed out that fiscal pressure on states, state–elite conflict, and popular mobilization potential varied systematically over time, and in accord with population pressure. He argued that in states with relatively inflexible agrarian economies, population growth generally produced price inflation. Where states also relied on fairly rigid traditional systems of taxation and elite recruitment, the combination of population increase and rising prices eroded tax revenues and heightened competition for elite positions. Population growth and inflation also raised mass mobilization potential by creating a more youthful population, spurring urbanization, depressing real wages, and creating a shortage of land and jobs for peasants and workers. Demonstrating the links between population change, price inflation, and pressures on states, elites and popular groups, Goldstone was able to explain the occurrence of major revolutions and rebellions in Europe, the Middle East and China in the centuries 1550–1650 and 1750–1850, and the relative absence of such events in the intervening century. Goldstone also added to Skocpol's analysis by stressing the importance of intra-elite conflicts and urban uprisings in the revolutionary process.

The currently prevailing view of the causes of revolution, following Skocpol and Goldstone, is known as 'structural' theory. In this view, revolutions will occur only when a *combination* of factors creates a structural situation favourable to revolution. This situation includes a weakened government; elites in conflict with the state and each other over resources; and a basis for popular mobilization through village and/or urban communities. The combination of these factors – when brought to a head by an acute fiscal or military crisis – is likely to produce a broad-based revolution along the lines described by the natural history school. However, as Trimberger (1978) pointed out, where elite opposition to the state is fairly united and comes primarily from elites with a strong base in the military or civil administration and the bases for popular mobilization are weak, an elite revolution stopping at stage 4 in the natural history schema (see p. 1051) is the more likely result. In either case, the key explanatory variable is the distribution of material and organizational resources among the state, elites and popular groups. Revolutionary ideologies – which might include communism, liberalism or Islamic fundamentalism – are considered to be capable of gaining wide appeal only when a structural situation arises which favours revolution.

However, this theory, like that of the 'natural history' scholars, was developed chiefly to account for the great revolutions that occurred in large, predominantly agrarian countries from the seventeenth to the early twentieth century. Recently, a number of writers (Dix 1983; Goldstone 1986a; Shugart 1989;

Goldstone *et al.* 1991) have pointed out that post-Second World War revolutions show a number of differences from earlier revolutions. First, the vulnerability of contemporary states has depended greatly on the actions of the superpowers, namely the United States and the Soviet Union. Second, as Eisenstadt (1978) pointed out, contemporary states are often undermined by their attempts to impose a foreign, secular ideology – such as communism or liberalism – on societies with deeply rooted religious cultures: for example, Roman Catholicism in Eastern Europe and Islam in the Middle East. A similar instability owing to the conflict between state policy and strong indigenous cultural and ethnic claims undercut colonial and white-settler regimes in Asia and Africa. Third, contemporary states are more urbanized and industrial than earlier states; they are thus less vulnerable to peasant uprisings. Instead, social revolutions generally have depended on a cross-class coalition of urban popular and elite groups against the state. Fourth, the vulnerability of contemporary states to revolution is greatest in neo-patrimonial, or personal, states. In such states, a single individual has captured the state and wields patrimonial power over it (for example, Batista in Cuba, Marcos in the Philippines, Anastasio Somoza Debayle in Nicaragua). The dependency of the state on that individual is then so great that opposition to the leader tends to take the form of a revolutionary alliance, and the inability of that leader to maintain support (owing to economic setbacks, withdrawal of superpower patronage, or struggles over succession) tends to produce a disintegration of military and civil institutions that is conducive to revolutionary change.

These findings do not directly overturn the social-structural theory of revolutions; they are still consistent with the view that revolutions only occur in a structurally favourable situation including state weakness, state-elite conflicts, and a basis for popular mobilization. However, these findings do require modification of the theory as developed for pre-Second World War revolutions by Skocpol (1979) and Goldstone (1991), who stressed the vulnerability of states to international military pressures, peasant rebellions and long-term population growth. Though these factors have played some role in recent years, the development of revolutionary situations in the decades after 1945 has depended to a far greater extent on the withdrawal or limiting of superpower support, ideological impositions by secularizing states, the growth of urban cross-class coalitions for change, and the rise and weakening of neo-patrimonial states.

UNSUCCESSFUL REVOLUTIONS AND REBELLIONS

History displays many examples in which elite conflicts and bases for popular mobilization arose, but without substantial fiscal or military weakening of the state. Such cases generally provide instances of failed revolutions, revolts or rebellions (Walton 1984). For example, South Africa has experienced recurrent episodes of rebellion, but state strength has prevented the outbreak of revolution.

The outcomes of rebellion or revolt appear to depend on the degree of elite conflict. Where rebellions are led by marginal elites, and the vast majority of elites are united in support of the state, rebellion is likely to produce a ruthless reaction against the rebels and against further change, as occurred in many early anti-colonial revolts. However, where elites are more evenly divided, and significant and powerful elite factions are sympathetic to the revolt, it is more likely that the state will engage in significant reforms, as followed the '*La Violencia*' revolt in Colombia and the Revolution of 1848 in Germany.

There is considerable debate among scholars as to whether revolutions are sharply distinct from, or in many ways similar to, unsuccessful revolutions and rebellions. Skocpol (1979) has argued that rebellions and revolts are endemic to pre-industrial nations, and that analysis should therefore focus on the conditions of state weakness that create a potential for revolution. However, Walton (1984) and Goldstone *et al.* (1991) emphasize that the nature of elite alienation and popular grievances are similar in both revolts and revolutions; therefore both kinds of events can be embraced in a common analytic framework. This debate can only be decided by further research on revolts and rebellions; the latter have generally been neglected by scholars in comparison with the voluminous work on revolutions.

COUNTER-REVOLUTION

Opposition to revolutionary regimes comes from two sources: first, members of the elite of the old regime – generally from the military as well as from groups that benefited economically from the old order – who seek simply to undo the revolution; and second, members of groups who originally supported the revolution, or were neutral, who seek to prevent the revolution from moving too far in a direction they deem undesirable. For example, in France after 1789 there were counter-revolutionaries among the former nobility who wanted a restoration of traditional aristocratic power; but there were also counter-revolutionaries among the leadership of major towns and peasant and landlord groups in western France, who opposed such specific revolutionary actions as the administrative reorganization and centralization of power in Paris and the nationalization of Church property. In the Iranian Revolution of 1979, there were a small number of counter-revolutionaries who wished to restore the Pahlevi monarchy; but there were also counter-revolutionaries among the moderate technocrats who, though they supported the removal of the Shah, opposed the development of a theocratic Islamic state.

As both of these examples demonstrate, the most serious threat of counter-revolution is not from those attached to the pre-revolutionary order, but rather from those moderate groups seeking to slow or limit the pace of revolutionary change. The counter-revolutionary wars in western France, and the struggles with secular or socialist groups in Iran, were far bloodier and more threatening than struggles with those seeking to restore the monarchies.

Counter-revolutionary movements have never succeeded by themselves in overturning a revolution by force. However, they have often succeeded in a variety of ways. First, military action against the revolutionary state by allies of counter-revolutionaries may produce a restoration of the old monarchy, although generally in modified form, or may lead to a more moderate regime (for example, the defeat of Napoleon resulted in the restoration of the Bourbons; US support for the counter-revolutionary Nicaraguan 'contras' – who were counter-revolutionaries of the second kind, opposing the extreme measures of the Sandinista revolutionary government rather than seeking restoration of the Somoza regime – helped pressure the Sandinistas into an election which resulted in their defeat by more moderate forces). Second, a failure of succession in a revolutionary regime may provide an opportunity for counter-revolutionaries to reclaim power, as happened in England after the Puritan Revolution, when Cromwell's failure to produce a powerful successor led to the restoration of the Stuart monarchy. Third, counter-revolutionary forces may 'capture' the institutions of a revolutionary regime, and use them to halt or moderate change. For example, following the Turkish Revolution of 1921, conservative landlords gained control of the new secular government and prevented any further radical social change.

However, such successes have been historically rare. In general, counter-revolutionary efforts have simply led revolutionary states into massive civil wars, whose main result has been to increase the coercive power and authority of the revolutionary state. For example, the counter-revolutionary movements led by General Kornilov in the Russian Revolution, and that led by General de la Huerta in the Mexican Revolution, gave rise to ruthless military and political terror by the Bolshevik and Constitutional forces, respectively, to crush their counter-revolutionary opponents. Indeed, Gurr (1986) has argued that the more active the counter-revolutionary opposition, the more likely it is that a revolution will have a highly authoritarian outcome.

THE OUTCOMES OF REVOLUTION

Research on the outcomes of revolution is less advanced than research into its causes. Only two conclusions seem well established. First, revolutions generally produce a growth of state power, as post-revolutionary regimes tend to attack the problem of state weakness by building states with larger armies and bureaucracies than the pre-revolutionary regime. Second, revolutions generally increase the likelihood of international wars, since the change of regime usually results in a change of international alliances. This often leads to tests of the strength of the new regime or the new alliances via international aggression, whether initiated by the new regime or its opponents.

On a host of other important issues, such as whether revolutions can create stable democracies, reduce inequality or enhance economic development, the evidence is highly ambiguous. Systematic study of these matters has only just begun.

In general, revolutions have not succeeded in producing stable democratic regimes. The reason for this failure is that the process of revolutionary power struggles leads to the concentration of power in the hands of revolutionaries, and the persecution and purging of their opponents. This process is highly inimical to the toleration and compromise between contending parties that is essential to stable democracy. Thus the most common political outcome of revolutions has been one-party states. Multi-party democracies are likely to emerge from revolutions only when the revolutionary process has involved minimal internal struggles against counter-revolutionary opponents, as was the case in the American Revolution of 1776 and may be the case in the Eastern European Revolutions of 1989.

Revolutions have been far more successful in changing patterns of inequality. Their gains, however, tend to be limited to eliminating the specific inequalities that prevailed between pre-revolutionary elites and the general population, rather than reducing or eliminating inequality in general. Inequalities between dominant and minority ethnic groups, between men and women, and between urban and rural populations, tend to persist after revolutions, and may even be exacerbated (Goldstone 1986b). In addition, inequality between the revolutionary elite and general population has a tendency to increase and grow more rigid over time. However, the level of income inequality seems to be less in nations that underwent socialist revolutions (such as the Soviet Union, China and Eastern Europe) than in nations that underwent capitalist revolutions (such as Mexico and Bolivia).

With regard to economic development, the impact of revolutions has been mixed. Socialist revolutions have been notably successful in providing the foundations of economic development: heavy industrial capacity, universal health care and literacy, and universal access to minimal standards of diet, clothing and shelter. However, such revolutions have been relatively unsuccessful in building a further superstructure of development – a viable consumer economy, individualized education and housing, and a rich and diversified diet. Capitalist revolutions – such as those of France in 1789 and Mexico in 1910 – have done more poorly than socialist revolutions with respect to extending literacy, health care and minimal living standards to their entire populations, but have done equally well with regard to building a heavy industrial capacity, and have been far more successful in providing a diversified, individualized consumer economy.

With regard to gains in per capita living standards, neither kind of revolution has allowed nations to escape their relative positions in the world economy as a whole. That is, countries that were relatively developed or underdeveloped compared to leading industrialized nations, and dependent on debt or foreign assistance, have generally remained in the same relative position after revolutions. For example, England and France remained major economic powers after their revolutions; the Russian Empire was a dominant military power but a weak economy in the nineteenth century, as was the Soviet Union in its last years; China, Mexico, Cuba and Nicaragua have remained semi-peripheral or peripheral economies after their revolutions (Eckstein 1982).

Ideological conflicts and cultural frameworks appear to play a major role in directing the outcomes of revolutions. Sharp repudiations of traditional social and political institutions have only occurred in societies that have absorbed ideologies with apocalyptic or eschatalogical imagery, either in Christian or secular (Enlightenment or Marxist) forms. In societies whose cultures lacked such imagery – such as traditional India, China, Japan and Islamic states – successful popular movements to overthrow governments have generally resulted in new regimes that sought to restore traditional virtues, rather than proclaim radical change. By contrast, societies with such eschatological imagery in their cultural framework have generally drawn on such imagery to symbolize revolutionary movements. Thus the English Revolution of 1640, the French Revolution of 1789, the Russian Revolution of 1917 and the Iranian Revolution of 1979 are notable for their world-remaking imagery, articulated by Puritan, Enlightenment, Marxist and Shi'ite publicists. Though revolutionary ideologies might spread and acquire salience only when the structural conditions arise that create a revolutionary situation, once such a situation has developed these ideologies assume great importance in setting the direction of change sought by revolutionary elites.

FUTURE PROSPECTS OF REVOLUTION

In the early and mid-twentieth century, when revolutions were viewed as the product of popular emotional response to the stresses of modernization, it was expected that revolutions would become less common as the world grew more rational and developed. However, the realization that revolutions are grounded in rational pursuit of political objectives, and arise when there occur shifts in power between states, elites and popular groups, has altered this expectation. Changes in technology, international politics and the world economy bring new resources into the hands of various groups, while strengthening some states and weakening others. Such shifts have been particularly marked in those countries heavily involved in the strategic competition between the United States and the Soviet Union. Thus revolutions (and attempted revolutions) have been frequent in the late twentieth century – in Iran, Nicaragua, Afghanistan, Poland, the Philippines and Eastern Europe. Resource shifts and changing patterns of superpower support are strongly affecting South Africa, Cuba, China, and various states in Central America, Africa and the Middle East; states in these regions are also being pressed by growing populations. The internal politics of the republics of the former Soviet Union and the states of Eastern Europe are currently in varying but early phases of revolutionary processes. It is therefore likely that revolutionary situations will occur and develop frequently in the coming decades. Thus, as they have in the past century, revolutions will play a major role in shaping world politics in the future.

REFERENCES

Brinton, C. (1938) *The Anatomy of Revolution*, New York: Vintage (revised and expanded 1965).

Dix, R. (1983) 'Varieties of revolution', *Comparative Politics* 15: 281–93.

Eckstein, S. (1982) 'The impact of revolution on social welfare in Latin America', *Theory and Society* 11: 33–94.

Edwards, L. P. (1927) *The Natural History of Revolution*, Chicago: University of Chicago Press.

Eisenstadt, S. N. (1978) *Revolution and the Transformation of Societies*, New York: Free Press.

Goldstone, J. A. (1986a) 'Revolutions and superpowers', in J. A. Goldstone (ed.) *Superpowers and Revolution*, New York: Praeger.

——(ed.) (1986b) *Revolutions: Theoretical, Comparative, and Historical Studies*, San Diego and New York: Harcourt Brace Jovanovich.

——(1991) *Revolution and Rebellion in the Early Modern World*, Berkeley and Los Angeles: University of California Press.

Goldstone, J. A., Gurr, T. R. and Moshiri, F. (eds) (1991) *Revolutions of the Late 20th Century*, Boulder, Colo.: Westview Press.

Gurr, T. R. (1970) *Why Men Rebel*, Princeton: Princeton University Press.

——(ed.) (1980) *Handbook of Political Conflict*, New York: Free Press.

——(1986) 'Persisting patterns of repression and rebellion: foundations for a general theory of political coercion', in M. P. Karns (ed.) *Persistent Patterns and Emergent Structures in a Waning Century*, New York: Praeger.

Huntington, S. P. (1968) *Political Order in Changing Societies*, New Haven, Conn.: Yale University Press.

Johnson, C. (1966) *Revolutionary Change*, Boston: Little, Brown & Co.

LeBon, G. (1913) *The Psychology of Revolutions*, New York: Putnam.

Moore, B., Jr. (1966) *Social Origins of Dictatorship and Democracy: Lord and Peasant in the Making of the Modern World*, Boston: Beacon Press.

Paige, J. (1975) *Agrarian Revolution*, New York: Free Press.

Pettee, G. S. (1938) *The Process of Revolution*, New York: Harper & Row.

Popkin, S. (1979) *The Rational Peasant: The Political Economy of Rural Society in Viet Nam*, Berkeley and Los Angeles: University of California Press.

Shugart, M. S. (1989) 'Patterns of revolution', *Theory and Society* 18: 249–71.

Skocpol, T. (1979) *States and Social Revolutions: A Comparative Analysis of France, Russia, and China*, Cambridge: Cambridge University Press.

Tilly, C. (1973) 'Does revolution breed modernization?', *Comparative Politics* 5: 425–47.

——(1978) *From Mobilization to Revolution*, Reading, Mass.: Addison-Wesley.

Trimberger, E. K. (1978) *Revolution from Above: Military Bureaucrats and Development in Japan, Turkey, Egypt, and Peru*, New Brunswick, NJ: Transaction Books.

Walton, J. (1984) *Reluctant Rebels: Comparative Studies of Revolution and Underdevelopment*, New York: Columbia University Press.

FURTHER READING

Adelman, J. R. (1985) *Revolution, Armies, and War: A Political History*, Boulder: Lynne Rienner.

Arjomand, S. A. (1986) 'Iran's Islamic revolution in comparative perspective', *World Politics* 38: 383–414.

Brinton, C. (1938) *The Anatomy of Revolution*, New York: Vintage (revised and expanded 1965).

Dix, R. (1983) 'Varieties of revolution', *Comparative Politics* 15: 281–93.

Goldstone, J. A. (ed.) (1986) *Revolutions: Theoretical, Comparative, and Historical Studies*, San Diego and New York: Harcourt Brace Jovanovich.

——(1991) *Revolution and Rebellion in the Early Modern World*, Berkeley and Los Angeles: University of California Press.

Goldstone, J. A., Gurr, T. R. and Moshiri, F. (eds) (1991) *Revolutions of the Late 20th Century*, Boulder, Colo.: Westview Press.

Moore, B., Jr. (1966) *Social Origins of Dictatorship and Democracy: Lord and Peasant in the Making of the Modern World*, Boston: Beacon Press.

Shugart, M. S. (1989) 'Patterns of revolution', *Theory and Society* 18: 249–71.

Skocpol, T. (1979) *States and Social Revolutions: A Comparative Analysis of France, Russia, and China*, Cambridge: Cambridge University Press.

Tilly, C. (1978) *From Mobilization to Revolution*, Reading, Mass.: Addison-Wesley.

Trimberger, E. K. (1978) *Revolution from Above: Military Bureaucrats and Development in Japan, Turkey, Egypt, and Peru*, New Brunswick, NJ: Transaction Books.

Walton, J. (1984) *Reluctant Rebels: Comparative Studies of Revolution and Underdevelopment*, New York: Columbia University Press.

67

TERRORISM

DAVID C. RAPOPORT

The concept of terrorism, as distinguished from the phenomenon, is associated with the origin of modern democracy. The word, originally French, became part of the English political language (1795) after the Reign of Terror. It meant a system of terror and referred to the activities of a government, i.e. 'government by intimidation', 'a policy intended to strike with terror those against whom it is adopted' (*Oxford English Dictionary*). A 'terrorist' implemented these activities.

Later the terms took on new meanings. By the 1890s a terrorist was a rebel who, in the tradition of the Russian *Narodnaya Volya* (the People's Will, 1879), attempted to destroy a system by assassinating its major office holders. Subsequent usage depended on the dominant concerns in particular periods. After the rise of the totalitarian states in the 1930s, terrorism most often referred to practices of those states, but by the 1950s it became identified almost exclusively with rebels again. State terrorism received some attention (Walter 1969; Dallin and Breslauer 1970; Rapoport 1982; Stohl and Lopez 1984), but rebel terrorism, the major focus here, still preoccupies academics.

The purpose and methods of the French Terror distinguished it from that of previous arbitrary governments. With regard to purpose, Robespierre proclaimed 'either virtue or the terror', meaning that monarchy had so corrupted France that terror had to be the midwife of democracy (Talmon 1970: 114). Similarly, *Narodnaya Volya* saw terror as the people's instrument, an emergency measure to create mass consciousness (Figner 1927).

The method of the French Terror was embodied in the practices of the 'Revolutionary Tribunals' ('People's Court'), which operated without rules. 'Enemies of the People' possessed 'impure hearts'; legal rules impeded understanding of motives. The fate of an 'Enemy of the People' was, moreover, a didactic lesson for the public, to show that the normal conception of guilt and innocence was irrelevant. Similarly, Russian terrorists chose their victims for 'symbolic' reasons, i.e. political effect, and understood too that their struggle could not be governed by any conceivable rules governing criminal or military activity.

Despite this tolerably clear initial characterization emphasizing both purpose and method, defining terrorism in recent years has become a serious issue. Schmid and Jongman (1988) discovered more than a hundred definitions, and Laqueur (1987), whose text is the most widely read, finds the question of an appropriate definition so vexing that he refuses to provide one! Many circumstances contribute to this confusion. There has been a multiplication of terrorist forms. More important, the experience with terror has given the term abusive connotations creating such political liabilities that now no one admits to being a terrorist. Earlier, terrorists proudly declared themselves as such, but the last group to describe itself this way was *Lehi* (the 'Stern Gang'), a participant in the fight for Israel's independence in the 1940s. Afterwards, rebels always characterized their enemies, the governments which opposed them, as such – a charge which sometimes had an element of truth, if only because in every struggle combatants tend to adopt similar tactics.

Immediately after the Second World War, terrorists struggling for independence against a colonial power were often called 'freedom fighters', even in the West. Later, in the public discourse of Third World and communist countries, the two terms became mutually exclusive, meaning in effect that no matter what methods rebels employed, they could not be terrorists if they struggled against Western influence, a position which greatly impeded international co-operation on the problem.

In the 1970s the media, apparently not wishing to be seen as blatantly partisan, corrupted the language further (Rapoport 1977). A common American convention was to describe identical persons in the same account alternatively as terrorists, guerrillas and soldiers. Similar inconsistencies plague academic accounts; noble causes may be pursued by terrorist means, but it is difficult to describe a group as terrorist if one sympathizes with its cause (Dugard 1988; Romanov 1990).

Credible, consistently applied, contemporary definitions focus on means and not purpose as the distinguishing criterion. The principal difference between definitions is that some distinguish terror as a distinctive form of violence while others minimize differences. Walter's study of Zulu state terror (Walter 1969) provided the most useful and influential account for the first group. Terror is extra-normal violence, one which goes beyond the informal and formal rules which govern coercion particularly in the explicit refusal to distinguish between combatants and non-combatants, guilty and innocent. The 'target' is not the victim, but the public as a whole. Thornton (1964), Hutchinson (1972), Rapoport (1977) and Schmid and Jongman (1988) had similar views. This definition conforms to conceptions the original terrorists had of themselves, provides a good way to link the various forms, and allows one to anticipate direction in terrorist activities. Objections are that it is too difficult to determine the meaning of 'extra-normal'.

In the second, less satisfactory view terrorism is synonymous with all forms of illegal rebel violence; hence, persons like George Washington and Robert E. Lee would be described as terrorists (Russell *et al.* 1979). Most legal definitions reflect this view, for instance those in the UK in 1974 and West Germany in 1985 (Schmid and Jongman 1988). Sympathy for some rebels is created inadvertently when the law refuses to acknowledge moral distinctions between acts of violence which the public recognizes (Rapoport 1988a).

HISTORY AND FORMS

No good history of terrorism exists; Schmid and Jongman's monumental study of the literature does not even list a history of the phenomenon. This absence reflects the conventional academic wisdom that terrorism dates from the 1960s, and is, hence, *sui generis*. If some recognize that modern terror derives from the late nineteenth-century Russians, virtually no attention is paid to rebel groups which existed earlier, nor to the relationships between movements in time.

Prior to the French Revolution, no secular principle of legitimacy could justify terror. Only religion had this power. Few studies of sacred terror exist. Rapoport (1984) compares groups from different religious traditions, the Assassins (Islam) during the eleventh to thirteenth centuries, the Zealots (Judaism) in the first century AD, and the Thugs (Hinduism) from the thirteenth to the nineteenth centuries, showing that despite reliance on primitive technologies, they were more destructive and durable than present-day secular terrorist groups. Their effectiveness depended on extraordinary commitment, organizational ingenuity, appropriate methods, and favourable public responses including international support.

Rebel secular terrorism was a feature of American history before the Russians made the world aware of terrorism. The barn-burnings and tar-and-feather mobs organized by the Sons of the American Revolution helped drive enormous numbers of suspected Loyalists from the country. The Ku Klux Klan used terror to force Federal troops to leave the South after the Civil War, frustrating the plans of the Radical Republicans. But the Americans did not try to explain their success or develop a logic for terror; they did their dirty work in secret and kept their 'mouths shut' afterwards.

The Russians (i.e. Nechaev 1971; Mozorov 1880; Stepniak 1883; and Kropotkin 1927) explained the logic of terror, described societies most vulnerable to it and indicated appropriate strategic principles. Their theory emerged out of debates on how to generate revolution when the traditional method, spontaneous mass uprisings, either would not work or emerged at times which made the process too costly and bloody (Mozorov 1880). Mass uprisings required clearly defined class hostilities, but modern society was characterized by latent and diffused tensions. How could one bring those tensions to the surface, and focus their expression towards the proper objects? Relying wholly on the written and spoken word was counter-productive, for the reputation of revolutionaries as 'idle word spillers' undermined credibility and self-respect. Bold, dramatic and heroic *action* demonstrating unconditional commitment would give revolutionaries belief in themselves, attract attention, excite admiration, draw followers, and infuse potential supporters with hope, the essential lubricant of revolution. 'Provocation' would produce the denouement. Terrorized officials would lash out indiscriminately against those it could not find, making the oppression of the masses so visible that a revolutionary insurrection would be inevitable (Nechaev 1971), or a government would be 'compelled for many years running, to neglect everything and to do nothing, but struggle with . . . [terrorists who] will render its position untenable' (Stepniak 1883: 257). Rapoport (1977: 46) characterizes this theory as 'a politics of atrocity', where atrocities are deliberately calculated to produce counter-atrocities redounding to the advantage of the original assailant. The original theory describes how to manipulate the emotions of an ambivalent, potentially sympathetic people while frightening a government and its supporters. It 'explains' how to kill and also how to die, often by explaining one's reasons in court, in order to extract maximum empathy. 'The terrorist is noble, terrible, irresistibly fascinating because he unites the two sublimities of human grandeur, the martyr and the hero' (Stepniak 1883: 39–40).

In the ancient sacred terrorist form, where dying also received intense attention, divine precedents always determined ends and usually means; humans lacked authority to alter either. In the secular form the group determines ends and means, altering them as the requirements of the situation dictate. This conception of secular terror has remained unchanged for a century. Secular terrorists have produced a 'culture' in which participants feel free to take their lessons from anyone, a tradition without binding precedents, one that caricatures a much-observed tendency in the larger society to subject all activities to standards of utility and efficiency. Striking features of this 'culture' are tendencies to expand the range of both means and ends.

Since the late nineteenth century there have been four major waves of terror, each closely connected to political turning-points which excited the hopes of potential terrorists, seemed to expose vulnerabilities of the establishment, and defined new issues. In each wave, at least three of four major rebel types appear: revolutionary, separatist, right wing and sacred.

The initial terror of the 1880s was precipitated by massive Russian reform efforts, exciting expectations which could not be fulfilled, and it ended with the assassination of the Austrian Archduke leading to the First World War.

Systematic assassination of highly placed officials, the principal strategy, served two major aims. In Russia and in Western Europe (via the Anarchists) the purpose was revolutionary. In the Ottoman Empire a separatist type (Federation of Armenian Revolutionaries, 1890, and Internal Macedonian Revolutionary Organization, 1893) seeking national independence emerged.

After the First World War a second wave began, reaching its climax after the Second World War. Separatists predominated, stimulated by a major war aim of the victors, national self-determination, an aim which unintentionally undermined the legitimacy of retaining colonial possessions. As Western colonial empires were dismantled and new states created (i.e. Ireland, Israel, Cyprus, Yemen and Algeria), the wave receded. Tactics included guerrilla-like actions with concealed weapons and without identifying insignia against troops, assassination campaigns against police forces, and often assaults against civilians.

A third wave in the late 1960s was intimately related to the Vietnam War. The effectiveness of Vietcong terror rejuvenated hopes that audacity could overwhelm modern technology. The war, moreover, severely undermined America's moral credibility, creating doubts among some NATO allies, and enabling groups elsewhere with a true indigenous grievance to attribute it to American 'imperialism', opinions encouraged by the Soviet bloc. The Revolutionary ethos, largely absent in the second wave, re-emerged in the Marxist-Anarchist (i.e. 'counter-culture') groups, such as Weather Underground (United States), Red Army Fraction (Germany), Red Brigades (Italy), Tupamaros (Uruguay), Montoneros (Argentina) and Direct Action (France). Separatist groups often had revolutionary elements too; but compared to the ethnic base, they played a subsidiary role, i.e. the Basque Nation and Liberty (ETA – Euzakadi ta Azakatsuna; Spain), the Armenian Secret Army for the Liberation of Armenia, and Northern Ireland. When the Vietnam war ended, the Palestine Liberation Organization (PLO), a confederation which contains revolutionary and separatist groups, but also has so many unique elements it defies classification, replaced the Vietcong as the heroic model for European terrorists (Baumann 1977). The PLO itself developed in the aftermath of the Six Day War when the extraordinary collapse of Arab armies gave credibility to those arguing that terror was the only remaining alternative.

International support materialized in every modern terrorist wave, and was the indispensable ingredient for the successes achieved in the second wave. But in the third wave the term 'international terrorism' was coined, suggesting a significant transformation (Rapoport 1988a). For the first time some groups conducted most assaults abroad; the PLO, and related groups, were often more active in Europe than European groups were. Even national groups operating locally sought targets with international significance, and attacks on Americans outside the United States were especially common. Different national groups and teams composed of separate nationals co-operated for attacks in third countries (i.e. the Munich Olympics 1972; the kidnapping of Ministers of the Organization for Petroleum Exporting Countries, Vienna 1975; Entebbe 1976; and Mogadishu 1977). Airline hijacking was introduced and it symbolized the international character of this wave, for the tactic requires secure foreign landing fields.

The rather visible physical support given a variety of groups by various states, especially Libya, Syria and Iraq, gave rise to the term 'state-sponsored terror'. The third wave began receding as victimized states developed co-operative mechanisms, the Israeli invasion of Lebanon (1982) deprived the PLO of facilities used to train foreign terrorist groups, and the disintegration of the Soviet bloc occurred.

A third type of rebel terror, often called right wing, and normally generated in reaction to revolutionary and separatist groups, became conspicuous in this period. Earlier counterparts existed in the Russian pogroms (first wave) and the Secret Army Organization (OAS) of French colonists in Algeria (second wave). They are distinctive because they usually shun publicity, and sometimes governments, particularly police and military personnel, have contributed direct support. Arguably, the most important have been neo-Fascist Italian groups (i.e. the New Order, the National Vanguard) which have caused more casualties and been more indiscriminate than their better-known revolutionary counterparts (Weinberg and Eubank 1989). In Latin America they often took the form of anonymous 'death squads' (as in El Salvador) which drew up extensive assassination lists, lists which included *inter alia* many persons 'too critical' of government. Some identified themselves, i.e. Communist Hunting Command (Brazil), and Secret Anti-Communist Army (Guatemala). The Grey Wolves plagued Turkey, and in Spain the Apostolic Anti-Communist Alliance operated. Northern Ireland has the Protestant Ulster Defence Association (UDA).

Religious elements were often present in earlier cases (i.e. Macedonia, Cyprus, Israel, Algeria, Northern Ireland); but in the fourth wave a new form of sacred terror, where tactics and targets are shaped by religious precedents, emerged primarily in the Third World (Rapoport 1990). The fourth wave began in the mid-1970s and became truly conspicuous after the successful 1979 Iranian Revolution. Compared to those of preceding waves the attacks were particularly brutal and deadly (Hoffman 1989). Encouraged by Iran, Shia terror materialized in neighbouring Middle Eastern states with large Shia populations, and less significantly in Europe. A novel feature was suicide bombing against Western targets in Lebanon (the importance of accepting death had largely disappeared in the third wave).

Sunni terrorists were also active, i.e the storming of the Grand Mosque in Mecca (1979) and Egyptian President Sadat's assassination (1981). Sunni terror has also shaken Syria, Tunisia, Morocco, Algeria, the Philippines,

Indonesia and other states. Outside Islam, Sikh terrorists seek a separate religious state in the Punjab. Religious differences between Hindus and Buddhists justify a persistent and extraordinarily bloody struggle in Sri Lanka. Jewish sacred terrorists have attempted to blow up a sacred Islamic site, the Dome of the Rock in Jerusalem, and waged a campaign against Palestinian mayors. Christianity produced examples also, particularly in the United States (Barkun 1989).

Initially, only the idea of a perfect society, or a total revolution, could be powerful enough to justify extra-normal violence or attacks on the unarmed or innocent – a politics of atrocity. But today virtually all contemporary states experience terrorism; and a vast array of groups, other than the four major types, employ terror. Their common sentiment is a strong feeling about the lack of attention to alleged injustices. Terror is used even by groups organized around a 'single issue', such as abortion, animal rights, environmentalism or 'guest workers', the last being particularly significant in Western Europe. Private persons with personal concerns have followed suit.

Underground violent groups are small. Few terrorist groups number more than fifty; and for each member four to six persons outside are required to provide essential logistic support. At their peaks, effective groups like the Irgun, the National Organization of Cypriot Struggle for Union with Greece (EOKA – *Ethniki Organosis Kypriakou Agonos*), the Irish Republican Army (IRA) and ETA had between 200 and 400 members. The Montoneros, who in the Argentine chaos operated openly, used over 1,500 members in operations during 1974. The PLO in Lebanon before the Israeli invasion numbered 25,000, but no other terrorist organization has ever been allowed to operate so freely, and much of its energy was consumed by an effort to establish a regular army.

Modern terrorist organizations, in contrast to their ancient counterparts, do not survive long. Perhaps as many as 90 per cent last less than a year. Nearly half of those which persist beyond the first year are out of existence by the tenth. On the other hand, successor groups generally continue the struggle, and some groups endure for generations: the IRA and the PLO have operated for over seventy and thirty-five years, respectively. Durability depends upon a constituency to supply the constant need for new recruits or secure foreign sanctuaries.

On the whole, terrorists fight a 'poor person's war'; but larger, more durable organizations increasingly need significant sums. Fund are 'expropriated' in bank robberies, forced donations, ransoms, protection rackets and services. A much larger source of income is derived from private parties and foreign states; in the case of the PLO, legitimate investments are crucial (Adams 1986).

The only demonstrable common characteristic of active terrorists is that they are young; very few reach the age of thirty. The reasons are obvious. The activity attracts persons at the peak of their physical strength, individuals with enormous enthusiasm, little patience, and willing to take great risks. Beyond that, attrition rates are very high.

Males predominate, but revolutionary groups attract many females; Vera Figner was the second commander of *Narodnaya Volya*, women dominated the Weather Underground and the Red Army Fraction, and 40 per cent of the Tupamaros in its final stage were women (Knight 1979; Lopes-Alves 1989; Weinberg and Eubank 1989). In right-wing groups and in those separatist organizations which lack a revolutionary component, women are insignificant.

Initially, the Russian terrorists were middle-class university students; over time the social composition diversified to approximate society more as a whole, though minor national groups, especially Jews and Poles, had disproportionate influence (Naimark 1990). Insufficient data prevent a conclusive picture, but a similar pattern appears in later revolutionary terrorist groups, although minority influence is not so great, and middle-class student predominance is less marked in the early phase of separatist and right-wing groups. Weinberg and Eubank (1989) discovered that the social profiles of leaders and followers in the Italian revolutionary and right-wing terrorist groups resemble those of left- and right-wing parties. Although information on contemporary sacred terror groups is sparse, social profiles seem to vary greatly with particular contexts. In Egypt, middle-class university students with technological interests are highly represented (Ibrahim 1980); but in Lebanon and Iran, the poor led by religious clerics predominate (Taheri 1987). Women generally play no role.

EFFECTS

Terrorists enjoy so few successes and inflict so few casualties that some (Falk 1988) argue that the terrorist problem is insignificant. Although the overall impact is quite difficult to gauge, this view is ill-considered. Some obvious effects can be measured precisely, like the cost of airport surveillance, which has become an omnipresent feature of our lives. Other important features are scarcely known and not easily measured when identified; for example, most undercover police forces (i.e. Russian Okhrana, the Federal Bureau of Investigation, Scotland Yard, etc.) were created initially to cope with terrorist threats.

In discussing effects, one must distinguish immediate victims and the various political audiences, systems and policies influenced. Intended consequences must be separated from unintended ones in both the short and long run. An estimate of effects must distinguish those where terror is the principal tactic, as in the case of the *Narodnaya Volya*, from those where it is either part of a larger, comprehensively organized political and military effort, as in Vietnam, or a tactic of one group for an objective that independent, competing groups struggle for too (for example, the Irgun). In every case, the alternatives must be considered too. No systematic discussion of effects exist; the most one can provide here are illustrations and general observations.

Only victims, largely with regard to their mental anguish, have been seriously studied. Statistical information on attacks is inadequate; cumulative figures are available only for international incidents since 1968. The statistics for domestic terror, which is many times deadlier for particular states than for the entire international scene, are unevenly collected, and often countries which have the most victims (such as Peru and Sri Lanka) keep the least reliable statistics.

Different data sources employ different definitions; consequently, the gross numbers for international terror vary widely (Jongman 1992; Weinberg and Davis 1989). Still, the data bases reveal common patterns. Western Europe is the geographical locale of most attacks, followed by the Middle East and Latin America. As in the nineteenth century, the overwhelming number of assaults involve bombings. Over 40 per cent involve property, 20 per cent involve attempts to kill persons, and 10 per cent involve kidnapping and hostage taking. More than half of the victims are government officials – mostly diplomats – and one-third represent business interests. Approximately one-third are Americans (since the 1960s the United States has had virtually no domestic terror), with the Israelis, French and British (who experience local terror problems) far behind in that order. American casualties average 350 annually, and an American is as likely to die from an animal bite (Rapoport 1988a) and more likely to be hurt taking a bath (Falk 1988)!

The real aim, however, is to produce public effects, and striking terrorist successes do exist. When they have a national base distinctly different from that of the government, and the major participating parties define the situation as colonial, terrorist activity has sometimes helped to establish new states.

When the dominant community does not perceive itself as a colonial power, terrorists achieve more limited results even when their organization commands serious international support. A United Nations Observer status for the PLO and recognition by many states that it represented the Palestinians were significant achievements, though ultimately frustrating ones in the light of its ambitious objectives. However, the special status that the German-speaking Trento-Alto-Adige region achieved in northern Italy in the 1960s disarmed the terrorists. In the hopes of satisfying or defusing ETA, Spain has given the Basques greater regional autonomy, a concession which has led some to lay down their arms and may ultimately bring peace.

The theory of terror was 'invented' by revolutionary groups, but without a distinct nationalist or ethnic base they always fail, as Latin American experiences in the 1970s and those in Europe in the 1980s demonstrate (Hewitt 1990). Revolutionary terrorists have altered political landscapes decisively, but not in ways intended. Tsarist efforts to reform Russia, and perhaps create a parliamentary government, were abandoned. In the wake of Tupamaro attacks, a Uruguayan military junta (1974) took over the 'Switzerland of Latin America'. Similarly, Argentine (1976) and Turkish armies (1980) aborted fresh attempts at democratic government. In all four cases, the terrorists were destroyed.

Terrorist activity normally hardens its essential nationalist constituency, creating willy-nilly even greater gaps between neighbouring ethnic groups, often making it impossible either to achieve the larger objective sought or to live with the more limited alternative achieved. EOKA, by eliminating British rule, hoped to consummate a union with Greece. It accepted an independent Cyprus (1952) as the only entity that frightened Turkish Cypriots would tolerate; but the hatreds and anxieties that EOKA atrocities had exacerbated has made a single state for that island impossible so far. In Algeria the fear of the European population was so great that flight was the only solution. PLO terror tactics achieved something, but the distrust evoked is a major, perhaps insuperable, obstacle for gaining more. Two decades of Provisional IRA terror has made the Protestant majority in Northern Ireland only more implacable.

In the international world, terrorist activity generally creates and exacerbates tensions between states. The most dramatic example is the assassination of the Austrian Archduke Ferdinand, which precipitated the First World War, transforming the political maps of Europe and the world. The issue was the extent of Serbian involvement, an issue which may always be raised when borders are crossed, even when the terrorists act wholly on their own. In the wake of President Kennedy's assassination the American government's most pressing problem was to convince its people that no foreign power was implicated. The Israeli–Egyptian War (1956) and the Six Day War (1967) were occasioned partly by terrorist raids, and the Israeli invasion of Lebanon (1982) was justified as a response to the attempted assassination of an Israeli diplomat in Britain. Iraq cited Shia terrorist attacks to justify war against Iran in 1980. The American raid on Libya (1986) was a direct response to a series of terrorist attacks implicating the Libyan government. In the same decade Britain severed diplomatic relations with Syria and Libya for sponsoring terrorism on British soil, France broke with Iran when Iran refused to let its embassy members be interrogated, the United States broke with Iran when fifty-two members of the American embassy staff were taken hostage in 1979, and the Iranian encouragement of Shia groups in Lebanon to hold Europeans and Americans hostage intensified tensions between Iran and the West. In the wake of the Gulf War, Iran decided that a more desirable relationship required that it use its considerable influence to get the Lebanese hostages released (1991).

Even friendly states find that terrorism creates frictions between them. France has refused to extradite some PLO, Red Brigade and ETA suspects to West Germany, Italy and Spain. Italy spurned an American request for the alleged organizer of the seizure of the *Achille Lauro* by Palestinian terrorists in 1985; and, in its turn, the United States refused British requests concerning IRA suspects. Such events will continue to occur as long as the laws and interests of separate states do not coincide.

Using foreign terrorists as surrogates in the international sphere for acts a state is otherwise too weak to undertake is enticing but rarely productive. Only Iran and Syria acting jointly have been successful in a strategic sense, and then only in one country, Lebanon (1984), where after a series of dramatic suicide attacks the multinational forces withdrew. In that unusual case, the sponsors hid their involvement well, local elements were deeply committed and the confused objectives of the multinational forces had little support. Normally surrogates are unreliable, because they have their own agenda and eventually may expose the sponsoring state to retaliation at the enemy's discretion (Wardlaw 1988). The limited power of the state-sponsored international terror is indicated also by the failure of Iraq to use it during the Gulf War, despite widespread predictions that Saddam Hussein would. Had he done so, bringing him to trial for war crimes would have been an objective of the war.

International state-encouraged terror can create enormous domestic problems for other states. Hostages held by the Iranians after the Shah escaped to the United States humiliated President Carter and caused, as spectacular terrorist acts always do, excessive and harmful obsessions with the issue. Carter's crisis management probably wrecked his bid for re-election in 1980. In the complicated Iran–Contra Affair, precipitated by efforts to get hostages in Lebanon released, the Reagan administration nearly unravelled, but the hostage holders did not benefit from these events.

CONDITIONS

The explosion of rebel terrorism in the 1960s surprised everyone, and no scholarly consensus emerged to explain it, in part because counter-terrorist tactics received most attention, few agreed on the definition of the phenomenon, and good hard data was sparse. Three explanations for the explosion, however, are favoured. These explanations may be offered singly or in combination. The 'technological theory' saw terrorism as a by-product of innovations in transportation, weapons and communication technologies that make it easier and cheaper to travel, find and destroy targets, and transmit messages quickly to large numbers (Kupperman and Trent 1979; Ketcham and McGeorge 1986). Psychological explanations treated terrorists as abnormal personalities with identifiable character traits. The conspiratorial theory (Possony and Bouchay 1978; Sterling 1981) explained terrorism as a Cold War product, a Soviet-inspired and Soviet-organized 'surrogate war'. The conspiratorial theory grossly underestimated the strength of local autonomy and concerns, the psychological theory became more and more inadequate as the data accumulated (Russell and Miller 1977; Hubbard 1971; Crenshaw 1981; Taylor 1988). All three theories betrayed little interest in the history of terrorism and its associated political circumstances, the best context for testing their propositions.

Undeniably, features of the modern world since the 1960s influenced terrorist practices. But a truly political account would see it as part of the French revolutionary tradition, a constituent feature of our political life for two centuries. In specific periods, different methods (mass uprisings, terrorism, *coups d'état* and guerrilla wars) have supplanted each other as the magic tool for successful revolution (Billington 1980).

Certain conceptions bequeathed by the French Revolution had their influence. In separating the conception of the sovereign, the 'People', from the institutions designed to embody it, the rebel's claim to represent the 'People' was always conceivable and, to some, often credible. Moreover, the Revolution 'promised' that a perfect world was possible by remaking social institutions, which in effect created 'guilt' when injustice was pointed out. At the minimum, these themes could create serious ambivalences in the community, leading often to indecision and, hence, to potential terrorist advantage.

Domestic terrorist activity occurs most often in states that are already democratic, states that are moving towards democracy, and states that have suddenly arrested a significant move towards democracy. The most oppressive states may contain the most injustices, but they also destroy the hope terrorists require. In Russia, rebel terror began after dramatic reforms, it ceased after an attempt on Lenin provoked savage repression, and 'incidents' auspiciously began again after the introduction of *perestroika*.

Total war was a by-product of the French Revolution. The crucial but quite artificial distinctions between combatants and non-combatants, and between permissible and impermissible military methods, became precarious when the life of the community was at stake – the justification for war that states depending on universal conscription require. After 1945 the implications of this transformation were visible for the first time in peace, embodied in terrifying weapons of mass destruction. The rules of combat inhibited earlier rebels; now they are less compelling, and, ironically, the actions terrorists cite for authority are those which democratic states take when they go to war!

The 'right' to use terror, moreover, is claimed as an entitlement of the 'weak', a startling perversion of democratic egalitarianism. Hence, the rebel who is understood to be weak normally 'claims responsibility' for acts of terror while states that are understood as being 'strong' normally conceal reponsibility. When states acknowledge terror practices, they are in the initial phase of a revolutionary take-over, a point at which states are known to be weak.

The concern for the sanctity of life is another feature of the democratic state, one that conflicts with the propensity to total war. In placing a high premium on the lives of hostages, for example, democratic states become vulnerable in ways that other states are not. Iraq found, for example, that Iran would not negotiate for .hostages and took no more. Lebanese Maronites, likewise, stopped taking Shia hostages after 1986. The tactical success of terrorists depends upon abilities to turn the antagonists' moral strength into political weakness.

Ever since *Narodnaya Volya* recognized the importance of the press, terrorists have struggled to dominate the communications network. Opportunities are maximized in democratic states because the public finds terrorist activity interesting and the media are generally free to satisfy that interest. For sixteen days in July 1985, some 65 per cent of national TV coverage in the United States was concerned with the hijacking of TWA Flight 847, and between 1981 and 1986 terrorism received more national TV attention than poverty, unemployment and crime combined (Martin and Walcott 1988; Atwater 1987; Weimann and Winn unpublished).

COUNTER-TERRORIST POLICIES

There may be no 'solutions' to terrorism without altering contemporary perceptions of legitimacy. But the ebb and flow of terrorist activity and the rise and fall of particular movements indicate that specific conditions and particular public responses are pertinent.

Terrorism normally combines criminal and political (or religious) activity with a mode of warfare. As a highly peculiar phenomenon, it eludes ordinary conceptual categories. Terrorists cannot be treated as soldiers because they reject traditional military norms. Yet in regarding terrorists simply as criminals, one sometimes creates martyrs. Focusing exclusively on the political question is unrealistic; the precedents set by the terror for other groups cannot be ignored and political demands often cannot be met without generating terror from those who oppose them (for example, Northern Ireland). Sometimes there is simply no ability to meet stated demands (for example, the demand for the Netherlands to create a South Moluccan state). Yet all three categories may be relevant, and in particular cases either the first or the second has considerably more weight.

Governments often make concessions initially, especially when hostages are involved, but each succeeding instance strengthens support for policies of breaking terrorist organizations via carrot-and-stick methods. Administrations obtain enlarged surveillance powers and special pardon powers for those who repent and help. The assumptions are that terrorists have exploitable ambivalences and that the pool of potential recruits is exhaustible (Hewitt 1984).

For domestic terror groups, especially revolutionary and right-wing ones with minimal international support, these assumptions often are appropriate; and Italian experiences with the Red Brigades and neo-Fascist groups provide strikingly successful illustrations. But separatist groups, especially those with important international resources, require more political attention.

Enlarging police powers can be costly. Sympathies for the terrorists may result. Yet democratic governments unable to use the powers needed have been overthrown by military forces more determined to 'get on with the job'. In every case, the enlargement of powers is at the expense of traditional civil liberties, and the question is always whether powers taken will be restored or whether other uses will be found for them.

A matter of special concern ever since the early Russian experiences has been the media's role in encouraging terrorist activity. British Prime Minister Margaret Thatcher said that publicity was the oxygen terrorists need. The unhealthy tendencies of democratic governments to become preoccupied with terrorist incidents and to make policy promises they cannot keep partly reflects pressures which media preoccupation with terrorists create. Media restrictions have been imposed often, even in the most genuinely liberal states like Britain. Yet the media, as terrorists themselves stress, affect groups adversely too. Unflattering portraits of persons and causes are painted. Media opportunities distract terrorists from more important questions. If media coverage helps multiply the number of terrorist groups, it also helps shorten their life expectancy.

Significant international support enables some terrorist movements to succeed. On the other hand, groups normally go to the international sphere to compensate for serious domestic weaknesses; and often that decision compounds their weakness, making them dependent on forces with distinctly different, often conflicting, interests (Rapoport 1988a).

Particular groups, like the Kurds and South Moluccans, may find the international environment hostile, but others will always find support because sovereign states have separate interests, and different traditions of political dissent. Three basic ways to deal with terrorism on the international level more effectively exist; changing the law, better co-operation in enforcing the law, and reprisals.

Attempts to change crucial rules exempting political offences have a long history. Assassination attempts against heads of state were held to be criminal not political acts in the mid-nineteenth century, and in the 1890s two influential British court decisions limited the exemption further. The League of Nations (1937) drafted two striking conventions establishing an international court with jurisdiction over all international terrorism cases; but war broke out before the conventions went into effect.

Since 1970 many bilateral, regional and UN agreements affecting aircraft, diplomats, hostages and the transportation of nuclear materials have been concluded. Only those regulating hijacking have clearly made a difference, helping to reduce the number of incidents enormously since the high-point in the late 1960s and early 1970s. Increased difficulties in hijacking may, ironically, have promoted a tendency to destroy aircraft in flight (Air India, mid-Atlantic, 1985, and Pan Am, Lockerbie, 1988).

Since the nineteenth century, police forces have intermittently and informally co-operated. The dramatic upsurge in Middle Eastern terrorism in Europe in the mid-1980s created an impetus for formal mechanisms to transmit information regularly through Interpol (which has 142 member states). In 1986, TREVI (*terrorisme, radicalisme, extrémisme et la violence internationale* – the 1975 European Community system of informal consultations between ministers of the interior on matters pertaining to extradition and prosecution) established a formal permanent body.

Ever since sacred terror groups emerged long ago, the willingness of foreign states to allow or provide terrorists with sanctuaries, training facilities and logistic support has produced reprisals. Normally, aggrieved states act alone, and sometimes their response is overwhelming. When in the nineteenth century everything else failed to stop the Thugs, the British incorporated hitherto independent Hindu states into British India. Significantly, no international reaction materialized. However, political considerations limit the military options of twentieth-century states. Rescue operations like Entebbe (1976) and Mogadishu (1977) are generally acceptable, but punitive reprisal raids are less so. During the Algerian war when France attacked FLN (*Front de Liberation National*) bases in Tunisia and Morocco, adverse international reactions made the raids counter-productive. Israeli raids in Egypt, Jordan and Syria deprived the PLO of its bases. The tactic was much less successful in Lebanon, and because the bases were deliberately placed in refugee camps the attacks incurred a difficult-to-estimate cost in world opinion.

Multinational sanctions have been rare, but the 1986 US air raid against Libya received British aid and was followed by a European Community arms embargo. Libya subsequently seemed to reduce its involvement with terrorist clients or at least reduce the more overt signs of that connection, a decision forced also because Libyan diplomats and students were expelled by European governments and Libya became increasingly isolated in the Arab world. Evidence that Libyan officials were involved in the Pan-Am Lockerbie crash (1988) led a unanimous UN Security Council to demand Libya extradite the suspects (1992). The step was wholly unprecedented in UN history and signifies perhaps a new era of internatonal co-operation against terrorism.

Although various states have imposed measures against individual state sponsors, no consistent policy of serious sanctions against *all* identified sponsors has been followed, not even by the United States whose citizens have been attacked most often, and even though, in 1980, then Secretary of State Alexander Haig described terrorism as the United States' most important international problem (Rappoport 1982). Clearly, other concerns and interests are more important.

Terrorism will remain a feature of our political landscape indefinitely, though we cannot forecast its ebb and flow. The transformation of the Soviet bloc is one more great political watershed in terrorist history, but its significance is unclear. The importance of the 'spontaneous mass insurrection' has been revived, and the extensive Soviet support given to international terrorist groups will vanish. But it is also true that appetites evoked by the reforms are unsatisfied, and a potentiality for many new separatist movements, which normally produce the most tenacious terrorist groups, exists.

The most frequently voiced anxiety about the future concerns the possibility of terrorists employing weapons of mass destruction. The possibility cannot be ruled out, but so far the desire to win public support has been a major inhibition and one that is likely to persist (Hoffman and de Leon 1986; Simon 1989).

REFERENCES

Adams, J. (1986) *The Financing of Terror*, New York: Simon & Schuster.

Atwater, T. (1987) 'Network evening news coverage of the TWA hostage crisis', *Journalism Quarterly* 64: 25–52.

Barkun, M. (1989) 'Millenarian aspects of "white supremacist" movements', *Terrorism and Political Violence* 1 (4): 409–34.

Baumann, M. (1977) *Terror or Love*, New York: Grove.

Billington, J. (1980) *Fire in the Minds of Men: Origins of the Revolutionary Faith*, New York: Basic Books.

Crenshaw, M. (1981) 'The causes of terrorism', *Comparative Politics* 13 (4): 379–97.

——(1986) 'The psychology of political terrorism', in M. Hermann (ed.) *Political Psychology*, San Francisco: Jossey-Bass.

Dallin, A. and Breslauer, G. (1970) *Political Terror in Communist Systems*, Stanford, Calif.: Stanford University Press.

Dugard, J. (1988) 'International terrorism and the just war', in D. C. Rapoport and Y. Alexander (eds) *The Morality of Terrorism*, 2nd edn, New York: Columbia University Press.

Falk, R. (1988) 'The overall terrorist challenge in international political life', in H. Kochler (ed.) *Terrorism and National Liberation*, Frankfurt: Peter Lang.

Figner, V. (1927) *Memoires of a Revolutionist*, New York: International Publishers.

Hewitt, C. (1984) *The Effectiveness of Anti-Terrorist Policies*, New York: University Press of America.

——(1990) 'Terrorism and public opinion: a five country comparison', *Terrorism and Political Violence* 2 (2): 145–70.

Hoffman, B. (1989) 'The contrasting ethical foundations of terrorism in the 1980s', *Terrorism and Political Violence* 1 (3): 360–77.

Hoffman, B. and de Leon, P. *et al.* (1986) *A Reassessment of Potential Adversaries to US Nuclear Programs*, Santa Monica, Calif.: Rand Corporation, R3363–DOE.

Hubbard, D. G. (1971) *The Skyjacker: His Flights of Fancy*, New York: Macmillan.

Ibrahim, S. (1980) 'Anatomy of Egypt's militant Islamic groups: methodological note and preliminary findings', *International Journal of Middle East Studies* 12: 423–53.

Jongman, A. J. (1992) 'Trends in international and domestic terrorism in Western Europe, 1968–1988', in *Terrorism and Political Violence* IV (forthcoming).

Ketcham, C. and McGeorge, H. (1986) 'Terrorism violence, its mechanisms and countermeasures', in N. Livington and T. Arnold (eds) *Fighting Back: Winning the War Against Terrorism*, Lexington, Mass.: Lexington Books.

Knight, A. (1979) 'Female terrorists in the Russian revolutionary party', *Russian Review* 38 (2): 139–59.

Kropotkin, P. (1927) *Revolutionary Pamphlets*, New York: Benjamin Blom.

Kupperman, R. and Trent, D. (eds) (1979) *Terrorism, Threat, Reality, Response*, Stanford: Hoover Press.

Laqueur, W. (1987) *The Age of Terrorism*, Boston: Little, Brown & Co.

Lopez-Alves, F. (1989) 'Political crises, strategic choices, and terrorism: the rise and fall of the Uruguayan Tupamaros', *Terrorism and Political Violence* 1 (2): 202–41.

Martin, D. and Walcott, J. (1988) *Best Laid Plans*, New York: Harper & Row.

Mozorov, N. (1880) *Terroristic Struggle*, London.

Naimark, N. (1990) 'Terrorism and the fall of imperial Russia', *Terrorism and Political Violence* 2 (2): 171–92.

Nechaev, S. (1971) 'The revolutionary catechism', reprinted in D. C. Rapoport, *Assassination and Terrorism*, Toronto: CBC.

Possony, S. T. and Bouchay, L. F. (1978) *International Terrorism, the Communist Connection, with a Case Study of West Germany Terrorist Ulrike Meinoff*, Washington, DC: American Council for World Freedom.

Rapoport, D. C. (1971) *Assassination and Terrorism*, Toronto: CBC.

——(1977) 'The politics of atrocity', in Y. Alexander and S. M. Finger (eds) *Terrorism: Interdisciplinary Perspectives*, New York: John Jay Press, pp. 46–59.

——(1982) 'State terror', Part 2, in D. C. Rapoport and Y. Alexander (eds) *The Morality of Terrorism*, New York: Pergamon, pp. 127–216.

——(1984) 'Fear and trembling: terror in three religious traditions', *American Political Science Review* 3: 658–77.

——(ed.) (1988a) *Inside Terrorist Organizations*, New York: Columbia University Press.

——(1988b) 'Messianic sanctions for terror', *Comparative Politics* 20 (2): 195–213.

——(1990) 'Sacred terror: a contemporary example from Islam', in W. Reich (ed.) *The Origins of Terrorism: Psychologies, Ideologies, Theologies, States of Mind*, Cambridge: Cambridge University Press.

Romanov, V. A. (1990) 'The United Nations and the problem of combatting international terrorism', *Journal of Terrorism and Political Violence* 2 (3): 289–304.

Russell, C. A. and Miller, B. H. (1977) 'Profile of a terrorist', *Terrorism* 1 (1): 17–34.

Russell, C. A. Banker, L. J. and Miller, B. H. (1979) 'Out-inventing the terrorist', in Y. Alexander, D. Carlton and P. Wilkinson (eds) *Terrorism: Theory and Practice*, Boulder, Colo.: Westview Press, pp. 3–42

Schmid, A. P. and Jongman, A. J. *et al.* (1988) *Political Terrorism: A New Guide to Actors, Authors, Concepts, Data Bases and Literature*, 2nd edn, New York: North-Holland.

Simon, J. D. (1989) *Terrorists and the Potential Use of Biological Weapons*, Santa Monica, Calif.: Rand Corporation, R-3771 – AFMIC.

Stepniak. S. (1892) *Underground Russia*, New York: Charles Scribner's Sons.

Sterling, C. (1981) *The Terror Network*, New York: Holt Rinehart.

Stohl, M. and Lopez, G. (eds) (1984) *The State as Terrorist*, Westport, Conn.: Greenwood Press.

Taheri, A. (1987) *Holy Terror: Inside the World of Islamic Terrorism*, Bethesda, Md.: Adler & Adler.

Talmon, J. L. (1970) *The Origins of Totalitarian Democracy*, New York: Norton.

Taylor, M. (1988) *The Terrorist*, London: Pergamon Brassey.

Thornton, T. P. (1964) 'Terror as a weapon of political agitation', in H. Eckstein (ed.) *Internal War*, New York: Free Press.

Walter, E. V. (1969) *Terror and Resistance*, New York: Oxford University Press.

Wardlaw, G. (1982) *Political Terrorism: Theory Tactics and Counter-Measures*, Cambridge: Cambridge University Press.

——(1988) 'Terror as an instrument of foreign policy', in D. C. Rapoport (ed.) *Inside Terrorist Organizations*, New York: Columbia University Press.

Weimann, G. and Winn, C. (unpublished) *The Theatre of Terror: The Mass Media and International Terrorism*.

Weinberg, L. B. and Davis, P. B. (1989) *Introduction to Political Terrorism*, New York: McGraw-Hill.

Weinberg, L. B. and Eubank, W. (1987) *The Rise and Fall of Italian Terrorism*, Boulder, Colo.: Westview Press.

——(1989) 'Leaders and followers in Italian terrorist groups', *Terrorism and Political Violence* 1 (2): 156–78.

Wilkinson, P. (1983) *The New Fascists*, London: Pan.

FURTHER READING

Finn, J. (1978) 'Public support for emergency (anti-terrorist) legislation in Northern Ireland', *Terrorism* 10 (2): 113–24.

Gal-Or, N. (1985) *International Cooperation to Suppress Terrorism*, New York: St Martin's Press.

Gaucher, R. (1968) *The Terrorists*, London: Secker & Warburg.

Hardman, J. B. (1934) 'Terrorism', in E.R.A. Seligman and A. Johnson (eds) *Encyclopaedia of the Social Sciences*, Vol. 14, London: Macmillan, pp. 575–80.

Hutchinson, C. M. (1972) 'The concept of revolutionary terrorism', *Journal of Conflict Resolution* 16 (3): 383–95.

——(1978) *Revolutionary Terrorism*, Stanford: Hoover Institution.

Israeli, R. (ed.) (1983) *PLO In Lebanon: Selected Documents*, London: Weidenfeld & Nicolson.

Jaszi, O. and Lewis, J. (1967) *Against the Tyrant*, Glencoe: Free Press.

Jenkins, B. M. (1975) *International Terrorism: A New Mode of Conflict*, Los Angeles: Crescent Press.

Lewis, B. (1967) *The Assassins: A Radical Sect in Islam*, New York: Oxford University Press.

Lodge, J. (ed.) (1981) *Terrorism: A Challenge to the State*, New York: St Martin's Press.

Merkl, P. (ed.) (1986) *Political Violence and Terror*, Berkeley: University of California Press.

Miller, A. (ed.) (1982) *Terrorism, the Media and the Law*, Dobbs Ferry, NY: Transnational Publishers.

Mommsen, W. and Hirschfeld, G. (eds) (1982) *Social Protest, Violence and Terror in Nineteenth and Twentieth Century Europe*, New York: St Martin's Press.

O'Brien, C. C. (1986) *The Siege*, New York: Simon & Schuster.

Pacifici, R. and Wagner, E. (1986) *The Moro Morality Play*, Chicago: University of Chicago Press.

Rubinstein, R. E. (1987) *Alchemists of Revolution*, New York: Basic Books.

Venturi, F. (1960) *Roots of Revolution*, New York: Knopf.

Walzer, M. (1977) *Just and Unjust Wars*, New York: Basic Books.

Wilkinson, P. (1979) *Terrorism and the Liberal State*, 2nd edn, London: Macmillan.

Wright, R. (1986) *Sacred Rage: The Wrath of Militant Islam*, New York: Simon & Schuster.

PART X

MAJOR ISSUES IN CONTEMPORARY WORLD POLITICS

68

SUPERPOWER RELATIONS SINCE 1945

MIKE BOWKER

The superpower relationship since 1945 has been an area of considerable academic debate. This essay will concentrate on two areas which have elicited most attention: namely the course and causes of the US–Soviet rivalry. To do this, the following analysis has been divided into three sections: the Cold War, 1945–62; competitive co-existence, 1962–89; and co-operative co-existence, 1989 to the present day. The aim of this subdivision is to emphasize the progression – albeit, very unsteady – towards an improved US–Soviet relationship.

THE COLD WAR 1945–62

There are different definitions of the Cold War. The one adopted here is a general one: the existence of high East–West tension with the threat of an escalation to direct superpower conflict. According to this definition, the Cold War is taken up to 1962 and the Cuban Missile Crisis, the time when the world came closest to nuclear war. Thereafter, the level of tension has varied, but the threat of superpower conflict has declined fairly steadily. Since 1962, superpower competition has found expression through the arms race and proxy wars in the Third World.

There are three main explanations for the origins of the Cold War: the Western orthodox view (Schlesinger 1967); the revisionist view (Williams 1962) and the Soviet view (Sivachev and Yakovlev 1979), which are here taken together; and the post-revisionist view (Gaddis 1982). A rough outline of the different positions is given below.

The orthodox view

This view places the blame for the Cold War on the Soviet Union's aggressive and expansionist tendencies. These tendencies were heightened by its totalitarian political system and messianic ideology. The role of Marxist-Leninist ideology in Soviet foreign policy making is a highly contentious issue. Ideology is an important, but not sufficient, reason to explain the Cold War, for US–Soviet rivalry only began in earnest almost thirty years after the Bolshevik Revolution of 1917, when both states attained great power status.

The orthodox school focuses, in particular, on Eastern Europe as evidence of Soviet expansionism in the immediate post-war period. By 1948, Moscow had imposed Stalinist systems, by force, throughout most of the region. The American response – remembering the lessons of appeasing Hitler – was containment. This policy was outlined by the diplomat George Kennan in his famous 'X' article, and articulated by the US government in 1947 as the Truman Doctrine (Kennan 1947). It consisted of two main elements. The first was the military containment of Soviet communism through an active and global US foreign policy. The North Atlantic Treaty Organization (NATO) was set up in 1949 as part of this policy. The second element was economic containment, through aid to areas of need and of vital strategic importance to the USA. Thus in 1947 Marshall Aid started being distributed to West European countries, and proved highly successful in rebuilding their war-torn economies.

The Soviet and revisionist view

The orthodox view is concerned with Soviet strength. The Soviet and revisionist view emphasizes the power of the United States, and its dominance of the international system in the early post-war period. The USA lost 400,000 lives in the Second World War, the USSR 27 million. Much of the western part of the Soviet Union was devastated by Nazi occupation; no part of the American mainland was attacked by the Axis powers. The United States, alone among the protagonists, found its economy had grown during the course of the war, and accounted for over 50 per cent of world economic output by the time the war ended in 1945. Its domination of the military sphere was less complete. The Soviet Union, at the end of the war, had a formidable land army in occupation of much of Eastern Europe. This potential threat to the West, however, was offset by America's monopoly of the atomic bomb between 1945 and 1949. Washington had shown itself willing to use the bomb against Japan in August 1945. Many revisionists see the bombing less as a means to defeat the Japanese, and more a threat to Moscow in the post-war world.

Revisionists are also more willing to accept Eastern Europe as a legitimate security zone for the Soviet Union. They suggest, however, that Stalin had no initial plan to impose communist dictatorship on the region as a whole. They point to the three-year delay, 1945–8, before uniform Stalinist systems were imposed. In the interim, communist-led coalitions were permitted in some countries, such as Czechoslovakia. In this view, the Soviet Union was reacting to Western pressure, for Stalin soon became suspicious of America's intentions. Lend-lease to the USSR ceased immediately after the war, and Harry S Truman, the new American president, took a tougher line towards Moscow. The American offer of Marshall Aid to Eastern Europe was perceived by Stalin as a ploy to undermine Soviet influence in the region and to create a cordon sanitaire around the USSR. Stalin rejected the Marshall Plan on this basis. In sum, through its economic, military and scientific advantage, Washington was viewed in Moscow as an intimidatory force. In response, the socialist camp cut itself off from the Western world, Stalin tightened his grip over Eastern Europe, and the Soviet Union built up its military capacity.

The post-revisionist view

Despite a resurgence of support recently for the orthodox approach, post-revisionism remains the dominant view in the West – and it is now emerging in the USSR too (Trofimenko 1988). It is a broad school, which is still developing. Nevertheless, it has two elements which differentiate it from the other approaches. Both are linked. First, post-revisionism attempts to avoid the apportionment of blame. The action–reaction concept of both the orthodox and revisionist views is dismissed as simplistic. Instead, decisions and actions of both sides are seen as inextricably interwoven. Therefore, any attempt to discover who started the Cold War is bound to fail.

Second, post-revisionism places stress on 'systemic' factors. A new international system had emerged struggling from the ashes of war. It soon became clear that the post-war world would be bipolar, with the two centres of power in Washington and Moscow. Any radical shift in the international system is prone to cause uncertainty and tension. This was especially so in 1945. Two major powers, Germany and Japan, which had traditionally contained Russian expansionism, were both defeated and occupied. Britain and France were also inexorably in decline, and soon began shedding their colonies. As a result, innumerable power vacuums were opened up in an impoverished and unstable world. Peace may have been desired by all after the destruction of the war, but both the United States and the Soviet Union wanted to influence the future configuration of the new international order. Washington sought to encourage free trade and private enterprise, and feared the Marxist-Leninist refutation of both concepts. For its part, Moscow sought greater security through a military and ideological buffer zone in Eastern Europe.

No peace treaty was signed after the war; the Yalta and Potsdam agreements had to serve as substitutes. They were, however, interpreted differently. Moscow saw Yalta as the Western acceptance of a divided Europe. The West, on the other hand, emphasized the clauses, ignored by Stalin, on self-determination and free elections. Orthodox historians vigorously criticized the Yalta agreement for seeming to legitimize Soviet expansionism in Europe. Nor could the post-war agreements prevent tension arising over the contours of a divided continent. For example, the status of West Berlin inside East Germany became the source of the eleven-month blockade which started in June 1948. The following year, the Soviet Union tested its own atomic bomb, and China fell to the communists. As a result, a feeling of paranoia gripped America at the prospect of a communist monolith, armed with the bomb, stretching from Berlin to Shanghai. This atmosphere allowed McCarthyism to flourish in America in the early 1950s, and in part accounts for Washington's decisive response to North Korea's attack on the South in 1950.

Most commentators speak of this period, 1950–3, as the height of the Cold War. The Korean war was certainly a most dangerous time. American troops served under the flag of the United Nations (UN), and Soviet pilots secretly aided the North Koreans. From this time too, the Cold War became heavily militarized. US troops flooded into Western Europe, fearing the Korean War presaged a new Soviet move on Berlin. At the same time, the arms race really took off. In 1952 and 1955, the USA and the USSR, respectively, tested their hydrogen bombs, which gave both sides a dramatically improved destructive capability.

After the death of Stalin in 1953, relations between the two superpowers improved. In 1953, the Korean War armistice was signed, followed two years later by the Austrian State Treaty in which the great powers withdrew their occupying forces in return for Austrian neutrality. Then, at the 20th Party Congress in 1956, Khrushchev introduced some theoretical innovations, which displeased Peking but were well-received in the West. First, Khrushchev denounced Stalin. Second, he announced there were different roads to social-ism. Finally, he declared war with the West was no longer inevitable, and claimed the two social systems could live in 'peaceful co-existence'. This did not indicate an abandonment of the cause of international communism. Moscow simply believed it could be achieved without superpower conflict, which would be apocalyptic in the era of nuclear weapons.

These shifts in ideology were important, but were insufficient to end the Cold War. The positive aspects of the interim period, 1953–62, outlined above, were balanced by more negative elements. Most important of all, the structures and organizing principles of the Cold War remained in place. The two systems remained in competition. Khrushchev had not abandoned the international class struggle, any more than Eisenhower or Kennedy had abandoned the US policy of containment. As a result, the divide in Europe was not weakened, but further consolidated during this period. West Germany, in the fear it might be tempted to emulate Austrian neutrality, was brought into NATO in 1955, while the Warsaw Pact was formed in the same year. Moscow, under Khrushchev, still held to the view that its security in Eastern Europe could only be guaranteed by Soviet-style systems. So, when Hungary moved towards neutrality and a multi-party system in 1956, Soviet troops invaded and overthrew Nagy and his government. The West did nothing to aid the rebels, in effect giving *de facto* recognition to the Soviet occupation of Eastern Europe.

In the Third World, Khrushchev's greater ideological flexibility provided the West with a new challenge. Stalin had been relatively uninterested in the Third World. He saw little prospect of these backward, often tribal societies progressing to communism in the foreseeable future. Khrushchev, however, utilizing the doctrine of different roads to socialism, supported anti-Western, non-communist states in the Third World. Thus, Khrushchev fostered good relations with states such as Egypt and India from the 1950s onwards.

Two major crises of the Khrushchev–Kennedy era finally belied the notion of the Cold War being over. The first was the 1958–61 crisis over the status of Berlin. As tension mounted, emigration from the East soared. The crisis ended with the construction of the Berlin Wall, and Soviet and American tanks pointing guns at each other. The second occurred in 1962, when Khrushchev was forced to withdraw nuclear weapons from Cuba under the threat of American attack. On both occasions, the world held its breath, as direct superpower conflict looked a distinct possibility.

COMPETITIVE CO-EXISTENCE 1962–89

Competitive co-existence, unlike the Cold War, is not a term commonly used in political texts. It has been chosen to emphasize the break in world politics after Cuba, the ongoing competitive nature of the superpower relationship, and the continuities in the period itself. For convenience, the period has been divided into three sections: the thaw; superpower *détente*; and the abandonment of *détente*.

The thaw

There had been a growing realization in Moscow and Washington that the destructive capacity of nuclear weapons had changed the nature of international relations. This view had been crystallized by the experience of the Cuban Missile Crisis. Khrushchev and Kennedy realized that in the nuclear age the superpowers had to co-exist. As a result, steps were taken by both sides to stabilize the relationship. In 1963, the Hot Line, a communications link between the White House and the Kremlin, was set up. In the same year, the Partial Test Ban Treaty was signed, and some five years later, the Non-Proliferation Treaty.

In Europe, in the 1960s, tension declined, as both sides found the division of the continent less unacceptable, and living standards, East and West, rose appreciably. The German signature on the Non-Proliferation Treaty, and its moves towards *Ostpolitik* in the late 1960s, further stabilized the international position in Europe. In the Third World, however, superpower competition intensified after the US intervention in Vietnam in the mid-1960s. The American intervention was justified in terms of the containment of Soviet communism. Moscow condemned the American action, and gave military aid to the anti-US forces, but it was careful not to become directly involved in the war. The arms race heated up too. In fact, one result of the Cuban Missile Crisis was a strengthened Soviet commitment to build up its military capacity in order to challenge American hegemony more effectively.

Superpower *détente*

The thaw of the 1960s had only been a limited success, but in the 1970s the superpowers embarked on the more ambitious policy of *détente*. The reason for this shift in policy differed in the two superpower capitals.

The United States, under President Nixon, became concerned at the growing military power of the Soviet Union at a time when America was weakened by involvement in Vietnam. Nixon saw that the United States could no longer effectively play the world policeman role required by the original concept of containment. Therefore Nixon, together with his National Security Adviser, Henry Kissinger, introduced the complex notion of co-opting the Soviet Union into the international system. The United States would seek to co-operate more with the Soviet Union by offering arms control, trade agreements and so on, in the hope that Moscow would refrain from undermining US interests worldwide. The policy of containment was replaced in Washington by the hope of Soviet self-containment. In other words, the aim of the Nixon–Kissinger strategy of *détente* was the maintenance of American hegemony.

The Soviet Union had a quite different view of *détente*. Brezhnev could not accept the idea of continuing American hegemony. Since the war, Moscow had sought to challenge the status quo which favoured Washington. As the 1970s approached, the USSR, at last, had the military power to do just that. Why then did Moscow support the policy of *détente*? First, the hardliners in the Kremlin believed *détente* was a means to make Soviet expansionism in the Third World safer, by reducing the risk of nuclear war. Second, the regulation of the arms race reduced the risk of America using its technological advantage to leap ahead. Arms control simply made defence planning simpler. Third, East–West trade was perceived as a boost to the Soviet economy. *Détente* did not presage domestic reform in the USSR. On the contrary, East–West trade was seen as a substitute for economic reform, and political repression was tightened under Brezhnev. Finally, the United States was no longer perceived as the primary threat to Moscow. That role had been taken over by Maoist China. The Sino-Soviet split began in Khrushchev's time, but in 1969 it had erupted into war along the Amur-Ussuri border. Despite a stabilization of the situation in the 1970s, Brezhnev still sought *détente* with the West to impede an anti-Soviet Peking–Washington axis.

From the above outline, it is clear that the *détente* of the 1970s had little real chance of success, due to the different conceptions of the process in Moscow and Washington. For this reason, some commentators have dismissed the US–Soviet relationship of the 1970s as a 'false *détente*' (McGeehan 1990: 18). The reality may have been more complex. With the benefit of hindsight, superpower *détente* could be regarded as a necessary learning process on the road to the *entente* of the 1990s. To show this, it is useful to consider in more detail the strengths and weaknesses of the US–Soviet rivalry in the *détente* period.

The substance of *détente*

The arms control agreements of the 1970s covered the superpowers' strategic nuclear weapons under SALT (Strategic Arms Limitation Treay) I (1972) and SALT II (1979), and their defensive weapons under the ABM (Anti-Ballistic Missile) Treaty (1972). In 1977, President Carter did propose deep cuts, but on the whole the arms control process was not aimed at stopping the arms race, merely regulating it and making nuclear deterrence more credible. In these limited aims, arms control was a qualified success. However, the defence lobbies in both capitals constantly feared that technological or quantitive gains by the other side could prove decisive. Both superpowers built up the military to guard against such an eventuality. As a result, the arms control process was less stabilizing than had been hoped.

Crisis management and prevention began with the Hot Line in 1963, but more ambitious attempts were negotiated in May 1972 and June 1973 – the Basic Principles Agreement and the Agreement on the Prevention of Nuclear War, respectively. These documents pledged the USA and the USSR to consult at times of regional crisis to prevent such crises escalating into super-power conflict.

Moscow placed a lot of emphasis on these agreements, but there is little evidence that they served much of a practical purpose. Only months after the Agreement on the Prevention of Nuclear War had been signed, the Middle East war of October 1973 broke out, in which the two superpowers came closest to direct conflict since Cuba. The crisis was defused, but only after Brezhnev had threatened intervention, and Nixon had gone on nuclear alert to prevent it.

Washington quickly became disillusioned with *détente*, as the Soviet Union began to expand its influence in the Third World, especially in Africa and Indo-China. It seemed Moscow was taking advantage of Washington's relative weakness, which was a result of its defeat in Vietnam and the Watergate scandal. In the eyes of America, the Soviet invasion of Afghanistan in December 1979 was merely the most dramatic example of Soviet expansionism in this period. It had become clear that the Nixon strategy of Soviet self-containment had not worked.

Crisis prevention was more successful in Europe. Crises did erupt, most notably in Czechoslovakia in 1968 and in Poland for much of the 1970s and 1980s, but they were contained at the local level. There was never any danger, unlike the Berlin or Cuba crises earlier, of such instabilities leading to a superpower confrontation. This was due to the political division of Europe, which was formalized by the bilateral German *Ostpolitik* in the early 1970s and the multilateral Helsinki Final Act of 1975 (which started the whole Conference on Security and Co-operation in Europe (CSCE) process). In these agreements, the Soviet dominance of Eastern Europe was recognized in return for Western demands of improved human rights in the region. Stability was further enhanced by rising living standards, a product of increased East–West trade. The benefits were short-lived. Due to gross inefficiencies and elite corruption, by the late 1970s the socialist economies were plunged into debt and crisis. The economic collapse, combined with a lack of basic human rights – in spite of Helsinki – led to the East European revolutions of autumn and winter 1989.

The abandonment of *détente*

Both sides had reason to be disillusioned with the process of superpower *détente*, but it was the Americans who abandoned it after the Soviet invasion of Afghanistan in December 1979. Washington believed that *détente* had become a one-way street favouring Moscow. Throughout the period, the Soviet Union had continued to seek advantages in the Third World and superiority in the arms race. Ronald Reagan, who became President in 1981, believed the only effective method of defending America's global interests was through a revival of the policy of containment based on American military strength. As a result, the rhetoric of the Cold War returned, military spending in both superpower capitals rose dramatically, and President Reagan adopted a more activist foreign policy line in the Third World.

Many commentators said that the Cold War had returned (Halliday 1983: 19–23). Certainly, relations between Washington and Moscow cooled markedly. Yet the differences between the 1970s and the 1980s are easily exaggerated. Despite a reduction in East–West contacts, trade continued to flow and negotiations below leadership level on arms control and Europe were maintained for most of the period. It is true that these negotiations met with little success during Reagan's first term in office, and Moscow broke off Strategic Arms Reduction Treaty (START – the successor to SALT) negotions in 1983–4, in response to the deployment of cruise and Pershing II in Western Europe. Nevertheless, both sides observed SALT II until a small technical breach by the United States in 1987, and this despite the non-ratification of the treaty by Senate.

In fact, the so-called Second Cold War had an unreal quality. Only the military, along with a handful of academics and politicians, seemed truly engaged by it. Only they seemed to take the ongoing superpower threat seriously. For the Second Cold War was a rarefied beast. It was full of arcane arguments, but with few crises to compare with earlier times. American politicians still talked about the Soviet desire for world revolution, the military of both sides worried over 'first strike survivability', but the public remained largely unmoved. It is true that majority opinion rejected unilateral nuclear disarmament, but it also rejected the more alarmist propaganda of their respective governments. The overwhelming majority in all countries, East and West, simply wanted a return to less conflictual policies. Reagan realized this when he began his re-election campaign in 1984. After its abortive walk-out of START, the Kremlin too was eager to get back to the negotiating table.

CO-OPERATIVE CO-EXISTENCE 1989 TO THE PRESENT

By the late 1980s, the superpowers had moved through three discernible stages: from open competition, through regulated competition, to a co-operative relationship. This shift to *entente* affected every aspect of international relations.

The most dramatic change occurred in Europe. The collapse of communism in 1989 reunited the continent, as well as the German nation. This necessitated a radical reassessment of all European organizations. On 5 July 1990, NATO declared the two military blocs were no longer adversaries, and called for a non-aggression treaty with the Warsaw Pact. The East European response was even more radical. The Warsaw Pact was formally dissolved on 1 July 1991, and with it collapsed the entire structure of Cold War European security. In early 1992, leaders are groping for a new European order which might guarantee continued peace and stability. It is possible that the European Community, the CSCE or the Western European Union (WEU) may come to play a more dominant role in European defence matters. One thing is certain. The former stability based on the structure of a divided Europe has gone.

The new superpower relationship also had an impact in the Third World. The Soviet Union withdrew its troops from Afghanistan in February 1989, and subsequently reduced its commitment to Marxist-Leninist regimes around the world. Washington and Moscow also sought greater superpower co-operation to encourage peaceful solutions to crises as far apart as the Middle East, Cambodia and Afghanistan.

Defence policy has also been radically reviewed. Arms control has been superseded by arms cuts. Thus, the Intermediate Nuclear Forces (INF) Treaty was signed in 1987, followed by the Conventional Forces in Europe (CFE) Treaty in 1990 and the START Treaty in the summer of 1991. The significance of these treaties has been reduced by the collapse of the USSR and the Warsaw Pact. Nevertheless, the likelihood of East–West conflict in the post-Cold War world is now negligible, and these arms agreements played an important part in improving superpower relations.

In sum, there is little doubt that the shift to co-operative co-existence has been a decisive one. Why did this shift occur? Why did it happen in the late 1980s? The most commonly accepted view is in line with the orthodox view of the Cold War. This argument runs: the Cold War was started by the Soviet ideology of expansionism. When Gorbachev renounced the ideology and started to withdraw from Soviet positions in Europe and the Third World, the need for Western containment disappeared. There is a lot of truth in this explanation. Gorbachev introduced major reforms in Soviet domestic and foreign policy. Gorbachev made the major concessions including the abandonment of the Brezhnev doctrine, the refutation of the international class struggle, and the acceptance of unilateral and asymmetrical cuts in defence.

However, this begs the question: why did Gorbachev adopt these policies when he did? One plausible explanation concerns the state of the Soviet economy when Gorbachev came to power in 1985. By this time, the Soviet economy could no longer sustain its superpower status. Moscow's allies in Eastern Europe and the Third World had become a considerable drain on the Soviet Union's limited resources. Furthermore, any attempt by the Kremlin to match the latest American technological innovations, such as the Strategic Defence Initiative (SDI) and smart weapons, were only likely to bankrupt the economy. The Soviet gross national product was less than half that of the United States, but Moscow spent perhaps 25 per cent of gross national product on defence, compared to Washington's 6 per cent.

Such arguments suggest another question. To what extent did Reagan's revival of containment force Gorbachev's new political thinking? This is a far more contentious issue. Most Soviet scholars still resist the idea (Podlesny and Kortunov 1988: 84–8). However, at a minimum, it can be stated that Reagan's tough policies made Soviet actions more costly. Reagan's declared aim of 'arming the Soviet Union to death' was more successful than many supposed at the time. Moreover, the American supply of Stinger anti-aircraft missiles to the Mujaheddin in 1986 increased Soviet casualties, and made continued occupation of Afghanistan less politically supportable. This is not to suggest that Reagan's Soviet policy was an unqualified success, but it did force the USSR to urgently reassess its political priorities (Cox 1990).

Nevertheless, the Soviet leadership had been prepared to bear severe costs in the past. Why did this change in the 1980s? Gorbachev himself had stated that he would never sacrifice security for military cuts (Gorbachev 1987: 20). Why, then, was Gorbachev prepared to withdraw from an area, such as Eastern Europe, which had always been considered of vital strategic interest to Moscow? The answer for this can also take account of revisionist and post-revisionist views. For the fact was, by the time Gorbachev became General Secretary in 1985, the international system was very different to that of the 1940s and 1950s. Despite the Cold War rhetoric, neither side perceived the other as a major threat. Communism was in decline. The re-Stalinization of the USSR under Brezhnev, the invasion of Czechoslovakia and the failure of the command economy alienated even erstwhile supporters. Eurocommunism declined in influence, and the Third World increasingly forsook the Soviet Union as an alternative model of development. Furthermore, the military gains of the Soviet Union in the 1970s looked less impressive a decade later. Only the most impoverished and often war-torn states, such as Afghanistan, Ethiopia and Angola, continued to uphold the precepts of Marxism-Leninism.

The United States and the Soviet Union retained massive military arsenals, which remained a potential threat to each other. However, in reality a stalemate had been reached at absurd levels of overkill. The military will always be important, but it became clear that additions to the firepower of the two countries no longer led to an equivalent increase in either national security or global influence. The arms control process of the 1970s had been of limited success, but its temporary abandonment in the early 1980s had been no more successful in affording either side a decisive military advantage. In fact, the massive defence spending of the United States and the Soviet Union had diminished their international standing, due to the detrimental effects on the civilian economy. The effect was most visible in the Soviet Union, but by the late 1980s the United States also faced severe economic problems. Thus the hegemonical position of the United States in 1945, stressed so much by the revisionists, had been reduced. America remains a dominant power. But in the late 1950s, the American mainland became vulnerable, for the first time, to Soviet nuclear attack. In the 1970s, Moscow achieved strategic parity with Washington. Since then, many Third World states, such as India and Iraq, have been narrowing the gap with the developed nations, in terms of the size and quality of their armed forces. At the same time, in the economic field, the United States has found itself being effectively challenged by countries such as Japan and Germany.

As a result, the modern world has become more complex. Problems have arisen which could not be dealt with inside the Cold War structures. The

Cold War worked in a narrow bipolar world, where Manichaean zero-sum games operated. Reagan's image of the Soviet Union as 'the focus of all evil' had only obfuscated the issues and made solutions to new problems more difficult. The threat to the United States in the 1990s came not so much from Soviet communism, but from greater Japanese and German economic power. Sources of global instability were less Soviet communism, more world poverty, national and religious differences, and ecological and resource problems. The world had become more multipolar and the United States and Soviet Union had to learn to play a less central role in this new international system. Great-power co-operation looked a better option than competition to solve the problems of the modern world.

Prospects

Some believe the new superpower relationship could be short-lived. Even after the failure of the August coup of 1991, and the subsequent dissolution of the Soviet Union at the end of that year, a return to power of military hardliners is still thought possible by some commentators. However, even if that were to happen a revival of Cold War policies is likely to be only short term. This survey has attempted to show that the new, more co-operative relationship between Moscow and Washington has deeper roots than the pessimists allow. Gorbachev was important in creating the conditions for co-operative co-existence; there are grounds to hope, however, that it will survive his political demise.

Co-operative co-existence represents a positive shift in the international system. The chances of conflict have been further reduced. Deep cuts in defence are underway, and the great powers have shown a willingness to co-operate to encourage the resolution of regional and global problems. Nevertheless, co-operation can only be seriously expected where interests do not clash. In the post-Cold War era, these interests can be expected to clash less than in the past, but disputes between Moscow and Washington are certain to arise in the future. Furthermore, co-operative co-existence does not mean an end to all conflict. There is a need for a far more fundamental change in the behaviour of states before world peace is even a remote possibility.

CHRONOLOGY OF THE US–SOVIET RELATIONSHIP
1945–1991

February	1945	Yalta conference takes place.
April	1945	President Roosevelt dies and is replaced by Harry Truman.
May	1945	War ends in Europe.

August	1945	Atomic bombs dropped on Hiroshima and Nagasaki, Japan surrenders.
March	1947	Truman Doctrine is announced.
June	1947	Marshall Plan is announced.
February	1948	The Communists take over in Czechoslovakia.
June	1948	The Berlin Blockade begins.
April	1949	NATO is formed.
May	1949	The Berlin blockade ends.
August	1949	The Soviet atomic bomb is tested.
September	1949	The Federal Republic of Germany is formed.
October	1949	The communists are victorious in China; the German Democratic Republic is formed.
June	1950	The Korean War starts.
November	1952	The USA tests its hydrogen bomb.
January	1953	Dwight D. Eisenhower becomes US President.
March	1953	Stalin dies.
July	1953	The Korean War is ended.
September	1953	Nikita Khrushchev replaces Stalin.
May	1955	West Germany joins NATO; the Austrian State Treaty is signed; the Warsaw Pact is formed.
November	1955	The USSR tests its hydrogen bomb.
February	1956	The 20th CPSU Congress takes place.
November	1956	The USSR invades Hungary
January	1961	John F. Kennedy becomes US President.
August	1961	The Berlin Wall is put up.
October	1962	The Cuban Missile Crisis takes place.
August	1963	The Hot Line is set up; the Partial Test Ban Treaty is signed.
November	1963	Kennedy is assassinated; Lyndon Johnson becomes President.
October	1964	Khrushchev is ousted and replaced by Leonid Brezhnev.
March	1965	US marines are deployed in Vietnam.
July	1968	The non-proliferation treaty is signed.
August	1968	The Warsaw Pact invades Czechoslovakia.
January	1969	Richard Nixon becomes US President.
March	1969	Sino-Soviet border clashes take place.
August	1970	The West German–Soviet Union Treaty is signed, setting Willy Brandt's *Ostpolitik* in motion.
December	1970	Food riots break out in Poland; Gomulka is ousted in favour of Gierek.

May	1972	SALT I, the ABM Treaty and the Basic Principles Agreement are signed.
January	1973	The Paris agreement is signed ending direct US participation in the Vietnam War.
June	1973	The agreement on the Prevention of Nuclear War is signed.
October	1973	The Arab–Israeli war takes place.
August	1974	Nixon resigns over Watergate and is replaced by Gerald Ford.
April	1975	Saigon falls to the North Vietnamese.
August	1975	The Helsinki Final Act is signed.
September	1976	Mao Zedong dies.
January	1977	Jimmy Carter becomes US President.
June	1979	SALT II is signed.
November	1979	American hostages are taken in Iran.
December	1979	The USSR invades Afghanistan.
August	1980	Solidarity is recognized by the Polish government.
January	1981	Ronald Reagan becomes US President.
December	1981	Martial law is declared in Poland, and remains in force until 1983.
June	1982	START negotiations begin.
November	1982	Brezhnev dies and is replaced by Yuri Andropov.
December	1983	The USSR breaks off talks on INF and START.
February	1984	Andropov dies and is replaced by Konstantin Chernenko.
March	1985	Mikhail Gorbachev replaces Chernenko, and talks on arms control begin again.
November	1986	Irangate breaks.
December	1987	The INF Treaty is signed.
April	1988	The Geneva accord is signed on USSR withdrawal from Afghanistan.
January	1989	George Bush becomes US President.
February	1989	Last Soviet troops withdrawn from Afghanistan.
April	1989	Solidarity in Poland is legalized.
May	1989	Gorbachev meets Deng Xiao Ping in Peking.
June	1989	Popular uprising in China is brutally suppressed; Solidarity wins a landslide election victory in Poland.
November	1989	The Berlin Wall comes down following East German protests and increased emigration to the West.
December	1989	Nicolae Ceauşescu is overthrown in Romania after a bloody revolution, bringing the first phase of East European revolutions to an end.

June	1990	German monetary reunion takes place; the Warsaw Pact declares itself to be a political, not military, alliance.
July	1990	NATO London declaration states the Warsaw Pact is no longer an adversary.
August	1990	The USA and USSR issue a joint communiqué condemning the Iraqi invasion of Kuwait.
November	1990	CFE signed.
Jan-Feb	1991	USA and USSR co-operate in war against Iraq.
June	1991	Civil War breaks out in Yugoslavia as Slovenia and Croatia declare independence; Soviet troops leave Hungary and Czechoslovakia ahead of schedule.
July	1991	The Warsaw Pact is dissolved.
August	1991	START is signed; an attempted coup in the USSR fails; Moscow formally recognizes the independence of the Baltic Republics.
December	1991	Formal disintegration of the Soviet Union begins.

REFERENCES

Cox, M. (1990) 'Whatever happened to the Second Cold War? Soviet–American relations, 1980–1988', *Review of International Studies* 16: 155–72.

Gaddis, J. L. (1982) *Strategies of Containment: A Critical Appraisal of Post-War American National Security Policy*, New York and London: Oxford University Press.

Gorbachev, M. S. (1987) *Perestroika: New Thinking for Our Country and the World*, London: Collins.

Halliday, F. (1983) *The Making of the Second Cold War*, London: Verso.

Kennan, G. F. (1947) 'The sources of Soviet conduct', *Foreign Affairs* 25: 566–82.

McGeehan, R. (1990) 'Sparring partners – the record of superpower relations', in M. Pugh and P. Williams (eds) *Superpower Politics: Change in the United States and the Soviet Union*, Manchester and New York: Manchester University Press.

Podlesny, P. and Kortunov, A. (1988) 'The 1980s – towards a new model', in P. Podlesny (ed.) *Soviet–American Relations: Past and Present*, Moscow: Nauka Publishers.

Schlesinger, A. M. (1967) 'The origins of the Cold War', *Foreign Affairs* 46: 22–52.

Sivachev, N. V. and Yakovlev, N. N. (1979) *Russia and the United States: US–Soviet Relations from the Soviet Point of View*, Chicago: Chicago University Press.

Trofimenko, G. A. (1988) 'Towards a new quality of Soviet–American relations', *International Affairs* (Moscow), (December): 13–25.

Williams, W. A. (1962) *The Tragedy of American Diplomacy*, rev. edn, New York: New York Publishing.

FURTHER READING

Armstrong, D. and Goldstein, E. (eds) (1990) *The End of the Cold War*, London: Frank Cass.

Bowker, M. and Williams, P. (1988) *Superpower Detente: A Reappraisal*, London: Sage Publications.

Gorbachev, M. S. (1988) *Address at the United Nations, New York, December 7th 1988*, Moscow: Novosti Press.

Kennedy, P. (1988) *The Rise and Fall of Great Powers: Economic Change and Military Conflict from 1500–2000*, New York: Random House; London: Unwin Hyman.

LaFeber, W. (1991) *America, Russia and the Cold War, 1945–1990*, New York: John Wiley.

69

IMPERIALISM

MICHAEL PARENTI

Imperialism has been the most powerful political force in world history over the last four or five centuries, carving up whole continents and colonizing and impoverishing entire civilizations. 'Imperialism' is used here to mean the process whereby the dominant economic and political elements of one nation expropriate for their own benefit the land, labour, raw materials and markets of another nation. Imperialism can occur between European nations, as centuries of continental conflict testify. The most recent and virulent example of intra-European imperialism was the Nazi conquests during the Second World War, which gave the German cartels the opportunity to plunder the natural resources and exploit the labour of occupied Europe, including the slave labour of concentration camps (Mayer 1988; Ferencz 1979). But the preponderant global thrust of imperialism has been 'outward', perpetrated by European, North American and, more recently, Japanese powers against the lands and peoples of Africa, Latin America and Asia.

Imperialism is, of course, older than capitalism. Alexander the Great was not a capitalist, nor were the Roman emperors capitalists, nor were the Spanish conquistadors. They did not systematically accumulate capital through the rationalized exploitation of free labour and the expansion of private markets. Their interest was mainly in plunder and tribute. Capitalist imperialism differs from these earlier forms in the range of raw materials it expropriates, the systematic ways it invests in other countries, and the ways it shapes the productive forces, penetrates the markets, and transforms the economies, cultures and political development of the colonized nations, integrating their financial and productive structures into an international system of capital accumulation.

The process of expropriating the natural resources of the Third World began around the start of the sixteenth century and continues to this day. Along with gold, silver, furs, silks and spices, the colonizers soon took flax, hemp, timber, molasses, sugar, rum, rubber, tobacco, calico, cocoa, coffee, cotton, copper, coal, palm oil, tin, iron, ivory and ebony, and, later on, oil, zinc, columbite, manganese, mercury, platinum, cobalt, bauxite, aluminium and uranium. In addition, there was the forceful abduction of millions of human beings from Africa for slave labour in the New World.

By the nineteenth century, the industrial nations saw the Third World as not only a source of raw materials but as a market for manufactured goods. By the twentieth century, they were exporting not only their goods but also their capital, in the form of machinery, technology, investments and loans. Rather than exporting vehicles to a Third World country, capitalist manufacturers today export entire automotive factories to take advantage of cheap labour markets. To say that we have entered the stage of capital export and investment is not to imply that the plunder of natural resources has ceased, only that it is now conducted in ways that differ somewhat from earlier days of colonization.

Capitalism contains within itself an inherently expansionist dynamic. Investors will not put their money into anything unless they can extract more than they invested. Increased earnings can only come with an increase in the size of the undertaking. A central law of capitalist motion and development is expansion. The capitalist is engaged in a ceaseless search for profitable enterprise, for ways of making money in order to make still more money. One must always invest to realize profits, gathering as much strength as possible in the face of competing forces and unstable markets. Given its expansionist nature, capitalism has little inclination to stay home. More than 140 years ago, Marx and Engels described a bourgeoisie that 'chases . . . over the whole surface of the globe. It must nestle everywhere, settle everywhere, establish connections everywhere' (Marx and Engels 1969).

Today the enormous capital concentrations of US and other Western corporations are strikingly international in scope. Some 400 companies control about 80 per cent of the capital assets of the entire non-socialist world (and are extending their control into former socialist countries of Eastern Europe). The larger portion of these investments is still in industrial countries, but more and more is going into the Third World. Citibank, for instance, earns about 75 per cent of its profits from overseas operations, mostly in less developed countries. US and other Western corporations have acquired control of more than 75 per cent of the known major mineral resources in Asia, Africa and Latin America. Given the low wages, low taxes, non-existent workers' benefits and non-existent occupational and environmental protections, US multinational profit rates in the Third World are 50 per cent greater than in developed countries. While profit margins at home have tended to shrink in the post-war era, earnings abroad have risen dramatically. It is this combination that has induced the development of the multinational corporation.

Some writers question whether imperialism is a necessary condition for capitalism, pointing out that most Western capital is invested in Western nations, not in the Third World. If corporations lost all their Third World investments, most of them could still profitably survive on their domestic markets (Miller *et al.* 1970). It is probably true that capitalism could exist without imperialism – but is it inclined to do so? Is it apt to discard its enormously profitable enterprises in Asia, Africa and Latin America? Imperialism may not be a necessary condition for capitalist survival but it seems to be an inherent tendency and a natural outgrowth of advanced capitalism. Imperial relations may not be the only way to obtain vital raw materials or overseas markets and investments, but they are the most lucrative way (Magdoff 1970; Szymanski 1981).

With the advent of the Western colonizers, the countries of Africa, Asia and Latin America were not only kept technologically backward and impoverished, they were actually deindustrialized, set back in their development – sometimes for centuries. The tremendous profits that have been extracted from them should remind us that there are few really poor nations in the Third World. Countries like Brazil, Indonesia, Chile, Bolivia, Zaire, Mexico, Malaysia and the Philippines are rich in resources. Only the people are poor. Of course, some lands have been so thoroughly plundered as to be desolate in all respects. But most of the Third World is not 'underdeveloped', only over-exploited. Western investments have brought a lower rather than a higher living standard. Thus, from 1850 to 1900, India's per capita income dropped by almost two-thirds. The value of the commodities the Indians gratuitously sent to Britain amounted yearly to more than the total sum of income of the 60 million Indian agricultural and industrial workers (Marx 1968). Formerly an exporter of finished textile goods to much of the world, India was forced by British tariffs and British gunboats to deindustrialize early in the nineteenth century and become the provider of raw materials for British manufacturers. Similar bleeding processes occurred in Egypt, China, and throughout much of the Third World (Stavrianos 1981).

The poverty of the 'underdeveloped' nations is not an original historical condition but something that has been imposed by imperialism. Economic wealth and impoverishment are interrelated in that each is caused by its relation with the other (Frank 1967). Wealth is transferred by direct plunder; by the expropriation of natural resources; the imposition of ruinous taxes, rents and royalties; the payment of poverty wages for native labour; and the forced importation of finished goods at highly inflated prices into domestic markets that remain unprotected by tariffs and import quotas. The colonized country is denied the freedom of trade and the freedom to develop its own natural resources, markets, capital and industrial capacity.

In the history of imperialism there have been few, if any, peaceable colonizations. The imperial usurpers often encountered desperate resistance from indigenous peoples. Only by using force and violence and establishing military supremacy were the invaders able to steal the lands and natural wealth of other peoples, extort tribute, undermine their cultures, destroy their townships, eliminate their crafts and industries, and indenture or enslave their labour. This was done by the Spaniards in Latin America; the Portuguese in Angola, Mozambique and Brazil; the Belgians in the Congo; the Germans in South-West Africa; the Italians in Libya, Ethiopia and Somalia; the Dutch in the East Indies; the French in North Africa, West Africa and Indo-China; the British in Ireland, China, India, Africa and the Middle East; the Japanese in Korea, Manchuria and China; and the Americans in the Philippines, Central America, the Caribbean and Indo-China.

Carving up the world has often been treated by the apologists of imperialism as a 'natural' phenomenon, involving an 'international division of labour' and 'specialization of markets'. But what really is distinctive about imperialism is its highly unnatural quality, its repeated reliance upon coercion and repression. Empires do not emerge naturally and innocently 'in a fit of absent-mindedness', as was said of the British empire. Rather they are welded together with deceit, fraud, greed, ruthlessness, blood and sorrow. They are built upon the sword, the whip, the torch and the gun (Stavrianos 1981; Parenti 1989; Drechsler 1966). The history of imperialism is no less dreadful for being conveniently ignored and untaught in most Western nations.

Empire does not come cheap. Burdensome expenditures are needed for military conquest and prolonged occupation, for colonial administration, for bribes and arms to native collaborators, and for the development of a commercial infrastructure to facilitate capital penetration and accumulation. Consequently, the governments of imperial nations almost always spend more than they take in. From this, some observers mistakenly conclude that empire is 'irrational', not worth the cost and effort. In fact, imperialism is not a losing proposition for everyone. As Thorstein Veblen pointed out in 1904, the gains of empire flow into the hands of a privileged business class while the costs are extracted from 'the industry of the rest of the people' (Veblen 1932: 217). Marx made the same observation about British rule in India, noting that while the costs exceeded the benefits, the former were 'paid out of the pockets of the people of England' (Marx and Engels 1972: 168) while considerable profits went to a small coterie of rich investors.

By the end of the Second World War, the costs of empire had proved too burdensome for the Western powers left financially insolvent by the war. Growing popular resistance within the Third World countries made direct rule still more difficult. The European powers eventually recognized that indirect rule was less costly and politically more expedient than outright possession. So in the post-war era, they adopted a strategy of what is now called 'neo-colonialism' or 'neo-imperialism'. First utilized a half-century earlier in

Cuba by the US colonialists, neo-imperialism entailed granting the over-exploited country its formal independence while preserving control over the more lucrative sectors of its economy and trade.

The removal of a conspicuously intrusive imperial power makes it more difficult for nationalist elements within victimized countries to mobilize anti-imperialist movements. The newly independent government is far from being completely independent of the former colonizers, yet it will enjoy – at least for a while – a somewhat greater legitimacy in the eyes of its populace than an administration directly controlled by the imperial power. The native government must take up the costs of administering the country while the imperialist interests continue to skim the cream.

For example, when the United States granted the Philippines its 'independence' in 1946, American citizens, under laws passed by the US Congress, were given equal rights with Filipinos in the development of the islands' natural resources and the operation of public utilities. Free-trade agreements deprived the Filipinos of any protective wall behind which they could build their own industries. US companies engaged in competitive dumping of commodities, driving out scores of pioneering Filipino entrepreneurs. Large sums of local credit were siphoned off by US banks to finance American investments in the islands. The Philippine peso was fixed to the dollar at a 2 to 1 rate with any change requiring the approval of the US president. The United States was granted leases for major land and naval bases, which it still occupies to this day. The relationship between the two countries resembled classical imperialism, minus the flag. The United States retained much of 'the economic and military advantages for colonial power, while it was relieved of the burden of administration and of direct responsibility for Philippine welfare' (Jenkins 1954: 69).

Still, neo-imperialism carries certain risks and costs of its own. The achievement of *de jure* independence eventually fosters expectations of complete independence and social betterment among the populace and sometimes even among national leaders. The imperialists have a more difficult time justifying domination and asserting that Third World people are incapable of equality and self-government when, in fact, these same people have attained some semblance of self-rule. Therefore, the change-over from colonialism to a world of distinct, albeit still dependent, nation-states is not without significance and represents a net gain for popular forces in the world.

Imperialism must build an armed security system to safeguard its overseas interests. Here the state plays an essential role. Sometimes state power is used to protect advantages won by private capital and sometimes the state stakes out a claim on behalf of private interests well before investors are prepared to do so. The state thus acts as an initiator and not just protector of overseas ventures. US President Woodrow Wilson made this clear when he observed that the government 'must open these [overseas] gates of trade, and open them wide, open them before it is altogether profitable to open them, or altogether reasonable to ask private capital to open them at a venture' (Williams 1976: 28).

The state must protect not only the capital that has been invested by particular firms but also the capital accumulation process itself. This entails the systematic suppression of revolutionary and populist-nationalist movements that seek to build alternative economic systems along more egalitarian, collectivist lines. Today, the United States is the foremost antagonist of revolutionary change in the Third World. Emerging from the Second World War relatively unscathed and greatly strengthened in wealth and productive capacity, the United States became the guardian of global capitalism. Judging by the size of its financial investments and military force, judging by every imperialist standard except direct colonization, the US empire is the most formidable in history.

Despite the absence of direct colonization, conditions of imperialist – or neo-imperialist – domination still obtain between the industrialized nations and the Third World in the following ways.

Unequal trade relations The economy of a Third World nation is typically concentrated on the export of a few raw materials or basic labour-intensive commodities. One or two industrialized countries are often the poorer nation's only customers. In this instance, monopoly power is exercised not by the supplier but by the buyer, as the poor country remains highly dependent upon the markets of the rich one. The former is also likely to find itself in intense competition with other poor nations for metropolitan markets. Rich nations are able to set trading terms that are highly favourable to themselves. They are far more flexible and diverse and can easily fall back on domestic sources, find substitutes, or play one country off against another, should a poor nation try to hold out for better terms. Trade cessations inflict more injury upon poor nations than rich ones. Attempts by Third World countries to overcome their vulnerability by forming trade cartels are usually unsuccessful, for they seldom are able to maintain a solid front, given their political differences, overall dependency and lack of alternatives (Szymanski 1981; Stavrianos 1981).

Not only are Third World countries underpaid for their exports, they are also regularly overcharged for the goods they import from the industrial world – for the same monopolistic reasons stated above. Thus, their coffee, cotton, meat, tin, copper, oil, or whatever, is sold cheap in order to obtain – at painfully high prices – various manufactured goods, machinery and spare parts. According to a former president of Venezuela, Carlos Andrés Pérez: 'This has resulted in a constant and growing outflow of capital and impoverishment of our countries' (Parenti 1989: 21).

Discouraging industrialization Raw materials not produced in the United States or in short supply are usually allowed into the United States duty free. But goods that have been processed in any way are subjected to tariffs. Unprocessed coffee beans or raw timber are admitted with no charge, but processed coffee and sawn lumber face import duties. This inhibits the development of independently owned industries in the Third World. It also leads to the expropriation of about $2 billion a year in tariff revenues for the US treasury (Szymanski 1981). The big companies also discourage industrialization by restricting or prohibiting the transfer of technology and credit to locally owned enterprises. Western firms generally crowd out local enterprises through superior financing, high-powered marketing, brand identification and greater managerial resources. The more profitable the area of investment, the more likely the local bourgeoisie is to be pushed out by multinational corporations.

Capital exports and assets In many Third World countries over half the manufacturing assets are foreign-owned or majority-controlled by foreign companies. Even in instances where the multinational companies have only a minority interest, they often retain a veto control. And even when the host nation owns the enterprise in its entirety, the multinational will enjoy benefits through its control of technology and international marketing. Such is the case with petroleum. While the multinational companies owned only 38 per cent of the crude oil production in the world markets in 1975, they held 83 per cent of the refining capacity and 85 per cent of the distribution. In addition, they continued to manage almost all petroleum production and exploration in member countries of the Organization of Petroleum Exporting Countries (OPEC)

Overseas investments represent an export of capital rather than an export of manufactured goods to foreign markets. The profits accumulated from capital exports are much greater than the profits obtained from exporting goods. Lenin argued as much almost a century ago and it certainly seems to be the case today (Lenin 1937; Szymanski 1981).

Foreign aid The billions of dollars in aid granted by the United States and other industrialized nations to the Third World has some tight strings attached to it. Almost all US aid commits the recipient nation to buy US goods at US prices, to be transported in US ships. The United States does not grant assistance to state-owned enterprises, only to the private sector. Very little assistance filters down to the poorer populations of recipient nations. Much of it is used for large agribusinesses that specialize in cash-crop exports, at the expense of small farmers who grow food for local markets. The net result of foreign aid, as with most foreign investment, is a greater concentration of wealth for the few and greater poverty for the many (Parenti 1989).

Aid is also a powerful weapon of political control (Adams and Solomon 1985; Lopez and Stohl 1985). It is withheld when the poorer nation has the temerity to effect genuine reforms that might tamper with the distribution of class wealth and power. Thus, in 1970 when the democratically elected Allende government in Chile initiated economic reforms that benefited the working class and encroached upon the privileges of wealthy investors, all US aid was cut off – except for assistance to the Chilean military, which was increased.

Debt domination   Given the disadvantageous trade and investment relations, Third World nations have found it expedient to borrow heavily from Western banks and from the International Monetary Fund (IMF), which is controlled by the United States and other Western member nations. By the 1990s, Third World debt was approaching US $2 trillion, an unpayable sum. The greater a nation's debt, the greater is the pressure to borrow still more to meet the deficits – often at higher interest rates and on shorter payment terms. An increasingly larger portion of the earnings of indebted nations goes to servicing the debt, leaving still less for domestic consumption. For example, by 1986, 80 per cent of Paraguay's export earnings went to pay the interest on its $2 billion foreign debt. Most other debtor countries must devote anywhere from one-third to two-thirds of their earnings to service their debts. By 1983 the money collected by foreign banks in the form of interest payments on Third World debts was three times higher than their profits on direct Third World investments.

Nations that default on their debts run the risk of being unable to qualify for short-term credit to fund imports. They may find their overseas accounts blocked, their overseas assets seized, and their export markets closed out. To avoid default, they must keep borrowing. But to qualify for more loans from the IMF, a country must eventually agree to the IMF's 'stabilization' terms, which invariably include cutting back on domestic consumption while producing more for export. By earning more and consuming less, the debtor nation presumably can pay off more of its debt. As part of the 'stabilization' programme, the debtor nation must make cuts in food subsidies, housing and other already insufficiently funded human services, thereby further penalizing the common population. In addition, the debtor nation is likely to be asked to devalue its currency, freeze wages and raise prices so that its populace will consume still less. And it must offer generous tax concession to foreign companies and eliminate favourable treatment or subsidies to locally owned or state-owned enterprises (Payer 1975). Debt payments today represent a substantial net transfer of wealth from the working poor of the Third World to the rich investors of the industrial world.

Most foreign aid monies and loans that go from rich to poor nations never reach the needy. Some of the money is actually used to subsidize foreign corporate investment and some of it finds its way into the pockets of corrupt rulers. The pattern of a growing national debt and a self-enriching local elite that complies with US counter-revolutionary policies could be observed in Chile under Pinochet, Nicaragua under Somoza, the Philippines under Marcos, Zaire under Mobutu, and Indonesia under Suharto, to name a few.

Maldevelopment What prevails in the Third World is not 'underdevelopment' as such but maldevelopment. The poorer nation's economic development is distorted, concentrated around a few extractive industries that are most profitable for the multinational investors. The corporations do not invest necessarily to obtain raw materials for their home country's market, but to make monopoly profits from underpriced resources and cheap labour. The resources extracted and the finished goods produced by cheap labour are sold to whatever country is the highest bidder and not just to the home country. The poor nation's maldevelopment is manifested in high-rise luxury hotels in the capital city instead of housing for the poor, cosmetic plastic surgery clinics for the rich instead of hospitals for the people, rich export crops for agri-business instead of food for local markets, highways that go from the mines and latifundia to the refineries and ports instead of roads that reach isolated villages. Some political scientists call this 'modernization'.

Cultural imperialism Imperialism exercises control over the ideational environment as well as the material one. No country enjoys such ideological hegemony over the world as does the United States (Parenti 1989). American films, television shows, music, fashions and consumer products inundate Latin America, Asia and Africa – not to mention Western and Eastern Europe. US advertising agencies dominate the advertising industries of the world. Millions of news reports, photographs, commentaries, editorials, syndicated columns and feature stories from US media sources saturate the Third World each year. The average Third World nation is usually more exposed to US viewpoints than to those of neighbouring countries or its own hinterland. Millions of comic books and magazines containing anti-communist or pro-US themes are published and distributed by US information agencies. The US Central Intelligence Agency (CIA) alone owns outright over 200 newspapers, magazines, wire services and publishing houses in countries throughout the world. The Ford Foundation and other US foundations help maintain Third World universities, providing money for academic programmes, courses, textbooks and scholarship that are supportive of a US ideological perspective. Rightwing Christian missionary agencies preach political quiesence and anti-communism to native populations. The American Institute for Free Labor Development (AFILD), an agency of the American Federation of Labour–Congress of Industrial Organizations (AFL–CIO) with ample state department funding, has actively infiltrated Third World labour organizations or created tame unions that are more anti-communist than anti-management. AFILD graduates have been linked to *coups* and counter-insurgency work in various countries. Similar AFL–CIO undertakings operate in Africa and Asia.

Political infiltration Washington has financed conservative political parties in Latin America, Asia, Africa, and Western and Eastern Europe. The major qualification of these parties is that they be anti-socialist and friendly to Western capital penetration. (But in the United States itself, the integrity of the electoral process is presumably safeguarded by a law that makes it illegal for any foreigner to make a campaign contribution.) The CIA has infiltrated important political organizations in numerous countries and has maintained agents at the highest levels of various governments, among heads of state, military leaders and opposition political parties (Agee 1975).

Military domination Military force is no less important today than during the era of colonial conquest and direct military occupation. The United States maintains the most powerful military machine on earth, with bases around the world, supposedly to protect democracy from communist aggression. However, with the dissolution of the communist bloc, the US showed no sign of abandoning its global military network. The purpose of a US military presence in or around the Third World – as demonstrated by the direct use of US military forces in Vietnam, Cambodia, Laos, Lebanon, the Dominican Republic, Grenada and Panama – is not to ward off Russian or Chinese invasions but to prevent indigenous revolutionary or populist-nationalist governments from prevailing, ones that might develop more egalitarian and collectivist social orders that encroach upon multinational corporate interests.

Military force is also widely exercised indirectly. Third World armed forces, gendarmerie, and intelligence and security units – including death squads – are financed, supplied, trained, advised and equipped by the United States, not to safeguard their autocratic governments from communist invasion but to suppress and terrorize rebellious elements within their own populations. The CIA has organized *coups* or trained and equipped armies to attack governments – including some democratically elected ones – hostile to multinational interests, as in Guatemala, Cuba, Indonesia, Iran, Chile, Brazil, Angola, Mozambique, Nicaragua and Afghanistan.

Of the various notions about imperialism circulating today in the United States, the dominant view is the one that says imperialism does not exist. It is not recognized as a legitimate concept, certainly not by US political leaders or major news commentators or mainstream academicians and intellectuals, particularly if applied to US foreign policy. One may speak acceptably of 'nineteenth-century British imperialism' or 'Soviet imperialism', but *US* imperialism – a term that enjoys vigorous currency throughout much of the world – is dismissed as leftist ideological blather.

The dominant theory of the last half-century, enunciated repeatedly by writers like Barbara Ward (1962) and Walt Rostow (1962), and afforded wide currency in the United States and other parts of the Western world, states that the rich nations of the North will help uplift the 'backward' nations of the South, teaching them proper work habits, bringing them technology and development. It is an updated, sanitized version of imperialism's ideology about the white man's civilizing role. The backward economic sectors of the poor nations will release its workers, who then find more productive employment in the modern sector at higher wages. As capital accumulates, business reinvests its profits, thus creating still more productivity, jobs, buying power and markets. Eventually a modern and prosperous economy evolves.

As this entire discussion of imperialism has indicated, this 'development theory' or 'modernization theory', as it is sometimes called, bears little relation to reality. What has developed in the Third World is a particularly pernicious and exploitative form of dependent capitalism. If anything, economic conditions in the 'developing' nations have worsened drastically with the growth of multinational corporate investment. The problem is not poor lands, nor unproductive populations, but foreign exploitation and class inequality. Investors go into a country not to uplift it but to benefit themselves. Left out of this arrangement and victimized by it are the bulk of the populace, who live without proper health care and other basic human services; who endure increasingly desperate conditions of poverty, malnutrition and inflation; who, when fortunate enough to find employment, toil at underpaid jobs without benefit of occupational safety laws, environmental protections, or disability, retirement and unemployment benefits.

The common people of the imperialist countries are also victimized, albeit to a lesser degree, by having to pay for the costs of empire in heavy taxes, and in seeing their jobs exported to cheaper labour markets abroad. Americans pay for their empire with an overblown military establishment, cutbacks in human services, the neglect of environmental needs, the deterioration of transportation, education and health care systems, and a public debt that is larger than the entire Third World debt combined. As in Rome of old and in every empire since, the centre is depleted in order to fortify the periphery. The treasure of the people is squandered so that patricians can pursue their far-off ventures. The instability of such arrangements at home and abroad are contained by a growing technology of repression and violence and by a more penetrating ruling-class cultural hegemony.

Nothing has been said thus far about 'Soviet imperialism', a subject that has preoccupied Cold War analysts for decades. In fact, if imperialism is a system of economic expropriation, then it is hard to describe the Soviets as imperialistic. They did not own an acre of land, nor a factory or oil well in the Third World or in Cuba or Eastern Europe. If anything, through most of the post-war era, certainly after 1956, Moscow's trade and aid relations with other socialist countries were decidedly favourable to those countries, contrary to the imperialist pattern in which wealth flows from the client states to the dominant nation. A report in the *New York Times* (Clines 1990) notes that the Soviet Union was seeking ways to relinquish its traditional position of subsidizing the economies of other Comecon members, like Bulgaria, Cuba, Czechoslovakia, Poland and Romania. The report noted that Moscow typically offered valuable oil and gas to these members but 'received in return relatively inferior products with little world market value'. In effect, the Soviets were subsidizing the other Comecon nations, permitting them to trade their better goods with the West and dispose of the rest through Moscow in return for much-needed fuel supplies often at below world market prices. The same kinds of fuel subsidies were long extended to restless republics within the Soviet Union, such as Lithuania. Again, this is the reverse of what imperialist relations have been throughout history.

The contrast between US and Soviet hegemony shows up in the substantial differences in economic conditions between US client states of the Third World and Soviet bloc nations – as measured by overall health and education standards, job security, work conditions and availability of human services. While communist nations may have been economically stagnant, bureaucratic, and politically repressed, material conditions for the common populace were superior to those found in most of the Third World. However, by 1990, there were signs that this was less true. The collapse of communist governments in Eastern Europe brought an increasing privatization of economies and greater reliance on market forces. It also meant the end for many state subsidies in food, housing and clothing, bringing conditions of hardship that began to resemble the Third World. Thus, while Poland dreamed of becoming another capitalist America, it seemed more likely to end up another capitalist Mexico.

All this is not to deny that until the *glasnost* and *perestroika* policies of the late 1980s the Soviets were hegemonic in their dealings with Eastern Europe, as evinced by their military interventions to suppress uprisings in Hungary in 1956 and Czechoslovakia in 1968. Throughout the post-war era, the Soviets had a record of intervening politically in Eastern Europe, a region that repeatedly has been an avenue of invasion and mortal threat to them. The Soviet goal was to prevent anti-communist regimes from re-emerging on their borders, even if this entailed committing interventionist and undemocratic abuses. By 1990 this hegemonic policy seemed to have come to an end, as Soviet troops withdrew from Czechoslovakia and Hungary and strongly anti-communist regimes re-emerged throughout Eastern Europe. Within the Soviet

Union itself, hegemonic conflicts arose between the central government and various Soviet republics, some of which took overtly secessionist routes.

Another country that does not have a markedly imperialist history, as the word is used here, is China. Yet, China, too, both in its pre-revolutionary and post-revolutionary stages, has acted in a hegemonic fashion toward such countries as Tibet and Vietnam. Claiming an age-old suzerainty over Tibet, China occupied and to some degree repopulated that country, demolishing its feudal theocratic rule, incurring the enmity of devout Buddhist elements and much of the indigenous population. It is said that Vietnam, too, has acted in a hegemonic fashion toward Laos and toward Cambodia, and that China has pursued a hegemonic interest in Cambodia.

In sum, the absence of the kind of imperialist relations that involve capital penetration and capital extraction does not guarantee the absence of hegemonic power relations. These latter continue to characterize the affairs of nations, be they capitalist or socialist. Hegemonic relations are motivated by competition for territory and scarce resources, boundary conflicts, a desire to seek security and national advantage through dominance, a desire to prevent the dismemberment of the nation-state by ethnic dissidents, and other such considerations.

With the dissolution of the communist bloc nations, hegemonic conflicts may increase within the capitalist world, both in Europe and between such large commercial powers as Japan and the United States. Whatever these developments, imperialism will not soon disappear, not in the way existing communism seems to be doing. The capitalist interests that own the land, markets and natural resources, and control the labour of so much of the world, including increasing portions of the erstwhile socialist world, are not about to dissolve themselves and democratize their global relations with weaker, less fortunate peoples. Imperialism is still very much with us, and so are the struggles against it.

REFERENCES

Adams P. and Solomon, L. (1985) *In the Name of Progress: The Underside of Foreign Aid*, Toronto: Energy Probe Research Foundation.

Agee, P. (1975) *Inside the Company: A CIA Diary*, London: Penguin.

Clines, F. X. (1990) 'Soviets and partners say Comecon needs repair', *New York Times* 9 January: A13.

Drechsler, H. (1966) *Let us Die Fighting*, Berlin: Akademie-Verlag.

Ferencz, B. (1979) *Less Than Slaves*, Cambridge, Mass.: Harvard University Press.

Frank, A. G. (1967) *Capitalism and Underdevelopment in Latin America*, New York: Monthly Review Press.

Jenkins, S. (1954) *American Economic Policy Toward the Philippines*, Stanford: Stanford University Press.

Lenin, V. I. (1937) *Imperialism: The Highest Stage of Capitalism* (1916), New York: International Publishers.

Lopez, G. and Stohl, M. (eds) (1985) *Development, Dependence, and State Repression*, Westport, Conn.: Greenwood Press.

Magdoff, H. (1970) 'The logic of imperialism', *Social Policy* 1 (September-October): 21–9.

Marx, K. (1968) Correspondence (1881), in *Karl Marx on Colonialism and Modernization*, ed. S. Avineri, New York: Doubleday.

Marx, K. and Engels, F. (1969) *Manifesto of the Communist Party*, reprinted in *Selected Works*, Vol. 1, Moscow: Progress Publishers.

———————(1972) *On Colonialism (Selected Writings)*, New York: International Publishers.

Mayer, A. (1988) *Why Did the Heavens Not Darken: The 'Final Solution' in History*, New York: Pantheon.

Miller, S. M., Bennett, R. and Alapatt, C. (1970) 'Does the US economy require imperialism?', *Social Policy* 1 (September-October): 20–7.

Parenti, M. (1989) *The Sword and the Dollar: Imperialism, Revolution, and the Arms Race*, New York: St Martin's Press.

Payer, C. (1975) *The Debt Trap*, New York: Monthly Review Press.

Rostow, W. W. (1962) *The Stages of Economic Growth: A Non-Communist Manifesto*, Cambridge: Cambridge University Press.

Stavrianos, L. S. (1981) *Global Rift: The Third World Comes of Age*, New York: William Murrow.

Szymanski, A. (1981) *The Logic of Imperialism*, New York: Praeger.

Veblen, T. (1932) *The Theory of the Business Enterprise* (1904), New York: Charles Scribner's Sons.

Ward, B. (1962) *The Rich Nations and the Poor Nations*, New York: W. W. Norton.

Williams, W. A. (1976) 'American interventionism in Russia: 1917–20', in D. Horowitz (ed.) *Containment and Revolution*, Boston: Beacon Press.

FURTHER READING

Ake, C. (1981) *A Political Economy of Africa*, Harlow: Longman.

Berberglu, B. (1987) *The Internationalization of Capital: Imperialism and Capitalist Development on a World Scale*, New York: Praeger.

Blum, W. (1986) *The CIA: A Forgotten History*, London: Zed Books.

Hobson, J. A. (1902) *Imperialism*, reprinted 1965, Ann Arbor: University of Michigan Press.

Kolko, G. (1988) *Confronting the Third World: United States Foreign Policy, 1945–1980*, New York: Pantheon Press.

Lenin, V. I. (1937) *Imperialism, the Highest Stage of Capitalism*, New York: International Publishers.

Marx, K. and Engels, F. (1972) *On Colonialism (Selected Writings)*, New York: International Publishers.

Parenti, M. (1989) *The Sword and the Dollar: Imperialism, Revolution, and the Arms Race*, New York: St Martin's Press.

Polyansky, F. (1973) *An Economic History: The Age of Imperialism (1870–1917)*, Moscow: Progress Publishers (available from Chicago: Imported Publications).

Stavrianos, L. S. (1981) *Global Rift: The Third World Comes of Age*, New York: William Murrow.

Szymanski, A. (1981) *The Logic of Imperialism*, New York: Praeger.

70

NATIONALISM

ANTHONY D. SMITH

Nationalism is a term with four main usages:

1 as a general process of the formation of nations, sometimes called 'nation building' (although that term often includes processes of 'state-making');
2 as 'national sentiment', or sentiments, attitudes and consciousness of belonging to a 'nation', and aspirations for its well-being, strength and security;
3 as a movement with political goals for the attainment or maintenance of the status of 'nation' and all that it implies, entailing one or more organizations and activities designed to achieve those goals; and
4 as a doctrine or, more loosely, an ideology which places the 'nation' at the centre of its concerns and which seeks its autonomy, unity and identity.

In addition, some writers have distinguished between 'political' and 'cultural' nationalism, the first focusing on the attainment and maintenance of independence and sovereignty for a nation, the second on the nation's identity and culture. For some, cultural and political nationalism entail each other; for others, they may vary independently (Hutchinson 1987).

No clear-cut definition of nationalism, even in its narrower senses, 3 and/ or 4 above, has emerged. Some, like Kedourie (1960), see it as a doctrine of the will; others, like Breuilly (1982), as a political argument; still others, like Kohn (1967), as a set of collective sentiments. The difficulty is that as a movement or ideology, let alone a sentiment, 'nationalism' covers a wide variety of ideals, beliefs and symbols, which no definition can hope to pinpoint, let alone comprehend. It is, however, possible to isolate from the words and actions of self-styled 'nationalists' certain common motifs: these include ideals of identity or distinctiveness of the nation, unity and fraternity of its citizens, and autonomy and autarchy of the territorial community. From these themes, an initial working definition of nationalism, the movement and ideology, may be derived. Thus nationalism becomes an ideological movement for the attainment and maintenance of identity, autonomy and unity for a social group, some of whose members consider it to be an actual or potential 'nation' (Smith 1973; 1983a: chapter 7).

The ideology of nationalism can be broken down into 'core' and 'secondary' elements. The 'core doctrine' may be summarized in the following propositions:

1 the world is divided into nations, each with its own distinctive character;
2 all political power derives from the nation;
3 loyalty to the nation overrides every other loyalty;
4 true freedom can only be realized through identification with a nation;
5 global peace and freedom depend on the liberty and and security of all nations;
6 nations can only be 'free' in their own sovereign states.

Though early nationalists like Herder and Bolingbroke did not draw the inference in point 6, and some nations have stopped short of demanding their own sovereign state (for example, Catalonia and Scotland), the other propositions figure in every nationalist ideology and movement. Because of their general character, however, specific nationalisms find it necessary to add 'secondary' elements or 'supporting theories', like Atatürk's Sun Language theory of Turkish origins or the German Romantic concept of a *Volkseele*, or more generally, linguistic or 'racial' theories. We can also distinguish recurrent ideological varieties of nationalism, along the lines of Hans Kohn's 'Western' and 'Eastern' nationalisms, the first of which sees nations as 'associations' of territorial populations governed by a single set of laws and institutions, while the second regards nations as organic wholes with a fixed culture and character, which stamps the individual forever (Kohn 1967).

There is even more disagreement over the definition of the 'nation'. A few scholars tend to equate the nation with the state, and nationalism with state-grounded and state-orientated movements (see Geertz 1963). Most, however, would accept that the nation belongs to the cultural and/or social psychological spheres. For some it constitutes a more or less artificial construct, a sovereign, but limited 'imagined community' (Anderson 1983); for others a large-scale, anonymous, unmediated, co-cultural unit (Gellner 1964: chapter 7); while others regard it as a self-aware ethnic group (Connor 1972, 1978). For such people, the 'nation' as a principle of socio-cultural organization or as a cultural concept, needs to be sharply distinguished from the state as an autonomous set of public institutions (Tivey 1980). On the other hand, purely subjective definitions run into the problem that any group of people who claim the status of 'nation' in virtue of their will or desires, must be accorded legitimacy; not only would such a criterion fail to discriminate between all kinds of aspirant collectivities, it would immeasurably complicate an already difficult international scene. Even more circumscribed cultural definitions encounter problems, being either too restrictive to accommodate the various types of nation and nationalism, or too vague and general to be useful (see Gellner 1983: chapter 5).

Nevertheless, it is along the lines of a 'culturalist' definition that progress is most likely to be made, for here 'objective' and 'subjective' elements which comprise the nation are intertwined. Two criteria appear to be essential to the definition of a nation: the first is cultural, the existence among some (if not all) of the population of an increasingly distinctive culture and history; the other is territorial, the possibility for a population (or part of it) to locate itself in a particular stretch of territory, a historic 'homeland'. This suggests the importance of historical myths and memories, related to the 'homeland' and fostering a particular culture. It also suggests the need for a population to be mobile throughout its homeland and have a single division of labour in that territory. This in turn implies the existence of a single set of laws, specifying common rights and duties for members of the nation. We may therefore initially define a nation as a community of common history and culture, occupying a given historic territory, and possessing a single economic system and a single code of rights and duties for all members. Where such nations also have their own sovereign states, the members will be citizens, and usually a single state education system prevails.

We are, however, dealing with an 'ideal-type' construct. Given nations will approximate to this touchstone; for example, some members may well be 'second-class' citizens, or only part of a historic territory may now be occupied by the members, or the historic culture may cover only part of the membership, and even then only superficially.

On this definition, a 'nation-state' is a nation with a sovereign state to itself alone; by such a criterion, most present-day 'nation-states' would fail the test, allowing plenty of scope for minority ethnic nationalisms when conditions are favourable (see Connor 1972).

THEORIES OF NATIONALISM

Despite earlier neglect, there has recently been a spate of systematic attempts to explain the causes, nature and consequences of nations and nationalism. Such explanations fall into three main groups: 'perennialist', 'modernist' and mixed 'symbolic' theories.

As the name implies, 'perennialists' view nations as 'always there', part of the fabric of history from its first records. This is what most nationalists believed (see Snyder 1954), as did an earlier generation of scholars (see Walek-Czernecki 1929; Tipton 1972). The even more radical 'primordialism' of many nationalists, who saw nations as fixed, 'natural' units, like human speech or physiognomy, has been discredited, though it has been applied to ethnicity by some socio-biologists (Van den Berghe 1979) in a challenging manner. Others have used a 'weak' primordialism to explain the strong and durable attachments to ethnic communities and nations on the part of many populations (Fishman 1980). In general, however, a blanket 'perennialism' does not square with the facts of collective cultural identities in history; we may, if we so desire, choose to call the ancient Persians and Assyrians 'nations', but we shall then need new terms to specify the considerable differences between such ancient collectivities and modern ones such as the French or Poles. We shall also have to recognize that such 'nations' may dissolve or be absorbed, or may radically change their character; modern Egyptians and Persians are both culturally and demographically different from their 'forebears' (Brass 1979).

Recent theories of nations and nationalism have been largely 'modernist'. They have located the nation firmly in the modern world, and explained its appearance in terms of 'modernization', a wide concept covering such processes as the rise of capitalism, industrialization, urbanization, political mobilization, secularization, mass education and the rise of science. Karl Deutsch (1966) pioneered a socio-demographic approach to nationalism, charting the rise of social mobilization and its concomitant, cultural assimilation, through such indices as urbanization, literacy, mass media and voting patterns. Benedict Anderson (1983: 40–9) has added some important cultural dimensions. Focusing on nationalism's ability to provide an alternative community and faith to those of a declining religion and dynastic realm, Anderson highlights the role of new conceptions of empty, homogenous, calendrical time, and of the technology of 'print-capitalism'. Printing made it possible to turn the book into the first commodity, and so break up the inherited clerical linguistic monopolies (of Latin, in particular) and substitute secular works in indigenous languages. Books, journals, newspapers, reports, novels, plays and articles were able to conjure up the image of communities which were sovereign but limited in space, while moving along the flow of calendrical, linear time, among people who would never meet each other. The nation is therefore essentially an imagined and narrated category, suited to an era of cultural publics bounded by language and territory, and to those administrative or intellectual elites whose 'pilgrimages' to their respective cultural centres enabled them to imagine themselves and their provinces or colonies as potential 'nations.'

A similar concern with the modernity and artificiality of the nation and nationalism is found in the work of scholars on the 'invention of tradition'. Hobsbawm and Ranger (1983), in particular, see the 'nation' as serving important cohesive functions in rapidly industrializing societies undergoing mass democratization. Hence the spate of 'invented' national traditions in the period 1870–1914 in Europe, the immense stress on symbolism and ritual, in flags, parades, monuments, societies, anthems and dress, all of which help to counteract the divisive class conflicts of industrial capitalism. This emphasis is quite compatible with the claim that nationalism as a political argument emerges in a period of alienation induced by the growing split between the state and civil society that has been widening in Europe since the sixteenth century (Breuilly 1982).

All of this suggests that the nation, apart from being 'modern', may be most fruitfully viewed as an imagined construct. It is easy, then, to slide into regarding it as 'imaginary', a device of intellectuals or other self-interested elites for the acquisition of power and wealth. Similarly, an undue emphasis on invented traditions and the novelties of print-capitalism may obscure important links between nations as 'constructs' and pre-existent ethnic ties (see the essays in Glazer and Moynihan 1975).

Similar objections can be made to the diffusionist, and often psychological, models of some historians of nationalism, such as Trevor-Roper (1961) and Kedourie (1960). The latter offers a sophisticated account of the philosophical background of nationalism as a European doctrine 'invented' at the beginning of the nineteenth century, especially in the Germany of Kant and his Romantic successors, Fichte, Schlegel and Muller. For Kedourie, this Romantic nationalism is basically a doctrine of the will, decked out with linguistic trappings, which render it even more incoherent and implausible. Though owing something to the example of the French revolution, this doctrine was essentially a product of an intelligentsia alienated by its exclusion from power in the petty German principalities. Nationalism fitted with the *Zeitgeist*, one of restless ambition and breakdown of political habits and viable communities like the family and religion. Striving after an unattainable perfection in this world, such 'children's crusades' could only unleash terror, atrocity and war, especially in ethnically mixed areas such as Eastern Europe and the Middle East.

For Kedourie, human beings need to 'belong' in a stable community, and nationalism's success lay in its ability to provide such a community, albeit one of desire and imagination, in the place of eroded traditional faiths. In Africa and Asia, too, European imperialism had pulverized traditional societies and brought literacy and colonial bureaucracy, which discriminated against the indigenous intelligentsia. In their ensuing discontent, African and Asian intellectuals had adapted European ideas of the nation to indigenous ethnic realities, invoking the 'dark gods' of their ancestral faiths to mobilize, and manipulate, the illiterate masses. But the origins of nationalism's appeal lay not only in the insults and destruction of imperialism but also in the peculiar messianic character, the promise of political salvation, of nationalism. This, in turn, Kedourie (1971) traces to the millennial doctrines of medieval Christendom, to Joachim of Fiore, the Franciscan Spirituals and the Munster Anabaptists, and ultimately to the Book of Revelations, which proclaimed the imminent advent of the Kingdom of Christ and his Saints to rule a 'new heaven and earth' for a thousand years. Nationalism must be seen as the secular heir of medieval millennialism, whose object was to destroy the barriers between private and public spheres and create a new elect on earth, by destroying the old order.

Not every scholar would agree with such an evaluation of nationalism. While many would concede the incoherence of the doctrine and its often baneful influence in world affairs, few would see it as millennial in character. Nationalism is, after all, an optimistic, human-centred and auto-emancipatory ideology, while millennialism is fundamentally pessimistic and world-denying. Its appeal is usually to the poorest, the most ignorant and marginal sectors of society, whereas nationalism tends to appeal to more educated, urban groups – intelligentsia, bureaucrats, bougeoisie, officers, lower clergy, gentry and, on occasion, skilled workers. Historically, too, there is no line of filiation between millennialism and nationalism: we find millennial movements that spawn no nationalism, and nationalist movements that are neither born of, nor preceded by, millennial outbursts, as in Finland, Armenia and Egypt, for example (Smith 1979: chapter 2).

Other 'modernist' theories of nationalism also emphasize the disruptive nature of European modernization. J. H. Kautsky, for example, sees modernization as a solvent of the old order in Asia and Africa, and as the creator of new social groups – bourgeoisie, workers, intellectuals – who seek modernization without the fetters of colonialism. Intellectuals, in particular, are attuned to the values and skills of modernity, and their nationalism is essentially a bid for leadership of a new social order in which their ideals and skills can flourish. Their kind of nationalism, in contrast to the European model, is really an anti-colonialism, which all too easily seeks the communist route to rapid industrialization (Kautsky 1962).

'Modernization' also provides the key to the most comprehensive theory of nationalism to date. Ernest Gellner (1964: chapter 7; 1983) claims that it is the 'uneven' character of the tide of modernization and industrialization, as it spreads out from its Western heartlands, that ensures a nationalist response. On the one hand, modernization erodes the role relationships of traditional societies, replacing their 'structure' by a new linguistic and literary 'culture'. Today all men and women are 'clerks': they have to be literate as well as numerate to run an industrial society, they have to be mobile and educated, and they have to communicate in a common idiom, usually a common literary language. In one sense, nationalism is the process whereby low oral cultures are turned into high literate ones through a public, standardized, compulsory mass education system. Since only the state has the resources to provide such an education system, today's nations tend to be large in scale and numbers. There is, however, an upper limit to the nation which makes it smaller than earlier empires or world-faiths: namely, the uneven and hence divisive character of the process of modernization. This creates a new system of stratification in urban centres, as the old-established city-dwellers try to keep down, or out, new arrivals from the countryside, uprooted by the 'push' and 'pull' of modernization. If the new arrivals look different, have a different religion or speak a different language, cultural discrimination will soon be imposed upon class conflict, and the 'proletariat' of ex-peasants will heed the calls of their 'intellectuals' to secede and form a new state.

In his later work, Gellner (1983) explained why pre-modern societies could have no room for nations and nationalism, while modern societies had to have both. Essentially, it was a question of the need for cultural homogeneity. In 'agro-literate' societies, elites had a different culture from the mass of food-producers, who were themselves divided into a series of discrete cultures. There was no need to unify these separate cultures or social strata, and there was enormous obstacles in the way of doing so. In modern industrial societies, it was both possible and necessary to unite different cultures and social groups, because of the homogenizing needs of industrialism. The only exceptions were those 'ancient chasms' of colour and textual religion, which would not disappear in the 'sea of industria'; they usually generated new nations as the disprivileged seceded from their oppressors.

The idea that modernization is jagged and uneven also looms large in the theory of Tom Nairn (1977). He argues that Western imperialism, by its uneven character, generates resistance by the elites in the 'periphery', and that, given their underdevelopment and helplessness, they are forced to 'invite the masses into history' (Nairn 1977: 340). Given the vernacular cultures of the peasant masses, romantic nationalism takes on a populist character, as it extols the virtues of the 'folk'. Nations and nationalism, therefore, must be seen as logical responses to the 'machinery of world political economy' (ibid.: 335). Today, such nationalisms are being exported back to the Western 'core' in the form of ethnic 'neo-nationalisms' among Western minority groups and nations from the Basques and Scots to the Occitanians and Frisians.

The central difficulty with such developmental theories is their determinism. They locate a multifaceted and elusive phenomenon like nationalism in the logic of capitalism or industrialism, relying on its 'uneven' mechanisms to explain every variation. But this is to put too heavy an explanatory load on a single dimension. It is not possible to derive the incidence, differing intensities and timings of nationalisms from the needs of the industrial system, or its uneven diffusion. This is quite apart from the fact that several Western nations emerged prior to industrialism, and even to the capitalist system. What such theories neglect is not only the central role of the bureaucratic state, both in the West and in the colonies, but also the importance of pre-existing ethnic ties, which so often provide the sites and impetus to the formation of nations. This is also true to some extent of the model of 'internal colonialism', which has been used to explain the rise of ethnic autonomy movements in Britain and, by implication, in the Western industrialized societies (Hechter 1975). Here, also, too much weight is accorded to relative deprivation of spatial 'regions', following industrialization, in explaining why 'peripheral sectionalism' persists, while too little is accorded to the presence (or absence) of a strong sense of ethnic identity and 'ethno-history' (see the essays in Stone 1979; Smith 1981: chapter 2).

In contrast to all these 'modernist' theories, a number of scholars have emphasized the pre-modern roots of modern nations. While they do not deny that several components of the nation are modern, including a centralized economy and common legal rights and duties, they also point to the persistence of pre-modern components – myths of ancestry, historical memories, elements of a common culture, perhaps a name and a homeland. These no doubt experience changes of content and even form over the long term, but they often continue to possess sufficient force and vibrancy to lend the ensuing nation its distinctive character and sense of identity. This is especially true of language, which Fishman (1972, 1980) argues is the most potent and emotive of social bonds. The same could be claimed for religion, which has experienced something of a 'nationalized' revival in many areas, particularly Islamic ones but also in India, Poland, Ireland and Latin America. More generally, the enduring power of ethnicity in the modern world, and its independence of economic and even political forces, suggests that we must look elsewhere for an adequate account of so complex a phenomenon as nationalism (Connor 1984; Smith 1981).

Some scholars have gone on to explore the pre-modern 'symbolic' background of nationalism in pre-existing ethnic communities. John Armstrong (1982) proposed a social interaction model of ethnic boundaries and persistence, following the lead of Fredrik Barth (1969), and applied it to ethnic identities in medieval Islam and Christendom. Claiming that, while the content of a group's culture may change, its boundaries are often preserved by symbols which act as 'border guards' against outsiders, Armstrong analysed the impact of various factors on the formation and preservation of ethnic boundaries. By examining their 'myth-symbol' complexes, he argued, one could see how ethnic identity was shaped by lifestyles, world religions, urban milieux, imperial *mythomoteurs* and administrations, religious organization and linguistic codes. Despite his phenomenological position, Armstrong in fact underpins the tenacity of ethnic ties and the potency of many communities, despite often shifting perceptions of their members.

In a similar vein, A. D. Smith (1986, 1988) traced the locations and character of several modern nations back to pre-existing ethnic communities (*ethnie*) whose myths, memories, symbols and values continued, in varying degrees, to bind and inspire populations in given areas. While agreeing with the 'modernists' that nations are in important respects 'modern', he points to the ways in which a 'returning intelligentsia' has recreated communities out of pre-existing motifs, including the 'poetic spaces' and 'golden ages' of heroes of a selectively rediscovered ethnic past. It is these motifs – myths, symbols, memories and the like – that give otherwise 'civic' nations their specific atmosphere and character, and attach their members to a nation that is felt to be venerable, if not primordial. Hence it is necessary to examine the nature and types of pre-modern *ethnie*, and their dynastic, communal and sacral *mythomoteurs*. It is particularly important to distinguish two types of pre-modern *ethnie*, the one 'lateral', extensive and aristocratic, the other 'vertical', intensive and demotic. In these two types lie the seeds of modern nations, and the dual character of the modern nation, at once civic and genealogical. Here too lie the origins of the different routes by which nations are formed. Interestingly enough, it was the 'lateral' type of *ethnie* which, by helping to create an incorporating bureaucratic state in the West (under the right conditions), provided the basis and 'core' of the first national states, and hence modern nations. Elsewhere, it was more a question of mobilizing demotic *ethnie*, politicizing and activating them, and thereby creating nations. In fact, ethnic nations based upon 'demotic' *ethnie* have become the most numerous class of nation, and the attempt to create political communities or 'civic' territorial nations in sub-Saharan Africa has met with very variable and qualified success (Neuberger 1986; Smith 1983b). A world of small ethnic nations is inevitably a precarious one. Combined with the uneven distribution of ethno-history and of capitalism, this makes it unlikely that we shall witness the 'withering away' of nations or nationalism in the foreseeable future.

THE COURSE AND CONSEQUENCES OF NATIONALISM

From this perspective, a history of nationalism must commence with the first records of ethnic community and identity in the ancient Near East, and examine the ways in which the example and incidence of 'lateral' and 'demotic' *ethnie* such as the Egyptians, Assyrians, Persians, Greeks, Jews and Armenians have helped to accustom and influence humankind to the idea and reality of ethnicity, as well as providing some of the myths, memories and traditions which later *ethnie*, and even modern intelligentsias, could make use of. Even if we cannot accept the antiquity of nations and of 'nationalism', the sentiments and ties of ethnicity were very real and sometimes politically significant, as in Roman Judaea, Greece and some early medieval *regna* (Fondation Hardt 1962; Brandon 1967; Reynolds 1984).

While there have been cases of pre-modern 'ethnic states' (ancient Egypt, Japan, Safavid Persia), it was in the West that *ethnie* were able to provide the cultural base for bureaucratic states that incorporated both outlying regions and *ethnie*, and middle and lower social classes. It was here that we meet the first nations, or what Seton-Watson (1977) has called the 'old, continuous nations', which antedated the rise of nationalism.

The eighteenth century marked a watershed in the history of nation formation. While nations were being formed in France, Spain, England, Holland, Sweden and Russia from the fourteenth century, it was in the late eighteenth century that the ideology of nationalism emerged, first in revolutionary France and then in Germany, Spain, Poland, Greece and Latin America, as well as the newly formed United States of America. Such ideological movements were preceded by at least a century of gestation, in which the idea of 'national character' and 'national genius' became widespread among the European educated classes (Kemilainen 1964). After 1800, many more nations were created, by design, as part of a conscious nationalist programme, but usually on the basis of pre-existing ethnic ties – myths, memories, symbols and traditions harking back to the medieval period.

During the nineteenth century, nationalisms appeared as unification movements in Germany and Italy, and as secession movements in Hungary, Romania, Bulgaria, Poland, Serbia and Croatia, and among Czechs, Slovaks and others in Eastern Europe and Russia. By the early twentieth century, nationalist movements led by native intelligentsias and backed by a variety of social groups had emerged in the Middle East, India, China, Japan and South East Asia, and after 1918 they flowered in sub-Saharan Africa, where they soon became movements of decolonization.

In inter-war Europe, however, while some nationalisms were partially satisfied by the Treaty of Versailles, others succumbed to the challenge of a much more radical, and often racist, fascism (Smith 1979: chapter 2; but see Breuilly 1982). Subsequently, spurred perhaps by the example of African and Asian decolonization, a wave of ethnic 'neo-nationalism' surged over the old-established, industrial states of the West, with Quebecois, Bretons, Scots, Welsh, Basques, Catalans, Flemish and Corsicans demanding much greater autonomy and regional control (Esman 1977; Smith 1981: chapter 9). This has been characterized as an 'ethnic revival', but some would prefer to think of it as another extension of ethno-nationalism, or the revitalization of surviving premodern ethnic ties (see Connor 1977).

Outside Europe, movements of ethnic secession and irredentism have appeared in the wake of colonial liberation among *ethnie* or coalitions of *ethnie* such as the Tamils, Nagas, Moro, Shan and Karen, Sikhs, Kurds, Eritreans, Tigre, Ibo and BaKongo. In addition, there have been many more cases of heightened ethnic competition leading to ethnic violence in states like Malaysia, Indonesia, Burma, India, Angola, Uganda, Yugoslavia, the Soviet Union, Trinidad and, in respect of Black and Hispanic populations, the United States, to name only the more salient outside western Europe. For Horowitz (1985), these conflicts are the products of estimations of differential worth, and of comparisons of relative 'backwardness' of both ethnic groups and the regions they occupy. They are endemic wherever formerly relatively isolated groups have been brought together by colonialism, whose main effect has been to create much larger territories under unitary governments able to distribute scarce resources along ethnic lines, so aggravating the competition for power.

More generally, political scientists and scholars of international relations have been disturbed by the destabilizing potential of a global nationalism. Not only are the most intractable regional conflicts likely to possess an ethnic or national character, with a dangerous 'demonstration effect': the fragility of many new states, and regional and global inequalities in the division of labour, tend to exacerbate existing ethnic cleavages and sharpen national tensions within regions, often with the moral and material support of overseas ethnic kinsmen (see Said and Simmons 1976 and the essays in Lewis 1983). But, though the great and/or regional powers may support particular ethnic movements, they are loath to threaten existing state boundaries, given their own often multiethnic composition and their 'guardian' and 'beneficiary' roles in the global distribution of power and wealth. Most states have therefore had a free hand to suppress secession or irredentist movements among their minority *ethnie*, and have often been aided by the other *ethnie*, who feel threatened by a breakup, especially if they become 'stranded minorities', as in the Biafran case. As a result, few movements of secession since 1945 have met with success (only Singapore, Bangladesh and the Baltic States can be cited, although Cyprus and Lebanon could perhaps still move in that direction), nor has any irredentist movement.

Despite this lack of overt political success (measured solely by the criterion of independence), nationalism in both its forms (territorial-bureaucratic and ethno-cultural) remains a powerful and self-renewing force, given both the number and strength of *ethnie* in the world, and the political conflicts and economic inequalities off which they can feed. Whether we regard the long-term future as a 'post-industrial' era, or one of advanced capitalist industrialism, the chances of a diminution of nationalism are remote, despite wide variations in its intensity. The 'nation' as the basic unit of social and cultural organization is also unlikely to wither away, despite wider regional economic and political co-operation. Even the European Community is unlikely to override the profound sentiments of French, Italian and British national identity, despite a slow growth of a wider European feeling in some sectors of the populations. But then national sentiment can comfortably co-exist with other levels of identification, or even appear at more than one level, as Ghanaian identity can co-exist with, and even find sustenance in, pan-Africanism. Given the structure of regional interstate systems, the unevenness of capitalism and the number and diversity of 'ethno-histories', whose myths and memories inspire submerged as well as more satisfied *ethnie*, there is little likelihood of an early 'supersession' of the nation and nationalism by a global cosmopolitanism (Richmond 1984; Smith 1990).

REFERENCES

Anderson, B. (1983) *Imagined Communities*, London: Verso Editions/New Left Books.
Armstrong, J. (1982) *Nations Before Nationalism*, Chapel Hill: University of North Carolina Press.
Barth, F. (ed.) (1969) *Ethnic Groups and Boundaries*, Boston: Little, Brown & Co.
Brandon, S. G. F. (1967) *Jesus and the Zealots*, Manchester: Manchester University Press.
Brass, P. (ed.) (1979) 'Elite groups, symbol manipulation and ethnic identity among the Muslims of South Asia', in D. Taylor and M. Yapp (eds) *Political Identity in South Asia*, London: SOAS/Curzon Press.
Breuilly, J. (1982) *Nationalism and the State*, Manchester: Manchester University Press.
Connor, W. (1972) 'Nation-building or nation-destroying?', *World Politics* 24: 319–55.
——(1977) 'Ethno-nationalism in the First World', in M. Esman (ed.) *Ethnic Conflict in the Western World*, Ithaca, NY: Cornell University Press.
——(1984) 'Eco- or ethno-nationalism?', *Ethnic and Racial Studies* 7: 342–59.
Deutsch, K. W. (1966) *Nationalism and Social Communication*, 2nd edn, New York: MIT Press.
Esman, M. (ed.) (1977) *Ethnic Conflict in the Western World*, Ithaca, NY: Cornell University Press.
Fishman, J. (1980) 'Social theory and ethnography', in P. Sugar (ed.) *Ethnic Diversity and Conflict in Eastern Europe*, Santa Barbara, Calif.: ABC-Clio.
Fondation Hardt (1962): *Grecs et barbares*, Entretiens sur l'antiquité classique VIII, Geneva: Foundation Hardt.
Geertz, C. (1963) 'The integrative revolution', in C. Geertz (ed.) *Old Societies and New States*, New York: Free Press.
Gellner, E. (1964) *Thought and Change*, London: Weidenfeld & Nicolson.
——(1983) *Nations and Nationalism*, Oxford: Basil Blackwell.
Glazer, N. and Moynihan, D. (eds) (1975) *Ethnicity: Theory and Experience*, Cambridge, Mass.: Harvard University Press.
Hechter, M. (1975) *Internal Colonialism: The Celtic Fringe in British National Development, 1536–1966*, London: Routledge & Kegan Paul.
Hobsbawm, E. and Ranger, T. (eds) (1983) *The Invention of Tradition*, Cambridge: Cambridge University Press.
Horowitz, D. (1985) *Ethnic Groups in Conflict*, Berkeley, Los Angeles and London: University of California Press.
Hutchinson, J. (1987) *The Dynamics of Cultural Nationalism*, London: Allen & Unwin.
Kautsky, J. H. (ed.) (1962) *Political Change in Underdeveloped Countries*, New York: John Wiley.
Kedourie, E. (1960) *Nationalism*, London: Hutchinson.
——(ed.) (1971) *Nationalism in Asia and Africa*, London: Weidenfeld & Nicolson.
Kemilainen, A. (1964) *Nationalism: Problems Concerning the Word, Concept and Classification*, Yvaskyla: Kustantajat Publishers.
Kohn, H. (1967) *The Idea of Nationalism*, New York: Macmillan.

Lewis, I. (ed.) (1983) *National and Self-determination in the Horn of Africa*, London: Ithaca Press.

Nairn, T. (1977) *The Break-up of Britain*, London: New Left Books.

Neuberger, B. (1986) *National Self-determination in Post-colonial Africa*, Boulder, Colo.: Lynne Rienner.

Reynolds, S. (1984) *Kingdoms and Communities in Western Europe, 900–1300*, Oxford: Clarendon Press.

Richmond, A. (1984) 'Ethnic nationalism and post-industrialism', *Ethnic and Racial Studies* 7: 4–18.

Said, A. and Simmons, L. (eds) (1976) *Ethnicity in an International Context*, New Brunswick: Translation Books.

Seton-Watson, H. (1977) *Nations and States*, London: Methuen.

Smith, A. D. (1973) 'Nationalism: a trend report and annotated bibliography', *Current Sociology* 21(3): 1–178.

——(1979) *Nationalism in the Twentieth Century*, Oxford: Martin Robertson.

——(1981) *The Ethnic Revival in the Modern World*, Cambridge: Cambridge University Press.

——(1983a) *Theories of Nationalism*, 2nd edn, London: Duckworth.

——(1983b) *State and Nation in the Third World*, Brighton: Harvester.

——(1986) *The Ethnic Origins of Nations*, Oxford: Basil Blackwell.

——(1988) 'The myth of the "modern nation" and the myths of nations', *Ethnic and Racial Studies* 11: 1–26.

——(1990) 'The supersession of nationalism?', *International Journal of Comparative Sociology* 31 (1–2): 1–31.

Snyder, L. (1954) *The Meaning of Nationalism*, New Brunswick: Rutgers University Press.

Stone, J. (ed.) (1979) 'Internal colonialism', *Ethnic and Racial Studies* 2 (3).

Tipton, L. (ed.) (1972) *Nationalism in the Middle Ages*, New York: Holt, Rinehart & Winston.

Tivey, L. (ed.) (1980) *The Nation-State*, Oxford: Martin Robertson.

Trevor-Roper, H. (1961) *Jewish and Other Nationalisms*, London: Weidenfeld & Nicolson.

Van den Berghe, P. (1979) *The Ethnic Phenomenon*, New York: Elsevier.

Walek-Czernecki, M. T. (1929) 'Le rôle de la nationalité dans l'histoire de l'antiquité', *Bulletin of the International Committee of Historical Science* 2: 305–20.

FURTHER READING

Anderson, B. (1983) *Imagined Communities*, London: Verso Editions/New Left Books.

Armstrong, J. (1982) *Nations Before Nationalism*, Chapel Hill: University of North Carolina Press.

Breuilly, J. (1982) *Nationalism and the State*, Manchester: Manchester University Press.

Connor, W. (1972) 'Nation-building or nation-destroying?', *World Politics* 24: 319–55.

——(1978) 'A nation is a nation, is a state, is an ethnic group, is a . . .', *Ethnic and Racial Studies* 1: 377–400.

——(1984) *The National Question in Marxist-Leninist Theory and Strategy*, Princeton: Princeton University Press.

Deutsch, K. W. (1966) *Nationalism and Social Communication*, 2nd edn, New York: MIT Press.

Esman, M. (ed.) (1977) *Ethnic Conflict in the Western World*, Ithaca, NY: Cornell University Press.

Fishman, J. (ed.) (1968) *Language Problems of Developing Countries*, New York: John Wiley.

——(1972) *Language and Nationalism*, Rowley, Mass.: Newbury House.

Gellner, E. (1983) *Nations and Nationalism*, Oxford: Basil Blackwell.

Glazer, N. and Moynihan, D. (eds) (1975) *Ethnicity: Theory and Experience*, Cambridge, Mass.: Harvard University Press.

Hechter, M. (1975) *Internal Colonialism: The Celtic Fringe in British National Development, 1536–1966*, London: Routledge & Kegan Paul.

Hobsbawm, E. and Ranger, T. (eds) (1983) *The Invention of Tradition*, Cambridge: Cambridge University Press.

Horowitz, D. (1985) *Ethnic Groups in Conflict*, Berkeley, Los Angeles and London: University of California Press.

Kautsky, J. (ed.) (1962) *Political Change in Underdeveloped Countries*, New York: John Wiley.

Kedourie, E. (1960) *Nationalism*, London: Hutchinson.

——(ed.) (1971) *Nationalism in Asia and Africa*, London: Weidenfeld & Nicolson.

Kohn, H. (1967) *The Idea of Nationalism*, 2nd edn, New York: Collier-Macmillan.

Nairn, T. (1977) *The Break-up of Britain*, London: New Left Books.

Seton-Watson, H. (1977) *Nations and States*, London: Methuen.

Smith, A. D. (1981) *The Ethnic Revival in the Modern World*, Cambridge: Cambridge University Press.

——(1983) *Theories of Nationalism*, London: Duckworth.

——(1986) *The Ethnic Origins of Nations*, Oxford: Basil Blackwell.

——(1991) *National Identity*, Harmondsworth: Penguin.

71

THE INTERNATIONAL DEBT CRISIS

BARBARA STALLINGS

The current international debt crisis formally began on Friday, 13 August 1982, when the Mexican finance minister journeyed to Washington to announce that his country could not continue to service its foreign debt as originally contracted. In the months that followed, many other Third World nations followed suit, mainly in Latin America and sub-Saharan Africa. Although by many measures the African countries suffered more under the debt burden, the Latin American region was of greater immediate concern to policy makers. On the one hand, Latin America's debt (US $333 billion as of end-1982) was almost five times that of sub-Saharan Africa ($70 billion).[1] On the other hand, Latin America's debt was largely held by private banks, while Africa's was almost all owed to official (bilateral and multilateral) creditors. These differences meant that Africa's debt was more 'manageable' from the viewpoint of policy makers in the advanced industrial countries and multilateral agencies. Thus the notion of a debt *crisis* came to focus primarily on Latin America and a handful of countries from other regions.[2]

This focus is indicative of the way the industrial countries defined the crisis: it was a crisis that endangered the international financial system. If major Third World debtors could not pay the banks, the weaker banks might go bankrupt and set off an international chain reaction. US institutions were especially vulnerable. They were the major creditors of the Latin Americans; indeed, the nine largest US banks had lent more than their entire capital and reserve base to Latin America. The Third World development crisis, which was both reflected in the debt crisis and exacerbated by it, was of much less concern to the officials of the US government and multilateral agencies who gathered to deal with the Mexican problems in August 1982. The result was that the perception of the crisis was very different from the creditor and debtor perspectives.

This essay will concentrate on the group of most heavily indebted countries, primarily located in Latin America. It will first examine the origins of the debt crisis and the response during the 1980s. Then it will survey possible solutions. Finally, it will look at the theoretical issues raised by the crisis. Here we will return to the development questions as well as power relations in the international political economy.

ORIGINS AND HISTORY OF THE DEBT CRISIS

The immediate causes of the debt crisis date back to the lending binge of the private international banks during the period 1970–82. In the early 1970s, for the first time in four decades, business cycles in the United States and Western Europe coincided on the down-swing. Consequently, multinational corporations slowed their borrowing, and the banks began to look around for new clients in order to maintain their loan volume and thus their profit rates. In this context, certain Third World countries appeared increasingly attractive. The banks' problems were greatly exacerbated by the 1973–4 oil price rises as a serious recession hit the advanced capitalist world, further dampening loan demand, and members of the Organization of Petroleum Exporting Countries (OPEC) deposited the majority of their new revenues in US banks. The banks' growing need to make loans generated fierce competition for borrowers, and normal caution was abandoned as the process of 'recycling petrodollars' got under way. Several authors (Kindleberger 1978; Darity and Horn 1988; Devlin 1989) argue that this supply-side push caused Third World governments to take on debt beyond their means or desires.

While valid, the argument overlooks the fact that these governments had independent reasons for wanting to borrow. During the post-war period, expectations of rapid growth and improved living standards had emerged, and governments were increasingly seen as responsible for providing them. This was especially true for the military governments in power during the 1970s. To generate legitimacy, they stimulated growth by borrowing and investing in large-scale industrial projects. Also, of course, substantial sums went for arms purchases. Even the rich oil exporters took advantage of the opportunity to gain access to additional revenues to cover rising expenditures without having to alienate citizens with new taxes.

The complementary growth of supply and demand led to an unsustainable buildup of debt that ultimately led to the crisis of the 1980s. The high volume of debt, however, was a necessary but not sufficient cause. Other problems triggered it. Some were external (declining terms of trade, high interest rates, recession in the advanced industrial countries); others were internal (overvalued exchange rates, enormous budget deficits, capital flight). Exacerbating the situation in all cases was the cessation of foreign loans on which many Third World countries had come to depend.

Initially, it was thought that the crisis would be short-lived, but such predictions proved false, and most observers now expect the crisis to continue at least until the end of the century. The first decade can usefully be divided into three sub-periods. The first, lasting from 1982 to 1985, consisted mainly of crisis management. Although a temporary solution was devised for the Mexican case (Kraft 1984), it was quickly followed by other Third World governments who announced that they could not continue to service their debts either.

To deal with these problems, the US government, after some consultation with its allies and the international financial institutions, devised a basic strategy that was patterned after the Mexican experience. The strategy had four main elements: rescheduling of payments, usually with a grace period; new money from the private banks; additional finance from the international institutions; and policies on the part of debtor countries to cut budget deficits and produce trade surpluses. The reason for the emphasis on new loans, which would enable interest payments to continue, arose from the requirements of US banking regulations. These regulations specify a variety of penalties for overdue loans that have the effect of cutting bank profits. Since the US banks had very low reserves in 1982, a strategy that did not provide for prompt debt service could have caused chaos in the financial system.

Based on this strategy, three overlapping rounds of negotiations took place in 1982–5. During this period, thirty-four countries in Africa, Asia, Latin America and Eastern Europe rescheduled loans with the commercial banks (Watson *et al.* 1986). Two trends were evident. On the one hand, maturities lengthened. Initial reschedulings were for one year only; by 1984 multi-year rescheduling agreements (MYRAs) were introduced. On the other hand, financial terms softened. In the first negotiations, the interest spreads and commissions were substantially higher than those agreed for the original loans, so the banks were making money on the reschedulings. Eventually charges came down as it became clear that the countries could not pay, but there was an increasing reluctance on the part of the banks to provide new money, even though most of the 'new money' was going to pay interest.

The process followed in each of these rounds was similar. The banks organized themselves into creditor committees, one for each debtor nation. The committees were composed of about a dozen large banks from the United States, Europe and Japan; they negotiated on behalf of all creditor institutions. In other words, the creditors united but the debtors did not, despite some attempts in that direction (Roett 1989).

The second period began in late 1985, as it became clear that the debt crisis was still unresolved. Even those countries that were successful in running trade surpluses were mired in recession. The stagnation was mainly the result of the very policies that permitted debt service to continue. On the one hand, the principal source of the trade surpluses was a lower volume of imports, which often brought a fall in production. On the other hand, the combination of high debt service payments and low capital inflow led to large net transfers from debtor to creditor countries, and thus a decline in both investment and consumption.

The widespread call for policies focusing on renewed growth found a response in the new US Treasury Secretary, James Baker. At the annual meeting of the World Bank and the International Monetary Fund (IMF) in Seoul in October 1985, he announced the so-called Baker Plan, which was to provide $29 billion to fifteen heavily indebted countries over three years. The money was to come from the international financial institutions and the private banks; governments of the advanced industrial countries were not directly involved. In order to get access to these funds, debtor countries were to implement a set of policies to open their economies, promote exports and cut back on government economic activities. Together, the measures were expected to restore growth in contrast to the previous policies that had centred on austerity. The Baker Plan never received enthusiastic support. Critics charged that it was insufficient to deal with the problems at hand, and they pointed to the lack of a role for the governments of the advanced industrial countries as a major drawback. Its only apparent success was the Mexican negotiations of 1986, which provided new money and the most favourable terms since the debt crisis began (Bogdanowicz-Bindert 1985–6; Roett 1986; Conway 1987).

Although the Baker Plan, as modified by a 'menu approach' to increase banks' options, continued to be supported by the executive branch of the US government, congressional alternatives multiplied. Best known was the proposal introduced in June 1986 by Senator Bill Bradley. This would have cut interest rates by three points over a three-year period and forgiven 3 per cent of principal per year over the same period. No new money would have been required from the private banks, but the international institutions would have been responsible for the same amount as under the Baker scheme. Bradley calculated that his plan would provide $57 billion of debt relief over three years, while Baker's would offer $29 billion of new debt.

The time for debt relief, however, had not yet arrived because the large banks were still too vulnerable. That began to change in the late 1980s through several mechanisms. The banks increased their capital base through new equity offerings; they set aside more reserves against losses; and they began selling some of their Third World loans on the secondary market. The overall result was a sharp decline in the weight of Third World debt as a share of the banks' capital/reserve base, so they could survive losses without a crisis ensuing (ECLAC 1990).

The third period began with the inauguration of George Bush as US President in January 1989, but was anticipated by a Japanese proposal the previous year. Known as the Miyazawa Plan after Japan's then finance minister, the proposal was designed to restore growth to the indebted countries by limiting the negative transfers of foreign exchange. In order to cut down on service payments, a part of the debt was to be 'securitized'. The idea was to trade old loans for new long-term bonds with lower interest rates. Although earning less, the new bonds would arguably be safer assets, since they would be guaranteed by reserves to the debtor countries. The Miyazawa Plan was presented as complementary to the Baker Plan, and its voluntary and case-by-case nature was stressed, but it was not welcomed by the outgoing Reagan administration. At the IMF/World Bank annual meeting in September 1988, it was openly attacked by Treasury Secretary Brady (Stallings 1990a).

Six months later, as Treasury Secretary for President Bush rather than President Reagan, Brady adopted the main elements of the Miyazawa Plan and labelled them the Brady Plan. The Brady Plan, however, had some additional features. First, Brady proposed that the IMF, the World Bank and creditor governments lend money to debtor nations to help them finance debt reduction. Second, he suggested that creditor governments review their accounting, regulatory and tax codes to reduce disincentives for bank participation in debt reduction. Third, the plan encouraged a more flexible IMF policy to allow disbursement of its funds to governments that still had arrears with the private banks. The Brady Plan was rapidly transformed into action; Mexico, as usual, was the test case. Although the negotiations were long and turbulent, and many economists are dubious about whether the resulting cut in debt service is sufficient to restore growth, other nations have already begun to participate. By September 1990, the banks had also reached agreements with Costa Rica, the Philippines and Venezuela. In the process, the policy itself has continued to evolve.

POSSIBLE SOLUTIONS FOR THE DEBT CRISIS

Opinions about appropriate solutions for the debt crisis have shifted over the decade as the interpretation of the crisis has changed. In the early days, when the diagnosis centred on lack of liquidity, the answer was generally seen to be stretched-out payments and new loans. Later, as analysis began to suggest solvency problems, debt-reduction proposals became more prominent. This evolution can be seen in the US government position, which changed from crisis management to the Baker Plan to the Brady Plan. Nevertheless, certain principles have been maintained: case-by-case treatment, voluntary negotiations and market-oriented solutions.

Debt reduction, of course, can be achieved in many ways. The voluntary, market-based approaches have centred on three main techniques: debt-for-debt swaps, debt-for-equity swaps and buybacks. (See Williamson 1989 for a review of such proposals.) Trading debt for debt is the mechanism embodied in the Brady Plan, whereby medium-term loans are exchanged for long-term bonds. The latter have either a lower face value than the original loan or a lower interest rate. To make the arrangement attractive to the creditor, and therefore voluntary, a guarantee is given that the new bonds will indeed be serviced; one form of guarantee is money deposited in a special account held by an international agent. The main criticism of debt swaps is the added inflexibility they give to a nation's debt, since the bonds are more difficult to reschedule, and the need to put up reserves or obtain additional loans to finance the guarantees.

More controversial are debt-equity swaps, used extensively by the Chilean government and to a lesser extent by other debtor nations. This technique involves a prospective investor purchasing some of the target country's debt paper at a discount and then redeeming it at full face value from the country's central bank. The proceeds are used to make an equity investment in the country. Many criticisms have been levelled at debt-equity swaps, but the banks have frequently insisted that they be included in renegotiation packages. One type of criticism is the inflationary impact resulting from central bank emissions to redeem the debt. Another is the possibility that direct investment, which would have come into the country in any case, will have a reduced value because of the discount provided. In addition, the investment may quickly leave the country once the discount is obtained, or the profit outflow from the investment may exceed the debt service payment that it replaces. Finally, debt-equity swaps are criticized because they provide a vehicle for the denationaliz-ation of domestic assets; this has been an especially volatile issue when the asset in question is a state corporation that is being privatized (Ffrench-Davis 1987).

Buybacks, a third type of market-based transaction, operate through the secondary market that has developed for Third World debt. The debt of countries with serious problems is traded at heavy discounts, ranging from 4–5 cents on the dollar for a 'bad' debtor like Peru to 85–90 cents for a 'good' debtor like Chile. This situation obviously offers the temptation for a country to purchase its own debt at deflated value. In the world of voluntary transactions, however, a government must get permission from its creditors to engage in buybacks. The major user of this technique has been Bolivia, which repur-chased about half of its commercial bank debt with funds specifically provided by multilateral agencies and creditor governments. Criticism of buybacks cen-tres on the inefficient use of scarce foreign exchange, especially if only a small percentage of the debt is repurchased (Bulow and Rogoff 1988).

Beyond particular criticisms of the individual techniques just described, more fundamental critiques – and alternate proposals – have also been advanced. Underlying the alternatives are disagreements with the main tenets behind the existing approach, i.e. the voluntary, case-by-case, market-based characteristics. One important type of alternative is an international debt agency, which would purchase loans from the banks at a discount and then reschedule or reduce payments to debtor countries. Although such an agency could operate in many different ways, it would at least partially challenge the case-by-case treatment by establishing a common set of procedures for all countries (Fishlow 1978; Kenen 1983; Dornsbusch 1989). A complementary critique/proposal derives from the problem of 'free riders', or banks that do not provide debt relief in the hope that others will do so, thus increasing the probability of their own loans being fully serviced. The proposed solution would be for all governments to require their banks to participate in debt relief measures. The influential United Nations Economic Commission for Latin America and the Caribbean (ECLAC) has recently suggested amendments to the Brady Plan that would incorporate a debt agency, obligatory participation and related proposals (ECLAC 1990).

Finally, there is a more radical approach that suggests unilateral moratoria on debt payments.[3] Again this proposal takes a variety of forms. At its broadest, it includes all creditors over a lengthy period. A more moderate alternative is a temporary and selective moratorium, often focused on commercial banks. Bolivia, Costa Rica and Brazil have all imposed moratoria at one time or other. A variant was used by the García government in Peru and the Kaunda government in Zambia, where only 10 per cent of export revenues was allowed for debt service. Although the moratoria mentioned above were officially declared policy, a more common and less confrontational approach is to build up arrears without officially announcing a policy. ECLAC (1990: 81) estimates that fifteen of twenty Latin American countries had payments arrears of some type during 1989; most of these were not formal policy.

The variation in proposed solutions to the debt crisis reflects differing views on who should pay and, ultimately, on what caused the crisis. Thus, for example, those who believe that 'rapacious' banks seduced Third World governments into borrowing are more likely to favour solutions that penalize the banks. These would include deep discounts in debt reduction or even moratoria. Those who see 'irresponsible' Third World governments at fault lean toward austerity and adjustment as the proper remedies. If a shared responsibility is assumed, including creditor governments and multilateral agencies that encouraged private banks to lend in the 1970s, then a solution that distributes costs is considered most equitable.

Despite differences with respect to individual policy prescriptions and even underlying assumptions, most analysts of the debt crisis agree on some basic contextual factors that would substantially improve the possibility for improved performance. One such factor is a higher growth rate in the advanced industrial countries. Together with less protection, this would increase export revenues for Third World countries, debtors and non-debtors alike. Another factor is lower international interest rates, which are often linked to a lower budget deficit in the United States. The US twin deficits are also related to a third factor that would help Third World countries. If those countries that have adjusted their economies were able to regain access to the international financial markets, it would provide an important incentive for them and others to continue to put their economies in order. In this regard, the large capital imports by the United States may be hindering capital access for the Third World (Feldstein *et al.* 1987; ECLAC 1990; Williamson 1990).

THEORETICAL DEBATES WITH RESPECT TO THE DEBT CRISIS

In addition to disagreement about the proper response to the debt crisis, there are several other debates that have emerged in the context of the crisis. One concerns the actual (rather than the proper) response of debtor countries. A second involves power relations among debtors and creditors. And a third looks at the implications for development in what has been known as the Third World.

Policy response

Policy response to the debt crisis of the 1980s can be analysed in two different ways. One is to look at the responses that Third World governments actually adopted to try to explain the variation among them. This approach provides a spectrum ranging from Chile under Pinochet to Peru under García. Chile followed highly 'orthodox' macroeconomic policies and maintained cordial relations with the banks and international financial institutions. Peru followed self-defined 'heterodox' domestic policies and refused to make payments to the commercial banks or to deal with the IMF. Other responses can be located between these two extremes.

Several variables have been suggested to account for the differences. Frieden (1988) follows a rational-choice approach to argue that the impact of the crisis on different social groups, the distinction between liquid and fixed asset-holders, and the availability of a sympathetic government or attractive oppositional coalition partners can explain the varying responses of different countries. Kaufman and Stallings (1989) pay more attention to political variables, in particular the role of political regimes. They suggest that, for the 1980s, the presence of authoritarian governments, consolidated democracies or transitional democracies will go a long way towards differentiating among economic policies, including policies toward the banks and the IMF. Nelson (1990) outlines a much broader array of variables that are said jointly to determine response to the crisis: nature of the crisis, state capacity, political structure, political circumstances and the role of external agencies.

An alternative way of analysing policy response is broader. Its focus is the possible responses rather than the actual ones. This argument has been developed in theoretical (Eaton and Gersovitz 1981; Sachs 1984; Cohen and Sachs 1986) and historical terms (Stallings 1990b). In the latter version, policies in earlier debt crises are compared with current ones. Rather than asking why Pinochet's policies were different than García's, the question becomes: why were all policies in the 1980s remarkably conservative? Why were there no complete, long-term moratoria or even repudiations of the debt? Why did all governments seek to maintain their links with the international financial system, even at the cost of large-scale capital export? Stallings's answer to these questions focuses on the greater power of international actors in the 1980s compared to earlier periods, while Frieden (1990) again privileges domestic variables, especially different interests among debtors.

A closely related debate concerns why no debtor cartel was formed in the 1980s. Tussie (1988) stresses the pattern of creditor manipulation to prevent a cartel, while Feinberg (1988) and Whitehead (1987) emphasize lack of debtor organization, including leadership. O'Donnell (1985) describes a prisoner's dilemma-type situation in the face of lack of information about other countries' intentions and lack of confidence in them. The success of the cartel in reducing debt to manageable proportions is the reward if all co-operate, while stiff sanctions are the punishment if all defect. Side payments from creditors are the promised rewards for individual defectors.

Power relations

A second set of debates concerns power relations, both between debtors and creditors and within the group of creditors. While some of the literature discussed above relates to the power of creditors over debtors, this issue is more fully joined in the work of Wood (1984, 1986). His argument is that the 1980s have seen a return to a new version of dependency based on debt. Just as Third World analysts have turned their attention away from external forces, events conspired to force a reconsideration. The restructuring of the 'aid regime' is said to have provided increased leverage over Third World countries, as creditors united to impose conditionality and to harden terms on debtors. Although coming from a different ideological position, Lipson (1981) arrives at surprisingly similar conclusions. Writing before the debt crisis struck, he is interested in how creditors were able to keep debtors paying. His answer points to the 'debt regime' that, unlike other regimes, centres on private actors and their capacity to impose sanctions. The influence of the IMF is important for both Wood and Lipson.

An alternative to the structural approach to power relations is the bargaining model, which has become increasingly popular for analysing debtor–creditor relations. Griffith-Jones and colleagues (1988) used a bargaining framework to examine the outcomes of negotiations between banks and debtor governments during the 1980s. Their main concern was to explain why these outcomes were much closer to the interests of creditors than debtors. The answer centred on greater resources, both economic and political, on the creditors' side. Similar bargaining approaches have been explored by Mosley (1987) and Mosley *et al.* (1991), with particular reference to negotiations with multilateral agencies. Putnam (1988) elaborated a complementary theory about 'two-level games' to enrich our understanding of the process through which bargaining positions are established and the resulting deals are implemented.

Power relations in the context of the debt crisis are not limited to relations between creditors and debtors. The debate on international hegemony, and particularly the shifting relationship between the United States and Japan, has also become intertwined with the debt crisis. At the outset of the crisis, governments of other advanced industrial countries ceded leadership on debt policies to the United States in collaboration with the International Monetary Fund. The particular characteristics of the US banking industry meant that US-led policies toward the debt focused on maintaining interest payments to the detriment of growth in debtor nations. Unlike earlier debt crises, national and international, no 'breathing space' was given to debtors to recover their productive capacity and thus their ability to service debt over the long run. The feared international financial crisis was averted, but the development crisis was exacerbated.

This situation became ever more obvious during the time in which Japan increased its international economic strength at the expense of the United States. Japan's longer-term view of economic relations suggested that the US policy was not appropriate, and eventually public and private officials in that country began to suggest alternative approaches. The clearest example was the Miyazawa Plan of 1988, which was later incorporated into the Brady Plan (Stallings 1990a). Although the Japanese themselves go to great lengths to deny that they are displacing the United States, some outside observers see the lack of US initiative on debt issues – especially since debt problems are concentrated in Latin America, traditionally regarded as the US sphere of influence – as both an indicator of declining US power and a step in that direction (Hollerman 1989). As in the more general debate on hegemony, others reject the idea of declining US power in the debt sphere (Nye 1990).

Development problems

A third area of debate coming out of the debt crisis turns from the international ramifications to the domestic problems in debtor countries. Of course, the two are not unrelated, but there is an important difference of emphasis and therefore a different group of people involved.

Virtually no one denies that the 1980s were a disastrous decade for most of the Third World. The term 'lost decade' symbolizes the fact that many countries in Africa and Latin America have now returned to per capita income levels of the 1970s or even 1960s. What is less often recognized is that the very term 'Third World' has also lost much of its meaning in the course of the decade as differentiation has occurred among countries once included under that label. Some of the East Asian countries, which barely suffered any symptoms of the debt crisis, now have much more in common with the advanced industrial nations than with their Third World colleagues. At the same time, many Latin American countries are sinking toward development levels that had previously only been found in Africa.

This difference in performance between East Asia and Latin America, which were often jointly hailed as the 'newly-industrializing countries' (NICs) in the 1970s, has led to the single most important development debate of the post-war period. Many development experts have attributed Latin America's poor performance to its inward-oriented development strategy which was developed during the depression of the 1930s. This is then contrasted with the performance of the Asian nations with their greater emphasis on export capacity. The debt crisis enters this debate as both cause and effect. On the one hand, the existence of the crisis is linked to the failure of Latin America to generate sufficient export revenue to service its debt. On the other hand, the crisis is a major cause of Latin American economic and social decay. Some say that the answer is obvious: Latin America must emulate East Asia and change its development strategy (Belassa et al. 1986). Others argue that increased openness will only increase Latin America's vulnerability and further widen the gap between rich and poor (Pastor 1987; Weeks 1989). A different but related debate is over why Latin America and Asia took different paths and, by extension, whether Latin America would be able to adopt the Asian model (Gereffi and Wyman 1990; Haggard 1990).

A more directly political discussion concerns the effect of the debt crisis on the newly emerging democracies in Latin America and in some cases in Africa. One side of this debate emphasizes the dangers that the debt crisis poses for democracy (Roett 1989). If economies continue to decay, they may generate support for populist leaders and, when populism fails, for military intervention. The other side claims that there is little or no relationship between political and economic trends. Remmer (1990) argues that there is no evidence to show that economic issues are the main cause of political problems; on the contrary, democracy provides governments with greater legitimacy to deal with difficult economic problems.

As the first decade of the debt crisis draws to a close, the relative importance of these debates has shifted. In the early and mid-1980s there was substantial interest among international relations experts – both economists and political scientists – because the crisis was seen as a major problem for the international economy and for North–South relations. More recently, as the vulnerability of the international financial system has lessened, the saliency of the debate within international relations has correspondingly declined. Development concerns, by contrast, have increased as the destructive power of the crisis continues to erode economic and social – and perhaps political – capabilities in Latin America and Africa. Discussion of the debt crisis in the 1990s, therefore, is more likely to find a prominent place in the literature on development than international relations.

NOTES

1 These figures are from the World Bank's annual publication, *World Debt Tables*. Various sources of debt statistics have surprisingly different figures. For a comparison of sources, see International Working Group on External Debt Statistics (1988).

2 The so-called Baker 17 are the highly indebted middle-income countries of most concern to policy makers. They include Argentina, Bolivia, Brazil, Chile, Colombia, Costa Rica, Côte d'Ivoire, Ecuador, Jamaica, Mexico, Morocco, Nigeria, Peru, the Philippines, Uruguay, Venezuela and Yugoslavia.

3 Virtually no one in the 1980s suggested outright repudiation of the debt. The only exceptions were specific loans, such as those obtained by Somoza in the final days of the war against the Sandinistas to purchase the bombs used against the civilian population.

REFERENCES

Belassa, B., Bueno, G., Kuczynski, P. and Simonsen, M. (1986) *Toward Renewed Economic Growth in Latin America*, Washington, DC: Institute for International Economics.

Bogdanowicz-Bindert, C. (1985–6) 'World debt: the United States reconsiders', *Foreign Affairs* 64 (2): 259–73.

Bulow, J. and Rogoff, K. (1988) 'The buyback boondoggle', *Brookings Papers on Economic Activity* 2: 675–98.

Cohen, D. and Sachs, J. (1986) 'Growth and external debt under risk of repudiation', *European Economic Review* 30: 529–60.

Conway, P. (1987) 'The Baker Plan and international indebtedness', *World Economy* 10 (2): 193–204.

Darity, W. and Horn, B. (1988) *The Loan Pushers*, Cambridge: Ballinger Press.

Devlin, R. (1989) *Debt and Crisis in Latin America: The Supply Side of the Story*, Princeton: Princeton University Press.

Dornbusch, R. (1989) 'The Latin American debt problem: anatomy and solutions', in B. Stallings and R. Kaufman (eds) *Debt and Democracy in Latin America*, Boulder, Colo.: Westview Press.

Eaton, J. and Gersovitz, M. (1981) 'Debt with potential repudiation', *Review of Economic Studies* 48: 289–309.

ECLAC (1990) *Latin America and the Caribbean: Options to Reduce the Debt Burden*, Santiago: UN Economic Commission for Latin America and the Caribbean.

Feinberg, R. (1988) 'Latin American debt: renegotiating the adjustment burden', in R. Feinberg and R. Ffrench-Davis (eds) *Development and External Debt in Latin America: Bases for a Consensus*, Notre Dame, Ind.: University of Notre Dame Press.

Feldstein, M., de Carmoy, H., Narusawa, K. and Krugman, P. (1987) *Restoring Growth in the Debt-Laden Third World*, New York: Trilateral Commission.

Ffrench-Davis, R. (1987) 'Conversión de pagares de la deuda externa en Chile', *Colección Estudios CIEPLAN* 22: 41–62.

Fishlow, A. (1978) 'A new international economic order: what kind?', in A. Fishlow, C. Díaz-Alejandro, R. Fagen and R. Hansen (eds) *Rich and Poor Nations in the World Economy*, New York: McGraw-Hill.

Frieden, J. (1988) 'Classes, sectors, and foreign debt in Latin America', *Comparative Politics* 21 (1): 1–20.

——(1990) 'Comment', in D. Felix (ed.) *Debt and Transfiguration? Prospects for Latin America's Economic Revival*, New York: M. E. Sharpe.

Gereffi, G. and Wyman, D. (eds) (1990) *Manufacturing Miracles: Patterns of Development in Latin America and East Asia*, Princeton: Princeton University Press.

Griffith-Jones, S. (ed.) (1988) *Managing World Debt*, New York: St Martin's Press.

Haggard, S. (1990) *Pathways from the Periphery: The Politics of Growth in Newly Industrializing Countries*, Ithaca, NY: Cornell University Press.

Hollerman, L. (1989) 'The role of Brazil in Japan's economic strategy: implications for the United States', paper presented at the Latin American Studies Association National Meeting, Miami, December.

International Working Group on External Debt Statistics (1988) *External Debt: Definition, Statistical Coverage, and Methodology*, Paris: World Bank, International Monetary Fund, Bank for International Settlements, and Organization for Economic Co-operation and Development.

Kaufman, R. and Stallings, B. (1989) 'Debt and democracy in the 1980s: the Latin American experience', in B. Stallings and R. Kaufman (eds) *Debt and Democracy in Latin America*, Boulder, Colo.: Westview Press.

Kenen, P. (1983) 'A bailout plan for the banks', *New York Times* (6 March).

Kindleberger, C. P. (1978) *Manias, Panics and Crashes*, New York: Basic Books.

Kraft, J. (1984) *The Mexican Rescue*, New York: Group of Thirty.

Lipson, C. (1981) 'The international organization of Third World debt', *International Organization* 35 (4):603–31.

Mosley, P. (1987) *Conditionality as Bargaining Process: Structural Adjustment Lending*, Princeton: Princeton Studies in International Finance.

Mosley, P., Harrigan, J. and Toye, J. (1991) *Aid and Power: The World Bank and Policy-Based Lending*, London: Routledge.

Nelson, J. (ed.) (1990) *Economic Crisis and Policy Change: The Politics of Adjustment in the Third World*, Princeton: Princeton University Press.

Nye, J. S. (1990) *Bound to Lead: The Changing Nature of American Power*, New York: Basic Books.

O'Donnell, G. (1985) 'External debt: why don't our governments do the obvious?', *CEPAL Review* 27: 27–33.

Pastor, M. (1987) *The International Monetary Fund and Latin America: Economic Stabilization and Class Conflict*, Boulder, Colo.: Westview Press.

Putnam, R. (1988) 'Diplomacy and domestic politics: the logic of two-level games', *International Organization* 42 (3): 427–60.

Remmer, K. (1990) 'Debt or democracy? The political impact of the debt crisis in Latin America', in D. Felix (ed.) *Debt and Transfiguration? Prospects for Latin America's Economic Revival*, New York: M. E. Sharpe.

Roett, R. (1986) 'Beyond the Baker initiative', *SAIS Review* 6 (2): 27–37.

——(1989) 'How the "haves" manage the "have-nots": Latin America and the debt crisis', in B. Stallings and R. Kaufman (eds) *Debt and Democracy in Latin America*, Boulder, Colo.: Westview Press.

Sachs, J. (1984) *Theoretical Issues in International Borrowing*, Princeton: Princeton Essays in International Finance.

Stallings, B. (1990a) 'The reluctant giant: Japan and the Latin American debt crisis', *Journal of Latin American Studies* 22 (1): 1–30.

——(1990b) 'Debtors versus creditors: power relations and policy response to the 1980s crisis', in D. Felix (ed.) *Debt and Transfiguration? Prospects for Latin America's Economic Revival*, New York: M. E. Sharpe.

Tussie, D. (1988) 'The coordination of Latin American debtors: is there a logic behind the story?', in S. Griffith-Jones (ed.) *Managing World Debt*, New York: St Martin's Press.

Watson, M., Mathieson, D., Kincaid, R. and Kalter, E. (1986) *International Capital Markets: Developments and Prospects*, Occasional Paper no. 43, Washington, DC: International Monetary Fund.

Weeks, J. F. (ed.) (1989) *Debt Disaster? Banks, Governments, and Multilaterals Confront the Crisis*, New York: New York University Press.

Whitehead, L. (1987) 'Latin American debt: renegotiating the adjustment burden', paper presented at British International Studies Association Annual Conference, Aberystwyth, Wales.

Williamson, J. (1989) *Voluntary Approaches to Debt Relief*, rev. edn, Washington, DC: Institute for International Economics.

——(ed.) (1990) *Latin American Adjustment: How Much Has Happened?*, Washington, DC: Institute for International Economics.

Wood, R. (1984) 'The debt crisis and North–South relations', *Third World Quarterly* 6 (3): 703–16.

——(1986) *From Marshall Plan to Debt Crisis: Foreign Aid and Development Choices in the World Economy*, Berkeley: University of California Press.

FURTHER READING

Cline, W. (1984) *International Debt: Systemic Risk and Policy Response*, Washington, DC: Institute for International Economics.

Cohen, B. J. (1986) *In Whose Interest? International Banking and American Foreign Policy*, New Haven: Yale University Press.

Devlin, R. (1989) *Debt and Crisis in Latin America: The Supply Side of the Story*, Princeton: Princeton University Press.

ECLAC (1990) *Latin America and the Caribbean: Options to Reduce the Debt Burden*, Santiago: UN Economic Commission for Latin America and the Caribbean.

Eichengreen, B. and Lindert, P. H. (eds) (1990) *The International Debt Crisis in Historical Perspective*, Cambridge, Mass.: MIT Press.

Feldstein, M., de Carmoy, H., Narusawa, K. and Krugman, P. (1987) *Restoring Growth in the Debt-Laden Third World*, New York: Trilateral Commission.

Griffith-Jones, S. (ed.) (1988) *Managing World Debt*, New York: St Martin's Press.

Husain, I. and Diwan I. (eds) (1989) *Dealing With the Debt Crisis*, Washington, DC: World Bank.

Kahler, M. (ed.) (1986) *The Politics of International Debt*, Ithaca, NY: Cornell University Press.

Kaletsky, A. (1985) *The Costs of Default*, New York: Priority Press.

Lancaster, C. and Williamson, J. (eds) (1986) *African Debt and Financing*, Washington, DC: Institute for International Economics.

Makin, J. (1984) *The Global Debt Crisis*, New York: Basic Books.

Marichal, C. (1989) *A Century of Debt Crises in Latin America*, Princeton: Princeton University Press.

Nelson, J. (ed.) (1990) *Economic Crisis and Policy Choice: The Politics of Adjustment in the Third World*, Princeton: Princeton University Press.

Pastor, R. (ed.) (1987) *Latin America's Debt Crisis: Adjusting to the Past or Planning for the Future?* Boulder, Colo.: Lynne Rienner.

Sachs, J. (ed.) (1989) *Developing Country Debt and the World Economy*, Chicago: University of Chicago Press.

Stallings, B. (1987) *Banker to the Third World: US Portfolio Investment in Latin America, 1900–86*, Berkeley: University of California Press.

Stallings, B. and Kaufman, R. (eds) (1989) *Debt and Democracy in Latin America*, Boulder, Colo.: Westview Press.

Weeks, J. F. (ed.) (1989) *Debt Disaster? Banks, Governments, and Multilaterals Confront the Crisis*, New York: New York University Press.

Williamson, J. (ed.) (1990) *Latin American Adjustment: How Much Has Happened?*, Washington, DC: Institute for International Economics.

World Bank (1990) *World Debt Tables 1991–91*, Washington, DC: World Bank.

72

EUROPEAN INTEGRATION

SONIA MAZEY

The past few years have witnessed a relaunching of the European Community (EC) – a development which has given fresh impetus to the long-running debate on the aims and objectives of European integration. At the 1983 Stuttgart summit the ten EC Heads of Government publicly declared their commitment to the achievement of European Union. This announcement was followed by the 1986 Single European Act (SEA) committing EC member states to the completion of the single European market by January 1993, the establishment of economic and monetary union and the introduction of institutional reforms designed to facilitate faster European decision making. These changes are potentially far-reaching: achievement of the internal market will require the introduction of some 300 harmonizing measures; economic and monetary union implies the establishment of an EC-wide macroeconomic policy, whilst the extension of majority voting in the Council of Ministers has effectively removed the national veto from key policy areas. Meanwhile, the dramatic collapse of the Soviet-backed regimes in Eastern Europe during the autumn of 1989 and German reunification have prompted a rediscovery of Europe and forced crucial questions about the future dimensions, powers and international responsibilities of the European Community to the forefront of political agendas throughout Europe. Against this background, the EC Heads of Government meeting at the Dublin Summit in April 1990 agreed to hold an intergovernmental conference in December to discuss ways of achieving European political union.

Yet, just as there has never been a consensus within the Community as to the precise meaning of European Union, there exists no agreement over the implications of political union. For the so-called 'maximalists' (i.e. the Commission, most Members of the European Parliament (MEPs), the Italian, Belgian, Spanish, Portuguese and French governments), European Union necessarily implies further steps towards social and political union within the framework of a supranational European federal state. However, for the 'minimalists' (whose position was most strongly defended by the former British Prime Minister, Margaret Thatcher, but shared also by the Danish, Luxemburg and Greek governments), European Union means the establishment of the single economic market with only limited co-operation between sovereign, independent states on other issues. This disagreement is not a new phenomenon; its origins lie in the post-war debate on European integration. Then as now the key issues were what kind of European Community should prevail – economic, social or political? What kind of institutional arrangement? And how might European integration be achieved? The 1957 Rome Treaties establishing the European Communities provided no unambiguous answers to these questions. To some people, the European Coal and Steel Community (ECSC), the European Economic Community (EEC) and the European Atomic Energy Community (EURATOM) were simply functional agencies set up to co-ordinate national strategies in specified policy sectors. However, European federalists, impressed by the supranational characteristics of these authorities, hoped they would serve as the basis for more comprehensive political integration. The tension between these two competing visions of European integration is the leitmotiv of the European Community, underpinning explanatory theories of European integration, the institutional framework of the Community and the current debate on the future of European integration.

EUROPEAN FEDERALISM AND THE ORIGINS OF EUROPEAN INTEGRATION

The origins of the European Community lie in the post-war debate on European federalism and the federalists' belief that the establishment of a federal European state would put an end to the long-established and dismal pattern of war between European sovereign states. The idea was not a new one. In the aftermath of the First World War the idea of a 'United States of Europe' had been propounded by the Austrian Count Koudenhove-Kalergi, leader of the Pan Europa movement, as well as by leading European politicians such as Aristide Briand, French Foreign Minister (1925–32) and Gustav Streseman, his German counterpart (1923–9). The Second World War gave fresh impetus to this debate: after 1939 federalist movements and publications proliferated throughout Europe, particularly among national resistance movements in Italy, France, Spain, Belgium and Luxemburg. International meetings of resistance organizations during the war culminated in the 1944 Draft Declaration of the European Resistance Movements, proposing the creation of a post-war Federal Union with a supranational government, single federal army and a supreme federal court (Vaughan 1979).

The immediate post-war period witnessed a further upsurge in public opinion in favour of European integration. But, from the outset, the debate was ambiguous. Whilst the general idea of European co-operation attracted widespread support, no similar consensus existed with regard to the precise form this co-operation should take. European federalist movements, united within the Union of European Federalists (UEF) established in 1946, and the new Christian Democratic parties in Western Europe campaigned for the establishment of a supranational European federal state. They were opposed by Conservative politicians (led by the British Prime Minister, Winston Churchill), the British Labour Party and the Scandinavian administrations who recommended the creation of a loose, confederal association as a means of facilitating economic recovery and serving as a bulwark against Soviet communism. At the 1948 Hague Congress on European co-operation, organized jointly by the federalist UEF, Churchill's United Europe Movement and the European League for Economic Co-operation, the federalists were defeated. The Congress approved a vaguely worded communiqué demanding 'a United Europe throughout whose area the free movement of persons, ideas and goods is restored' (cited in Vaughan 1979), a Charter of Human Rights, a Court of Justice and a European Assembly. In concrete terms, the outcome of the meeting was the Council of Europe, established in 1949, which provided a forum for voluntary co-operation between national governments and MPs.

European federalists made one further attempt in 1952 to establish a European Political Community with federal institutions as part of an ambitious proposal for a European Defence Community (EDC) entailing the creation of a single European defence force. In fact, the EDC idea was the French government's response to US demands that West Germany be permitted to re-arm in order that it might contribute to the defence of Western Europe. Though supported by both the West German Chancellor, Konrad Adenauer, and the US government, the whole project collapsed in August 1954 with the refusal of the French National Assembly to ratify the project. The failure of the EDC project marked an important turning-point in the European integration process. In the immediate post-war period the socio-economic and political situation in Europe was so fluid that it was just conceivable that the radical federalist strategy – the introduction of a European federal constitution and institutional framework – might have succeeded. In the event, nationalism and commitment to the nation-state proved an insurmountable obstacle to such a massive step. Nevertheless, one should not underestimate the importance of federalism in the context of European integration; though the federalists were defeated in the 1950s, the federalist model of European integration remains an important goal for many EC policy makers.

Meanwhile, so-called 'functional-federalists' – notably the founders of the European Community, Jean Monnet (French *Commissaire du Plan*), Robert Schuman (French Foreign Minister) and Alcide de Gasperi (Italian Prime Minister) – sought to achieve federalist objectives by a different route. Whilst sharing the aspirations of the federalists they disagreed with their head-on approach, believing instead that the best way to achieve European integration was by incremental steps in sectors where the issue of national sovereignty was less contentious. This strategy formed the basis of the Schuman Plan, which recommended that all aspects of French and German coal and steel production be placed under the control of a supranational High Authority in a European Coal and Steel Community (ECSC) open to other European countries. Undoubtedly, a major reason for the initiative was French concern at the threat to the weakened French economy posed by the steady post-war increase in German industrial productivity. For the West German Christian Democratic government, membership of the ECSC offered a means of re-establishing its international position and demonstrating its Europeanism. Notwithstanding the appeal to national self-interest that lay behind the ECSC, Schuman made it clear that he personally regarded the organization as nothing less than the first concrete step towards a much deeper 'European Federation' (Groeben 1986: 22).

Six countries (Belgium, the Netherlands, Italy, Luxemburg, West Germany and France) signed the 1951 Paris Treaty establishing the ECSC. The British government, though invited to participate, refused to join. Though Britain eventually joined the European Community in 1973 (having had its first two membership applications vetoed in 1963 and 1967 by the French President, General de Gaulle), successive British governments have been criticized for their lack of commitment to the Community and European integration. Three factors relating to the post-1945 situation help to explain this deep-rooted ambivalence towards European integration. First, the British wartime experience had strengthened rather than weakened nationalist sentiment (due largely to the absence of an occupying power, physical isolation from the rest of Europe, and war victory). Second, British foreign and defence policy in the immediate post-war period was based upon the Churchillian concept of three overlapping circles: the special relationship with America; the Empire and Commonwealth; and – lastly – Europe. In Churchill's words Britain was with Europe, but not part of it. Third, the majority of British politicians – Conservative and Labour alike – were united in their opposition to any supranational European authority which they believed would constrain British policy makers and undermine the doctrine of Parliamentary sovereignty. Post-war economic and imperial decline rather than commitment to European integration prompted Britain's application to join the Community. This instrumental motivation, combined with the fact that Britain does not share the cultural, administrative and legal traditions of continental Europe has often left Britain isolated within the Community (Camps 1964; Wallace 1980).

The establishment of the ECSC was followed by the creation of two other supranational, functional agencies – the European Atomic Energy Association

(EURATOM) and the European Economic Community (EEC), both of which were created by the 1957 Treaties of Rome. The former was intended to promote European co-operation in the development and promotion of nuclear energy, whilst the latter committed member states to the establishment of a common market involving the abolition of internal trade tariffs and the intro-duction of a Common External Tariff (CET), the establishment of a Common Agricultural Policy (CAP), the co-ordination of member states' economic and monetary policies and the partial harmonization of their fiscal and social policies. In 1967 the institutions of the three separate European Communities were merged and the ECSC, EEC and EURATOM (which are discrete communities) collectively became the European Community (EC).

THE INSTITUTIONAL FRAMEWORK OF EUROPEAN INTEGRATION

The institutional arrangement established by the Rome Treaties was designed to facilitate co-operation between member states in the policy sectors outlined above (pp. 1146–7). Whilst this was not a federalist structure, the founders also hoped that it would facilitate further European integration. In practice, however, for the reasons outlined below (pp. 1148–9), the institutional balance of power within the Community has proved to be a major obstacle to European integration.

Based in Brussels, the European Commission (successor to the High Authority) is the Community's executive. There are seventeen commissioners – two each from Britain, France, Germany, Italy and Spain, and one from each of the other member states. The commissioners are appointed by their national government for a four-year (renewable) period, but once appointed swear an oath of allegiance to the Community in which they promise not to put national interests before those of the Community. The Commission, which is serviced by some 15,000 administrators, is formally accountable to the European Parliament (EP), which by a vote of censure could force all seventeen commissioners to resign. Individual commissioners, however, are not account-able and cannot be dismissed either by the EP or their national governments during their period of office. The Commission President (currently the French Socialist, Jacques Delors) is elected for a two-year (renewable) period by the commissioners. Perceived by the founders as an embryonic European government, the Commission is guardian of the Treaties and responsible for the initiation and implementation of all EC policies.

The Council of Ministers consists of national government ministers and is the Community's legislature; its principal function is to accept or reject pro-posals put to it by the Commission, taking into account the views of the EP and the Economic and Social Committee (a consultative assembly representing corporatist interests). It does not have a permanent membership; participants change according to the subject under discussion. The presidency of the Council rotates among the member states every six months in (French) alphabetical order. In fact, the bulk of work within the Council is done not by ministers but by the Committee of Permanent Representatives (COREPER). Established in 1958, COREPER comprises civil servants of ambassadorial rank from the member states, whose role is to liaise with each other and the Commission in order to arrive at mutually acceptable policies. In contrast to the Commission, the Council of Ministers is essentially an 'intergovernmental' body; the primary objective of each participant is to get the best deal for his/her country (or a deal which is electorally popular back home!).

The Treaties state that voting in the Council of Ministers may be by unanimous vote or by either an absolute or qualified majority. In the case of a vote by absolute majority each member state has one vote and a simple majority is binding. In a qualified majority vote each member state has a number of votes proportionate to its size: Britain, France, Germany and Italy have ten each; Spain has eight; Belgium, Greece, Portugal and the Netherlands have five each; Denmark and Ireland three each; and Luxemburg has two votes. Fifty-four votes out of the seventy-six constitutes a qualified majority. Under the Treaties, majority voting was to come into force automatically in January 1966 in a range of policy areas. In fact, this timetable was overturned by the six-month French boycott of the Community in 1965, undertaken in protest against the Commission's growing assertiveness and the supranationalist implications of majority voting in the Council. The conflict was resolved by the 1966 'Luxemburg Compromise', which effectively granted each member state a veto in the Council of Ministers if 'very important (national) interests' are at stake. The agreement marked an important turning-point for the Community and European integration. The Luxemburg Compromise slowed down the policy-making process as the Commission was forced after 1966 to tailor its proposals to accommodate the interests of all member states (usually by working out complicated 'package deals' offering member governments favours in one policy area in return for their co-operation on another issue). More fundamentally, this agreement shifted the institutional balance of power within the Community decisively away from the Commission and supranationalism in favour of national governments and national interests.

Though institutional analyses of the EC stress the importance of the Commission–Council axis, the EP has gradually become more influential within the context of EC policy making and is likely to become more important in the future (see p. 1158). The European Treaties established a European Assembly composed of delegates from the national parliaments of member states. Since 1979, this body has been elected by universal suffrage and is now formally called the European Parliament. Since the entry of Spain and Portugal into the EC in January 1986, the EP has contained 518 representatives elected for a period of five years. Hitherto, the EP has enjoyed few formal powers. In addition to the right (never yet exercised) to dismiss the Commission, the Parliament has since 1975 exercised joint control (with the Council of Ministers) over the Community's budget and – since the 1986 SEA – very limited legislative powers. Formerly, though MEPs were consulted over legislative proposals, the Council of Ministers was under no obligation to take their views into account. However, the SEA has introduced a new 'co-operation procedure' which grants the EP the right to a second reading of Community legislation related to the single market, and aspects of social policy and social and economic cohesion (i.e. regional policy). This permits the Parliament to propose amendments to the 'common position' agreed by the Council of Ministers, which may then either accept the EP's amendments, acting on the basis of a qualified majority vote, or, by acting unanimously, reject the EP's views. Whilst the co-operation procedure does not amount to full legislative power, it has significantly increased the Parliament's capacity to exert leverage over both the Commission and COREPER officials at an early stage in the legislative process since both the Commission and the Council have a vested interest in allowing the EP to delay legislation at the second reading stage (Fitzmaurice 1988; Bogdanor 1989).

Nevertheless, the title 'European Parliament' is in many respects a misleading one. Certainly, the EP performs the traditional parliamentary functions of scrutiny, representation and public debate. It also exercises limited budgetary powers, the power to delay the adoption of legislation (since the Council of Ministers must await its opinion on proposed legislation before making a decision) and, since 1987, increased legislative powers with regard to policies relating to the internal market (covered by Article 100A of the SEA). Yet, constitutionally speaking, the EP is an anomalous institution. Unlike national parliaments in liberal parliamentary regimes, it does not sustain an executive, it is not elected to carry out a comprehensive programme and it has no effective control over either the Commission (appointed by national governments) or the Council of Ministers (nationally elected government ministers). The fact that the Community's only directly elected body wields the least power has prompted growing disquiet within member states, and debate over how to remedy the EC's 'democratic deficit' is a major theme of the present debate on institutional reform and political union.

The European Court of Justice (not to be confused with the European Court of Human Rights in Strasbourg, which is a Council of Europe body, or the International Court of Justice in The Hague) sits in Luxemburg and comprises thirteen judges (assisted by six advocates-general), including at least one from each member state, who are appointed for six years. The court is an appellate court whose task is to interpret and enforce the application of

Community law in cases of dispute and to ensure that national laws are compatible with those of the EC. Though the Treaties did not specify the supremacy of EC law over national law, a number of key rulings have firmly established the two legal principles of 'primacy' and 'direct effect' upon which the supranational authority of the EC rests. Whilst the principle of 'primacy' ensures that EC law overrides national legislation in the event of a conflict, that of 'direct effect' means that individuals may rely upon EC laws in the court of a member state irrespective of whether or not those laws have been incorporated into national legislation. Though the powers of the court are limited (it has no power of sanction), its rulings have generally been respected by member states. In consequence, the court has played a major role in the process of European integration as the extension of EC legislation into more and more policy areas has gradually eroded the degree of legislative autonomy enjoyed by member states. Indeed, the current Commission President, Jacques Delors, recently predicted that by 1995, 75 per cent of all European economic and social legislation would emanate from the Commission.

The founders of the European Community hoped that the institutions of the Community would evolve into a federal structure. In practice, decision-making power became concentrated in the hands of national governments within the Council of Ministers, with the result that EC policy making became a slow and tortuous process. Protracted negotiations, crisis summits and unsatisfactory policy compromises thus became the hallmark of the European Community. Since the early 1970s, the Community has repeatedly sought to redress the situation by means of institutional reform. Agreement over institutional reform has, however, proved difficult for the simple reason that it raises the contentious issue of the aims and objectives of European integration. Successive reports commissioned by the Council of Ministers during the 1970s and early 1980s recommended that the powers of the Commission and the EP should be strengthened and that majority voting should become the norm within the Council of Ministers. Whilst welcomed by the Commission, MEPs and some member governments (notably the Italian administration), other member states such as Britain, Greece and Denmark have consistently resisted any attempt to abolish the national power of veto within the Council of Ministers. The debate on institutional reform culminated in the 1986 Single European Act which introduced majority voting in the Council of Ministers for legislation relating to the internal market, marginally increased the EP's legislative powers in these areas and strengthened slightly the Commission's authority in certain specified areas. These changes have nevertheless left unresolved the fundamental issue of whether the Community should have a federal structure. That question is now at the top of the Community's agenda (see p. 1158).

FUNCTIONALISM, NEO-FUNCTIONALISM AND INTERGOVERNMENTALISM

The piecemeal approach to European integration adopted by Monnet and Schuman (see Monnet 1976; Bromberger 1969) fits neatly into the 'neo-functionalist' theory of regional integration developed by Haas (1968) and Lindberg (1963) in the context of post-war European integration, which now dominates studies of the Community and its policy-making process. This theory is itself based upon a sympathetic critique of the functionalist theory of integration put forward by David Mitrany (1966) as a means of promoting international conflict. Mitrany was, in fact, opposed to regional government, believing that it would merely reproduce national rivalries on a larger scale. Instead, he advocated the linking of authority to a specific function, thereby breaking the traditional link between authority and territory. The functionalists argued that politically sensitive and potentially divisive issues such as defence and foreign policy were unsuitable starting-points for international co-operation. Welfare issues, however, were a fruitful area for such collaboration because they were essentially technical in nature and, in consequence, it was easier to identify universal expectations and reach agreement over ends and means. Policy making within international functionally based organizations is thus perceived to be a non-political process within which issues are resolved according to 'technical' as opposed to 'political' criteria. Since the aim of the functionalist strategy is to avoid political conflict, political elites do not figure in the process. Instead, problems are solved by 'experts' acting in a rational manner. Integration occurs because successful co-operation in one sector stimulates demands for further co-operation in another area.

Functionalist theories of integration attracted widespread criticism. First, the theory assumes that policy makers share a common set of values which enables them not only to identify a common problem, but also to agree upon an internationally co-ordinated strategy for dealing with the matter. In reality, however, there is no reason why experts (such as planners or scientists) and socio-economic interest groups (such as farmers or industrialists) should not opt for a national solution on the grounds that such a strategy is simpler and/or potentially more lucrative. Second, the theory is premissed upon the naïve belief that it is possible to distinguish between 'technical' and 'political' policy sectors. This assumption simply cannot be sustained. Since 1945, national governments throughout Western Europe have come to be regarded as welfare agencies, whilst their intervention into most areas of the economy adds a political dimension to apparently functional sectors such as coal and steel. It is, for instance, impossible to imagine national governments remaining indifferent to EC negotiations on the future of the coal industry given the political significance of nationalized interests and regional socio-economic development. In short, welfare issues cannot be divorced from politics because there is no universally acceptable criteria for 'just' and 'efficient' allocation of resources (Webb 1977: 11).

Functionalism attracted critical support from Haas and Lindberg, who further developed the model in the context of the ECSC experience (see Haas 1968; Lindberg and Scheingold 1970). In contrast to functionalist theory, which stressed the importance of an underlying social consensus as the primary feature of society, neo-functionalist theory is premissed upon the assumption of a pluralistic society and competition between self-interested groups. European integration is perceived as the most efficient way of managing conflict. This shift in emphasis marks an important theoretical development since it not only acknowledges the existence of politics, but actually introduces political conflict as an essential element in the integrative process. As sectors are brought under supranational control, organized interests, political parties and national governments are increasingly drawn into the regional (i.e. European) policy-making arena. This development, it is argued, is followed by the transfer of loyalties (in return for interest satisfaction) from the national to the regional level authority.

Central to the neo-functionalist thesis is the concept of 'spillover' which has two aspects – functional and political. Functional spillover refers to the process whereby a given action related to a specific objective creates a situation in which the original goal can be met only by taking further action in a contiguous policy area. Full monetary union, for instance, requires full economic union including fiscal harmonization, whilst a common transport policy implies the existence of an integrated regional policy. 'Political spillover' involves the buildup of domestic political pressures in favour of further integration. For example, Haas (1968) argued that when the ECSC assumed responsibility for coal and steel production, national representatives associated with these industries (employers, trade unions and consumer groups) switched at least part of their lobbying activities away from national governments to the High Authority. Once aware of the benefits available to them from the ECSC, these organizations became advocates of further sectoral integration (George 1985). National politicians and civil servants would, according to the neo-functionalist thesis, then come under pressure from organized interests to participate fully in European policy making (Harrison 1975).

As Webb (1977: 12) points out, the neo-functionalist theory of European integration owes much to pluralistic models of politics. Community institutions and agreement among participants on the 'rules of the game' provide the framework within which political elites, organized interests and bureaucrats compete. Coalition-building, horse-trading and package deals are perceived by the neo-functionalist studies of Community policy making as the key to conflict resolution and integration. In this context, both Haas and Lindberg emphasized the Council–Commission relationship as the principal innovative feature of EC decision making, with the Commission's capacity to initiate and mediate providing the means of securing policy agreements which go beyond merely identifying the lowest common denominator (Webb 1977: 13). Acceptance by national governments and interest groups of the Commission's status and capacity to negotiate thus facilitates consensual policy making and piecemeal integration.

Neo-functionalist models of European integration which focus upon the strategies of self-interested groups and individuals have come to dominate analyses of the EC and undoubtedly provide a useful framework within which to examine the policy process. There is also considerable evidence of functional spillover within the Community; since 1957, the Community has gradually extended its activities into an increasing range of related policy areas. The Common Agricultural Policy, for instance, has since its establishment in the 1960s steadily become more extensive, embracing an increasing range of products and activities. This development has in turn affected EC budgetary policy and – in the Commission's view at least – demonstrated the need for monetary union (in order to eliminate the need for the Green exchange rate which is at present used to standardize agricultural payments between member states). Similarly, the planned completion of the internal market has persuaded the Commission and most member states of the need to strengthen EC social policy (which is primarily concerned with employees' rights and working conditions) in order to harmonize labour market conditions throughout the Community. Perhaps the most significant example of functional spillover has been the recognition since the early 1970s of the foreign-policy connotations of the Community's external trade relations. Realization of this fact led to the establishment of European Political Co-operation (EPC), which takes the form of regular meetings between the EC foreign ministers. EPC was formally acknowledged in an Appendix to the 1986 Single European Act, which also extended the Community's sphere of competence to include new policy sectors such as the environment and research and development.

As George (1985) points out, the record of political spillover has been slower and more uneven. In short, the attitude of interest groups towards the EC has varied from positive support to widespread opposition. Though the predicted increase in pressure-group activity at the European level has occurred, it has been far from uniform. Not surprisingly, interest-group activity is most evident in those areas where there is a well-established EC policy – i.e. where policy-making power has shifted from the national to the Community level. The fact that the agricultural lobby is the most influential of the Euro-lobbies, for example, owes much to the existence of the Common Agricultural Policy. Other prominent lobbies include the financial services sector, retailers, liberal professions, industrial employers and trade unions, all of which are directly affected by much EC legislation (for example, on industrial, competition and social policies) (Butt-Philip 1985). The 1992 programme has given a further boost to EC interest-group activity (Mazey and Richardson 1992). The chemical industry, for example, has been prompted into action by the Community's growing interest in environmental protection (Grant 1989), whilst the Commission's proposed Social Action Programme, designed to strengthen workers' rights, has provoked a swift reaction from the European Employers' Federation. However, as Nugent (1989) observes, most non-producer groups (for example, those representing consumer interests, welfare causes, women's rights, environmental issues, etc.) are generally less influential at the EC level due to problems of organization and funding. The pluralistic image of EC policy making portrayed by neo-functionalists should, therefore, not be exaggerated; not all groups are equally powerful. Indeed, the close working relationships which often exist between Commission officials and some groups (notably between officials and the agro-industrial lobby) have given rise to concerns that EC policy making is excessively corporatist in style. Marxist commentators, such as Holland (1980), who point to the interests of private capital as the driving force of European integration, go even further and stress the determining role played in EC policy making by the capitalist interests (multinationals, banks, industrial groups). According to this view of European integration, the neo-functionalist thesis that economic union will lead to political union is misguided since it fails to recognize that the supranational powers granted to the Commission are geared primarily to serving the interests of private capital rather than to the establishment of a citizens' Europe.

The neo-functionalist theory of integration has also been criticized from the perspective of 'intergovernmentalism' for failing to take sufficient account of the need for and difficulties of coalition building within the Community between national governments of different political ideologies. Both Stanley Hoffman (1966) and Ralf Dahrendorf (1972) have argued that national governments are nowhere near as 'obsolete' as neo-functionalists have implied. Taking up the two related issues of nationalism and political leadership, Hoffman argued that as soon as the EC attempted to progress from 'low politics' issues (technical and economic issues) to 'high politics' (foreign and defence issues), nationalism would rear its ugly and insurmountable head as governments sought to retain their sovereignty. This 'realist' view of European integration denies the uniqueness of the EC as a forum for international co-operation, able to go further than existing international agencies in the undermining of national sovereignty. It also denies that the national political, social and economic systems of the EC member states are becoming so interdependent and subject to Commission authority that national governments will lose ultimate control over key policy decisions. According to inter-governmentalist interpretations of European integration, the coalition building which characterizes EC policy making represents a refined version of conventional international diplomacy. According to Hoffman, governments distinguish between those areas where they are willing to concede part of their authority to the Community and those in which the preservation of national control is perceived as crucial to national independence (Webb 1977: 20).

Intergovernmentalism seeks to explain the establishment of the EC, its subsequent enlargement and the development of common policies in terms of national governments acting to protect and further their domestic (and/or electoral) interests. Clearly, national governments, their (often conflicting) political ideologies and perceptions of national interests have played an important role in determining the pace and direction of European integration. Alongside General Charles de Gaulle, both the current French, socialist President, François Mitterrand, and the former British, Conservative Prime Minister, Margaret Thatcher, have played a key role in the present debate on European integration. The former played a critical role in extending the 1992 programme to include monetary union and the so-called social dimension (i.e. the strengthening of EC social policy) in line with his personal commitment to Europe and social democracy. Meanwhile, Thatcher will be remembered for her steadfast opposition to European social and political integration which she claimed will, if achieved, undermine the economic benefits of the internal market, restore socialism in Britain and undermine national sovereignty.

Moreover, as indicated above (p. 1148), the institutional balance of power within the EC underwent a decisive shift with the 1966 Luxemburg Compromise which effectively granted each member state a veto over Community policy proposals. This development in turn increased the importance of negotiations between national COREPER officials within the Commission whose role is to prepare package deals to attract the support of national politicians in the Council of Ministers. The establishment of EPC and the introduction in 1969 of regular European Summit meetings between the EC Heads of Government lend further support to the intergovernmentalist view of the Community. Major policy initiatives such as the internal market programme, institutional reform and monetary union have emanated not from the Commission, which is formally responsible for policy initiation, but from meetings of the Heads of Government. However, it would be incorrect to assume that national governments have consistently opposed European integration. Paradoxically, summit meetings between the EC Heads of Government have not infrequently accelerated the process of integration. The 1986 Single European Act, the Delors Package on monetary integration and the decision to introduce political union were all agreed at such meetings.

Federalism, neo-functionalism and intergovernmentalism constitute the three principal approaches to the study of European integration. Federalist arguments and movements played a vital role in the early post-war period in opening up the whole debate on European integration. Even after the collapse of the EDC project demonstrated the unrealistic nature of the federalists' strategy, federalist aspirations continued to motivate the founders of the EC, and for many people still represent the ultimate form of European integration. Neo-functionalist theories of integration meanwhile are helpful in explaining the incremental development of Community policies and the discernible increase in interest-group activity at the European level. However, it is necessary also to bear in mind the consequences for European integration of the institutional weight of national governments within the EC, which inevitably necessitates intergovernmental policy compromises. In addition, it is necessary to take into account the impact upon European integration of external pressures such as overt American support for European integration during the 1950s, the prolonged economic recession of the 1970s and early 1980s, and, more recently, developments in Eastern Europe which impinge directly on the EC (see p. 1157). In short, the evolution of the Community does not fit neatly into any single explanatory model because there is no agreement on the goal to be achieved. Since 1957, important developments have occurred which have slowly nudged the Community further along the road towards social and political union. However, this course is far from predetermined; European integration is an ongoing process, the pace and direction of which depends upon a changing constellation of pressures pulling in different directions.

CURRENT ISSUES AND FUTURE DEVELOPMENTS

The European Community has undergone many stages in its metamorphosis from a mere customs union between six European states to a *de facto* political organization of states and 320 million inhabitants. Further European integration will depend crucially upon how member states respond to the internal and external pressures for change bearing down upon the Community. The most obvious catalyst of change is the 1986 Single European Act. The completion of the single European market will result in far-reaching and wide-ranging socio-economic changes within the Community. The dismantling of trade barriers, harmonization of standards and free mobility of persons, goods and services within the world's largest trading bloc will directly or indirectly affect the whole of the Community. Nor will the impact of the single market be confined to Europe: the 1992 programme has given rise to complaints from the United States and Japan that the Commission is building a protectionist 'Fortress Europe' which contravenes the principles of the General Agreement on Tariffs and Trade (GATT). Equally, the 1989 agreement by the EC Finance Ministers to implement the Delors three-stage plan for economic and monetary union marks a major step in the direction of a federal Europe. The introduction of a single European currency and a European central bank logically implies central co-ordination of member states' macroeconomic strategies and interest-rate policies. In short, it implies political integration (Owen and Dynes 1989).

In addition to the momentum unleashed by the 1992 programme, recent external developments have added fresh urgency to the debate on the future status of the EC. The pulling down of the Berlin Wall in November 1989 and the reunification of Germany has changed the dimensions of the Community. Despite the fact that it is the wealthiest member of the EC, the costs of reunification will undoubtedly place strains upon the West German economy which may in turn destabilize the European Monetary System which is heavily dependent upon the strength of the Deutschmark. The Community will also be expected to provide aid for East German industry and infrastructure development. Some EC leaders, including Mrs Thatcher, argued that the debate on political union should be postponed because of German reunification. This, however, was a minority view. Other states (notably France) have voiced concern at the prospect of an economically powerful Germany and are anxious that the process of reunification should be closely monitored by the EC and that a reunified Germany should be integrated into a strengthened, democratic European Community.

The EC also has to respond to the collapse of the Soviet-backed regimes in other East European countries. Though the Community has since the early 1970s sought to establish closer trading links with some COMECON countries, the situation has now changed dramatically. As an interim measure the EC approved an aid package for Eastern Europe and signed co-operation agreements with Poland, Hungary, Romania, East Germany and the Soviet Union. However, Hungary, Czechoslovakia and Poland have indicated that this is not enough and have already applied for full membership of the Community. Though in theory any 'democratic' nation-state may apply to join the EC, the Commission has declared that it does not envisage any further enlargement until after 1992. In fact, it is difficult to see how the Community, having just absorbed East Germany, could afford to embrace the crippled economies of Eastern Europe at present. Nevertheless, these applications represent a declaration of intent and the EC will eventually have to make a decision about where the boundaries of the Community – and European integration – lie. Indeed, recognition of the changes now underway within the Community has also prompted interest in EC membership from elsewhere, including Cyprus, Turkey, Norway, Finland, Sweden and Austria. This new interest in EC membership from economically and culturally diverse states has given rise to speculation about a future 'two-tier' European Community comprising different degrees of membership.

The changes which have occurred in Eastern Europe have also raised important questions about the future defence needs of Europe and given new life to the long-running debate about the role of NATO within Europe. Formally speaking, foreign and defence matters lie, for the moment at least, beyond the remit of the EC. Within the framework of European Political Co-operation, the EC foreign ministers have sought to establish a common position on international developments such as the Arab–Israeli conflict and apartheid in South Africa. European security and defence matters have, however, up until now been dealt with mainly within the framework of NATO. Whilst NATO is unlikely to disappear, its role may be adapted to suit the changed international situation in Europe. If such a change were to occur and to coincide with the achievement of European political union, it is at least possible that the EC might be given new powers in the areas of European defence and foreign policy. As Palmer (1987, 1988) points out, whilst the obstacles to such a development should not be underestimated, there are some grounds for thinking that European defence co-operation might be a feasible alternative.

The cumulative effect of the above pressures has been to push to the forefront of the Community's agenda once again the two interrelated issues of European political union and EC institutional reform. The first of a series of tripartite meetings leading up to the December 1990 summit (where Heads of Government discussed the issue) between the EP, the Council of Ministers and the Commission took place in Strasbourg in May 1990. At this meeting the two conflicting visions of European integration were once again defended. On the one hand, the West German, French, Italian, Spanish, Belgian and Portuguese governments supported the EP's view that the Commission should become a political executive, accountable to a strengthened European Parliament. In addition to the right to dismiss individual commissioners, the EP is also demanding the right to initiate legislation and co-equal legislative power with the Council of Ministers (which would become the second chamber of the Parliament). In opposition to this view, the British government, supported by Luxemburg and Greece, argued that the Council of Ministers should become a more powerful European executive, accountable not to the European Parliament, but to the national Parliaments. Thus the debate on the proper aims and objectives of European integration continues. The question now is whether the spillover effects of the 1992 programme combined with the integrative pressures of German reunification will carry the EC further in the direction of political union.

REFERENCES

Bogdanor, V. (1989) 'The June 1989 European elections and the institutions of the Community', *Government and Opposition* 24 (2): 199–214.
Bromberger, M. (1969) *Jean Monnet and the United States of Europe*, New York: Coward McCann.

Butt-Philip, A. (1985) *Pressure Groups in the European Community*, Occasional Paper No. 2, London: University Association for Contemporary European Studies (UACES).

Camps, M. (1964) *Britain and the European Community 1955–63*, Oxford: Oxford University Press.

Dahrendorf, R. (1972) 'A new goal for Europe', in M. Hodges (ed.) *European Integration*, London: Penguin.

Fitzmaurice, J. (1988) 'An analysis of the European Community's co-operation procedure', *Journal of Common Market Studies* 26: 389–400.

George, S. (1985) *Politics and Policy in the European Community*, Oxford: Clarendon Press.

Grant, W. (1989) *Pressure Groups, Politics and Democracy in Britain*, Hemel Hempstead: Philip Allan.

Groeben, H. von der (1986) *The European Community: The Formative Years*, Luxemburg: European Perspectives.

Haas, E. (1968) *The Uniting of Europe*, 2nd edn, Stanford, Calif.: Stanford University Press.

Harrison, R. (1975) *Europe in Question*, 2nd edn, London: Allen & Unwin.

Hoffman, S. (1966) 'Obstinate or obsolete: the fate of the nation-state, and the case of Western Europe', *Daedalus* 95: 862–915.

Holland, S. (1980) *The Uncommon Market*, London: Macmillan.

Lindberg, L. (1963) *The Political Dynamics of European Economic Integration*, Stanford, Calif.: Stanford University Press.

Lindberg, L. and Scheingold, S. (1970) *Europe's Would-be Polity: Patterns of Change in the European Community*, Englewood Cliffs: Prentice-Hall.

Mazey, S. and Richardson, J. J. (1992) 'British pressure groups in the European community: the challenge of Brussels', *Parlimentary Affairs* 45 (1): 92–107

Mitrany, D. (1966) *A Working Peace System*, Chicago: Quadrangle Books.

Monnet, J. (1976) *Memoires*, Paris: Fayard.

Nugent, N. (1989) *The Government and Politics of the European Community*, London: Macmillan.

Owen, R. and Dynes, M. (1989) *The Times Guide to 1992*, London: Times Books.

Palmer, J. (1987) *Europe Without America? The Crisis in Atlantic Relations*, Oxford: Oxford University Press.

——(1988) *Trading Places: the Future of the European Community*, London: Radius.

Vaughan, R. (1979) *Twentieth-Century Europe*, London: Croom Helm.

Wallace, W. (ed.) (1980) *Britain in europe*, London: Heinemann.

Webb, C. (1977) 'Variations on a theoretical theme', in A. Wallace, H. Wallace and C. Webb (eds). *Policy-Making in the European Communities*, London: John Wiley.

FURTHER READING

European Commission (1989) *Forging Ahead: European Parliament 1952–88*, Luxemburg: European Commission.

Haas, E. (1968) *The Uniting of Europe*, 2nd edn, Stanford, Calif.: Stanford University Press.

Lintner, V. and Mazey, S. (1991) *The European Community: Economic and Political Aspects*, London: McGraw Hill.

Lodge J. (1986) 'The Single European Act: towards a new Euro-dynamism?', *Journal of Common Market Studies*: 24: 203–33.
——(ed.) (1989) *The European Community and the Challenge of the Future*, London: Pinter Publishers.
Nugent, N. (1989) *The Government and Politics of the European Community*, London: Macmillan.
Owen, R. and Dynes, M. (1989) *The Times Guide to 1992*, London: Times Books.
Palmer, J. (1987) *Europe Without America? The Crisis in Atlantic Relations*, Oxford: Oxford University Press.
——(1988) *Trading Places: The Future of the European Community*, London: Radius.
Swann, D. (1988) *The Economics of the European Community*, 4th edn, London: Penguin.
Tugenhadt, C. (1987) *Making Sense of Europe*, London: Pelican.
Van Helmont, J. (1986) *Options européenes 1945–85*, Luxemburg: European Commission.
Wallace, A., Wallace, H. and Webb, C. (eds) (1977) *Policy-Making in the European Communities*, London: John Wiley.

73

THE MIDDLE EAST

BERNARD REICH

The Middle East is a large and diverse area whose precise geographical delineation remains a matter of some controversy, although the core is generally defined as the area from Egypt to the Persian (sometimes referred to as Arabian) Gulf, and from Turkey and Iran in the north to Yemen and Sudan in the south. The political units encompassed in this region represent a broad spectrum of political systems (from virtual theocracy to parliamentary democracy, with military and other forms of dictatorial regimes also represented). The region includes a number of ethnic and linguistic groups, varying socio-economic achievements and systems, and a range of international alignments.

GEOSTRATEGIC SIGNIFICANCE

The geostrategic significance of the region has made it an international focal point as external powers have competed for presence and power, for influence and control, and for access to resources and to markets throughout the region.

The international geostrategic significance of the area is a direct consequence of two overriding factors: location and resources. The Middle East lies at the intersection of Europe, Asia and Africa and thus is astride land, sea and air routes connecting these continents. The historical caravan routes were utilized for transporting silks and spices while their modern counterparts are used for oil and electronics. The numerous sea routes in the region create importance for such choke-points as the Turkish Straits, the Suez Canal, the Bab el-Mandeb and the Strait of Hormuz. At the same time lesser-known locations (such as the Gulf of Aqaba and the Strait of Tiran) are of vital importance to their littoral states. The location of the Soviet Union has had a dual effect. For centuries Tsarist Russia and, later, the Soviet Union, sought access to the warm waters of the Persian Gulf as an alternative to its own ice-choked ports as a means of access to the world's oceans. The Soviet Union, as Russia before it, sought to ensure its own security by carefully monitoring developments in bordering states and by seeking to influence their nature and policy in a direction favourable to the Soviet Union. Turkey, Iran and Afghanistan thus became regional actors of significance and remain so today. For many of the same general reasons the Western states have had interests in this northern tier of Middle Eastern states. The Eastern Question of the nineteenth century developed a modern counterpart in the twentieth. Throughout the post-Second World War Cold War era the United States sought to counter a Soviet role and to establish one of its own in the northern tier of Middle Eastern states. A military and intelligence presence became a goal and a means of United States and allied policy and interest in the region. The construction of the Baghdad Pact (later the Central Treaty Organization or CENTO) and Turkey's inclusion in the North Atlantic Treaty Organization (NATO) were elements of this approach.

Increasingly the Middle East is synonymous with oil, possessing most of the world's proven reserves and serving as the largest oil-exporting region. Although the area has produced oil for much of the twentieth century, the region's oil industry and production has assumed significant international proportions only since the Second World War, and truly dramatic international levels only since the Arab–Israeli war of October 1973 and the concomitant oil crisis. The Middle East has emerged as the focal point of the international trade in oil and is likely to retain and probably enhance that position into the twenty-first century.

The members of the Organization of Petroleum Exporting Countries (OPEC) and of the Organization of Arab Petroleum Exporting Countries (OAPEC) increasingly control the reserves, production and export of the world's oil. Within OPEC, Saudi Arabia and, following closely, Iraq, Kuwait, Iran and the United Arab Emirates (UAE) hold a growing proportion of the world's proven oil reserves. Saudi Arabia itself possesses more than 25 per cent of the total and is the world's largest exporter of oil. These data provide some indication of the growing power of the Gulf members of OPEC to determine the production, availability and price of oil worldwide. Associated with this is a growing economic and political role and capability in the international system.

There is also an international economic dimension to Middle Eastern oil. Oil exports – a function of high levels of reserves and production and low levels of domestic consumption – generate revenues at high levels of magnitude. In general the costs of production, especially in the Gulf sector (for example, Saudi Arabia), are very low, and thus much of the selling price constitutes earnings for the state-owned oil companies. The earnings from oil sales grew dramatically following the oil price increase of 1973–4 associated with the October 1973 Arab–Israeli war and subsequently with other price booms. But, especially in the mid-1980s, there were also declines in price due to over-production and competition among oil producers. Nevertheless, the major oil-producing states of the Middle East have earned huge sums of money from their vital resource and this has, in turn, created international economic power. The oil-rich states have become a major market for goods and services in virtually every economic sector. Infrastructure construction, industrial development, military purchases and education and training have drawn countries and companies from every geographic area of the globe. At the same time the oil revenues – sometimes referred to as petrodollars – have led states in the region to invest surplus funds in companies and other investments worldwide. These states have purchased government bonds and notes, and in other ways have become a factor in the international economic and financial system. The international competition to earn revenues in, or gain investments from, the Middle East has continued unabated since the mid-1970s, although the participants both in and outside the region have varied over time as has the focus of economic activity.

THE ARMS TRADE

Increasingly the Middle East has emerged as a primary venue for the international arms trade. This is a consequence of two essentially unrelated factors – regional instability and conflict, and substantial resources to acquire military equipment, facilities and training.

Conflicts abound in the Middle East – some have been essentially continuous since the Second World War, while others have been of shorter duration. The continuation of local and regional conflicts has generated an interest in and concern for the acquisition of armaments and military capability by the parties to conflict. Middle East arms acquisition has involved virtually every state and many levels of both sophistication and quantity. Arms suppliers are numerous and virtually all forms of military equipment, military infrastructure and construction, and training of personnel are available. Limits on weapons desired and weapons supplied are few and generally self-imposed, if imposed at all.

In the first decade after the Second World War there was little sophisticated modern military equipment in the region but this began to change, especially in the Arab–Israeli sector, with the provision of arms by the Soviet Union to Egypt (and somewhat later to Syria) and by France to Israel in the early 1950s. Further acquisition by these and other states, and supplies by additional arms producers, developed apace in the 1960s and early 1970s. With the massive revenues earned from dramatically increased oil prices at the time of the 1973 Arab–Israeli war, and the consequent availability of huge sums of money for Iran and the Arab states, a vast new market for arms developed. Coupled with the availability of funds there was a regionally perceived need for weapons and military capability. The meshing of a perceived need with available financial resources generated a new and, in many respects, uninhibited military equipment supply–acquisition relationship. Modern high-technology weapons systems (with accompanying facilities and trained personnel) began to become a characteristic of many of the (richer) states of the region. Drawn by the opportunity for sales, profits and perceived accompanying influence, the group of possible supplying powers grew significantly. While the superpowers remained the major regional suppliers for a wide variety of reasons, numerous smaller and internationally less powerful states joined in the effort to develop regional links.

The arms regime in the Middle East was and is overwhelmingly conventional in nature and extra-regional in source of supply. Nevertheless, the regional states have begun to develop and expand their own arms production capabilities and to expand their efforts to produce and/or acquire non-conventional military equipment. Within the region, defence industries have developed a wide range of weapons systems both for use by the producing state and for export to earn revenues. Although the full range of locally produced weapons is not always publicly known, it is clear that some states have advanced capabilities that include missiles, aircraft, tanks and other sophisticated weapons systems.

Several critical issues have developed as it has become clear that regional states had, or could acquire, non-conventional weapons systems, some with mass destruction capabilities. At the same time the willingness of some states to use missiles to strike civilian targets (such as Tehran and Baghdad) and poison gas to strike even at segments of their own populations (for example, Baghdad against its Kurdish population) posed additional questions about the potential of more widespread use of these capabilities in other conflicts or to deal with different adversaries. Chemical-biological warfare puts the Middle East in the dubious forefront of modern military activities and the likely expansion of its use further exacerbates regional and international tensions.

At the same time there remains a concern about nuclear capabilities and their development and use in the region. Israel is seen as the pioneer of nuclear research in the region and is widely believed to possess a nuclear capability, although it has yet to be used, even in combat. Iraq has expressed a desire to develop such a capability and there is clear evidence that progress had already been made towards this goal prior to the Gulf War.

It must be remembered, however, that arms are neither produced nor purchased nor acquired simply to have them. The development of regional military capabilities is directly related to issues of security and potential conflict.

THE ARAB–ISRAELI CONFLICT

To many observers, the Middle East is synonymous with the continuing Arab–Israeli conflict. The centrepiece of this issue remains the ultimate status of the territory that was known throughout history by many names but which now consists of Israel, the West Bank and the Gaza Strip. The territory, a part of the Ottoman Empire from the sixteenth century until the end of the First World War, became a League of Nations Mandate under British control after the allied powers severed it and other areas from the Ottoman Empire in the post-war peace settlements. Partly in an effort to fulfil the pledges it made in the course of the First World War, Britain divided the Palestine Mandate along the Jordan River and created, in the territory east of the river, a new entity known then as Transjordan and subsequently as the Hashemite Kingdom of Jordan. Arabs of Palestine and Jews in the Yishuv (the Jewish community in Palestine) clashed over the future of the territory west of the river from the inception of the Palestine Mandate in 1922. For the Jews of Palestine and the Zionist movement that encouraged and supported them, the goal was the creation of a Jewish state in Palestine in accordance with the concepts of Zionism and the pledge of the Balfour Declaration of November 1917. For the Arabs of Palestine and their Arab world supporters, the objective was to retain Palestine as an Arab state within the broader Arab world as they believed they had been promised in the Hussein–McMahon exchange of correspondence during the First World War.

Tensions, demonstrations and armed clashes between the rival camps in Palestine were commonplace throughout the British Mandatory period (1922–48). Although various concepts for the ultimate disposition of the territory were put forward during the period between the world wars, the final decision awaited the United Nations in 1947. The British turned the matter of the future of the Palestine Mandate over to the United Nations, and in November 1947 its General Assembly adopted the majority plan of the United Nations Special Committee on Palestine (UNSCOP), which called for the partition of Palestine and the creation of a Jewish state and an Arab state, with Jerusalem under an international regime. The Zionists responded in the affirmative (with reluctance); the Arabs rejected the plan.

The adoption of the partition plan served as a prelude to different forms of conflict not, as had been hoped, as a means of resolution of previous difficulties. Local fighting continued and escalated to a fully-fledged Arab–Israeli war in May 1948 when Britain terminated its Mandatory government and withdrew its military forces from Palestine.

Since the end of the Mandate and the declaration of independence by Israel, the Jewish state in Palestine proposed by the partition plan, and in the absence of a similar declaration by a Palestinian state until four decades later, the international community has focused on the subsequent Arab–Israeli wars as well as on the efforts to resolve the conflict and to achieve peace. Six major Arab–Israeli wars were fought in the first four decades after the adoption of the partition plan and the establishment of Israel. Israel's War of Independence (1948–9) was fought by Israel against Egypt, Jordan, Syria, Lebanon, Iraq and the Palestinian Arabs with lesser participation by the other Arab states. The West Bank and Gaza Strip came into existence as separate territories, although the former was soon annexed by Jordan while Egypt retained military control over Gaza. Jerusalem was divided *de facto* between Israel and Jordan, with the latter holding the old walled city and East Jerusalem. Armistice agreements established formal frontiers between Israel and each of its neighbours (Egypt, Jordan, Syria and Lebanon), but peace negotiations did not follow and preparations for a next round of hostilities were soon underway.

The Sinai/Suez War of 1956 between Israel and Egypt resulted in no geographical or substantial political alterations in the regional situation and no real movement toward peace, although a United Nations Emergency Force (UNEF) was installed along the Israel–Egypt frontier to prevent cross-border attacks and to forestall conflict between the two antagonists. During the decade between the spring of 1957 and the spring of 1967 the Egypt–Israel frontier remained quiet, but efforts to achieve an Arab–Israeli peace were few and unsuccessful. Growing tensions and clashes between Israel and its eastern neighbours replaced those along Israel's frontier with the Gaza Strip and the Sinai Peninsula.

The June 1967 Six Day War dramatically altered the strategic-political situation. In a brief period Israel won a major military victory over a combined Arab war effort that involved Egypt, Syria, Jordan, Iraq and elements of the armed forces of other Arab states, as well as the Palestine Liberation Organization (PLO), and gained control of substantial Arab territory, including the Sinai Peninsula of Egypt, the Gaza Strip, the West Bank, the Golan Heights of Syria and East Jerusalem. The magnitude of the Israeli victory and of the Arab defeat suggested to some that the altered environment might provide a basis for peace efforts. Some moves followed, including the articulation of positions by Israel, by the Arab states at the Khartoum Arab Summit, by the Soviet Union and by the United States. The adoption of United Nations Security Council Resolution 242 in November 1967 provided the basis for subsequent peace efforts and specifically for the mission of Ambassador Gunnar Jarring, who was charged with implementing the resolution to establish peace. Jarring achieved an exchange of prisoners of war and the reiteration of some policy positions by the parties, but these moves were not followed by more general successes.

The War of Attrition launched by President Gamal Abdul Nasser of Egypt against Israeli forces along the Suez Canal in April 1969 was not ended until

August 1970. By then peace efforts launched by the United States, the Soviet Union, England and France and by the superpowers bilaterally, as well as continued United Nations efforts, were unable to prevent an escalation of regional tensions and a direct role by the Soviet Union in the air defence of the Suez Canal zone. The level of conflict and the commitment of new weapons systems – especially United States Phantom F-4 Jets to Israel, and Soviet anti-aircraft missiles to Egypt – led to Henry Kissinger's observation that the Soviet Union should be expelled from Egypt and to President Richard Nixon's comment that the region was as dangerous as the Balkans in 1914. The defusing of tension and the ceasefire of August 1970 was followed by some efforts to resolve the broader issues, but these produced little and could not prevent the next round of war.

The October (Yom Kippur or Ramadan) War of 1973 proved to be a watershed in many respects with regard to the international relations of the region. Egypt and Syria could reclaim Arab honour as a consequence of their initial achievements in combat. Nevertheless, the hostilities ended with Israel clearly in command of the situation, albeit under external pressures to terminate its actions prior to the humiliation of Egypt's President Anwar Sadat. The unusual configuration of troop locations at the termination of hostilities and the efforts of United States Secretary of State Henry Kissinger soon combined with modifications in regional perspectives to generate significant moves towards peace. Within weeks of the end of hostilities, negotiations for military disengagement began at Kilometre 101 on the Cairo–Suez road, and these soon gave way to a Peace Conference convened in Geneva in December 1973. The United States and the Soviet Union served as co-chairs of the Geneva Conference at which the parties essentially restated their perspectives and policies. Nevertheless, the conference provided the context for Kissinger's shuttle diplomacy between Egypt and Israel which led to the agreement in January 1974 for the disengagement of their military forces in the Sinai Peninsula, and for his subsequent shuttle in the spring of 1974 between Israel and Syria to secure a military disengagement in the Golan Heights to be monitored by the United Nations Disengagement Observer Force (UNDOF).

Further moves and an effort to secure an Israel–Jordan agreement encountered a series of political road-blocks that led Kissinger to concentrate on a second disengagement between Egypt and Israel. The Sinai II agreement in the fall of 1975 went beyond a simple military disengagement. Ultimately the barriers to peace were broken by Egyptian President Anwar Sadat's initiative in 1977 to deal directly with Israel on the substance of Arab–Israeli peace, a procedure formally rejected by the Arab states at the 1967 Khartoum Summit meeting and reaffirmed subsequently. Sadat violated the Arab consensus and elevated the peace process to a new level that made progress possible. The resultant Camp David Accords (1978) and the Egypt–Israel Peace Treaty of

March 1979 (the first Arab–Israeli peace treaty) established peace and a normalized relationship between Israel and its largest and then most powerful neighbour. However, peace between Egypt and Israel, and the autonomy talks that followed, did not induce other Arab states or the Palestinians to join the process.

A sixth Arab–Israeli war in 1982 resulted from Israel's Operation Peace for Galilee, which sought to eliminate the threat to Israel's northern sector resulting from PLO military/terrorist attacks originating in Lebanon. The destruction of the PLO's military bases and presence in Lebanon was the primary objective of Israel's invasion. The termination of hostilities through United States efforts was followed by United States-brokered Lebanese–Israeli negotiations that led to an agreement on 17 May 1983. This was ultimately abrogated by Lebanon under Syrian pressure, but otherwise would have become a second move toward a peaceful resolution of the conflict. The failure of the 17 May accord and other regional and extra-regional developments essentially precluded further moves towards peace in the zone in the ensuing period. At the same time war seemed to become increasingly unlikely.

A major change in the Arab–Israeli sector developed from regionally initiated moves. The Palestinian uprising (*intifada*) which began in December 1987 and Yasser Arafat's acceptance of the three 'yesses' of Geneva (recognition of Israel's right to exist, renunciation of terrorism, and acceptance of United Nations Security Council Resolution 242) in December 1988 generated international attention but also set in motion new efforts to move in the direction of a settlement of the Arab–Israeli conflict. The *intifada* seemed to galvanize Palestinians' demands for an end to Israeli occupation of the West Bank and Gaza and the creation of an independent Palestinian state. The Arab world and the PLO soon rallied to the support of the Palestinians and their objectives. Although spurred by the installation of the Bush administration in Washington in January 1989, and again by the successful results of the United States-led coalition to oust Iraq's invading forces from Kuwait in the spring of 1991, regional and international developments did not lead to major and significant moves toward peace in the short term. Identifying the proper combination of negotiating parties provided the initial agenda for peace efforts, but the determination of the agenda and, more importantly, of the solutions to agenda items acceptable to the parties and their external patrons remained formidable obstacles. Nevertheless, the United States was able to convene a peace conference in Madrid in October/November 1991 at which Israelis met face-to-face in direct public negotiations with Arab delegations.

The basic issues continue to be the ultimate division of the territory that was called Palestine and sovereignty over it. The borders of the state of Israel and its right to exist in peace and security, the status of Jerusalem and the rights of the Palestinians, as well as a host of essentially technical problems, are component elements that have yet to be addressed substantially, let alone resolved.

LEBANON

The civil war in Lebanon is a conflict of multiple dimensions and levels involving not only the various religious groups in the country but also their regional and international supporters and patrons. Shifting alliances in the country, combined with alterations in regional and international involvement, have contributed to the continuation of the conflict and acted as impediments to its resolution.

Modern Lebanon is essentially a creation of great power (that is, primarily French) actions. In their effort to create a viable, Western-oriented, predominantly Christian state out of parts of the Syrian sector of the Ottoman Empire, the French added other groups to the Christian base centred on Mount Lebanon. Ultimately the disparate nature of these religious groups included in the Lebanese state was reflected in a compromise – the national pact – which formed the political basis for the independent state of Lebanon after the Second World War. An uneasy arrangement at best, there were numerous clashes between and among the groups that constituted modern Lebanon.

The establishment of Israel to Lebanon's south and the continuation of the Arab–Israeli conflict contributed to the tensions within a Lebanon seeking to establish its own identity in an overwhelmingly Muslim Arab World. Lebanon participated in the first Arab–Israeli war but avoided formal participation in succeeding conflicts, although its territory often was utilized as a base for operations directed against Israel. For Lebanon, the Arab–Israeli conflict posed a basic dilemma – the extent to which Lebanon was or should be identified as an Arab state in an Arab world, and the extent to which its Christian communities were able to avoid Lebanon's identification with a predominantly Muslim Arab world. Lebanon's ability to master its fence-straddling posture was undermined by events not of its making or subject to its control. The Jordan civil war of September 1970 (Black September) resulted in the ejection of the PLO from its bases and facilities in Jordan, where it had endangered Jordanian security by provoking Israeli retaliations for its actions and endangered the King's control by acting outside his governing system. The PLO's move from Jordan to Syria was of relatively short duration and it then shifted to Lebanon, where it eventually established its own state in all but formal name. This move threatened the balance within Lebanon, invited Israeli response and retaliation to PLO strikes against Israel, and ultimately contributed to and exacerbated the civil war.

The conflict in Lebanon formally traces its origins to an incident in April 1975 in which Maronite church worshippers were attacked by unknown gunmen. Since that early date, however, the conflict has continued with virtually all political and religious factions playing a role within a collage of constantly changing military and political coalitions composed of the various factions. Adding to the complexity of the situation is the involvement of external powers, most notably Syria and Israel. Syrian forces first entered the country in July 1976, ostensibly on behalf of the Arab League, but have remained there ever since. The initial intervention was on behalf of the Maronite forces, but Syria subsequently altered its position on a number of occasions.

Over the decade of the 1970s the PLO gained in power and position within Lebanon and its forces moved closer to the border with Israel. This increased the tensions in southern Lebanon as the factions continued their battles elsewhere in the country. Israel supported Major Saad Haddad and his Christian militia forces in southern Lebanon as a counterweight to the growing PLO and radical Muslim strength in that sector and in response to the growing Syrian presence in the country. As the Syrian and Israeli presences and activities in Lebanon grew, the potential of a Syrian–Israeli clash seemed to dominate much of the strategic/political thinking about the country. A 'red line' was drawn in southern Lebanon, suggesting a point across which Israel would not tolerate the movement of Syrian troops in its direction, although this position never emerged in reality and both Syria and Israel were careful not to create a situation where their forces might clash. Southern Lebanon, along the border with Israel, became a base of PLO operations against Israel (often known as Fatahland) and a zone of conflict among the supporters of Saad Haddad, the PLO and the Shi'ite population of the sector. Clashes in the south were echoed by partisans elsewhere in the country, and this contributed to the civil war.

In the spring of 1978 Israel launched Operation Litani to clear southern Lebanon of the PLO and its supporters. The invasion led ultimately to a temporary reduction in tension and to the establishment of the United Nations Interim Force in Lebanon (UNIFIL) as a force designed to help prevent regional clashes. Despite Operation Litani and UNIFIL, the civil war continued throughout Lebanon and the PLO succeeded in establishing itself as a 'state within a state' in much of southern Lebanon in the ensuing years. This led to tensions and clashes with the resident Shi'ite community as well as with the Israelis across the border and the militia of Saad Haddad. Various efforts to prevent the PLO from using Lebanon as a base against Israel and to end the civil war ended in failure, despite some short-term successes and variations in the scope and level of the civil war.

In June 1982 Israel launched a full-scale invasion of southern Lebanon. This achieved a number of objectives including the expulsion of the PLO from Lebanon, a substantial United States (and to some extent multinational) effort to restore Lebanon's sovereignty, and negotiations to achieve another agreement between Israel and a warring neighbour that would move the Arab–Israeli conflict in the direction of peace. Although Israel and Lebanon reached agreement on the withdrawal of Israeli forces from Lebanon, the accord subsequently was abrogated by Lebanon under Syrian pressure. The president-elect of Lebanon, Beshir Gemayel, was assassinated and there were Christian massacres of Palestinians at the Sabra and Shatilla refugee camps outside Beirut in the autumn of 1982. A major United States effort that included the despatching of Marines to Lebanon to support the government of President Amin Gemayel and the launching of a Reagan 'fresh start' initiative to deal with the Arab–Israeli conflict all came to naught. There was no major progress as a consequence of these efforts toward restoring Lebanon to its place as a stable and tranquil state in the Middle East.

The civil war continued into the decade of the 1990s with an ever-changing series of military-political coalitions among the warring parties and their external patrons and supporters. Within the several factions additional tensions developed. All significant efforts at reconciliation of the parties seemed to fail and Lebanon remained divided into a series of military-sectarian cantonments, each reflecting fear, mistrust and animosity toward the others at one time or another.

The Taif agreement and the selection of Elias Hrawi as President provided an opportunity for a positive turn in the civil war. However, General Michel Aoun, the Maronite Christian commander of the Lebanese army, prevented Hrawi from assuming control. The Iraqi invasion of Kuwait created a framework in which President Assad of Syria was able in mid-October 1990 to move militarily against General Aoun and oust him from control, and to extend Syria's control further into Lebanon. The Lebanese government began to extend its authority, under the patronage of Syria, and sought to end the control of portions of the country by the militia forces and, thereby, to bring stability to Lebanon.

THE IRAN–IRAQ WAR

Conflict and combat across the Shatt-al-Arab and the Persian (Arabian) Gulf can be traced back many centuries, although the identity of the contestants has varied. In the twentieth century conflict has erupted and settlements have been achieved on a number of occasions.

The Iran–Iraq (or Persian Gulf) war which erupted in September 1980 marked the latest but probably not the last of the wars to be fought over the question of boundaries in the Gulf and associated political-economic issues. Iraq initiated the conflict with the clear intention of rectifying what it regarded as the inequitable situation created by the 1975 accord imposed on a then relatively weak Iraq. The subsequent overthrow of the Shah, the Iranian

Revolution with its accompanying internal disarray, the decimation of Iran's armed forces and military capability, and other regional and international factors resulting from the Iranian revolution weakened Iran and made it vulnerable to a stronger Iraq, which saw an opportunity to reorder the situation in the Shatt and the Gulf to its advantage. Iraqi President Saddam Hussein apparently calculated that Iran was weaker militarily and more isolated internationally than before and acted decisively, if impulsively. After some initial successes, Iraq soon lost its advantage, and developments in Iran and in the conflict itself veered from the presumed and expected course. There were periods in which each side appeared to achieve an advantage, but eventually the hostilities settled down to a seemingly endless stalemate.

The war later escalated as the two parties began to attack oil tankers sailing to and from the Gulf. Iraq began, in May 1984, by declaring a sector around the Iranian port at Kharg Island as a war zone and began to attack tankers sailing to and from that location. Iran began striking at tankers calling at Arab states' ports in the Gulf.

The Arab states in general and the members of the Gulf Co-operation Council (GCC) in particular grew increasingly concerned about the threat from Iran that took several forms. The GCC states worried about the export of the Islamic revolution to their Shi'ite minorities, they were anxious about subversion emanating from Iran, and they were concerned that they would be targets for Iran's broader ambitions if Iraq was defeated. The tanker war, and particularly the attacks on ships bound to and from the Arab gulf ports, served to confirm the fears of the GCC states about Iran's intentions and their vulnerability. Thus, although the GCC states generally were wary of Iraq and its threat to their sovereignty (such as a long-standing claim to Kuwait) and a substantial military capability that could be employed against them, they supported Iraq financially and politically against Iran.

External parties benefited from roles as military suppliers and more general provision of required goods and services, but some were negatively affected by disruptions in oil production and export. An occasional act expanded the hostilities beyond the parties' territory to that of other regional states, but more generally the main external targets became the international oil trade as the tankers carrying oil from the Gulf soon were targeted. The tanker war ultimately led to more direct external involvement as both the United States and the Soviet Union became involved in efforts to ensure freedom of navigation. Reflagging of Kuwaiti ships became one of the mechanisms not only for ensuring safety of shipping but also for superpower involvement. Ultimately this programme achieved its goals of ensuring the safety of Gulf shipping, but only after clashes between the United States and Iran.

The acceptance by Iran of the United Nations Security Council ceasefire resolution in the summer of 1988 ended the major hostilities but did not foreshadow a quick or clear resolution of the conflict or any of its major issues. Iran's acceptance of a ceasefire a year after its adoption by the United Nations Security Council seemed to be a direct consequence of a number of factors that included the Iraqi missile launchings against the civilian population of Tehran, the disastrous state of the Iranian economy, that state's increasingly poor showing in the hostilities, and Iran's growing international isolation.

The hostilities ceased but movement toward resolution of the underlying issues was not achieved. The United Nations Iran Iraq Military Observer Group (UNIIMOG) and various envoys helped to sustain the ceasefire, but the underlying issues and the hostility as a consequence of eight years of fighting and generations of discord were not susceptible to amelioration in the short term.

Iraq remained the only substantial military power in the Gulf. However, its decision to invade Kuwait soon created a very different situation in the Gulf and other sections of the Middle East.

THE GULF CRISIS

The unexpected invasion of Kuwait by Iraq on 2 August 1990 generated a major crisis that culminated in a war and a subsequent ceasefire in early 1991. The crisis was a complicated event and the first major challenge in the Middle East since the end of the Cold War.

In the early summer of 1990 Iraq threatened its neighbours, especially Kuwait, over oil pricing and revenues. Despite pledges to settle oil (and territorial) disputes by peaceful means and despite some (generally ambiguous) warnings by the United States and others to Iraq not to take military action, Iraq invaded Kuwait. It proclaimed an end to an independent Kuwaiti identity and the incorporation of Kuwait and its oil riches into Iraq as its nineteenth province.

The reaction of the United States and many of its major allies, as well as a large number of other states, was swift and ultimately uncompromising. An international coalition was constructed and a United Nations Security Council framework for resolution of the crisis was adopted.

An international grouping, under United States leadership, devised a multi-faceted policy that included economic, political, diplomatic and military elements. The basic goal was the unconditional and complete withdrawal of Iraqi forces from Kuwait and the restoration of the legitimate government. These would precede a post-crisis effort to assure the security and stability of the Persian Gulf. The means to achieve these ends were unusual, if not unique. The United Nations, generally viewed as moribund on issues of this ilk, provided an important venue if not mechanism for responding to the crisis. A series of United Nations resolutions condemned Iraq's actions and called for their reversal. An embargo of Iraq was to help achieve these ends. The United States-led multinational coalition of some thirty states mounted a strong diplomatic effort to isolate Iraq and to put further pressure on Iraqi President Saddam Hussein to comply with the United Nations resolutions.

The embargo and the diplomatic-political efforts were supplemented by the creation of a multinational military force in the region to confront Saddam Hussein and to act, if needed, to end the invasion and occupation of Kuwait. Ultimately, a force numbering more than half a million troops was deployed to the area, along with modern and sophisticated equipment.

The hope was that the combined international political, diplomatic and economic efforts would achieve the stated objectives without the need to resort to force. This proved to be an elusive goal. Conflict began soon after the expiration of the 15 January 1991 deadline in United Nations Security Council Resolution 678 which authorized the use of force.

The war against Iraq involved two stages – the initial air war phase was followed by a brief ground war that was terminated after some 100 hours of hostilities. Iraq was forced to withdraw from Kuwait and its military forces suffered substantial losses of personnel and equipment.

The termination of hostilities was followed by a United Nations Security Council ceasefire resolution that laid out the requirements for a permanent ceasefire. It reversed the annexation of Kuwait and sought to create conditions that would prevent Iraq from being able to take similar actions in the future. The termination of hostilities was also followed by internal uprisings in Iraq against Saddam Hussein by the Shi'ites in the south and the Kurds in the north, but these initial efforts were soon subdued.

Despite the successes of the United States-led coalition against Iraq and Iraq's consequent losses, the nature and extent of Iraq's actions against Kuwait left a situation that would require substantial time and resources in order to restore the pre-war situation. Hopes for regional security and resolution of the problems in the Gulf and elsewhere in the region soon emerged, but the extent of the problems and the slow pace of initial accomplishments did not suggest that the Bush administration's proclaimed new world order would soon emerge in the post-war Middle East.

RELIGION AND POLITICS: THE ROLE OF ISLAM

The contemporary conflicts in the Middle East have often been seen by external observers as a consequence and/or a demonstration of religious disagreement and animosity. Although this discord often gains significant attention, it should be recognized that the interrelationship of religion and politics has been a feature of the Middle East throughout its history. The region came to prominence as the birthplace and centre of three major monotheistic religions – Judaism, Christianity and Islam. Each has played an important role in the history and politics of the area.

Christianity helps to explain the Vatican's links to the Christian communities of Lebanon. The French desire to ensure a Christian presence, a factor that can be traced to the Crusades, led to the creation of the modern state of Lebanon, essentially a Christian enclave carved from greater Syria. The Vatican's interest in the Holy Land, and especially in the city of Jerusalem, has coloured its approach to the termination of the Palestine Mandate, as well as its view toward the internationalization of Jerusalem, the creation of an independent Jewish State of Israel, and the relationship it has established over time with Israel and its position concerning the Palestinians, some of whom are linked to Rome through Church affiliation.

The Jewish connection to the Holy Land can be traced to the origins of the Jewish people and the Bible's record of the promise of God that the children of Abraham (i.e. the Jews) shall inherit the area. The promised land concept and the Jewish connection to Zion (Jerusalem) remains at the centre of the Jewish faith, and is a primary element of Zionism, which sees the solution to the Jewish question as the creation of a Jewish state in Palestine, i.e. Israel.

In many respects, Islam's impact has been even greater than Judaism and Christianity in shaping the nature and consciousness of the states and peoples of the region. Much of the region now known as the Middle East has been under Islamic domination for more than a thousand years, and the impact of Islam on the people and their lives cannot be overestimated. Islam is not simply a religion, but a way of life affecting all aspects of the activities of its adherents. It has a religious doctrine but also provides patterns of social and political relationships. Islam's inherent simplicity of doctrine and theology, combined with the ease of conversion to the fold, has helped to facilitate a universalism that has allowed dramatic and relatively rapid expansion of the faith. It can be adopted by virtually anyone, anywhere, because there are no inherent limits to such an action.

Over time, Islam's impact has been different in each of the states in which it has manifested itself, in the Middle East and elsewhere. The traditional impact was modified in the Middle East after the Second World War in a number of ways. More recently, a concept broadly and popularly (but not always properly) labelled 'Islamic fundamentalism' has cast its shadow on the region. It is not a monolithic, unified and coherent movement, although each of the approaches seeks to return to the basic or fundamental truths of the religion as a means of resolving contemporary political, social, economic and other problems. There is no necessary link between fundamentalism and revolutionary political or military action. Indeed, many of the movements that speak in the name of Islam are often political groups with an Islamic façade.

Perhaps the most significant of the fundamentalist phenomena, and certainly the most widely observed, is the Islamic revolution in Iran which began in the 1970s and has had a major impact on the regional and international scene since its overthrow of the Shah in 1979. Within Iran, the Islamic revolution was both a political and a religious movement with a blurred division between the two elements. In its foreign policy it has sought to use Shi'ite Islamic doctrine to launch efforts at the replacement of illegitimate rulers and regimes. A primary concern of the revolutionary Islamic Republic of Iran has been exporting its revolution. In pursuit of this goal it has become a force for revolutionary change in the Persian Gulf, by example and by propaganda with attractive ideas and concepts. Among other appeals it represents the victory of Islam and demonstrates the value of Islam and Islamic ideas in the modern world. Some of the appeals of the Iranian revolution have been well received among the oppressed and disaffected masses in the other Gulf states.

The threat of Islamic fundamentalism to Middle Eastern political stability comes from several factors. It is an ideology of protest and provides a viable alternative to leftist ideologies that have gained adherents in some parts of the Arab world. However, it draws on local traditions and historical values and seems to gain in appeal because of its local base. There is concern that the Iranian revolutionaries will connect with the dissident groups and may therefore develop threats to local regimes. There is also the possibility that the success of the transfer of Islamic fundamentalist ideas might force local regimes to give up on development and modernization schemes as secular rather than Islamic in nature. There have been more violent methods utilized by those who seek to advance Islam's grasp in the region. At the same time, variants have developed a rationale for terrorism and other efforts to remove and punish opponents of the system. Despite these factors, no other 'Islamic Republic' of the Iran model has been established in the Middle East.

FUTURE PROSPECTS

The Middle East will remain if not gain in significance in the decade of the 1990s and into the twenty-first century. The various components of international, regional and national politics continue to mesh as the main political themes are interwoven. The region's oil, essential for much of the world's future industrial growth and improved living standards, will grow in proportional significance and will continue to generate petrodollars that will allow the region to retain its role as a market for goods and services. The sense of insecurity and instability which characterizes many of these states due to recent histories of *coups*, revolutions and other changes of regime, and perceived (whether real or imagined) threats, makes the area one where continued development of regional military and arms capabilities will be supplemented by the efforts of regional states to acquire arms from abroad, in part by utilizing oil wealth to acquire such weapons systems. The superpower interest, although modified by the 'end of the Cold War', will continue unabated as has past superpower interest continued from previous centuries to this.

The region will see itself affected by religion and the political manifestations of religious movements. But secular-oriented political movements will also influence the nature and direction of the region's politics. Terrorism in and from the Middle East, or supported by regional state sponsors, will continue to be a matter connected to the various conflicts and developments in the region, and while one might anticipate occasional changes, the patterns will be sustained. The factors that have made the Middle East a major focus of international attention in the period since the Second World War will assure an even more central place for the region in the international system in the future.

FURTHER READING

Bill, J. A. and Springborg, R. (1990) *Politics in the Middle East*, 3rd edn, Glenview, Ill. and London: Scott, Foresman/Little, Brown Higher Education.

Brown, L. C. (1984) *International Politics and the Middle East: Old Rules, Dangerous Game*, Princeton: Princeton University Press.

Davison, R. H. (1960) 'Where is the Middle East?', *Foreign Affairs* 38: 665–75.

Drysdale, A. and Blake, G. H. (1985) *The Middle East and North Africa: A Political Geography*, New York: Oxford University Press.

Esposito, J. (1989) *Islam: The Straight Path*, New York: Oxford University Press.

Goldschmidt, A., Jr. (1988) *A Concise History of the Middle East*, 3rd edn, Boulder, Colo.: Westview Press.

Long, D. E. and Reich, B. (eds) (1986) *The Government and Politics of the Middle East and North Africa*, 2nd edn, Boulder, Colo., and London: Westview Press.

Ramazani, R. K. (1988) *The Gulf Cooperation Council: Record and Analysis*, Charlottesville: University Press of Virginia.

Reich, B. (ed.) (1987) *The Powers in the Middle East: The Ultimate Strategic Arena*, New York, Westport, Conn., and London: Praeger.

——(ed.) (1990) *Political Leaders of the Contemporary Middle East and North Africa: A Biographical Dictionary*, New York, Westport, Conn., and London: Greenwood Press.

Smith, C. (1988) *Palestine and the Arab–Israeli Conflict*, New York: St Martin's Press.

74

AFRICA

TIMOTHY M. SHAW

African states and studies are in a profound period of revisionism as the 'crisis' decade of the 1980s yields to the 'adjustment' of the 1990s. The relative optimism and expansion of the initial independence years have long since been superseded by pessimism and contraction as successive energy, drought, debt and devaluation shocks have resulted in impoverishment and inequalities. The former has affected 'vulnerable groups' – in particular women, children, the elderly and peripheral communities – while the latter has occurred both within and between states. A few classes and countries have thrived despite or because of the continental crisis – more bourgeois fractions and more informal sectors on the one hand and, on the other, Botswana, Mauritius and Zimbabwe. Africa at the end of the 1990s will likely be more marginal, vulnerable and unequal than ever, hardly the revolutionary, nationalist scenario anticipated after the Second World War, but more realistic and realizable none the less.

This essay concentrates on a 'Fourth World' continent in a New International Division of Labour and Power at the end of the twentieth century (see Onwuka and Shaw 1989). Its perspective is informed by the continuing continental crisis of the 1980s and the surprising global conjuncture at the end of the same decade: the structural adjustment policy conditions insisted upon by the International Bank for Reconstruction and Development (IBRD or World Bank) and International Monetary Fund (IMF) on the one hand and, on the other, the strategic *détente* achieved by the two superpowers with its profound implications for ideology and diplomacy everywhere, including Africa. In short, the debt syndrome has been joined by the democracy shock of contemporary Eastern Europe and Soviet Union. African socialism was under attack from both adjustment conditionalities and *détente* correlates as the new decade dawned.

The new global context and continental condition have engendered a mood of revisionism in both analysis and praxis. First, neither orthodox moderniz-ation nor orthodox materialism – i.e. belief in unilineal progress and in inevitable contradictions, respectively – have been able to explain the causes and characters of Africa's divergent political economies: from hitherto ubiquitous state socialisms to contemporary (state) capitalisms. And, second, post-independence state controls have been superseded by post-crisis structural adjustments: the familiar mix of devaluation, deregulation, removal of subsidies and privatization. The latter has impacted upon the former: political economies under intense conditionalities and contradictions have compelled revisionist political economy approaches. Hence the imperative of transcending orthodoxies of analysis and praxis in the final decade of the twentieth century. To be sure, some continuities of assumption and condition remain, yet the emerging response is both post-modernization and post-materialism, now reinforced by the series of democratic transformations in Eastern Europe.

The new contexts confronting academic analysts and policy makers alike mean that established explanations and prescriptions are no longer valid. In particular, the orthodox paradigm of modernization and orthodox policy of one-party state control are in the process of being superseded by, first, more radical approaches which treat gender, ecology, culture and informal sectors as well as constitutions, organizations, classes and formal sectors; and second, more pragmatic ideologies which advance agriculture, innovation and accumulation rather than industry, conformity and consumption. If scholars, indigenous and international alike, facilitated the initial nationalist direction of one party, state-dominated and over-regulated political economies, then policy makers have since advocated and advanced the revisionist, post-nationalist orientation espoused by the World Bank and other external agencies. If the motif of the 1960s was, the familiar claim of African nationalist Kwame Nkrumah's 'Seek ye first the political kingdom' (Nkrumah 1965), that of the 1980s became that of American economist Elliot Berg (1981) to deregulate: from *Neo-colonialism: The Last Stage of Imperialism* to *Accelerated Development in Sub-Saharan Africa: Agenda for Action*.

The analysis of African politics in the post-nationalist period was dominated by orthodox American political science concerns with parties, ideologies, leaders and policies, overly influenced by the behaviouralist fashions of the time. By contrast, post-behavioural analysis of African political economy in the post-crisis era is characterized by a mix of both materialist and non-materialist perspectives which combine policy with production, ideology with interest and national with global interactions. Yet despite the stand-off between modes of political economy, analysis at the level of superstructure alone is hard to sustain: economic realities and relations are central and integral, affecting if not determining forms of participation as well as production. Thus the continent enters the 1990s in a more revisionist yet realistic mood: political economy can hardly be wholly excluded nor readily manipulated given contemporary contradictions and constraints.

PAST: FROM DECOLONIZATION TO DEPENDENCE

The post-colonial era in Africa's political economy has been marked by two interrelated transitions: from expansion to contraction in economic perform-ance and from optimism to pessimism in political analysis. Whether these evolutions are cyclical or unilineal remains debatable. They are undeniably unfortunate in their impact and uneven in their incidence. Moreover, there is a dialectical quality to the relationship between praxis and analysis as policy changes have responded to political difficulties. In general, there has been a trend away from a preoccupation with superstructure towards a concentration upon substructure: if political preferences alone have not generated develop-ment then perhaps economic constraints need to be prioritized. An intermedi-ate level of investigation is to focus on the state as either bureaucracy or oligarchy, and always as patriarchy (Stichter and Parpart 1988). This focus on the styles and structures of governance led to the one-party state and on to decentralization, but never to popular participation. Meanwhile, political concentration tended to coincide or correlate with economic contraction, so serving to reinforce patterns of exclusion and accumulation.

The initial modernization project assumed that all African states could and would become more developed and democratic as foreign capitals, tastes and values spread. Likewise, the early materialist genre believed that all such political economies would become more capitalist, industrialized and contradic-tory, generating more socialist forms of production and distribution. Thus, both these orthodox approaches revealed, despite their apparent differences, rather idealistic, optimistic and Eurocentric 'stages' assumptions. In a rather mechanistic or rationalistic way, they assumed that indigenous leaders would and could manage and manipulate social forces in preferred directions. There was little sense of structural or global constraints – dependence – in either formulation.

The initial reaction to the deficiencies of analysis and praxis came in the late 1960s and early 1970s in the guise of a nationalist, dependency rejoinder: the reason for the lack of progress in the direction of either modernization or materialism was external structures rather than internal failures. Thus the logical policy response, reviving previous Latin American prescriptions, was national and collective self-reliance. But this was problematic given colonial inheritances and post-independence inclinations. Some efforts were made, at least at the level of rhetoric and declaration, to advance such self-reliance, continuing into the 1980s. But these formulations were typically top-down and were essentially inseparable from established personalities and ideologies. Lacking popular input or support, they were rarely implemented or insti-tutionalized. Along with notions such as life presidency and African socialism, they now exude a somewhat dated aura. Moreover, the policy pressure today lies in a contrary direction, towards rather than away from external integration and interaction.

The most familiar symbol of such claims for external redistribution and disengagement was the New International Economic Order (NIEO). This set of demands from the leaders of the South coincided with the last period of economic expansion and optimism: the mid-1970s. Africa's oil exporters benefited from the series of energy shocks which seemed to open up vistas of enhanced export earnings and industrial development along with South–South exchange and influence; and, initially, any costs to the continent's oil importers were disguised by increased external loans. However, in the absence of a successful strategy to generalize oil to other commodity cartels, Northern resilience soon exposed Southern vulnerabilities. In the African case, the reappearance of drought in the Sahel, Horn of Africa and southern regions coincided with the incidence of economic contraction and debt repayments. Such difficulties came to symbolize the whole decade of the 1980s in which expectations of development and self-reliance receded along with the NIEO debate. Indeed, subsequent reform conditionalities constituted the North's response, even revenge.

Not only is Africa now the most marginal of the Southern continents, it is becoming more so (World Bank 1989b). It has endured the lowest levels of gross domestic product (GDP) per capita, yet even these declined in the first half of the 1980s (see Table 1). It was always the least industrialized but the proportions of GDP in industry, investment and saving continue to fall (see Table 2). Given the colonial commodity character of its exports, it was hit hardest by declining terms of trade before adjustment and by imported inflation after devaluation (see Figure 1).

The increasing elusiveness and unevenness of development served in turn to reinforce insecurities and instabilities. Thus notions of 'one person, one vote' gave way to one-party, even one-person, regimes in which 'one person, one election' was more apposite. Military *coups* proliferated as old solutions appeared not to work, and a variety of special police and intelligence forces

Table 1   Developing nations: 1980s growth (average annual percentage change in GDP per capita)

Region	1980–5	1986	1987
All developing nations	1.2	2.8	2.3
Sub-Saharan Africa	−3.6	−0.5	−5.1
East Asia	6.2	5.7	7.0
South Asia	3.1	2.4	0.5
Europe, Middle East, North Africa	0.6	2.0	1.1
Latin America, Caribbean	−2.0	1.6	0.4

Source: World Bank

Table 2 Comparative economic indicators

	Sub-Saharan Africa	All low-income LDCs	All LDCs
Growth of per capita GDP, 1980–6 (% yearly)	−3.1	5.6	1.8
Growth of per capita private consumption 1980–6 (% yearly)	−2.4	3.5	0.9
Gross domestic saving as % GDP, 1986	11.0	25.0	24.0
Gross domestic investment as % GDP, 1986	14.0	29.0	24.0
Central govt. fiscal balance as % GDP, 1986	−6.0	...	−6.0
Growth of export volumes, 1980–6 (% yearly)	−2.1	6.5	4.8
Growth of import volumes, 1980–6 (% yearly)	−7.5	7.2	0.5
Change in terms of trade, 1980–6 (%)	−13.0	−9.0	−7.0
Gross international reserves in months of import coverage, 1986	2.1	4.2	3.5

Source: World Bank, *World Development Report*, 1988, and IMF, *World Economic Outlook*, 1989.

were created to ensure regime or presidential survival. To be sure, some military governments successfully set in motion processes for return to civilian rule, but given the continued condition of contraction such 'second generation' constitutions rarely lasted for long. Access to power and privilege became ever more of an imperative as alternative avenues for accumulation were absent, given small and shrinking private sectors. The only remaining prospect for survival if not affluence was the informal sector.

Modernization perspectives tended, then, to lose their salience as the 1960s gave way to the 1970s and the continent appeared to be stagnating or regressing rather than developing. Moreover, such orthodox approaches were losing their dominance elsewhere, especially in Latin America, so that critiques of them in Africa were part of a broad current. That of Nzongola-Ntalaja (1987: 15) reflects the trend: 'modernization theory is ahistorical, astructural and ethnocentric'.

Likewise, dependency approaches tended themselves to be displaced if not discarded as the 1970s gave way to the 1980s because of divergent development directions on the continent. Moreover, with the combination of oil, then debt and now democracy shocks throughout the Third World as well as Africa, dependency has become at best a starting-point for analysis rather than a comprehensive perspective. In particular, the conception of all African leaders as compradors was quite misleading given their ability to be corrupt, authoritarian, arbitrary and influential. As Ben Turok cautions, 'The notion that the bourgeoisie, the state bourgeoisie and the *petit-bourgeoisie* are simply intermediaries for imperialism with no interests or agenda of their own is both inaccurate and unhelpful' (Turok 1987: 80). Obviously, some states and presidents are more vulnerable and attractive at different times, but to treat them all as homogeneous is incorrect and misleading.

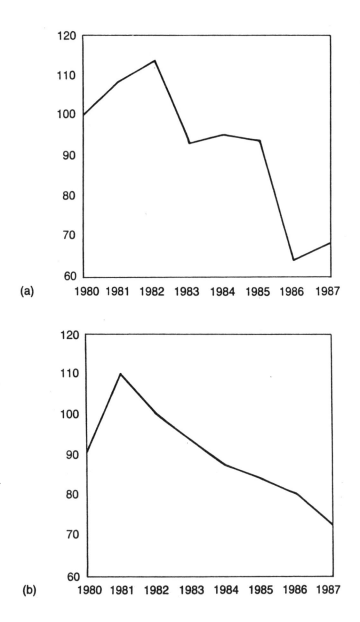

Figure 1 (a) Africa's terms of trade (index 1980 = 100); (b) Africa's volume of imports (index 1980 = 100)

Source: UNCTAD

The demise of the NIEO and rise of structural adjustment served to marginalize the former's theoretical correlate and to reinstate the latter's theoretical antecedents. For, in many ways, reform is but an applied form of modernization for the late twentieth century: external models are still attainable although the terms for realizing them have become even more arduous.

The more nuanced, contemporary studies of political economy do not focus only on policy and economy; they also treat state, class, gender and now participation. First, as Nzongala-Ntalaja asserts, 'no political economy is intelligible without the analysis of the crucial role the state plays in the economy' (Nzongala-Ntalaja 1987: 20). And the character of the 'African state' has generated considerable debate and disagreement. Second, as Turok cautions, 'Compared to the advanced capitalist states, the identification of classes and their alliances in Africa is a much more speculative matter' (Turok 1987: 67). In particular, the range of bourgeois fractions and the roles of the peasantries are crucial, especially in an era of adjustment. Third, despite the central place of women in social and economic production, gender has largely been ignored in both modernization and materialist genres. And, fourth, issues of democracy, both formal and informal, proliferated at the end of the 1980s because of the cumulative human-needs consequences of adjustment inside Africa (Sandbrook 1988) and the unanticipated human-rights examples of Eastern Europe outside.

Any persuasive, neo-materialist political economy for Africa in the 1990s must, then, include at least three salient elements, all of which involve revisionism around established perspectives. First, it should situate the continent's political economies in the global context of a New International Division of Labour in which novel technologies are transforming patterns of production, distribution, consumption and accumulation. Second, it must recognize the transformed policy context in which the conditionalities of structural adjustment have come to undermine assumptions about one-party, state-dominated systems of power and privilege. And third, it should incorporate changing social contexts: the dynamics and dialectics of the continent's distinctive political economies, particularly the expansion of informal and rural sectors, the contraction of industrial and state sectors, the recognition of female production and consumption, and the creation of novel forms of democratic participation and organization. All of these interrelated contexts have been reinforced in terms of their revisionist potential by the dramatic transformations in Eastern Europe, both democratic and diplomatic.

In short, Africa has entered a new period following that of decolonization: one in which new class contradictions and coalitions are apparent, as revealed in patterns of advocacy of and opposition to structural adjustment and one in which there are enhanced prospects for African capitalisms and corporatisms, especially those in which the national fraction of the indigenous bourgeoisie is hegemonic.

Africa was not, in any case, entirely resourceless and passive as the crises intensified at the end of the 1970s. The nationalist claim to collective self-reliance had generated a continuing concern for continental co-operation. Thus, in response to the demise of any NIEO, Africa's leaders, intellectual as well as political and economic, had come to organize and orchestrate the first continental economic summit. Basing their proposals on an earlier Monrovia consultation, the Lagos Plan of Action for the Economic Development of Africa, 1980–2000 (LPA) called for compatible levels of self-reliance in which Africa's resources were to be used for its own development first. Thus its leaders were in principle agreed on a collective economic direction as the successive energy, ecology and economic crises hit. But most of the continent's peoples and many of its regimes had minimal reserves through which to withstand such external shocks and subsequent policy reforms and political reactions.

PRESENT: FROM CRISES TO CONDITIONALITIES

The dominant policy context in the 1980s, like the prevailing paradigm of the 1960s, has been external in origin and orientation. Although African intellectuals had advocated self-reliance in response to perceived dependence, so emboldening the continent's leadership to espouse the LPA, the dominant direction was in fact determined by Washington, not so much by the United States as by the IMF and the World Bank. The intense series of crises in the early 1980s thus led to the conditionalities of adjustment in which longer-term development was postponed and replaced by shorter-term reform. The LPA was substituted as the outdated African reaction to the absence of an NIEO. It was rapidly overtaken by a set of economic and diplomatic events: drought and debt on the one hand and, on the other, the controversial but authoritative 'Berg report', *Accelerated Development* (Berg 1991).

The decade of the 1980s has thus been marked by an incremental yet cumulative retreat from the idealism of self-reliance and the irresponsibility of dependency towards the pragmatism and inevitability of adjustment. The Economic Commission for Africa (ECA), let alone the Organization of African Unity (OAU), lacked the resources to effect the LPA, whereas the World Bank and the IMF can enforce their definition of reform both directly and indirectly, such as through 'cross-conditionality' under which no major bilateral aid donor (or, in practice, private capital investor (United Nations 1988a)) will provide resources unless an agreed programme is in place.

Thus, although little of the analysis of Africa has begun to recognize the profound current and continuing impacts of such adjustment sequences

(Campbell and Loxley 1989), even by the end of the decade, the realities are that, first, all policies, national, regional and continental, have to take adjustment effects into account, and second, any perspective, whether modernization or materialist, has to incorporate these into its analysis. In short, the reforms insisted upon by Bank and Fund for each African state have come to determine not only policy directions but also theoretical parameters over the last decade. It is symptomatic of the continent's vulnerability that international financial institutions can come to set political and intellectual frameworks for policy and decision makers. As John Ravenhill has recently lamented, '*Accelerated Development* subsequently has effectively taken the *Lagos Plan* off the agenda' (Ravenhill 1988: 179).

However, despite the Bank's series of reports and sets of conditions being supported by the major Western economies, it has not monopolized the policy arena without challenge. Reactions to the deficiencies and drawbacks of its prescriptions come from three interrelated sources. First, predictably, the ECA has maintained its opposition, on the grounds that adjustment does not advance development. Through its own series of annual and occasional reports, particularly its 1983 and 1988 perspectives studies and scenarios, the Commission has criticized Bank methodology and criteria. Whilst being a party to mid- and end-decade attempts at consensus within the United Nations (UN) system, the Commission's reservations were articulated in a pair of 1989 documents: *African Alternative Framework* (Economic Commission for Africa 1989a) and *Statistics and Policies*, the latter being a direct rejoinder to the controversial World Bank and UN Development Programme (UNDP) tract (World Bank and UNDP 1989).

Second, several other development agencies within the UN system have expressed similar reservations about the apparent disregard for development, notably the United Nations International Children's Emergency Fund (UNICEF) with its 'human face' preference. Such 'human dimension' critiques tend to reflect much non-governmental organization (NGO) thinking also.

Third, a set of academic evaluations of adjustment has pointed not only to the human costs but also to (a) indefensible assumptions that Africa can export its way out of recession given demand and price patterns in the New International Division of Labour; (b) inaccurate comparisons because the supposedly non-statist 'models' of the newly industrializing countries (NICs) are in general examples of judicious intervention instead; and (c) unfounded generalizations that if other African states would follow 'success stories' like Ghana (the only plausible one left?) then capital would flow in (Campbell 1989). But as the eminent and non-partisan 'Wass' report from the United Nations (1988a) indicated, the continent needs at least US $5 billion more in official assistance and private investment each year to enable it even to return to economic performances achieved in the 1970s, hardly an over-ambitious

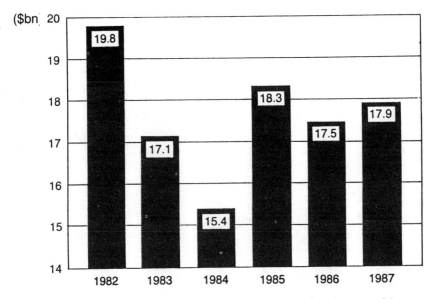

Figure 2 Net resource flows to sub-Saharan Africa (billion US dollars, at 1986 prices and exchange rates)

Source: OECD

goal (see Figure 2). The *de facto* 'contract' of the mid-decade UN special session – external assistance in exchange for internal reform (United Nations 1986) – was never consumated. Very few regimes have received sufficient resources, and then only for strategic or demonstration purposes, such as Ghana, Kenya or Zaire. And such 'generosity' could never be proffered on a continental scale.

Predictably, the structural adjustment project has received minimal support and considerable opposition within Africa. Yet because of the perceived imperative of access to foreign aid and exchange, regimes continue to renegotiate impossible packages, which internal resistance or external reluctance tend to undermine. Novel social coalitions have arisen to resist such prepackaged formulas.

Adjustment is unfortunate as well as unworkable because it reinforces Africa's colonial divisions and retards any prospects for regional co-operation. National reforms are incompatible with regionalisms. Collective as well as national self-reliance is eroded, although both may become inevitable in the future as adjustment terms become unbearable; literally, self-reliance by default.

The continental crisis has not only spawned new approaches, it has also generated new categories of states and peoples. Typologies of the former have multiplied from low and middle income and from less and least developed

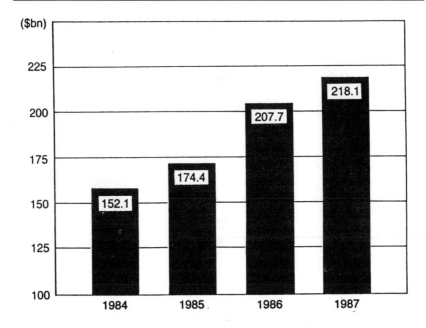

Figure 3 Africa's external debt

Source: ECA

countries to Third and Fourth Worlds, Most Seriously Affected and now 'debt distressed'. The debt-distressed category has been applied by the World Bank only to Africa: to thirty out of fifty countries (see Figure 3). The Bank has also unilaterally reclassified African governments into 'strong' (nineteen) or 'weak' (twelve) reformers and 'non-reformers' (the remaining nineteen?) according to its definitions (World Bank and UNDP 1989) (see Figure 4). Africa contains just three of the Bank's seventeen 'highly indebted countries' (Côte d'Ivoire, Morocco and Nigeria). Structural adjustment loans have been reformulated as enhanced 'facilities'. The other side of such economistic typologies are new categories of people – vulnerable groups and economic or ecological refugees – as reflected in the more progressive perspectives (see Figure 5).

PROSPECTIVE: FROM REGRESSION TO RENAISSANCE?

The series of African crises over the 1980s has served to concentrate attentions and to advance solutions, so generating the decade-long debate over causes and consequences already examined. Although the origins and orientations of adjustment are controversial, at least the new discourse about reform conditionalities has transformed the context for analysis (Campbell and Loxley

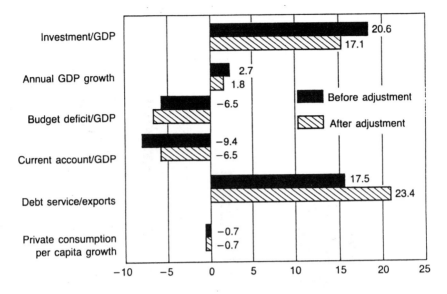

Figure 4 Sustainability of adjustment (annual average percentage changes in indicators for fifteen sub-Saharan countries with SAPs)

Source: World Bank, *Adjustment Lending: An Evaluation of Ten Years of Experience,* 1988

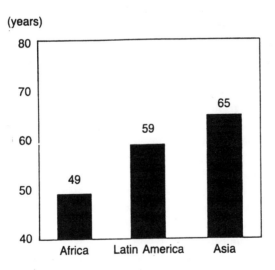

Figure 5 Life expectancy (mid-1980s)

Source: R. L. Sivard, *World Military and Social Expenditures,* 1986

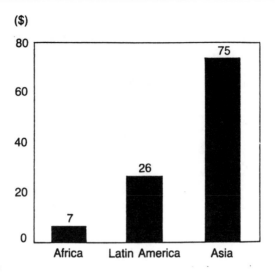

Figure 6   Public health expenditure (per capita, mid-1980s)

Source: R. L. Sivard, *World Military and Social Expenditures*, 1986

1989). As noted above, African scholars and statespersons began this process in Monrovia at the end of the 1970s and have continued it at major continental gatherings at Abuja (June 1987), Khartoum (March 1988) and Arusha (February 1990). Although the main source of revisionist ideas has been Washington, doctrinaire adjustment has been discredited because of problematic economic results and politically unacceptable social costs. So, notwithstanding the misplaced optimism and dubious methodology of the World Bank's 1989 tract, it had been preparing in a careful and consensual manner a major decade-end report, *A Long-Term Perspective Study* (World Bank 1989b). As expected, this treated a wider range of issues than the reform project, including hitherto neglected industrialization and regionalism as well as infrastructure and human resource development: 'an enabling environment'. Nevertheless, the World Bank and the IMF remain reluctant to recognize the full social dimensions of adjustment packages (see Figure 6).

If Africa is to recapture minimally acceptable rates of development, then a more comprehensive approach must be adopted because its political economies are more complex than either Bank or Commission admits. In particular, any transition beyond adjustment to more sustainable patterns of development must recognize the resilience of informal sectors, the imperative of popular participation, the ubiquity of female production, and fragility of the continental ecology.

If the resourcefulness of Africa's populations is recognized and encouraged then the continent may yet progress from regression to renaissance by the end of the century, in terms of participation as well as production. I treat this dialectic in conclusion by reference to the prospects for African capitalisms and corporatisms. Elsewhere (Shaw 1988), I have identified and contrasted three alternative medium-term scenarios – optimistic, realist and pessimistic – broadly related to World Bank, Commission and revisionist perspectives, respectively. Here I concentrate on the last, historically rooted preview, given the limited purview of official agencies whether they be global or continental in scope.

First, informal sectors of unrecorded and untaxed economic activity, often unregistered and illegal, and always small in scale and capital, have proliferated and prospered as formal sectors have contracted. Although they were historically female-dominated and concentrated in food production and distribution, they have since diversified into small-scale manufactures and repairs, along with cross-border trade in a variety of products, particularly high-value electronics and, now, drugs. Informal sectors exist in every economy in North and South but they have prospered in Africa as formal employment and production have stagnated and regressed. Thus they may now be larger than formal sectors in states like Ghana, Nigeria, Uganda and Zaire. These activities exist in an ambiguous relation to both formal economy and the state as some connection and protection are often essential. In turn, officialdom is ambivalent towards them, seeking both to eliminate – police or inspectors' raids – and to graduate – small-scale loans, infrastructures, training and employment. Until the formal sectors are large and dynamic enough to absorb growing generations of school-leavers, however, their informal counterparts will flourish: the ultimate, populist form of privatization?

Second, popular participation is once again being recognized as integral to redirection and reinvigoration. But notions of democratic development are no longer restricted to occasional acts of formal voting. Rather, they emphasize and encourage continuous informal involvement in policy and decision making at local and higher levels, such as communities, co-operatives, religions, unions, etc. Such people-defined structures have expanded in response to the decline or exclusiveness of the state and have drawn strength from the international rise of NGOs. Although some African regimes have been quite ambivalent about the presence and roles of such organizations, they are protected somewhat by their transnational associations and internal advocates (Bratton 1989b; United Nations 1988b).

Democratization in Africa is different from redemocratization in Latin America because the latter involved a return to earlier patterns of participation in a continent in which military rule had become well institutionalized. In Africa, by contrast, although democratic structures have rarely taken root (except in a few cases like Botswana, Senegal, Tanzania and Zimbabwe), military influences have also been tentative. Therefore, current demands from both inside and outside the continent for greater degrees of democracy, both formal and informal, involve fewer precedents but also fewer obstacles. The distinctive styles of democratic transition in Eastern Europe may not be repeated in the different environment of Africa although they will have profound indirect as well as direct impacts and implications.

Democratization in Africa is, then, of two distinct types, which are not necessarily compatible. First, formal participation involves the (re)establishment of state-sanctioned processes of organization, election, decision and protection at the level of politics. These have been advocated and advanced from both modernization (Diamond *et al.* 1988; Oyugi and Gitonga 1987) and materialist (Nyong'o 1987) perspectives: either liberal democratic or radical proletarian genres. By contrast, informal participation involves the establishment of extra-state patterns of participation typically at the level of economics. As indicated already, these involve novel forms of non-governmental, often co-operative, organization, sometimes building on pre-crisis institutions but now with post-crisis mandates. Such informal democracy occurs at the level of society rather than the state and both exploits and encourages the shrinkage of the latter under adjustment. It symbolizes and reinforces shifts in the political economy of Africa away from state-centrism and towards more open politics and economics, as recently reviewed by Michael Bratton:

> The harsh reality of state formation in post-colonial Africa is that, in many countries, the apparatus of governance has begun to crumble before it has been fully consolidated. There is a crisis of political authority that is just as severe as the well-known crisis of economic production. . . .
>
> Because of the shallow penetration of society by weak state institutions, there is a relatively larger realm of unoccupied political space in Africa than anywhere else in the world.
>
> (Bratton 1989a: 409, 427)

Third, there has been belated acknowledgement, even encouragement, of female production, typically within informal sectors. Women in Africa have always produced most of the foods (and beers) along with the children, but have rarely enjoyed much of the consumption or accumulation. Their roles in households and economies have been particularly strong in West African urban and peasant communities and in southern African mining and migratory societies. As adjustment has exacerbated male unemployment and underemployment so female resourcefulness has been essential to familial and national survival. Male (and some female) conservatives and chauvinists may not appreciate encouragement of feminist organizations – which now include credit and sexual-abuse centres as well as more traditional agricultural and rural co-operatives – but these are now protected by their economic centrality and transnational networks.

And fourth, African political economies must return to a sustainable balance

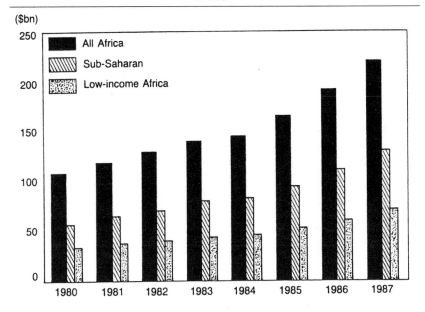

($bn)

Figure 7 Africa's total debt

Source: World Bank, *World Debt Tables*, 1988–9

with the continental ecology as the combination of population pressure, uneven and unreliable water and energy resources, exponential erosion, and a variety of pollutants has jeopardized future development. There are ongoing debates over the causes as well as consequences of Africa's droughts – internal or external, environmental or economic – but the realities are incontrovertible: spreading deserts and shrinking arable, grazing, forest and wildlife lands. Yet some of the solutions are already at hand – solar and other renewable energies, biotechnologies, resistant seeds, etc. – even if their implementation is limited (Harrison 1989; Timberlake 1988). Traditional African societies had to live in harmony with nature and the gods. Extroverted economies have satisfied export demand first and debt repayments now. Until basic human needs are Africa's effective priority and are met in a sustainable manner, the continental ecology – water and soils rather than animals and resorts – will continue to deteriorate at an exponential rate. Although Africa's debt of some $240 billion (see Figure 7) was just 10 per cent of the global total in 1987; the influence of its repayments on already fragile economies and ecologies is very intense, even more so than for Latin America (see Figure 8).

In short, the privatization of state and society in Africa is not an uncontroversial process in either policy or politics. First, there has been a radical response to policy pressures to deregulate or dismantle the state on the grounds of its continued centrality to longer-term national development in Africa and

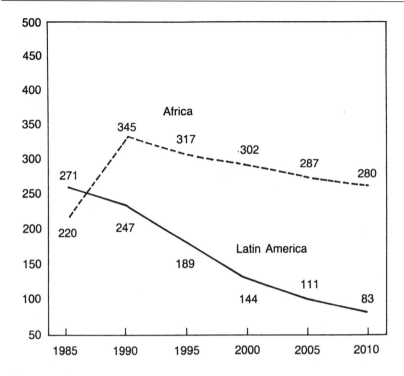

Figure 8 African and Latin American debt (projection of debt/exports ratios)

Source: UNCTAD, assuming current trends and policy formulations

its apparent centrality in the economic success of the NICs (Bienefeld 1989). And second, there has been a traditional caution to political demands to downgrade or dismiss the government on the grounds of historical or organiz- ational inevitability. As Bratton warns, 'The state in Africa may be incompletely formed, weak and retreating, but it is not going to wither away' (Bratton 1989a: 425).

Likewise, there may have been exaggerated projections of both decline and response over the last decade: doomsday and miracle. Clearly, a few countries and classes have survived and even prospered. Most have not, but innovative informal responses have enabled some to survive better than aggregate data indicate. Yet, even relatively optimistic World Bank projections at the end of the 1980s do not anticipate particularly attractive scenarios. Thus, in the first half of the 1990s, given sustained structural adjustments, it predicts GDP growth of just 3 per cent a year (see Figure 9). And, 'with population growing at nearly the same rate, per capita real income in the region stagnates. Even with an optimistic view of adjustment, the region's per capita income will not

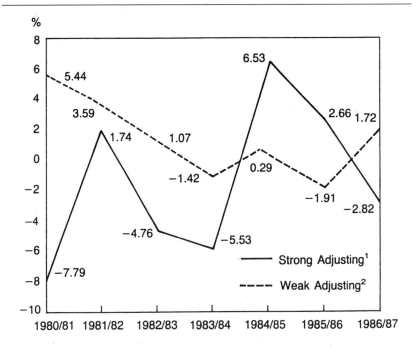

Figure 9 Growth of GDP in Africa (constant 1980 US dollars, market prices)

Source: Derived by ECA from World Bank data files

Notes: 1 As defined by the World Bank, includes Burundi, Central African
Republic, Congo, Cote d'Ivoire, Gambia, Ghana, Guinea, Guinea-
Bissau, Kenya, Madagascar, Malawi, Mauritania, Mauritius, Niger,
Nigeria, Senegal, Tanzania, Togo and Zaire

2 As defined by the World Bank, includes Benin, Burkina Faso, Com-
oros, Equatorial Guinea, Ethiopia, Liberia, Mali, Sierra Leone, Somalia, Sudan, Zambia and Zimbabwe

return to the level of the mid-1960s over the projection horizon' (World Bank
1989a: 21), i.e. until after 1995.

There are some other salient realities which need to be incorporated into
such scenarios but are typically excluded because of their sensitivity or elusiveness, notably AIDS, foreign exchange (forex) and crime. First, although most
orthodox demographic projections point towards exponential increases until
well into the next century, based on historic ±3 per cent trends – up from a
population of 443 million in 1987 to 659 million in 2000 and 1259 million in
2025 in sub-Saharan Africa, according to the World Bank (1989a: 215) – the
economic crisis combined with the AIDS virus may yet lead to static or even
declining numbers, especially in the 'more infected' countries of Eastern
Africa, particularly Kenya, Malawi, Tanzania, Uganda, Zaïre and Zambia.

Africa cannot afford the present 5 million conflict, economic or ecological refugees, nor can it afford the direct and indirect costs of AIDS, which, although it affects society at all levels and through all classes, seems to concentrate on 'endangered' middle-aged generations of middle-class male professionals.

Second, the preoccupation with foreign exchange, exacerbated by widespread devaluations of local currencies, leads to corruption of individuals and institutions. The combination of conspicuous consumption and external accumulation means that rich and poor seek external goods and monies. The ubiquity of taste and technology transfers means that Africa is increasingly dependent on foreign foods and fashions, a syndrome exacerbated by liberalization. And the lack of confidence in the continent's economies leads to transfer pricing, capital flight and external savings. The proliferation of forex shops and imports means that foreign currencies sell at a premium, further increasing the attraction of black markets and drug smuggling.

And third, the intensification of inequalities in many African societies has led to crime waves. The more affluent elements are both visible and vulnerable, protecting their property with alarms, dogs and guards, even guns and vigilante groups. Africa's cities are more dangerous than its countrysides, but nowhere is unaffected as cattle theft, even with automatic rifles, spreads. Gangs snatch purses and jewellery and invade and strip houses, sometimes with the connivance of guards and police. Security operations, from concrete fences to private detectives, flourish, sometimes as branches of multinational companies, and they now include contracts to protect industries and infrastructures. Life can be even more brutal in the high-density shanty towns. And domestic violence, mainly directed at women, continues to increase. The social dimensions of structural adjustment are visible and palpable.

In conclusion, reflective of continuing debates and directions, the continent's crises and conditionalities have together generated new possibilities for African capitalisms and corporatisms. First, *African capitalisms* are a correlate of structural adjustments in which state interventions are contained and private interests advanced. They remain a controversial notion for both the modernization – why 'capitalism'? – and materialism – why 'African'? – perspectives. Yet, in a post-one-party state and leadership-code era, new regimes' association with capitals is once again a respectable ambition, legitimized by a permissive global context and national prospects of privatization, commercialization, etc. In a period in which bureaucratic, comprador and technocratic, if not military, fractions of the indigenous bourgeoisie are somewhat endangered, the national fraction is encouraged. Conditionalities advance national as well as international capitals. Given the well-established, if sometimes latent, entrepreneurial and acquisitive inclinations of many African societies, a revival of capitalisms, both big and small, is quite feasible (Kennedy 1988).

But second, *African corporatisms* represent a statist response to such conditionalities and capitalisms: how to rearrange and recapture state control through patterns of social inclusion and exclusion. In short, how can endangered indigenous fractions reassert their hegemony in a period of adjustment? Various forms of corporatism – authoritarian, bureaucratic, military, etc. – constitute one possible means in which regime, capital and labour reach trilateral accommodations to resist more progressive or populist pressures. Such 'defensive radicalism' (Ake 1981: 189) represents a conservative response to economic contractions and related political conflicts: a means to retain or restore regime control in a period in which orthodox patterns of patrimonialism are either not acceptable or effective (Chazan 1988). Alternative strategies of corporatism offer one means for incumbent yet insecure interests to circumvent or contain the political if not social costs of adjustment (Nyang'oro and Shaw 1989). Again, the current spate of organizational experiments in Eastern Europe may be of some relevance to Africa during the 1990s.

Given the status and relentlessness of the intellectual and political 'counterrevolution' in Africa, emanating in the first instance from Washington, there is a unique opportunity for creative synthesis, as Richard Sklar suggests:

> In sum, socialism needs capital and lacks a theory of incentive; capitalism needs the state and lacks a theory of social responsibility. The African economies need private capital, purposeful state participation, powerful incentives, and public responsibility for the general standard of living. These common requirements for social progress can only be met by judicious mixtures of capitalism and socialism. . . . Challenged by social problems of unprecedented severity, development theorists in Africa need to question the validity of restrictive political conceptions.
>
> (Sklar 1988: 18)

Thus, at the start of the 1990s, Africa was in a revisionist mood, a mix of pessimism and optimism in which a selective mixture of modernization and materialist explanations and prescriptions was being sought (Spark 1989). Naomi Chazan captures the essence of this moment of apprehension yet not defeatism:

> The crisis of the 1980s in Africa invites policy alterations because previous formulas have proved to be either unworkable or unsatisfactory and because the complexities of the present situation raise questions that heretofore were not anticipated, let alone addressed. . . .
>
> Few crises in the contemporary world have engendered the kind of fundamental political reassessment necessitated by the confrontation with economic collapse.
>
> (Chazan 1988: 7, 2)

The 1990s may, then, yet represent a conjuncture for the continent at the levels of both analysis and praxis, politics and economics.

REFERENCES

Ake, C. (1981) *A Political Economy of Africa*, London: Longman.

Berg, E. (1981) *Accelerated Development in Sub-Saharan Africa: An Agenda for Action*, Washington, DC: World Bank.

Bienefeld, M. (1989) 'Dependency theory and the political economy of Africa's crisis', *Review of African Political Economy* 43: 68–87.

Bratton, M. (1989a) 'Beyond the state: civil society and associational life in Africa', *World Politics* 41: 407–30.

——(1989b) 'The politics of government–NGO relations in Africa', *World Development* 17: 569–87.

Campbell, B. K. (ed.) (1989) *Political Dimensions of the International Debt Crisis: Africa and Mexico*, London: Macmillan.

Campbell, B. K. and Loxley, J. (eds) (1989) *Structural Adjustment in Africa*, London: Macmillan.

Chazan, N. (1988) 'Ideology, policy and the crisis of poverty: the African case', *Jerusalem Journal of International Relations* 10: 1–30.

Diamond, L. Linz, J. J. and Lipset, S. M. (eds) (1988) *Democracy in Developing Countries*, Vol. 2: *Africa*, Boulder, Colo.: Lynne Rienner.

Economic Commission for Africa (1989a) *Statistics and Policies: ECA Preliminary Observations on the World Bank* [sic] *Report 'Africa's Adjustment and Growth in the 1980s'*, Addis Ababa, April.

Harrison, P. (1989) *The Greening of Africa: Breaking Through in the Battle for Land and Food*, London: Paladin.

Kennedy, P. (1988) *African Capitalism*, Cambridge: Cambridge University Press.

Nkrumah, K. (1965) *Neo-colonialism: The Last Stage of Imperialism*, London: Nelson.

Nyang'oro, J. E. and Shaw, T. M. (eds) (1989) *Corporatism in Africa*, Boulder, Colo.: Westview Press.

Nyong'o, P. A. (ed.) (1987) *Popular Struggles for Democracy in Africa*, London: Zed Books.

Nzongola-Ntalaja, G. (1987) *Revolution and Counter-revolution in Africa: Essays in Contemporary Politics*, London: Institute for African Alternatives/Zed Books.

Onwuka, R. I. and Shaw, T. M. (eds) (1989) *Africa in World Politics: Into the 1990s*, London: Macmillan.

Oyugi, W. D. and Gitouga, A. (eds) (1987) *Democratic Theory and Practice in Africa*, Nairobi: Heinemann; London: James Currey.

Ravenhill, J. (1988) 'Adjustment with growth: a fragile consensus', *Journal of Modern African Studies* 26: 179–210.

Sandbrook, R. (1988) 'Liberal democracy in Africa: a socialist-revisionist perspective', *Canadian Journal of African Studies* 22: 240–67.

Shaw, T. M. (1988) 'Africa in the 1990s: from economic crisis to structural readjustment', *Dalhousie Review* 68: 37–69.

Sklar, R. L. (1988) 'Beyond capitalism and socialism in Africa', *Journal of Modern African Studies* 26: 1–21.

Spark, D. (1989) 'Review article: What chance of change in Africa?', *Development Policy Review* 7: 193–8.

Stichter, S. and Parpart, J. L. (eds) (1988) *Patriarchy and Class: African Women in the Home and Workforce*, Boulder, Colo.: Westview Press.

Timberlake, L. (1988) *Africa in Crisis: The Causes, the Cures of Environmental Bankruptcy*, London: Earthscan.

Turok, B. (1987) *Africa: What Can Be Done?*, London: Institute for African Alternatives/ Zed Books.

United Nations (1986) *UN Programme of Action for African Economic Recovery and Development 1986–90*, New York: United Nations.

——(1988a) *Financing Africa's Recovery: Report and Recommendations of the Advisory Group on Financial Flows for Africa*, New York: United Nations.

——(1988b) *Africa Four Years On: Overview of UN–NGO Conference, Geneva, April 1988*, Geneva: United Nations.

World Bank (1989a) *World Development Report 1989*, Washington, DC: World Bank.

——(1989b) *Sub-Saharan Africa: From Crisis to Sustainable Growth: A Long-Term Perspective Study*, Washington: World Bank.

World Bank and UNDP (1989) *Africa's Adjustment and Growth in the 1980s*, Washington, DC: World Bank and UNDP.

FURTHER READING

Adedeji, A. and Shaw, T. M. (eds) (1985) *Economic Crisis in Africa*, Boulder, Colo.: Lynne Rienner.

Ake, C. (1981) *A Political Economy of Africa*, London: Longman.

Brown, R. (1992) *Public Debt and Private Wealth: Debt, Capital Flight and the IMF in Sudan*, London: Macmillan.

Chazan, N. and Shaw, T. M. (eds) (1988) *Coping with Africa's Food Crisis*, Boulder, Colo.: Lynne Rienner.

Chazan, N., Mortimer, N. R., Ravenhill, J. and Rothchild, D. (1988) *Politics and Society in Contemporary Africa*, Boulder, Colo.: Lynne Rienner.

Economic Commission for Africa (1989b) *Economic Report on Africa 1989*, Addis Ababa, April.

——(1989c) *African Alternative Framework to Structural Adjustment Programmes for Socio-Economic Recovery and Transformation*, Addis Ababa, July.

Harris, B. (1992) *The Political Economy of the Southern African Periphery*, London: Macmillan.

Lancaster, C. (1989) 'Economic restructuring in sub-Saharan Africa', *Current History* 88 (May): 213–16 and 244.

Lehman, H. P. (1992) *Indebted Development: Strategic Bargaining and Economic Adjustment in the Third World*, London: Macmillan.

Markovitz, I. L. (ed.) (1987) *Studies in Power and Class in Africa*, New York: Oxford University Press.

Martin, M. (1991) *The Crumbling Façade of African Debt Negotiations: No Winners*, London: Macmillan.

Nyang'oro, J. E. and Shaw, T. M. (eds) (1992) *Beyond Structural Adjustment in Africa: The Political Economy of Sustainable and Democratic Development*, New York: Praeger.

Onimode, B. (1988) *A Political Economy of the African Crisis*, London: Institute for African Alternatives/Zed Books.

Parfitt, T. W. and Riley, S. P. (1989) *The African Debt Crisis*, London: Routledge.

Parpart, J. L. and Staudt, K. A. (eds) (1989) *Women and the State in Africa*, Boulder, Colo.: Lynne Rienner.

Ravenhill, J. (ed.) (1986) *Africa in Economic Crisis*, London: Macmillan.

Rothchild, D. and Chazan, N. (eds) (1988) *The Precarious Balance: State and Society in Africa*, Boulder, Colo.: Westview Press.

Sandbrook, R. A. (1985) *The Politics of Africa's Economic Stagnation*, Cambridge: Cambridge University Press.

Sender, J. and Smith, S. (1986) *The Development of Capitalism in Africa*, London: Methuen.

Shaw, T. M. (ed.) (1982) *Alternative Futures for Africa*, Boulder, Colo.: Westview Press.

——(1985) *Towards a Political Economy for Africa: The Dialectics of Dependence*, London: Macmillan.

——(1987) 'Security redefined: unconventional conflict in Africa', in S. Wright and J. Brownfoot (eds) *Africa in World Politics*, London: Macmillan.

——(1988) 'Africa's conjuncture: from structural adjustment to self-reliance', in *Third World Affairs, 1988*, London: Third World Foundation.

——(1989) 'The UN Economic Commission for Africa: continental development and self-reliance', in D. P. Forsythe (ed.) *The United Nations in the World Political Economy*, London: Macmillan.

——(1992) *Reformism and Revisionism in Africa's Political Economy in the 1990s: The Dialectics of Adjustment*, London: Macmillan.

Shaw, T. M. and Aluko, O. (eds) (1985) *Africa Projected: From Recession to Renaissance by the Year 2000?*, London: Macmillan.

United Nations (1989) *African Debt*, United Nations Africa Recovery Programme briefing paper, 1 June.

Whitaker, J. S. (1988) *How Can Africa Survive?*, New York: Harper & Row.

75

ASIA

ROBERT C. OBERST

Student unrest in China, South Korea and Burma, as well as youth-led insurrections in Sri Lanka and the Philippines and urban youth unrest in Papua New Guinea, all reflect a trend towards political violence and unrest by youth in Asian societies. Although the motivations of the movements vary from country to country, there are some common threads which link the nature of the movements to each other.

Over the last decade, the nations of Asia have found the pursuit of political stability to be much easier than the nations of Africa and Latin America have. However, the Asian nations now face serious problems in maintaining stable and peaceful political environments. The failure of a number of nations to establish internal peace has raised questions about the nature of political stability. It has become popular in social science literature to explain such violence and instability as a result of frustration and aggression (Gurr 1972; Gurr and Lichbach 1986), but nagging questions remain over what the frustration-aggression theorists do not explain about political violence (Eckstein 1980; Finkel and Rule 1986).

The diversity of Asia makes specific comparisons between countries difficult to draw. With over 40 per cent of the world's population and hundreds of cultural groups, the vast population of the region shares little in common. One area where there is very little similarity is economic development. In East Asia, the decade of the 1980s offered a great deal of hope as the economic take-off of the newly industrializing nations continued. Yet for the vast part of Asia there was little economic change. In South Asia and China, hopes for rapid economic development faded as these nations grappled with political crises. In India, the 1985 euphoria surrounding the election of Rajiv Gandhi and his technocrat advisers evaporated as his government was unable to deliver on its promises. In China, the opening of the society was rapidly brought to an end by the massacre at Tiananmen Square on 3 June 1989 and the isolation of the country which followed the deaths. A common denominator in both the newly industrializing nations as well as the poorer nations of Asia was the continuing high levels of political violence in their societies.

Economic growth and development, or the lack of it, both appeared to be increasing the tensions among ethnic communities and classes in all of the Asian states, with the exception of Japan. It would appear that the challenge of the 1990s and beyond would be to stem the political disintegration of the Asian states.

The forces of disintegration fall into three categories. The first of these are the student movements of discontent found in such countries as South Korea, China and Taiwan where students faced with severe problems in their economies find that job opportunities are restricted and thus begin political agitation for change. The ethnic and religious conflicts within Asian societies comprise the second category. The continuing crises in the Indian states of Kashmir and the Punjab, and the Sri Lankan civil war are examples of these types of conflict. Egalitarian revolutionary movements are the third area of conflict. Most of these movements since the Second World War have been Marxist inspired. Although at the moment they do not seem to be spreading, they still persist in the region, as shown by the Philippine insurrection. As long as poverty persists in Asia, these movements will have a captive audience to appeal to.

The remainder of this essay will examine three varieties of conflict in Asia and the implications they have for further economic and political development in the region.

ETHNIC CONFLICT

Traditionally, observers of the political systems of the Third World have attributed much of the political instability in these states to the ethnic divisions within their societies. Donau Horowitz has stated that 'the fear of ethnic domination and suppression is a motivating force for the acquisition of power as an end. And power is also sought for confirmation of ethnic status' (Horowitz 1985: 187). Economic deprivation appears to be an important factor in the persistence of this fear of ethnic domination and suppression. It is also an important motivating factor in the use of ethnicity to confirm one's ethnic status. Differences in income levels between different ethnic groups in society can create a sense of deprivation on the part of some groups. As economic development progresses, ethnic differences will be accentuated and stressed in the Asian states. As Horowitz has noted, the need to define one's ethnicity, as well as the fear of domination, will fuel secessionist and political movements to protect ethnic minorities. The lack of resources and the feelings of deprivation that accompany ethnic relationships in most of the nations do not offer hope for the future.

Ethnically based separatist movements are a particular problem in South Asia. Countries such as India have faced the unenviable job of uniting diverse languages, cultures and religions into a coherent nation-state. Since independence, India has appeared to be an unmanageable amalgam of differing ethnic groups facing many separatist movements. Today there are several movements in India which are agitating for separatism. In the eastern Indian state of Assam, the Bodoland agitation has demanded a separate state for the Bodo people in the narrow area that connects India to its north-east. In central India, the tribal Jharkhand movement has sought to create a separate state from adjacent districts in four Indian states (West Bengal, Madhya Pradesh, Orissa and Bihar).

The most serious areas of concern in India, however, are the Sikh separatist movement in north-west India and Muslim militants in Kashmir. In the Indian state of the Punjab, militant leaders among the Sikhs seek to create an independent state of Khalistan. The Sikhs not only fear Hindu domination, but are concerned that they are subsidizing the poorer areas of India where the people are not as economically successful as the Punjabis. In Kashmir, to the north-west of the Punjab, Kashmiri separatists have been agitating for the creation of an independent Muslim nation-state. The population of Kashmir is overwhelmingly Muslim, and support for the militants is strong. Once again the fear of domination in an overwhelmingly Hindu-dominated society frightens many of the youthful Muslim leaders. Across India in the north-east, tribal groups such as the Nagas and the Mizos have been in a perpetual state of rebellion since the British era. Although most of these movements have been quiet in the last years of the 1980s, these tribal groups offer a continuing threat to India's territorial integrity as they seek to protect and promote their cultural identity.

Complicating these separatist movements has been the rise of Hindu nationalist sentiment in India which has increased tensions between Muslims and Hindus. Militant Hindus have made claims to religious sites such as the Babri Masjid mosque in the state of Uttar Pradesh, built on the site where the Hindu Lord Rama is believed to have been born. Hindu militants want to tear down the mosque to build a Hindu temple on the site. Related to Hindu militancy has been increased caste conflict. In 1990, the Indian government established quotas in government hiring for lower-caste Indians. Fifty per cent of government jobs were reserved for untouchables. This resulted in widespread student unrest by upper-caste Hindus who resented the fewer job openings which would be made available for upper-caste students.

In neighbouring Pakistan, Pathan and Baluchi tribal minorities have been agitating for additional influence in the Pakistani government. In addition, with the apparent end of the Afghanistan war in sight, the possibility of Baluchi separatists reactivating their campaign for an independent state is very likely during the 1990s. Pakistan has also been supporting Kashmiri separatists in India. This policy could backfire because of the possibility of a separatist movement among Pakistan Kashmiris to join an independent Kashmir, if one is created.

In Sri Lanka, ethnic conflict has also had Indian involvement and has been threatening the territorial integrity of Sri Lanka. The Tamil minority group in Sri Lanka has been at war against the government to create an independent nation of Eelam since the early 1980s. The large Tamil population in the Indian state of Tamil Nadu has pressured the Indian government to support the demands of the Sri Lankan Tamils. At different times during the conflict, both the Tamil Nadu and the Indian national governments have provided financial support, military training and a staging area to carry out attacks in Sri Lanka for the Sri Lanka Tamil rebels. The conflict entered a new stage in the early 1990s when a Sri Lankan government offensive against the Tamil guerrillas was unable to dislodge the guerrillas from their control of the Tamil heartland on the Jaffna peninsula in the north of the country. The success of the resistance of the Tamil guerrillas implies a long conflict between the two sides.

In Bangladesh, a relatively homogeneous nation ethnically, ethnic violence in the Chittagong Hills Tracts continues to pose serious problems for the government. The main demand is for the removal of all non-tribal people from the tracts. Increased autonomy, which has already been granted, has not satisfied the demands of the movement. In addition to this conflict, the government must deal with a movement centred in India that has been calling for the creation of a Hindu state from areas of Bangladesh.

Ethnic conflict is found in South-East Asia as well, although the greater economic success of the region appears to have alleviated some of the tension between ethnic groups. The Philippines faced two serious insurrections during the 1980s. The first of these is the Moro revolt, an ethnic conflict based on religion – Islam. The second is a communist-led insurrection by the New People's Army and will be mentioned in the next section (p. 1205). In the case of the Moro movement, youth gangs and unrest have been common in the Moro areas (Wurfel 1988: 156–7). The Islamic Moros want greater autonomy in the largely Christian Philippines. The issue of Moro autonomy has increased tensions between the old Moro elite and a new, younger, Arab-educated elite. The more militant youths are unwilling to compromise with the government in Manila and have continued the conflict.

The nations of East Asia are ethnically more homogeneous and have not experienced as many ethnically related problems. However, even China has not escaped ethnic strife. Continuing unrest in Tibet and Muslim rioting in Sinkiang province in the north-east pose serious threats to Chinese government rule in these areas. Both of these areas are geographically remote from the rest of China and are dominated by non-Chinese ethnic groups.

There appears to be little hope that these ethnic conflicts will come to an early end. As economic development progresses, especially in the poorer nations of the region, there will be an increased likelihood that disparities in the distribution of the benefits of that growth will result in increased tensions between ethnic groups within the nations of the region.

REVOLUTIONARY VIOLENCE

Throughout the 1950s, 1960s and 1970s, the United States and its European allies were concerned with Marxist revolutions in Asia. Since the end of the Vietnamese war, revolutionary movements have not been a significant force in most of Asia. Communist-led movements in Malaysia and Thailand have disappeared while in India the violent Naxalite movement in Orissa, Madhya Pradesh and Maharastra in central India has declined in significance. In the Philippines, however, the communist rebellion controls most of the countryside throughout the nation. With the decline of militant support for such movements in the Soviet Union, it can be expected that these types of revolutions will disappear or undergo a severe change.

Theories to explain the prevalence of this type of violence have usually been associated with the frustration-aggression school of thought. Most of these approaches have stressed the importance of economic factors which increase the possibility of revolutionary changes (see Davies 1962). Sudden economic downturns in societies that are developing rapidly are liable to create revolutionary movements. It can be argued that this pattern was followed in the Philippines where the economic growth and success of the 1960s and early 1970s led many to believe that this country was going to follow the example of South Korea and Taiwan in transforming its economy. Unfortunately, the late 1970s and 1980s ended this optimism as the country stagnated economically. The consequence was the rise of a rebellion which is now believed to control most of the countryside. The New People's Army was the product of dissatisfaction of younger Communist party members with the leadership of the party in the 1960s (Wurfel 1988: 226). The rapid growth of the movement (Manning 1985: 401) reflects its appeal to Filipino youth. In addition to this insurrection and the Moro revolt discussed earlier (p. 1204), the mass movement which led to the collapse of the Marcos regime had a strong youth-based component and reflected the widespread dissatisfaction in the society.

One reason for hope that revolutionary movements would decline has been the economic success of the East Asian nations of Taiwan, South Korea and Singapore. The economic success of these nations reduces the likelihood that revolutionary movements will develop. Other nations such as Malaysia and Thailand appear to be following these countries to economic success.

One possible area of concern about revolutionary violence is that much of it in the future may be inspired by China or Maoist ideology. This pattern can be seen in the emergence of Maoist movements such as the Khmer Rouge in Cambodia and the People's Liberation Front in Sri Lanka. However, at this time there is no clear trend or indication that these types of movement will become more prevalent in other countries.

In Cambodia, the Khmer Rouge revolt against the North Vietnamese supported government of Heng Samrin appears to be very close to regaining control of the government it held in the 1970s. Although the Khmer Rouge is part of an alliance with several non-communist groups, it dominates the opposition to the Cambodian government. The Khmer Rouge continues to obtain support from China and no end to this support is in sight. The Khmer Rouge has been consolidating its rural base of support and seems to have overcome the fears and opposition that resulted from the millions of deaths during its rule in the 1970s. The Khmer Rouge has benefited from Western pressure, especially from the United States, in the 1980s on the Vietnamese government to withdraw its troops from Cambodia. The United States also supplied military support and money to the non-communist guerrillas in the Khmer Rouge alliance. The combination of this military and diplomatic pressure finally resulted in a Vietnamese troop withdrawal from Cambodia. The Heng Samrin government in Cambodia lacks the military strength to defend itself from the Khmer Rouge and a Khmer Rouge return to power appears likely.

In Sri Lanka, a Maoist revolt by the People's Liberation Front (more commonly known by its initials in the Sinhalese language, JVP) was severely damaged by the capture of all of the politburo and most of the second-level leaders in November and December 1989. This revolt appears to have no outside support and was an indigenous response to nationalistic and economic factors. However, the revolt was not completely eliminated by the capture of its leaders. Sporadic attacks by the Front continued despite the activities of government-supported death squads which killed suspected members of the Front and their families.

It is obvious that an end to the Cold War has not stopped the social forces that have fuelled revolutionary insurrections in the past. It can be expected that although the Soviet Union may not be actively involved in revolutionary movements around the world, these movements will continue with or without outside support in the poorer societies of South and South-East Asia.

YOUTH-LED VIOLENCE

The incidence of youth-led violence appears to be increasing in the Asian nation-states. The demographic transformation of many developing nations has created large youth cohorts which have been a major source of violence or political instability in the developing world (Keyfitz 1973; Wriggins and Jayawardene 1973; Fuller and Pitts 1990).

Rapidly growing populations require a rapidly growing economy to support the increased numbers of consumers in the society. To prevent declines in the economy, a society's economy must grow as rapidly as its population. However, population growth also creates a large age cohort who grow up together through adolescence. The sheer size of this cohort forces a society to focus its energies and attention on them. In addition, the economy of that society must expand rapidly to meet the demand for jobs as the youths come of age. It has been noted that the sheer size of a youth cohort may destabilize social and political institutions (Moller 1972). Peter Loewenberg (1974) has even argued that the large number of people born in Germany from 1900 to 1914 fuelled the growth of the Nazi movement in that country.

Rapid population growth in all of the Asian societies during the 1960s and 1970s helped to produce large numbers of youths who today are trying to enter the job markets of their societies. This problem has been compounded by the success of the Asian societies in developing educational opportunities and the growth in the number of young people holding secondary and university degrees. When they graduate they find that the job market does not provide the kinds of white collar jobs that they had hoped to qualify for with their education. The consequence is a growing pool of educated, unemployed youths who find high competition for jobs commensurate with their educational level.

Complicating this problem is the existence of generational dissonance and demographic discontinuity. Generational dissonance is the condition in which the communication between the generations has been so disrupted by the demographic, educational and social changes in the society that they cannot communicate with each other. This condition will frequently lead to the development of new value systems among the youth age cohorts through a process Braungart (1984: 117) calls the deauthorization of the older generation. In this process, the younger generation rejects the authority and value systems of their elders.

Santmire (n.d.) has described demographic discontinuity as the consequence of events or conditions that change the circumstances under which a child's socialization takes place. These may include traumatic events such as changes in family size, changes in the status of women in the society, urban migration, or changes in the birth rate. All of these changes have been experienced by Asian societies in the 1980s. These changes further amplify the differences between the generations and the experiences of the generations. For instance, parental interaction may differ between first- and second-born children or between parents and their children (Santmire n.d.: 5–12). In addition, changes in cohort size in school may also affect the impact that education may have on the socialization of the students (ibid.: 22). Thus, demographic discontinuity may amplify the effects of generational dissonance on the development of the younger generation.

The baby boom that most Asian societies experienced (Japan is an exception) resulted in forces leading to demographic discontinuity and generational dissonance. Rapid expansion of the educational system has led to larger numbers of youths contesting for educational and career resources. Thus, the educational systems of most Asian societies have not been able to accommodate the increased demand for access to higher education. In addition, the economies have often not been able to expand quickly enough to create new jobs for the increased numbers of youths entering the job market. This led to a sense of frustration as educational and career opportunities failed to appear. The sense of frustration felt by the unemployed young people was augmented by the sense of generational dissonance. The failure of the older generation to provide an acceptable quality of life for the younger generation, and in many cases to act out the value system that they had taught to the younger generation, amplified these changes.

All of these factors can lead to a youth subculture which may reject the values of the older generation. The main features of this subculture can be adjustment problems, suicides and most importantly the propensity to join revolutionary movements.

Demographic changes play an important part in the emergence of the youth subcultures in Asian societies. Gary Fuller and Forrest Pitts (Fuller and Pitts 1990) have argued that when the 15–24-year-old age cohort exceeds more than 20 per cent of the population, there is a strong likelihood of political unrest. Table 1 shows those Asian societies with the largest age cohorts among 15–24-year-olds. The population data from which the table was compiled (United Nations 1989) reflect the period from 1983 to 1986.

It should be noted that the size of this age cohort is not only the consequence of the birth rate in earlier years but is also the consequence of different mortality rates, changes in life expectancy, the increase and decrease of the size of age cohorts over the age of 50, and finally, the rate of population growth of those youths born after this age cohort. For instance, reduced birth rates and increased life expectancy have resulted in the small size of the Japanese age cohort (see Table 1).

Seven nations in Asia have exceeded 20 per cent of the total population in this age cohort. These countries are the Philippines, Thailand, Malaysia, Sri Lanka, South Korea, Papua New Guinea and Burma. In all but two of

Table 1 Youth cohorts

Country	Percentage of population aged 15–24
Philippines	22.4
Thailand	22.1
Malaysia	22.1
Sri Lanka	21.0
South Korea	21.0
Papua New Guinea	20.2
Burma	20.2
China	19.9
India	19.8
Indonesia	19.8
Singapore	19.6
Pakistan	19.5
Bangladesh	19.0
Nepal	18.2
Afghanistan	17.5
Japan	15.0

Source: United Nations, *1986 Demographic Yearbook*, pp. 190–223, New York: United Nations, 1989.

these countries (Thailand and Malaysia) there have been extensive youth-led violence in the last five years. In addition, two countries just below the 20 per cent cut-off mark, India and China, are also experiencing youth unrest.

However, rapid population growth alone is not the only factor which affects the likelihood of youth subculture development. Rapid expansion of the educational system also plays a role in the development of violent youth movements. The educational systems of Asia have been expanding rapidly to accommodate the education of the younger generation. This educational expansion results in a generation of young people who are better educated than their parents.

Table 2 shows the percentage of youths in the 15–19 age cohort attending secondary school and the percentage in the 20–24 age cohort receiving a post-high-school university or technical education between the mid-1970s and mid-1980s. The crucial statistic is the percentage of youths in secondary school. Because the number of university students is still low in most Asian countries, this is not as important a factor as the expansion of secondary education. As would be expected, Japan and South Korea had the highest percentage of young people in secondary and tertiary education, with Afghanistan and Papua New Guinea at the low end of the scale. The development of violent youth movements is intensified by the combination of educational expansion and the growth in the size of youth cohorts.

Table 2 also shows the average annual percentage increase in the number

Table 2   Growth of students*

Country	Percentage of age group Secondary	Tertiary	Yearly percentage increase Years	Secondary	Tertiary
Afghanistan	10.0	2.3	1976–84	−6.1	7.5
Bangladesh	37.0	6.5	1976–81	7.0	52.1
Burma	30.7	4.6	1974–84	3.9	19.4
China	38.7	1.9	1977–82	−5.2	13.9
India	41.2	7.7	1976–86	3.2	6.9
Indonesia	41.5	6.5	1976–84	10.5	31.5
Japan	113.9	27.2	1977–85	1.8	0.3
South Korea	105.1	28.1	1977–86	3.7	29.6
Malaysia	78.0	6.2	1977–84	5.4	18.4
Nepal	27.1	3.3	1977–86	8.1	11.7
Pakistan	30.3	2.4	1977–81	4.6	9.0
Papua New Guinea	13.3	2.1	1976–85	1.9	1.3
Philippines	55.3	25.8	1977–84	5.9	12.1
Singapore	86.6	12.6	1976–86	0.4	5.6
Sri Lanka	80.8	3.9	1977–85	5.3	42.0
Thailand	35.9	21.4	1976–85	8.2	83.9

Source: United Nations, *1986 Demographic Yearbook*, pp. 190–223, and *1985/86 Statistical Yearbook*, pp. 253–75, New York: United Nations, 1989.
* The calculations used in compiling these figures allow total percentages to exceed 100.

of secondary school and tertiary level students for selected years. The rapid growth of the educational systems can be seen in these figures. Although the growth of secondary school students is slowing down, it still remains very high in most of the countries, especially Indonesia, Thailand, Nepal and Bangladesh. However, the growth in the number of university-level students has been exceptional. Thailand, Sri Lanka and Bangladesh have been expanding the number of students at this level at a phenomenal rate of increase.

In the case of Sri Lanka, no other nation in Asia has faced as severe a threat from youth-led social movements. A youth-led insurrection in 1971 led to a large loss of life (Wriggins and Jayawardene 1973; Kearney and Jiggins 1975). Since 1983, two youth movements have emerged. As has been already discussed (p. 1204), the Tamil ethnic minority have been in open rebellion against the government since 1983. This conflict has resulted in over 10,000 deaths.[1] Since 1987, members of the Sinhalese ethnic majority led by the People's Liberation Front have been in rebellion against the government. Both rebellions have utilized large numbers of university and secondary school students who at least sympathize with the movement. Over 10,000 deaths have resulted from the People's Liberation Front conflict. In both cases, rapid population growth was followed by a rapid expansion of the educational system. This results in high levels of unemployed youth, especially among educated youth.

According to Table 1, two other countries have a high propensity for youth-led violence: South Korea and Thailand. Throughout the early 1980s, Korea faced widespread student unrest. However, the demographic data found in Korea should be viewed with caution. The population data used to produce the table reflect the Korean population in 1986. Population projections for the 1990s indicates that Korea will show a sharp decline in the size of the 15–24-year-old age cohort. It can also be expected that South Korea's economic growth will continue. As a result the pressures creating the demographic problems in Korea are rapidly declining.

Thailand also appears to be a likely case for youth-led violence. However, Thailand has not experienced the high levels of violence and unrest that Sri Lanka and the Philippines have experienced in the 1980s. Yet the student movement in Thailand was extremely active in the 1970s and still continues to play an important role in the political system. The rapidly growing economy in Thailand and the country's increasing democratization may have helped to alleviate the social forces leading to the demographic trap. In any case, although Thailand may at first appear to defy the demographic trap, there is evidence that the country has youth unrest.

This analysis offers little hope for those societies which are trying to maintain political stability and have experienced a baby boom in the last five to thirty years. The failure to control population can lead to possible political instability fifteen to thirty years later. Attempts to alleviate the problem may be futile. Widespread economic development is needed to create jobs for rapidly expanding work-forces. Beyond expanding the economy, which may not be possible, there is relatively little that can be done to alleviate the social pressures described in this analysis. One possible solution may be to create institutions which give young people an active and useful role in the society. Beyond this, there is little that can be done to minimize the impact of the demographic trap once the baby boom has occurred. Because of baby booms years earlier, increased political instability among youths may be an important part of the political future of South and South-East Asia over the next few years.

SUMMARY

This analysis presents a less than optimistic prospect for the political stability and internal peace of Asian societies. Two patterns emerge for the future prospects of Asian nations. The first is reflected by the economically successful nations of East and South-East Asia which have been able to develop their economies and appear to be close to alleviating many of the social forces which lead to political violence. This category includes South Korea, Taiwan and Singapore. In addition, Malaysia and Thailand appear to be joining this group. Among the former three nations, there is a great deal of ethnic homogeneity and, as a result, ethnic conflict has not restricted their growth. In Malaysia and Thailand there is extensive ethnic diversity and this may become an important factor in their future stability.

The second pattern can be found among the other countries of Asia. These are poorer nations where economic growth has been limited and most of them have faced sharp ethnic divisions in their societies. Thus, for these nations, economic growth has only acted to increase the social forces leading to political violence and instability. Ethnic rivalries and large numbers of educated, unemployed youths will exacerbate political unrest in these societies. The interrelationship of the forces at work is very complicated. This makes predictions difficult. However, if economic growth remains sluggish, it can be expected that ethnic tensions and disaffected youths will remain in these societies.

The challenge of the 1990s in these societies will be to alleviate the ethnic divisions while reducing youth dissatisfaction with the political and economic system. This is no easy task. Ethnic divisions will be widened by competition for scarce resources. Nations such as India will face increased unrest among its many minorities. Sri Lanka may find it impossible to subdue ethnic violence permanently. Beyond this there will be a need to assimilate the educated young people and ethnic minorities into the society. This process would leave them with the feeling that they are playing an integral part in the future of the nation, but such a process is difficult to achieve and, if economic development remains slow, would probably be impossible. This prospect should make the decade of the 1990s an era of serious challenges to political stability in the region. The remaining democracies may find it hard to maintain their political systems while the autocratic regimes in the area may be joined by other nations that have been taken over by the military or one-party states.

NOTES

1 These and later death statistics are from the author's own tabulation of deaths in the conflict.

REFERENCES

Braungart, R. (1984) 'Historical generations and youth movements: a theoretical perspective', in R. E. Ratcliff (ed.) *Research in Social Movements, Conflicts and Change: A Research Annual*, Vol. 6, Greenwich, Conn.: JAI Press.

Davies, J. C. (1962) 'Toward a theory of revolution', *American Sociological Review* 27: 5–18.

Eckstein, H. (1980) 'Theoretical approaches to explaining collective political violence', in T. R. Gurr (ed.) *Handbook of Political Conflict*, New York: Free Press.

Finkel, S. E. and Rule, J. B. (1986) 'Relative deprivation and related psychological theories of civil violence: a critical review', in K. Lang and G. E. Lang (eds)

Research in Social Movements, Conflicts and Change: A Research Annual, Vol. 9, Greenwich, Conn.: JAI Press.

Fuller, G. and Pitts, F. (1990) 'Youth cohorts and political unrest in South Korea', *Political Geography Quarterly* 9: 9–22.

Gurr, T. R. (1972) *Why Men Rebel*, Princeton: Princeton University Press.

Gurr, T. R. and Lichbach, M. I. (1986) 'Forecasting internal conflict: a competitive evaluation of empirical theories', *Comparative Political Studies* 19: 3–38.

Horowitz, D. L. (1985) *Ethnic Groups in Conflict*, Berkeley: University of California Press.

Kearney, R, N. and Jiggins, J. (1975) 'The Ceylon insurrection of 1971', *Journal of Commonwealth and Comparative Politics* 13: 40–64.

Keyfitz, N. (1973) 'The youth cohort revisited', in H. Wriggins and J. F. Guyot, *Population, Politics and the Future of South Asia*, New York: Columbia University, pp. 231–58.

Loewenberg, P. (1974) 'A psychohistorical approach: the Nazi generation', in A. Esler (ed.) *The Youth Revolution*, Lexington, Mass.: D. C. Heath.

Manning, R. A. (1985) 'The Philippine crisis', *Foreign Affairs* 63: 392–410.

Moller, H. (1972) 'Youth as a force in the modern world', in P. K. Manning and M. Truzzi (eds) *Youth and Sociology*, Englewood Cliffs, NJ: Prentice-Hall.

Santmire, T. E. (n.d.) 'Demographic discontinuity and psychosocial development', unpublished paper, University of Nebraska at Lincoln.

United Nations (1989) *1986 Demographic Yearbook*, New York: United Nations, pp. 190–223.

Wriggins, H. and Jayawardene, C. H. S. (1973) 'Youth protest in Sri Lanka (Ceylon)', in H. Wriggins and F. Guyot (eds) *Population Politics and the Future of Southern Asia*, New York: Columbia University.

Wurfel, D. (1988) *Filipino Politics: Development and Decay*, Ithaca, NY: Cornell University Press.

FURTHER READING

Brake, M. (1985) *Comparative Youth Culture: The Sociology of Youth Cultures and Youth Subcultures in America, Britain, and Canada*, London: Routledge & Kegan Paul.

Braungart, R. (1984) 'Historical generations and youth movements: a theoretical perspective', in R. E. Ratcliff (ed.) *Research in Social Movements, Conflicts and Change: A Research Annual*, Vol. 6, Greenwich, Conn.: JAI Press.

Eckstein, H. (1980) 'Theoretical approaches to explaining collective political violence', in T. R. Gurr (ed.) *Handbook of Political Conflict*, New York: Free Press.

Finkel, S. E. and Rule, J. B. (1986) 'Relative deprivation and related psychological theories of civil violence: a critical review', in K. Lang and G. E. Lang (eds) *Research in Social Movements, Conflicts and Change: A Research Annual*, Vol. 9, Greenwich, Conn.: JAI Press.

Francis, C.-B. (1989) 'The progress of protest in China', *Asian Survey* 29: 898–915.

Gurr, T. R. (1972) *Why Men Rebel*, Princeton: Princeton University Press.

Kearney, R. N. (1980) 'Youth protest in politics of Sri Lanka', *Sociological Focus* 13: 293–309.

Keniston, K. (1968) *Young Radicals: Notes on Committed Youths*, New York: Harcourt Brace.

Manogaran, C. (1987) *Ethnic Conflict and Reconciliation in Sri Lanka*, Honolulu: University of Hawaii.

Mead, M. (1977) *Culture and Commitment: The New Relationships Between the Generations in the 1970s*, New York: Anchor Press.

Oberst, R. C. (1988) 'Sri Lanka's Tamil Tigers', *Conflict* 8 (2/3): 185–202.

Wurfel, D. (1988) *Filipino Politics: Development and Decay*, Ithaca, NY: Cornell University Press.

Yitri, M. (1989) 'The Crisis in Burma: back from the heart of darkness?', *Asian Survey* 29: 543–58.

76

LATIN AMERICA

GEORGE PHILIP

During the past decade there have been three major political developments in Latin America. On the positive side democracy has returned (one hopes more than temporarily) to most countries in the region; the democratic credibility of some countries is greater in 1990 than it has ever been. On a less positive note the 1980s were a decade of considerable violence and conflict in Central America; the US invasion of Panama in December 1989 and the election of Violetta Chamorro in Nicaragua in February 1990 have certainly changed many perspectives, but by no means have all outstanding issues been resolved. There is also considerable political violence in both Colombia and Peru – much of it, directly or indirectly, drug related. A second adverse factor is that for most Latin American countries the 1980s were a decade of great economic difficulty. In 1990, of all the Latin American countries, only Chile and Colombia had a level of per capita income higher than in 1980. Indeed inflation, debt and other manifestations of economic crisis continue to pose great problems for policy makers across the region. In 1980 an observer would probably have concluded that Latin America had succeeded in maintaining a respectable level of economic growth, but at a very high price in terms of both inequality and political repression. A decade later there is less repression (which is not to say none), but economic conditions for the majority of Latin Americans range from precarious to dismal. As the reality has changed, so obviously have ways of analysing it.

To talk of 'the region' in this way does, of course, presuppose that the eighteen different republics involved have enough in common to make generalization worthwhile. This has at times been questioned, particularly by citizens of one or other of these republics objecting to the idea of their own country being lumped in with the others. Indeed it is true that there are major differences between the various Latin American republics. Cuba retains a Marxist-Leninist form of government, while many South American countries have had recent experience of military rule. There is, moreover, a considerable difference in per capita income and other 'life chance' indicators between, for example, Honduras and Venezuela.

Nevertheless, there are enough similarities to make it useful to talk of a Latin American region. Allowing for variations between countries, there are a number of generalizations which hold true across most countries of the region. There is also the common background of language, religion and law. Although the Catholic Church is less a force than it was, as well as being less monolithic, the historical impact of Catholicism has been considerable. The heritage of Roman Law, with the absence of judicial review and the emphasis on executive power, has also mattered. Let us begin, however, with a discussion of the political institutions themselves.

GOVERNMENT AND POLITICS

A decade ago, most Latin American governments were military dictatorships and there was a significant scholarly literature which purported to show that there was, at least, an 'elective affinity' between a certain stage of economic development and authoritarian rule. Indeed, one of the main scholarly debates was between those who sought to find some kind of 'structural' reason for the increase in the number of authoritarian governments after 1960, and those who preferred to stress more voluntaristic or accidental factors. In retrospect, the debate seems to have been won convincingly by the latter. However, discussions of this kind, at least in the social sciences, do not so much end with the emergence of a new, reasoned consensus as with a shift of view which relates as much to change in the outside world as to debate within the scholarly community. This is what seems to have happened in this case.

No Latin American country is today under direct military rule. Although the military is now out of the presidential palace, military officers continue to play an influential behind-the-scenes role in many countries. They are involved in combating insurgencies in Peru, Colombia, El Salvador and Guatemala. In at least the last two mentioned cases the military wield substantial political power, to the point where it has seriously been suggested that democracy is largely a façade. Elsewhere military power is less, but still significant. The military and police forces sometimes participate in the narcotics traffic. The military continues to play a significant role in state industries in several countries – most notably in Brazil. Although military influence has waned during the past decade, it is by no means obvious that military involvement in politics belongs solely to the past. One area in which further research seems appropriate concerns the role of the military under recently established democratic governments.

Meanwhile what of the newly re-established democratic institutions themselves? Institutional studies of Latin American politics are relatively rare, and this is another field which seems open to further research. No Latin American country has a fully parliamentary political system; there are only different forms of presidentialism. Moreover, without a strong US-style Supreme Court exercising the right of judicial review, the presidential institution is particularly strong and centralizing. By this I do not mean that Latin American presidents are necessarily successful in policy-making terms – very often they are not. The point is, rather, that the presidency acts as a focal point within the political system. Individual charisma is raised above party loyalty, and there is always the unfortunate possibility that a Latin American republic may find itself governed by an intensely controversial or manifestly incompetent figure who is virtually immune from removal by constitutional means. In the past there was more than a superficial relationship between this kind of presidential institution and the Latin American military *coup*, since opposition figures who despaired of their ability to remove a president by constitutional means tended to 'knock at the doors of the barracks' instead.

Democratic politics is naturally about far more than governing institutions. There are also electorates and voting behaviour. There is a considerable literature on the (imperfect) democracies that existed in a number of countries prior to the military interventions of the 1960s and 1970s. It is generally accepted that successful candidates for office tended to be 'populists' – a term which generations of scholars have spent much time trying to define. In essence it seemed to involve the ability of some fairly conservative politicians to sound radical at election time. That is, they produced a rhetoric which raised expectations and attracted mass support without precluding the compromise and bargaining that was necessary for the candidate to be tolerated by economic elites and the military. 'Give me a balcony' said Velasco Ibarra of Ecuador 'and I will govern.' When the balancing act failed (and it often did), the result was growing polarization and military intervention.

Now that democratic politics is back, can it be said that the age of populism is over? In one sense the answer seems to be yes. There has been a general worldwide change, in Latin America as much as elsewhere, from a politics of parties, organizations and mass rallies to a politics of television. Media candidates win elections – in Peru and Brazil, formerly almost unknown figures recently won the presidency fundamentally on the basis of televisual appeal. Televisual politics is more bland and less potentially confrontational than the politics of mass demonstrations.

There is another sense, however, in which the era of televisual politics promises more of the same. Populism, like presidentialism, tended to elevate a dominant individual above his or her party and colleagues. It may even be said that presidents do not have colleagues as such. Television further emphasizes the paramount role of a particular individual, whose strengths and weaknesses can have a far greater effect on policy (and even political stability) than would otherwise be the case. Politics is about personalities everywhere, but perhaps especially so in Latin America.

Nor does any Latin American country have a professional, 'British-type', civil service that might to some extent offset the tendency toward extreme personal rule. Instead there is clientelism; presidents appoint not merely their cabinets but also (at least nominally) the entire public sector bureaucracy. It is, indeed, widely recognized that a clientelist system of public administration can make a contribution to social stability. Allied to the extended family, it can bring a wide range of society into the outer circles of power. The judicious use of public subsidy and appointment by the post-revolutionary Mexican authorities did much to replace political turmoil with an enviable record of stability. On the other hand, there is a cost in terms of efficiency. People appointed to positions on the basis of political loyalty may not be ideal when it comes to carrying out complex professional tasks.

Of perhaps even greater importance is the difference between the universalist notions that lie behind professional recruitment, at least in theory, and the unavoidably arbitrary (some would say neo-patrimonialist) operation of a clientelist system. According to the former concept, every citizen has certain rights, including above all the right to impartial administration; corruption, though it undoubtedly occurs, is widely regarded as being wrong. According to the latter concept, everything is a matter of knowing the right people, being on good terms with the government, or (alternatively) threatening disruption until one's claims are met; agreements, when they are reached, are not always written down or formalized and formal documents do not always reflect the genuine reality. Obviously, European bureaucracies are not fully 'rational' in the Weberian sense, while Latin American public administration is not entirely arbitrary. Nevertheless, there is a difference of emphasis, and it is an important one.

This combination of a formally strong and largely unaccountable presidency and a clientelist bureaucracy is far from ideal in terms of policy making or even, perhaps, of democratic stability. Commentators have often considered that many (though perhaps not all) Latin American countries have suffered from weak political institutions which have not always been able to withstand the strains imposed by serious social conflicts. Too much depends upon the single personality of the president of the day. There is another factor in this equation and that is the military itself. In most (though not quite all) Latin American countries the military has developed a bureaucratic structure which operates more effectively, and at times more ruthlessly, to protect its corporate interests than do most civilian organizations. This fact led some observers, rather more in the past than today, to adopt the fallacious argument that military rule in Latin America might be more effective than rule by civilians because (as is often true) senior military officers are generally more technically qualified than many senior civilian policy makers.

While it is difficult at present to see how informed public opinion in Latin America could again be led to believe that authoritarian governments offer solutions, rather than worse problems, it remains true that there are policy-making weaknesses in these political systems. What is often lacking is that consistency which is the basis of bureaucratic effectiveness. Instead a rather typical pattern of policy making in Latin America is one in which incoming presidents offer a 'new broom' approach.

This leads to a brief period of enthusiasm and apparent success. Then problems start to emerge and the politically weakened president finds it difficult to resolve them; he/she is likely to have used up much political capital with the original scheme. A relatively unpopular president cannot control Congress easily, if indeed at all, while the bureaucracy cannot be trusted to implement policy consistently without continued prodding from above. Too often, things are then allowed to drift and the president increasingly becomes a lame duck. The initial euphoria dissipates and there is nothing to replace it. This either leaves effective policy making to await the next presidential election, after which the cycle is repeated or else the president is forced to take increasingly radical (and at worst politically destabilizing) measures in an attempt to regain credibility. In some systems, the next presidential election begins within days of the presidential inauguration. The political system, in other words, makes especially difficult the step-by-step ('incremental') approach to change which tends to be the hallmark of parliamentary systems. Instead, short periods of frenetic action are followed by longer periods of drift.

This may not have mattered greatly when governments were not expected to do much except distribute moderate amounts of patronage to their supporters. However, we now live in a world in which government is pervasive and policy error can trigger capital outflows amounting to many billions of dollars within days, so that the effect of policy mismanagement is far more serious. The United States operates a public sector which is substantially clientelist, but the United States has an independent central bank, relatively powerful local and state governments and an ethic which is hostile to over-powerful and over-ambitious government. Most Latin American countries have none of these things.

POLITICAL SOCIETY

Problems of policy making also contribute to and result from broader social issues of various kinds. There are some kinds of difficulty from which Latin America is mercifully free. Religious conflict is not really a source of concern; the Catholic Church is both more tolerant and weaker than it once was and there is certainly no Latin American counterpart to Islamic fundamentalism. Ethnic conflicts do simmer in places and occasionally burst out (the most notable and tragic example being Sendero Luminoso in Peru), but there is less overt racism in Latin America than in many other parts of the world. There is no violent secessionism or irredentism. Moreover, war between states is rare. Internal conflict is more frequent, but the extremely violent situation in Central America since 1979 has been a departure from the normal historical pattern. As state socialism has come to look increasingly unattractive, and the Soviet Union increasingly implausible as a source of foreign aid for left-wing Latin American governments, so the issues involved in the Central American conflict have become less pressing; it seems that the Reagan administration greatly exaggerated what was at stake in any event. Certainly Marxist-Leninist revolution is not seriously on the agenda in the Latin America of the 1990s.

The most serious problems in Latin America relate to the unequal distribution of wealth; there are few regions of the world in which political life is seen as being so unambiguously about money. There is a fairly wide gap between the richest and poorest countries in Latin America. Nevertheless, the similarities in social structure across the region are again striking. Argentina was once considered to have virtually a developed country standard of living, but has now slipped back towards the Latin American average. On the other hand only Bolivia, Honduras and perhaps Nicaragua rank alongside the poor countries of Africa and South Asia; given the importance of illegal exports in Bolivia, one doubts whether that country really belongs with the very poor. In other words, most of Latin America shares a similar level of per capita gross national product to the East Asian newly industrialized countries (NICs). There is a significant degree of industrialization – both Brazil and Mexico export more manufactured goods than anything else – but also a tremendous unevenness between the more progressive and advanced parts of each economy and the (often rural) backwaters in which a substantial part of the population continues to live.

Partly for this reason, income distribution in Latin America is, in general, far worse than it is in the Asian NICs; the problem is, if anything, becoming even more difficult. The worst poverty in Latin America is rural, and policy has done little to alleviate this. Most Latin Americans now live in cities and urban electorates demand (and get) the bulk of public resources. At the same time the population of Latin America is still relatively young. Birth rates are quite high, although they have come down from their peaks. The most dramatic phase of the 'population explosion' and the rush to the cities now appears to be over; what remains is how to live with the consequences. With the notable exception of the Southern Cone countries (Chile, Argentina and Uruguay) which urbanized earlier, most of Latin America is 'first generation urban'. The majority of citizens live in cities, but many migrated there. The majority is literate, but not especially well educated. There are more university students than ever, but the number of jobs available for them has expanded far more slowly. There is, in consequence, a disaffected intelligentsia in many countries.

This set of characteristics has made Latin America particularly interesting to political sociologists of various kinds. Thirty years ago there was an assumption that the Latin American republics would, on the whole, enjoy a gradual increase in per capita living standards along with a consolidation of democratic systems. It was generally believed that the two things went together. Conservative social theorists reacted by hypothesizing that first generation urbanization is a time of maximum danger to the social order. Traditional social institutions weaken; the generally controllable rural vote is replaced by the volatile and unpredictable urban mass. City dwellers enjoy freedoms for the first time, which is a heady experience. Moreover, sections of the middle class suffer status deprivation as their educational qualifications become devalued by the sheer expansion of the education system, and as high-status employment opportunities expand more slowly than the numbers of those qualified to fill them. 'Lumpen' sectors are created, more volatile and dangerous to political order than the organized working class in which orthodox Marxism once placed its trust.

It is indeed true that the majority of social revolutions in the world have occurred during early 'modernization'. However, South America has remained relatively immune to revolution or major social upheaval, although the same cannot be said of Central America or the Caribbean. The relative immunity of South America is partly because the organized military has been ready and willing to step in and put an end to 'disorder', where this has occurred. Revolutions have been far more likely when the military itself was undermined from within and turned into the personal machine of a particular despot; obvious examples are provided by Batista in Cuba, Somoza in Nicaragua and (in the early part of the century) Porfirio Díaz in Mexico. Yet repression, while certainly a part of the explanation, is by no means the whole story. South American politics has almost never been as violent as pre-war Spain or post-war Greece – let alone Nazi Germany or the USSR under Stalin. It may well be precisely that the personalism, flexibility and plasticity of South American political institutions, combined with the coherence of power elites, has usually proved an effective barrier against social revolution. Certainly social revolutions rarely if ever occur under even partially democratic systems.

Unfortunately this flexible institutional structure has exerted a cost both in terms of economic efficiency and social policy – which together make up most definitions of development. Public resources are distributed mainly to those willing to push hardest for them – rather than according to any principle of universal entitlement. Public policy in many ways tends to reinforce inequality. Huge amounts of money have, for example, been spent in many countries on subsidizing the price of petrol – although there is clear statistical evidence that this is overwhelmingly a subsidy to the middle class.

The relationship between political institutions and economic progress is a large theme and it remains to be seen whether the idea, currently fashionable in Latin America as elsewhere, of returning to market liberalism and limiting the role of the state will live up to its current promise. It may well be that rolling back the frontiers of the Latin American state will prove even more effective, in terms of its economic consequences, than similar policies in other parts of the world because the gap in efficiency between public and private sectors is particularly great.

In sum, therefore, the debate between liberal optimism and the pessimism of traditionalist conservatives is in a sense being re-run at the beginning of the 1990s. It is true that communist revolution seems less of a threat (or a hope) than ever before, more because of changes within communism than because of any specifically Latin American developments. There is also far less enthusiasm – both among Latin Americans and influential foreigners – for authoritarian rule in any form. On the other hand, the threat of lawlessness in its various guises (for example violence associated with the narcotics traffic) has increased. Although Latin America has changed very considerably since the 1960s, therefore, the central question informing the 'politics of development' has changed far less. Are the democratic leaderships that hold power in most Latin American countries capable of making the very difficult policy choices that will be necessary if the region is to recover its economic balance and meet pressing social demands? And what are the appropriate policy choices to bring this about?

LATIN AMERICA AND THE EXTERNAL ENVIRONMENT

Some of the most salient issues here relate to what might be called the international economic relationships of the region. Latin American intellectuals have always been keenly aware of these – possibly even to the point of exaggerating their importance. An important current of opinion within Latin America has been sceptical of, if not hostile towards, excessive foreign influence. It has resented 'big stick' US diplomacy (which has certainly been evident on occasion), and felt that commercial relationships between Latin American countries and the developed world have been unequally in the interests of the latter. To this is sometimes added a cultural disdain which, while now on the decline, may be summed up as an attitude toward the United States that 'you may have the strongest economy, but we have the more artistic sensibilities'. (It is, incidentally, true that educated Latin Americans tend to take cultural and artistic concerns far more seriously than do their opposite numbers in Britain or the United States.) Prior to 1945 this attitude of insularity (as aspiration, not as fact) was mainly to be found among the region's conservatives. Subsequently, perhaps in reaction to the world hegemony enjoyed by the capitalist USA, it came to be found mostly on the left.

An early landmark in this evolution is to be found in the work of Raúl Prebisch. Although fairly conservative in his politics, Prebisch became concerned that the most advanced Latin American countries were seeing the benefits of their raw material exports disproportionately enjoyed by the developed country importers of these products. The 'terms of trade' issue, which Prebisch raised, has generated a huge literature and relatively few firm conclusions. There is some suggestion that he based his generalizations on the possibly untypical period of the Great Depression and Second World War. However, many Latin American policy makers found his arguments convincing and tended to de-emphasize exports in favour of stimulating domestic industrialization through import controls and public sector subsidies.

There is a vast literature on import-substituting industrialization (ISI) which is beyond the scope of this discussion. It is clear that at least some Latin American countries enjoyed a relatively rapid growth of manufacturing during 1950–70 but that the distortions introduced by ISI became increasingly apparent as time went on. By 1970 it was clear that Latin America had de-emphasized exports to the point of losing a significant part of its share in world trade, and that this de-emphasis involved not only raw material and mineral exports but also those manufactured and other 'non-traditional' exports which the Asian NICs were increasing so successfully. Development capital, instead of being earned by dynamic exports, was raised by attracting, first, multinational corporations and, later, international loans, on terms which were not obviously advantageous to Latin Americans.

The difficulties facing ISI (particularly its tendency to generate inflationary and balance-of-payments crises) had the effect of polarizing academic debate within Latin America. According to one perspective, ISI can be seen as a halfway house between separation from and integration with the imperatives of international markets. Imports of manufactured goods were discouraged, but opportunities were held out to foreign companies either to manufacture locally or to provide local economies with the necessary means to do so. Much the same could be said within the oil and mineral sector, where the trend of policy was to nationalize production but to continue to rely on international sources of finance and technology.

From around the mid-1960s, arguments of two kinds came to be heard. On the one side were those who believed that attempts to use state controls to control liberal capitalism were likely to fail. Consequently it was argued that policy should move towards import liberalization, limiting the role of the public sector and ensuring that public-sector prices reflected real costs. There was a brief and half-abandoned market experiment under Castello Branco in Brazil

(1964–7) and another one under Juan Carlos Ongania in Argentina (1966–70), but the real thrust of these economic liberal policies could be seen most clearly under Augusto Pinochet in Chile after 1973. All of these governments, however, were dictatorships – a point not lost on left-wing critics of free-market policies.

On the other side were those who believed that it was necessary to achieve a far more decisive break with international markets. Policy should be 'anti-imperialist' and, to the extent that political reality permitted, socialist. The dependency paradigm, which began to be elaborated around the mid-1960s and was virtual orthodoxy on the left a decade later, was consistently hostile to international markets and the governments of the rich democracies – particularly the United States government. The government that many dependency writers most admired was Castro's Cuba.

It now appears that dependency writers were far too optimistic about the degree of material progress (to say nothing of political democracy) that could be expected from a policy of autarkic socialism. Castro's Cuba is now generally seen in Latin America as an example of what to avoid, rather than (as it often was a generation ago) what to emulate. Moreover, with the increased public recognition (post-Gorbachev) of the drastic shortcomings of East European-style state socialism, the Latin American left needed to embark on a serious process of rethinking. This is still going on.

One issue which might be considered 'left-wing' (though not everybody would see it as such) is that of greater Latin American integration. There have certainly been moves towards closer diplomatic relations, but the real need is for closer economic ties. Few Latin American countries trade much with each other, while the banks have retained an ability during the whole process of debt renegotiation to 'divide and rule' by dealing separately with each country.

Meanwhile the debt crisis has further encouraged a very necessary degree of economic rethinking on the right. Prior to about 1980, most Latin American conservatives identified the key policy requirement as being to maintain tight (fiscal and political) control at home in order to encourage the inflow of finance from abroad. In one respect, of course, this policy was brilliantly successful. Latin America did attract a huge inflow of foreign lending during the 1970s. Unfortunately this did not seriously benefit Latin American economies and the debt crisis which followed did very great damage to the whole region.

It may well be that the most appropriate response to this setback would be for Latin American states to seek to reorganize themselves (and their economies) along the lines which have evidently proved helpful for the development of several Asian countries. Instead of the false polarity of 'states versus markets', the important task may be to find a way of organizing co-operation between the two in order to stimulate exports, develop local capacities and improve the distribution of income.

A BRIEF CONCLUSION

It is ironic and somewhat unfortunate that the civilian governments which came to power in Latin America during the 1980s were left, in most cases, with the extremely difficult task of reducing the damage created by their authoritarian predecessors. It says something that these civilian governments have survived and, in most cases, performed well under some very difficult circumstances. Nevertheless, Latin America as a whole has not yet recovered from the economic setbacks of the early 1980s, although there are signs that some countries may now be beginning to do so. In some countries, moreover, there is still a problem of civil conflict although it may well be that the worst of the violence in Central America is now over.

It is very difficult to resolve social and political problems of any kind at a time of acute economic crisis. These may appear somewhat less formidable once economic growth resumes. However, we have seen that Latin American political systems remain heavily personalized, clientelistic and difficult to manage; it may be that success in public policy terms is likely to require some degree of rethinking on purely constitutional matters. In the last decade many countries have achieved the important task of replacing authoritarian with democratic rule; it remains to be considered how these systems can be further adapted to deal with the challenges of the next decade.

BIBLIOGRAPHY

Latin America is a difficult field to cover partly because of the sheer pace of political change and partly also because, quite understandably, many scholars prefer to concentrate on one or two countries. The best general introductory textbook is that of T. Skidmore and P. Smith, *Modern Latin America* (Oxford: Oxford University Press; various editions), but there is something to be said for starting off with more challenging literature.

Controversies surrounding the emergence and behaviour of military governments in South America are well covered in D. Coller (ed.), *The New Authoritarianism in Latin America* (Princeton: Princeton University Press, 1979) and J. Linz and A. Stepan (eds), *The Breakdown of Democratic Regimes; Latin America* (Baltimore: Johns Hopkins University Press, 1978). More recent, on the transition from military to civilian government, is G. O'Donnell, P. Schmitter and L. Whitehead (eds), *The Transition to Democracy in Latin America* (Washington, DC: Woodrow Wilson Institute, 1988). G. Philip, *The Military in South American Politics* (London: Croom Helm, 1985) is in the nature of a general survey. An outstanding account of the Brazilian government is T. Skidmore, *The Politics of Military Rule in Brazil 1964–85* (Oxford: Oxford University Press, 1989).

General studies of Latin American policy making were frequent enough in the 1960s. Among the best are C. Anderson, *The Politics of Economic Change in Latin America* (Princeton: Van Nostrand, 1967) and various works of A. Hirschman, many of which are compiled in his *Essays in Trespassing* (Cambridge: Cambridge University Press, 1981). More recent writing has tended to concentrate more on macroeconomic policy making and the debt issue. Here there is P. Kuczynski, *Latin American Debt* (Baltimore: Johns Hopkins University Press, 1988), R. Thorp and L. Whitehead (eds), *Latin America and the Adjustment Crisis* (London: Macmillan, 1986) and E. Duran (ed) *Latin America and the World Recession* (London: Royal Institute of International Affairs, 1985).

Institutional studies of democratic Latin America are still relatively few although more are likely soon. On Mexico there is G. Philip, *The Presidency in Mexican Politics* (London: Macmillan, 1991). On the continuing influence of the military in Brazil see A. Stepan, *Rethinking Military Politics* (Princeton: Princeton University Press, 1988).

Conversely the literature on political-economy questions is vast. The problem is to keep it to manageable proportions. The Prebisch thesis can be approached through J. Love, 'Raul Prebisch and the origins of the doctrine of unequal exchange' *Latin American Research Review* 15 (3): 45–73 (November 1980). I discuss dependency theory more fully in G. Philip, 'The political economy of development', *Political Studies* 38: 485–302 (September 1990). An exposition of some key arguments of the New Right can be found in T. Congdon, *Economic Liberalism in the Southern Cone of South America* (London: Trade Policy Research Centre, 1986).

77

EASTERN EUROPE

ZORAN ZIC

The sweeping changes in Eastern Europe in the autumn of 1989 opened up many bright prospects for this region and for Europe as a whole. It is becoming clear that the East European revolution of 1989, as the events of that year were soon named by the media, amount to nothing less than a complete turnaround and remaking of the post-war European order. The centrepiece of that order had been the division of Europe and Germany between the two adversarial alliances based on antagonistic ideological beliefs and political systems. The bipolar division of Europe provided the continent with forty-five years of stability and peace, one of the longest periods in European history without a major war, but exposed it to unprecedented levels of ideologically based animosity and military confrontation, severing many traditional routes of cultural communication and economic exchange.

The events of 1989 in Eastern Europe could therefore prove to be among the most dramatic developments in the modern history of the European continent, creating the conditions for the political harmonization and closer economic co-operation or integration in accordance with the desires of the founders of the European movement. The potential for bringing back some of the old rivalries that led to the outbreak of two world wars on the European continent in the twentieth century also exists, especially given the fact that Central Europe will again be dominated by a united and economically and politically assertive Germany. Traditional, ethnically based, antagonisms of Eastern Europe could also act as a major unsettling factor in the creation of the new Europe.

In their other aspect the changes in Eastern Europe can also have a broad historical impact because they spell out the demise of communism as one of the leading ideologies and political systems of the nineteenth and twentieth centuries. As a combination of misapplied theoretical utopianism, practical authoritarianism and a secular belief system, communism failed to deliver on its promises and did not prove to be a functional and productive system that can contribute to the increased well-being and prosperity of nations. Both its introduction and its demise in Eastern Europe were conditioned by the evolution of Russia/the Soviet Union and by the Soviet security and foreign policy interests and have to be analysed in that light. The Soviet Union, which as a hegemonic power in post-Second World War Europe sponsored the communist experiment in Eastern Europe, has to be credited at the same time for allowing and even encouraging its end once it realized that not only did it not enhance the Soviet best interests but it also involved increasingly unsustainable burdens for the Soviet state and economy. This, on the other hand, speeded up the process of political change in the Soviet Union, contributing to the ultimate abandoning of both Stalinist and communist legacies and, indirectly, even to the disintegration of the Soviet Union.

Although the term revolution has been almost universally accepted for the East European upheaval of 1989, the processes underway are essentially a restoration of democracy from communism as a type of modern authoritarianism; thus the term transition would appear to be better suited. Regardless of whether they came about as a result of the self-initiated moves of the East European communist regimes or whether they were forced on them through popular protest, or even an armed *coup* (as in Romania), the changes in Eastern Europe are a gradual process of restoration of the democratic order, 'a controlled transformation of illiberal states into liberal ones' (Dahrendorf 1990: 134).

In the post-Second World War period, the term Eastern Europe was understood to refer to the communist-dominated countries of East Central Europe. Most often the term implied the countries of this region, members of the Soviet bloc (of the Warsaw Treaty Organization (WTO) and the Council for Mutual Economic Assistance (CMEA)) – Poland, the German Democratic Republic (GDR), Czechoslovakia, Hungary, Romania and Bulgaria. Often, but not always, the term also referred to Yugoslavia and Albania, the countries that initially belonged to the Soviet bloc but have since abandoned it (Yugoslavia, in 1948, and Albania, practically in 1961 and formally in 1968), although preserving their own types of communist systems.

The proper geographical term for the region outlined would more likely be East Central (or Central East) Europe (Halecki 1952: 4–5; Rothschild 1989: ix). The term Eastern Europe, denoting essentially East Central Europe, was introduced during the Cold War, reflecting the division of Europe between the East and the West. It has to be understood, therefore, as a political or politicized term that carries with it in the first place the notion of East Central Europe ruled by the communist parties and part of the bipolar world under the domination of the Soviet Union (with the exception of Yugoslavia and Albania). With the dismantling of the bloc barriers it is possible that the term

East Central Europe (as well as Central Europe) will once again be more widely used.

During the Second World War, Soviet demands regarding Eastern Europe were limited to the formation of 'friendly regimes' in the region which would prevent any possibility of future aggression on Soviet territory coming from or across Eastern Europe. As such, these demands were acceptable to the Western allies. With the intensification of Cold War hostilities, with the rising distrust and suspiciousness between the former allies, Soviet demands escalated to a requirement of a fully-fledged sphere of interest. Given the character of the Soviet political system and ideology, especially during Stalin's rule, it should be understandable that, under worsening conditions in world politics, Soviet designs to create a security buffer zone could not be limited just to the establishment of 'friendly regimes' in Eastern Europe, which would pledge non-aggressive foreign policies toward the Soviet Union but would retain a full measure of internal political autonomy. According to the then prevailing Soviet frame of mind, the East European regimes could not be trusted in fulfilling a promise to conduct non-aggressive policies towards the Soviet Union. The Soviet Union had to make sure that they were effectively prevented in doing so by imposing a full Soviet control. This necessitated the introduction of the Soviet model of political system based on and run by the communist parties unquestionably loyal to the Soviet party. This procedure again, according to the Soviet experience, would not be limited just to politics; it had to entail every sphere of social and cultural life (Rothschild 1989: 78).

The creation of the so-called people's democracies in Eastern Europe in the years 1945–8 did not mean, therefore, the establishment of a new specific political order – one that supposedly, according to the Soviet theoreticians, would be in between the bourgeois democracies and Soviet socialism as a higher form of political system. In practice, it meant the remoulding of the East European societies and their politics into faithful replicas of the Soviet model and under total Soviet control. It amounted to a Sovietization and satellization of Eastern Europe which was carried out through the main vehicles of the political authority and repression in the Soviet Union – the Communist Party, the secret police and the army. In East European countries this process was implemented at two distinct levels: first through the domestic communist parties and their agencies, and second through the Soviet ones – acting as sponsors, supervisors and, sometimes, direct enforcers.

A question often asked in the analyses of the Soviet bloc (as the Soviet quasi-alliance in Eastern Europe came to be called) is whether its establishment and preservation was motivated on the Soviet side primarily by security concerns or by political and ideological reasons of maintaining the same type of system and ideologies in Eastern Europe as a factor of support and prestige. Judging by the origins of the Soviet hegemony in Eastern Europe, it was security interests that initiated the whole undertaking, although later the two dimensions of the East European protective axis became more narrowly interconnected and mutually interdependent. The domestic systems and ideologies, having over time become a factor of prestige, always appeared instrumental in keeping the security network in place and ensuring the loyalty of the East European governments and East European armies.

The successive crises that shook Eastern Europe after the imposition of Soviet domination, usually starting with economic grievances, escalating to demands for change in the political and economic system and tending to evolve towards demands for the abandonment of the Soviet bloc, only reinforced Soviet suspicions and fears. From the East European point of view it could be argued, in turn, that it was exactly because of the stringent character of imposed Soviet control, which denied any amount of real political autonomy to East Europeans, that crises and rebellions occurred. Based on the rigid rules of the game that the Soviet Union imposed in Eastern Europe, it was only through the rejection of any control whatsoever, including the areas of foreign policy and security, that the East European countries could aspire to any degree of freedom and autonomy. The total denial of freedom led to attempts at a complete rejection of control (most notable in the Hungarian uprising of 1956). Even if the attempts at reform had more limited goals, they were apt to be read by the Soviet Union as being a result of a more far-reaching intention to undermine the bloc and leave it. This was shown on several occasions and especially in Czechoslovakia in 1968 when the officially proclaimed aims in both domestic policy and foreign affairs, more so in the latter, were quite limited in character; the Soviets nevertheless suspected the worst.

It was only with Gorbachev's 'new thinking' that the basic Soviet approach to Eastern Europe outlined above was changed. The critical assumption that no Soviet leadership prior to Gorbachev's wanted to accept was introduced – namely, that there can be a realistic hope that sufficient security arrangements can be made with domestically free and even non-communist authorities in Eastern European countries only when they are given full autonomy and freedom to shape their political and economic systems as they wish. Concomitant with this was a realization by Soviet leaders, although by no means by all in the Soviet establishment, that the high cost the Soviet Union had to pay economically, militarily and politically in imposing and reinforcing its control in Eastern Europe did not pay off any more. The background to this psychological evolution had been furnished by the dismal performance of the Soviet communist concept both in the Soviet Union and in Eastern Europe. This finally induced the Soviet leadership to try to change it radically and in the process revise the basic conceptions of the country's security and, consequently, its foreign policy, and, more generally, political and developmental priorities.

This realization, however, did not come easily. It was the result of almost half a century of trial and error in attempts to maintain and reimpose, if necessary by force, the tight Soviet system of regional hegemony against East European attempts to reshape and adjust it, or occasionally reject it.

After Mikhail Gorbachev took office in March 1985 there was no immediate or rapid change in Soviet policy in Eastern Europe. Two months later, the Warsaw Treaty was renewed for another period of thirty years. This appeared to be a sign of the willingness of the new Soviet leader to maintain the status quo. In reality it was more a reflection of a lack of consensus among the WTO member countries and within the Soviet leadership on whether the changes should be made and in what way. In 1984, a round of for the first time more or less open polemics on the quality of relations in the bloc was initiated, involving a number of countries. On one side the GDR, Hungary and Romania argued for more flexibility and autonomy in foreign policy and in intra-bloc relations, each for its own reasons. On the other, the Soviet Union, Bulgaria and Czechoslovakia resisted, in accordance with the limited sovereignty doctrine, stressing the importance of respect for the agreed-upon (in practice Soviet-imposed) foreign policy guidelines within the bloc (Dawisha 1988: 160–2). Some time into Gorbachev's tenure Soviet attitudes began to shift, first being polarized themselves and subsequently, with Gorbachev's personal contribution, assuming the 'liberal' attitude and carrying it considerably farther than the East European countries initially dared to hope.

This line of policy led to the formulation of the 'common European home' concept, although it remained for some time a rather vague idea, and was treated therefore by the West as just another Soviet propaganda campaign. Ultimately, after some hesitation, with very cautious and gradual shifts in the tone of official pronouncements, the Soviet Union announced in the autumn of 1989, the time at which the communist regimes of Eastern Europe were already being overturned, that it was abandoning the Brezhnev doctrine. Shortly afterwards (in December 1990) came the Soviet and WTO collective apologies for the 1968 intervention in Czechoslovakia as a wrong and damaging move. Pledges by the WTO that there would be no future interference in the internal affairs of East European countries and that they would be free to pursue the policies of their own choice had already been made earlier (in July 1989).

Changing Soviet attitudes in and about Eastern Europe in the period 1985–9 provided a favourable background for democratic experiments and liberalizing trends in the region. However, not all the communist regimes in Eastern Europe decided to avail themselves of the newly found opportunities. Some of them still tried to resist the changes. As before (in the 1950s), it was obvious that the new Soviet leniency might lead to convulsions and perhaps serious social and political crises that could eventually tempt the Soviet Union, and especially its military, to try to restore order and protect the integrity of the Soviet sphere of interests by force. That these were not vain speculations was proved more recently in the open criticisms of Soviet policies and accusations against Gorbachev for 'losing Eastern Europe' by Party hardliners and high-ranking military officers at the founding congress of the Russian Communist Party and at the 28th congress of the Communist Party of the Soviet Union (CPSU) (June–July 1990).

The East European communist regimes were therefore slow, and some of them even recalcitrant, in responding to the expanding limits of freedom and implicit calls for innovation and reform coming from Moscow.

One exception to this attitude has been Poland. Polish society has to be credited for its remarkable record of a sustained and persistent resistance to both the communist system and Soviet domination. Despite the dire experience in the hands of both German and Soviet oppressors in the twentieth century, Poland has shown a resilience and craving for independence. It has been the only East European country to experience several severe crises during the period of communist rule (1956, 1970, 1976 and 1980–1) but also has been the only one that managed to avoid Soviet military intervention on these occasions through an exceptional demonstration of national unity despite bitter domestic political confrontations.

Poland is also the country where the process of unravelling the communist system and Soviet hegemony in Eastern Europe started. During the 1980–1 crisis, Solidarity, as a new and unique political organization – a combination of the independent trade unions and a massive anti-communist and national movement, almost completely eclipsed the power and authority of the Polish United Workers' Party (PUWP). The effects of this first *de facto* pluralism and sharing of power in Eastern Europe were only deferred by the imposition of martial law in December 1981, but the previous system and the PUWP's influence and control over the society could not be restored. The Polish army and party bureaucrats showed a novel sense of realism by relegalizing Solidarity in January 1989 and entering round-table negotiations with its representatives.

Through the accords that resulted from the round-table talks in April 1989 and were successfully tested in the partly free multi-party elections in June 1989, Poland became the first country in Eastern Europe and the first communist-ruled country to embark on the road of decommunization. What happened in practice in the period from August 1980 to December 1981 was thus affirmed and legalized eight years later. Still, when it came to the implementation of the election results that at the very start undermined the balance of the carefully crafted round-table accords (Solidarity won all the 35 per cent of the seats in the lower house of parliament that it was allowed to contest, and all but one of the 100 seats in the recreated Senate that were open for contest), the Communists balked at the possibility of a Solidarity-dominated government and tried to block the process of transition. At that crucial moment in August 1989 it was the Soviet Union and Mikhail Gorbachev personally who intervened, this time in favour of democratization and the abandonment of the one-party communist system, thus opening the door for the ensuing chain reaction of liberalization in other East European countries.

Subsequently, the timing of full democratization in Poland lagged somewhat behind that of most other East European countries. Solidarity leader Lech Walesa was elected the first non-communist president of Poland in December 1990. The first fully free elections in Poland, held in October 1991, produced a fragmented parliament without a clear majority, setting the stage for a rather unstable political life. A check on this may be the fact that Poland adopted a rather authoritative presidential system, the only East European country (aside from some Yugoslav republics) to have done so. Starting from 1 January 1990, Poland introduced a very ambitious 'shock therapy' programme of transition to a market economy. The programme, which made Poland a pioneer in economic transition in Eastern Europe, achieved some notable results, such as improving the supply side of the economy and lowering the inflation from 2,000 to just 40 per cent. Accompanying social and economic strains, especially unemployment, were not eliminated, however, and the state-owned sector of the economy could not be transformed as quickly as desired.

Aside from Poland, Hungary was the only East European country that experimented with reforms during the 1980s, relaunching some of the programmes it was forced to abandon in the previous decade because of Soviet pressure (Brown 1988: 210–18; Goldman 1987: 155–8), and developing them further. In 1988, after the removal of the old-time communist leader Janos Kadar, the pace of the reforms quickened, spreading from the areas of economy and foreign policy to the crucial spheres of the political system. The rising reformist majority within the Hungarian communist party (Hungarian Socialist Workers' Party) set the grounds for the evolution towards multi-party democracy, introduced the necessary constitutional and legislative changes, authorized the reassessment of the 1956 crisis which was now proclaimed a popular uprising, and opened up a dialogue with opposition parties and groups. Finally, the party decided to reconstitute and rename itself (as the Hungarian Socialist Party) in October 1989. In the first free multi-party elections, held in March–April 1990, the centre-right Hungarian Democratic Forum won, ousting the reformed communists from power.

Throughout the 1980s and prior to the dramatic change that overthrew the dogmatic communist leaderships in the GDR, Bulgaria, Czechoslovakia and Romania in October, November and December 1989, only Poland and Hungary could qualify for the label 'liberal'. The distinction between the liberal and conservative communist regimes, according to the character of the domestic policies, did not, however, coincide with a similar distinction in the area of foreign policy. Here, some of the most conservative regimes, such as the GDR or Romania, advocated 'liberal' views, hoping to defend old-style communist authoritarianism at home through a greater degree of autonomy in foreign policy. On the eve of the radical change in Eastern Europe, independence in foreign policy had thus paradoxically become the means of last resort to some communist establishments in defending their entrenched positions and withstanding pressures to reform coming from the Soviet Union. Some regimes (the GDR and Romania) openly rejected and condemned the Soviet-style reforms, while others (Czechoslovakia and Bulgaria) adopted a wait-and-see attitude, hoping that perhaps the Soviet conservatives could solve their problems by defeating Gorbachev and ending Soviet reform.

In this situation of polarization within the bloc, Hungary played a crucial role in accelerating the pace of change and enabling the process of democratization to expand further and engulf all of Eastern Europe. By deciding to allow the East German asylum-seeking tourists to emigrate to West Germany in September 1989, Hungary contributed to new waves of emigration that kept adding pressure on the East German regime to democratize. Massive anti-regime protests followed in October and November 1989. Left this time without effective Soviet military support for the defence of the regime, the East German communist elite had to bow to popular pressure by making one concession after another. The major one was to open the borders to West Germany and allow free movement of people, including free emigration. This included the symbolic 'downfall' of the Berlin Wall (on 9 November 1989), erected in 1961 with the purpose of preventing the constant drain of population from East to West Germany. In the process, the East German party (Socialist Unity Party of Germany – SED) purged itself of old leaders, reformed itself and agreed to the multi-party elections held in the spring of 1990 and to the sharing of power with the opposition parties in the meantime. The victory of the Christian Democratic Union (a counterpart of the ruling party in the Federal Republic of Germany) in the first free elections (February 1990) paved the way for a quick unification which came into effect on 3 October 1990. Despite the vigour of the West German economy the difficulties of absorbing the GDR and remodelling and resuscitating its economy proved a challenging task, and its cost turned out to be higher than expected (over US $70 billion). The process of unification was not free of political and social strains, or of some second thoughts in both parts of Germany. Certain adverse effects, especially in the former GDR, resulting from economic difficulties and clashes of social values, will probably continue to be felt for a long time to come.

In Czechoslovakia, the regime was likewise overturned by rising popular pressure and the basic elements of transition were achieved in an even shorter period of time, in November and December 1989, starting with the overthrow of the top Communist Party and state leaders and the consolidation of the umbrella opposition movement Civic Forum, formed from the former dissident groups. The Civic Forum forced the Communist Party to share power and soon emerged as the leading political force in the country. It has to be recognized that in both the GDR and Czechoslovakia, aside from the impact of the Polish and Hungarian developments and the new situation created in the bloc by innovative Soviet policies, the Soviet Union played a crucial role in initiating the democratic process. The Soviet Union did so not only by adhering to the earlier-announced policies of non-interference but also, as some indications tend to confirm, by demanding that the East German and Czechoslovak leaderships allow the democratization and reform to unfold freely and without obstruction. Although the process of transition in Czechoslovakia was, together with that in Hungary, perhaps the most orderly and peaceful in Eastern Europe, with the first free elections (held in April 1990) confirming a clear and total break with the communist past, the ethnic tensions, especially in the form of the autonomist and even secessionist demands by some parties and groups in Slovakia, have continued to pose problems for the new democracy. As a result, Czechoslovakia was officially renamed the Czech and Slovak Federative Republic (CSFR). The final agreement on its future constitutional form is still pending. It is possible that the issue of whether Czechoslovakia will remain a unified, federated state or disintegrate into completely independent Czech and Slovak states will have to be determined in a referendum.

The transition in Bulgaria was started by the reformist faction in the Bulgarian Communist party that managed to oust the long-time Bulgarian leader Todor Zhivkov and his main supporters in November 1989, initiating the process of evolution towards multi-party democracy and a market economy. At the later stages of this evolution the reformed Bulgarian Communist Party had to face further challenge from the emerging opposition parties. Its victory in the first free elections in June 1990 only contributed to the rising tensions and resulted in a protracted stand-off with the leading opposition bloc (Union of Democratic Forces (UDF)), during which the urgent social and economic needs of the country could not be properly addressed. This situation was only gradually changed, first by the victory of the UDF candidate Zhelyu Zhelyev in presidential elections (August 1990), and finally by a narrow UDF victory in the new parliamentary elections (October 1991), opening the way for speedier and more thorough changes of the system.

In Romania, events took a different turn and the personal dictatorship of Nicolae Ceauşescu was swept away within a few days of violent revolution in December 1989, with the army, backed by popular support, switching to the side of the rebels and fighting and defeating the secret police units loyal to the dictator. The first multi-party elections in May 1990 were won by the National Salvation Front (NSF), a broad political organization led by the reformed communists opposed to the Ceauşescu dictatorship, which had established the interim government following the downfall of the Ceauşescu regime. In time there was a growing disillusionment with the NSF government, and charges that it had 'stolen' and betrayed the revolution of December 1989, monopolizing power and opposing a full democratization, were becoming more assertive. After a period of continued political tensions, social unrest, mass protests and violent clashes, the NSF gave in to the demands of the opposition parties, appointing a new government in the autumn of 1991 and promising more representative parliamentary elections.

The processes of political change in the Eastern bloc affected Yugoslavia as well, although this country, having been outside the bloc since 1948, had evolved specific political, economic and federal systems of its own. Yugoslavia therefore faced some specific problems not found elsewhere in Eastern Europe. Nevertheless, a great many of the political, economic and social difficulties that Yugoslavia experienced in the 1980s were similar or common to those of other East European countries. While the federal government braced itself towards the end of 1989 finally to adopt resolute measures of economic reform, and the ruling League of Communists decided in principle to give up its monopoly of power in January 1990, the differences among the various federal units and animosities between several of the country's nationalities threatened both the reforms and the very integrity of the federal state. The first multi-party elections were held in all six Yugoslav republics during 1990. In four (Slovenia, Croatia, Bosnia-Herzegovina and Macedonia), the elections brought to power, or turned into dominant political actors, non-communist parties or party coalitions. In the remaining two republics (Serbia and Montenegro), communists, or reformed communists, won the elections. All winning parties, regardless of their political differences and in varying degrees and forms, espoused nationalism, which soon emerged as the most destructive political agent and a threat to an orderly transition into a post-communist society. The resurgence of nationalism in Yugoslavia was compounded by a lack of agreement between the federal units and nationalities on the make-up of the future state. Slovenia and Croatia, the two westernmost and economically most developed republics, favoured a loose confederation or, rather, a union of sovereign states; Serbia, the most populous and traditionally politically dominant republic, and Montenegro, ethnically close to Serbia, gave preference to a strong, centralized federation, which would automatically guarantee Serbia a dominant role; the two remaining republics, Bosnia-Herzegovina and Macedonia, tried to argue for a compromise, opting for a confederation. Failure to achieve agreement, with the ever more assertive policies on the part of Serbia bent on preserving a strengthened federation and satisfying its national goals of keeping all ethnic Serbs in one state, led Slovenia and Croatia formally to declare full independence in June 1991. (Macedonia followed suit in September and Bosnia-Herzegovina in December 1991.)

The aftermath of Slovenia's and Croatia's declarations of independence saw the outbreak of a fully-fledged civil and ethnic war in which a special role was played by the Yugoslav Federal Army. Acting initially as a protector of the integrity of the federal Yugoslav state, the army, composed in the majority of ethnic Serbs, was increasingly siding with Serbia and fighting for the achievement of Serbia's national goals. The conflict between the army and Slovenia ended, in a relatively short period of time in early July 1991, with the army agreeing to pull out its troops from the republic.

The war that started after that in Croatia has been fought on a much greater scale, between the federal army and local Serb militias, on one side, and the Croatian army and militias, on the other. It dragged on past the end of 1991, despite the repeated efforts of the Conference on European Security and Co-operation (CSCE), the European Community (EC) and the United Nations (UN) to mediate between the warring parties and achieve a cease-fire agreement as a prelude to a more lasting political solution. Fourteen cease-fire agreements negotiated by the European Community were subsequently violated. The war resulted in several thousands of killings or disappearances, many more wounded persons and more than half a million Serb and Croat refugees.

With the joint decision of the EC (in December 1991) to recognize Slovenia and Croatia, and possibly Bosnia-Herzegovina and Macedonia, in early 1992, and Serbia's gradual takeover of the remains of the federal government and preparations to create a new Serbian dominated rump federation, the disintegration of Yugoslavia seems virtually assured. Important differences on territorial issues (with Serbia wanting to incorporate areas with a Serb majority and/or areas with a mixed population that were seized by the federal army or local Serb militias in the republics of Croatia and Bosnia-Herzegovina, and those republics stiffly opposed to such a scenario) and on the final issue of the constitutional form of the Yugoslav successor state(s) have to be resolved.

The war in Yugoslavia as the first and only war in Europe after the end of the Second World War spells out a grave warning on the perils of the post-communist transition in multi-ethnic states, where the explosion of nationalism and ethnic conflicts are almost inevitable after decades of suppression of national feelings under communism.

Albania, as the most isolated and most repressive East European country for years, with a self-styled dogmatic version of communism, was the last to join the process of democratization. After a series of upheavals, violent protests and clashes, with several thousands of Albanians fleeing abroad or attempting to do so, the first multi-party elections were finally held in April 1991. Albanian communists managed to win the elections amid accusations of violations and intimidation of voters. As the socially and economically most backward European country, Albania will certainly face serious difficulties on its road to democracy and a market economy, with the developments of 1991 marking only the very beginning of this process.

The year of 1989, especially the last three months, marked the crucial change by which the communist regimes and political systems that had been established in Eastern Europe were either radically self-reformed or overthrown and replaced by interim coalition governments. This was, however, only the beginning of the democratic transition. The formidable tasks of reforming both the political and economic systems still awaited all these countries and their new governments. In order for this to be possible, the immediate requirement was to stabilize the new democracies by providing them with the political and legal foundation through elections for new parliaments and adoption of new constitutions and other legal acts. At the same time, there had also to be a gradual but resolute dismantling of the very elaborate and complex structure of power built over decades by the communist parties – their network at the work-place that extended to government agencies at all levels, including the secret police and the army, as well as the dissolution of the secret police itself as the main mechanism of control and repression developed by the communist parties.

By the end of 1991, the process of systemic transition in Eastern Europe had progressed considerably, reaching new levels of consolidation, assuring the new democracies much better prospects and making the transition practically irreversible. In all Eastern European countries, multi-party elections had been held, new pluralistic parliaments elected, and new governments and heads of state, reflecting the changed domestic balance of forces, appointed or elected.

The new political landscape of Eastern Europe, aside from resting on the crucial concept of pluralism, offered a variety of solutions and political orientations and preferences. Nevertheless, it is possible to discern a number of common and typical political and social trends and features in the emerging East European democracies. In addition, the East European developments of 1989–1991 pose a variety of practical and theoretical problems and offer new experiences in carrying through and studying the processes of democratic transition.

This is the first time that there has been a transition to democracy from the communist system, made possible by favourable external circumstances (adoption of a consenting attitude on the part of the Soviet Union). The changes in Eastern Europe were initiated either by the ruling communist parties, or by their majority reformist factions (Hungary, Bulgaria, Yugoslavia's republics and Albania), or by peaceful popular and opposition group pressures (Poland, the GDR and Czechoslovakia). Only Romania experienced violent conflict and an armed *coup d'état* because of the unwillingness of Ceauşescu's regime to give in to popular demands.

In the interim period between the overthrow of former leaderships and the conduct of free elections, governmental affairs were managed either by coalitions of the former ruling communist parties and the opposition groups and parties (specifically in Poland, the GDR, Czechoslovakia and Romania) or by the reformed communist parties alone (Hungary, Bulgaria, Yugoslavia's republics and Albania). In most cases the transition during this period was reasonably smooth and the elections conducted properly and fairly. Only in Romania, Albania and, to a lesser degree, Bulgaria, have there been instances of violations of electoral procedures favouring the ruling parties.

The scope and pace of political and economic change differ from country to country. The processes in some countries started earlier, were smoother and accomplished more. The causes of the variations in this respect can be found in the different position of the ruling communist parties in individual East European countries, and in the quality of the legitimacy (or a lack thereof) they enjoyed. In the countries in which the legitimacy of the communist regimes has been precarious or non-existent and perceived as being imposed by the Soviet power, and also in the countries that experienced at some point a military intervention or a serious threat of intervention or another critical upheaval, the regimes were ousted swiftly once conditions became favourable, regardless of whether the transition was initiated by the ruling parties or forced on them (i.e. Poland, the GDR, Czechoslovakia and Hungary). In the countries where the regimes were authentic and independent (Yugoslavia and Albania), or have over time acquired a degree of independence (Romania), the ruling power structures were more resistant to change or accepted the democratization at a later date (although this is partly contradicted by the cases of Slovenia and Croatia).

Additional explanations can be sought in the traditions of political culture, distinguishing the north-western parts of Eastern Europe, which have enjoyed longer periods of Western political cultural influences and longer periods of parliamentary democracies, from south-east Europe, where the above-mentioned legacies of Western civilization were largely lacking. Many authors point also to a predominant confessional divide between the two sub-regions into the mainly Catholic–Lutheran north-west and the Orthodox–Muslim south-east as compounding the differences in the cultural heritage (Linz 1990: 145). Although these aspects can provide part of the explanation, one should refrain from generalizing when drawing conclusions because exceptions can be easily identified in each case and new turns of events can alter the picture dramatically.

The new East European political scene is still very much in flux. Predictably, as in every case of democratic transition or restoration, there is a variety of political parties, groups and movements whose political programmes differ in orientation as well as in scope. The classical left–right continuum of the political spectrum has been obscured under the communist system, and in some cases reversed (with conservative-rightist meaning dogmatic communist, and leftist referring to liberals and reformists with socialist or social democratic proclivities).

In a number of East European countries the transition has been championed and managed by broad umbrella political movements and organizations, incorporating many smaller groups and organizations, whose main commitment was the overthrow of the communist system and the rebuilding of democracy (Solidarity in Poland, Civic Forum and Public Against Violence in Czechoslovakia, as well as, in a way, National Salvation Front in Romania; a similar possibility of several opposition groups coalescing into a broader movement was offset in the GDR by the emergence of the counterparts of the leading West German parties). Such movements have organized as political parties and won elections, completing the first phase of transition. Some of them have already splintered into several parties along more traditional divisions on the left–right continuum.

The intelligentsia and, within it, the former dissidents in particular, have played a prominent role in the East European transition, with its representatives leading some of the most influential parties and movements and subsequently being elected or appointed to key functions in the new governments (as in Poland, the GDR, Czechoslovakia and Hungary) (Schopflin 1990: 6). In some East European countries there are signs of the new class cleavages in which the working class (and peasantry) increasingly oppose the government led by intellectuals (especially in Poland). In other countries (Romania and Bulgaria) the opposition parties initially expressing mainly the interests of the intelligentsia and the urban class have been defeated in elections by communist successor parties supported by the majority of mainly rural and working-class strata of the population. As a result, political polarization and social tensions have grown in some East European countries in the aftermath of elections, threatening the stability of the democratization process.

The left–right continuum has re-emerged in other East European countries that have held elections, in a yet incomplete way, with the victory going to the centre and centre-right parties (the GDR, Hungary, Slovenia and Croatia) or to the former communist parties (Bulgaria, Albania, Serbia and Montenegro). Some victorious as well as other parties have displayed varying degrees of nationalist rhetoric and goals.

In the wake of the political change in Eastern Europe many concerns have been raised about the possibility of the region falling back into ethnic animosities and being torn by the violent ethnic conflicts both between and within states (Geremek 1990: 130; Deak 1990: 53). Given the repressive character of the East European regimes as well as a tight regional system of control that the Soviet Union had imposed on its satellites, it should not come as a surprise that in the initial period of liberalization nationalist feelings strongly coloured both regional and domestic politics in most East European countries.

Latent or actual interstate and internal ethnic conflicts abound in Eastern Europe (some of the major ones in the first group being German–Polish, Czechoslovak–Hungarian, Hungarian–Romanian and Bulgarian–Yugoslav; the other group includes tensions and conflicts between the Czechs and Slovaks, between Hungarians and Romanians in Romania, between Bulgarians and Turks in Bulgaria, and those between several nationalities in Yugoslavia). If the foundations of the democratic process prove firm enough they could serve as the best guarantee that nationalism will gradually decline in importance and appeal and be marginalized as a politically significant factor. This would, however, require political wisdom and skill as well as a resolute commitment to the cause of democratization. In addition, a successful economic transition to productive market economies would be needed in order to assuage social tensions that can easily translate into ethnic animosities in an ethnically hetero-geneous and antagonized environment. In an alternative scenario, nationalism could become a major challenge to democratization and generate new forms of authoritarianism as it naturally tends towards non-pluralistic forms of political organization and expression (Geremek 1990: 130).

The developments in Yugoslavia, and the tensions in Czechoslovakia and between Rumanians and Hungarians in Romania underline such a bleak pros-pect. However, it may also prove that these conflicts, including the war in Yugoslavia, will be successfully contained and in the end peacefully resolved. Although many governments were reluctant to endorse requests for the full independence and realization of the right to self-determination of the parts of the former multi-ethnic communist states, fearing the derailment of the democratic process and threats to international security, the developments in Yugoslavia and in the Soviet Union seem to suggest that denial of the right to self-determination and the forcible preservation of the multi-ethnic com-munities, when there is no longer an overwhelming support for this, may hurt even more the interests of democracy and international security and produce more violence and destruction.

What makes the transition to democracy in Eastern Europe unique histori-cally is not only the fact that this is the first transition from communism to democracy but also that in addition to political transition there has to be an economic one – a transition from the centrally planned and state-ownership-based economies to market economies. Due to the character of communist systems and communist economies, the first impetus in the process of econ-omic transition has to be made in the sphere of politics so that the basic preconditions can be created for a complete overhaul of the economy. What

is known, and is more or less accepted by most new East European governments, is that the economic transition will of necessity involve many strains.
Some of the major tasks that all East European countries will carry through
include: decontrolling prices and abolishing state subsidies for a range of
products; allowing bankruptcies and layoffs; reforming the bank system;
creating a stock exchange market and making the national currencies convert-
ible.

At the same time, it is necessary to create new opportunities for private
initiative through appropriate political and legal reforms. In order to do this,
the bans and restrictions on private property have to be lifted, allowing for a
reprivatization of significant sectors of the economy. The immediate adverse
effects of this process must certainly be a rise in prices, growing inflation and
unemployment. Poland, which under the Solidarity-led government adopted
early on a very austere programme of economic transition and recovery, has
already been experiencing some of these problems.

The prospects of reprivatization present the new East European governments with some hard choices regarding the scope of this measure as well as
the way in which it should be carried out – should state property be put up
for auction and, if so, who should be the bidders; or should its value be
distributed in some form among the population? The politically more palatable
solutions in this area may not be the most rational and efficient ones economically, and vice versa.

It appears certain that, regardless of the approaches chosen by individual
East European governments in the process of economic transition, East European societies will have to endure more hardship in the immediate future.
This raises the problem of the political stability and viability of the new
democracies. Any mishandling of the economic aspects of the transition could
easily jeopardize political democratization. On the other hand, it has been
proven on several occasions that, with a democratic government enjoying solid
support and legitimacy, the population may be willing to sustain more economic
difficulties than might be the case otherwise (Linz 1990: 160). This is certainly
one crucial difference between communist and post-communist Eastern
Europe. It appears unlikely, even under increased social and economic strains,
that East European societies would opt for a return to communism, although
a different form of authoritarianism should not be ruled out.

As a result of both political and economic changes, these societies are
likely to undergo some alterations of their very fabric and composition. With
privatization and the introduction of free enterprise, and under even a modicum
of success, East European societies, while becoming wealthier on the whole,
will also be more differentiated – inequalities in terms of income and wealth
will probably be on the increase. Although most East Europeans were ready
to reject communism, for large segments of society the enforced, artificial and

low-level social equality introduced under the communist system, accompanied by lax labour discipline and low productivity requirements, was something that they became accustomed to and something that was accepted over time as a part of core social values. This aspect of the changes caused by democratization may cause dissatisfaction in certain social strata, especially among manual workers, and therefore result in political instabilities.

An additional aspect of social change in the emerging East European democracies is the need to create or recreate civil society (Dahrendorf 1990: 135) based on the traditions of liberal democracy in respective countries. After decades of often brutal repression, with the resulting demoralization and loss of values, this will not be an easy task and may require a protracted period of time. For the countries that had little if any tradition in this respect (primarily those in south-east Europe) the task will be even more formidable.

A related and very sensitive issue that all new East European democracies must deal with is that of the treatment of members and/or collaborators of the former regime. The temptations of revanchism will be strong, the more so the more repressive the communist rulers were. In all new democracies there have been instances of purges or demonstrated intentions to conduct purges, coupled with disqualifications of political figures from holding office for having co-operated with the former authorities, especially with the secret police agencies. If the new democratic governments want to establish themselves as such and remain true to the ideals of building a liberal democracy and a civil society they should not repeat the mistakes of their communist predecessors, no matter how strong the urge for justice or revenge may be, or how justified in some cases. Therefore, although personnel changes in the state administration should be regarded as a logical ingredient of any change of government, there have to be limits for the sake of upholding the very principles for which the new democratic parties stand and for which they were rewarded with electoral victories. Most new East European governments and election-winning parties have accepted this pragmatic orientation. Some of them have called for national reconciliation as the best indication that their countries are entering a new era of respect for human rights and civil liberties.

The future evolution of Eastern Europe's international position and of individual countries' foreign policies is open to many questions. It is clear that the bipolar system in Europe has dissolved, but it is far from certain what may supersede it.

In the early phase of the transition the East European countries pledged allegiance to the alliance with the Soviet Union and paid lip-service to respect for all the bloc mechanisms. There was a unanimous agreement among Soviets and East Europeans that bloc institutions would have to undergo fundamental change in their character and organizational structure. These changes were, however, only vaguely addressed at the joint meetings of the bloc organizations during 1990, although it became apparent that the views of the individual member countries differed considerably. As the processes of democratization got underway and the new democracies were stabilized after the parliamentary elections in the spring of 1990, the fate of both the WTO and the CMEA was becoming increasingly a matter of speculation.

An issue of utmost importance that had to be dealt with before tackling the future of the European security was the fate of Germany: will it be reunited and, if so, what will its security status be? Although the Soviet Union tried initially to slow down German unification and to prevent membership of the unified Germany in NATO, it gradually gave up on both goals when provided with assurances that the Western alliance would become a more defensive and political institution and that the armed forces of unified Germany would be reduced and would adopt some other restrictions. The agreement between the former four occupying powers in Germany (the United States, the United Kingdom, France and the Soviet Union) and the two German states ('two plus four agreement'), concluded in September 1990, removed the last obstacles and unknowns on the path of German unification. The western allies agreed that the Soviet troops could remain on the territory of the former East Germany until they are finally withdrawn by 1994 and that until that time NATO troops would not be deployed there. In the aftermath of the German unification (October 1990) it became clear that there was no longer any justifiable reason for the preservation of the Eastern Bloc institutions – the WTO and the CMEA. The East European states were now openly calling for their dissolution. Although this certainly went beyond the initial Soviet expectations of a more liberal Eastern Europe, the Soviet leadership went along with it. Thus, the CMEA was formally dissolved in January 1991, followed by the military structure of the WTO in March and its political institutions in July of the same year. Based on the previously reached bilateral agreements, the Soviet Union pulled out its troops from Hungary and Czechoslovakia in the summer of 1991, agreeing to do the same in Poland by 1993. These steps formally marked the end of the Soviet political and military control of Eastern Europe and of the Cold War division of Europe.

The real political and diplomatic efforts in and around Eastern Europe are therefore no longer focused on relationships with the Soviet Union or its successor states (although this will obviously have to be treated as a long-term but strategically less important aspect of East European as well as broader European security arrangements), but rather on finding a proper place for the new, democratic Eastern Europe in a European and global context.

There is, undoubtedly, a need for an all-encompassing security system in Europe that can replace the hostile blocs of the Cold War and establish the newly agreed rules of international conduct and guarantees for the democratic political systems of member countries. At the same time, and perhaps even more vitally, there is also a need for a new network of intensified economic co-operation and integration that can absorb the shocks of economic transition in Eastern Europe and thus ensure political transition as well.

A number of proposals and scenarios have been suggested regarding future security arrangements in Europe and the place and role of Eastern Europe in such arrangements. In these suggestions, four organizations have featured most prominently: the CSCE, the EC, NATO and the Western European Union (WEU).

There is a broad agreement and support for the expansion of the CSCE into an all-European system of security that would in due course replace the two military alliances and in the meantime act as a hub for the existing European and East–West security arrangements. This proposal has had the support of most East and West European countries, the Soviet Union and the United States, although US support appears to be less enthusiastic and is qualified by a strong insistence on the preservation of NATO as a vital institution for promoting Western security and political interests.

The CSCE summit conference (November 1990 in Paris) formally ushered in the post-Cold War Europe and marked a significant breakthrough in expanding the CSCE's political role and stature. The conference adopted the Charter which proclaimed the beginning of the new era in European history, with an emphasis on higher requirements for the respect of human rights and the rights of ethnic minorities, economic freedoms and equal security standards for all participants. The conference introduced the regular meetings of heads of states and foreign ministers and established for the first time rudimentary permanent bodies of the CSCE: a Crisis Prevention Centre in Vienna, a Secretariat in Prague and a monitoring Office for Free Elections in Warsaw. The CSCE is thus evolving towards a tentative collective security organization for Europe, with the participation of the United States and Canada. The CSCE can be an important diplomatic forum for Eastern Europe, offering a broad political and security framework, and support and mediating services in cases of conflicts. The CSCE's institutional foundation is, nevertheless, still too weak and incomplete, and its mandate too vague, for it to provide East European states with effective and specific assistance or protection in cases of serious crisis.

The EC may be an even more important player in the stabilization of the new democratic Europe. The prospects and the challenges opened by the democratic transition in Eastern Europe initially gave the impression of having the potential to undermine the continuity of the integration process in the EC. The EC was in the midst of the latest, ambitious phase in its integration drive, with the aim of achieving a unified internal market and laying grounds for the political union of member countries, when the upheaval in Eastern Europe occurred. The democratization of Eastern Europe presented new opportunities of expansion for the EC but also demanded increased financial assistance efforts and exposed imperfections in its institutional mechanisms and political co-operation. An overarching dilemma is whether the EC will be able to maintain the momentum of its integration as well as a recently reinvigorated political mission in a depolarized Europe, without the protective security shield it enjoyed from the Western alliance. With the demise of the Soviet power the real dilemma is more and more one of choosing between further and faster integration on the one side and greater expansion on the other, as a growing number of former communist as well as neutral countries have announced their plans to apply for full or at least associate membership. An additional uncertainty for the EC concerns the policies of the united Germany: will the new, more powerful Germany gradually abandon the integration goals of the EC, turning itself more inward and simply pursuing policies of its own, unwilling to sustain the growing burden of the expanding EC institutions, or will it, on the contrary, remain committed to the EC's proclaimed goals of integration, trying at the same time to use its greater leverage within the EC for the enhancement of its own specific interests?

By the end of 1991, some tentative answers to these questions seemed to be emerging. The EC Summit in Maastricht, the Netherlands (December 1991), ended with a strong support for the continuation of economic as well as social and political integration, despite British reservations. Co-operation in the areas of foreign and defence policies will be further enhanced, and the role of the WEU upgraded for this purpose. It is likely, therefore, that the EC will in due course become a defence organization of European states, possibly by incorporating the still fledgling mechanisms of the WEU. After its unification, Germany was among the staunchest supporters for the continuation of the integration process and its expansion into social, political and defence areas, thus denying any speculations that its enthusiasm for the EC might slacken. This, however, gave rise to the other type of suspicion: namely, that Germany would try increasingly to dominate the EC, using it as a vehicle for the realization of its own policy goals.

On the issue of the expansion of membership, the EC has been following a different, more cautious approach. The reason for such a choice was obviously based on the understanding that the furtherance of integration goals might be hampered and 'diluted' by a too speedy expansion of membership. The EC has concluded agreements on associate membership with three East European countries: Hungary, Czechoslovakia and Poland, all of whom manifested a strong interest in expanding their ties with the 'twelve' and at the same time could demonstrate that democratization and the transition to a market economy were proceeding at a steady pace and with firm political guarantees. As for the other interested aspirants, which includes virtually all the other East European countries, as well as the Yugoslav and Soviet successor states, the prospects of extending assistance and co-operation are conditional upon an orderly and genuine democratization and a transition to a market economy.

There is little doubt that the EC will operate, economically and politically, as the most significant actor in post-Cold War Europe, and will be the most relevant source of stability, assistance and support for Eastern Europe. It is the organization best equipped to play such a role, because of its closeness, its resources and its developed institutional mechanisms.

The relative ineffectiveness with which both the CSCE and the EC dealt with the war in Yugoslavia, necessitating in the end the involvement of the UN, proved that both organizations are still not appropriate for addressing emergency situations and serious crises on the continent. However, the Yugoslav crisis has been a learning process and the EC, in particular, has maintained steady monitoring and mediating efforts, trying at the same time to smooth out differences on the issues involved between its own members, and working towards defining a joint compromise policy, which was finally agreed on in December 1991.

Given the fact that neither the CSCE nor the EC are for the time being fully evolved and equipped security organizations, the immediate problem that Eastern Europe faces is that after the demise of the Soviet hegemony the region was left with no satisfactory security arrangements or institutions, and this has led to a kind of power vacuum or strategic limbo (Binendijk 1991: 70). There were suggestions, especially before the disintegration of the Soviet Union, that NATO was the only organization capable of offering the necessary guarantees to the East European countries, and that it should therefore extend its protective role over Eastern Europe. Some East European countries, notably Hungary, Czechoslovakia and Poland, fearing the resurgence of Soviet expansionism or a spill-over effect from the internal conflicts in the Soviet Union and other areas (Yugoslavia), expressed an interest in becoming members of NATO, or at least in obtaining a special protection in cases of crisis. Similar concerns and interests were expressed by the three Baltic states once they regained full independence from the Soviet Union in the autumn of 1991.

At the same time, NATO has been undergoing an identity crisis, trying to determine its proper role and strategy in the changed circumstances of post-Cold War Europe. This process has been compounded by differences among some of the most significant member states in this respect. While high-level NATO meetings in this period reached a compromise on a number of issues, such as on the need to preserve NATO for the time being as the organization that can provide both Europe and the world with the necessary stability in times of changing security arrangements, there was no willingness to extend NATO membership to East European states or to offer any explicit security guarantees to them at this stage.

The NATO Summit Conference (November 1991, Rome) decided only to establish the consultative council of foreign ministers in which all East European countries, the Baltic states and the Soviet Union (or the Soviet successor states) could participate. The first meeting of this new body was held in December 1991. Pending further clarification of the strategic situation in Europe, and a more precise redefinition of NATO's role and policies, the allies were not willing to extend any firm commitments of protection to East European states. Thus, NATO remains on the outside of the new East Central European security zone, acting only as an indirect source of support and stability.

Regional security organizations formed by the East European states themselves have also been suggested as a possible solution to the region's security dilemmas. Italy and Austria championed the 'Pentagonal', a group of five countries which would also include Yugoslavia, Hungary and Czechoslovakia. (Following the outbreak of hostilities in Yugoslavia, its position is uncertain; its place in the organization could be taken by the two western republics – Slovenia and Croatia.) Poland has also shown some interest in joining this group. Another proposal referred to the creation of the 'Baltic Group', which would consist of the Scandinavian states, the Baltic states and Poland. There were also suggestions that Hungary, Czechoslovakia and Poland form a separate organization, since they have many things in common and have already acted as a group (for associate membership in the EC, one of the most impressive achievements in the transition process). The states of Eastern Europe have never been able historically to form stable organizations and to overcome their mutual conflicts of interests. Although that does not mean that a major breakthrough in this respect is impossible, it seems that the regional organizations in Eastern Europe could only act mainly as supportive actors and could not, on their own, provide the region with the necessary security guarantees or with safe mechanisms for conflict prevention and crisis management.

Eastern Europe will have to cope with several factors of risk and uncertainty. The major ones include future internal developments in the former Soviet Union, relations between the leading West European nations, and their impact on the future of the EC, and, perhaps most crucially, relations between and within the East European countries – in particular, ethnic tensions and conflicts. A reassuring factor could be that in post-Cold War Europe and Eastern Europe, especially since a remarkably smooth and peaceful process of disintegration and transformation of the Soviet Union got under way in December 1991, there is no longer an overwhelming source of threat. This should make it easier for the existing international organizations (the UN, the CSCE, the EC, NATO and the WEU), and for the East European states themselves, to deal successfully with the ongoing and potential new crises, despite institutional weakness and political uncertainties, building at the same time the structures and rules of the new security order for Europe that would in time give the whole continent, including Eastern Europe itself, more solid and lasting security guarantees.

It appears that in the 1990s Europe will have better chances than it has had in decades, perhaps centuries, to overcome its historical cultural and civilizational divisions, as well as its political and ideological divisions from the more recent past (Howard 1990: 32), and to unite around the ideas of liberal democracy and civil society, based on modern democratic capitalism tempered with the achievements of the welfare state. These ideas have been generated and nourished on the European continent persistently in the course of the last two centuries and they appear to have won a historical victory despite all the set-backs produced by nationalism and totalitarianism and by the destructions of the two World Wars. This would also represent the realization of the dream that the founders of the European integration movement cherished in the aftermath of the Second World War and for which their successors in the EC continued ardently to strive – to have a Europe without divisions, united and built on the democratic and humanitarian values of its common civilization. Eastern Europe would in this process finally be integrated with the rest of the continent, ceasing to be its culturally and economically backward part and joining in sharing the guiding principles and ideals of the Western civilization, to which its most progressive and enlightened people have always aspired but to which it could ill-afford to belong fully.

REFERENCES

Binendijk, H. (1991) 'The emerging European security order', *Washington Quarterly* 14 (4): 67–81.

Brown, J. F. (1988) *Eastern Europe and Communist Rule*, Durham, NC: Duke University Press.

Dahrendorf, R. (1990) 'Transition: politics, economics, and liberty', *Washington Quarterly* 13 (3): 133–42.

Dawisha, K. (1988) *Eastern Europe, Gorbachev and Reform*, Cambridge: Cambridge University Press.

Deak, I. (1990) 'Uncovering Eastern Europe's dark history', *Orbis* 34 (1): 51–65.

De Michelis, G. (1990) 'Reaching out to the East', *Foreign Policy* 79: 44–55.

Geremek, B. (1990) 'Postcommunism and democracy in Poland', *Washington Quarterly* 13 (3): 125–31.

Goldman, M. I. (1987) *Gorbachev's Challenge: Economic Reform in the Age of High Technology*, New York: Norton.

Halecki, O. (1952) *Borderlands of Western Civilization: A History of East Central Europe*, New York: Ronald Press.

Howard, M. (1990) 'The springtime of nations', *Foreign Affairs* 69 (1): 17–32.

Linz, J. J. (1990) 'Transition to democracy', *Washington Quarterly* 13 (3): 143–64.

Rothschild, J. (1989) *Return to Diversity: A Political History of East Central Europe Since World War II*, Oxford: Oxford University Press.

Schopflin, G. (1990) 'The end of communism in Eastern Europe', *International Affairs* 66 (1): 3–161.

FURTHER READING

Abel, E. (1990) *Behind the Upheaval in Eastern Europe*, Boston: Houghton Mifflin.

Banac, I. (1990) 'Political change and national diversity' *Daedalus* 119: 141–59.

Brown, J. F. (1991) *Surge to Freedom: The End of Communist Rule in Eastern Europe*, Durham, NC: Duke University Press.

Bugajski, J. and Pollack, M. (1989) *East European Fault Lines: Dissent, Opposition and Social Activism*, Boulder, Colo.: Westview Press.

Connor, W. (1988) *Socialism's Dilemmas: State and Society in the Soviet Bloc*, New York: Columbia University Press.

De Nevers, R. (1990) *The Soviet Union and Eastern Europe: The End of an Era*, Adelphi Paper no. 249, London: International Institute for Strategic Studies.

Dienstbier, J. (1991) 'Central Europe's security', *Foreign Policy* 83: 119–27.

Fejto, F. (1971) *A History of People's Democracies*, New York: Praeger.

Garton Ash, T. (1990) *The Uses of Adversity: Essays on the Fate of Central Europe*, New York: Vintage Books/Random House.

Gati, C. (1990) *The Bloc that Failed: Soviet-East European Relations in Transition*, Bloomington: Indiana University Press.

——(1990) 'East-Central Europe: the morning after', *Foreign Affairs* 69: 129–45.

Gremion, P. and Hassner, P. (eds) (1990) *Vents d'est: vers l'Europe des états de droit?*, Paris: Presses Universitaires de France.

Holloway, D. and Sharp, M. O. J. (eds) (1984) *The Warsaw Pact: Alliance in Transition*, Ithaca, NY: Cornell University Press.

Jones, C. (1980) *Soviet Influence in Eastern Europe: Political Anatomy and the Warsaw Pact*, New York: Praeger.

Mlinar, Z. (1983) *Krisen und Krisen Bewaltigung im Sowjetblock*, Cologne: Bund-Verlag.

Nelson, D. (1989) *The Soviet Alliance: Empirical Studies of the Warsaw Pact*, Boulder, Colo.: Westview Press.

Orme, J. (1991) 'Security in East Central Europe: seven futures', *Washington Quarterly* 14 (3): 91–105.

Rakowska-Harmstone, T. (ed.) (1984) *Communism in Eastern Europe*, Bloomington: Indiana University Press.

Remington, R. A. (1971) *The Warsaw Pact: Case Studies in Communist Conflict Resolution*, Cambridge, Mass.: MIT Press.

Rupnik, J. (1990) *The Other Europe: The Rise and Fall of Communism in East-Central Europe*, New York: Schocken Books.

Schopflin, G. and Kovrig, B. (1989) *Eastern Europe in the Gorbachev Period*, Boulder, Colo.: Westview Press.

Seton-Watson, H. (1962) *The East European Revolution*, New York: Praeger.

Sugar, P. (ed.) (1980) *Ethnic Diversity and Conflict in Eastern Europe*, Santa Barbara, Calif.: ABC-Clio.

Terry, S. M. (ed.) (1984) *Soviet Policy in Eastern Europe*, New Haven: Yale University Press.

Tismaneanu, V. (1988) *The Crisis of Marxist Ideology in Eastern Europe*, London: Routledge & Kegan Paul.

Whetten, L. (1989) *Interaction of Political and Economic Reforms Within the East Bloc*, New York: Crane-Russak.

White, S., Gardner, J., Schopflin, G. and Saich, T. (1990) *Communist and Postcommunist Systems*, New York: St Martin's Press.

78

NUCLEAR
PROLIFERATION

P. EDWARD HALEY

The discovery of nuclear weapons a half-century ago profoundly and permanently altered international diplomacy and strategy. As former United States
Secretary of Defense, Robert McNamara, observed: 'A few hundred [powerful
nuclear weapons] could destroy not only the United States, the Soviet Union,
and their allies, but through atmospheric effects, a major part of the rest of
the world as well' (McNamara 1987: 5). To Bernard Brodie, a pioneering
strategist of the atomic age, nuclear weapons 'changed not merely the destructiveness but the very nature of war' (Kaplan 1983: 25). Few if any national
interests would justify going to war if the fighting might lead to a nuclear
exchange that obliterated cities and incinerated millions.

Despite the unique destructiveness of nuclear weapons, the changes they
have brought to diplomacy and strategy resemble the effects of other transformations in military technology, such as gunpowder, steam-driven sailing ships,
aircraft, tanks, and radar (Schilling 1968: 589–98). Each of these innovations
contributed to unforeseen and far-reaching diplomatic, military, political and
social developments.

Seen in this light, nuclear proliferation – the spread of the knowledge to
build nuclear weapons and the capacity to attack other countries with them –
should be expected to occur and to be affected by the same factors that
limited or promoted the spread of earlier military revolutions. Governments will
acquire nuclear weapons if they have the resources and if they conclude they
must have them to counter threats and exploit opportunities. An observer with
this point of view is not surprised that five countries have publicly announced
they have the capacity to attack others with nuclear weapons; that two other
countries have developed nuclear explosives; and that a half-dozen others are
engaged in nuclear research and development projects that would favour 'going
nuclear'. At the same time, many policy makers and analysts take it for granted

that nuclear proliferation increases the risk of nuclear war and should be prevented by international agreement.

Opponents of nuclear proliferation have argued that, even if the United States and the Soviet Union avoided entanglement, the use of nuclear weapons in a conflict would result in terrible loss and destruction. Within a region, a nation that acquired nuclear weapons ahead of its neighbours might attempt to intimidate them and coerce them into concessions they would not otherwise make. As the number of nuclear weapons increases so also does the likelihood that they could fall into the hands of terrorists or escape governmental control during a profound domestic crisis (Spector 1984: 3–4).

One of the most persuasive arguments against nuclear proliferation was made around the time of the French decision to develop an independent nuclear arsenal. An American strategist, Albert Wohlstetter, argued that it is far more difficult to deter a major nuclear power than proponents of independent national nuclear forces imagine it to be. Building a force able to survive an attack is hard and costly, and it is far more difficult to disarm a major nuclear power to such a degree that it would be possible to escape devastating retaliation. There are great difficulties, as well, in preserving command and control while under nuclear attack. Independent nuclear forces are sometimes justified in light of an alleged reduced credibility of American (or Soviet) nuclear protection, but if the credibility of these huge arsenals is diminished how credible are the smaller national forces? The spread of nuclear weapons increases the risk of nuclear war by mistake, increases ambiguity as to source of attack, and increases the probability of purposeful use, because additional governments are involved in nuclear decision making. If responsible use of nuclear power is to be maintained, Wohlstetter concluded, it is 'vital to keep that power under centralized control. For deterrence and responsibility, [the United States] must do what [it] can to inhibit the diffusion of nuclear weapons' (Wohlstetter 1961: 386).

Despite the widespread acceptance of this line of argument, the number of countries armed with nuclear weapons has increased significantly. With the dates of the first explosion, the states that publicly admitted to possessing nuclear weapons are: the United States (1945); the Soviet Union (1949); Great Britain (1952); France (1960); and China (1964). Although India conducted what its government termed a 'peaceful nuclear explosion' in 1974, expert opinion remains uncertain as to whether India has developed a nuclear arsenal. In 1974 the United States Central Intelligence Agency also reported that 'Israel has already produced nuclear weapons' (Reiss 1988: 155). Two mysterious flashes off the coast of South Africa detected by a US reconnaissance satellite suggest that Israel may have tested a nuclear device in co-operation with South Africa in September 1979 and again in December 1980 (Walters 1987: 41–61). Four other states – Argentina, Brazil, Pakistan and South Africa

– are on the 'threshold' of nuclear proliferation. All maintain unsafeguarded nuclear reactors, reserve the right to carry out nuclear explosions, and are able to build or acquire effective delivery systems (Simpson 1987: 24–36). Libya, Iraq, Iran, Taiwan and South Korea have all sought nuclear weapons (Spector 1988: 5).

Plainly the arguments in favour of nuclear proliferation are powerful ones and have persuaded many political and military leaders. The arguments are based on the perceived benefits of possessing nuclear weapons, the logic and apparent success of nuclear deterrence, and the example of other nations that have gone nuclear, such as France.

The United States worked closely with Great Britain during the Second World War to develop nuclear weapons ahead of Nazi Germany. Germany surrendered before the weapons had been tested. However, the United States dropped two atomic bombs on Japan in a successful attempt to hasten the end of the war and to save the lives of the allied soldiers who would otherwise have had to invade the Japanese home islands in pursuit of unconditional surrender.

To Stalin and his successors, nuclear weapons served a number of vitally important purposes: to protect the Soviet Union against attack and coercion by the United States and its allies, which Marxist theory predisposed Soviet leaders to expect; to allow the projection of Soviet influence around the world; and gradually to cause a shift in favour of the Soviet Union in what Soviet leaders term the global 'correlation of forces' (Holloway 1983; Leebaert 1981; Nerlich 1983). A favourable correlation of forces was seen as essential to the triumph of the Soviet system around the world.

Great Britain's decision to acquire nuclear weapons was intended to maintain that country's great-power status and its place at the negotiating table with the Soviet Union and the United States. Similar concerns played an important part in the French decision, but French strategists also developed an elaborate rationale for their nuclear forces. The fundamental criticism of France, and indeed of any country that chose to build an independent, small nuclear force, was that smaller nuclear powers would always be deterred by the Soviet Union or the United States except in the most extreme case, where the weaker country faces a total loss of freedom, and perhaps even then.

The French rebuttal held that while this might have been true in a bilateral context, it was not valid in the actual working of multilateral relations between allies and adversaries. Because the two superpowers had established an uneasy but stable nuclear equilibrium and could destroy one another regardless of the weight of an initial attack, according to the French strategists, the Soviet Union and the United States had to take great care to avoid collisions that might have resulted in the use of nuclear weapons. During a crisis, their fear of escalation would have made them ready to compromise about areas of marginal interest. The problem for small nuclear power was that in their eyes what was at stake may have been vital rather than marginal. In this situation, according to the French strategists, the existence of a small nuclear force would be a great advantage, because it would unavoidably link the interests of the small nuclear country to its superpower ally. To avoid a nuclear showdown with one another, the superpowers would settle the conflict in a way that would work to the advantage of the small nuclear ally (Beaufre 1966: 102).

China and India were the next two countries to develop nuclear weapons. China was a Soviet ally when it started its nuclear weapons programme in 1955, and India has been an ally of the Soviet Union. In this sense, the arguments of the French strategists help explain the Indian and Chinese decisions. However, China soon dropped out of its alliance with the Soviet Union, and Chinese and Indian political leaders and strategists may be forgiven if they do not necessarily think of their countries as 'small' or 'weak' powers on the scale of France or Great Britain.

Following the Korean War, the defeat of France in Indo-China, and a clash with the United States over Taiwan, Mao Zedong and his associates in the Chinese government decided to acquire nuclear weapons. These events provided, in the words of John Wilson Lewis and Xue Litai, the 'proximate cause' of China's decision to acquire nuclear weapons. But Lewis and Litai believe that the Chinese leaders' nationalism, ideology and concepts of force and diplomacy would have led them to build nuclear weapons regardless of the immediate strategic situation (Lewis and Litai 1988: 35). In 1963, the Chinese government published a summary of the reasons behind its nuclear weapons programme, which emphasized the usefulness of nuclear weapons as a means of avoiding nuclear blackmail and nuclear war and of preventing the Soviet Union, the United States, or any other nuclear powers from dictating to the rest of the world.

India's decision to start its nuclear weapons programme was also deeply influenced by immediate strategic and military considerations. These were China's defeat of India in the Himalayas in 1962 and China's nuclear explosion in 1964. In the wake of the Chinese explosion, Indian leaders and strategists addressed the moral, financial, strategic and diplomatic aspects of acquiring nuclear weapons (Reiss 1988: 211–13). The moral concern over weapons of mass destruction was met by the assertion that India would seek a nuclear capability for deterrent purposes only. Costs were minimized by the Chair of India's Atomic Energy Commission, Homi Bhabba, who advised that India could test a nuclear device within eighteen months and could acquire fifty atomic bombs for around $20 million and fifty hydrogen bombs for $30 million (Reiss 1988: 214). Proponents of the nuclear programme stressed that only a nuclear India could escape China's nuclear coercion. Ten years after Bhabba's promise of a test within eighteen months, the Indian government allowed a single 'peaceful nuclear explosion'. India apparently has not gone on to develop nuclear weapons (Reiss 1988: 243; Spector 1988: 105–6).

Pakistan's nuclear weapons programme was meant to offset India's conventional superiority and its nuclear potential (Spector 1988: 121). Within a year of Pakistan's overwhelming defeat and dismemberment by India in 1971, Prime Minister Zulfikar Ali Bhutto began moving his country towards the acquisition of nuclear arms. In the years that followed, through a variety of imaginative (and unimaginative) subterfuges and smuggling escapades, Pakistan manoeuvred to obtain the machinery and other devices necessary for weapons production, such as the extremely high speed electric switches known as krytons. By 1977 Pakistan lacked only a reprocessing or enrichment capability. Finally, in 1986, the Reagan administration informed the news media that Pakistan was believed to have produced weapons-grade uranium and to have the capability to build nuclear weapons. Under United States law the American government must suspend all aid in the event that Pakistan acquires nuclear weapons. A halt to aid would destroy a vital part of the coalition opposed to Soviet domination of Afghanistan and destroy Pakistan's coalition against India. For these reasons Pakistan continued to claim innocence, and President Reagan, and later President Bush, continued to certify that Pakistan had not actually assembled nuclear weapons (Spector 1988: 142).

The Middle East remains a cauldron of political tension. Only Egypt has concluded a peace treaty with Israel. Uneasy armistice agreements obtain between Israel and Jordan, Syria and Lebanon, while a state of war and rebellion exist between Israel and the Palestinians, who are represented by the Palestinian Liberation Organization. Thus, vital national security concerns have dominated Israeli politics and policy debates throughout the four decades of the state of Israel's existence. In this context, it is not surprising that Israel would choose to develop nuclear weapons.

Israel's nuclear weapons programme began in 1952. In 1953 Israel and France joined in intimate co-operation to develop nuclear weapons. French support included help in constructing a large reactor and a facility for extracting plutonium from the reactor's fuel after it had been used, both located at Dimona in the Negev desert. According to Israeli nuclear technician Mordechai Vanunu, whose spectacular revelations to the London *Sunday Times* in October 1986 confirmed Israel's nuclear capabilities, much of Israel's critically important facilities were built underground for concealment and security. France also collaborated with Israel on the design of nuclear weapons and on the development of a short-range nuclear-capable missile (Spector 1988: 168).

Israel obtained uranium with French help from mines in French-controlled Africa (the present states of Gabon and the Central African Republic), perhaps from Argentina, and also from its own phosphate deposits. In 1959, when Israel's co-operation with France was at its height, Norway supplied Israel with 22 tons of heavy water, apparently in full knowledge of its intended use to produce nuclear weapons, and declined for many years to invoke its right of inspection. After the 1967 war Israel apparently acquired some 200 tons of processed uranium ore or 'yellowcake' from European suppliers, obtained 1.5 tons of additional heavy water from Norway in 1970, and by 1972 had built three phosphoric-acid plants which would provide it with a significant indigenous supply (100 tons annually) of uranium (Spector 1988: 171–6).

The capacity of the reactor at Dimona has not been conclusively established. Israel only admitted to its existence under pressure from the United States in December 1960. At the time, the then Prime Minister, David Ben Gurion, put its capacity at 24 megawatts. The reactor may have started operation as early as 1962, and the plutonium plant may have begun production in 1968 or 1969 (Spector 1988: 392 n. 46). The United States government began to assume that Israel possessed nuclear weapons from 1968.

Mordechai Vanunu's revelations and the disclosures of a French journalist, Pierre Pean, who in 1982 interviewed many of Israel's French nuclear collaborators, have shed light on the size of Israel's nuclear arsenal (*Sunday Times* 1986; Pean 1981). The arguments are complex and turn on a number of highly technical and ambiguous developments, including: an apparently advanced bomb design photographed by Vanunu that might allow the production of nuclear weapons with about half (8.8 pounds) the assumed standard amount; and the augmentation of the Israeli reactor to levels ranging from 40 megawatts upward, which would significantly increase the available irradiated uranium. Vanunu indicated that the extraction plant yielded 2.6 pounds of weapons-grade plutonium each week, or 88 pounds in a year, allowing time off for plant maintenance. Using the estimate of 8.8 pounds of plutonium for each weapon would mean that Israel could have produced approximately 80 weapons from August 1975 to November 1985, when Vanunu worked at Dimona. At this rate, Israel may have produced from 100 to 200 nuclear weapons, according to a US weapons designer, Dr Theodore Taylor, and a British physicist, Dr Frank Barnaby (*Sunday Times* 1986).

Other estimates give a lower total. Doubting that the Dimona reactor could have been augmented so massively, some US analysts have adopted 40 megawatts as a working estimate of its capacity. Over the quarter-century of its operation, the reactor and extraction plant would therefore have produced some 440 pounds of plutonium. By this scheme, Israel would have fifty weapons. Other analysts have taken 70 megawatts as the reactor's capacity from the outset, which would put the number of weapons closer to 100 (Spector 1988: 179–83). Others have wondered if the Vanunu affair were a hoax, and the revelations intended to intimidate Israel's enemies by inflating its nuclear capabilities. The most that can be said with certainty is that Israel's arsenal appears to be substantially larger than the twenty to twenty-five weapons with which it was usually credited before the Vanunu affair. The larger number of weapons is significant because it would allow Israel considerable freedom in choosing targets and, in particular, to strike military targets instead of cities in the event of a conflict with its Arab neighbours.

As important as national security considerations have been in the decision to 'go nuclear', the relative technical ease of the undertaking has also played a major part. Obtaining supplies of fissile material is a much greater obstacle to proliferation than bomb design: college students working from unclassified materials have designed crude but workable nuclear weapons, designs which obviously could be bettered by teams of trained scientists working, for example, in a developing country's nuclear power laboratories (Wohlstetter et al. 1977: 33–46).

The destructive force of nuclear weapons is derived from nuclear fission (the bombs dropped on Japan in the Second World War), nuclear fusion ('hydrogen bombs' or 'H-bombs'), and from a combination of fission and fusion. In fission weapons, a nuclear chain reaction – the sustained release of enormous amounts of energy as a result of the splitting of atomic nuclei – occurs in uranium-235 or plutonium-239. A minimum of 55 pounds of uranium-235 and 18 pounds of plutonium – or, with more sophisticated design, as little as 32 pounds of uranium and 11 pounds of plutonium – would normally be needed for the core of a fissile weapon. In fusion weapons, the nuclei of deuterium and tritium combine, releasing huge amounts of energy. Fusion can occur only at extremely high temperatures, and this is produced by an initial fission explosion (Spector 1988: 447–54).

Uranium-235 constitutes only 0.7 per cent of natural uranium. Before it can be used in weapons, it must be separated from uranium ore by a highly complex and expensive process relying on gaseous diffusion or gas centrifuge to separate heavier from lighter molecules. Plutonium is created as a nuclear reactor uses its fuel. The plutonium must be extracted from the spent fuel for use in weapons, but this is done by a chemical process, which although difficult and costly is less so than the separation of uranium-235 from uranium ore.

Not surprisingly, those nations which have acquired nuclear weapons recently, or are tempted to acquire them, focus their research and engineering efforts on the production and extraction or 'reprocessing' of fissile material. Bomb design and delivery means are also of critical importance. Together, these stages in the development, production and deployment of nuclear weapons offer those concerned in blocking their spread opportunities for intervention and regulation.

The combined efforts to stop the spread of nuclear weapons are often called 'the non-proliferation regime', a somewhat inflated wording, which refers to a loose collection of shared assumptions, goals, expectations of behaviour, bilateral and multilateral agreements, and unilateral policies. The underlying approach of the non-proliferation 'regime' is the control of what Stephen M. Meyer called the 'technical means' of going nuclear. The threats, circumstances and problems that incline nations to acquire nuclear weapons – their motives or 'nuclear propensities' in Meyers's term – are not directly addressed (Meyer 1984: 112–66).

At the heart of the non-proliferation regime are the 'safeguards' of the International Atomic Energy Agency (IAEA). Established in 1957, the IAEA has more than 110 members. Its headquarters are in Vienna, and it is affiliated with the United Nations. The IAEA 'monitors the flow of nuclear materials at nuclear installations by auditing plant records and conducting physical inventories. Seals and cameras are used to ensure materials are not diverted while IAEA inspectors are not present' (Spector 1988: 456).

There are a number of serious limitations to the effectiveness of IAEA safeguards: not all nuclear installations, particularly those for enrichment and reprocessing, are subject to IAEA inspection; small amounts of nuclear fuels, especially plutonium and enriched uranium, could be diverted without detection; the IAEA is short of money and therefore of the inspectors it needs; unannounced inspections are essentially impossible to make.

Another weakness in the IAEA safeguards is that it is possible to combine the operation of safeguarded and unsafeguarded installations in such a way as to produce fissile material. Before Israel blew up its reactor in an air attack on 7 June 1981, Iraq appeared to be showing how this might be done. In the autumn of 1980 Iraq expelled the French technicians who were building its 70-megawatt nuclear reactor. Iraq then announced that it could not allow IAEA inspections until the end of its war with Iran. The Iraqi plan may have been to make unsafeguarded 'yellowcake' (concentrated uranium oxide) suitable for irradiation into plutonium at its unsafeguarded Italian-built 'hot cell' (shielded remote-equipped facility for handling radioactive materials); to irradiate the uranium at its reactor; and to return the irradiated uranium to the hot cell for reprocessing or extraction of the plutonium (Sweet 1988: 169–72). The chief contributions of the safeguards system would, therefore, appear to serve less as a deterrent than as an early warning of intention to acquire nuclear weapons.

The full extent of the weaknesses of the non-proliferation regime became apparent in the aftermath of the defeat of Iraq's attempt to annex Kuwait in the Gulf War (August 1990 to April 1991). To make certain that Iraq's nuclear capabilities had been destroyed, the UN Security Council inserted provisions in cease-fire resolution 687 requiring Iraq to accept UN/IAEA on-site inspections to verify the destruction of all weapons of mass destruction and ballistic missiles by 2 July 1991.

In June the Bush administration said that an Iraqi nuclear scientist had defected and reported that Iraq's nuclear programme was continuing, that there were secret nuclear sites that had escaped UN/IAEA notice, and that Iraq possessed 40 kilograms (88 pounds) of uranium that had been enriched through magnetic isotope isolation (using devices called calutrons) – enough to build two bombs comparable to those used against Japan in the Second World War (*Facts on File* 1991a). After threats by the UN coalition to resume military action, Iraq admitted in July that it had been producing enriched uranium in secret. Iraq also admitted to possessing thirty calutrons, which were theoretically capable of producing 75 kilograms (180 pounds) of enriched uranium per year. Although inefficient, calutrons can be used to produce enriched uranium without requiring sophisticated imports.

In September 1991, UN inspectors reported that by the mid-1990s, had its programme continued unimpeded, Iraq would have been able to build two or three nuclear weapons a year (*Facts on File* 1991b). (See also *Newsweek* 1991; *New York Times* 1991; *Washington Post* 1991.) By implication, other small nations, could and perhaps already had escaped the restraints of the non-proliferation regime. This bad news was offset to some extent by the unprecedented international co-operation in the destruction of Iraq's nuclear capabilities. But there remained the possibility that, like the Gulf War itself, the co-operation among outsiders and the unimpeded access to Iraqi territory were unique; they would not make a solid precedent for non-proliferation efforts in the year ahead.

The Treaty on the Non-Proliferation of Nuclear Weapons (NPT) is a second obstacle to the spread of nuclear weapons. Negotiations for the NPT were led by the Soviet Union and the United States under the general umbrella of the Eighteen Nation Disarmament Committee of the United Nations. Signed on 1 July 1968 by the United States, the Soviet Union, Great Britain, and fifty-nine non-nuclear states, the treaty has since been signed by more than 130 countries. Some notable non-signatories are China, India, France, South Africa, Brazil, Argentina and Chile.

Under the Non-Proliferation Treaty non-nuclear signatories agree not to manufacture or receive nuclear weapons, and decline to develop or use peaceful nuclear explosives. They are not prohibited from accumulating fissile material provided the material is subject to IAEA inspections. Non-nuclear states also undertake to allow IAEA safeguards on all their nuclear activities. Nuclear and non-nuclear signatories promise not to help others acquire nuclear weapons and to allow IAEA safeguards and inspections on all exports of nuclear material and equipment. All signatories also promise to share peaceful nuclear technology. Although all signatories are bound, the provision to seek a negotiated end of the nuclear arms race has applied primarily to the nuclear states and especially to the Soviet Union and the United States (Spector 1988: 459).

Multilateral commitments to stop nuclear proliferation have been adopted in Latin America and the South Pacific. In addition, an anti-nuclear aspiration for a Zone of Peace, Freedom and Neutrality (ZOPFAN) has received widespread publicity in South-East Asia. The Latin American undertaking is in the form of a Treaty on the Prohibition of Nuclear Weapons in Latin America (Treaty of Tlatelolco). It creates a nuclear-free zone by prohibiting all signatories from acquiring nuclear weapons in any way and from allowing other nations to bring nuclear weapons on to their soil. All signatories pledge to allow IAEA safeguards to be enforced, and, in addition, have established the Agency for the Prohibition of Nuclear Weapons in Latin America, which is to conduct inspections if there are grounds to suspect the treaty has been violated. Twenty-two nations have signed and ratified the Treaty; Argentina has signed but not ratified; Brazil and Chile have ratified, but have declined to waive the requirement for universal membership before the Treaty may come into force. Cuba has refused to sign or ratify until the United States withdraws from Guantanamo naval base.

Two protocols to the treaty concern countries outside the region. Protocol I asks nations with territories in the region to refrain from introducing nuclear weapons into their territories. The United States, Britain, France and the Netherlands – all the countries with Latin American territories – have agreed. By Protocol II no nuclear state may use or threaten to use nuclear weapons against a signatory of the treaty. The Soviet Union, the United States, China, France and Britain have ratified Protocol II.

The Treaty of Raratonga, signed in 1985 by Australia, New Zealand, the Cook Islands, Papua New Guinea and other islands, creates a nuclear-free zone in the South Pacific. Its provisions are similar to the Treaty of Tlatelolco, but it also seeks to prohibit nuclear testing in the region by all nations. China and the Soviet Union accepted all relevant provisions, but Britain, France and the United States refused to ratify any part of the treaty. In addition, France continues to test nuclear weapons at its sites in the South Pacific.

Several co-operative arrangements have been established to prevent exports of nuclear supplies from contributing to the spread of nuclear weapons. The first of these, the NPT Exporters Committee (or Zanger Committee after its first Chair), brought together Australia, Denmark, Canada, Finland, West Germany, the Netherlands, Norway, the Soviet Union, the United Kingdom and the United States in an agreement to subject their nuclear exports to IAEA safeguards in compliance with the NPT. In addition, each of the parties agreed to a 'trigger list' of materials which could be exported only with IAEA safeguards (Spector 1988: 468). Eventually, Austria, Czechoslovakia, East Germany, Ireland, Japan, Luxembourg, Poland and Sweden also accepted the arrangement.

However, the Exporters Committee was limited to signatories of the NPT. In an attempt to tighten the limits and, in particular to draw in the French, a second arrangement was concluded in London in 1976. In keeping with the indirect, technical character of the non-proliferation regime, the Nuclear Suppliers Group, as the arrangement came to be known, adopted guidelines that apply to the recipients rather than the exporters of nuclear materials and technology. Recipients agree not to use their imports to make nuclear weapons; to apply agreed safeguards indefinitely on all transferred material and technology; and not to pass the material or technology to third countries unless the original exporter agrees or the new recipient has accepted the initial safeguards. The original participants in the negotiations were Canada, West Germany, France, Japan, the Soviet Union, Britain and the United States. They have so far been joined in the new arrangement by Belgium, Italy, East Germany, the Netherlands, Sweden, Switzerland, Czechoslovakia, Poland, Australia, Finland, Denmark, Greece, Luxembourg, Ireland and Bulgaria (Spector 1988: 468–73; Council on Foreign Relations 1986: 122–6).

A number of other unilateral and multilateral measures have been taken regarding nuclear proliferation. A convention for the physical protection of nuclear material was concluded in 1980, and has been signed by more than a dozen nations, including the principal nuclear manufacturers. China, in particular, may have made a sharp turn away from its earlier hostility to non-proliferation. China has joined IAEA, and partial IAEA safeguards now apply to China's nuclear transfer agreements with Japan, Argentina and Brazil, and cover re-transfers of nuclear materials and equipment from Britain, the United States and Germany (Council on Foreign Relations 1986: 144).

US statutes and the statutes of other countries opposed to proliferation reflect the technical and indirect character of the non-proliferation regime. The Atomic Energy Act of the United States prohibits sharing of nuclear information and technology, although exceptions have been made for Britain and France. There are, in addition, US laws forbidding aid to countries that import uranium enrichment technology; that import plutonium extraction technology; that receive, transfer or detonate nuclear explosives; and that import items from the United States for use in nuclear explosives. These laws obviously affect Pakistan as it proceeds with its nuclear development programme; some were written with Pakistan specifically in mind. In 1985 the US Congress allowed military and economic aid to go to Pakistan only if the President certified that Pakistan did not 'possess a nuclear explosive device' (Spector 1988: 142). To date, the Reagan and Bush administrations have made the necessary certification. But misgivings have increased. In his letter to the Congress in October 1989, President Bush noted that 'Pakistan has continued its efforts to develop its unsafeguarded nuclear program', and added that he remained 'extremely troubled' about the development of a nuclear arms race in South Asia (New York Times 1989).

In the fifth decade of the nuclear era, optimists about nuclear proliferation would be inclined to agree with a leading participant in the French nuclear programme, Bertrand Goldschmidt, who argued that 'three miracles' have forestalled the worst fears of proliferation: safeguards have been widely accepted; the rate of proliferation has declined – three countries acquired nuclear weapons in the first decade after the Second World War (the United States, the Soviet Union and Britain), two in the next decade (France and China), two in the third decade (India and Israel), and none in the fourth or fifth decades (assuming a bright flash between South Africa and Antarctica on 22 September 1979 was not a bomb); and five countries that could easily have built nuclear weapons have refrained: Japan, Italy, Canada, Sweden and Germany (Walters 1987: 41–61).

Pessimists might respond that the non-proliferation regime is close to reaching the limits of its indirect, technical approach, and that growing economic pressures on suppliers and the increased resourcefulness and determination of the near-nuclear nations may reverse the happy trend Goldschmidt identified. By lowering international tensions, the warming of relations between the Soviet Union and the United States addressed some of these concerns and will, if continued, contribute to a changed international climate that will be hostile to nuclear proliferation. Further progress in the effort to slow nuclear proliferation may depend on the willingness of the nations concerned to address the specific circumstances in which nuclear proliferation could occur – such as the conflict between Israel, the Palestinians and the Arab states, or that between Pakistan and India, or South Africa and its neighbours – and to develop approaches that are tailored to the unique conflicts and threats that lie behind the motives of the parties to acquire nuclear weapons.

REFERENCES

Beaufre, A. (1966) *Deterrence and Strategy*, New York: Praeger.

Council on Foreign Relations (1986) *Blocking the Spread of Nuclear Weapons: American and European Perspectives*, New York: Council on Foreign Relations.

Facts on File (1991a) Chicago: Rand McNally, 20 June: 455.

——(1991b) Chicago: Rand McNally, 19 September: 686.

Holloway, D. (1983) *The Soviet Union and the Arms Race*, New Haven: Yale University Press.

Kaplan, F. (1983) *The Wizards of Armageddon*, New York: Simon & Schuster.

Leebaert, D. (ed.) (1981) *Soviet Military Thinking*, London: Allen & Unwin

Lewis, J. W. and Litai, X. (1988) *China Builds the Bomb*, Stanford: Stanford University Press.

McNamara, R. (1987) *Blundering into Disaster*, London: Bloosmbury.

Meyer, S. M. (1984) *The Dynamics of Nuclear Proliferation*, Chicago: University of Chicago Press.

Nerlich, U. (1983) *Soviet Power and Western Negotiating Policies*, 2 vols, Cambridge, Mass.: Ballinger.

New York Times, (1989) 12 October.
____(1991) 4 June 3A; 15 July: 1A; 6 August: 1A; 9 November: 1A.
Pean, P. (1981) *Les deux bombes*, Paris: Fayard.
Reiss, M. (1988) *Without the Bomb: The Politics of Nuclear Nonproliferation*, New York: Columbia University Press.
Schilling, W. (1968) 'Technology and international relations', *International Encyclopedia of the Social Sciences*, Vol. 15, New York: Macmillan, pp. 589–98.
Simpson, J. (ed.) (1987) *Nuclear Non-Proliferation: An Agenda for the 1990s*, New York: Cambridge University Press.
Spector, L. S. (1984) *Nuclear Proliferation Today*, New York: Vintage.
____(1988) *The Undeclared Bomb*, Cambridge, Mass.: Ballinger.
Sunday Times (1986) 'Revealed: the secrets of Israel's nuclear arsenal', 5 October: 1a, 4a.
Sweet, W. (1988) *The Nuclear Age: Atomic Energy, Proliferation, and the Arms Race*, 2nd edn, Washington, DC: Congressional Quarterly.
Walters, R. W. (1987) *South Africa and the Bomb: Responsibility and Deterrence*, Lexington, Mass.: D. C. Heath.
Washington Post (1991) 24 August: A18; 5 October: A1.
Wohlstetter, A. (1961) 'NATO and the N + 1 country', *Foreign Affairs* 3: 355–87.
Wohlstetter, A., Brown, T. A., Jones, G., McGarvey, D. C., Rowen, H., Taylor, V. and Wohlstetter, R. (1977) *Swords from Plowshares: The Military Potential of Civilian Nuclear Energy*, Chicago: University of Chicago Press.

FURTHER READING

Albright, D. (1986) 'Israel's nuclear arsenal', Federation of American Scientists, *Public Interest Report* (May): 4–6.
Barnaby, F. (1987) 'The nuclear arsenal in the Middle East', *Technology Review* 90 (May–June): 27–34.
Bolt, R. (1988) 'Plutonium for all: leaks in global safeguards', *Bulletin of the Atomic Scientists* 44 (December): 14–19.
Cobban, H. (1988) 'Israel's nuclear game', *World Policy Journal* (Summer): 4115–433.
Cohen, S. (ed.) (1991) *Nuclear Proliferation in South Asia: The Prospects for Arms Control*, Boulder, Colo.: Westview Press.
Dan, C. (1989) 'Exporting trouble: West Germany's free wheeling nuclear business', *Bulletin of the Atomic Scientists* 45 (April): 21–7.
Desjardins, M. and Rasif, T. (1988) 'Nuclear subs: a new proliferation concern', *Arms Control Today* 18 (December): 13–18.
Flournoy, M. and Campbell, K. (1988) 'South Africa's bomb: a military option?', *Orbis* 32 (Summer): 385–401.
Kapur, A. (1987) *Pakistan's Nuclear Development*, London: Croom Helm.
Karp, A. (1988) 'Frantic Third World quest for ballistic missiles', *Bulletin of the Atomic Scientists* 44 (June): 14–20.
Looney, R. E. (1988) *Third World Military Expenditure and Arms Production*, New York: St Martin's Press.
Moore, J. D. L. (1987) *South Africa and Nuclear Proliferation*, New York: St Martin's Press.

Scheinman, L. (1987) *The International Atomic Energy Agency and World Nuclear Order*, Washington, DC: Resources for the Future.

Spector, L. S. (1987) 'Nuclear proliferation: who's next?', *Bulletin of the Atomic Scientists* 43 (May): 17–20.

Stone, J. (1988) 'Argentinian/Brazilian nuclear cooperation', Federation of American Scientists, *Public Interest Report* (May): 3–4.

United States Congress, Senate Committee on Foreign Relations (1988) *Nuclear Proliferation in South Asia: Containing the Threat*, Washington, DC: Government Printing Office.

Weissman, S. and Krosney, H. (1981) *The Islamic Bomb*, New York: Times Books.

Zaloga, S. (1988) 'Ballistic missiles in the Third World: Scud and beyond', *International Defence Review* 21 (November): 1423–7.

79

ARMS CONTROL AND DISARMAMENT

MICHAEL SHEEHAN

The terms 'arms control' and 'disarmament' describe both the means and ends of policy, the desired state of affairs and the suggested mechanism for attaining that objective. The two expressions are often used as if they were synonymous, but in fact they represent significantly different approaches to the achievement of security in an anarchic international system. In broad terms, the period 1919–36 saw significant efforts to achieve disarmament, while the years 1959–86 were dominated by the arms control approach. After 1986, security in the northern hemisphere was pursued through an amalgam of the two approaches in which the key assumptions of arms control remained intact, but the methods adopted emphasized disarmament.

DISARMAMENT

Classical disarmament theory is based upon certain key assumptions – that the central problem of international relations is war, that war is a barbaric and illegitimate tool of policy, and that the obvious way to abolish war is to abolish the weapons with which it is waged. Proponents of disarmament argue that weapons themselves are a cause of war in that they deepen the tension between states warily watching each other for signs of hostile intent. Unless the relationship between a pair or group of states is one characterized by traditionally friendly relations, states will tend to fear that a rival's weaponry has been acquired for use against them. Critics of weaponry also allege that their possession makes a state more likely to resort to the use of force in times of crisis (Claude 1964: 262–3).

In terms of policy, disarmament can be total or partial. The total form, known as 'general and complete disarmament', requires the reduction of armed forces down to the absolute minimum required for domestic policing purposes. The United States and the Soviet Union committed themselves to this goal as a long-term aim in the 1961 Agreed Statement of Principles. This agreement, which embraced the abolition of all weaponry, disbanding of their armed forces and abolition of all other military organizations, has to date been pursued more through faith than by good works.

The second approach to disarmament is that of partial disarmament, in which certain numbers or classes of weapons are eliminated, while others are retained. This approach seeks significant reductions rather than abolition. Thus in Bull's classic definition, 'disarmament is the reduction or abolition of armaments. It may be unilateral or multilateral, general or local, comprehensive or partial, controlled or uncontrolled' (Bull 1965: ix). Two examples of disarmament occurred during the late 1980s, both involving bilateral agreements: the first a tacit understanding, the second a formal treaty. Between 1985 and 1988 the People's Republic of China cut its army by one million troops and sharply reduced its forces on the Sino-Soviet border. In response, between 1988 and 1990 the Soviet Union cut its forces by 500,000, including 260,000 troops based on the Sino-Soviet border. In 1987 the United States and the Soviet Union signed the Intermediate Nuclear Forces treaty, eliminating a complete category of nuclear weapons from their respective arsenals.

The key element in both approaches to disarmament is reduction, without which disarmament cannot be said to be occurring. In Booth's paraphrase of Clausewitz, 'disarmament is a continuation of politics by a reduction of military means' (Booth 1975: 89).

ARMS CONTROL

Arms control is not the same thing as disarmament. The two approaches have different historical origins and are inspired by quite different sets of assumptions. The arms control approach in fact emerged because of a loss of faith in the disarmament process as it had operated in the first half of the twentieth century. In the late 1950s Western academic strategists unleashed a damning critique of the disarmament route to security, arguing that it had not only failed during the inter-war period, but had directly contributed to Hitler's diplomatic victories over the poorly armed British and French prior to 1939. In addition to this alleged failure, by the late 1940s the emergence of nuclear weapons and of the 'Cold War' changed the context of the debate about disarmament. At the same time as these developments created 'shapeless fears' about nuclear armageddon, they raised critical new obstacles to disarmament. Disarmament agreements had been difficult enough to negotiate prior to 1945, but in the nuclear era the implications of poorly drafted or unilaterally broken treaties became more profound. If a nuclear-armed state violated a disarmament agreement, it could mean annihilation for its victims.

The question of verification thus acquired a critical new salience. Verification is 'the process by which states utilize their intelligence gathering and interpretation capabilities for the purpose of satisfying themselves that their treaty partners are abiding by the terms of the agreements they have signed' (Sheehan 1988: 123). By the 1950s the French and Soviet governments accepted that no verification regime could be devised that could account for all the fissile material then in existence and that total disarmament would therefore demand absolute trust in the other parties. In the context of the Cold War that degree of trust was clearly unattainable and therefore disarmament was an unrealistic objective (Frye 1961: 73–5). From this point onwards arms control began to replace disarmament as the goal of the NATO and Warsaw Pact states.

The new arms control approach differed in crucial respects from that of disarmament. Whereas disarmers opposed weaponry and the use of the military instrument *per se*, arms controllers promoted a balance of military power in which arms control complemented unilateral force improvements as a means to achieve security (Lefever 1962: 122). Unlike disarmers, the proponents of arms control argued that there was no simple cause-and-effect relationship between the possession of weapons and the outbreak of war. They believed armaments were a normal part of the peacetime environment (Bull 1961: 8). Weapons were seen as a symptom rather than a cause of distrust between states and their possession merely reflected the naturally differing interests of states whose promotion or protection would periodically necessitate the use of the military instrument. Thus the problem was not to abolish weapons but to control their use (Booth 1975: 145). Arms controllers therefore sought the creation and maintenance of a stable balance of power, acceptable to both sides, in which neither was tempted to attack by the weakness of the other.

Such an environment requires a high degree of 'military transparency' so that legitimate defensive activities do not trigger the fear of attack in potential adversaries. While a balance of power was deemed stabilizing, it was recognized that certain weapons or deployments would jeopardize this stability and that a common interest therefore existed in creating a negotiated environment in which such destabilizing influences were controlled. Arms control therefore sought to discriminate between 'those kinds and quantities of forces and weapons that promote the stability of the balance of power, and those which do not; to tolerate or even to promote the former and to restrict the latter' (Bull 1965: 61). Whereas disarmament necessarily involves reductions, arms control may do so, but might just as easily require a freeze at existing levels or even, in certain circumstances, an actual increase in numbers.

This acceptance of the utility of military power extended to the realm of nuclear weaponry. Unlike the disarmers, the arms controllers did not see nuclear deterrence as an immoral expedient. On the contrary, they eulogized nuclear deterrence as a means of war prevention and saw the abolition of nuclear weapons as something to be avoided, while working to refine the deterrent balance and render it more accident-proof. Arms control was thus in fundamental opposition to the whole ethos of disarmament since it concerned the strengthening of the military balance of power. It was not, as the general public seemed to feel, disarmament in easy stages. Indeed, arms controllers favoured balances at high rather than low levels. This was because at low levels marginal advantages to one side were militarily significant, whereas at high levels marginal differences were of no practical consequence. The absolute level of weaponry was therefore deemed as significant for stability as the ratios involved. Beyond a certain point, therefore, arms reductions were seen as increasing the risk of war, an outlook that fundamentally separated the approach from that of disarmament, which favoured reductions at all times. The arms control approach did not reject the possibility of reductions, but it sought these only insofar as they did not threaten stability.

The operational result of this approach was that arms control sought to make the world safe for nuclear deterrence rather than to abolish nuclear weapons. However, it was recognized that a great deal of military effort is expended simply matching the weaponry of the other side and that there therefore exists a common interest in determining the extent to which mutual deterrence might be attainable at lower levels of deployment and expenditure. It was felt that it would in any case be a beneficial exercise to 'educate the Soviets in mutually desirable strategies and armament policies' (Brennan 1961: 40). Unlike disarmers, however, arms controllers did not feel that the activity was beneficial purely for its own sake. If other benefits flowed from it so much the better, but unless a deal enhanced stability it should be rejected (Lefever 1962: xii).

In their important work on the subject, Schelling and Halperin declared the objectives of arms control to be 'reducing the likelihood of war, its scope and violence if it occurs, and the political and economic costs of being prepared for it' (Schelling and Halperin 1961: 2). Subsequent experience demonstrated that these objectives might conflict with one another: for example, increasing the number of survivable nuclear weapons, as happened during the 1960s, reduced the likelihood of war, but increased its likely violence if it broke out. Complex verification regimes such as those surrounding the intermediate nuclear force (INF) agreement of 1987 reduced the likelihood of war, but generated additional financial burdens.

In proposing methods to achieve arms control, early theorists explored a larger number of possibilities than did subsequent practitioners. It was emphasized that formal treaties were only one possible route (Bull 1965: xi). Others included executive agreements, informal understandings and contingent self-restraint. The arms controllers left open the question of whether increase in weaponry and technical improvements to weapons would be the optimum arms control strategy in certain situations (Schelling and Halperin 1961: 2). The passage of time has led to a narrowing of the definition of what constitutes arms control, so that unilateral force improvements, while perfectly consistent with the theory of arms control, no longer constitute it in public parlance. Early theorists also noted the value of unilateral initiatives (Schelling 1961: 174), whereas subsequent political discourse has tended to treat unilateral moves as a feature of disarmament but not of arms control.

The arms control approach also differed from disarmament in laying stress upon initiatives which did not directly constrain the weaponry possessed by each side. Thus, for example, information exchanges were encouraged. This, it was felt, would ameliorate the 'worst-case' assumptions usually built into each side's threat assessment. It also held out the possibility of reducing the dangers of nuclear war by establishing communication procedures, information exchanges and even confidence-building visits to each other's military facilities. Such efforts, by increasing confidence, would enable the levels of military power deemed prudent to be lower than would otherwise be the case.

THE RECORD OF ARMS CONTROL

Arms control has taken a variety of forms since its inception, and the various negotiations and agreements can be subdivided into a number of categories. The first of these comprises the non-armament treaties, which are accorded pride of place only in so far as the 1959 Antarctic Treaty, which falls into this category, was also the first post-1945 arms control treaty. The non-armament treaties are attempts to prevent military competition from being introduced into a region which had hitherto been free of such activity. The 1959 Antarctic Treaty prohibited the establishment of military bases in Antarctica as well as banning weapon tests and military manoeuvres on that continent.

There are three other agreements in this category. In 1967 the Treaty of Tlatelolco established a Latin American nuclear weapon free zone. The same year saw the signing of the UN-sponsored Outer Space Treaty, which among other things banned the testing or deployment of 'weapons of mass destruction' in Earth-orbit or on other bodies in the solar system. In 1971 the Sea-Bed Treaty was signed, which banned the emplacement of weapons of mass destruction on the ocean floor.

The value of such agreements is questionable since, with the exception of Tlatelolco, they banned activities for which the parties either had no need, or for which they lacked the technology to carry out. Experience with the Outer Space Treaty demonstrated that when these self-restraining factors were no longer present the superpowers were scarcely inhibited in pressing the treaty limits. In 1968, only a year after signing the Outer Space Treaty, the Soviet Union introduced weaponry into Earth-orbit by initiating an anti-satellite (ASAT) weapon test programme. Because the kill-mechanism used conventional explosives the USSR argued that not being 'a weapon of mass destruction' the ASAT did not contravene the 1967 treaty. The United States began a similar programme in the 1980s. These programmes, while adhering to the letter of the 1967 treaty, clearly contravened its spirit. The preamble refers to 'the common interest of mankind' in the use of space 'for peaceful purposes', and the majority of the signatories clearly interpreted it as a ban on all weapons in space. This willingness to side-step the constraints of a treaty once it became technically feasible or militarily desirable to do so casts doubt upon the utility of all the non-armament treaties.

A second cluster of agreements was inaugurated by the 1963 'Hotline' Treaty. Early arms control theorists had stressed the desirability of clear and rapid communication between the superpowers, and the 1962 Cuban Missile Crisis had reinforced the wisdom of this. The 1963 agreement established a duplex wire-telegraph link between the Pentagon and the Kremlin. It was updated in 1971 to create a system based on two satellite communication circuits, and a 1984 protocol to the agreement modified the technology further to allow it to transmit pictures and diagrams as well as text. The Soviet Union subsequently established similar facilities with Britain and France. This desire to enhance 'crisis management' capabilities also lay behind such accords as the 1971 US–Soviet agreement on 'measures to reduce the risk of outbreak of nuclear war', the 1972 superpower treaty on the prevention of military incidents on and over the high seas, and the 1976 Franco-Soviet agreement on the accidental or unauthorized use of nuclear weapons. The 1971 agreement, for example, provided for immediate notification of the other party in the event of incidents which involved a possible nuclear detonation, immediate notification of missile warning alerts and advance notification of test launches. Both sides also pledged themselves to improve their own 'fail-safe' technologies and techniques to reduce the risk of accidental or unauthorized nuclear release.

Multilateral 'confidence-building measures' (CBMs) took rather longer to achieve. CBM's are designed to provide 'credible evidence of the absence of feared threats' (Abbott 1980: 382). Proposals of this nature, exemplified by the 1986 Stockholm Agreement, have concentrated on measures related to the reduction of the dangers of surprise attack. The Stockholm Agreement, for example, provided for forty-two days' notification of major military activities; an annual 'calendar' of planned military activities for the year ahead, with a ban on activities involving 40,000 troops or more if they have not been mentioned in the calendar; detailed advance notification of any activities involving 13,000 troops or 300 tanks, or amphibious or parachute operations involving 3,000 troops; and mandatory verification. The verification regime included three 'challenge' inspections per year on each state's territory and mandatory invitation of observers to any manoeuvre involving more than 17,000 troops. Such confidence-building measures address not so much the weapons of war as the intentions behind the possession of such weapons. They are designed to reduce the risk of a misunderstanding in times of crisis which might lead to war, by increasing the transparency of each side's legitimate defensive preparations in peacetime. They also have the effect of making it more difficult for states to utilize their armed forces for the purpose of political intimidation.

Europe was the focus for two other sets of arms control negotiations: those on conventional forces and those on chemical weapons. Negotiations on 'mutual and balanced force reductions' (MBFR) began in 1973, but neither NATO nor the Warsaw Treaty Organization (WTO) were committed to bringing the talks to a successful conclusion. This lack of political will, coupled with an inability to agree on such crucial matters as the types of weapons to be counted, the numbers of troops and weapons each side actually possessed, and the verification regime required to police any agreement led the talks into a dead end, although they were not formally ended until 1989. They were replaced by a new set of negotiations, on Conventional Forces in Europe (CFE), which began in March 1989. In the CFE negotiations both sides adopted a positive attitude. In particular, the advent of Mikhail Gorbachev as Soviet leader had meant that in all the areas that had blocked agreement during the MBFR talks a new Soviet approach prevailed. The Soviet Union, for economic and political reasons, was sincerely committed to making large-scale reductions in its conventional forces. For the first time the USSR accepted that in almost all areas it held a numerical advantage and would therefore have to make proportionately greater cuts than the NATO allies. *Glasnost* or 'openness' in the USSR also meant that for the first time the WTO provided reliable data on its force levels and that the intrusive verification methods required would not be an insurmountable obstacle to agreement as they had been during MBFR. Effectively the WTO abandoned its MBFR goal of reductions that would not 'disturb the existing balance of power in central Europe' in favour of the NATO objective of 'a more stable military balance at lower levels of forces with undiminished security for all participants'. CFE embraced a wider area, from Portugal to the Urals, than its predecessor and was far more ambitious in terms of the reductions sought.

Difficult as the conventional arms control negotiations were, they faced lesser problems than those surrounding chemical weapons. In 1972 an agreement was concluded between the superpowers banning biological weapons, but chemical weapons control remained elusive. The only existing agreement is the Geneva Protocol signed on 17 June 1925. Since most of the signatories to this added a caveat reserving the right to retaliate in kind against a state attacking them with chemical weapons, the Geneva Protocol is little more than a no-first-use agreement. It allows states to produce and stockpile chemical munitions. Unlike biological weapons, chemical weapons are of proven military utility, a fact reinforced by Iraq's successful use of chemicals to defeat Iran's offensives during the Iran–Iraq War of the 1980s. Their proven record makes armed forces reluctant to discard them. A second major obstacle to their control is the peculiar difficulties involved in verifying compliance with any chemical weapons agreement. Chemical agents are produced in factories that are externally indistinguishable from civil chemical facilities. Even inside the plant the technologies are virtually identical. Any verification regime must of necessity, therefore, be extremely intrusive. In the pre-Gorbachev Soviet Union such intrusive verification was out of the question. Since 1985, however, the chemical weapons talks have moved slowly but steadily closer to agreement, thanks largely to a new Soviet willingness to countenance intrusive on-site inspection.

When in 1987 the Soviet Union accepted the principle of mandatory on-site inspections, the negotiations being held under the auspices of the UN Conference on Disarmament in Geneva entered a new phase. Whereas until that point chemical arms control had appeared to be essentially a NATO–WTO issue, after 1987 the question of chemical proliferation also became crucial. This was both because more states were acquiring chemical weapons and because since 1987 a chemical treaty has appeared an attainable goal, therefore prompting states who had previously taken little serious interest in the proceedings at Geneva to begin manoeuvring to protect their particular interests. Between 1960 and 1990 the number of chemical weapons states rose from five to twenty (Flowerree *et al.* 1989: 4), and while such proliferation has made the desirability of a chemical weapons treaty greater it has made the verification problems associated with a treaty more demanding also.

More than any other issue, the control of nuclear weapons dominated the arms control agenda after 1960. Efforts at control focused on three areas: horizontal proliferation (the spread of nuclear weapons technology to other countries); vertical proliferation (the increase in the numbers of nuclear weapons deployed by the existing nuclear powers); and attempts to constrain the technical development of nuclear weapons through limitations on nuclear weapons tests.

The first example of the latter occurred in 1963 when Britain, the United States and the Soviet Union signed the Limited Test Ban Treaty. This agreement restricted the signatories to testing their nuclear weapons under-ground, with tests in the atmosphere, in outer space and under water being banned. China and France refused to sign the treaty, but by the late 1980s both countries were restricting their tests to below ground. In 1974 the super-powers signed a follow-up agreement, the Threshold Test Ban Treaty. This limited the size of individual nuclear test explosions to a yield of 150 kilotons, well below the yield of the largest nuclear weapons in existence, though still ten times the power of the weapons that destroyed Hiroshima and Nagasaki in 1945. In order to prevent a state circumventing the treaty by designating a nuclear test a 'peaceful nuclear explosion' for engineering purposes, in 1976 a further treaty was signed. The Peaceful Nuclear Explosions Treaty extended the provisions of the 1974 treaty to tests designated non-military. The upper yield limit was again 150 kilotons for a single explosion, though 'group explosions' could exceed this limit to a maximum yield of 1.5 megatons. The two states agreed to abide by the terms of these treaties, though in 1990 the US Senate had still not ratified either agreement.

Efforts to control the spread of nuclear weapons found form in the negotiations to conclude a non-proliferation treaty during the 1960s. While most of the nuclear arms control treaties are bilateral agreements between the superpowers, the Non-Proliferation Treaty (NPT) of 1968 was fully multilateral, open to signature by all states. In many ways, however, the NPT remains an agreement between two parties – the nuclear weapons states on one side and the non-nuclear weapons states on the other. The former pledge to 'pursue negotiations in good faith on effective measures relating to cessation of the nuclear arms race at an early date and to nuclear disarmament' (Article VI), and also to make available to the non-nuclear states the technology for the production of nuclear energy for peaceful purposes (Article IV). In return for this the other signatories give up their right to acquire nuclear weapons (Article II) and agree to accept a system of safeguards and monitoring of their nuclear facilities. The treaty came into effect in 1970, and by 1990 over 120 states had signed it.

Although the NPT is not as constraining as some states would have liked, it remains a significant disincentive to proliferation. Though a number of important 'threshold' states (i.e. states verging on the capability to produce nuclear weapons) refused either to sign or to ratify the treaty, proliferation has been remarkably slow. Only one additional state, India, has carried out a full-scale nuclear test since the treaty came into effect. While states such as Argentina, Brazil, Iraq, Israel, Libya, Pakistan, South Africa, South Korea and Taiwan have the capability to acquire nuclear weapons, and in the case of Israel and South Africa are suspected of already having done so, proliferation has been neither as inevitable nor as widespread as was feared in the early 1960s, and for this the NPT must be given some credit. Criticisms of the treaty remain, and the International Atomic Energy Agency has had some of its power of inspection strengthened to meet those criticisms. The main criticism of the non-nuclear states, that Article VI, requiring significant nuclear disarmament by the superpowers, has not been lived up to, still remains potent.

While the *détente* agreements of the early 1970s went some way towards mollifying the non-nuclear states, this was only true for a brief period. The nuclear confidence-building agreements and the threshold test ban treaties were a positive development but they were clearly no substitute for the nuclear disarmament promised in Article VI of the NPT. The superpowers sought to

achieve this through the SALT (Strategic Arms Limitations Treaty) negotiations of the 1970s and the follow-on START (Strategic Arms Reduction
Treaty) talks of the 1980s and 1990s.

Talks on the limitation of strategic nuclear weapons between the super-
powers began in Helsinki on 17 November 1969. With one short hiatus
between November 1983 and January 1985 (caused by a Soviet 'walkout' in
protest against NATO INF deployments), they have been going on ever since.
By 1971 the superpowers had agreed to complete a treaty on Anti-Ballistic
Missiles (ABM) and an interim agreement on strategic offensive weapons.
These two agreements were concluded in May 1972 as the SALT I treaties.
The ABM Treaty sharply restricted each side's ability to defend itself against
the nuclear missiles of the other. Each country was allowed only two ABM
sites. A July 1974 protocol reduced this still further to one site each, with 100
interceptor missiles. The associated radars were also restricted and the treaty
prohibited the development, testing or deployment of sea-based, air-based,
space-based or mobile land-based ABMs. Conversion of other defence systems
to ABM capability was also banned. Modernization was permitted but deployment of 'exotic' ABM systems 'based on other physical principles' was banned.

The Interim Agreement on Strategic Offensive Arms limited the two sides'
intercontinental ballistic missile (ICBM) and submarine-launched ballistic
missile (SLBM) launchers to those currently operational or under construction.
The agreement was to last for five years, during which time a more comprehensive agreement of longer duration would be negotiated.

The SALT I agreements represented a significant breakthrough in arms
control and were of major significance. The agreement of two political and
ideological rivals, potential adversaries in a future war, to restrain their offensive capabilities while limiting their abilities to defend themselves was historically unprecedented. The nature of the constraints upon this critical technology
meant that the two sides were doing far more than just limiting weapon
numbers: they were defining the nature of their strategic relationship and
moving toward a shared view of the nature and purpose of the deterrent
relationship in the nuclear age. The ABM Treaty represented an acceptance
by the Soviet Union of the logic of mutually assured destruction, that adequate
deterrence requires the capability to inflict, regardless of the circumstance,
assured destruction on a potential attacker. By limiting their defensive capabilities to levels that were barely more than symbolic, the two sides ensured that
if nuclear war did break out mutual annihilation would be assured – and by
so doing they enormously reinforced the deterrent effect of their offensive
arsenals.

By limiting the growth of those offensive arsenals the superpowers averted
a pointless arms race, made unquantifiable savings from deferred future spending and, most importantly, introduced considerably enhanced stability and

predictability into the strategic competition. 'Worst-case analysis' could now give way to predictions based on known capabilities within the lifetime of the treaty. Since SALT was a process, an ongoing activity without a foreseeable end-point, that predictably would be long lasting.

SALT I represented failure as well as success, however. It evolved no method for containing the qualitative improvement in strategic nuclear weaponry. In particular MIRVs (Multiple Independently Targetable Re-entry Vehicles) were neither banned nor limited, so while the number of launchers was capped, the number of warheads carried by those launchers increased dramatically during the 1970s.

None the less, SALT was envisaged as a process. The shortcomings of any one agreement could be addressed in the subsequent negotiations. SALT I was crucially important in establishing the framework for all subsequent strategic nuclear negotiations. A mutually understood vocabulary evolved, the critical issues were identified, data bases exchanged, acceptable methods for verifying the agreements using remote sensing techniques (mainly satellites) were agreed and mechanisms for facilitating the operation of the agreements, such as the standing consultative commission to discuss complaints about compliance, were established. These procedures would be available for use in the subsequent negotiations and agreements.

SALT II, signed in June 1979, attempted to go beyond the constraints imposed by its predecessor. SALT I had legitimized strategic parity between the superpowers, but had done so at very high numbers. The freeze on missile numbers restricted the competition, but critical strategic programmes such as MIRV were unaffected and an array of new weapons and delivery vehicles were under development by both sides. SALT II limited each party to 2,400 strategic missiles and bombers. New sub-limits were imposed on warhead numbers, each side being limited to 1,320 weapons equipped with MIRV warheads or air-launched cruise missiles. No more than 1,200 ballistic missiles could be carried by MIRVs, and ICBMs would be limited to a maximum of ten warheads per delivery vehicle. SLBMs would be restricted to fourteen warheads. In order to slow the rate of technological development each party would only be permitted to deploy one new ICBM type during the lifetime treaty. The treaty also banned certain types of technology which were feasible but had not yet been deployed, such as ballistic strategic nuclear missiles on surface ships. There was also a specific ban on the Soviet SS-16 ICBM. The agreement also committed the superpowers to negotiating a SALT III treaty which would further reduce the number of strategic offensive arms and introduce additional qualitative limitations.

SALT II represented a modest but significant advance over SALT I. The brake on the strategic nuclear arms race touched lightly in 1972 was being pressed firmly by 1979. While the United States would have been only marginally affected since its forces were within the SALT II limits, the Soviet Union would be required to dismantle 10 per cent of its strategic nuclear arsenal to get down to the SALT II ceilings. Surprisingly, given this, it was the United States rather than the Soviet Union which refused to ratify the treaty. SALT II was overtaken by the wider breakdown of the *détente* relationship, brought into sharp focus by the Soviet invasion of Afghanistan in December 1979. However, even though it remained unratified by the US Senate, both countries agreed to abide by its terms, even after it had technically expired on 31 December 1985.

President Reagan, who condemned SALT II as 'fatally flawed', renamed the strategic negotiations START and insisted on a more radical approach, emphasizing both deeper numerical reductions and more significant qualitative restraints. Until 1986 he had little success in convincing his Soviet counterparts, particularly after the announcement of the Strategic Defence Initiative (SDI) in 1983, which both threatened the ABM Treaty and created a rationale for continuing, even increasing, high levels of Soviet ballistic nuclear weaponry. However, at the Reykjavik summit in 1986, President Reagan and General Secretary Gorbachev agreed to pursue the goal of deep cuts in strategic nuclear weaponry to 1,600 delivery vehicles and 6,000 warheads. These would represent reductions of almost 40 per cent. The complexities of the issues prevented a treaty from being concluded while President Reagan was still in office and it was left to his successor to finalize the agreement in 1991.

The strategic nuclear negotiations were critically interrelated to those on INFs in Europe. During the 1960s NATO had adopted a doctrine known as 'flexible response', which called for the ability to respond to aggression in whatever form and at whatever level it occurred. The enormous expense involved meant that the policy had not been fully implemented, but since the USA had greater strategic firepower than the USSR this was not seen as a major problem. In the final analysis, deficiencies at other levels could be compensated for by the threat to escalate to all-out strategic nuclear warfare, where the USA held the cards. With the advent of 'parity' legitimized in the SALT I treaty, the superiority of NATO at the strategic level disappeared. It became more important, therefore, to ensure that deterrence remained intact at the lower levels. The next 'rung' down, INF, showed signs of needing bolstering. With its ageing bombers no longer up to the task, NATO decided in 1979 to deploy a new generation of intermediate-range missiles in Europe. The Soviet Union had taken a similar step with its new SS-20 three years earlier. These developments triggered an arms spiral in Europe which was finally and dramatically broken by the 1987 INF treaty. The advent of Mikhail Gorbachev to the Soviet leadership and the 'new thinking' on Soviet security policy produced the most dramatic treaty of the arms control era. The US–Soviet treaty 'on the Elimination of their Intermediate-Range and Shorter-Range

Missiles' signed on 8 December 1987 committed the superpowers to eliminating their entire force of intermediate- and medium-range missiles and launchers within three years of ratification and to eliminate all short-range INF within eighteen months of ratification. The treaty was unprecedently detailed, comprising 127 typed pages, and most of these dealt with the issue of verification of the agreement. The treaty mandated the destruction of nearly 2,700 guided missiles capable of carrying nuclear warheads – about 3 per cent of the global total. In addition, all associated equipment and facilities were to be dismantled and all production and flight testing of new INF missiles, missile stages or launches banned for all time (ACDA 1987: 21). Destruction and non-production was to be verified by intrusive on-site inspection and continuous monitoring of designated missile production facilities for a period of thirteen years after the treaty came into force. Destruction of the missiles was completed on schedule within three years of the treaty being signed.

METHODS AND PROBLEMS

The experience with arms control during the 1960s and 1970s led to a major debate over the methods most likely to achieve success. It produced a major critique by Thomas Schelling, one of the founders of arms control, who argued that the shift from concern about the *character* of weapons to concern about their *numbers* was the crucial difference between arms control negotiations before and after 1970 (Schelling 1985–6: 224). Indeed, Schelling argued that arms control was being pursued without reference to its original guiding philosophy and that reductions in numbers only really mattered if the ultimate goal was zero, 'but hardly anyone who takes arms control seriously believes that zero is the goal' (Shelling 1985–6: 226).

The implications of this difference are profound. Arms control as pursued during the 1970s tended to concentrate upon negotiability. Weapons were divided up for bargaining purposes into manageable categories such as strategic nuclear weapons or biological weapons. Criteria for control emerged that were based upon negotiability; that is, those weapons were identified which could be controlled without placing inordinate burdens upon the negotiating process. But sometimes the weapons which could be so controlled were not necessarily those that most needed controlling. Thus 1970s arms controllers frowned on sea-launched cruise missiles (SLCMs), because their numbers were hard to verify with confidence. Yet these weapons were too slow to be used in a first strike, were difficult to defend against, hard to locate on station and comparatively cheap to produce. In 'traditional' 1960s arms control terms, SLCMs did not need to be controlled since they could neither pre-empt themselves nor be the subject of a successful pre-emptive strike by an adversary.

In a purely intellectual sense Schelling was right, but in political terms his view was no longer a feasible option. The manner in which arms control has been conducted for thirty years and the way in which politicians have geared the public to expect arms control to freeze or reduce numbers means that a central original tenet of arms control has effectively been buried.

The arms control approach also evolved in other unpredicted ways. Rather than pursuing the variety of approaches advocated by early theorists, political leaders became obsessed by the pursuit of comprehensive accords. These took years to conclude since they embraced so many complex issues. Whereas the Partial Test Ban Treaty took only weeks to negotiate, SALT I took four years, SALT II took seven years and START I was a decade in the making. Dissatisfaction with the ponderous nature of the SALT process led arms controllers to advocate more limited but more frequent agreements – 'small steps or large steps for a short duration' (Pierre 1980: 192). Sceptics suggested that since comprehensive negotiations produced such limited outcomes, limited negotiations might produce nothing at all (Kruzel 1985: 128). Nor did unilateral initiatives play the part that Schelling and Halperin in 1960 had suggested they should. What did become a feature of the politics of arms control was a perceived need to sustain 'momentum'. Arms control was seen very much as a process rather than an event, and new mechanisms such as more frequent superpower 'summits' evolved to provide the political pressure which would sustain the momentum of arms control. So much did arms control dominate the agendas of superpower summits during the 1970s and 1980s that its success or failure became a barometer of the superpowers' relationship. This ultimately imposed too great a burden of responsibility upon arms control, progress in which always remained hostage to the vicissitudes of the wider superpower and indeed East–West relationship.

The dissappointment of the 1970s did not lead to any notable evolution in arms control thinking; on the contrary there remained a striking absence of innovative proposals. Honourable exceptions existed, such as Christoph Bertram's suggestion that the obsession with numerical parity be dropped in favour of an approach which focused instead upon the missions that weapon systems were designed to implement – an emphasis upon 'who could do what' rather than 'who had what' (Bertram 1978: 15–31). However, while the record of arms control was disappointing in terms of the number and significance of the agreements signed, the process itself did bring a number of advances, laying the foundations upon which future success could be built. There were permanent gains which created an infrastructure into which subsequent negotiations could be fitted with comparative ease.

To argue that between 1960 and 1990 arms control was a failure because little significant disarmament occurred is simplistic for a number of reasons. In the first place, as has already been noted, arms control need not encompass disarmament. Nevertheless, it must be said that the rhetoric with which politicians have advocated arms control has inextricably associated it in the public mind with the goal of disarmament. It is not unreasonable, therefore, to ask why arms control produced so little in the way of meaningful ceilings or reductions. In answering this question, however, it should be borne in mind that states engage in arms control negotiations for a variety of reasons. These include the desire to make propaganda points, to highlight the military pro-grammes of the adversary, to be seen negotiating 'at the top table' thereby gaining status, to deflect domestic or international criticism of one's own defence efforts, to constrain the adversary for actions in other areas of the relationship, to sustain a desired non-belligerent image, and so on. Moreover, military power itself is an instrument with far more varied uses than simply deterring a single adversary. All these factors impinge upon the conduct of arms control negotiations by producing clear limits to each side's desire to reduce their own weaponry if doing so would reduce the flexibility of their military capabilities. Arms control negotiations are part and parcel of the wider struggle for influence in international relations and are often just another diplomatic battlefield on which states seek to outwit their opponents (Spanier and Nogee 1962: 176–81).

The critical nature of security relationships and the complexity of the issues discussed at arms control negotiations makes arms control a demanding enter-prise. Even so, many proponents of arms control after 1970 argued that the manner in which it was being pursued was almost counter-productive. For political reasons, numerical parity in the relevant weapon categories was taken as the objective of the negotiations. Yet given the dissimilar strategic situations of the protagonists and the differing weapon requirements this generated, aggregate force levels or even aggregate capabilities were what needed matching rather than 'optical parity' in weapon systems (Krepon 1984: 130). Unfortunately a balance which matched overall capabilities was far harder to explain to domestic publics than was one based upon straightforward numerical parity (Schlesinger 1974: 41). Prospects for disarmament were also held back by the strategy of 'negotiating from strength'. Proponents of this logic argued that states only made concessions if the other side gave up 'virile' military systems, therefore only if both sides had something to offer could talks succeed.

Thus in the early 1980s the United States argued that it needed an anti-satellite weapon programme of its own to convince the USSR to abandon the Soviet programme. Binary chemical weapons and modernized INF systems were justified by a similar rationale. The pursuit of arms control in these instances led to increases in weaponry rather than the reverse. However, while the 'bargaining from strength' argument is logical, the record demonstrates that states are often willing to do deals when no matching capability exists (Einhorn 1985). An example of this was the 1972 Biological Weapons Treaty.

Pursuit of comprehensive accords also limited progress. Talks such as SALT

II, which took several years to conclude, were particularly vulnerable to the mood-swings of international relations. Critics argued that frequent, modest gains were better than infrequent substantial achievements, because they carried fewer political risks, made the progressive nature of the exercise more obvious and produced regular pay-offs (Makins 1985: 174). Moreover, as the new atmosphere that followed the 1986 Stockholm Agreement and 1987 INF Treaty showed, success in one area can lead to accelerating progess in other sets of negotiations. Frequent, limited agreements offered a route which the major powers remained reluctant to follow, however, with comprehensive agendas such as START and CFE continuing to be the norm.

In the 1970s domestic impediments to arms control received far more attention than had previously been the case. This was partly the result of the example of the rise and decline of *détente* and partly a result of application to the arms control realm of the fruitful insights offered by the 'decision-making analysis' approach following the publication of Graham Allison's *Essence of Decision* in 1971. The domestic debate influences progress in arms control negotiations in a number of ways. The need to mollify political opposition, reassure sceptics in one's own party, maintain the support of the armed forces, allay fears concerning the economic impact of potential reductions and so on means that the bargaining process within each state is as complex and as necessary for success as that between states. Again, the interplay of domestic forces may lead to arms control negotiations increasing rather than reducing weapons totals: for example, by the need to placate the armed services by giving them new weapons systems to offset those lost through the arms control negotiations (Kissinger 1979: 1240). Given the number of special interest groups that may be affected by the outcome of arms control negotiations, it is inevitable that building a domestic consensus behind an arms control policy is a complex and time-consuming process. Recognition of this is crucial, for overcoming domestic obstacles to arms control is as critical to success as is achieving a consensus with other states.

The value of arms control should not be judged simply in terms of the agreements arrived at. The real value of arms control is political rather than technical and its pursuit generates a variety of second-order benefits, of which the maintenance of a dialogue on critical security issues is by no means the least. Arms control cannot be a substitute for adequate defences, but it can play a crucial role both in influencing each side's perceptions of what constitutes 'adequate' defence and in sustaining public support for legitimate defence efforts. Arms control, intelligently pursued, is capable of reducing the economic burdens of maintaining a mutual security regime, of reducing the risk of misperception increasing the possibility of war, and of mobilizing public support for national security objectives.

THE GORBACHEV REVOLUTION AND THE RE-EMERGENCE OF DISARMAMENT

In its original formulation, arms control was seen as a method of helping to sustain the balance of power by constraining military competition and anticipating and foreclosing threats to strategic stability. Arms control was the handmaiden of strategic deterrence and it was in terms of the technical requirements of deterrence theory that it was pursued. The arms control approach accepted the validity of deterrence doctrine and worked to sustain it. Deterrence theory, however, is itself a contributing factor in arms build-ups since it creates a need for ever more numerous and more varied weapons in order to ensure that deterrence can be sustained under any conceivable circumstance. One of the rationales for arms control in the late 1950s was that disarmament required too great a degree of trust between states. From 1960 to 1985 that trust simply did not exist. Given that the 'threat' posed by another state is defined in terms of both capabilities and perceived intentions, in an era characterized by massive military build-up and intense mutual suspicion, the possibility of disarmament was non-existent and even the scope for arms control was limited.

The emergence of Mikhail Gorbachev as Soviet leader in 1985 was therefore an event of historical importance. The promotion by Gorbachev and Foreign Minister Schevadnadze of 'new thinking' in Soviet foreign policy led to a revolution in the Soviet approach to achieving security and, in doing so, triggered a paradigm-shift, bringing disarmament back to centre stage after thirty years of apparent obsolescence. Gorbachev argued that in the nuclear age it was a mirage for one state to pursue security at the expense of another's. Security had to be mutual. Moreover, military threats were denounced as an illegitimate policy instrument while ideological confrontation was criticized, with emphasis placed instead upon self-determination and 'equal-security'. As the evolution of *perestroika* began to demonstrate that Gorbachev's words were based on conviction and were not just rhetoric, so the possibilities for arms control and disarmament improved out of all recognition. An array of factors made this possible. Recognizing that the huge size of its armed forces generated so much suspicion abroad that it diminished rather than enhanced Soviet security, the USSR began a series of unilateral reductions and withdrawals. These cuts, in reducing the scale of the threat, also modified foreign perceptions of Soviet intentions and led to compensating reductions in the size of the Chinese army and a softening of NATO's military posture. The Soviet withdrawal from Eastern Europe and Mongolia accelerated these trends. Pressure for real reductions was also created by the economic difficulties of the superpowers, seen in the enormous American budget deficit and the Soviet Union's chronic economic weakness. Both looked to major savings in their military budgets to ease their economic burdens. Finally, the political changes in Eastern Europe, the emergence of pro-Western democratic governments, combined with *glasnost*, the new openness in Soviet society, meant that verification was no longer the bug-bear it had once been. Eastern Europe had become as militarily transparent as the West, while the Soviet Union itself developed a relaxed attitude to intrusive verification techniques that it would have deemed an unacceptable breach of its sovereignty a few years earlier.

All these changes helped produce an environment in which disarmament rather than arms control was the objective once more. In practice the evolution of arms control thinking after 1970 had meant that the two approaches were no longer the distinct schools they had been in 1960. What had emerged was a new synthesis. The values of arms control remained intact – the centrality of stability, of mutual deterrence, of predictability in military matters. Onto this was grafted the goal of disarmament as a fundamental objective. General and complete disarmament down to zero in all categories remained outside this new consensus, but it did embrace the pursuit of zero in certain categories and minimal optimum levels in all others. Whereas ceilings at high levels had sufficed for the 1970s, radical reductions were on the agenda for the 1990s.

However, the very scale of the changes in 1985–90 which made so many things possible also served to act as a brake on some of the more ambitious proposals. Arms control and disarmament require a high degree of stability and predictability to succeed. In order to know what cuts can safely be made and what new levels and types of weaponry will be optimum in terms of security, there must be a high degree of consensus on strategic matters. There must, for example, be agreement on what kinds of weapons are or are not destabilizing, and there must be stability in the political framework within which the negotiations are occurring. Neither of these conditions was fulfilled at the beginning of the 1990s. The superpowers remained at odds over whether ballistic missile defences, such as the American SDI programme, should be encouraged or opposed. The sweeping political changes in Eastern Europe, the unification of Germany and the disintegration of the Warsaw Pact left the Soviet Union unsure as to what residual forces it would require in the changed and unpredictable circumstances of the century's final decade.

This hesitancy, which was shared to an extent on the NATO side, made it clear that while the 1990s would see more arms control agreements than preceding decades and that those agreements would be far more radical than their predecessors, involving significant reductions in all categories of weaponry, the final result would be neither denuclearization nor total disarmament. Arms control retains its function of constraining military-political competition between rival states and alliances within stable limits short of open conflict. The central goal remains what it has been for forty years: the avoidance of nuclear war.

REFERENCES

Abbott, B. A. (1980) 'Confidence building measures in European Security', *The World Today* (October).

ACDA (US Arms Control and Disarmament Agency) (1987) *Understanding the INF Treaty*, Washington, DC: ACDA.

Bertram, C. (1978) 'Arms control and technological change: elements of a new approach', *Adelphi Paper* no. 146.

Booth, K. (1975) 'Disarmament and arms control', in J. Bayliss, K. Booth, J. Garnett and P. Williams (eds) *Contemporary Strategy: Theories and Policies*, New York: Holmes & Meier.

Brennan, D. G. (ed.) (1961) 'Setting and goals of arms control', in D. G. Brennan (ed.) *Arms Control, Disarmament and National Security*, New York.

Bull, H. (1965) *The Control of the Arms Race*, New York: Praeger.

Claude, I. (1964) *Swords into Ploughshares: The Problems and Progress of International Organization*, New York: Random House.

Einhorn, R. J. (1985) *Negotiating from Strength*, New York: Praeger.

Flowerree, C. C., Harris, E. and Leonard, J. (1989) 'Chemical arms control after the Paris Conference', *Arms Control Today* 19 (1).

Frye, W. R. (1961) 'Characteristics of recent arms control proposals and agreements', in D. G. Brennan (ed.) *Arms Control, Disarmament and National Security*, New York.

Kissinger, H. (1979) *The White House Years*, London.

Krepon, M. (1984) *Strategic Stalemate: Nuclear Weapons and Arms Control in American Politics*, London: Macmillan.

Kruzel, J. (1985) 'What's wrong with the traditional approach?', *Washington Quarterly* 8 (2).

Lefever, E. W. (1962) *Arms and Arms Control*, New York.

Makins, C. J. (1985) 'The superpowers' dilemma: negotiating in the nuclear age', *Survival* 27 (4).

Pierre, A. J. (1980) 'The diplomacy of SALT', *International Security* 5 (1).

Schelling, T. C. (1961) 'Reciprocal measures for arms stabilization', in D. G. Brennan (ed.) *Arms Control, Disarmament and National Security*, New York.

——(1985–6) 'What went wrong with arms control?', *Foreign Affairs* (Winter): 219–33.

Schelling, T. C. and Halperin, M. (1961) *Strategy and Arms Control*, reprinted 1985, Oxford: Pergamon.

Schlesinger, J. (1974) *Hearing on US–USSR Strategic Policies*, Sub-committee on Arms Control, International Law and Organization, Senate Committee on Foreign Relations, 93rd Congress, 4 March 1974, Washington, DC.

Sheehan, M. (1988) *Arms Control: Theory and Practice*, Oxford: Blackwell.

Spanier, J. W. and Nogee, J. L. (1962) *The Politics of Disarmament: A Study in Soviet–American Gamesmanship*, New York.

FURTHER READING

Bertram, C. (1980–1) 'Rethinking arms control', *Foreign Affairs* 59 (2): 352–65.

Blechman, B. (1980) 'Do negotiated arms limitations have a future?', *Foreign Affairs* 59 (1): 102–25.

Borawski, J. (1988) *From the Atlantic to the Urals. Negotiating Arms Control at the Stockholm Conference*, Oxford: Pergamon.

Brennan, D. G. (ed.) (1961) *Arms Control, Disarmament and National Security*, New York.

Bull, H. (1965) *The Control of the Arms Race*, New York: Praeger.

Flowerree, C. C. (1983–4) 'The politics of arms control treaties: a case study, *Journal of International Affairs* 37 (2).

Garnett, J. (1979) 'Disarmament and arms control since 1945', in L. W. Martin (ed.) *Strategic Thought in the Nuclear Age*, London: Heinemann.

Gelb, L. H. (1979) 'A glass half-full', *Foreign Policy* 36: 21–32.

Goldblat, J. (1983) *Arms Control Agreements: A Handbook*, London.

Krepon, M. and Umberger, M. (eds) (1988) *Verification and Compliance: A Problem Solving Approach*, London.

Kruzel, J. (1986) 'From Rush-Bagot to START: the lessons of arms control', *Orbis* 30 (1): 193–216.

Luttwak, E. N. (1978) 'Why arms control has failed', *Commentary* 65: 19–28.

Meyer, S. M. (1984) 'Verification and risk in arms control', *International Security* 8 (4): 111–26.

Miller, S. E. (1984) 'Politics over promise: the domestic impediments to arms control', *International Security* 8 (4): 67–90.

Perry-Robinson, J. P. (1985) *Chemical Warfare Arms Control: A Framework for Considering Policy Alternatives*, London: Taylor & Francis.

Potter, W. C. (ed.) (1985) *Verification and Arms Control*, Lexington, Mass.: Lexington Books

Schelling, T. C. (1985–6) 'What went wrong with arms control?', *Foreign Affairs* (Winter): 219–33.

Schelling, T. C. and Halperin, M. H. (1961) *Strategy and Arms Control*, reprinted 1985, Oxford: Pergamon.

Scribner, R., Ralston, T. J. and Metz, W. D. (1985) *The Verification Challenge*, Boston.

Sheehan, M. (1988) *Arms Control: Theory and Practice*, Oxford: Blackwell.

80

THE POLITICS OF
LIMITED RESOURCES
AND NORTH–SOUTH
RELATIONS

TOIVO MILJAN

The Industrial Revolution ushered in almost two centuries of increasing abundance of goods and services for human use. This growth, based on increasingly sophisticated exploitation of resources, has never been uniform nor linear across time and space. Although at times it has threatened to stop, so far the trend continues, despite the intellectual community's sporadic cries of alarm. Dennis Pirages's statement, that 'Growth in population and consumption of resources, once considered desirable signs of industrial and economic progress, are now considered to be major global problems in light of limited resources' (Pirages 1989: 291), is still more an expression of concern than one based on empirical observation.

In the two decades since the publication of *The Limits of Growth* in 1972 (Meadows *et al.* 1972), a major qualitative change has taken place in the Western intellectual communities' concerns with resource utilization.[1] We have moved from the age-old preoccupation with particular scarcities, such as Plato's fear of overgrazing and deforestation, or Malthus's notion that population grows at geometric rates while food supply expands at an arithmetic rate, or the focus in *The Limits of Growth* on exhaustion of mineral resources to an understanding that nature forms a comprehensive interdependent ecological system. Today our emphasis is on attempting to conserve the conditions under which the different interrelated components of the ecosystem are able to sustain human life at a level of maximum freedom of individual choice for the majority of the world's population. But the new global view of people as an integral part of the ecological chain of nature is far from universally accepted. The same old division of optimists and pessimists argues over permissible rates of exploitation to sustain life as we know it. Likewise, the same phalanxes of have-nots oppose the haves over what 'reasonable' exploitation means in the context of poverty within global economic and ecological interdependence.

Clearly, the Western developed economies and their intellectual communities have been successful in bringing the issue into the political consciousness of their electorates. Increasing numbers of laws are passed to control air and water pollution, and governments co-operate in reducing the cross-border flows of these pollutants. Recycling and conservation programmes of certain resources, on the other hand, appear mainly to be the result of cost factors and the NIMBY (not in my backyard) syndrome. Nevertheless, whatever the contributing reasons, ecological consciousness is a political and economic factor today in the First World. Ironically, one of the more lasting impacts on the publics of the Western world of the opening up of Eastern Europe that began in late 1989 may be the demonstration effect of large-scale destruction of ecosystems from pollution brought about by politically irresponsible planning. The new freedom of access to these countries and their desperate need for assistance to contain the ecosystemic disasters will dramatically increase Western electorates' understanding of the fragility of the ecology. It is likely that in the near term the public at large will become more activist and demand further action by governments.

THE NOTION OF RESOURCE LIMITS

High mass consumption, the most advanced stage of the optimistic modernization models of the first three decades of the post-war era, began to falter as the tripling of oil prices by the Organization of Petroleum Exporting Countries (OPEC) in 1973–4 sent political shock-waves through the industrialized West. Widespread doubts arose whether the good times of the 1950s and 1960s were indefinitely sustainable, as had been blithely assumed. It was necessary to rethink the optimistic assumptions of continuous economic growth and its impact on social and political development. Indeed, the very meaning of the concept of 'development' needed to be clarified. The shift from a secure world full of optimism to an uncertain one tinged by pessimism raised a host of questions, all focusing on the newly rediscovered conundrum of growth and its limits. Suddenly, the buzzword on every lip was 'scarcity'.

Two fundamental questions associated with this shift in attitudes required answers: was the world really running out of everything; and who decides what resources should be utilized and at what rates of exploitation?

But questions beget more questions. Given the accepted patterns of resource exploitation and utilization in an increasingly interdependent world system, the following specific questions arise: first, does the world at large face a period of growing scarcity of mineral resources; second, in what sense does the problem of First World access to Third World mineral resources arise; and third, do Third World demands on the future use of their resources conflict with the general objective of world economic expansion (i.e. is there, or should there be, a New International Order with respect to non-renewable resources)?

In considering these questions the following definition of resources is used: a *resource* is anything needed by a nation to maintain or increase growth of population and living standards. Fossil fuels, including coal, petroleum and natural gas, are currently the most essential natural resources because they are the main source of energy used to transform other resources into useful products. It should be noted that the popular conception of resource scarcity erroneously equates resource scarcity with reserves. Part of the problem stems from the use of the term 'non-renewable resources'. However, mineral resources are not fixed quantities, they change over time. The standard definition of reserves clarifies this confusion. *Reserves* are the subset of total resources which are identified as recoverable in a given period of time under existing economic and technological conditions. Hence, the magnitude of recoverable reserves is constantly changing: their sizes are reduced by downward price changes, increases in costs, restrictive regulations, etc.; and enlarged by new discoveries and by new political, economic and technological developments that make it possible to produce from deposits previously left unexploited.

We must also distinguish between particular scarcities and scarcity in general. Scarcity in one commodity (such as oil) is a planning instrument. In the hands of the manager, controlled scarcity is a political opportunity to discipline the market, justify high prices and solidify monopolistic power. Scarcity in general is another matter altogether. Actual physical limits on resources are difficult to quantify in any meaningful sense and represent a 'world *problématique*', one that implies the need to consider such concepts as the 'equilibrium' or 'steady-state' society.[2] Optimists, of course, view scarcity or constraint more as theoretical constructs than as guiding principles or policy prerequisites. Their usual rejoinder is: the next generation of technology will correct the shortsightedness of the last one.

The notion of 'limited resources/scarcity' is indebted to the dismal teachings of Malthus. Thomas Malthus developed the doctrine that the increase in population is greater than the increase in the supply of food and that unless the birth rate is controlled poverty and war will become the natural regulators of the size of the population. He based this pessimistic conclusion on the population explosion that was taking place in Europe at the beginning of the Industrial Revolution. Within a few decades his conclusions were shown to be wrong. The railways opened up the North American prairies for grain growing and ushered in the era of food abundance in the North Atlantic basin that shows no sign of ending a century and a half later. Nevertheless, his pessimistic views received such widespread publicity that they became doctrine quoted authoritatively to the present. The current version of Malthusian scarcity sees the quantity of natural resources remaining constant as economic development progressively requires ever-increasing extraction of resources. As an aside it bears repeating that ideas of economic scarcity have changed little over two millennia, for as pointed out earlier (p. 1286), Plato was worried about the same problems of food scarcity that Malthus made into a modern doctrine.

David Ricardo's notion of scarcity of natural resources differs from the Malthusian one in that it does not assume the quantity of resources to be constant. Because economic development forces people to use resources of progressively inferior quality, resources are not exhausted all of a sudden but the cost associated with extracting them rises. Relative scarcity implies the possibility of successive adjustment to new resource situations. W. Stanley Jevons, another early economist concerned with limited resources, argued in 1865 that Britain could not long sustain its current rate of industrial production because of the finite deposits of coal. Like Malthus, he based his predictions on the assumption of a static technology.

It is clear that the arguments of limits to resources in the above references, except for Ricardo, are based on theoretical projections of particular current trends. Even today, the objective and scientific method applied to project the impact of growth on the ecosystem and its resource base is invariably rooted in the same problems of lack of actual knowledge of what the real limits of a particular non-renewable resource are, or at what prices a substitute will be found, or whether and when technological innovation will render the utility value of a particular resource sufficiently low that it will be deemed plentiful again. That certain resources have been exhausted in particular locations, even with updated technology, does not invalidate the fact that so far we have been unable to project future resource utilization with any confidence. All we have been able to do is fall back on modelling beliefs or assumptions, with the results reflecting the parameters of the models. Thus the cry of despair voiced by Caldwell in 1977: 'The ultimate absurdity of contemporary political-economic debate is the growth-no-growth controversy' (Caldwell 1977: 135). To make its meaning clear, the concept of growth invariably requires a modifier. Thus Club of Rome studies distinguish between 'organic' and 'cancerous' growth; other studies have distinguished 'selective' from 'undifferentiated' growth and have identified various forms of controlled growth as cyclical, renewed, guided and ecological.

The conservation movement in the United States during the first years of the twentieth century was primarily concerned with the conservation of natural resources and steps to prevent their exhaustion. The movement was not founded on economic theory. It was based on the perceived axiom that since the exploitation of resources was rising dramatically, the dwindling of resource stocks was inevitable. The simple conclusions drawn from this analysis concerned the point at which a resource would 'run out'. In its day the movement was criticized as being overly moralizing. But, have we during the intervening seven decades improved on the movement's approaches? Are not our present-day ecological or green movements across Europe, the United States and Canada voicing exactly similar sentiments? The one difference may be that the opposing voices are themselves wrapped up in the controversy over the quest for 'rational' levels of growth to preserve the ecosystem in which both 'green' and 'rational' industrialists live. An added, but crucial, difference in the long run in the division of supporters and critics of the current ecological movement is the disappearance of heavy industry and the rapid and continuing decline of the share of manufacturing in our economies. Hence, we no longer focus on the finite amounts of coal or iron or even copper and manganese, since we use relatively little of them. In any case we have discovered and mapped large fields of mineral-rich 'manganese nodules' on the ocean bed; their exploitation is a function of price, demand and supply of conventional reserves. Instead, our most widespread concern is the preservation of the environment to permit us to enjoy the benefits of both post-industrial technology and clean air, water and relatively clean land and seascapes to which to escape from polluted or partially polluted urban concentrations. It is largely a matter of lifestyle for both the moralist and the critic, who agree that they want the same result, but disagree on the means.

THE CONTINUUM OF VIEWS: PESSIMISTS AND OPTIMISTS

The current debate over resource availability was ushered in by the globalization of the technology of communications and transportation that took place in the 1960s. Rapid economic growth in a reconstructed Europe, a maturing Japan, the phenomenon of the newly industrialized countries (NICs) and the spreading of mass consumption to all corners of the world had brought about a period of sustained economic growth which began slipping into recession and inflation at the end of the decade. Disillusionment with the policies of growth that had brought with them urban blight, increasing levels of pollution and the creation of an ideology of unrestrained growth, especially in the NICs, alienated large numbers of intellectuals in the First World and led to calls for a re-evaluation of the role of industrial society worldwide. Among the high-profile actions undertaken in the 1970s were a large number of conferences on global issues, many sponsored by the United Nations.[3]

Between 1967 and 1977 an avalanche of reports and books appeared, produced by either prominent economists or under the aegis of prominent political and business figures. *The Limits to Growth* (Meadows *et al.* 1972), subtitled *A Report for the Club of Rome's Project on the Predicament of Mankind*, was among the most pessimistic in its projections, and received such wide publicity that its title became the slogan for the new conservation movement, the ecology movement. In 1978 Sam Cole examined the great limits-to-resources debate of the previous decade (Cole 1978). He discovered that 'each of the current views of the future' in the eighteen major contemporary works reviewed 'had its precursor in the nineteenth century or before' (Cole 1978: 11). Moreover, most were pessimistic variations of the Malthusian doctrine of absolute scarcity of resources, especially food resources, which presage an end to population and economic growth.

Several of these works merit brief mention. Arguably the most famous, *The Limits to Growth* (1972) forecasts the collapse of the world economy and world population sometime within the next hundred years unless the world stops economic growth now and achieves equilibrium of population.[4] In considering the effect of technology-driven growth on the use of metals the authors of *The Limits to Growth*, typical of the confirmed pessimists, applied exponential growth rates and predicted that the earth's supply of aluminium would last just thirty-one years (or until the year 2001); copper would last only twenty-one years (or until 1991) at the then current rates of growth. Moreover, according to the model, the authors found that even if five times as much copper were discovered as was known to exist, the resource would last only forty-eight years (Meadows *et al.* 1972: 54–69).

Robert Heilbroner (1974, 1976), author of two doomsday books, predicts a grim Malthusian outcome in poor countries which will lead to either worldwide totalitarianism or anarchy; only major disasters will slow the pace of growth. There is a slim possibility that we may be able to stave off the disasters if we move immediately and constructively to preserve the environment. Mesarovic and Pestel (1974), the authors of the Second Report of the Club of Rome, predict a crisis in the Third World with regional resource catastrophes which could spread worldwide and paralyse future orderly development. In fact, the survival of the world system itself is in question, and can be saved only by restraining technology and re-orienting social and institutional lifestyles away from technology dependency (Cole 1978: 12–16).

Listed among the optimists are conventional economists and Marxist ideologues who seem to be either inherently optimistic, or largely unconcerned about future prospects for resource availability and the practical difficulties of allocation. This unlikely group (Modrzhinskaya and Stephanyan 1973; Beckerman 1974; Kosolapov 1976; Simon 1981; Simon and Kahn 1984) sees scarcity occurring as the result of political intervention and economic irrationality rather than physical limits. In short the causes of scarcity are faulty allocation of actual or potential abundance of resources.[5]

Among the less optimistic are the 'technologists' – those who see technology as a 'good thing' and the source of human salvation, at least so far – who more readily concede the eventual exhaustion of natural resources. They make statements such as: 'Technology will find ways to substitute one substance for another', and 'Technology will find ways to do more with less'. Are these testaments of faith or science? 'Unfortunately, no evidence supports the belief that technology can or will provide solutions to all problems of resource depletion' (Caldwell 1977: 141). On the other hand, neither is there any technical reason why technical advances should not continue indefinitely.

Although tempting, in the end it is probably inappropriate to reduce the debate over scarcity to one pitting optimists versus pessimists. The optimists, while not afraid of resources running out, are usually apprehensive of the growth of world population (a tacit element of pessimism). The pessimists, on the other hand, contribute constructive suggestions as to how problems may be solved, thus indicating a certain degree of optimism concerning the future. Gordon MacDonald (1978) places participants in the debate along a continuum – at one extreme is the pessimistic pessimist who believes that catastrophic exhaustion of resources is inevitable unless economic growth is brought to a stop by drastic measures; at other end of the spectrum is the optimistic optimist who views the future as one in which non-renewable resources are economically and physically infinite. Between these two extreme points of view we find what may be termed optimistic pessimists and pessimistic optimists. Most analyses, including this paper, fit in the broad middle.

RESOURCE AVAILABILITY: AN EVALUATION

On the basis of empirical evidence (limited as quantitative assessments of the world's resource endowments may be) Malthusian and neo-Malthusian definitions of absolute scarcity must be resisted. These myths of scarcity lead us to a dead end. The Malthusian world order governed by absolute physical limits is as hopeless a prospect as a world order guided by Adam Smith's invisible hand. Rather, most researchers agree that absolute physical limits, in terms of the contents of the earth's crust, are not a problem. Problems are more likely to arise from the availability of factor inputs in the extraction function – energy, capital, etc. To be sure, logic dictates that both the planet and its resources are finite and exhaustible, but there is little concrete evidence to support the position that the world faces a period of growing scarcity. The alarmist theses are based on modelling a single assumption, and consequently are simplistic in the extreme. Jan Tinbergen (1976), the author of one of the more complex studies of the world economy, concludes that overall shortage of minerals does not appear to be a real danger for the near future. With the sole exception of limited petroleum, metals, minerals, and other useful elements contained in the first 1,000 metres of the earth's crust and sea-beds represent several million times the world's present annual consumption.

The complex studies (Tinbergen 1976; Leontieff *et al.* 1976) conclude that physical obstacles are not the issue. Technology transfers, social, political and institutional changes in the developing countries, plus adjustments in the world economic order are the real impediments to sustained world economic growth.

What stock of materials, then, is actually present on earth? This question represents a source of great confusion – some resource economists contend that fairly accurate figures are available and that it is simple to estimate the total stock of elements; others suggest that almost all past attempts at quantification of resource stocks have been inadequate or misleading. Be that as it may, it is possible to fix a theoretical estimate of the total stock of various elements in the earth's crust. Such theoretic estimates indicate that, with the exception of fossil fuels, human beings are using an inappreciable fraction of the amount of elements that are physically near at hand. As Feinberg puts it:

> At present rates, because of the limited span of time in which virtually all human artifacts remain in use, the integrated use-time of elements is such that men will never deplete any significant fraction of the earth's upper crust by mobilizing it for human purposes.
>
> (Feinberg 1977: 156).

Of course, there are those who are tempted to reject the technological-optimist approach represented by Feinberg because of its emphasis on technology as the problem solver *par excellence*. Nevertheless, the classical scarcity hypotheses are not borne out by developments: historically the principal counteracting influences have been technological progress and the possibility of substituting one raw material for another. The life expectancies of selected world mineral reserves have been calculated at different times, but have turned out to be wrong in all cases because of the two main factors already discussed above, (p. 1288): the meaning of the term 'reserves' and the fluctuating rates of demand for minerals. In addition, many factors will push up these outward usage limits: new deposits are discovered; previously unexploited deposits become economic through new processes of extraction, recycling and/or substitution; technological advances take place; and mineral deposits from the bottom of the deep sea-bed become recoverable. As a result of these factors in general there is a tendency for reserves to grow despite increasing exploitation. Table 1 clearly shows that this has been the case for the majority of the commonly used non-fuel minerals, and it applies equally to oil and gas. World petroleum reserves, for example, increased from 569 billion barrels in 1974 to 681 in 1982, after dropping slightly to 567 in 1978, and increased again to 717 billion in 1986, when production stood at an all-time high of 57 million barrels a day (Pirages 1989: 60).

Table 1   Known reserves for selected minerals (metric tons), 1950, 1974, 1980

Mineral	1950 Reserves (mt)	1974 Reserves (mt)	1980 Reserves (mt)
Bauxite	1,400	16,000	26,000
Chromium	100	1,700	3,360*
Cobalt	0.79	2.4	1.5*
Copper	100	390	498
Iron	19,000	88,000	93,000
Lead	40	150	127*
Manganese	500	1,900	1,675*
Nickel	14	44	60*
Tin	6	10	10
Tungsten	2.4	1.6	2.0
Zinc	70	120	155

Sources: Compiled from Tilton 1977: 10; Chapman and Roberts 1983: Appendix 1.
* 1978 figures

UNEQUAL DISTRIBUTION AND UTILIZATION PATTERNS

While the world supply of the most important industrial minerals seems almost inexhaustible, the problem for the developed countries is that they are becoming increasingly dependent upon imported non-fuel minerals; some of the most crucial ores are to be found within the territories of their former colonies. This concentration of resources in certain geographical areas is one fact of life in the conflict over resources. The other is the gross inequality of the consumption/use pattern of resources in the world. While the average Costa Rican or Sudanese makes a negligible demand on the world's store of resources, because he or she is very poor, every man, woman and child living in the USA requires 40,000 pounds of minerals a year to maintain their standard of living. Put another way, Americans, who account for only 5 per cent of the world's population, have been consuming 27 per cent of the world's annual production of minerals.

Examples of unequal distribution and use patterns of resources are easy to find. Figure 1 displays a selection of nine minerals with the regions that are currently major sources of supply. These critical minerals have been identified as being so important to the security of the developed countries, so limited in supply, and located in such volatile areas of the world that they are classified as strategic minerals (Pirages 1989: 122). All of these minerals are imported in large quantities by the developed countries. Table 2 indicates the levels of import dependence for ten industrial minerals. Clearly, Japan continues to be highly dependent on other countries. The United States, while comparatively better off than either Japan or the European Community, also imports increasingly large quantities of some minerals from the less-developed countries.

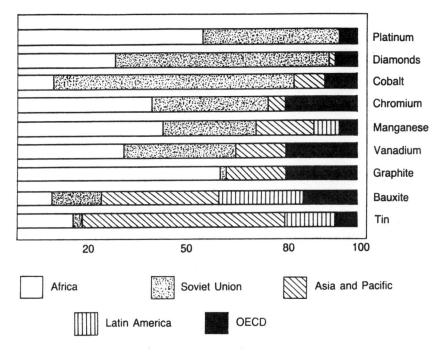

Figure 1   Regional distribution of selected mineral resources: major sources of supply

Source: Adapted from Pirages 1989: 124

A general assessment, based on existing data and global studies conducted over the past two decades, leads to the conclusion that while the use of physical resources cannot grow indefinitely on a finite planet, there is no physical or technical reason why the basic human needs of individuals throughout the world cannot be met today and into the foreseeable future. The problem of resources revolves primarily around their unequal distribution and consumption. 'It is not the absolute amount of a resource but the manner in which that resource is distributed geographically, and how (and by whom) it is used, that in the latter part of the twentieth century affect the ability of the global community to provide basic human needs' (Harf and Trout 1986: 235).

NORTH–SOUTH RELATIONS AND RESOURCE SCARCITY

In North–South relations the issue of scarcity of natural resources is important because of the close link between the availablity of resources and economic growth. Historically, growth had depended on, and indeed demanded,

Table 2   Import dependence for selected minerals (net imports as percentage of consumption)

	United States		EEC		Japan	
	1972	*1987*	*1972*	*1986*	*1972*	*1986*
Bauxite and alumina	88	97	51	52	100	100
Chromium	100	75	100	96	100	98
Copper	17	25	93	98	90	88
Iron ore	32	28	37	94	94	99
Lead	19	15	75	84	76	66
Manganese	95	100	98	98	90	100
Nickel	90	74	89	41	100	100
Tin	100	73	96	56	97	96
Tungsten	42	80	100	46	100	73
Zinc	55	69	61	63	80	61

Source: Pirages 1989: 114

abundant natural resources, particularly energy. This is a crucial consideration for both the developed countries, which need to maintain economic growth, and the developing countries which are attempting to increase and expand their economic potential. This relationship gives rise to what may be termed 'lateral pressure': growth gives rise to demands for resources; once domestic resources have been exhausted (from an economic point of view), growth gives rise to lateral pressures to obtain them from other sources.[6] Responses to lateral pressure can be either benevolent (such as trade) or malevolent (such as war, conquest or colonialism). When the growth of interdependence that has led to the emergence of the global system is factored in, it is easily understandable that economic matters, of local or regional concern only a few decades ago, are 'automatically' transformed into global issues that threaten the future stability of the international system. This interrelationship is dramatically demonstrated in Figure 2, which shows that the less developed the country the greater the role that commodity exports play as a source of economic well-being. The interaction of US economic health and the well-being of the Third World may be seen by comparing Table 2 with Figure 2.

The literature of the past two decades has led to the definite conclusion that there is a real need to develop comprehensive resource policies for the globe. There appears to be near unanimity on this generally, although there is no agreement on how this should be carried out, nor is there agreement on what the policies should contain (MacDonald 1978; Wionczek 1982).

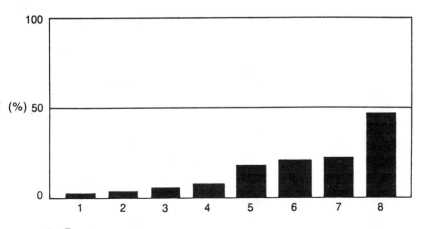

1 Europe
2 OECD
3 US and Canada
4 Asia
5 Africa
6 Third World (excludes major petroleum exporters)
7 Latin and Central America
8 Least Developed Countries

Figure 2   Basic commodity exports: eighteen basic commodities as a percentage of merchandise exports, 1983

Source: Adapted from Pirages 1989: 148

THE DISMAL RECORD OF CO-OPERATION

Unfortunately, to date the First World has shown little inclination at the intergovernmental level to co-ordinate even an attempt to chart resource exploitation, not to mention develop any proposals for co-operating with the Third World on resolving the issues raised by the intellectual community. Part of the reason is a disillusionment with the Third World resulting from its inability to co-operate politically and follow up on its initial success in placing its concerns on the inequitability of the present world economic system on the United Nations' agenda at the beginning of the 1970s. In the face of a small, tightly knit First World the badly split disparate Third was only able to agree on radical demands unacceptable to the leading industrial states. Part of the reason for the First World's lack of urgency to co-operate with the Third World is an ongoing euphoric faith in the industrialized world in the magic powers of technological invention to solve all our problems. And indeed, concerted political action by the public and technological advances in combating air and water pollution, as well as recycling to conserve land-fill sites and forests, has become widespread across Western Europe and North America in a few short years since the mid-1980s.

The recalcitrance of Third World political leaders to join the First World and jump on the conservation bandwagon has turned off a great deal of the goodwill of the North's electorates. The negative attitude towards the South is exacerbated by their endemic inability to rise to levels of economic efficiency, political democracy and bureaucratic incorruptibility expected by Northern electors. The South's debts and the North's budget overruns, necessitating psychological and economic retrenchment by Western governments and tax-payers alike, have underscored not only the relative inefficiency of the South but their inability to convince the North that the interdependence of the world economic system means that the proverbial chain is only as strong as its weakest link. Indeed, a backlash appears to be developing in the North against the South. Business investment is falling off as investors have become disen-chanted with the political instability and the financial woes of the Third World. Instead, they are turning to the democratizing Eastern Europe that promises to provide large returns as it switches over to capitalism. The taxpayers of the First World are also disenchanted enough with the Third World that their own chronic budget deficits are forcing cut-backs in aid transfers.[7]

Moreover, the fears of the 1970s of strategic shortages of resources available only from the South have been replaced by confidence that the conservation movement will reduce demand to manageable proportions, and by growing awareness of the utter failure of the cartel power of the Third World. The promise of OPEC as the model whereby the Third World would be able to create particular scarcities to raise commodity prices to levels that would redress the long-term decline in the terms of trade for them was totally dashed by the ability of the technology of the North to demonstrate rapidly the truism of the inverse relationship between prices and demand.[8] Cartel power did not work because of lack of political cohesiveness and cheating. It must be noted that the Third World is not unique in demonstrating these truisms in oil, cocoa, coffee, sugar, tin, etc.; historically, cartel power has lasted only as long as the political will has been stronger than particular members' economic differences. The only hope is that both consumers and producers have a political commitment to maintain prices. Hindsight tells us that this hope was premature even at the beginning of the decade of negotiations between the First and the Third Worlds: even the agenda at the New International Econ-omic Order negotiations at the United Nations between 1974 and 1980 was never agreed. It was merely adopted 'without vote' to permit discussion, but without agreement by the North that the agenda or the discussion were even necessary.

SCARCITY, INEQUALITY AND CONFLICT BETWEEN
NORTH AND SOUTH: PROSPECTS AND PROBABILITIES

Some years before the publication of *The Limits of Growth*, President Lyndon Johnson told the troops in Vietnam: 'There are three billion people in the world. They want what we have' (Barnet 1980: 296). Although Johnson's objective was to provide an easily understood metaphor for the American GI to fight harder to 'contain communism' in Asia, his words unwittingly stated the basic foundation that prevents agreement and co-operation between the Third and the First Worlds: the First is unwilling to share its abundance with the Third, all the statements of interdependence notwithstanding. At the same time, the Third World, in its attempts to catch up, is exploiting its natural resources with the reckless abandon that characterized the industrial states not long ago, thus adding to the pollution of the globe's air and water at a rate alarming to the West. It is also cutting down forests and desertifying marginal agricultural land in the pursuit of rapid development.

Unfortunately, the economic inequalities between the First and Third Worlds are not decreasing (except for a handful of NICs). The uneven social and economic development characteristic of any developing country, exacerbated by the increasingly declining terms of trade for the Third World, are actually increasing the gap of well-being between the two worlds. 'Over the last twenty years the industrial economies have been growing at a real per capita rate of 2.4 percent each year, while the least industrialized economies have been plodding along with growth of less than 1 percent' (Pirages 1989: 145). However, the ubiquitous omnipresence of New York-centred telecommunications is making the poorest peasant in Asia familiar with life in the fast lane of conspicuous consumption. Politicians, prone to promise the rainbow throughout history, are raising expectations in the Third World that they will never be able to deliver. The continuing mismanagement of the international commercial banking system on a grand scale has, in a few years, led to a concentrated and immense net drain of resources from the poor South to the wealthy North. The year 1989, for example, saw over US $50 billion net transfer of wealth to the North from Asia and Latin America to pay for the debts incurred between 1973 and 1981; and still the net debt grew.

Midlarsky, writing in 1982 when the debt problem's dimensions were much smaller than at the beginning of the 1990s, analysed the relationship between scarcity and inequality as a basis for the occurrence of mass revolutions. Historically, scarcity has been demonstrated to be a contributing factor to mass revolution in Third World countries. Examined empirically, the process is one where scarcity directly leads to increased inequalities, which create, 'zero-sum conditions ... with their consequences for the increased probability of revolution'. Incidentally, while inequality is shown to be less of a factor in industrial societies, their future stability may be threatened as well: 'At the same time, the added inequality attendant upon scarce resources, a diminishing equality of opportunity, and an increased differentiation of function in the world's most industrial societies may portend badly for the stability of these countries in the years ahead' (Midlarsky 1982: 33).

The conflict over resource allocation in the South, in conjunction with the axiom that the globe is interdependent (while vertically cleaved into at least three levels and horizontally riven into a myriad of shifting camps), poses the question, 'What will happen when the resource supplying countries begin to withhold resources because they foresee the day when their own demand will require the available supplies?' (Forrester 1971: 27). Will a new era of international conflict grow out of pressures from resource shortages? Will it lead to industrial countries disassociating themselves from the least-able developing countries (both economically and politically)?

The latter point finds considerable support in the literature. Caldwell (1977), for example, suggests that Third World 'euphoria' over newly found political and economic advantage (i.e. resource endowments) might stimulate just such a countervailing reaction by the industrial countries. Indeed, as the past decade demonstrates, they have spurred efforts to reduce their dependence on external sources of essential fuels and materials. According to Caldwell, the present state of affairs in the world 'does not indicate that the distribution and demand for natural resources will inevitably compel a greater international interdependence' (Caldwell 1977: 132) Accordingly, conclusions regarding the implications of uneven distribution and demand for resources should be drawn with caution. For some countries, and for some particular resources, interdependence may increase; for others, dependence on external sources might be dramatically reduced. Equally important, if indeed scarcity marks the future, then, given the unequal distribution of non-renewable resources across the world, at least some countries will be given an opportunity to embark on development strategies on the basis of resource revenues. Others will not have this opportunity.

Even if the foregoing analyses are badly skewed, common sense decrees that there is only one prescription to prevent future conflicts: develop a harmonious basis for joint management of an asymmetrical economic interdependence. Put plainly, we must work out the ground rules before Third World attitudes harden and 'extreme policies' undermine the relationship. Such an approach implies that market forces alone are not sufficient to bring about a constructive reciprocal relationship between industrial North and developing South. Moreover, all nations must be encouraged and enabled to feel part of the world system.

Any view of the future from the perspective of the periphery makes it clear that the Third World cannot follow extremely conservationist policies. Third

World countries 'badly need resource export proceeds for financing economic growth and sometimes also for participating in the international power game, and are little interested in a zero growth strategy' (Wionczek 1982: 305).

Nevertheless, in the foreseeable future although conflicts over resources will increase, since nature has so badly skewed their endowment, 'resource wars' are unlikely unless, of course, political and economic relations between the two segments of the world economy degenerate into a series of confrontations. It bears reiterating that realities have changed since the first half of the century when First World resource consumers used to enjoy a 'divine right' of unconditional access to Third World resources under traditional concessions.

A SUMMING-UP

There is little doubt that the vast reserves of the First World in knowledge and in technical competence cannot be 'redistributed' in any manner acceptable to both worlds. This was shown dramatically by the total failure of the UN Conference on the Transfer of Technology in 1978, and by the impossibility to achieve any real agreement on a Code of Conduct for Transnational Corporations, even after half a decade of negotiations. Realities of power intruded in each case. Moreover, as Caldwell puts it, 'If the basic sources of wealth today are knowledge and energy, then transfers of natural resources among nations will not, in themselves, decisively influence the distribution or intensity of political power' (Caldwell 1977: 143).

This view, general among power-brokers in the First World's corporate and political elites, implies that in addition to 'knowledge' we also have much of the one natural resource, energy, that is needed to lead a life of abundance and comfort in the post-industrial, information-oriented era that the First World has already entered.

Despite the equanimity shown by the power-brokers, in the long run common sense again shows that real resource scarcity will affect all nations in the future. An almost universal effect on the industrialized countries has already appeared: periodically increased vulnerability and instability follows from the discovery by some Third World countries that they can use their supply capabilities for political purposes. The OPEC case is not unique. Similar attempts to 'corner' the market to jack up prices have been made from time to time by coffee, sugar, cocoa and copper producers, to name a few. Because of complex internal interdependence in industrialized economies, the effects of any constrictions in the flow of materials quickly spreads through the system. The developing countries, under the threat of food shortages and rapidly expanding populations, are dependent on a flow of critical materials to and from the developed world. The currency to pay for these inputs has largely been derived from the sales of raw materials. Moreover, inability or unwillingness within the developed world to buy these materials restricts the options of the Third World suppliers. Lastly, the continuing decline in prices of minerals in real terms (the terms of trade for minerals have been declining steadily for three decades) exerts pressure to exploit these resources as quickly as possible to maximize the economic rents from their extraction.

The resource policies and declarations of the Third World show a paradoxi-cal ambivalence. On the one hand they are highly critical of the developed countries for depleting Third World resources. One popular response has been to nationalize resource sectors and apply legal and extra-legal forms of pressure on transnational corporations to obtain concessions. Chief among the targets is the USA, which is widely criticized as an inordinate drain on the world's resources. On the other hand, Third World countries fear that developed countries might cease to purchase their resources and substitute synthetic substances for natural materials. A decade ago Julian Simon, despite the label of optimist, concluded his analysis with words to which most of us in the broad middle can subscribe. They sound uncommonly realistic today:

> Is a rosy future guaranteed? Of course not. There always will be temporary shortages and resource problems where there are strife, political blundering, and natural calamities – that is, where there are people. But the natural world allows, and the developed world promotes through the marketplace, responses to human needs and shortages in such manner that one backward step leads to 1.0001 steps forward, or thereabouts.
>
> (Simon 1981: 348)

NOTES

1 *The Limits of Growth* was researched and written by a research group at MIT for the Club of Rome, under the direction of Dennis Meadows (Meadows *et al.* 1972)

2 In defining scarcity, David Novick, in *A World of Scarcities* (1976), notes that 'practi-cally all materials are scarce under most circumstances in the sense that, if they were available without cost, more would be demanded than could be supplied' (Novick 1976: 68). Obviously, scarcities can be the result of either too small a supply or too great a demand – on both sides of the equation existing data are inadequate. However, 'we know that all historic projections of scarcity have turned out to be wrong' (ibid.: 69).

3 For example: the Human Environment (UN Environment Programme, Stockholm, 1972), Population (UN, Bucharest, 1974), Food and Agriculture (Food and Agri-culture Organization, Rome, 1975), Habitat Conference on Human Settlements (Vancouver, 1976), Conference on the Law of the Sea (UN, New York, 1976–), and Trade and Development (UN Conference on Trade and Development, Nairobi, 1976).

4 In the authors' own words: 'if the present growth trends in world population, industrialization, pollution, food production, and resource depletion continue unchanged, the limits to growth on this planet will be reached sometime within the

next one hundred years. The most probable result will be a rather sudden and uncontrollable decline in both population and industrial capacity' (Meadows *et al.* 1972)

5 For example, Simon and Kahn (1984) 'are confident that the nature of the physical world permits continued improvement in mankind's economic lot in the long run, indefinitely' (ibid.: 3). However, they are less sanguine about the constraints imposed on 'material progress' by political and institutional forces. Calls for subsidies and price controls, government ownership and management of resource production, and government allocation of the resources that are produced are constraints that will increasingly act as a brake on progress.

6 Choucri and North (1975) use the term 'lateral pressure' to characterize the growth dynamic that led to Western European expansion into foreign territories. As they put it, 'When demands are unmet and existing capabilities are insufficient to satisfy them new capabilities may have to be developed. . . . Moreover, if national capabilities cannot be attained at reasonable costs within national borders, they may be sought beyond' (ibid.: 16).

7 The Canadians, among the most consciously generous of aid donors, have been reducing their official development-aid budget since 1988. Public opinion polls taken in January 1990 show an even split (48 for; 47% against; 3% don't know) for additional cuts in official aid (*The Toronto Star*).

8 The failure of OPEC is most dramatically shown when we examine its share of the non-Communist world's energy supply in the pre- and post- 'oil shock' periods. By 1983 oil production in the Western world comfortably exceeded OPEC's exports, whereas in 1973 the latter were almost double the former. In percentage terms imports of OPEC oil accounted for 36.5 per cent of non-Communist energy use in 1973. By 1983 this figure had dropped to 19.5 per cent. (Odell 1986: 78).

REFERENCES

Barnet, R. J. (1980) *The Lean Years: Politics in the Age of Scarcity*, New York: Simon & Schuster.

Beckerman, W. (1974) *In Defence of Economic Growth*, London: Jonathan Cape.

Caldwell, L. K. (1977) 'Global resource transfers: a scientific perspective', in G. Garvey and L. A. Garvey (eds) *International Resource Flows*, Lexington, Mass.: Lexington Books.

Chapman, P. F. and Roberts, F. (1983) *Metal Resources and Energy*, London: Butterworth.

Choucri, N. and North, R. (1975) *Nations in Conflict*, San Francisco: W. H. Freeman.

Cole, S. (1978) 'The global futures debate 1965–1976', in C. Freeman and M. Jahoda (eds) *World Futures*, London: Martin Robertson.

Feinberg, G. (1977) 'Material needs and technological innovation: some hopes – and some doubts', in G. Garvey and L. A. Garvey (eds) *International Resource Flows*, Lexington, Mass.: Lexington Books.

Forrester, J. W. (1971) *World Dynamics*, Cambridge, Mass.: Wright-Allen.

Harf, J. E. and Trout, B. T. (1986) *The Politics of Global Resources*, Durham, NC: Duke University Press.

Heilbroner, R. L. (1974) 'An inquiry into the human prospect', *New York Review of Books* (24 January).

——(1976) *Business Civilization in Decline*, London: Marion Boyars.

Jevons, W. S. (1865) *The Coal Question*, London: Macmillan.

Kosolapov, V. (1976) *Mankind and the Year 2000*, Moscow: Progress Publishers.

Leontief, W. *et al.* (1976) *The Future of the World Economy*, preliminary report, New York: United Nations.

MacDonald, G. J. (1978) 'Long-term availability of natural resources', in H. J. McMains and L. Wilcox (eds) *Alternatives for Growth: The Engineering and Economics of Natural Resources Development*, Cambridge, Mass.: Ballinger.

Malthus, T. R. (1817) (1963) *Principles of Population*, Homewood, Ill.: Irwin.

Meadows, D. H., Randers, J. and Behrens, W. W. (1972) *The Limits to Growth*, New York: Universe Books.

Mesarovic, M. and Pestel, E. (1974) *Mankind at the Turning Point*, New York: Dutton/ Readers Digest.

Midlarsky, M. I. (1982) 'Scarcity and inequality: prologue to the onset of mass revolution', *Journal of Conflict Resolution* 26: 3–38.

Modrzhinskaya, Y. and Stephanyan, C. (1973) *The Future of Society*, Moscow: Progress Publishers.

Novick, D. (1976) *A World of Scarcities*, New York: John Wiley.

Odell, P. R. (1986) 'Draining the world of energy', in R. J. Johnston and P. J. Taylor (eds) *A World in Crisis?*, Oxford: Basil Blackwell.

Pirages, D. (1989) *Global Technicopolitics*, Pacific Grove, Calif.: Brooks/Cole.

Rees, J. (1985) *Natural Resources*, New York: Methuen.

Ricardo, D. (1817) (1962) *Principles of Political Economy and Taxation*, London: J. M. Dent.

Simon, J. L. (1981) *The Ultimate Resource*, Princeton: Princeton University Press.

Simon, J. L. and Kahn, H. (eds) (1984) *The Resourceful Earth*, New York: Basil Blackwell.

Tilton, J. E. (1977) *The Future of Nonfuel Minerals*, Washington, DC: Brookings Institution.

Tinbergen, J. (1976) *Reshaping the International Order: A Report to the Club of Rome*, New York: Dutton.

Wionczek, M. S. (1982) *Some Key Issues for the World Periphery*, Oxford: Pergamon.

81

INTERNATIONAL TRADE AND THE NEW PROTECTIONISM

HELEN V. MILNER

INTERNATIONAL TRADE IN THE TWENTIETH CENTURY: AN OVERVIEW

The exchange of goods and services between nations has followed an uneven course during the twentieth century. By the end of the nineteenth century a true international economy had begun to emerge, as the separate trading blocs established by the European powers slowly formed a single network of world trade. From this time until the First World War, the volume and rate of growth of world trade grew phenomenally. Between 1881 and 1913, total foreign trade grew an average of 40 per cent per decade; per capita trade grew about 34 per cent in the same period (Kenwood and Lougheed 1983: 222). The First World War, the Depression, and then the Second World War dramatically hurt the international trading system. The growth of trade, especially relative to that of world production, and its volume dropped sharply in the inter-war period. In the early 1930s, the volume of world trade declined some 60 per cent (Kenwood and Lougheed 1983: 222–5; Kindleberger 1973: 172). Indeed, by the early 1950s the volume of international trade was at levels similar to those of 1913.

After the Second World War, with the establishment of a new multilateral world trade and payments system, international trade grew rapidly once again. Reconstruction, the revival of global economic growth, technological innovations, especially in transportation, and the lowering of trade barriers all stimulated foreign commerce. Between 1948 and 1960, the volume of world exports climbed by 6 per cent per year; between 1960 and 1973, this average annual growth rate reached almost 9 per cent (Kenwood and Lougheed 1983: 299). In this period the growth of trade also outstripped that of world production. Only after 1973 did world commerce again suffer, this time in the wake of the oil crises, inflation and the debt crises. Along with economic growth, international commerce has failed to grow as quickly or steadily in the late 1970s and 1980s as before. With the conclusion of new regional economic integration agreements, negotiations to reduce trade barriers and debt problems, and other economic reforms, it is possible that the world will see a resurgence in trade and growth in the 1990s and beyond.

Over the course of the twentieth century, the nature of world commerce has also changed. Three important alterations in the character of this trade are apparent. First, a change in the commodity composition of trade has occurred over the century. The shares of food and primary products have steadily declined, while that of manufactured goods has grown (Kenwood and Lougheed 1983: 302–3). Moreover, in the past few decades the share of trade in services has also increased, making it an ever more important focus for trade liberalization efforts.

Second, within manufacturing, trade has also developed a new character. Exchange of products within an industry, so-called intra-industry trade, has flourished (Grubel and Lloyd 1975: 41–5). In fact, such trade is now believed to account for a very substantial portion of all world trade. The growth of intra-industry trade reflects two facts about international commerce: in manufactured goods the developed countries trade most heavily with each other and, thus, factor endowments are of less influence in shaping their trade in these goods than are the presence of substantial scale economies and product differentiation.

Third, in this century direct foreign investment has grown appreciably, bringing with it new forms of trade. While some of this foreign investment may replace trade flows, those investments linked to the development of worldwide networks of production *within* firms have created trade – namely, global intra-firm trade. In the early 1980s, estimates showed that over 30 per cent of US, Japanese and British trade involved such intra-firm exports and imports (Centre for Transnational Corporations 1988: 92). The rise of such trade reflects the growing importance of large multinational firms in international production. It also signals that a sizeable proportion of international exchange is controlled internally by these firms and is not purely market-driven. These changes in the composition of international trade are coupled with one constant: that most trade occurs among the developed countries (Gilpin 1987: 177). These facts about the evolution of international trade in the twentieth century are essential for understanding the phenomenon of the 'new protectionism'.

TRADE POLICY AND THE 'NEW PROTECTIONISM'

Before examining the 'new protectionism', it is important to understand the concept of protectionism and the evolution of ideas and policies concerning protection. In its broadest connotation, protectionism can refer to any policy which insulates the home market from foreign competition. In particular, policies that raise the price of imports or lower the price of exports tend to have protectionist effects. A very wide range of policies, both micro and macro ones, can be employed to effect this. But, most commonly, protectionist policies are associated with import tariffs and quotas as well as export subsidies. Tariffs are, in effect, a tax levied upon imports, while quotas imply a quantitative restraint on their volume. Under conditions of perfect competition, equivalent tariffs and quotas have similar distributive effects. In imperfect markets, the two may have different consequences; and then tariffs are usually the economists' preferred instrument if protection must be used (Bhagwati 1965). These policies tend to affect trade flows directly – either by restricting imports or promoting exports – and to promote the affected domestic producers by increasing their prices and/or their production. These policies are, nevertheless, costly. Domestic consumers lose, as do other domestic industries; foreign producers often suffer as well.

Because of these and other costs, economists since the time of Adam Smith have generally opposed protectionism and supported free trade. Under certain conditions, free trade can be shown to maximize the efficiency of resource use and hence welfare. In standard economic analysis, it is considered to be the first-best policy. In the presence of various market imperfections, economists have long recognized the potential utility of interventionist trade policies, although even then they tend to advocate only the use of tariffs (Corden 1974). Protectionism is considered a second-best choice; other more direct policy measures, such as taxes or subsidies, are first-best.

Political disputes about the merits of protectionism have abounded. With the rise of the nation-state in the seventeenth century, protection of the domestic economy was often the favoured approach. Mercantilism, a doctrine promoting such protection, flourished at the time. Mercantilist writers advocated policies to encourage exports and restrict imports in the hope of securing a favourable balance of trade. This in turn would lead to the inflow of gold and other specie, which would contribute to the power of the nation. The goal here was to use trade policy to ensure the prosperity and strength of the nation (Heckscher 1983: vol. 1, introduction; vol. 2, chapter 1). Throughout much of the seventeenth and eighteenth centuries, many nation-states followed this doctrine and adopted protectionism widely.

At the end of the eighteenth century, Adam Smith in his celebrated *An Inquiry into the Nature and Cause of the Wealth of Nations* (1776) challenged mercantilism. Smith sought to show that free trade, and free markets in general, were the best means of maximizing a nation's wealth. For him, the extension of markets by deepening the division of labour enhanced efficiency and ultimately prosperity. Smith saw protectionism – except in certain cases related to national security, such as shipbuilding – as impeding the division of labour. Later writers, such as David Ricardo, also attacked mercantilism and established an even firmer base for the superiority of free trade. Ricardo, for instance, demonstrated that national wealth was enhanced by foreign trade (Ricardo 1821: esp. chapter VII). He used the idea of comparative advantage to show how trade promoted efficiency and hence wealth. The ideas of these writers seem to have influenced policy debates in the nineteenth century. By the middle of the century, many leading states had substantially reduced the levels of protection surrounding their economies, with Great Britain being the leader in this process.

The freer trade atmosphere of the mid-nineteenth century did not last long. In part, tariffs were the main source of revenue for many states at this time. Lowering them reduced the government's capacity to govern effectively. At a time of rising demands on governments due to a variety of causes (including wars, promotion of industry, depression, and rising labour unrest and organization), pressures arose to increase rather than decrease tariffs by the last third of the century. In addition, new arguments for mercantilist policies had arisen. The growing competition among states for industrial progress led once more to a connection between protection and national power. Mercantilist writers, such as Alexander Hamilton and Friedrick List, had argued early in the century that new industries must be protected from foreign competition and thus allowed to develop. Otherwise, in an environment of free trade, nations like Britain with well-developed industries would remain dominant forever. Protection of infant industries in 'backward' countries was necessary to enable their emergence as challengers to more advanced countries. Mercantilism here focused on industrial development, not the amassing of gold and other specie. National power was to be enhanced by the protection of new industries (Earle 1986: 217–61).

High tariffs and quotas remained prevalent throughout the first third of the early twentieth century. The First World War led to the suspension of much trade and increased intervention in the economy. The inter-war period saw some of the highest levels of protection ever, especially in peacetime. With the onset of the Great Depression, America helped to initiate a process of upwardly spiralling world tariffs with its Smoot–Hawley trade bill (1929–30). This bill raised American tariffs to their highest level yet, at around 50 per cent, and set off a spiral of retaliation in other countries (Pastor 1980: 77–84). As mentioned earlier (p. 1305), combined with the Depression, this surge in protectionism helped reduce world trade by almost 60 per cent in the early

1930s. While attempts were made in the 1930s to reduce protectionism – for instance, in the United States' Reciprocal Trade Agreements Act and negotiations – little change occurred before the 1950s. The approach and onset of the Second World War hindered efforts to lower tariffs and abandon quotas. In the aftermath of the war, however, the international trading system was dramatically altered.

At the end of the Second World War, under American leadership, a system based on the principle of non-discriminatory trade liberalization was developed primarily by the advanced industrial democracies of the West. After failing to agree upon an International Trade Organization with rules for all aspects of trade, these nations established the new international trading order on the basis of a less developed agreement, the General Agreement on Tariffs and Trade (GATT). GATT embodied a number of principles that were to guide trade. Countries were not to discriminate against other countries in their trade relations; this non-discrimination was embodied in the practice of unconditional most favoured nation (MFN) status. Reductions in trade barriers were to be mutually advantageous and to be extended to all members of the system (Spero 1985: 95–9). The pursuit of free trade in this system, however, was tempered by the requirements of domestic economic stability, full employment objectives and growth. GATT embodied a compromise between those arguing for the freest possible trade and those arguing for more protection of the domestic economy; it rested on the principle of 'embedded liberalism' (Ruggie 1982: 393–404). GATT thus contained a number of exceptions to the rule of free trade and non-discrimination, many of them intended to preserve domestic economic stability.

GATT has performed exceptionally well in the post-war period. Beginning in the late 1940s, a number of international trade negotiations held under GATT auspices helped to lower trade barriers worldwide. It should be noted, however, that GATT has worked mainly on trade in manufactured goods, not in either agriculture or services. Among the advanced countries, tariffs on industrial goods have been lowered from an average of about 25 per cent at the end of the Second World War to about 5 per cent today through successive GATT rounds (Whicker and Moore 1988: 26; IMF 1988: 9). The most important of these were the Kennedy Round negotiations (1964–67) and the Tokyo Round (1975–9). GATT has thus virtually eliminated the problem of tariffs from international trade, and herein lies a source of the 'new protectionism'.

As tariffs have progressively been negotiated away and 'bound' to their low levels by GATT commitments, countries have developed other means of protecting their economies. These non-tariff barriers (NTBs), often dubbed the 'new protectionism', have become increasingly salient since the 1970s. In part, they were always there, and now are just more noticeable due to the absence of tariffs. In part, though, they have been increasingly introduced to compensate for the protection lost through tariff reductions. Moreover, some of these barriers are simply the result of increased government intervention to deal with domestic problems.

The complex nature of these NTBs makes the new protectionism hard to measure, let alone to control. While often associated with domestic problems, these NTBs clearly violate the international trade principles embodied by GATT. They tend to be unilateral, discriminatory, and non-transparent in their effects. Many such NTBs are imposed by one country against the most efficient exporters of a product and in a manner that makes it most difficult to see their effects. This latter characteristic makes them particularly hard to deal with internationally. The 'new protectionism' then represents a serious threat to the liberal trade system that GATT has helped to establish.

The new protectionism refers to a wide variety of non-tariff measures which reduce the prices of exports and/or increase the prices of imports. They all, intentionally or not, insulate domestic markets from foreign competition. In their effect, they are much like the old protectionism. The most prominent of these measures are voluntary export restraints (VERs), orderly marketing agreements (OMAs), subsidies, and administrative practices that disrupt trade. VERs are quotas on exports that the exporting nation agrees to, usually in response to pressure from an importing nation. Administrative practices which entail challenging the legality of imports, such as many US trade laws, also contribute to protection by increasing uncertainty over future access to the foreign market. A wide range of other domestic policies also increasingly affect international trade. For instance, safety and anti-pollution laws imposed on domestic vehicle manufacturers may help to limit foreign imports. Industrial policy measures also have significant trade effects. As governments have come to intervene more in the economy to serve domestic objectives, these measures have naturally proliferated. Eliminating or harmonizing these policies with those of other countries requires changing domestic objectives and thus upsetting internal politics.

The use of NTBs seems to have grown greatly since the early 1970s. One study shows that 'managed trade' rose from 13 per cent of all world manufactured-goods trade in 1974 to almost 24 per cent in 1980 (Page 1981: 28–9). Including agriculture, over US $100 billion of trade was subject to NTBs in 1983, which represented a substantial increase since 1981 (Deardorff and Stern 1987: 27–32). Since the early 1980s further increases have been noted. For instance, among the industrial countries, NTBs rose from 19 per cent of their total (non-fuel) imports in 1981 to about 23 per cent in 1987 (IMF 1988: 1). It seems likely that about a quarter of all world trade is now affected by NTBs.

This new protectionism has been unevenly distributed within the economy.

Agriculture and other primary products have been the most controlled; in fact, they were never subjected to the liberalization of the post-war years. Manufactured goods remain less protected. Among manufacturing industries, however, some are more heavily protected by NTBs. Vehicles, steel, textiles and clothing, footwear and electronic products have received the most protection (IMF 1988: 2). The new protectionism is also distinctive in terms of the countries which use it and those which are its main targets. In the main, the advanced industrial countries, especially those in the European Community, have employed NTBs to keep out products from Japan, the East Asian NICs and Eastern Europe (IMF 1988: 2). In many ways, the new protectionism has simply replaced the old. As will be explained more fully below, these sectors would probably have been protected by tariffs before GATT, given their economic difficulties and importance. The new protectionism, then, may not be all that new. It is perhaps more invidious since it is less transparent than tariffs are and it violates GATT principles.

Many different factors can be seen as sources of this new protectionist trend in international trade. The beginning of the trend is usually dated around the early 1970s, about 1974. This date coincides with the serious economic difficulties and changes associated with the first oil crisis. The oil embargo of 1973–4 and the macroeconomic difficulties linked to the end of the fixed-exchange-rate monetary system – the Bretton Woods system – caused much worldwide economic turmoil. Serious recession, mounting inflation, rising unemployment and rapid shifts in comparative advantage upset the fairly stable, prosperous economic situation of many countries. These difficulties continued throughout the 1970s and were further aggravated in the early 1980s by a second oil 'shock', the debt crisis of many less developed countries, and another recession induced in part by very high interest rates in the USA.

Demands for protection have long been linked to periods of economic difficulty. Growing import competition, a recessionary environment and mounting unemployment are likely to be met with demands for protection from foreign competition by both firms and workers. For many governments, especially those facing imminent elections, such pressures may prove irresistible. This scenario seems to portray fairly accurately the situation of many advanced industrial countries in the late 1970s and early 1980s. As one economist notes, 'the "new protectionism" of the late 1970s followed closely the severe world recession of 1974–75 and the recent wave of protection in automobiles and steel is clearly related to the devastated level of activity in these sectors during the global stagnation of 1980–82' (Cline 1983: 9).

The economic difficulties of this period were further compounded by rapid shifts in comparative advantage. For labour-intensive industries, such as vehicles, steel and footwear, comparative advantage moved rapidly in the 1970s from the industrialized countries of the West to the low-wage, newly industrializing countries (NICs), mainly in the East. Western governments saw the loss of these large industries, which were once the basis for national prosperity and power, as gravely threatening. Many felt that they had to be protected. Since GATT prevented the use of tariffs, other means had to be found. And so economic difficulties and changes helped induce the use of the new protectionism.

The surge in protectionism has also been associated with macroeconomic and exchange rate problems. In particular, exchange rate instability and misalignments are seen as causes of protectionism. Rapid, significant swings in exchange rates can subject sectors to surges in imports and/or in changes in demand for exports, making long-term planning and investment in the industry very difficult. '[T]he volatility of flexible exchange rates – especially as experienced in practice – fosters protective trade policies due to the uncertainties which result for pricing, investment returns, and competitive position' (Bergsten and Cline 1983: 85). Exchange rate misalignments, especially if persistent, can also hurt industries and prompt demands for protectionism. Persistent overvaluation of a currency can undermine the competitiveness of industries and subject them to severe import competition. Both instability and misalignments have characterized the period since 1973. In particular, the surges of protectionism since the early 1970s in the USA have been attributed to serious overvaluations of the dollar. As several economists point out, 'The three postwar periods of most severe protectionist pressures in the United States – the early 1970s, 1976–77, and the present [i.e. the early 1980s] – followed promptly upon periods of overvaluation of the dollar' (Bergsten and Williamson 1983: 111).

These arguments have been challenged by other scholars on a number of counts, however. For one, the fact that the new protectionism is highly sector-specific makes it unlikely that broad macroeconomic factors, which should affect most industries, are responsible. Using econometric evidence, two economists note that the sectoral distribution of protection is poorly explained by the exchange rate argument. They conclude that 'The macroeconomic hypotheses appear to be incomplete explanations of protection. . . . The most significant explanatory variable . . . is the simple time trend, suggesting that long-run structural problems, more than macroeconomic factors, may be the root cause of protectionism' (Dornbusch and Frankel 1987: 111–12).

A more political source of the recent protectionism has also been discussed. Political scientists have suggested that the cause of rising protection since the 1970s is the decline of American power and prestige. The argument here is that as the world's strongest state in the 1950s and the 1960s, the United States organized and led the emerging free-trade system. It was willing to pay the costs of leadership and/or to coerce others into opening their markets. As American political and economic dominance have declined relative to other states, the United States itself has adopted protection and has been less willing and able to prevent others from doing so. The decline of US hegemony has thus released pressures for protection. As Robert Gilpin has speculated, 'With the decline of the dominant economic power, the world economy may be following the pattern of the latter part of the nineteenth century and of the 1930s: it may be fragmenting into regional trading blocs, exclusive economic alliances, and economic nationalism' (Gilpin 1975: 259). The worldwide dispersion of economic power since the late 1960s, then, may help account for the rise of the new protectionism.

Another political source of the new protection has its roots in domestic politics. Some have posited a link between the rise of the welfare state and this protectionism. The welfare state involves substantial government intervention within the market to achieve certain social objectives. In particular, these interventions serve 'to provide economic security for its citizens by protecting them from change that would adversely affect their economic positions . . . and to redistribute income (and economic power in general) from capital to labor' (Krauss 1978: xxi). These objectives require sustained intervention to alter market forces, and these interventionist policies constitute barriers to international trade flows.

While designed to protect and promote certain domestic groups, these policies also tend to distort trade flows, usually in a protectionist manner. Krauss claims that 'The new protectionism, in fact, refers to how the totality of government intervention into the private economy affects international trade' (Krauss 1978: 36). He stresses that 'The new protectionism is not a recent occurrence of an old phenomenon; it reflects new attitudes toward the proper role of government in the economy' (ibid.: xxi). In particular, 'The emergence of the new protectionism in the Western world reflects the victory of the interventionists, or welfare, economy over the market economy' (ibid.: 36). In quoting another economist, Krauss concludes that 'Now, as in the 1930s, protectionism is an expression of a profound skepticism as to the ability of the market to allocate resources and distribute incomes to societies' satisfaction' (ibid.: 36). This argument may explain some secular increase in protection since the rise of the welfare state. It has more trouble accounting for the rise in protectionism in particular sectors and in the 1980s when free-market ideology was dominant and leading a challenge to the welfare state. It is, nevertheless, true that increased state intervention to achieve various social goals has contributed to the new protectionism, especially in face of the declining salience of tariff barriers.

The new protectionism has many possible causes, but what have its effects been? These new policies appear now to affect about a quarter of all trade in manufactured goods and more than that in agriculture and services. An important and perhaps growing portion of international trade is thus being conducted outside GATT auspices and the market system. Despite this, the volume of world trade and the exports of the countries targeted by these restrictions have continued to grow fairly steadily. Even the rate of growth of trade has seemed relatively unaffected by this protection. As two economists point out,

> In view of the protectionist pressures, especially since the mid-1970s, it is tempting to attribute some of the slowdown in world trade to increased protection. However, a closer analysis suggests that virtually all of the slowdown can be explained by softer demand for imports associated with slower economic growth.
>
> (Bergsten and Cline 1983: 72–3).

This protectionism also does not seem to have prevented the global shifts in comparative advantage and in the location of industry from occurring. The rise of Japan and continuing ascendence of the NICs as large producers and exporters of manufactured goods have not been halted by the new protectionism, although they may have been slowed down. Indeed, a paradoxical effect of some VERs has been to encourage exporters to upgrade their industries and produce higher technology and higher value-added goods (Yoffie 1983).

The new protectionism has helped to reduce international trade and economic growth to some extent. It has certainly slowed down, but not stopped, long-term structural changes in comparative advantage. The new protectionism has also affected GATT and international trade negotiations. These measures have violated GATT principles, especially multilateralism and non-discrimination. They have undermined confidence in the GATT system. Moreover, the new protectionism has necessitated a change in the negotiation process. While most earlier GATT negotiations focused on tariffs, beginning with the Tokyo Round the negotiations have looked more and more at non-tariff barriers, such as subsidies. Indeed, the agenda for the current GATT round (the Uruguay Round) emphasizes such non-tariff measures and other heavily protected areas, like services and agriculture, rather than the traditional concerns of tariffs and the trade in manufactured goods.

Successful reductions in these 'new' types of trade barriers will be difficult to achieve. Many of these measures have legitimate and important domestic sources. Many are hard to identify and do not permit accurate estimates of their effects, thus making reciprocal reductions difficult. Many are also seen as legitimate responses to unfair trading practices by other countries. For these and other reasons, eliminating restrictive practices or altering policies to harmonize them among nations is a more painstaking process than reducing tariffs. The recent success of the European Community in its effort to create a unified market by 1992 through reducing and harmonizing policies that negatively affect international trade, however, should create some hope and perhaps even a model for such an effort worldwide.

The new protectionism in all its manifestations is certainly a cause for concern. It has all the makings of a challenge to the peaceful and prosperous free-trade-oriented international system of the early post-war period. The rise of the new protectionism is linked to new attitudes and theories about international trade. Increasingly, states that once were the backbone of the GATT system have come to believe that the system is deficient. A widespread sense that the trading game is being played unfairly exists among the Western nations. Concern abounds that Japan, the NICs, and other countries are manipulating the trading system through a variety of subtle means to the disadvantage of the United States and West European states.

Demands for an end to such unfair play have arisen; most call for the linking of the openness of one's own market to that of its trading partners. This type of specific, bilateral reciprocity violates all of the principles underlying the post-war trading system (Keohane 1986). In addition, some have claimed that in today's world comparative advantage itself is manipulable by governments. Government policies are viewed as being able to effect fundamental changes in the location of industries and the flow of goods and services internationally. Recent work in international trade theory has supported, at least partially, this idea. The so-called theory of strategic trade policy shows how, under certain conditions of imperfect competition, state intervention can benefit national firms and help them gain long-lasting comparative advantages in trade (Krugman 1986).

These types of ideas and their substantiation in economic theory have provided the justification for both aggressive policy measures to create such advantages and defensive interventions to force others to change their policies. A rationale for intervention and retaliation exists now. The 'new protectionism' thus could develop into something far more serious if states adopt this type of reasoning. The limited protectionism of the 1980s could become widespread, and its consequences far more deleterious, should the manipulation of comparative advantage and the pursuit of specific reciprocity become the dominant concerns in the trade policy-making process of states.

The future of the 'new protectionism' depends on a large number of factors. Economic conditions, exchange rate movements, US leadership, progress in the new GATT negotiations, and the reception of new ideas regarding trade policy may all affect the levels of protection in the international system. So far this essay has focused on the factors promoting protectionism. But some forces do exist that may mitigate the spread of trade barriers. These include fear of retaliation and a replay of the disastrous 1930s experience, concerns about inflation, the increasing importance of exports, multinational production and global intra-firm trade for all industrial economies, high levels of economic interdependence, the pressures of an ongoing GATT negotiation to reduce barriers, and broad foreign policy concerns about the impact of a trade war on relations among allies (Cline 1983: 9; Milner 1988: chapter 2). These forces may help limit the spread of the new protectionism, but it will require visionary leadership and much co-operative effort among nations to reduce substantially the new protectionism, as they did the old protectionism.

REFERENCES

Bergsten, C. F. and Cline, W. R. (1983), 'Trade policy in the 1980s: an overview', in W. R. Cline (ed.) *Trade Policy in the 1980s*, Washington, DC: Institute for International Economics.

Bergsten, C. F. and Williamson, J. (1983) 'Exchange rates and trade policy', in W. R. Cline (ed.) *Trade Policy in the 1980s*, Washington, DC: Institute for International Economics.

Bhagwati, J. (1965) 'On the equivalence of tariffs and quotas', in R. Caves (ed.) *Trade, Growth, and the Balance of Payments*, Chicago: Rand McNally.

Centre for Transnational Corporations (1988) *Transnational Corporations in World Development*, New York: UN.

Cline, W. R. (1983) 'Introduction and summary', in W. R. Cline (ed.) *Trade Policy in the 1980s*, Washington, DC: Institute for International Economics.

Corden, W. M. (1974) *Trade Policy and Economic Welfare*, Oxford: Clarendon Press.

Deardorff, A. V. and Stern, R. M. (1987) 'Current issues in trade policy', in R. M. Stern (ed.) *US Trade Policies in a Changing World Economy*, Cambridge, Mass.: MIT Press.

Dornbusch, R. and Frankel, J. A. (1987) 'Macroeconomics and protection', in R. M. Stern (ed.) *US Trade Policies in a Changing World Economy*, Cambridge, Mass.: MIT Press.

Earle, E. M. (1986) 'Adam Smith, Alexander Hamilton, and Friedrich List: the economic foundations of military power', in P. Paret (ed.) *Makers of Modern Strategy*, Princeton: Princeton University Press.

Gilpin, R. (1975) *US Power and the Multinational Corporation*, New York: Basic Books.

——(1987) *The Political Economy of International Relations*, Princeton: Princeton University Press.

Grubel, H. G. and Lloyd, P. J. (1975) *Intra-Industry Trade: The Theory and Measurement of International Trade in Differentiated Products*, New York: John Wiley & Sons.

Heckscher, E. F. (1983) *Mercantilism* (1935), 2 vols., New York: Garland Publishing.

IMF (1988) *Issues and Developments in International Trade Policy*, Washington, DC: International Monetary Fund.

Kenwood, A. G. and Lougheed, A. L. (1983) *The Growth of the International Economy*, London: Allen Unwin.

Keohane, R. (1986) 'Reciprocity in international relations', *International Organization* 40: 1–27.

Kindleberger, C. P. (1973) *The World in Depression, 1929–39*, Berkeley: University of California Press.

Krauss, M. B. (1978) *The New Protectionism: The Welfare State and International Trade*, New York: New York University Press.

Krugman, P. R. (ed.) (1986) *Strategic Trade Policy and the New International Economics*, Cambridge, Mass.: MIT Press.

Milner, H. V. (1988) *Resisting the Protectionist Temptation: Global Industries and the Politics of International Trade*, Princeton: Princeton University Press.

Page, S. A. (1981) 'The revival of protectionism and its consequences for Europe', *Journal of Common Market Studies* 20: 17–39.

Pastor, R. A. (1980) *Congress and the Politics of US Foreign Economic Policy, 1929–1976*, Berkeley: University of California Press.

Ricardo, D. (1821) *The Principles of Political Economy and Taxation* (1817), London: Everyman's Library.

Ruggie, J. G. (1982) 'International regimes, transactions, and change: embedded liberalism in the postwar economic order', *International Organization* 36: 379–415.

Smith, A. (1776) *An Inquiry into the Nature and Cause of the Wealth of Nations*, ed. Edwin Canaan, New York: Modern Library, 1937.

Spero, J. E. (1985) *The Politics of International Economic Relations*, New York: St Martin's Press.

Whicker, M. and Moore, R. (1988) *Making America Competitive*, New York: Praeger.

Yoffie, D. B. (1983) *Power and Protectionism*, New York: Columbia University Press.

FURTHER READING

Baldwin, R. E. (1970) *Non-Tariff Distortions of International Trade*, Washington, DC: Brookings Institution.

——(1986) *The Political Economy of US Import Policy*, Cambridge, Mass.: MIT Press.

Bauer, R. A., De Sola Pool, I., and Dexter, L. A. (1972), *American Business and Public Policy*, Chicago: Aldine-Atherton.

Bhagwati, J. (1988) *Protectionism*, Cambridge, Mass.: MIT Press.

Dam, K. W. (1970) *The GATT: Law and International Economic Order*, Chicago: University of Chicago Press.

Destler, I. M. (1986) *American Trade Politics*, Washington, DC: Institute for International Economics.

Hine, R. C. (1985) *The Political Economy of European Trade*, London: Wheatsheaf Books.

Hirschman, A. O. (1946) *National Power and the Structure of International Trade*, Berkeley: University of California Press.

Krasner, S. D. (1976) 'State power and the structure of international trade', *World Politics* 28: 317–43.

——(1985) *Structural Conflict*, Berkeley: University of California Press.

Lake, D. A. (1988) *Power, Protection, and Free Trade*, Ithaca, NY: Cornell University Press.

Lavergne, R. (1983) *The Political Economy of US Tariffs*, Toronto: Academic Press.

Lipson, C. (1982) 'The transformation of trade', *International Organization* 36: 417–56.

Ray, E. J. (1981) 'Tariff and nontariff barriers to trade in the US and abroad', *Review of Economics and Statistics* 63: 161–88.

Reich, R. (1983) 'Beyond free trade', *Foreign Affairs* 16: 747–72.

Strange, S. (1985) 'Protectionism and world politics', *International Organization* 39: 233–59.

——(1988) *States and Markets*, New York: Basil Blackwell.

Winham, G. R. (1986) *International Trade and the Tokyo Round Negotiations*, Princeton: Princeton University Press.

Zysman, J. and Tyson, L. (eds) (1983) *American Industry in International Competition*, Ithaca, NY: Cornell University Press.

82

HUMAN RIGHTS

ADAMANTIA POLLIS

Prior to the Second World War, nationalism, diplomacy, imperialism, war and treaties were major concerns of the Western world in the international arena, a concern reflected in the writings of scholars. By the end of the war human rights had been added to the international agenda. In turn, scholarly discourse on rights was revived, which, while deriving from the intellectual heritage of the past, developed human rights into a multi-disciplinary field more focused on contemporary issues. Rights theory, which had been largely the domain of philosophers, proliferated, engaging the attention of political scientists, international legal scholars, sociologists and anthropologists.

The first instance in modern history in which states were held accountable for not adhering to standards of internationally acceptable humane behaviour transcending the laws of individual states was during the Nuremberg trials. The victorious allies tried and convicted Nazis, and in separate trials Japanese, by charging them, in addition to war crimes, with 'crimes against humanity'. By holding individuals accountable for violating 'laws' above the state, implicitly the absoluteness of state sovereignty was challenged. Inevitably, however, the trials were severely criticized for being *ex post facto*, for imposing norms of international moral behaviour that had not existed at the time the inhuman acts were committed. Subsequently, the pressure for adherence to 'laws' above the state abated and the principle, if not always the practice, of state sovereignty continues to define the world order. This has been partly counterbalanced by efforts to formulate binding laws with human rights standards.

Before looking at the contemporary scholarly debates and controversies regarding human rights, a brief overview of the emergence of international and regional human rights instruments will provide the context for an analysis of diverse and controversial human rights theories. It is against this background that scholarly interest in issues such as the substance of fundamental human rights, their ideological underpinnings, their universality or their cultural relativity, the prioritization of rights and the relationship of rights to other social forces such as economic development, acquires greater salience.

THE INTERNATIONAL BILL OF HUMAN RIGHTS

The process of evolving an 'international bill of human rights' was gradual, extending over decades. The United Nations' first action was the adoption in 1948 by the General Assembly of the Convention on the Prevention and Punishment of the Crime of Genocide. The same year, on 10 December, it adopted the Universal Declaration of Human Rights. At this time the United Nations was dominated by the Western powers, yet even then the absence of consensus on human rights was evident in the abstention of eight countries, including the Soviet Union, Saudi Arabia and South Africa. While this Declaration articulates a set of principles and is not a treaty, it has been hailed as embodying the aspirations of a world committed to respecting the rights and dignity of human beings.

In the ensuing decades, UN conventions and covenants have proliferated. The two basic covenants, which set forth a complex of rights, the International Covenant on Civil and Political Rights, frequently referred to as the first generation of rights, and the International Covenant on Economic, Social and Cultural Rights, referred to as second generation of rights, were adopted in 1966 after years of controversy and compromise among the member states. The required number of ratifications for them to come into force, however, did not come about until ten years later. Despite the comprehensiveness of these two documents, their perceived insufficiency and an expanding conception as to the substance of human rights have led to further action. The highly politicized International Convention on the Elimination of all Forms of Racial Discrimination came into force in 1969, while the Convention on the Elimination of all Forms of Discrimination Against Women was not ratified until 1981. Despite the prevalence of torture, the Convention against Torture and Other Cruel, Inhuman and Degrading Treatment or Punishment did not become operative until 1987, while in 1990 the Convention on the Rights of Children was adopted. The more recent third generation of rights, such as those pertaining to the environment and development, have not, at least as yet, been incorporated into the 'international bill of human rights', nor have the rights of indigenous peoples, although they find their way in to declarations and/or discussions.

Paralleling the evolution of an 'international bill of human rights' by the United Nations, regional organizations have formulated their own legally binding human rights documents. The Council of Europe, consisting of Western European countries, adopted the European Convention of Human Rights in 1953. After much controversy, the Organization of American States enacted the Inter-American Convention on Human Rights in 1967, while in 1983 the Organization of African Unity adopted the African Convention on Human and Peoples' Rights (Banjul Charter). At the beginning of the 1990s there are few prospects for an Asian or Middle Eastern human rights document. In view of the widely divergent conceptions of human rights that prevail in different societies, it is noteworthy that all these documents are Western oriented and are modelled on the Universal Declaration rather than on indigenous values, thus reflecting at least at the legal, formal level a gradual universalization of Western norms. It should be noted, however, that while the provisions of the European convention are limited to civil and political rights, the other two incorporate some elements of economic, social and cultural rights while the African Charter also incorporates some traditional values.

The notion of universal applicability of the 'international bill of human rights' is diminished by the fact that a positive vote in the General Assembly is little more than a statement of support in principle. It is not necessarily indicative of a state's willingness to be legally bound or to accept the authority of a supranational organ, such as the UN's Commission on Human Rights. Since states are bound only by those treaties or international instruments they have ratified, it has been common practice for states to vote for a human rights convention in the General Assembly but fail to ratify it. The United States, for example, is notorious for having voted for numerous human rights conventions but having ratified only one, the Genocide Convention, and that not until 1987. The most frequently cited reason, as stated clearly by Senator Jesse Helms, is that such action would infringe on US sovereignty, and the United States is, moreover, a country which fully implements human rights. It should be stated, however, that in October 1990 the Senate Foreign Relations Committee voted to support ratifications of the Torture Convention. In contrast to the United States, the Soviet Union ratified all the basic UN covenants, except the optional protocol of the Civil and Political Rights covenant. Complaints against states for violations of human rights documents are normally brought by other states, but the latter protocol enables an individual to file a petition with the UN Human Rights Committee charging his/her state with violations. Since fewer than half of the states overall have ratified the UN human rights documents, the applicability and effectiveness of the 'international bill of human rights' is severely limited.

Furthermore, the absence of enforcement mechanisms limits the effectiveness of the 'international bill of human rights'. While machinery has been established both at the international and regional levels to monitor and to report violations, enforcement powers are weak; the strongest sanction is publicity and public opinion. The weakness of publicity as a tool for ensuring compliance is further attenuated by the confidentiality of many investigations and findings. Only the European Commission of Human Rights and the

European Court have had a measure of success in protecting and implementing rights. This is attributable to ideological and cultural consensus on the substance of rights, to the signatory states' shared interests and to a willingness on the part of the member states to abide by the decisions of these organs.

The one dramatic instance in which sanctions were imposed against a country charged with violating a human rights convention was the case of Greece. In 1968 Greece was under military rule and several Scandinavian countries brought charges against it for violations of the European Convention of Human Rights to which it was a signatory, in particular for torture. After conducting an investigation and after extensive hearings the European Commission of Human Rights found Greece in gross violation. The agreed-upon sanction was expulsion from the Council of Europe, but Greece withdrew from that body the day prior to the scheduled vote. The uniqueness of this case demonstrates both the rarity with which human rights bodies impose sanctions and their fundamental ineffectiveness in the face of a defiant sovereign state. The Greek case demonstrates the powerlessness of the international community to take effective measures against a state which, in the name of sovereignty, defiantly rejects legal and/or normative obligations to implement human rights.

Of equal importance in thwarting the furtherance of human rights is their politicization. In the international arena the predominance of 'politics' in dealing with human rights issues is overwhelming. State actors manipulate or exploit human rights concerns in light of their foreign policy objectives. Thus at the United Nations and at the East–West meetings, held in accordance with the 1975 Helsinki accord, human rights violations were often used as propaganda tools for the furtherance of the strategic and economic goals of the protagonists. At times, deals were struck between the United States and the Soviet Union whereby, to cite one instance, the former will refrain from raising the issue of Afghanistan in exchange for the Soviet Union not raising the issue of Chile in the UN Human Rights Commission. Even in Europe, despite consensus on the nature of rights, conflicting national interests often prevail. Thus, charges of gross violations of human rights lodged against Turkey in 1982 were dropped after an alleged agreement whereby Turkey was to release some political prisoners. The strategic interests of NATO and the economic interests of European countries were considered of greater magnitude.

Despite the severe limitations of international and regional organizations in effectively furthering adherence to and implementation of basic human rights, worldwide concern continues unabated. In recent decades, non-governmental human rights organizations (NGOs) at the local, regional and international level have proliferated and have become critical pressure groups. Their activities range from monitoring human rights developments, conducting investigations, preparing reports, providing legal assistance to those charged with political crimes and lobbying for the adoption of human rights instruments. Many have consultative status at the United Nations and/or at regional organizations where in addition to providing vital information, their lobbying often succeeds in placing human rights violations on the agenda. Most of these organizations, such as Watch Committees, Amnesty International and the Fédération des Droits de l'Homme, are Western oriented, emphasizing violations of civil and political rights to the neglect of economic and social rights. Their role is critical in keeping human rights issues in the forefront, in contributing to the abatement of torture and minimally to a reduction in violations. In the long run, of great importance is the emergence, particularly in Asia, Africa and Latin America, of grassroots NGOs, often affiliated with international NGOs, which advocate the implementation of human rights in their country, monitor violations and often provide legal defence for political prisoners.

The salience of human rights issues is also evident in the perceived need of Western European governments and the United States, at least at the rhetorical level, to incorporate human rights considerations into foreign policy formulation. However, the extent to which human rights concerns do influence foreign policy is contingent on a nation's national priorities. Strategic and economic interests invariably overshadow concern with human rights. The United States, despite its commitment to civil and political rights, has supported its allies on the basis of national interests and not rights practices. Neither US Congressional legislation prohibiting the granting of aid to gross violators of human rights nor ex-President Carter's human rights foreign policy impeded aid to countries such as South Korea. Security and/or economic considerations override human rights. It has been the lesser powers – Canada, the Netherlands and the Scandinavian countries – that have moderated their foreign aid policy in light of the state of human rights.

More than forty years since the adoption of the Universal Declaration of Human Rights and the continuing expansion of the 'international bill of human rights', massive violations not only persist but are ubiquitous. Charters, covenants and conventions proliferate in an effort to incorporate the totality of human rights and to achieve standardization and universality. A perception of progress, of an evolving international consensus on the substance of rights, is given credence by the increasingly voluminous body of legal documents. Unfortunately, this is an illusion. Standardization has not been achieved and state sovereignty continues to reign supreme, while millions are deprived of their dignity and are denied fundamental rights, are tortured and arbitrarily imprisoned. Multiple and complex factors account for the continued widespread violations of internationally accepted norms; among them, cultural and/ or ideological diversity as to the substance of rights, the primacy of state sovereignty and national interests, class conflict, the priority of the goal of economic growth in Third World states and the policies imposed on them by international financial institutions. In recent decades scholars have addressed these issues from differing perspectives in the endeavour to set a philosophic foundation of rights, to develop a rights theory and to ascertain which factors are conducive to adherence by a state to rights standards and which lead to gross violations. This scholarly discourse, as most scholarly discourses, stems from the need to explain and account for a particular social phenomenon.

WHAT ARE HUMAN RIGHTS?

Despite efforts to formulate and codify universal human rights norms, notions of human rights are grounded in different cultural, ideological and philosophic world views resulting in divergence both as to the substance of human rights and on the meaning and interpretation of agreed-upon rights. Intellectual thought is largely the outcome of a dialectical relationship between changing social reality and social theory whereby the latter provides an explanation, a justification and/or critique of social transformation. The social reality of contemporary societies is an intricate mosaic of distinctive patterns with a multitude of varying cognitive frameworks, value systems and socio-economic formations. Inevitably, differing conceptualizations of human rights emanate from the complex social dynamics of particular societies.

As it was stated earlier, the Cold War confrontation between the Soviet Union and the United States transformed the issue of human rights into a political propaganda tool. Underlying the controversy, however, was a sharp ideological divergence as to the nature of rights, whereby the West argued for civil and political rights and Eastern Europe and the Soviet Union for economic and social rights. While Gorbachev's *glasnost* and *perestroika* and the demise of communism in Eastern Europe have appeared at one level to be giving increased legitimacy to the Western notion of rights, the different conceptualizations regarding basic human rights which emanate from their different philosophic legacies and ideological premises will undoubtedly persist. The interconnection between individual civil and political rights and capitalism is not necessarily causal, except under historically specific conditions as in Western Europe. It does not follow that privatization and a market economy in Eastern Europe will be accompanied by the implementation of individual rights.

Nevertheless, despite ideological differences the East–West universe of discourse is shared, stemming from a common European intellectual heritage. By contrast, Asia, Africa and the Middle East not only diverge markedly among themselves but have no common intellectual history with either Eastern or Western Europe. To what extent the imposition by the colonial powers of Western institutional forms and legal codes, and the incorporation of colonies into the world economy, have resulted in the assimilation of the Western mode of thinking will be discussed later. It is clear, however, that rights in many Third World countries, both in their conceptualization and in practice, continue to bear little resemblance to those advocated either by the West or by the East; rather they are rooted in traditional cultural patterns. Overall, the persistence of tradition and its world view, even when modified by contemporary realities, appears to be relatively independent of a state's legal commitment to the 'international bill of rights' or for that matter to its espousal of the ideology of capitalism or socialism. Moreover, even in societies whose elites share the language of modern human rights, the universality and alleged consensus enshrined in the 'international bill of human rights' is belied by the reality. Hence an understanding of the underpinnings of the diverse notions of human rights is essential in order to begin accounting for the state of human rights in the world today.

INDIVIDUALISM: CIVIL AND POLITICAL RIGHTS

Advocates of the universality of human rights derive their beliefs historically from the writings of the modern political philosophers of Western Europe. Faced with radical social transformations of their societies, which came about as a result of industrialization, with Britain in the lead, and armed with the scientific revolution during the late eighteenth and nineteenth centuries, thinkers drew upon the works of Locke, Hobbes and Rousseau, borrowing arguments about the natural laws of society that parallel scientific discoveries and laws of the natural sciences. Adam Smith's formulation of the foundations of classical economics and political philosophers' doctrines of liberty were on the one hand explanatory of ongoing social change, specifically the emergence of capitalism, and on the other they were an elaboration of new philosophic and ideological premisses legitimating the new social order. Philosophic schools such as positivism and pragmatism came to authenticate such a new social order. The emerging middle class demanded political power, freedom from the constraints of centralized monarchical control and freedom to further their interests. The pursuit of individual self-interest, the acquisition of private property, competition, freedom of choice and the impartiality of the market, were the core ingredients of the new socio-economic order. Individual rights became crucial, both as a requisite to fulfil the needs of the new socio-economic order and as a vehicle for the attainment of political power by the bourgeoisie. Concurrently, the breakdown of traditional communal bonds in rural areas and the rise of an urban and rural proletariat atomized the person and facilitated the notion of individualism. The individual rather than some organic entity became the basic unit of society.

Integral to nineteenth-century intellectual thought, and consonant with the new social order, was the centrality of the notion of atomized individuals, mirroring the sundering of traditional feudal bonds. This autonomous individual was conceived by Locke and Hobbes from the analytic category of people 'in the state of nature' possessing certain inalienable, natural rights and joining together through a social contract or social compact to form civil society. Since for Locke human nature was benign while for Hobbes it was brutal, the former envisaged a liberal polity in which the individual retained natural rights, while Hobbes conceived a Leviathan in which most rights were delegated to the state. For both, however, the individual remained sacrosant. It was assumed that human nature was acquisitive and motivated by the pursuit of self-interest, a self-interest defined in terms of material wealth. The individual rights posited by these political philosophers, it should be noted, were restricted to persons who were rational beings in pursuit of self-interest. Women, servants and many others were viewed as less than human and devoid of the attribute of rationality, which was essential for the possession of these inherent individual rights. While it was presumed that the doctrines of the modern philosophers were scientific and hence universally valid, this universality was confined to a universe exclusive to Caucasian males. More than a century later, this philosophic premiss of exclusivity provoked social movements demanding equal rights for blacks, women and homosexuals in the United States and Western Europe.

The modern political philosophers did not elaborate a specific rights theory; it was developed later, albeit within the conceptual framework of individualism and rationality. In the contemporary era, the underpinning of inalienable rights has shifted from Locke's God-given rights in nature, and has become secularized, grounded in natural law. In recent years, however, the philosophic justification for the claimed universal individual rights appears to be floundering. By contrast to the uncertainty regarding the foundation of rights, a more precise specification of civil and political rights has evolved: freedom of speech, freedom of religion, freedom of association, freedom of contract, freedom of choice, the right to privacy, equality before the law, the rights of the accused (due process of law) and the right to private property, among others. All these are considered negative rights in that governments are proscribed from infringing on their exercise by individuals. They are the civil and political rights that many scholars continue today to view as both fundamental and as universal. Furthermore, it is frequently contended that other rights claims, such as economic and social ones, can be fulfilled through the exercise of civil and political rights. Freedom of association, for example, enables workers and the underprivileged to organize for the attainment of their economic well-being. Thus for many scholars, and in the international and regional human rights instruments, priority is assigned to civil and political rights. The primacy of civil and political rights, moreover, is buttressed by the writings of many legal scholars who contend that by contrast to economic and social rights, they are justiciable.

Over the decades, as the premisses of individual civil and political rights became internalized and became one element of Western political culture, scholarly probing as to the grounding of rights and their nature had abated. It was forcefully revived, however, in the aftermath of the Second World War, when, after the initial euphoria proclaiming the universality of individual rights, challenges were raised. Confronted with empirical evidence of cultures and societies for whom the notion of individual rights and even the concept of rights was alien (Pollis and Schwab 1979; Downing and Kushner 1988) and confronted with religious and philosophic traditions, such as Islam, Hinduism and Buddhism, which did not share in the ontology of the West (Rouner 1988), the certitude of universal, inalienable rights was shattered.

The internationalization of the world economy and increased awareness of diversity among societies did not, however, lead to the abandonment of the liberal tradition of individual rights. The core notion of rights inhering in the individual *qua* individual has persisted into the contemporary era, but numerous derivative schools have emerged which vary in their justification of individual rights. In none does a scientific pretence remain, and none argues forcefully that these rights are universal. Rather it is argued that they should be. The dominant contemporary school derived from the liberal tradition stems from analytic philosophy. Individual rights, for some, are derived from moral philosophy, thus positing a normative rather than a scientific basis, for which they nevertheless claim universality. And while this universality may not have become extant in the world as yet, its moral force, it is contended, will prevail in time (Donnelly 1985). Proponents of the analytic theory of rights, while differing among themselves as to the connection among moral, legal and human rights, share not only these concerns but also the view that inherent human rights *per se* are too fuzzy and should be codified into legal rights; in other words they have shifted the ground from negative rights to positive rights. Furthermore, emphasis remains on civil and political rights to the exclusion of economic and social rights. They advocate an abstract model, stemming from a notion of justice (which remains muddled) from which they logically and rationally derive a theory of rights (Dworkin 1977; Flatham 1980; Rawls 1971).

Most recent Western-oriented scholars, however, in contrast to the analytic school, take individual rights as given, addressing conditions that are necessary for their fulfilment and/or impediments to their implementation. For some, basic rights are inextricably dependent upon a democratic political system, while others argue that the primacy of state sovereignty impedes the implementation of rights (Falk 1981). Still other scholars consider the priority of economic development in Third World countries as a deterrent to human rights.

It is important to recognize that consensus in the West as to the substance of basic rights obfuscates differing philosophic premises with respect to the source of rights. Although the modern political philosophers were searching for universal laws, the rise of nationalism in Europe, with its imperative of national distinctiveness, led to multiple ideologies, cultures and histories. The notion of inherent, inalienable rights is essentially an Anglo-Saxon tradition which is not shared by most West European countries. The neo-Kantian German tradition, although concurring on the primacy of individual civil and political rights, is rooted in logical positivism which rejects the notion of rights as inhering in the individual. It is the state which is the source of rights, the state which is primary, and the rights which it grants are embodied in a constitution and/or legal codes (Kommers 1989). While sharing with the analytic philosophers the view of rights as positive and as embodied by statute, they repudiate the notion that an individual has the right to disobey the law if it violates human rights (Dworkin 1977). Moreover, whereas in Anglo-Saxon countries a legitimate claim can be made that a state can violate rights, such as privacy, which may not be specifically incorporated in any statute, in German legal thought such a claim is impossible since it is the state that grants rights. The French tradition, also rooted in logical positivism, adds another dimension, stemming from the French Revolution – namely, that the state, the giver of rights, must be a just state and the protector of individual rights. It should serve as a constraint on the emergence of authoritarianism and repression.

In sum, the various tendencies with the Western intellectual tradition, despite shared notions of individual civil and political rights, hold variant implications for the practice and implementation of rights. Notions of the state and state's rights in conjunction with the doctrine of legal positivism, which views rights as subordinate, can potentially legitimate authoritarian political regimes, as was the case in Nazi Germany, and, under certain conditions, rights can be seen as an impediment to the 'proper' exercise of state power. In France, in contrast to German legal positivism, while the state is the giver of rights, its power is circumscribed by its obligation to protect its citizens' rights. Consequently, opposition and rebellion against an unjust state are philosophically legitimate.

THE INDIVIDUAL AND THE COLLECTIVITY: ECONOMIC AND SOCIAL RIGHTS

Whereas Western Europe and the United States derived their conception of rights from the liberal philosophers, the Soviet Union and East European socialist states formulated their doctrine of rights from within the Marxist tradition. Nevertheless, both traditions, despite sharp divergence on the doctrine of rights, share a universe of discourse, a common intellectual heritage in which the individual is *the* object of philosophic speculation. However, whereas for the liberal philosophers the individual in pursuit of self-interest is an immutable given of human nature, for Marx human nature is unformed and malleable, being contingent on the extant mode of production. According to Marx, the liberal conception did describe human nature, but only when and where the capitalist mode of production prevailed. Consequently, the rights inhering in liberalism that emanated from human nature under capitalism, namely civil and political rights, were bourgeois rights designed to further the interests of this class (McPherson 1973). And while capitalism, according to Marx, was progressive in so far as it had solved the problem of material scarcity, simultaneously its emphasis on competition and individualism had resulted in the alienation of the individual from other human beings and from nature. Marx's theory of historical materialism suggested that in socialism, which would follow capitalism, the individual would no longer be atomized and alienated but would become an integrated person through membership in a collectivity. Under socialism, interpersonal bonds and mutuality would be re-established, thereby restructuring social relations. Each individual would possess reciprocal rights and obligations. The notion of an autonomous individual in lonely and isolated pursuit of self-interest and the corresponding social relations would be extinguished. In turn, humanity's basic rights of life and security, instead of being manifest in the panoply of civil and political rights, would be fulfilled through the implementation of economic and social rights. Subsistence, housing, clothing and all other basic needs would be attained for all. Yet these rights would become attainable because of the productive affluence resulting from capitalist development.

Just as the modern political philosophers did not have a specific theory of rights, neither did Marx. The theory of rights that has been derived from Marxism is grounded in his notion of humankind's basic need for security, leading to the articulation of fundamental rights as economic, social and cultural. People under socialism would not be hedonistically motivated but would be social beings in harmony with others and with their environment. In turn the satisfaction of basic needs within a communal context would lead to self-fulfilment. More than a century later, Marx's conceptualization was echoed, from a different perspective, by the psychologist Abraham Maslow in his theory on the hierarchy of human needs (Maslow 1970). Marx himself did not preclude individual self-expression as necessary for self-fulfilment, but argued that this would only be possible within a collectivity after the fulfilment of the reciprocal rights and duties which would provide for survival and security. Therefore, for Marx it was not solely that the substance of fundamental rights differed from those of liberalism, but that individual rights were inextricably interdependent and contingent on the individual's obligations to the group. An individual had the right to work, but he/she also had an obligation to engage in productive work which would make possible the satisfaction of economic rights. Central to Marx's thought was this reciprocity between rights and obligations, and the belief in fundamental rights as economic and social.

Marx's notion of rights was only one of several elements of his theory of historical materialism and class struggle that was adopted by the Soviet Union at the time of the Bolshevik Revolution. In contrast to social transformation in Western Europe during the seventeenth and eighteenth centuries which was directed against the monarchical state, the Russian revolution of the early twentieth century was anti-colonial and nationalist. Russia had not been colonized, but it had been penetrated by Western capitalism, and its revolution was comparable to post-Second World War nationalist movements in so far as one of its goals was to liberate itself from exploitation by the advanced capitalist countries. In order to eliminate exploitation and assert state sovereignty, rapid industrialization became a primary task of the new communist regime in the Soviet Union. No industrial, domestic, capitalist class had developed in Russia, and indigenous capital for productive investment was lacking. At the same time the capitalist states of the West were mobilizing to overthrow the new socialist regime in the Soviet Union. Under these conditions, the vehicle for industrialization, in contrast to the process in the West, was not the bourgeoisie but inevitably the state. Marxism, as further elaborated by Lenin, became the ideological and philosophic framework justifying and legitimating the newly emerging social order.

In the process of consolidating the new socialist order, the incipient theory of rights contained in Marx was recast so as to conform to the Soviet Union's social and political realities. Thus while Marx spoke of the mutuality and interdependence of members of a community with reciprocal rights and obligations, in the Soviet Union these obligations to others were transposed to the state. It was to the state, the new collectivity, and not to others in a social network, that duties were owed by individuals. In exchange the state became the guarantor, provider and implementor of the citizens' fundamental rights – the rights to life and security (Gonchavuk 1979). The substance of these latter rights, however, was not the civil and political rights of liberalism but the rights associated with fulfilling humankind's basic needs as set forth by Marx – the right to shelter, to employment, to clothing, to health care, to social security, in fact to all those economic and social rights set forth in the Convenant on Economic, Social and Cultural Rights. Civil and political rights were viewed as subsidiary and contingent on state action.

Whereas Western liberal thought concerning the justification of rights evolved and was modified as the initial paradigm was challenged, socialist doctrine on rights in the Soviet Union and Eastern Europe remained static. The denial of freedom of expression foreclosed intellectual discourse. The dissident movement on the whole advanced demands for Western freedoms, justifying them in the Soviet context by highly legalistic arguments that the Soviet Constitution provided for civil and political rights, which unfortunately the regime consistently violated. The rare voice that attempted to recast socialist rights by arguing for the incorporation and interdependence of economic/ social and civil/political rights was suppressed (Medvedev 1975). Significantly, despite the espousal of socialism as an alternative ideology and social system to capitalism/pluralism, the Soviet Union and Eastern Europe concurrently articulated a legal philosophy – legal positivism – comparable to that of continental European countries. As in Germany, it was the state that was the giver and definer of rights. The differences lay both in the prevailing concept of fundamental rights and in the ascribed role of the state. In the Soviet Union the state was perceived as either the instrument for transition to socialism or as the agent of the working class.

It is too soon to assess the potential impact on doctrines and practices of human rights that may be generated as a result of the revolutionary changes in Eastern Europe beginning in late 1989 and the dissolution of the Soviet Union at the end of 1991. A relatively recent debate in the West which postulates that both sets of rights – economic/social and civil/political – are essential for the satisfaction of either, in time may resonate and find roots in Eastern Europe.

While civil and political rights remain fundamental in the West, some non-Marxist scholars are increasingly arguing that economic and social rights, often labelled basic needs, are equivalent if not more fundamental (Galtung 1977). This rethinking of the nature and substance of rights in terms of basic needs has authenticated the socialist doctrine of rights in the minds of Western scholars at the very time they are being questioned in the East. While in Eastern Europe demands for freedom and individual liberties are in the forefront, Western analysts are discoursing on the dimensions of basic needs, on ascertaining valid distinctions between needs and wants, and disputing whether social rights or political/civil rights are primary. In fact, at a time when Eastern writers and politicians are abandoning their commitment to fulfilling basic needs, a body of literature has grown which delves into the relatedness and interdependence, if any, between these two sets of rights (Shue 1980).

In the euphoria of the transformations in Eastern Europe the cry for freedom is deafening, but it is an ill-defined freedom which, in addition to asserting liberation from Soviet domination, is largely articulated in terms of traditional Western liberties. The emphasis has been on capitalist economic rights – the right to private property, freedom of contract, and a market economy – ignoring the economic and social rights of socialism. A half-century of socialization into a socialist ideology in which economic and social rights were fundamental, limited as their implementation may have been, may pose a dilemma and engender tensions as the underlying notion of rights in Eastern Europe and the former Soviet Union is shifted towards Western individualism. Moreover, the rise of ethnicity has resurrected demands for self-determination which potentially pose a contradiction between the claims of individual rights and those of communal rights. It is premature, however, to speculate on what the long-run configuration will be both with regard to the practice of rights and to the possibility of the emergence of an alternative doctrine of rights emanating from new philosophic foundations.

COMMUNALISM AND RIGHTS

The revival of scholarly interest in the theory of rights during the post-Second World War era has had to confront a social reality in vast regions of the world where the very vocabulary of rights has been non-existent. During the course of the twentieth century, societies throughout the globe had been incorporated into the world system as colonies, semi-colonies and/or economic dependencies. The nationalist movements for independence following the Second World War were accompanied, as it had been half a century earlier in Russia, by demands for industrialization and modernization. The revolutionary leaders, largely educated in the West or the Soviet Union, had been profoundly affected by modernity. They created or inherited modern state structures from their former colonial masters and embarked on the task of economic development. While colonial rule and/or incorporation into the world economy had severely disrupted traditional societies and economies, the lifestyles of the vast majority of the population in Africa, Asia and the Middle East, as well as their identities, values, attitudes, behaviour and social relations, remained relatively unaffected.

In the West, prior to the rise of capitalism and the doctrines of liberalism, people's identity, their notion of self, was defined by their membership in a group and by their role and status in this group. Similarly, in much of today's so-called 'Third World', despite vast cultural and social diversity, a person's notion of self is in terms of an integral group, precisely which group depending upon a society's particular cultural configuration – extended family, kinship, tribe, village. It is this communal structure of society that has formed a person's self-definition, and not individualism. Independence and the mostly failed strategies of economic development have not brought about life experiences conducive to notions of individualism. In fact, as several African writers (Zvobgo 1979; Cobbah 1987) have pointed out, the concept of rights, and most definitively those of individual rights, does not exist linguistically in African languages. Nor does the ideology of individualism have much resonance in the Middle East (in Islamic societies) or in Asia (in Hindu and Buddhist communities). If the language of rights is superimposed on these communally based societies, as is done by many Western analysts, rights must be seen either as hierarchical, differential person-to-person rights whose exercise is inextricably connected with obligations, or as attributes of the communal group *per se.*

Inevitably, by contrast to Western intellectual thought, including both liberalism and socialism, the continued centrality of religious thought in much of Asia and the Middle East and imbedded cultural values in Africa have impeded the emergence of a secular contemporary doctrine of rights. A significant exception to this generalization regarding religious thought and individual rights is the recent doctrine of liberation theology, prominent in Latin America. Emanating from the Catholic notion of human dignity, liberation theology merges Marxian social rights with individual civil and political rights (Gutierrez 1973). Overall, however, the rights that are formally espoused by Third World political elites are either those embedded in the constitutional legacy of the colonial powers or in the international instruments of human rights to which these states have become signatories. These legal norms regarding rights do not constitute principles underlying and legitimating political regimes in the Third World.

Nevertheless, there are scholars from these regions who are reformulating, redefining and adapting traditional cultural and philosophic doctrines in such a manner as to incorporate and justify modern notions of rights within their tradition (An-Na'im and Deng 1990). Other analysts have attempted to recast and transpose traditional communal value systems which articulate interpersonal reciprocal relations to the national level of the modern state. Rather than assimilating Western notions of the atomized individual possessing civil and political rights, a fusion has been attempted between traditional communalism and the Marxian doctrine of economic and social rights. Historically a person had duties towards others within the social network – tribe, village, kinship, etc. – that structured his/her membership, in exchange for guarantees of the fulfilment of security needs. With the imposition of modern state structures the state replaced the communal group and assumed the traditional communal obligations for providing security while the person owed duties and obligations to the state. On this view, since Third World countries had not undergone the historical phase of capitalism and the consequent atomization of the individual, socialism was congruent and could be fused with traditional values (Nyerere 1968; Huang 1979).

Some Western analysts have countered the claim that human rights are culturally relative by contending that as Third World countries modernize, as development takes place, individuals will internalize the Western notion of individual human rights because the very process of industrialization will result in individual autonomy (Howard 1986). Others dispute this claim, arguing that Third World processes of development and modernization have not replicated those of the West and, perhaps of greater significance, modernity itself has been elusive. Hence, in the face of increasing impoverishment in some areas, urbanization dissociated from any industrial base, the destruction of subsistence economies, and mounting ethnic conflict, the various theories of individual rights and freedoms as set forth by Western political philosophers were and remain irrelevant. Significantly, even those states that in the post-Second World War decades have industrialized successfully, as judged by the standard measures of economic growth, have not assimilated either the doctrine of individual civil and political rights or that of economic and social rights. Repression and massive violations of the entire complex of rights persist. While South Korea and Taiwan have developed and have become industrial economies, they have failed to implement and adhere to human rights standards. This failure posits a severe challenge to the argument that modernization would be accompanied by the internalization of human rights precepts and implementation of their practice. The juxtaposition of theoretical models of individual human rights with social reality in newly industrialized states requires a rethinking of the issue of cultural relativism and its role in the articulation of conceptualizations of human rights.

In addition to questions concerning the applicability of doctrines of individual human rights to Third World countries, there is also debate on the impact of economic dependency on the implementation of human rights in non-Western states. The trade-off theory argues that, lamentable as it may be, the priority of the goal of economic development of necessity requires restrictions on the exercise of rights. Political stability and domestic cohesion are necessary preconditions, it is argued, for successful industrialization. Human rights will flow after growth is attained. The experience of the NICs would seem to invalidate this argument since rights implementation has not followed industrialization. In fact, it is contended that development and the practice of human rights can and should be complementary. The converse of the trade-off theory is argued by others claiming that it is not the priority of economic development *per se* and the alleged requisite of political stability that denigrate human rights but that strategies for economic development in themselves lead to gross violations of rights. Strategies that emphasize rapid industrialization result in neither political stability nor economic development. In fact the failed strategies, one of whose defining features is gross violations of economic/social rights, often lead to social discontent to which states respond in turn by increasing political repression (Lopez and Stohl 1989).

Moreover, other analysts argue forcefully that economic dependency structurally impedes and thwarts the implementation of human rights. Among the many forms of dependency on the industrialized countries, the reliance of Third World countries on external financing of their economies, in particular, has resulted in massive foreign debts which in turn subjects them to economic policies destructive of rights (Conklin and Davidson 1986). Foreign borrowing, initially designed to deal with balance-of-payments deficits and to obtain needed capital for industrialization, is now primarily used to service the foreign debt. Imposition of stabilization and austerity programmes by the international financial institutions, spearheaded by the International Monetary Fund (IMF), in the name of restructuring economies and controlling inflation, results in increased unemployment, a reduction in wage levels and consequently a further decline in the standard of living. Furthermore, the IMF's strict technical economic criteria and its insistence on political stability as a condition for granting loans mandate severe restrictions on the exercise of civil and political rights while simultaneously downgrading the fulfilment of economic/social rights. It should be noted that if human rights practices were to be judged in terms of the Third World's traditional values, the IMF's devastating impact on social rights grossly violates the tradition of providing for the basic needs of its peoples.

The issue of human rights, however defined and whatever the philosophic premises, remains problematic in most of the Third World. Analysts, both from the West and from the Third World, rather than formulating modifications of or advocating a particular theory of rights rooted in the abstract models of the analytic philosophers or the class-based notions of Marxism, have been wrestling with concrete problems. Accepting on the whole the validity of the substance of rights as set forth in the various international and regional human rights instruments, their inquiries focus on explaining the failure of Third World states to adhere to these standards and the persistent violation of rights, including such practices as torture and arbitrary arrests. Hypotheses that have been offered include the supremacy of state sovereignty, the constraints imposed by economic dependency discussed above (p. 1334), cultural diversity, and most recently the roots of state terrorism. Since on the whole, with the exception of those who espouse a socialist ideology, Third World countries have not articulated a set of principles underlying or governing their societies, they lack a doctrine of rights. Exceptions are China, Vietnam and Nicaragua (prior to the elections in 1989), which have espoused a modified Marxist theory of rights linked to the specifications of their traditions.

CONCLUSION

As stated at the outset, human rights as a subfield within political science has burgeoned, and in so doing it has frequently ventured beyond the boundaries of the discipline. Initially a philosophic concern primarily of liberal philosophers, it has become an interdisciplinary endeavour drawing the attention of legal scholars, sociologists, anthropologists and economists in addition to political scientists. Concern with human rights and their linkages to the state, society and economy have become matters of intense scholarly discourse. In recent years the never-ending dialectic relationship between social reality and intellectual thought has brought to the fore a new set of rights implicitly rooted in normative considerations but outside the scope of traditional liberal or Marxist rights theories. Often labelled the third generation of rights – as distinct from the first generation of civil and political rights and the second generation of economic and social rights – these rights encompass such diverse issues as the right to development and environmental rights. Disparate as these newly proclaimed rights may be, they share one common element: they are rights of a community, and not individual rights.

Environmental rights are often considered a prerequisite for the implementation of the right to life and survival. Without clean air, clean water and uncontaminated land, survival and the enjoyment of economic rights become precarious. But these are not rights that can be exercised by individuals, nor can they be provided for by a collectivity to individuals. They can only be attributes of communities *qua* communities. Similarly, while individuals can claim economic rights – the right to food, to shelter, and to health care – these rights are contingent on a society's available resources. World poverty has worsened in recent years, prompting analysts to argue that the enjoyment of individual economic rights necessitates development. While the economically privileged may enjoy individual economic rights, implementation for all is dependent upon development of the community, be it the state or local grassroots communal groups. Recently, in fact, a literature has emerged probing the meaning of development which implicitly or explicitly recasts the question of human nature by asserting that development is a holistic process in which human dignity is affirmed. For this end to be achieved, individuals must have control over their lives and participate in decisions leading not only to economic development but more fundamentally to the development of community structures and to the expression of their individual potential.

In summary, as the issues posed and scrutinized appear to be increasingly complex, the study of human rights has been moving in directions which encompass a greater range of phenomena normally considered the province of other fields or disciplines. Perspectives are multiple, as are theories. Some are broad ranging, aimed at a general theory; others are concrete, probing specific aspects of a human rights concern. The proliferation of studies is bound to continue in the search for consensus on the meaning of human rights and in the search for the determinants of rights violations. Particularly as the surge of ethnicity and ethnic conflict poses an increasingly acute challenge to human rights theories, more particularly to those grounded in individualism, the conflicting claims of individual rights and communal rights will have to be addressed.

REFERENCES

An-Na'im, A. A. and Deng, F. M. (eds) (1990) *Human Rights in Africa: Cross-Cultural Perspectives*, Washington, DC: Brookings Institution.

Cobbah, J. A. M. (1987) 'African values and the human rights debate: an African perspective', *Human Rights Quarterly* 9 (3): 309–31.

Conklin, M. and Davidson, D. (1986) 'The IMF and economic and social human rights: a case study of Argentina 1958–1985', *Human Rights Quarterly* 8 (2): 227–69.

Donnelly, J. (1984) 'Human rights and development: complementary and competing concerns?', *World Politics* 36 (2): 255–83.

——(1985) *The Concept of Human Rights*, New York: St Martin's Press.

Downing, T. and Kushner, G. (eds) (1988) *Human Rights and Anthropology*, Cambridge, Mass.: Cultural Survival.

Dworkin, R. (1977) *Taking Rights Seriously*, Cambridge, Mass.: Harvard University Press.

Falk, R. (1981) *Human Rights and State Sovereignty*, New York: Holmes & Meier.

Flatham, R. E. (1980) *The Practice of Political Authority: Authority and the Authoritative*, Chicago: University of Chicago Press.

Galtung, J. (1977) *Human Needs as the Focus of the Social Sciences*, Oslo: University of Oslo Press.

Gonchavuk, M. (ed.) (1979) *Socialism and Human Rights*, Moscow: USSR Academy of Sciences.

Gutierrez, G. (1973) *A Theology of Liberation*, Maryknoll, NY: Orbis Books.

Howard, R. E. (1986) *Human Rights in Commonwealth Africa*, Totowa, NJ: Rowman & Littlefield.

Huang, M. (1979) 'Human rights in a revolutionary society: the case of the People's Republic of China', in A. Pollis and P. Schwab (eds) *Human Rights Cultural and Ideological Perspectives*, New York: Praeger.

Kommers, D. (1989) *Constitutional Jurisprudence of the Federal Republic of Germany*, Chapel Hill, NC: Duke University Press.

Lopez, G. A. and Stohl, M. (eds) (1989) *Development, Dependence and State Repression*, Westport, Conn.: Greenwood Press.

McPherson, C. B. (1973) *Democratic Theory: Essays in Retrieval*, Oxford: Clarendon Press.

Maslow, A. (1970) *Motivation and Personality*, 2nd edn, New York: Harper & Row.

Medvedev, R. (1975) *On Socialist Democracy*, trans. and ed. E. Dakadt, New York: Knopf.

Nyerere, J. (1968) *Ujamma: Essays on Socialism*, Oxford: Oxford University Press.

Pollis, A. and Schwab, P. (eds) (1979) *Human Rights: Cultural and Ideological Perspectives*, New York: Praeger.

Rawls, J. (1971) *Theory of Justice*, Cambridge, Mass.: Harvard University Press.

Rouner, L. (1988) *Human Rights and the World's Religions*, Notre Dame, Ind.: University of Notre Dame Press.

Shue, H. (1980) *Basic Rights: Subsistence, Affluence and US Foreign Policy*, Princeton: Princeton University Press.

Zvobgo, J. M. (1979) 'A Third World view', in D. Kommers and G. D. Loescher (eds)

Human Rights and American Foreign Policy, Notre Dame, Ind.: University of Notre Dame Press.

REFERENCES

Bay, C. (1982) 'Self-respect as a human right: thoughts on its dialectics of wants and needs in the struggle for human community', *Human Rights Quarterly* 4 (1): 53–95.

Cranston, M. (1967) 'Human rights, real and supposed', in D. D. Raphael (ed.) *Political Theory and the Rights of Man*, Bloomington: Indiana University Press.

Gewirth, A. (1982) *Human Rights: Essay on Justification and Application*, Chicago: University of Chicago Press.

Henkin, L. (1978) *The Rights of Man Today*, Boulder, Colo.: Westview Press.

Lopez, G. A. and Stohl, M. (eds) (1984) *The State as Terrorist*, Westport, Conn.: Greenwood Press.

Schwab, P. and Pollis, A. (eds) (1982) *Toward a Human Rights Framework*, New York: Praeger.

83

REFUGEES

ELIZABETH G. FERRIS

The massive uprooting of people from their communities and countries has become a permanent feature of the international political landscape in the forty-five years since the Second World War. Today, refugees number over 17 million while the number of internally displaced persons is probably double that figure. In the years following the First World War and especially since the Second World War, the international system developed a number of institutions and a body of international law to protect and assist those forced to flee their countries of origin. In the last decade, this international system for the protection and assistance of refugees has been undergoing a major transformation as a result of changes in the character and duration of refugee movements. While it seems clear that a new international refugee system is in the process of formation, it is unclear what shape and direction the new system will take. Studying the ways in which the international community and national governments have responded to refugee movements offers considerable insight into the functioning of the international system.

THE STUDY OF REFUGEES

Traditionally scholars have paid little attention to refugee movements, largely interpreting such migrations as marginal to the central processes of inter-national conflicts. Refugees were typically seen as tragic but politically irrel-evant and temporary by-products of political violence between or within states. Most accounts of refugee situations were descriptive in nature, written by practitioners or journalists concerned with raising awareness about particular situations (see, for example, Shawcross 1984; Clay 1989). In the last five to ten years, however, the field of refugee studies has recognized the importance of studying refugees as both a cause and a consequence of conflict. As refugee situations become more complex, scholars have developed more sophisticated analytical tools to analyse refugee situations. Today, scholars in different disciplines – political science, sociology, economics, history and law, as well as anthropology, psychology, environmental studies and geography – are reassessing their theoretical tools for understanding refugee situations. The study of refugees and refugee policies raises many of the basic issues of political and social analysis – policy-making processes, human rights, international and national law, the nature of conflict, development and global institutional responses on particular issues.

One strand of research on refugees has focused on the individual level: why does a particular individual decide to leave his or her country at a particular point in time? What factors determine whether or not an individual refugee will successfully adapt to life in a new country? Keller (1975) analysed the stages of psychological change experienced by people uprooted from their countries, while Stein (1981) considered the processes by which individuals decide to leave their country of origin. He distinguished, for example, between acute and anticipatory refugees as a function of the time available for individuals to make their decisions.

A second approach has focused on the national level of analysis in seeking to understand the causes and consequences of refugee flows. What types of conflict produce mass exoduses? What are the determinants of refugee policies of receiving countries? How does treatment of refugees contribute to a resolution or intensification of conflict? A focus on the national level has been the most common approach to studying refugee situations. Zolberg, *et al.* (1989) consider the relationship between the types of conflict, the nature of refugee migrations and the policies of receiving countries. A number of studies have analysed the refugee decision-making processes in the United States, tracing the interplay of domestic and foreign policy interests. Thus Zucker and Zucker conclude that:

> when a particular group of refugees serves our foreign policy goals, does not threaten to overwhelm us with its numbers, and can be resettled with little cost or domestic resistance, the members of that group are usually assured of admission. Conversely, members of a group that does not meet any of these criteria may be certain that admission will be denied.
>
> (Zucker and Zucker 1987: xviii)

Other studies have focused on the interaction between various actors in the process of refugee policy formation and implementation. Thus Nichols (1988) traces the relationship between US government refugee policy and religious-based non-governmental organizations.

A third approach analyses refugee movements from a global or systemic perspective. How have changes in the international system affected refugee migrations? What are the systemic determinants of refugee migrations? What is the relationship between international forced migration and underlying economic and political characteristics of the international system? What is the capacity of the international community to respond to refugees? Zolberg *et al.* (1989) look at systemic trends in the cause of refugee migrations, while Hoffman-Nowotny (1981) sees migration as a societal mechanism for displacing the stresses produced by social change on the national level. A particular thrust of the international level of analysis has been on the role of international law and practice (Goodwin-Gill 1983; Jaeger 1983) and international organization (Gordenker 1987) in responding to the challenge of mass movements of people.

These three approaches are not mutually exclusive; increasingly scholars are realizing the benefits of multi-disciplinary approaches using multiple levels of analysis. The inauguration, for example, of the *Refugee Studies Journal* in 1988 is one manifestation of the growing commitment to a more comprehensive approach to the study of refugees.

Although the approaches used by scholars differ, central to all research on refugees is the increasingly thorny issue of how refugees are defined. It is generally recognized that accepted definitions of who is a refugee have been the product of particular historical developments. Moreover, the way in which refugees are defined in practice is a consequence of the particular situations producing refugees, as well as the international community's response to their plight.

WHO IS A REFUGEE?

Since the Second World War, the principal legal definition of refugees has been that incorporated into the 1951 United Nations (UN) Convention Relating to the Status of Refugees and its 1967 Protocol, which removed the Convention's geographic limitation of refugees as being those displaced by events in Europe before 1951. This definition of refugees was designed to meet the needs of individuals fleeing persecution in the post-war era. Certainly one of the current dilemmas facing the international system today is the inadequacy of this definition to respond to the needs of people uprooted by a different combination of causes than those present in Europe during the 1940s.

The Convention defines a refugee as:

> any person who, owing to a well-founded fear of being persecuted for reasons of race, religion, nationality, membership of a particular social group or political opinion, is outside the country of his nationality and is unable or, owing to such fear, is unwilling to avail himself of that country, or who, not having a nationality and being outside the country of his former habitual residence, is unable, or owing to such fear, is unwilling to return to it.
>
> (UN 1951)

Furthermore, the UN Convention provides a set of rights for individuals determined to be refugees, including the right of *non-refoulement* – that is, the right not to be forcibly repatriated to the country of origin.

Thus, the internationally accepted definition of refugees includes those who have been singled out for persecution for five reasons: religion, race, nationality, membership in a particular social group or political opinion. The definition excludes those individuals who are displaced by violence or warfare and who have not been singled out for individual persecution: the vast majority of today's refugees. As Elliott Abrams, former US Assistant Secretary of State for Human Rights and Humanitarian Affairs, stated, 'the key to the concept of asylum is targeting. It's not sufficient to note that the country [an applicant comes from] is repressive, violent or poor. You must show something about you as an individual that would make you a target of persecution – your religion, your race, or something' (*Washington Post* 1983).

In contrast to this narrow definition of refugee status, the Organization of African Unity (OAU) in 1969 developed a Convention Governing the Specific Aspects of Refugee Problems in Africa which expanded the UN definition to include those individuals displaced by generalized conditions of violence. The OAU definition of refugees includes:

> every person who, owing to external aggression, occupation, foreign domination or events seriously disturbing public order in either part or the whole of his country of origin or nationality, is compelled to leave his place of habitual residence in order to seek refuge in another place outside his country of origin or nationality.
>
> (OAU 1969)

These definitions exclude several important groups of people uprooted by forces beyond their control. Both the UN and the OAU definitions exclude those individuals who have been displaced or persecuted because of violence, but who, for one reason or another, have not left their country of origin. The protection and assistance needs of these 'internally displaced' populations are often more serious than those who are able to get out of the country where they are insecure or fearful. Although reliable data are lacking, the evidence suggests that those who are displaced internally are both more numerous and more vulnerable than those leaving the country. Unlike refugees, the internally displaced have no body of international law or practices to call upon.

A second major group excluded from this definition are those leaving their home countries for economic or environmental reasons. As governments increasingly use economic oppression as a tool of warfare, the distinction between political and economic motivations for flight breaks down. Where armies burn fields and destroy warehouses to deprive opposition forces of support – whether in Afghanistan, Guatemala or Cambodia – people's immediate motivation to flee may be 'economic' but the reasons behind the economic factors are political. Similarly, people are increasingly uprooted by environmental factors, frequently exacerbated by political decisions. Drought leads to famine in countries where certain political decisions have been made or where war disrupts normal mechanisms for food distribution. This has been the case in the Horn of Africa throughout the 1980s.

Related to the definition of refugees is the concept of asylum – the actual granting of protection to those fleeing persecution. Although the Universal Declaration of Human Rights (Article 14) states that 'individuals have a right to seek and enjoy asylum', they do not have an inherent right to be *granted* asylum. It is governments that award asylum, and thus national legislation and procedures largely determine whether or not a particular individual is to be considered a refugee. Within the last decade, governments, particularly Western governments, have faced dramatic increases in the number of asylum seekers reaching their borders and, as explained below (p. 1347), are taking measures to deter more arrivals of asylum seekers.

Most of the world's governments have ratified the Convention (although some have maintained geographical restrictions) and have incorporated elements of the Geneva Convention into their domestic legislation on refugees. However, the application of such laws has always depended on national domestic and foreign policy interests as well as on the particular situations. The United States Immigration Act of 1965, for example, limited refugee status to those fleeing communist-dominated countries or the Middle East (although the Attorney-General was given parole power to admit refugees from other regions). The adoption of the Refugee Act of 1980 eliminated this restriction and incorporated the language of the UN Convention on refugees, but the practice of awarding refugee status primarily to those fleeing communist regimes continued. As Loescher and Scanlan (1986) demonstrate, 95 per cent of those admitted as refugees to the United States since the Second World War have been from communist countries. But while asylum policy has always been applied in response to particular national situations, there has also been a serious effort to shape an international response to the needs of those displaced by factors beyond their control.

THE INTERNATIONAL COMMUNITY'S RESPONSE

Refugee movements are, by definition, international and require an international response. Around the time of the First World War, the number of refugees dramatically increased. The war itself produced large numbers of civilians fleeing combat areas. The Russian revolution and civil war produced 1.5 million refugees, while upheavals in Turkey uprooted hundreds of thousands of Armenians and Greeks. In response to these large-scale movements,

Fridtjof Nansen was appointed High Commissioner for Refugees of the League of Nations in 1921 in recognition of the need for a co-ordinated international response. During the inter-war period there was no institutionalized apparatus to respond to the material needs of refugees although the Nansen Commission did contribute to the development of international legal principles and instruments. During the Second World War, an Intergovernmental Committee on Refugees was constituted to deal with the flight of political and Jewish refugees from Germany and Austria and to seek their resettlement, but only helped around 4,000 refugees.

The United Nations Relief and Rehabilitation Agency (UNRRA) was established in 1943 with responsibility for emergency relief and repatriation. UNRRA helped some 7 million people return to their homes, but was hampered by its lack of a mandate for involvement in resettlement. By 1947, most of Europe's refugees had been repatriated and the task of facilitating the integration of the remaining 2 million people was transferred to the International Refugee Organization (IRO), which had a clear mandate to care for and assist refugees. Under the auspices of the IRO, almost 3 million refugees, mostly East Europeans, were given protection and assistance. In 1949 another international organization was established to deal with the special needs of the almost 800,000 Palestinians uprooted as a result of the establishment of the state of Israel. The United Nations Relief and Works Agency for Palestine Refugees in the Near East (UNRWA) was intended as a short-term response to a temporary problem. Its initial mandate was limited, requiring General Assembly approval for extension. In 1951, the IRO was dissolved although there were still refugees remaining in Europe. That same year, the office of the United Nations High Commissioner for Refugees (UNHCR) was created, initially for three years, with a small budget and a limited mandate. In 1952, the Intergovernmental Committee on European Migration (ICEM) was established by Western governments to provide assistance with transporting refugees.

These three institutions – UNHCR, UNRWA and ICEM (now IOM – International Organization for Migration) – were all created to deal with specific needs at a particular historical moment. In addition, a large number of non-governmental organizations (NGOs) provided essential services to refugees – sometimes in collaboration with the intergovernmental bodies or national governments, sometimes independently. In the years following the Second World War, NGOs controlled more relief funds for refugees than the intergovernmental institutions. In the immediate post-war period, the main challenges for both the intergovernmental and the non-governmental organizations were to repatriate and resettle those displaced by the war and by the changes taking place in post-war Europe. Although refugee movements were occurring in other parts of the world, notably as a result of the partition of the Indian subcontinent, the international institutions were not involved as their mandate was limited to specific geographic regions. However, the flow of refugees from Europe was substantial. Some 3.5 million Germans crossed into the West between 1951 and 1961, when the Berlin Wall was constructed (Marrus 1985). UNHCR's ability to respond was limited during this period by its small budget; indeed, as Gallagher (1989: 582) notes, only a $3 million grant from the Ford Foundation kept the institution alive until 1956. At that time, the arrival of 200,000 Hungarian refugees led the UN General Assembly to authorize UNHCR to respond to the situation – the first of many occasions where UNHCR was authorized to respond to needs of people who did not meet the formal definition. Also in 1956, the General Assembly renewed UNHCR's mandate for five years (and has renewed it at subsequent five-year intervals since then).

By the late 1950s and early 1960s, independence struggles in Africa had led to increasing numbers of refugees on that continent: by the end of 1963, there were some 400,000 refugees, mainly Angolans and Rwandans. Ten years later, the figure had jumped to over 1 million as a result of conflicts in Sudan, Congo, Portuguese Guinea, Ethiopia, Burundi and Equatorial Guinea. With the lifting of the geographic restriction to the convention definition in 1967 and the promulgation of the OAU definition in 1969, the international community began to respond to these needs. By 1980, the number of refugees in Africa had increased to 3.5 million and in 1990 the number had risen to some 5 million.

Until the mid-1970s, most of Asia's refugee population was cared for in the region: Tibetans in India, Chinese in Hong Kong, and most notably 10 million East Pakistanis who were able to return to their country after the creation of the state of Bangladesh in 1971. But in the mid-1970s, the outpouring of Indo-Chinese refugees led to a new dynamic. Governments in South-East Asia found themselves unable and unwilling to cope with the large numbers of refugees arriving on their shores and borders. They agreed to provide temporary asylum to the new arrivals only on the condition that the refugees would be resettled elsewhere. At the 1979 International Conference on Indo-Chinese Refugees, governments agreed to provide the necessary resettlement places; between 1975 and 1990 over 1 million Indo-Chinese refugees were resettled to third countries, primarily to North America and Australia. By the late 1980s, this international commitment to care for the Indo-Chinese refugees was breaking down. The second International Conference on Indo-Chinese Refugees in 1989 formulated a Comprehensive Plan of Action which maintains a resettlement option but also provides for repatriation of those found not to be refugees and calls on the government of Vietnam to take measures to prevent its citizens from leaving.

In the early 1960s large numbers of Cubans left for the United States, followed in 1981 by the Mariel exodus of 125,000 Cubans. However, the response to the Cuban exodus was dealt with bilaterally by the US government, which for both foreign policy and domestic reasons chose to implement a generous admissions policy. The late 1970s were also characterized by massive refugee migrations in Central America, the Horn of Africa and from Afghanistan. While Latin America had historically had a generous tradition of asylum, until 1974 this was extended to small numbers of political opponents. With the Chilean *coup* in 1973, the system was challenged with the need to provide for several hundred thousand refugees. With the outbreak of violence in Central America in the late 1970s, millions of Salvadorans, Guatemalans and Nicaraguans were displaced from their communities. But like the 5.5 million Afghan refugees, most of the Central Americans remained in their region, receiving assistance from governments, international agencies and NGOs. Similarly, the massive flows from Ethiopia, Somalia, and Sudan were largely dealt with in their region of origin.

The presence of large numbers of refugees in some of the poorest countries of the world challenged the international mechanisms for refugee protection and assistance. UNHCR's budgets underwent dramatic expansion and refugee 'bureaucracies' grew up in many countries. NGOs mobilized substantial resources to implement and complement efforts by governments and UNHCR to assist refugees. Increasingly too, NGOs were challenged to perform protection functions in areas where UNHCR was unable to do so.

The traditional three 'durable solutions' to refugee situations – voluntary repatriation, local integration and resettlement in third countries – seemed more and more inadequate to deal with the needs of 15 million people living in exile for years. As it became clear that most of the refugees would not be able to return home in the near future and that resettlement in third countries was not a viable option, the need for refugee self-sufficiency and development rose to the top of the international agenda. Two major International Conferences on Assistance to Refugees in Africa (ICARA I and II in 1981 and 1984, respectively) were held to affirm the link between refugee and development assistance. But the many far-sighted recommendations from these conferences were overtaken by major refugee emergencies in both the Horn of Africa and southern Africa.

By the mid-1980s, refugee situations in Africa, Asia, Latin America and the Middle East were characterized by mass numbers and a lack of durable solutions. As wars lasted longer, often supported by outside powers, refugees remained in camps or eked out an existence on the margins of large cities, waiting for conditions to change, which would enable them to return home. By the late 1980s, governments, largely Western governments, were questioning the extent to which the international community could continue to support seemingly permanent refugee populations for indefinite periods of time. In

1989, UNHCR faced its most serious financial crisis in its forty-year history and was forced to cut back on programmes assisting refugees in all regions.

While the refugee situation in the South was serious, the most dramatic challenge to the international system of refugee protection in the 1980s occurred in Western countries. As Widgren notes, during the first half of the 1970s an average of 13,000 persons applied for asylum in Western Europe each year (Widgren 1989: 601). By the late 1980s, the average number of asylum applications per year had climbed to 195,000 – fifteen times as many as the previous decade. Moreover, most of the increase was in arrivals of asylum seekers from countries in the South. The reasons for the increase seem obvious: the growing economic disparity between North and South, improved communication and transportation systems, and the deteriorating conditions of refugees remaining within their regions of origin. Increasingly those arriving in Western countries do not meet the criteria for refugee status as spelled out in the convention or under national laws. While Western governments had been generous in allowing many of these individuals to remain, the surge in new arrivals led to much more restrictive asylum policies. Criteria of proof of persecution, for example, are more rigidly applied, with the predictable result that rates of acceptance of asylum requests are declining significantly in virtually all Western countries. Moreover, governments are increasingly adopting measures intended to deter further arrivals of asylum seekers. Physical prevention of refugees from arriving, such as interdiction at sea of vessels carrying asylum seekers, has been used by the US government to prevent Haitians arriving in the United States as well as by South-East Asian governments seeking to prevent the arrival of Vietnamese asylum seekers. Today, Western governments are increasingly using visa requirements and sanctions against airlines to prevent asylum seekers from arriving at their borders. Other deterrence measures include detention of asylum seekers, and prohibitions against employment and language training, which cause particular difficulties when asylum procedures drag on for years.

The dramatic political changes in Eastern and Central Europe since late 1989 have further strained Western European willingness to accept asylum seekers. While the government of the Federal Republic of Germany maintained its open policy toward ethnic Germans, there is evidence that a backlash is being created as the numbers soar. Similarly, other Western European governments are concerned at the impact of such migration when unrestricted movement within Europe becomes a reality. On a larger scale, governments are concerned at the potential migrant and refugee flows resulting from resurgent ethnic conflicts in the East. These trends will undoubtedly have a negative impact on European receptivity to asylum seekers arriving from the South.

The financial problems of host governments and of UNHCR in caring for the bulk of the world's refugees living in the South and the policies of Western governments toward asylum seekers arriving at their borders are related. Western governments resisted efforts by UNHCR to denounce their restrictionist policies at the same time that they were being asked to contribute more to UNHCR's refugee programmes and to accept more Indo-Chinese refugees for resettlement. At the present time, the future of the international system for refugee protection and assistance is unclear. Most authorities acknowledge that the system itself is in a state of change, but there are few forecasts about the nature of the future international system which will emerge.

FUTURE CHALLENGES

The study of refugee situations cannot be viewed in isolation from the major international issues of peace, justice, economic structures and the environment. The major challenge facing the international refugee system is to prevent the uprooting of individuals from their communities and countries of origin. With the lessening of tension between the United States and the Soviet Union, and the subsequent dissolution of the Soviet Union at the end of 1991, there is increased hope that 'proxy wars' in the Third World will diminish in severity and scope. The changing governments in Eastern and Central Europe hold out the possibility that the number of people fleeing persecution from those regions will diminish, although this hope is tempered by the prospect of renewed ethnic conflict. But the causes of refugee movements are more complex than regional wars or non-democratic governments. As long as economic conditions in many of the countries of the South remain desperate, governments will be forced to use authoritarian methods and violence to maintain public order. Economic scarcity also increases the possibility of ethnic and religious conflict over scarce resources. While some social scientists and NGOs advocate development of early warning systems and models for forecasting refugee movements, efforts to address the root causes of refugee flows require political and economic solutions.

The complexity of the causes of refugee movements make it likely that the question of the definition of refugees will become an increasingly contentious issue in the future. The international consensus underlying the international refugee system has been that refugees – compared with migrants or other social groups – have a special claim on the international community's resources. But that distinction on humanitarian grounds breaks down when one considers the present situation in many countries of the South. Are the people fleeing starvation less in need of assistance and protection than those individuals who leave because they cannot practise their religion? Recent research on the global environment situation also gives rise to prediction of mass migrations as a result of environmental destruction. Moreover, the often desperate need of internally displaced persons illustrates the ambiguous and inconsistent treatment of people who manage to cross a national border versus those who are not able to leave. The forging of an international consensus on the internally displaced will be much more difficult than similar initiatives on behalf of refugees as the very notion of national sovereignty is challenged. Increasingly refugee advocates are seeking to use international human rights instruments to raise issues of protection and security of refugees.

If, as seems likely, the international refugee system changes in such a way as to reduce the financial commitment of the Western countries, the North–South split seems certain to intensify. Most of the world's refugees, perhaps 95 per cent, are in countries of the South where governments face increased pressures of survival and of providing a minimum standard of living to their own populations. The presence of refugees is accepted on the condition that their care will not pose an unacceptable burden on the host governments. If funds to care for refugees are not forthcoming from the international community, governments of the South will be forced either to strain their limited resources to care for the foreigners or to expel them. While the ICARA conferences were not successful in generating large amounts of development funds for refugee assistance, the need to recognize the role that refugees play in development remains serious. Refugees place substantial burdens on host societies and, as is increasingly recognized, on the environment. Insufficient international assistance, for example, to Mozambican refugees has led to massive deforestation in southern Malawi with the consequences that women are walking back to Mozambique to gather firewood while the Malawian government is considering the relocation of the refugees.

While the current tendency of governments is to see the responsibility of the international community to refugees in terms of short-term emergency response, the reality is that refugees must be understood in the broader context of national development policy. In evidence from refugee situations in all regions of the world, it is clear that the presence of refugees engenders resentment among national populations unless measures are taken to ensure that programmes designed to benefit refugees also benefit local communities.

The study of refugees offers a fascinating entry point into the larger political issues of conflict and conflict resolution, policy-making processes at both the national and international levels, and the interplay of domestic and international factors. Moreover, the study of refugees offers almost a unique opportunity to integrate the experiences of individual human beings into discussions of systemic international politics. In this respect, refugees are both a symbol of the violent world in which we live and a reminder that changes on the international and regional levels affect not only theoretical models, but also human lives. Given present trends, it seems likely that refugees will remain an integral part of the international political landscape and a subject of study by scholars in many different disciplines.

Presently, the international system for refugee protection and assistance – a system constructed in the aftermath of the Second World War by the liberal democracies of the world – is in a process of transformation. It is unclear what shape the new system will take, but it is certain that the new system will have to take more complex factors into account than the system it replaces.

REFERENCES

Clay, J. (1989) 'The West and the Ethiopian famine: implications for humanitarian assistance', in G. Loescher and B. Nichols (eds) *The Moral Nation: Humanitarian and US Foreign Policy Today*, Notre Dame, Ind., and London: University of Notre Dame Press.

Ferris, E. G. (ed.) (1985) *Refugees and World Politics*, New York: Praeger.

Gallagher, D. (1989) 'The evolution of the international refugee system', *International Migration Review* 23: 579–98.

Goodwin-Gill, G. S. (1983) *The Refugee in International Law*, Oxford: Clarendon Press.

Gordenker, L. (1987) *Refugees in International Politics*, London: Croom Helm.

Hoffman-Nowotny, H. (1981) 'Sociological approaches toward a general theory of migration', in M. M. Kritz, C. B. Kelly and S. M. Tomasi (eds) *Global Trends in Migration*, New York: Center for Migration Studies.

Holborn, L. W. (1975) *Refugees: A Problem of Our Time*, 2 vols, Methuen, NJ: Scarecrow Press.

Independent Commission on International Humanitarian Issues (1986) *Refugees: The Dynamics of Displacement*, London: Zed Books.

Jaeger, G. (1983) 'The definition of "Refugee": restrictive versus expanding trends', in *World Refugee Survey*, New York: US Committee for Refugees.

Keller, S. L. (1975) *Uprooting and Social Change: The Role of Refugees in Development*, Delhi: Manohar Book Service.

Krasner, S. D. (ed.) (1983) *International Regimes*, Ithaca, NY: Cornell University Press.

Kritz, M. M. (ed.) (1983) *US Immigration and Refugee Policy: Global and Domestic Issues*, Lexington, Mass.: D. C. Heath & Co.

Loescher, G. and Monahan, L. (eds) (1989) *Refugees and International Relations*, Oxford: Oxford University Press.

Loescher, G. and Nichols, B. (eds) (1989) *The Moral Nation: Humanitarianism and US Foreign Policy Today*, Notre Dame, Ind., and London: University of Notre Dame Press.

Loescher, G. and Scanlan, J. (1986) *Calculated Kindness: Refugees and the Half-Opened Door*, New York: Free Press.

Marrus, M. R. (1985) *The Unwanted: European Refugees in the Twentieth Century*, Oxford: Oxford University Press.

Mitchell, C. (1989) 'International migration, international relations and foreign policy', *International Migration Review* 23: 681–708.

Nichols, B. (1988) *The Uneasy Alliance: Religion, Refugee Work and US Foreign Policy*, New York: Oxford University Press.

OAU (1969) *Refugee Convention Governing the Specific Aspects of Refugee Problems in Africa*, Article 1, p. 1, Addis Ababa: Organization for African Unity.

Refugee Studies Journal (quarterly) Oxford: Oxford University Press.

Shawcross, W. (1984) *The Quality of Mercy: Cambodia, the Holocaust, and Modern Conscience*, New York: Simon & Schuster.

Stein, B. N. (1981) 'The refugee experience: defining the parameters of a field of study', *International Migration Review* 15: 320–30.

Suhrke, A. (1983) 'Global refugee movements and strategies of response', in M. M. Kritz (ed.) *US Immigration and Refugee Policy: Global and Domestic Issues*, Lexington, Mass.: Lexington Books.

Tomasi, L. F. (annual) *In Defense of the Alien*, New York: Center for Migration Studies.

UN (1951) *Convention Relating to the Status of Refugees*, Article 1, p. 1, Geneva: United Nations.

US Committee for Refugees (annual) *World Refugee Survey*, Washington, DC: US Committee for Refugees.

Washington Post (1983) 22 April: A13.

Widgren, J. (1989) 'Asylum-seekers in Europe in the context of South–North movements', *International Migration Review* 23: 599–605.

Zolberg, A. R., Suhrke, A. and Aguayo, S. (1989) *Escape from Violence: Conflict and the Refugee Crisis in the Developing World*, New York: Oxford University Press.

Zucker, N. L. and Zucker, N. F. (1987) *The Guarded Gate: The Reality of American Refugee Policy*, San Diego: Harcourt Brace Jovanovich.

FURTHER READING

Ferris, E. G. (ed.) (1985) *Refugees and World Politics*, New York: Praeger.

Gallagher, D. (1989) 'The evolution of the international refugee system', *International Migration Review* 23: 579–98.

Goodwin-Gill, G. S. (1983) *The Refugee in International Law*, Oxford: Clarendon Press.

Gordenker, L. (1987) *Refugees in International Politics*, London: Croom Helm.

Hoffman-Nowotny, H. (1981) 'Sociological approaches toward a general theory of migration', in M. M. Kritz, C. B. Keely and S. M. Tomasi (eds) *Global Trends in Migration*, New York: Center for Migration Studies.

Holborn, L. W. (1975) *Refugees: A Problem of Our Time*, 2 vols, Methuen, NJ: Scarecrow Press.

Independent Commission on International Humanitarian Issues (1986) *Refugees: The Dynamics of Displacement*, London: Zed Books.

Kritz, M. M. (ed.) (1983) *US Immigration and Refugee Policy: Global and Domestic Issues*, Lexington, Mass.: D. C. Heath & Co.

Loescher, G. and Monahan, L. (eds) (1989) *Refugees and International Relations*, Oxford: Oxford University Press.

Loescher, G. and Nichols, B. (eds) (1989) *The Moral Nation: Humanitarianism and US Foreign Policy Today*, Notre Dame, Ind., and London: University of Notre Dame Press.

Loescher, G. and Scanlan, J. (1986) *Calculated Kindness: Refugees and the Half-Opened Door*, New York: Free Press.

Marrus, M. R. (1985) *The Unwanted: European Refugees in the Twentieth Century*, Oxford: Oxford University Press.

Mitchell, C. (1989) 'International migration, international relations and foreign policy', *International Migration Review* 23: 681–708.

Nichols, B. (1988) *The Uneasy Alliance: Religion, Refugee Work and US Foreign Policy*, New York: Oxford University Press.

Shawcross, W. (1984) *The Quality of Mercy: Cambodia, the Holocaust, and Modern Conscience*, New York: Simon & Schuster.

Stein, B. N. (1981) 'The refugee experience: defining the parameters of a field of study', *International Migration Review* 15: 320–30.

Suhrke, A. (1983) 'Global refugee movements and strategies of response', in M. M. Kritz (ed.) *US Immigration and Refugee Policy*, Lexington, Mass.: Lexington Books.

Tomasi, L. F. (annual) *In Defense of the Alien*, New York: Center for Migration Studies.

US Committee for Refugees (annual) *World Refugee Survey*, Washington, DC: US Committee for Refugees.

Zolberg, A. R., Suhrke, A. and Aguayo, S. (1989) *Escape from Violence: Conflict and the Refugee Crisis in the Developing World*, New York: Oxford University Press.

Zucker, N. L. and Zucker, N. F. (1987) *The Guarded Gate: The Reality of American Refugee Policy*, San Diego: Harcourt Brace Jovanovich.

84

DEMOCRATIZATION

GEORGE MODELSKI

Democratization is the process by which democracy spreads across the world. First identified by Alexis de Tocqueville in 1835, it quietly shapes and reshapes the world system in an ongoing movement that, from time to time, as in 1989–90, looms prominently in the public consciousness. The process is observable and describable, from beginning to end, as a sequence, a forward progression, and it is capable of being explained in terms of broader concepts and the evolutionary principles governing it. Looking deeper, one may see a mechanism of structural change with substantial impact and ramifications, and not the least of them upon world politics.

This essay consists of four parts, and deals respectively with democratization and democracy; the democratic experience; explanation; and democracy and peace.

DEMOCRATIZATION AND DEMOCRACY

Alexis de Tocqueville is generally credited as being the author of the view that democracy is a universal phenomenon, capable of worldwide dissemination. His principal work, *Democracy in America* (1835) was a comprehensive study of the working of society in the United States, but it was also propelled by the idea that 'democratic institutions ... prudently introduced into society ... will subsist elsewhere than in America' (Tocqueville 1835: 309), that the same kind of society based upon the equality of conditions that he saw prevailing in America was also advancing towards power in Europe and throughout the world. 'A great democratic revolution is taking place in our midst' he wrote in the preface to the first edition (ibid.: 9), and in the twelfth edition, written fifteen years later, his conviction remained unshaken: 'this work was written ... with a mind constantly preoccupied by a single thought: the thought of the approaching irresistible and universal spread of democracy throughout the world' (ibid.: xiii).

We might observe immediately that this 'irresistible and universal' process is still underway, and not approaching imminent completion. Still, we cannot but marvel at the boldness of Tocqueville's conception and cannot be surprised that it attracted immediate attention and continues to fascinate to this day. But it has also been noted that although democracy's ultimate triumph is central to Tocqueville's argument, the reasons why democracy must prevail are never fully or adequately explained. John Stuart Mill noticed this in his first review of Tocqueville's work when he wrote, in the October 1835 issue of the *London Review*, that Tocqueille considers democracy's unstoppable progress 'an established truth, on the proof of which it is no longer necessary to insist' (Mill 1977: 50; Zetterbaum 1967: 4). Little wonder then that arguments on these matters have persisted to this day. Democracy's progress, moreover, has been neither unilinear nor unbroken. As a consequence, opinions on the prospects of democratization, in part as mirror of the temper of the times, have varied over the years.

Alexis de Tocqueville's 'inevitability thesis' has never had complete endorsement. Some commentators thought that he himself viewed it as no more than a 'salutary myth' that needed to be proclaimed in public but about which persistent private doubts were also unavoidable (Zetterbaum 1967: 19). As time passed, the fortunes of democracy rose and fell; after the Paris Commune, for instance, democracy appeared to Europeans as the 'entirely new disease' America was 'infecting the Old World with' (James R. Lowell 1884: 24). Two decades later, both M. Ostrogorski (1902) and Robert Michels (1915) discerned a 'crisis of democracy' caused by the excessive power of party organizations, which robbed the forms of democracy of the substance of liberty that they demanded. Ostrogorski himself decried as unwarranted by experience 'the blissful theory of necessary progress' (Ostrogorski 1902: 739).

Writing as a political scientist, Woodrow Wilson declared that 'democracy seems about universally to prevail.... [T]he spread of democratic institutions ... promises to reduce politics to a single form by reducing all forms of government to democracy' (Wilson 1918: 35), and, as President, he led the United States into the First World War to make the world 'safe for democracy'. But, writing at the same time, another scholar-politician, James Bryce, was more cautious. Having posed the question about 'whether the law of social progress' decrees 'a natural trend toward democracy', he answered: 'although democracy has spread ... we are not yet entitled to hold ... that it is the natural and therefore ... the inevitable form of government (Bryce 1921: 24, 42).

After the Second World War, which the United States first joined as 'an arsenal' for 'the democracies' (Franklin Roosevelt's 'Four Freedoms' message to Congress, 6 January 1941, in Modelski and Modelski 1988: 359), theories of political and economic development once again moved to the fore as part of efforts to master 'modernization'. But the failure of many newly instituted democracies in the Third World brought disillusionment, and once again chilled the climate of opinion. In the 1980s, Jean-François Revel published a book with the title *How Democracies Perish* and began it with the sentence: 'Democracy may, after all, turn out to have been a historical accident, a brief parenthesis that is closing before our eyes' (Revel 1984: 3).

This rapid overview suggests that the process of democratization, while prominent in political discourse, is hardly unambiguous, and stands in need of clarification and verification. Not only have the problems of democracy often appeared more severe than its prospects, but the accounts of the process and of its postulated end-point have also failed to command wide acceptance and often appeared inconclusive. Let us then pull together a few general points as the basis for an empirical account of the process and also for its explanation.

First, democracy has both formal and substantive aspects. The forms of democracy may be seen principally as a unique arrangement for making authoritative decisions ('the democratic process') (Dahl 1989; Sartori 1987). These procedural, or efficient, aspects become manifest in elections which are a complex, rule-bound process involving, among others, parties, voters, majorities and the media, competing around a number of representational devices. They are a form of macrodecision by which a community elects some individuals to positions of leadership and endorses the policies they offer. The substance of democracy centres on the conditions of equality, so forcefully highlighted by Tocqueville; they are constitutive of a unique type of community and they reflect the conditions without which democracy cannot operate effectively – a community of equals participating as free individuals (one person, one vote) in collective decisions. The early Greek definition of democracy as 'equality under law' combines these two aspects well.

Second, democratization, as the process of spreading or building democracy, likewise moves along two distinct, though parallel paths. In the first place, it appears as the diffusion of an efficient technology of collective choice, as when constitutional forms or practices such as presidential government, or the Westminster model, disseminate worldwide. Or else, less obviously, it is observed in the growth of democratic communities (for example, through greater inclusion and broader participation), and of a community of democracies (for example, through increased interdependence, and wider sharing in the resolution of issues at the global level). Considered as a global process, democratization is observable in particular when the development of relations and interactions between democratic communities reaches a higher degree of intensity and starts giving rise to new forms of social organization.

Third, democratization may be more or less *intensive* because the quality of the democratic experience for a given community varies over time and is subject to change in both positive and negative directions; it may differ from that experienced by other democratic communities. Countries become more democratic, such as through extensions of the suffrage; they also become less democratic, such as when power is seized by an armed minority. Thus they can be rated accordingly, not just as to whether or not they are democratic, but as to how democratic they are. In Freedom House publications (for example, Gastil 1989), every country in the world has been awarded, since 1972, annual freedom scores (ranging from 2 (highest) to 14 (lowest) that are meant to measure the level of both political rights and civil liberties. The Polity II survey (Gurr *et al.* 1989), which covers the years 1800–1986, uses a ten-point scale of 'institutional democracy', which scores the extent of party competition, the quality of the electoral system, and restraints on executive power, but not human rights. For instance, in the Polity II project, the United States scores a '7' between 1800 and 1837, and a '10' after 1870. Japan rates a '10' since 1950. The Polity II dataset on institutional democracy does, as the name suggests, emphasize the formal or procedural aspects of democracy, whereas Freedom House (and other surveys) lend greater emphasis to participation. Where comparisons can be made, the differences in ratings do not seem to be greater than, at most, some 10 per cent of the cases.

Fourth, *extensive* democratization asks how much democracy there is in the world at a certain basic level. For instance, Freedom House calls countries ranking 2–5 'free countries'; in Polity II we might take the threshold level to be a '6' and then ask how many countries there are at that level in any given year. Tocqueville's thesis of inevitable progress might then be assessed by reference to such a minimum criterion, even while we remain aware that a great deal of subjectivity remains in such measures, some of which we may not agree with.

THE DEMOCRATIC EXPERIENCE

What is the empirical support for Tocqueville's thesis? What is the world's actual experience of extensive democratization?

Robert A. Dahl (1989) has helped us organize our thinking about the evolution of the democratic process and the growth of self-governing communities of equals in terms of 'the three transformations'. The following is a brief account of his thesis.

The first transformation saw the creation (in about 500–400 BC) of the democratic city-state in ancient Greece, of which Athens was the principal exemplar. In a process compared by Dahl to the invention of the wheel, a new form of community arose in which a sovereign people proceeded to rule themselves. It meant that a citizen, as member of that sovereign community, was not only equal to all others in being subject to law, but was also himself, at the same time, a ruler, participating in the work of governing the city. This vision of democracy remains critical to this day.

The second transformation occurred when the idea of democracy shifted its locus away from the city-state, to the nation-state, a crucial part of modernity. The other essential element of the second transformation was the invention of representation. Originally devised to facilitate the working of systems of monarchical or aristocratic rule, representative forms gradually found new application on behalf of democratic aspirations. Through representation, the obvious and widely feared limitation of direct democracy could now be surmounted, and the feasibility of democracy for larger-scale communities could be confirmed. The process had its roots in the republican tradition, and in the ideas and practices of representative institutions; it took off strongly in the nineteenth century and gained significant momentum in the twentieth.

That is why, according to Dahl, a third democratic transformation is now on the horizon. Spurred by developments in information and telecommunications, and moving beyond the nation-state, democratic processes are now beginning to enter the transnational, the regional and global levels of social and political organization. Given, however, that 'the story of democracy is as much a record of failures as of success' (Dahl 1989: 312), and because the imperfections of existing democracies are 'so obvious and so enormous' (ibid.), Dahl argues that the prospects for the third transformation must be seen as, in the first place, a vision of future possibilities.

Dahl's scheme offers us the benchmarks for a broad look at democratization. He posits that democratic evolution proceeds from the smaller to the larger units and that each increase in unit size, from city-state to nation-state to world system, requires new types of democratic process and some form of structural change. It is a spacious conception that takes in the whole of human experience. But there is room also for a more detailed account of the second transformation on its own terms, and for tracing links of continuity between the second and third transformations.

The immediate source for modern democracy is the experience of the city-states of Renaissance Italy. The free, prosperous and active communes that sprang up – mostly in the northern and central portions of the peninsula, in cities such as Milan, Florence, Pisa, Genoa and Venice – and flourished in conditions of expanded trade, and in opposition to imperial and later papal rule, drew their models of social organization from the republican tradition, especially that of Rome. They flourished for a while but then gave way either to conquest or local tyranny. Spectacularly successful in the fifteenth century as a regional Mediterranean power, Venice alone retained a republican regime (until 1799). Proud of its Roman heritage, the city boasted of a mixed constitution that combined monarchical, aristocratic and democratic elements, in a manner that in turn became a model for later European and American developments. While stressing this Italian background to modern developments, we need also to take note of parallel and promising, though ultimately unsuccessful, stirrings at the other end of the Eurasian landmass. Sung China

(960–1279), then probably the most prosperous part of the world, was also the seat of much technical, social and political innovation and was engaged in extended interregional contacts. Developments in printing and education created public opinion and stirred partisan and political debate, but they were drastically set back by the Mongol conquest of the thirteenth century and failed to revive under the Mings.

In the early modern period after 1500, then, we observe two successive waves as laying the foundations for democratization: the spread of the republican model, and then the growth of the liberal tradition. The republican model spread from Venice and Florence and functioned as the primary alternative to princely rule. At the theoretical level the contrast between the two was first clearly developed in the writings of Niccolò Machiavelli, and in particular in *The Prince* and in *The Discourses*, written between 1513 and 1521 but first published in 1532. The most practical exemplar of the republican model was the Dutch Republic, which renounced its allegiance to the King of Spain in 1581 and had to fight a long war before its new status was finally acknowledged, but which emerged from that ordeal vigorous, with greatly increased strength and a prominent global role. The Dutch model stressed the rights of local and national assemblies, citizenship, and limited powers for the executive, and gave rise to proto-parties. Other related cases, so many experiments in free social and political organization, included the Swiss Confederation, the Polish Lithuanian Commonwealth, and (before it was absorbed by Moscow in 1478) the Republic of Novgorod.

Among these, only the Dutch Republic executed a successful transition to the second, liberal model of democratic development. Based on representative institutions and civil liberties, the Dutch model held the essentials of a modern constitutional system and helps explain why the ascent to the British throne of William III, the stadhtholder of Holland, in 1689, served to lay the foundations for the Glorious Revolution that reshaped the British political system and made Britain the model of the liberal state for the next two centuries. That transition had been prepared for by a number of Anglo-Dutch alliances in the previous one hundred years.

Historian R. R. Palmer (1959) has termed the period 1760–1800 'The Age of the Democratic Revolution', referring in particular to the events in the United States and France, and others related to them, such as in the Low Countries, Italy and Poland. Yet the American Revolution was, in the first place, a successful war of independence (not unlike the Dutch case) fought in the republican column, while the French Revolution soon lost its democratic colouration. The high point of 'democracy' in the latter was the March 1794 speech by Robespierre which launched the Terror, even while staking out the claim that 'the French are the first people in the world to establish a true democracy' (Palmer 1959: 16–17). Robespierre himself was guillotined six months later, and democracy was thus, by association, discredited for at least a generation. 'The Age of the Democratic Revolution' did indeed set in motion strong forces of change, notably in the United States, but it did not by itself create the democratic community.

It is in the nineteenth century that democratization took off as a major social and political process, on the basis of a maturing American democracy linked to a Britain transforming itself in the same direction. These two constituted the basic cluster around which other democracies gradually accrued.

Table 1 depicts the progress of democracy in twenty of the world's major countries. For the present purpose a 'major' country is one having a population of 25 million or more in the late 1980s, when there were altogether thirty-one such nations, accounting for more than 80 per cent of the world's inhabitants. Of these, twenty had three or more years of 'institutional democracy' in that period (as defined by Polity II criteria and with a score of '6' or more, see p. 1356). Eleven others had no such experience: Bangladesh, Burma, China, Egypt, Ethiopia, Indonesia, Iran, Mexico, the Soviet Union, Vietnam and Zaïre.

Table 1   Major democratic trajectories 1837–1990 (Polity II data)

	1837	1882	1927	1972
USA	○○○○○○○○○○○○○●●●●●●●	●●●●●●●●●●●●●	●●●●●●●●●●●●●	●●●●●●●●●●●●
UK	○○○○○○○○○○○○	○○○○○○○○○○○○○	●●●●●●●●●●●●	●●●●●●●●●●
France	○	○○○○○○○○○○○○○○○○○○	●●●○○○○○○○○○○○	
Canada		○○○○○○○○○○○○○○○○○○	●●●●●●●●●●●●●●	●●●●●●●●
Colombia		○○○○○	○○○○○	○○○○○○○○○●●●
Spain		○○○○○○○○○○○○○○	○○○	○○○○○○
South Africa*			○○○○○○○○○○○○○○○○○○○C○○○○○	
Poland			○○○	○
Germany (FRG)			○○○○	●●●●●●●●●●●●●●●
Philippines			○○	○○○○○○○ ○○○
Argentina	○			○ ○○
Turkey			●●○○○●●●	●●●
Brazil			○ ○	○○○
Italy				●●●●●●●●●●●●●●
Japan				●●●●●●●●●●●●●●
India				●●●●●●●●○○●○○○
Pakistan			○ ○	
Nigeria			○○○	○○
Thailand				○○○○○
South Korea				○○

Notes: ○ = three years of institutional democracy, score of 6 or higher in the Polity II dataset (1987–90 est.); ● = score of '10'.

Table shows all countries with a population of 25 million or more in late 1980s, with a minimum of three years of institutional democracy during 1837–1990.

*The editors wish to dissociate themselves from the depiction of South Africa as a democratic nation.

This rather general description is adequate for purposes of characterizing worldwide trends. Certain of these are immediately apparent:

1 the crucial role of the United States and Britain in its continuity and mutuality and as a baseline of the entire development;
2 the lack of continuity in the other cases – in thirteen out of eighteen cases we observe discontinuity;
3 the importance of the twentieth-century experience, especially since 1945;
4 the more recent spread of democratization outside North America and Europe, to Asia in particular.

The Polity II dataset used in constructing Table 1 measures 'institutional democracy' and might therefore be subject to the criticism that it neglects the substantive (or participatory) aspects of the subject. But if we are prepared to assume that over time the procedural and the substantive aspects tend to adjust to each other, because formal democracy without equality is a sham, and malfunctions, and substantive equality without procedural safeguards tends towards disorder, then in the long run 'institutional' will tend to correlate with 'participatory' democracy. That is why in a survey that takes the long view the divergences between the two become less significant.

In fact, Table 1 presents two measures of institutional democracy: a broad one (score of 6–10), and a narrow one (score of 10). Use of the narrower measure (●) highlights the full-blown democracies, each of which also satisfies the criteria of participation; it also reduces the number of democratic cases to ten, but it does not negate the broad trends just outlined. Vanhanen's study (Vanhanen 1984), which gives greater weight to electoral participation, points in the same direction.

An alternative way to summarize the progress of democratization is to determine the fraction (percentage) of the world population that has lived in democracies (see Table 2). That fraction has risen dramatically in the past 150 years, from less than 1 per cent in 1800, to just over 10 per cent in 1900, to a level of 43 per cent in 1990. The picture is one of a strong and determined process.

Table 2 Fraction democratic

Year	No. of countries	Fraction democratic
1800	1	0.6
1840	3	3.9
1890	12	11.9
1900	13	12.3
1920	29	20.6
1940	15	11.4
1950	29	34.4
1970	37	36.4
1990 (est.)	55	43.2

Note: Fraction democratic is the percentage of world population living in institutional democracies (Polity II scale, score of 6–10).

Source: Modelski and Perry (1991: 29)

The democratic transformations in Eastern Europe in 1989–90 have been striking and significant, not the least for their mostly non-violent character. Beginning with a real election in Poland in mid-1989, going on to the crumbling of the Berlin Wall and the collapse of the Czechoslovak and Romanian regimes, which were followed by other elections, these changes reshaped the social and political landscape of the area and added maybe 2 or 3 per cent to the 'fraction democratic' just mentioned. They also interacted with, and exerted an influence on, great changes in the Soviet Union itself. A process of democratization got underway there, too, and has brought, so far, greater 'openness', the rise of new political parties, elections to new representative institutions, and a renunciation of the Communist party's monopoly on power. The Baltic republics gained independence in August 1991, and the Soviet Union began formally to disintegrate in December of that year. A reshaped and democratic confederation to take the place of the Soviet Union is now conceivable. Were it to come to pass, it might move the world's population for the first time ever towards a democratic majority. This would mean a major structural change in the world system.

EXPLANATION

Our empirical survey shows democratization to be a pervasive social process with strong roots and significant antecedents that in the past century and a half has extended to a strategic portion of the world's population. How might we account for this phenomenon, anticipated but not explained by Tocqueville and discussed by historians and political scientists most commonly as a function of unique historical circumstances or individual country characteristics, functioning as preconditions?

We shall explore two avenues of explanation: viewing democratization both a process of technology diffusion and as one of community formation. Each has an evolutionary learning cast to it.

If democratization is conceived as a technology, that is, a means to an end, a technique of collective choice or a form of macrodecision making, then its dissemination may be subject to patterns observed in the diffusion of technological and other innovations. For societies unfamiliar with such practices, democracy is indeed a bundle of innovations. Rogers's synthesis of the technological literature (Rogers 1962) showed that the path of the adoption of innovations follows a bell-shaped curve over time and approaches normality; when plotted on a cumulative basis the distribution is essentially S-shaped, and on semi-logarithmic graph paper it forms a straight line.

One useful application of this approach, and a proven predictive tool, is the Fisher–Pry model of technological substitution (Fisher and Pry 1971). If technology is no more than one way of satisfying society's unchanging needs, then technological evolution consists in substituting new forms of satisfaction for old ones (such as solar power for oil as a means of generating energy, or cars for horsepower and airlines for buslines as forms of transportation). Similarly, social practices can be understood as means to an end: they meet essential needs for making authoritative choices; socio-political evolution then would consist in replacing old forms of organization by new ones. Democracy would become a substitute for autocracy or dictatorship just as, on a smaller scale, for example, improved electoral arrangements (such as the secret ballot, party conventions) replace earlier ones (such as open voting, closed caucuses).

The present application of the Fisher–Pry model makes the following assumptions: first, that democracy is a superior substitute for authoritarian society and is likely to have greater potential for improvement and cost reduction; second, that a substitution that has gone as far as a few per cent of its 'market', and has shown viability that will increase with rising volume and yield increasing returns to scale, will also proceed to completion – in other words, democratization will be the more successful the more democracies there are; and third, that the substitution process will proceed exponentially.

A test of such a model on Polity II data of institutional democracy for 1837–1986 (starting the data at the 4 per cent level) produces a high correlation (R^2 of 0.9), and shows that democratization has so far followed a course predicted by the model of technological substitution (Modelski and Perry 1991).

If the analogy between technology and democracy holds and if the assumptions governing the application of the Fisher–Pry model in this case are warranted, then one might expect that by the year 2003 one-half of the world's population will be living under democratic regimes. An extrapolation of the trendline in Figure 1 shows that the flexpoint of the process (that is, the predicted point in time when the 'fraction democratic' is 50 per cent) is the year 2003. The time constant (or take-over time) is 228 years, and 90 per cent saturation is expected toward the end of the next century.

Alternatively, democratization might also be seen as community formation (through inclusion and participation), and the spread of democracy as a form of clustering of communities. In as much as communities may also be seen as ends in themselves, this second 'cut' at democratization raises issues parallel to, but different from, those involved in democracy as a means or technology.

Robert Axelrod's model of the 'evolution of co-operation' (Axelrod 1984) shows how a set of 'nice' (that is, co-operative) strategies can survive in a 'mean' world (that is, among a set of uncooperative strategies); it can do so essentially by clustering, and mutual support of 'nice' strategies.

As applied to democracy, such an argument would run in three stages. First, democracy promotes co-operative behaviour, based on reciprocity of equals, and hence on strategies that are 'nice', retaliatory, forgiving and clear. Second, democracies will have initial viability (that is, a chance of survival in a hostile environment) if they appear in a cluster, or if there is kinship among them.

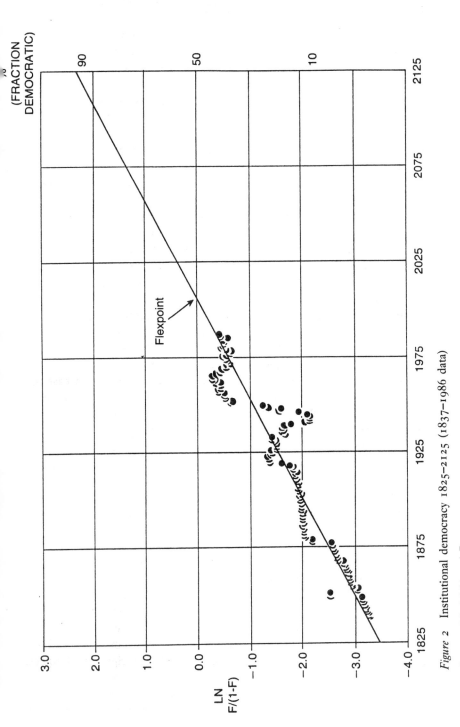

Figure 2 Institutional democracy 1825–2125 (1837–1986 data)

Source: Modelski and Perry 1991: 31

Third, democracies have evolutionary stability (and resist invasion by hostile strategies) when they have durability, and the shadow of the future is enlarged (that is, long-term interests are pursued).

The long-term process of democratization depicted here fits the model of evolution of co-operation. The world political process, over the past several centuries, generated a variety of experiments in social and political organiz-ation, and some of these have fashioned sets of co-operative strategies, as in the republican regimes of the early modern period. Those republican regimes that successfully survived in a 'mean' environment possessed characteristics of 'kinship' (as in the Anglo-Dutch case) and of clustering. The Anglo-Dutch alliance, from 1689 onwards, became the nucleus of the emerging global system. In due course it came to be absorbed, and superseded, by the Anglo-American special relationship, the axis of most of twentieth-century world politics, which in Table 1 appears as the durable anchor of democratization. Moreover, on the eve of the twenty-first century, the community of democrac-ies has shown significant durability and is well on its way toward attaining evolutionary stability.

These stages in the evolution of global co-operation correspond to the republican, liberal and democratic phases that we have observed in the preced-ing section (pp. 1357-9), and we also notice that they match the progress of long cycles in world politics (Modelski 1987, 1990). In a broader sense, they appear to be stages in the evolution of a global (democratic) community.

For we notice, too, that both our explanatory approaches, the Fisher–Pry model of technological evolution and the Axelrod model of the evolution of co-operation, must be what they say they are: models of a collective evolution-ary process. They give substance to the idea that democratization, viewed as a stage in the emergence of a global community, is such an evolutionary process. That is, unlike Tocqueville, who saw it as a democratic *revolution*, erupting upon the world with some suddenness and thoroughness, we need to think of it as a series of evolutionary changes, marked by peaks and valleys, and some crises, but in the main a gradual transformation.

To say that democratization is an evolutionary process is not to say that it is devoid of violence, or the use of force. Remarkably, all the major wars of the modern world system – most obviously the First and Second World Wars – and also the Napoleonic Wars, the Wars of Grand Alliance against Louis XIV, and the Dutch–Spanish Wars (particularly between 1580 and 1609) were strongly forwarding that process by defeating regimes of absolute power (Napoleon, the Sun King, the Spanish monarchy), giving advantage to key republican, liberal systems (the Dutch Republic), and confirming Britain as a model of political and economic development.

Yet the net effect of these processes has been to enlarge steadily the area within which democratic procedures ultimately prevailed, and where the incidence of violence gradually declined. The evolutionary paradigm counsels against the instant gratification of revolutionary rhetoric, and highlights the gradualness of the process (albeit punctuated by macrodecisions, such as elections, or wars which are occasions for trials of strength) and asks us to cultivate a long perspective.

This is not the only such evolutionary process in the global realm, and the burden of change does not rest with it alone. The long cycle of global politics just mentioned is another process of evolutionary learning (Modelski 1990), and both are members of the family of global evolutionary processes. Other members of that family are the Kondratieff waves of economic innovation and global lead industries, and the active zone process that has successively shifted the centre of global innovation and change from the Mediterranean, to the North Sea, on to North America, and now toward the Pacific Rim.

What was no more than a nucleus before 1945 has since then grown and spread into an increasingly weighty community of democracies, with the United States at its core but also becoming more substantial in Europe and in Asia. A progressively denser web of relationships now links these democracies, both in formal organizations and in informal networks (Huntley 1980). Proposals have been advanced for consolidating these networks, for example through the establishment of a League of Democracies, an international organization for the support of democracy (Fossedal 1989; Diamond 1989). As the balance of the world system increasingly tilts toward a democratic majority, the community of democracy is gradually becoming the operative framework of the global system.

DEMOCRACY AND PEACE

For students of international relations, the most interesting thing about democracy is the empirically documented fact that democracies do not fight wars with each other (Rummel 1983). Their war record is, of course, substantial and successful, witness the key role of the Anglo-American coalition in winning the Second World War. But the story of interdemocratic relations has generally been peaceful. The emerging democratic community has been marked by political intimacy and some sense of common purpose, in part because in global wars they fought on the same side, for common goals, as members of the same coalition. Their generally peaceful record might be confirmed by glancing again at Table 1. The twenty major countries in that table have never fought a war against each other while in a condition of institutional democracy. The only exception is the Spanish–American war of 1898, fought in Cuba and the Philippines, at a time when the United States ranked '10' and Spain ranked '7' on the Polity II scale. At other times, and prior to the establishment of democracy, such wars did, of course, occur.

Democratic countries not only abstained from war against each other but also maintained, and kept strengthening, maritime, commercial, communicative and social arrangements of an open kind that encouraged intimacy, and which perceived little threat in cross-border contacts and interchanges. A 'zone of peace' (Doyle 1986) has emerged within which higher standards of policy and behaviour have evolved, and in which positive peace (and not just the absence of war) is beginning to be something of a reality.

These developments vindicate Immanuel Kant's 1795 analysis of the structural conditions of general peace as outlined in his famous essay, *Zum Ewigen Frieden*. These included republican regimes, federal organization and universal hospitality.

By contrast with the experiences of democracies, the domestic record of non-democratic governments has been extremely poor. 'The most violent governments have been totalitarian, those least free' writes Rudolph Rummel (1988: 27–9), and his research shows indeed that, in the twentieth century, loss of life inflicted by absolutist governments upon their own people have been significantly greater than those experienced in all the international and civil wars put together. Little wonder that a substitution process has been strongly underway.

For such reasons, the progress of democracy opens up the possibility of significant change in the condition of world politics, within the zone of peace, away from the 'mean' strategies of the 'realists', toward the 'nice' strategies embedded in democratic societies. Within the zone of peace, the problem of security and defence would shrink in significance, not because of the absence of conflict and competition but because such competition would be conducted by democratic procedures, that is, by means other than those of war. Outside, it would shrink too because by definition that outside would then acquire a minority, hence an inherently weaker and less threatening character. World politics is still a long way from satisfying the conditions of a democratic process (as formulated, for example, by Dahl 1989: chapter 8) or operating in a democratic community, but democratization is moving it steadily closer to that state.

Tocqueville was right when he identified the progress of democracy as a major process of the world system. A century and a half later we can say that that progress has been steady and substantial, and that, if our understanding of it as an evolutionary process is correct, it is likely to continue, with important and salutary consequences especially for world politics.

REFERENCES

Axelrod, R. (1984) *The Evolution of Cooperation*, New York: Basic Books.
Bryce, J. (1921) *Modern Democracies*, London: Macmillan.

Dahl, R. A. (1989) *Democracy and its Critics*, New Haven: Yale University Press.

Diamond, L. (1989) 'Beyond authoritarianism and totalitarianism: strategies for democratization', *Washington Quarterly* 12 (1): 141–63.

Doyle, M. (1986) 'Liberalism and world politics', *American Political Science Review* 80 (December): 1151–70.

Fisher, J. C. and Pry, R. H. (1971) 'A simple substitution model of technological change', *Technological Forecasting and Social Change* 3: 75–88.

Fossedal, G. A. (1989) *The Democratic Imperative*, New York: Basic Books.

Gastil, R. (1989) *Freedom in the World: Political Rights and Civil Liberties 1988–1989*, New York: Freedom House.

Gurr, T. R., Jaggers, K. and Moore, W. H. (1989) *Polity II Codebook*, Boulder, Colo.: Center for Comparative Politics, University of Colorado.

Huntley, J. R. (1980) *Uniting the Democracies*, New York: New York University Press.

Kant, E. (1795) 'Eternal peace', in C. J. Friedrich (ed. and trans.) *Inevitable Peace*, Cambridge, Mass.: Harvard University Press, 1948, pp. 245–81.

Lowell, J. R. (1884) 'Democracy', in C. H. Gauss (ed.) *Democracy Today: An American Interpretation*, Chicago: Scott Forsman, 1917, pp. 19–48.

Michels, R. (1915) *Political Parties: A Sociological Study of the Oligarchical Tendencies of Modern Democracy*, New York: Free Press, 1962.

Mill, J. S. (1977) *Essays on Politics and Society*, ed. J. M. Robson, Toronto: University of Toronto Press.

Modelski, G. (1987) *Long Cycles in World Politics*, London: Macmillan.

——(1990) 'Is world politics evolutionary learning?', *International Organization* 44 (Winter): 1–24.

Modelski, G. and Modelski, S. (eds) (1988) *Documenting Global Leadership*, London: Macmillan.

Modelski, G. and Perry, G. (1990) 'Democratization in long perspective', *Technological Forecasting and Social Change* 39 (March–April): 23–34.

Ostrogorski, M. (1902) *Democracy and the Organization of Political Parties*, New York: Macmillan.

Palmer, R. R. (1959) *The Age of the Democratic Revolution*, 2 vols, Princeton: Princeton University Press, 1963.

Revel, J.-F. (1984) *How Democracies Perish*, New York: Doubleday.

Rogers, E. M. (1962) *Diffusion of Innovations*, New York: Free Press.

Rummel, R. (1983) 'Libertarianism and violence', *Journal of Conflict Resolution* 27 (March): 27–71.

——(1988) 'As though a nuclear war: the death toll of absolutism', *International Journal on World Peace* 5 (3): 27–43.

Sartori, G. (1987) *The Theory of Democracy Revisited*, Chatham, NJ: Chatham House.

Tocqueville, A. de (1835) *Democracy in America*, ed. J. P. Meyer, New York: Anchor Books/Doubleday, 1969.

Vanhanen, T. (1984) *The Emergence of Democracy*, Helsinki: Finnish Society of Arts and Letters.

Wilson, W. (1918) *The State: Elements of Historical and Practical Politics*, Boston: D. C. Heath.

Zetterbaum, M. (1967) *Tocqueville and the Problem of Democracy*, Stanford: Stanford University Press

INDEX

ABM (anti-ballistic missile) Treaty 1089,
1275, 1277
Abrams, Elliott 1342
Accelerated Development 1186
Achaean League 340
Achille Lauro 1071
Adam, H. 751
Adenauer, Konrad 148, 1145
administrative elites 490
Adorno, T. W. 159, 161, 488
advertising 415, 416, 417, 420, 434, 476
Afghanistan 221, 889, 995, 1090, 1187, 1277,
1346
Africa
  AIDS in 1195, 1196
  authoritarian regimes and 234
  boundaries in 572
  capitalisms 1184, 1191, 1196
  colonial legacies 540
  colonies in 578
  conflicts in 570
  corporations 1184, 1191, 1196, 1197
  coups d'état 119, 249
  debts 1128, 1178, 1181, 1182, 1185, 1188,
  1193
  decolonization 890
  democracy in 1191–2
  diglossia 590
  drought 1181, 1185, 1193, 1343
  elites in 496–7
  ethnicity in 570
  famine 1343
  federalism in 342
  human rights 1332
  ideology 1179
  languages in 590, 595
  liberation movements 622
  local government 327, 328
  materialism 1178, 1179, 1180, 1184, 1186
  migration in 720
  military rule 1181, 1182
  modernization 1178, 1179, 1180, 1182,
  1184, 1192
  oil and 1181, 1182
  parliamentary systems 540
  privatization 1193–4
  refugees in 1196, 1342, 1345, 1346
  socialism 1178, 1179, 1180
  SOEs in 830
  terms of trade 1181, 1183
African Charter 1321
agenda setting 651
Age of Enlightenment 472
Agranoff, R. 424
AIDS 696, 1195, 1196
air pollution 685, 686, 687, 688, 690, 691,
710
Ala al-Mawdudi, Allamah Abul 184
Albania 218, 225, 1237–8, 1239
Algeria 298, 1066, 1070, 1075
Algiers Accords 907, 909, 910
'Ali, Caliph 182
Allen, G. 444, 449
Allende, Salvador 963, 1106
Alliance for Progress 496
alliances
  attributes 1009–15
  balance of power 1002–4, 1017–18, 1019
  capabilities 1012–13
  coalition theories 1004
  collective security 1018–19
  conflict and 1019
  definition 1002
  disarmament and 1017
  effects of 1017–20, 1021
  foreign policy 1006
  formation, theories of 1002–7
  institutionalization of 878
  integration and 1020
  international system and 1015–17, 1020
  members' attributes 1008–9
  national attributes 1006–7
  performance 100–17
  prospects 1021–2
  size principle 1004–6, 1010–11
  war and 1018–20
Allison, G. T. 322, 649, 849, 850, 1281
Allport, G. W. 359
Almond, G. A. 33, 308, 309, 459, 508, 509,
510, 619, 623
Althusius, Johannes 340
Althusser, L. 162

French separatism 571
immigration 720
languages in 591, 593, 594, 596, 597, 598
law in 73, 295, 296, 299–301
legitimacy and 122
privatization and 823
welfare state 147
Cantwell-Smith, W. 184
capital
international 626, 627, 628, 629
urban policy and 777, 778, 780
capitalism
analysis of 156
contradictions of 624, 625
democracy and 623
international system and 854
urban policy and 778, 779, 783, 784, 785, 786
capitalist markets 33–4
capitalist societies
class and 56, 560
state and 547
carbon dioxide 682
Cardoso, F. H. 626
Carlyle, Thomas 366
Carnegie, Andrew 878
Carr, E. H. 879, 988
Cartegena Agreement 961, 962, 963, 964
Carter, President Jimmy 645, 784, 1071, 1089, 1323
Casanova, González 625
caste 85
Castro, Fidel 219, 220
Catholicism 522, 523
caudillos 248
Cawson, A. 48
Ceauşescu, Nicolae 222, 223, 1235, 1236, 1238
censorship 731
CENTO (Central Treaty Organization) 1021, 1162
Central America
conflict in 1215, 1216, 1219, 1220
refugees 1346
see also under names of countries
Central American Bank 960, 961
Central American Common Market (CACM) 958–61, 968
Centre for the Settlement of Investment Dispute 921
CFCs 685
Chad 994
Chamberlain, H. S. 147
Chamorro, Violetta 1215
Chapman, J. 454
'charisma' 274, 275
charismatic courts 293

Chazan, Naomi 1197
Cheema, C. S. 327, 328
chemical waste 690
chemical weapons 1272–3, 1280
Chernenko, K. 355
Chilcote, R. H. 620
children 88, 89, 92, 449, 450, 451, 452, 454, 455, 456, 457, 463, 464
Children, Convention on the Rights of 1320
Chile
ANCOM 963–5, 968
debts 1133
democracy overthrown 209
legislature 281, 282, 285
military governments 257, 260
privatization 827
Chilton, S. 617
China
alliance policy 1011, 1016
arms control and 1267, 1282
ASEAN and 991
changes in 224–5
conflict in 1204–5
democracy in 499
development 1201
ethnicity 568
imperialism 1111
India and 1015
Korean War and 888
Maoism 223
Marxism and 218
non-proliferation and 1262
nuclear weapons 1253, 1254
privatization and 827–8
revolution 1051, 1058
thought reform in 222
Tienanmen Square massacre 119, 225, 1201
UN and 456
chlorinated fluorocarbons 685
Chodak, S. 620
Christelow, A. 297, 298
Christianity 521, 523, 524, 528, 529, 531
Christie, R. 369
Churchill, W. S. 145, 210, 1145, 1146
cities see urban policy
citizenship, concept of 45
Citrin, J. 122
civil and political rights 1325–8, 1331
Civil and Political Rights, Covenant on 1320, 1321
civil law 294
class
conflict and 559, 563
nature of 555–6
political parties and 557, 558
politics and 555–66
significance of 555, 556

decolonization and 884
definitions 616–18
democracy and 617, 623
dependency and 625, 626
environment and 684
evolving perspectives 618–21
growth, stages of 621
health and 712
human needs 627
imperialism and 628
inward directed 625–6
literature on 619, 620
Marxism and 620
mode of production 627, 631
multi-faceted process 616, 617
nationalism 622–3
planning 617
politics and 616–32
socialism and 617, 618
strategies 629–31
sub-imperialism and 628
synthesis 631–2
underdevelopment and 624
unequal 626
women in 916
development, cognitive 457, 461, 465
devolution 319
'dictatorship of the proletariat' 111
dictatorships 117, 197
differentiation 523, 527–31
diplomacy
  anti-diplomacy and 1027
  coercive 1026
  contemporary 1033–7
  definition 1025
  failure of 1032–3
  force and 1026
  history 1027–31
  reconciliatory nature 1025
  war and 1027, 1035
direct action 609
disabled people 92
disarmament 1266–7, 1268, 1269, 1283 see
  also arms control
diseases 695, 696
displaced people 1339, 1342, 1348–9
Disraeli, Benjamin 142, 144, 396, 415
'divergent thinking' 589
division of labour, cultural 576, 577, 578, 580,
  581
division of labour, international 778, 780
Djilas, M. 493
Dogan, M. 516
Domhoff, G. W. 492
Domínguez, J. 619
dominium 56
Dornic, S. 589
Dos Santos, T. 625

Douglas, M. 510–12
Dowse, R. 445, 455
Drucker, Peter F. 826
drug abuse 710, 711
dual sovereignty 338
Dube, S. C. 620, 627, 629
DuBois, W. E. B. 534
Duguit, Leon 47
Dulles, John Foster 853, 1013
Durkheim, Emile
  grid-group therapy and 511, 512
  religion and 522, 523
  state and 47
  structural model 63
Dussel, E. 625
dust emissions 682
Duverger, Maurice 198–9, 396–7, 399, 400,
  408, 608
Dworkin, A. 605
Dworkin, R. 71, 74, 75, 76, 77, 84, 85, 90,
  136

East African Airways 966
East African Community 965–8
East African Development Bank 965
Eastern Europe
  changes in 210, 215, 225, 260, 350, 498,
    685, 710
  communism, collapse of 1091, 1227, 1233
  debts 1090
  democracy and 1228, 1229, 1238, 1241,
    1244, 1283, 1298, 1361
  economies of 644
  elections in 413, 1238
  environment 682, 685, 686, 688, 691
  ethnic conflict in 1240, 1241
  feminism 604
  human rights in 1328
  political parties and 393, 686
  privatization 1242
  revolution 1090
  security organization 1248
  social change 1243
  terror in 221
  USSR and 1228, 1229, 1230, 1231, 1234,
    1243, 1244
  see also under names of countries
Easton, D. 454
Eastonian systems theory 677
EC
  CAP 1147, 1153
  Committee of Permanent Representatives
    (COREPER) 1148, 1149, 1155
  confederation and 338
  Council of Ministers 1143, 1147–8, 1150,
    1155, 1158
  Eastern Europe and 1245–7
  economies 662